MILESTONE DOCUMENTS
OF AMERICAN LEADERS

Exploring the Primary Sources
of Notable Americans

MILESTONE DOCUMENTS
OF AMERICAN LEADERS

Exploring the Primary Sources
of Notable Americans

Volume 4
Powell – Young

Paul Finkelman
Editor in Chief

James A. Percoco
Consulting Editor

Schlager Group

CONTENTS

VOLUME 1: ABIGAIL ADAMS TO FREDERICK DOUGLASS

Volume 2: W. E. B. Du Bois to John Jay

MILESTONE DOCUMENTS
OF AMERICAN LEADERS

Exploring the Primary Sources
of Notable Americans

Adam Clayton Powell, Jr., addresses a crowd at the Lincoln Memorial in Washington, D.C., May 17, 1957. (AP/Wide
World Photos)

ADAM CLAYTON POWELL, JR.   1908–1972

U.S. Congressman

Featured Documents
◆ **Speech on Civil Rights (1955)**
◆ **"Black Power: A Form of Godly Power" (1967)**
◆ **"Black Power and the Future of Black America" (1971)**

Overview

Adam Clayton Powell, Jr., was born in New Haven, Connecticut, in 1908. After graduating from Colgate University, Powell became active in Harlem's Abyssinian Baptist Church, where his father was minister. He received a master's degree from Columbia University, followed by theological studies at Shaw University, and assumed leadership of the Abyssinian Baptist Church congregation in 1937. Powell, an ordained minister, used the church as his base of operations to provide free meals and clothing and to protest discrimination against African Americans in Harlem's white-owned businesses and segregated hospital. In 1941 Powell ran for the City Council of New York and won. Three years later he was elected as a Democrat to the U.S. House of Representatives, representing Harlem in the newly formed and predominantly black eighteenth congressional district—a position he used to advocate major civil rights legislation over the next two decades.

Rising to the position of chairman of the House Education and Labor Committee in 1961, Powell was instrumental in passing federal legislation that brought minimum wages to all black workers, desegregated public facilities, and re-enfranchised African Americans. In 1967 Powell was stripped of his chairmanship and expelled from Congress for misappropriation of funds. Two years later the U.S. Supreme Court reinstated him, but he was unable to return to his position as committee chair. A pioneer of both the modern civil rights movement and the Black Power movement that followed, Powell was married three times and had three children. He died in Miami on April 4, 1972.

Powell was loved by much of black America for his independence and audacity in the realm of politics; he was derided, if not feared, by his colleagues in Congress for the same reasons and was almost constantly at odds with Tammany Hall, the New York Democratic Party clubhouse. Charismatic and politically astute, Powell came to exude black pride, despite being so light-skinned that he was often mistaken for a white person in public. As a student at Colgate he initially had tried to hide the fact that he was African American. However, he was "exposed" as black after a rumor spread that he was trying to pass as white. Humiliated for trying to keep his blackness a secret, he decided from that point forward to fight for racial justice. He quickly developed leadership skills and spoke out wherever and whenever he could on behalf of black men and women.

Powell's commitment to the poor, with an emphasis on the black poor and working class, was virtually unquestioned—despite his flamboyant lifestyle. He was a respected Christian minister and preached a form of liberation theology to the downtrodden; he was also known as an avid night clubber, who dated a range of women, wore flashy designer clothes, and drove a Jaguar sports car. Politically, as in his personal life, he could not easily be categorized. Although he was a registered Democrat, Powell was never fully committed to any one party or faction within it. He remained largely independent. He won office with the support of Socialists, Communists, and the American Labor Party. He worked with Republicans and progressive northern Democrats but remained unyielding toward Dixiecrats (conservative southern Democrats) and lashed out at any liberals whom he perceived to be standing in his way or dragging their feet when it came to civil and political rights. In 1956 Powell endorsed the Republican presidential candidate Dwight D. Eisenhower; four years later, he endorsed the Democratic presidential candidate John F. Kennedy and, at various points in his career, threatened to either run as an independent for office or form a third party. His core base throughout his political career remained the Abyssinian Baptist Church—at the time, the nation's largest black congregation.

Powell's life was a source of fascination to his contemporaries and those who followed. Ultimately, his political legacy is that of a resilient rebel, a fierce and determined political operator, a public rabble-rouser against racial discrimination. He was the black congressman from Harlem who authored and helped enact some of the most sweeping legislation in American history—including the Civil Rights Act of 1964, which under Title VI, authorized federal agencies to withhold aid to any institutions that practiced racial segregation. The act embodied the long-standing "Powell Amendment," a rider that the congressman attempted to attach to any bill seeking federal funds in order to attack discrimination against African Americans.

Explanation and Analysis of Documents

Powell served in Congress during a period that saw great political advances in black self-determination around the world—from the black freedom movement in the United States, which succeeded in dismantling Jim Crow laws (the legal segregation and disfranchisement of African Americans in the southern states) to the anticolonial movements in Africa, which led to the independence of more than a dozen nations. Black America was putting itself forward, on the national and international stage, as linked to Africa and other parts of the diaspora, where people of African descent have been dispersed as a voice and force for democracy. Powell shaped and, in turn, was shaped by these historic events. While hundreds of thousands of Americans protested racial segregation, Powell pushed for dramatic legislative reforms from the seat of federal government and then took his message to the pulpit and onto the streets of Harlem. He traveled across the United States and overseas as an ambassador for black freedom, demanding even greater changes while acknowledging the progress that had already been made.

Three documents—a speech delivered in Congress in memory of President Franklin D. Roosevelt and chapters from two books authored by Powell—demonstrate the congressman's forcefulness on the issues of civil and political rights and articulate his particular conception of Black Power, which was neither black nationalist nor integrationist per se. "Black Power: A Form of Godly Power," in *Keep the Faith, Baby!*, is an expansion of Powell's 1965 "Black Position Paper for America's 20 Million Negroes." "Black Power and the Future of Black America" is a poignant passage from his autobiography, *Adam by Adam*.

◆ Speech on Civil Rights

Adam Clayton Powell, Jr., gave his speech concerning civil rights on the floor of the House of Representatives on February 2, 1955. It was a day set aside by the House to commemorate the life of Democratic President Franklin D. Roosevelt, known for formulating New Deal programs in the midst of the Great Depression of the 1930s, for assembling a "black cabinet" of African Americans chosen to fill advisory roles with respect to public policy, and for leading the nation during World War II. Eight and a half months before Powell gave his speech, the U.S. Supreme Court had ruled in *Brown v. Board of Education* that segregated schools were "inherently unequal." The landmark ruling overturned rulings dating back to *Plessy v. Ferguson*, the Supreme Court ruling of 1896 that sanctioned racial segregation under the doctrine of "separate but equal." Being the leading advocate in Congress for civil rights legislation, Powell used the occasion to advance a specific proposal regarding equal access to employment in the District of Columbia.

Powell begins his speech by castigating his fellow congressmen for not doing enough—indeed, he says, "absolutely nothing"—to advance civil rights legislation. He does so by simultaneously lauding the U.S. Supreme Court for "eradicating the concept of second-class citizenship," referring to the *Brown* decision, and the actions of Republican President Dwight D. Eisenhower. Eisenhower had appointed the pro–civil rights attorney Herbert Brownell, Jr., as U.S. Attorney General. Brownell would prove instrumental in advancing a range of civil rights cases. He also played a decisive role in the appointment of

Earl Warren as chief justice (who proved to be more liberal than Eisenhower had expected).

A decade before the *Brown* decision, Powell became the first black congressman of Harlem, the cultural and political capital of black America. While he was not the first African American to be elected to the House of Representatives since the late nineteenth century (Oscar De Priest of Chicago received that honor in 1929), Powell was far and away the most vocal spokesperson for black civil and political rights in the House. He represented a new kind of black congressional leadership and pointed to the significance of his fellow black Representatives Charles Diggs of Detroit and William Dawson of Chicago serving on the Veterans' Affairs Committee and the Committee on the District of Columbia—and there being thwarted by colleagues regarding proposed civil rights legislation.

Powell, the preacher and master orator, declares:

For 10 years, my colleagues and I have introduced civil rights amendment after amendment, civil rights bill after bill, pleading, praying that you good ladies and gentlemen would give to this body the glory of dynamic leadership that it should have. But you have failed and history has recorded it.

Drawing on notions of constitutional obligations while pointing to a higher moral standard, Powell goes on to offer concrete examples of efforts by colleagues to pass civil rights legislation in the face of overwhelming congressional opposition. He calls the actions of the House both "childish" and "immature"—reversing on those to whom he was directing his comments terms applied to African Americans regarding their supposed unpreparedness and immaturity in the political arena. Powell challenges his colleagues to move with the times and to get beyond their "19th century attitude."

Powell next implores his colleagues to support a Federal Employment Practices Committee (FEPC) bill for the District of Columbia, where the issue of states' rights, he believes, could not be argued. President Roosevelt had created the FEPC in 1941 by signing Executive Order 8802, which barred racial discrimination in defense industries. Roosevelt strengthened the FEPC with Executive Order 9346 in 1943, but Congress had never enacted the FEPC into law. Powell's tactic here was to invoke Roosevelt's legacy and set an important precedent in the District of Columbia that could help expand the realm of desegregation in the nation with federal enforcement measures.

Powell ends his speech in Congress by quoting Roosevelt, but not before invoking the life of the late Lieutenant Thomas Williams. Williams had offered testimony to the House Committee on Interstate and Foreign Commerce, which was considering legislation to end segregation in interstate travel. He had honorably served in the U.S. Air Force, but after being jailed and then fined for refusing to move from his seat on an interstate bus, he was dropped from the Air Force. Powell, whose eloquence was sometimes soaring, uses such concrete examples to make

Time Line

1969

■ **June 16**
The U.S. Supreme Court rules that Powell was illegally removed from the House of Representative.

1970

■ **November**
In a bid for reelection, Powell is defeated in the Democratic Party primary.

1971

■ Powell publishes his book *Adam by Adam*, which contains the chapter "Black Power and the Future of Black America."

1972

■ **April 4**
Powell dies in Miami, Florida.

his case, by presenting African Americans as patriotic and otherwise law-abiding citizens whose constitutional rights were being violated. It was the job of Congress, says Powell, to enact federal legislation that is not only morally correct but also in line with the Constitution as determined by the U.S. Supreme Court.

Within six months of the speech, a young African American, Emmett Till of Chicago, was killed in Mississippi for whistling at a white woman. The Till case brought national attention to the plight of black men and women in the South. Four months later, Rosa Parks, E. D. Nixon, and Jo Ann Robinson launched the bus boycott in Montgomery, Alabama, that propelled Martin Luther King, Jr., to international acclaim for his leadership role in the mass protest against segregation on the city's buses. For many, it would mark an opening moment of the modern civil rights movement. Decades earlier, however, Powell, among others, had engaged in protest actions in Harlem and pushed for legislation granting civil rights for African Americans both in New York and in the nation's capital. In essence, Powell had helped develop models of protest against racial discrimination in the North that were later applied in the South.

◆ **"Black Power: A Form of Godly Power"**

In the second chapter of Powell's book *Keep the Faith, Baby!*, the author reminds his readers of the position paper he had offered in Chicago in March 1965—one year before he wrote this book—in which he had laid out his vision of black social, economic, and political empowerment. Through a series of points, the thesis of the paper called for black empowerment by nonviolent means. Powell was so determined to get his "Black Position Paper" on record and into wider circulation that he had aspects of it almost immediately included in the *Congressional Record* His

Emmett Till, a black boy who was brutally murdered in Mississippi on August 31, 1955, after whistling at a white woman (AP/Wide World Photos)

chapter in the book was a further articulation of this thesis, and at the heart of it was his concept of what he would soon call "Black Power."

Powell helped coin the term *Black Power* in a major address at Howard University on May 29, 1966. He was among the earliest proponents of the use of the word *black* to positively describe African Americans; he did so in his speeches and writings nearly two decades before it became widely used to signify racial pride among men and women of African descent. As early as 1945 Powell published *Marching Blacks: An Interpretive History of the Rise of the Black Common Man*, which attacked the Jim Crow South and urged southern African Americans to leave the region and go north.

The term *Black Power* had other and earlier proponents: Robert F. Williams, the North Carolina chapter leader of the National Association for the Advancement of Colored People, began using it in the 1950s, and the author Richard Wright published a book in 1954 entitled *Black Power*, referring to African nations seeking their indepen-

dence. But it was Stokely Carmichael of the Student Nonviolent Coordinating Committee who popularized the term, beginning in June 1966, a month after Powell's Howard University address and in direct response to the shooting of the black civil rights activist James Meredith in Mississippi. Powell's definition of Black Power, however, was different from Carmichael's, which went beyond racial pride and began calling for physical resistance to racial oppression.

Black Power, the movement immediately following the modern civil rights era, sought more radical changes in the United States regarding men and women of African descent. It connoted pride in being black, and its adherents used more militant language than that of civil rights activists. *Black Power* did not necessarily imply that violence should be adopted, but virtually from its inception in 1966 the term was taken in the press and by many younger black activists in the nation to mean advocating violence and animosity toward white people. In this context, Malcolm X's 1965 declaration that black people were entitled to respect and human rights "by any means necessary" (the title of his biography) was quickly interpreted to mean a call to violent action, if needed.

In this essay Powell offers his own view of Black Power. As he notes, "Black power is not anti-white. Black power incorporates everybody who wishes to work together, vote together and worship together.... Black power simply reaffirms the integrity, dignity and self-respect of black people. White supremacy denies them." Powell had gained power of his own largely through black (African American and West Indian) support—first in the Abyssinian Baptist Church, which his father had grown to a congregation of eight thousand strong before handing over its reins to the younger Powell, and then in the electoral arena as a public official. However, Powell also worked with people from other backgrounds, including Puerto Ricans, Jewish Americans, and a variety of other white European Americans. After all, Powell's congressional district was not solely black; moreover, in order to advance black civil and political rights, as the congressman knew all too well, one *had* to work with other groups of people.

But like so many others living in Harlem during the 1920s, Powell was greatly affected by the sense of black pride espoused by Marcus Garvey, the Jamaican immigrant and black nationalist who amassed the largest following of black people in the era. As a youth, Powell had watched in awe from rooftop, doorway, and street corner as Garvey's Universal Negro Improvement Association paraded through Harlem. Garvey's association had chapters across the United States as well as in Central America, the Caribbean, and Africa itself. Millions of men and women adhered to Garveyism, whether or not they were themselves members of his short-lived organization. While Powell was not a black nationalist, he would never forget the symbolism and organizational might that the association's men and women displayed—dignified and deeply inspiring.

Powell expressed his own sense of black pride by taking the fight for racial justice into the halls of government. He attempted to pass legislation attacking segregation and discrimination against black people. Whether addressing his congregation at the Abyssinian Baptist Church, people on the streets of Harlem, or black and white audiences elsewhere in the nation, he spoke as a proud man of African descent. He also spoke as a man of deep religious faith. He begins to outline his vision of Black Power in this essay by saying, "Black Power is, *first and foremost*, Godly power." He draws on biblical passages in Psalms (62:11) and II Timothy (1:7) in stating, "Without the hand of God in man's hand, there can be no coming together of black and white in this world."

Part of his message came as a response to the rioting and violence that had recently taken place in cities across the United States, among large and largely poor black populations. His version of Black Power remained nonviolent. He saw the creation of more jobs as the necessary response to economic exploitation and marginalization among African Americans. As he put it, "A man's respect for law and order exists in precise relationship to the size of his paycheck. Find jobs for the black jobless in our cities and the cooling breezes of employment will lower the hot temperatures in our streets." He advocated black economic autonomy but also pressed government to do its part. Toward this end, he demanded "a proportionate share of the responsibilities of running the communities, the cities and the states in which [we black people] live"—in other words, he was calling for greater black political representation in order to change public policy even as he sought black economic independence through community-based action.

◆ "Black Power and the Future of Black America"

Powell's autobiography, published a year before he died, culminates with his central thesis of Black Power. In the chapter "Black Power and the Future of Black America," he reflects on the assassinations of Malcolm X and Martin Luther King, Jr.—the two best-known African American figures of the era but who Powell felt were given undue attention next to his own legislative achievements. He speaks of King and Malcolm X as having needed correction by him, the elder statesman. With respect to Malcolm X, a leader of the Nation of Islam, Powell claims to have given him "a better understanding of his religion." Malcolm X, he says, "thought that Christianity was the white man's religion and that Islamism…was the black man's religion." He goes on to say, "I pointed to the Coptic cross in the Abyssinian Baptist Church and said to him, 'This is where Christianity began—in Ethiopia.'" Powell could even boast of having been visited in 1954 by the emperor of Ethiopia (historically called Abyssinia), Haile Selassie. A year after Selassie's visit, Powell attended the Bandung Conference in Indonesia, where leaders from more than two dozen African and Asian nations met to discuss how to support one another politically and economically.

Long influenced by the spirit of third world leaders coming together to combat colonialism and neocolonialism, Powell would call for a united front among black leaders, whom he saw as fragmented in their perspectives and organizing strategies. He notes,

The one point on which we can all definitely afford to agree is unity on the basis of desegregation, regardless of whether we are joining with Black Muslims, Black Panthers, or the Negro bourgeoisie. After desegregation is accomplished, then we can afford the luxury of differences among ourselves. BLACK POWER! BLACK POWER!

Six years earlier, in September of 1966, Powell had organized a Black Power conference in the District of Columbia. The group released a position paper to the press, calling for better voting rights protection, more money for predominantly black municipalities, and a more aggressive stance among those who sought electoral political action. If black Americans could unite at the leadership level, their constituencies could vote more powerfully and effectively.

Even while he calls for desegregation as a key uniting point, Powell acknowledges that "the Civil Rights Act of 1964 had absolutely no meaning for black people in New York, Chicago, or any of the Northern Cities. De jure school segregation, denial of the right to vote, or barriers to public accommodations are no longer sources of concern to Northern blacks." To northern blacks, civil rights "means more jobs, better education, manpower retraining, and development of new skills." Still, he continues to press the issue of desegregation as a unifying theme, but not without politically differentiating it from integration: "Blacks must distinguish between desegregation and integration. Desegregation removes all barriers and facilitates access to an open society. Integration accomplishes the same thing but has a tendency to denude the Negro of pride in himself. Blacks must seek desegregation, thereby retaining pride and participation in their own institutions."

Powell's distinction between desegregation and integration expressed his view of Black Power as a form of black political independence, highlighting the ability to command one's own terms in the face of black exploitation and discrimination. In his words, he sought to "negotiate for a share of the loaf of bread, not beg for some of its crumbs." Negotiation would require greater electoral power for Powell—indeed, for all black people. He had lived to see enormous power and authority himself. As chairman of the House Committee on Education and Labor from 1961 to 1967, he had controlled the flow of key legislation in Congress that secured $1.5 billion for antipoverty programs in a single year and boosted minimum wages for some 8.1 million Americans. For Powell, blacks stood at the "dawn of a new day."

Impact and Legacy

Less than a month before Powell died, the National Black Political Convention was held in Gary, Indiana. Black leaders gathered from across the nation to discuss the best possible course of action for black empowerment: increasing the number of African Americans elected to office via the Democratic Party, forming an all-black third party, or establishing a multiracial independent political party. Ultimately, the strategy that came out of the Gary convention was to increase black representation in the nation through the Democratic Party. Powell did not live to see that strategy unfold, but he set a precedent by serving as an independent voice of black empowerment in Harlem and Washington, D.C. And he did so long before the use of the term *black* came into vogue, before African Americans exercised power at the ballot on a national level, and before Black Power developed into a movement.

Key Sources

There is no single repository for the collected papers of Adam Clayton Powell, Jr. The Schomburg Center for

---

Essential Quotes

"*Tremendous changes are taking place in our country eradicating the concept of second-class citizenship. Yet the United States Congress has done absolutely nothing in this sphere. We are behind the times. We are a legislative anachronism. In an age of atomic energy, our dynamic is no more powerful than a watermill.*"

(Speech on Civil Rights)

"*Black power simply reaffirms the integrity, dignity and self respect of black people. White supremacy denies them.*"

("Black Power: A Form of Godly Power")

"*A man's respect for law and order exists in precise relationship to the size of his paycheck. Find jobs for the black jobless in our cities and the cooling breezes of employment will lower the hot temperatures in our streets.*"

("Black Power: A Form of Godly Power")

"*The one point on which we can all definitely afford to agree is unity on the basis of desegregation, regardless of whether we are joining with Black Muslims, Black Panthers, or the Negro bourgeoisie. After desegregation is accomplished, then we can afford the luxury of differences among ourselves. BLACK POWER! BLACK POWER!*"

("Black Power and the Future of Black America")

"*Blacks must distinguish between desegregation and integration. Desegregation removes all barriers and facilitates access to an open society. Integration accomplishes the same thing but has a tendency to denude the Negro of pride in himself. Blacks must seek desegregation, thereby retaining pride and participation in their own institutions.*"

("Black Power and the Future of Black America")

Research in Black Culture of the New York Public Library; the Lyndon B. Johnson Presidential Library in Austin, Texas; and Columbia University's Rare Book and Manuscript Library, New York, hold scattered materials written either by Powell or about him. The Schomburg Center has on microfilm *The People's Voice* (1942–1948), a newspaper that Powell published and edited; sermons delivered by Powell from 1939; Powell's FBI file; and the papers of the black Tammany official Herbert L. Bruce and Powell's first wife, Isabel Washington Powell, which provide insights into Powell's life. *Keep the Faith, Baby!* (1967) is a compilation of Powell's speeches and sermons from the 1960s. *Marching Blacks: An Interpretive History of the Rise of the Black Common Man* (rev. ed., 1973) is Powell's call to action for African Americans to secure their civil and political rights. At the end of his life, Powell wrote *Adam by Adam: The Autobiography of Adam Clayton Powell, Jr.* (rev. ed., 1994), in which he delineates his view of Black Power.

Further Reading

■ Articles

Capeci, Dominic J., Jr. "From Different Liberal Perspectives: Fiorello La Guardia, Adam Clayton Powell, Jr., and Civil Rights in New York City, 1941–1943." *Journal of Negro History* 62 (April 1977): 160–173.

McAndrews, Lawrence J. "The Rise and Fall of the Powell Amendment." *Griot* 12 (Spring 1993): 52–64.

Nutting, Charles B. "The Powell Case and Separation of Powers." *American Bar Association Journal* 54 (May 1968): 503–505.

Pollock, Art, "'My Life's Philosophy' Adam Clayton Powell's 'Black Position Paper'." *Journal of Black Studies* 4, no. 4 (June 1974): 457–462.

■ Books

Alexander, E. Curtis. *Adam Clayton Powell, Jr.: A Black Power Political Educator.* New York: ECA Associates, 1983.

Dionisopoulos, P. Allan. *Rebellion, Racism, and Representation: The Adam Clayton Powell Case and Its Antecedents.* DeKalb: Northern Illinois University Press, 1970.

Hamilton, Charles V. *Adam Clayton Powell, Jr.: The Political Biography of an American Dilemma.* New York: Atheneum, 1991.

Hapgood, David. *The Purge That Failed: Tammany v. Powell.* New York: Holt, 1959.

Haskins, James. *Adam Clayton Powell: Portrait of a Marching Black.* New York: Dial Press, 1974.

Questions for Further Study

1. In his speech on civil rights, Powell makes the following remark: "We are derelict in our duty if we continue to plow looking backward. No man is fit for this new world, for this new kingdom of God on earth, who plows looking backward." What does Powell mean by "plow looking backward," and how does his speech as a whole attempt to persuade legislators to look forward?

2. In "Black Power: A Form of Godly Power," Powell articulates a definition of "black power" that was generally interpreted to be a call for black activism and militancy. Although Malcolm X did not use this specific term in "Message to the Grass Roots" or his speech "The Ballot or the Bullet," he, too, articulated a vision of black empowerment. Compare Powell's "Black Power" with the documents of Malcolm X. How were the visions of black empowerment articulated by these two leaders similar and how did they differ?

3. In "Black Power and the Future of Black America," Powell distinguishes between integration and desegregation. What, according to him, is the difference between the two? Why does Powell argue for desegregation but place less emphasis on integration?

4. Some black civil rights leaders have stressed economic development in the African American community. Review Jesse Jackson's article "The Fight for Civil Rights Continues" and compare his views of black economic development with those of Powell in "Black Power: A Form of Godly Power" and "Black Power and the Future of Black America."

Haygood, Wil. *King of the Cats: The Life and Times of Adam Clayton Powell, Jr.* New York: Houghton Mifflin, 1993.

Hickey, Neil, and Ed Edwin. *Adam Clayton Powell and the Politics of Race.* New York: Fleet Publishing, 1965.

Jacoubek, Robert E. *Adam Clayton Powell, Jr.* New York: Chelsea House, 1988.

Lewis, Claude. *Adam Clayton Powell.* Greenwich, Conn.: Fawcett Publications, 1963.

Paris, Peter J. *Black Leaders in Conflict: Joseph H. Jackson, Martin Luther King, Jr., Malcolm X, Adam Clayton Powell, Jr.* New York: Pilgrim Press, 1978.

Weeks, Kent M. *Adam Clayton Powell and the Supreme Court.* New York: Dunellen, 1971.

■ **Web Sites**

"Adam Clayton Powell, Jr." Black Americans in Congress Web site. http://baic.house.gov/member-profiles/profile.html?intID=33.

"Powell, Adam Clayton, Jr. (1908–1972)." Biographical Directory of the United States Congress Web site. http://bioguide.congress.gov/scripts/biodisplay.pl?index=P0004 77.

—Omar H. Ali

Speech on Civil Rights (1955)

Mr. Speaker, the United States Congress is a 19th century body in a 20th century world. In the field of civil rights we are still conducting ourselves along the pattern of yesterday's world. Tremendous changes are taking place in our country eradicating the concept of second-class citizenship. Yet the United States Congress has done absolutely nothing in this sphere. We are behind the times. We are a legislative anachronism. In an age of atomic energy, our dynamic is no more powerful than a watermill.

The executive and the judicial branches of our Government have passed us by so completely and are so far ahead that the peoples of our Nation do not even look to the United States Congress any longer for any dynamic leadership in the field of making democracy real. So many changes, tremendous changes, have taken place under our Supreme Court and under the leadership of President Eisenhower that many of the civil rights bills which I used to introduce are no longer of any value. This year, for instance, I did not introduce the bill to abolish segregation in the Armed Forces—it was not needed. Nor did I introduce the bill to guarantee civil rights in the District of Columbia—it was not needed.

I think it highly significant to point out that the appointment of my distinguished colleagues, Representatives Diggs, of Detroit, Mich., and Dawson, of Chicago, Ill., to the Veterans' Affairs Committee and the District of Columbia Committee, respectively, was due entirely to the changing climate.

Two years ago the leadership of this House, Republican or Democrat, would not have dared to place a Negro on either of these two committees because both were committees which dealt with segregation.

Our Veterans' Administration rigidly maintained the bars of segregation, especially in our veterans' hospitals. Two years ago, this Capital was a cesspool of democracy where not only I, as a Negro congressman, was banned from a public places but also visiting chiefs of state and their representatives, if their skin happened to be dark. But under the vigorous leadership of H. V. Higley, Administrator of Veterans' Affairs, there is no longer any segregation in any veterans' hospital. And under the leadership of District Commissioner Samuel Spencer, from Mississippi, if you please, this Capital has become a glorious place, truly representative of the finest of our American way of life. And, again I repeat, all of this was done without the help of the Congress and oft times done in spite of the opposition of the Congress.

For 10 years, my colleagues and I have introduced civil rights amendment after amendment, civil rights bill after bill, pleading, praying that you good ladies and gentlemen would give to this body the glory of dynamic leadership that it should have. But you have failed and history has recorded it.

I am proud to be a Member of the Congress of the United States. I am proud to be a Member of the legislative branch of the United States Government and I know you are too. But I beseech you to transform this emotion of pride into the deed of leadership. This is an hour for boldness. This is an hour when a world waits breathlessly, expectantly, almost hungrily, for this Congress, the 84th Congress, through legislation to give some semblance of democracy in action. Our President and our Supreme Court cannot do all this by themselves and, furthermore, we should not expect it. We are derelict in our duty if we continue to plow looking backward. No man is fit for this new world, for this new kingdom of God on earth, who plows looking backward. And it is coming with or without us. Time is running out, ladies and gentlemen; Asia has almost slipped from our grasp and Africa will be next. There is no guaranty of our position in Europe. Only a resolute three-pronged drive can make democracy live, breathe, and move now. Only legislative, judicial and executive action can completely guarantee the victory of the free world.

The legislative branch—this Congress—must immediately change its childish, immature, compromising, 19th century attitude and not just become a part of the 20th century world but a leader.

Therefore I ask all of you, on both sides of the aisle, to support this year the bill to eradicate segregation in interstate transportation; to support the omnibus civil rights bill offered by Representative Emanuel Celler, chairman of the Judiciary Committee. Prompt hearings on these bills should be held immediately and swift passage with a minimum of friction should be brought about. We should have a bipartisan approach to domestic democracy or our bipartisan foreign policy approach will be utterly meaningless.

The fair employment opportunities bill did languish in the Committee on Education and Labor, of which I am a member, under the chairmanship of both the Republican and the Democratic leaders, and that should immediately be considered.

The opponents of a fair employment opportunities bill state that they do not believe that the Federal Government should intrude in States rights. I do not agree with them, but until such time as we do pass a national FEPC, I am introducing today an FEPC bill for the District of Columbia. There can be no argument of violation of States rights now. An FEPC bill for the District of Columbia would automatically allow this Congress to become a part of the glorious, victorious, forward march of our executive and judicial branches in the District of Columbia.

We who believe in civil rights urge first: Unity of thought and action for the passage of an interstate antisegregation bill to ban segregation on all interstate carriers. This bill has been introduced by the gentleman from Massachusetts, Representative Heselton. Also I have introduced a companion bill.

Last year when the House Committee on Interstate and Foreign Commerce was considering legislation to end segregation in interstate travel, a 29 year old witness appeared. He was Lt. Thomas Williams, formerly of the United States Air Force. Lieutenant Williams had volunteered for duty when he was 19 years old. He served in the Air Force with merit until 1953 when he was dropped following his arrest in the State of Florida because he refused to move from a so-called white section of an interstate bus. That young man, in the uniform of his country, was jailed and fined even though the United States Supreme Court had told carriers to end racial segregation. That case is still before the courts on appeal. After he was dropped by the United States Air Force, Lieutenant Williams was so eager to serve his country that he enlisted in the New Jersey National Guard. He served for nearly a year. About 2 weeks ago, while flying a jet plane, he was killed serving his country before he had a chance to see democracy come to pass.

We believe in the second place in unity of thought and action towards the passage of an omnibus civil-rights bill.

We believe in the third place in unity of thought and action for the passage of a fair employment opportunities act.

I would like to serve notice that some of us intend after a reasonable time of waiting for our committees and our committee chairmen to act to use every parliamentary device we can to bring before this Congress civil-rights bills of worth and value. We intend to use, after a reasonable period of time, Calendar

Glossary

Calendar Wednesdays	the day of the week designated by legislative procedure to allow committees to call up bills of their choice, designed to curtail in part the power of the Speaker of the House of Representatives to control the progress of legislation
discharge petitions	legislative means by which a congressional committee brings a bill out of committee to the floor of the House for consideration without a committee report and often without backing of the party leadership
President Eisenhower	Dwight D. Eisenhower, thirty-fourth president of the United States
Representative Emanuel Celler	congressman from New York
Representative Heselton	John Walter Heselton
Representative Dawson	William L. Dawson
Representative Diggs	Charles Coles Diggs, Jr.
"So let us be strong…"	Loose quotation from the poem "Be Strong" by Maltbie Davenport Babcock, a nineteenth-century American minister, poet, and writer of hymns

Wednesdays and discharge petitions. I trust that the leadership will give us cooperation and that we will not be stymied by the use of counter parliamentary methods to prevent us from bringing Calendar Wednesday forward.

On this day, when we bow our heads and hearts in the memory of one of the greatest human beings that ever lived, Franklin Delano Roosevelt, may we not use some of the breadth of his greatness in our hearts and minds, realizing those great words of his that "We have nothing to fear but fear."

"So let us be strong.
We are not here to play, to dream, to drift.
We have hard work to do, loads to lift.
Shun not the struggle that is God's gift.
Be strong. It matters not how deep entrenched the wrong.
Nor how hard the battle goes, nor the night how long.
Faint not, fight on.
Tomorrow will come the dawn."

"BLACK POWER: A FORM OF GODLY POWER" (1967)

In the last year and a half, a number of statements about "power" and, more recently, "black power" have been made by me.

Others have embraced the phrase "black power," more for their own misguided and selfish ends than in any sincere attempt to help the black masses.

Let me go back to March 28, 1965, when I spoke in Chicago and presented a "Black Position Paper for America's 20 million Negroes."

At that time I called for black people to seek "audacious power." Audacious power is the power that begins with the stand-up-and-be-counted racial pride in being black and thinking black. "I am black, but comely, O ye daughters of Jerusalem," said the peasant girl in the Song of Solomon.

On that same day, I outlined a seventeen-point plan for black people to build this "audacious power" within the Great Society. It was a kind of "Black Operation Bootstrap."

I urged black people to mobilize their political, economic, financial and educational power to build their communities into neighborhoods of excellence.

Then on May 29, 1966, in the baccalaureate at Howard University, I urged my people to pursue excellence and to purpose our lives to the fulfillment of divine-souled human rights instead of the narrow-souled civil rights.

I declared on that day: "To demand these God-given human rights is to seek black power, audacious power—the power to build black institutions of splendid achievement."

Thus the phrase "black power" was born.

What is "black power"?

"Black power" has come to mean whatever any newspaper columnist, editorial writer, civil rights leader or white racist wants it to mean.

One of America's great statesmen, A. Philip Randolph, talks in terms of "coalition power."

Phrased another way, it is called by my beloved friend Rev. Martin Luther King, Jr., "striped power." (I called Martin the other day and told him that stripes are found on striped pants, which are worn by Baptist preachers and zebras. And nobody can ride a zebra.)

The National Urban League's Whitney Young conceptualized "black power" as the "green power" of the pocketbook. And indeed he should, because what organization has derived more green power from the civil rights movement than the National Urban League—the Wall Street of the civil rights movement? It can be rightfully said that the National Urban League has made a "killing" on the civil rights stock market with the more than $1 million it receives in grants from the federal government.

That fiery young radical [Stokely] Carmichael sees "black power" as the fuse for rebellions in America's cities.

I cannot pretend to speak for what others interpret "black power" to mean.

I can only speak for Adam Clayton Powell. And in so doing, I only remind millions of black people of my thirty-six years of commitment to the cause of freedom for the black man.

First of all, black power is not anti-white.

Black power incorporates everybody who wishes to work together, vote together and worship together.

Is black power white supremacy in reverse?

Black power makes no moral judgment. But white supremacy does. Black power simply reaffirms the integrity, dignity and self-respect of black people. White supremacy denies them....

Black power is, *first and foremost*, Godly power. "God hath spoken once; twice have I heard this; that power belongeth unto God." (Psalms 62:11) "For God hath not given us the spirit of fear; but of power …" (II Timothy 1:7)

Without the hand of God in man's hand, there can be no coming together of black and white in this world. The deterioration of white power is its failure to incorporate God in its way of life.

Unless man is committed to the belief that all of mankind are his brothers, then he labors in vain and hypocritically in the vineyards of equality.

Second, black power is black pride—"I am black, but comely, O ye daughters of Jerusalem."

It is this pride, this belief in self and in the dignity of the black man's soul that Senegal President Leopold Senghor emphasizes when he speaks of *"la negritude"*.

To Senghor *"la negritude"* is the cry of an in-gathering for all black people to be proud of their black culture, their black roots. This is where "black power" also begins.

Third, black power is black initiative—the arousing of black people from fear and the sad fatigue of idleness to take the initiative by lifting themselves up and changing their lives through the mobilization of the energies of millions of black people in black communities all over America.

Fourth, black power is black productivity—the increase of black jobs for black men and women, the contribution of black people to the gross national product, the beautification of black neighborhoods, and the expansion of black businesses.

In the ashen wake of San Francisco's recent riots, Mayor Shelley made history by his honest assessment of the underlying causes of those riots. The mayor implored President Johnson by telegram, "in the name of God and all human decency," to provide federal funds for jobs in his city.

Those riots, as have so many of the riots in our big cities, confronted us all with the ugly reality of one inescapable fact: while unemployment for whites has continued to decline, unemployment for black people has risen in the last twelve months.

A man's respect for law and order exists in precise relationship to the size of his paycheck. Find jobs for the black jobless in our cities and the cooling breezes of employment will lower the hot temperatures in our streets.

Fifth, black power is black responsibility—the recognition by black people that they must demand and have a proportionate share of the responsibilities of running the communities, the cities and the states in which they live.

This responsibility is more than more black Congressmen, black mayors, or more city councilmen and state assemblymen. It is individual responsibility—an active involvement by each individual in the political, educational, religious and economic life of his community.

In this era of black power—a peaceful and constructive approach to the problems of black people—and the so-called white backlash—a fear-ridden and destructive reaction to these problems—I am hopeful that America can rediscover its democratic soul to forge a new togetherness among all its citizens.

Whites must join hands with blacks to achieve the full freedom of the Guaranteed Society because they are determined to get their full measure of freedom.

Glossary

A. Philip Randolph	prominent civil rights activist and founder of the Brotherhood of Sleeping Car Porters, a labor union
Great Society	name given to President Lyndon B. Johnson's program for social reform and reduction of poverty
Leopold Senghor	Léopold Sédar Senghor, poet, political thinker, and first president of Senegal
Mayor Shelley	John Shelley, mayor of San Francisco in September 1966, when race riots erupted after a police officer killed a black youth
National Urban League	civil rights organization founded in 1910 to promote economic self-reliance among African Americans
President Johnson	Lyndon B. Johnson, thirty-sixth president of the United States
Song of Solomon	a biblical book of the Old Testament, often called the Song of Songs or the Canticles
[Stokely] Carmichael	black nationalist leader of the Student Nonviolent Coordinating Committee
Whitney Young	civil rights leader and executive director of the National Urban League

"Black Power and the Future of Black America" (1971)

Every single black leader in America with a strong national following has been bought off, assassinated, imprisoned, or exiled. While I know I was not directly responsible, in a way I have a deep sense of guilt concerning the assassinations of Martin Luther King, Jr., and Malcolm X.

Martin Luther King came to see me once in Washington, bringing with him Ralph Abernathy. Chuck Stone, my administrative assistant, and the chief investigator of the Education and Labor Committee, were also present.

King and I talked for about three hours. I told him that the concept of total nonviolence had become outmoded. I reminded him that when Gandhi died, even Nehru, his closest follower, gave up the concept in the course of the fratricidal war between the Hindus and Moslems that resulted in the creation of Pakistan....

Malcolm X, one of the great minds we black people lost, was a dear friend of mine. As time went on we became extremely close because I was able to give him a better understanding of his religion. At the time we became acquainted he thought that Christianity was the white man's religion and that Islamism, or Muslimism, was the black man's religion. I pointed to the Coptic cross in the Abyssinian Baptist Church and said to him, "This is where Christianity began—in Ethiopia. It wasn't until A.D. 329 that Constantine recognized Christianity, but long before that there was the Coptic Church."

I also taught Malcolm that his concepts of Muslimism were incorrect, and I urged him to go to the Arab countries and if possible to Mecca to find out what Islam really was. This he did. After his return from Mecca he held a press conference at which he stated that he had found outstanding leaders of the Muslim religion who were white, with blue eyes and blond hair, and that he knew he had been wrong in his previous thinking on that point. Evidently his changed attitude did not find favor with all his followers because two months after this Malcolm X was assassinated....

Black people need to make a decision, however, before they achieve this unity of the majority—they need to decide what they are going to believe about integration and separatism. My own opinion is that we cannot afford the luxury of differences among ourselves now. But the one point on which we can all definitely afford to agree is unity on the basis of desegregation, regardless of whether we are joining with Black Muslims, Black Panthers, or the Negro bourgeoisie. After desegregation is accomplished, then we can afford the luxury of differences among ourselves.

BLACK POWER!

BLACK POWER!

During 1968, 1969, and 1970 I made more than one hundred speeches all over the United States. I spoke to entirely white audiences in the South and to entirely black audiences in the North. And I found that no phrase strikes more terror to the hearts of white Americans than Black Power.

Black Power was founded half a century ago by Marcus Garvey, the semiliterate immigrant from Jamaica, at whose feet I sat as a youngster and listened while he talked. I held the first National Black Power Conference in this Republic. Therefore I write with authority.

Black Power does not mean antiwhite unless whites make blacks antiwhite....

Black organizations must be black-led. To the extent to which black organizations are led by whites, to that precise extent is their black potential for ultimate control and direction diluted....

The black masses must demand and refuse to accept nothing less than that proportionate percentage of the political spoils, such as jobs, elective offices, and appointments, that are equal to their proportion of the population and their voting strength. They must reject the shameful racial tokenism that characterizes the political life of America today. Where blacks provide 20 percent of the vote, they should have 20 percent of the jobs....

Black people must support and push black candidates for political office first, operating on the principle of "all other things being equal." This is a lesson Chicago Negroes might well learn. In a primary in the heavily black Sixth Congressional District, Chicago black people actually elected a dead white man over a live black woman. A young white candidate, who had going for him only the fact that he was young and white, defeated an intelligent, dedicated black woman who was backed by all major civil rights groups for alderman in a predominately black ward.

Black leadership in the North and the South must differentiate between and work within the two-pronged thrust of the black revolution: economic self-sufficiency and political power. The Civil Rights Act of 1964 had absolutely no meaning for black people in New York, Chicago, or any of the Northern Cities. De jure school segregation, denial of the right to vote, or barriers to public accommodations are no longer sources of concern to Northern blacks. Civil rights in the North means more jobs, better education, manpower retraining, and development of new skills. As chairman of the House Committee on Education and Labor, I controlled all labor legislation, such as the minimum wage, all education legislation, including aid to elementary schools and higher education, the manpower training and redevelopment program, vocational rehabilitation, and, of greater importance today, the "War on Poverty." This is legislative power. This is political power. I use myself as an example because this is the audacious power I urge every black woman and man to seek—the kind of political clout needed to achieve greater economic power and bring the black revolution into fruition.

Black masses must produce and contribute to the economy of the country in strength proportionate to their population. We must become a race of producers, not consumers. We must rid ourselves of the welfare paralysis that humiliates our human spirit.

Black communities of this country—whether New York's Harlem, Chicago's South and West Sides, or Philadelphia's North Side—must neither tolerate nor accept outside leadership, black or white. Each community must provide its own local leadership, strengthening the resources within its own local community.

The black masses should follow only those leaders who can sit at the bargaining table with the white power structure as equals and negotiate for a share of the loaf of bread, not beg for some of its crumbs. We must stop sending little boys whose organizations are controlled and financed by white businessmen to do a man's job. Because only those who are financially independent can be men. This is why earlier I called for black people to finance their own organizations and institutions. In so doing, the black masses guarantee the independence of their leadership....

Glossary

Black Muslims	a name often given to members of the Nation of Islam, a black nationalist movement
Black Panthers	more formally, the Black Panther Party, a group formed in the 1960s to promote black power and black self-defense
Constantine	Emperor Constantine I, the first Christian Roman emperor
Coptic church	a branch of Christianity prominent in Egypt, dating from the fifth century
Coptic cross	a symbol of Jesus' Crucifixion and Resurrection in the Coptic Christian Church
cotillions	balls at which young women are presented to society
de jure	by law
Gandhi	Mohandas Gandhi, often called Mahatma Gandhi, leader of the independence movement in India
Malcolm X	born Malcolm Little, assassinated civil rights leader
Marcus Garvey	black nationalist and founder of the Universal Negro Improvement Organization
Mecca	city in Saudi Arabia and Islam's holiest site
Negro bourgeoisie	the black middle class
Nehru	Jawaharlal Nehru, the first prime minister of India after its independence from Great Britain
Ralph Abernathy	civil rights activist and leader of the Southern Christian Leadership Conference after the death of Martin Luther King, Jr.

Blacks must distinguish between desegregation and integration. Desegregation removes all barriers and facilitates access to an open society. Integration accomplishes the same thing but has a tendency to denude the Negro of pride in himself. Blacks must seek desegregation, thereby retaining pride and participation in their own institutions, just as other groups, the Jews, Irish, Italians, and Poles have done. Negroes are the only group in America that has utilized the world "integration" in pursuing equality....

Black people must discover a new and creative total involvement with ourselves. We must turn our energies inwardly toward our homes, our churches, our families, our children, our colleges, our neighborhoods, our businesses, and our communities. Our fraternal and social groups must become an integral part of this creative involvement by using their resources and energy toward constructive fund-raising and community activities. This is no time for cotillions and teas. These are the steps I urge all of America's 25 million black people to take as we begin the dawn of a new day by walking together. And as we walk together hand in hand, firmly keeping the faith of our black forebears, we glory in what we have become and are today.

Colin Powell (AP/Wide World Photos)

COLIN POWELL   1937–

U.S. Military Officer and Secretary of State

Featured Documents
- ◆ "U.S. Forces: Challenges Ahead" (1992/1993)
- ◆ Remarks to the United Nations Security Council (2003)
- ◆ Opening Remarks on Intelligence Reform before the Senate Governmental Affairs Committee (2004)

Overview

The son of Jamaican immigrants to New York City, Colin Powell is best known as the first black secretary of state, a post he held under President George W. Bush from 2001 to 2005. Prior to that, he served for thirty-five years in the U.S. military, a career that began in the Reserve Officer Training Corps at City College of New York and led to two tours of duty in Vietnam—a war that would shape his views of military objectives decades later. He climbed the ranks to become the nation's third black four-star general in 1989, following two years as national security adviser under President Ronald Reagan. He became chairman of the Joint Chiefs of Staff under President George H. W. Bush, a post he held from 1989 to 1993. His tenure included the first Gulf War, also known as Operation Desert Storm, and the mission that led to the war, Operation Desert Shield. Powell's pragmatism and reputation as a reluctant warrior made him one of America's most admired public officials, and he was even mentioned as a potential candidate for the U.S. presidency in the 1990s.

Beginning under the Reagan administration, Powell was credited with developing the "Powell doctrine." The military principles Powell called for, articulated in an influential article in *Foreign Affairs*, included the use of decisive force, the need for clear objectives, and a thorough understanding of risks. But many say that Powell's legacy was tarnished by his February 2003 speech before the United Nations, making the case for a U.S.-led war against Iraq. Soon afterward, most of the speech's key assertions were publicly discredited as based on faulty intelligence information. Nonetheless, the speech had succeeded in galvanizing public opinion in support of a March 2003 invasion of Iraq that led to a conflict not entirely resolved by the time of the 2008 presidential election. Powell offered his resignation in 2004, but not before proposing reform in the intelligence community to prevent the type of mistakes made in the framing of his own speech.

Explanation and Analysis of Documents

Colin Powell spent much of his adult life under fire. The firing began with his tours of duty in Vietnam and continued in the political arena when he arrived in Washington, D.C., to serve Presidents Ronald Reagan, George H. W.

Bush, and George W. Bush. Particularly during the two Bush presidencies, Powell was at the center of geopolitical events that would, for better or worse, reshape the Middle East and redefine American foreign policy in these regions. The mission assigned to him was to lead wars—as chairman of the Joint Chiefs of Staff under the elder Bush during the Gulf War and then as secretary of state under the younger Bush during the invasion of Iraq.

Powell, however, was by no means a military hawk. His experience in Vietnam made him something of a reluctant warrior, and consequently he found himself at odds with administration officials about the need for war and, after the conflicts were launched, how to prosecute them. Some of his most significant documents reflect this reluctance, or at least a moderate, cautious approach to the use of American military might. The three documents reproduced here trace the arc of Powell's career, from a highly regarded and trusted shaper of military policy, to a key architect of the 2003 Iraq war, to a chastened public official seeking to correct the intelligence mistakes of the administration under which he served.

◆ "U.S. Forces: Challenges Ahead"

At the time he wrote his article "U.S. Forces: Challenges Ahead" for *Foreign Affairs*, published in the winter 1992/1993 issue, Powell was credited with formulating the "Powell doctrine," but this was a term created primarily by journalists and one he did not use himself. It was a strategy for warfare largely based on principles held by the former secretary of defense Caspar Weinberger, to whom Powell reported during the Reagan administration. Its essential principles are that military action should be a last resort, that the war must be justified by a clear risk to national security, that the military force used should be decisive and overwhelming, that there must be public and international support for the use of force, and that there must be a clear exit strategy from the conflict. The doctrine was also influenced by Powell's own wartime experiences in Vietnam—a war fought without a clear objective or a clear exit strategy and, most significantly, with rapidly eroding support at home. The doctrine was further influenced by the disastrous action by U.S. Marines in Lebanon in 1983, sent there by President Ronald Reagan as part of an international peacekeeping force to help stabilize a new Lebanese government in a situation highly muddled by warring factions. These troops were then hastily withdrawn when it became

Time Line

1937
- **April 5**
  Powell is born in New York City.

1958
- **June**
  Powell graduates from City College of New York and receives his commission as a second lieutenant in the U.S. Army.

1962–1963
- Powell serves his first tour of duty in Vietnam as an adviser.

1968–1969
- Powell serves a second tour of duty in Vietnam.

1971
- Powell obtains a master's degree in business administration from George Washington University.

1987
- Powell is named deputy national security adviser.
- **November 23**
  Powell becomes national security adviser to President Ronald Reagan, serving until January 20, 1989.

1989
- **October 1**
  Powell becomes chairman of the Joint Chiefs of Staff.

1992/1993
- Powell publishes "U.S. Forces: Challenges Ahead" in *Foreign Affairs*.

1993
- **September 30**
  Powell retires from the U.S. military.

1997
- Powell, with his wife, Alma, founds America's Promise Alliance, to help socioeconomically disadvantaged youth.

clear that they were more targets than peacekeepers, especially after a terrorist truck bomb killed more than two hundred Marines and other service personnel on October 23, 1983. Conversely, the success of the Persian Gulf War (1990–1991) in liberating Kuwait after an unprovoked invasion by the Iraqi dictator Saddam Hussein became his model for a war with clearly defined objectives.

In his autobiography *My American Journey*, Powell recalled being upbraided by then Secretary of Defense Dick Cheney after raising questions during an early meeting about the Gulf War: "Before we start talking about how many divisions, carriers and fighter wings we need, I said, we have to ask, to achieve what end?" (p. 465), adding that he was seeking to avoid the docility the Joint Chiefs showed during the Vietnam War. "I was not sorry…that I had spoken out at the White House. What I had said about giving the military clear objectives had to be said" (p. 466). Years later, in the run-up to the 2003 Iraq war, Powell and others faced more intense criticism about why they had not pursued Iraqi forces to Baghdad and unseated Saddam in 1991. Powell's defense in his 1992 article was that removing the dictator would have created instability in the region and forced U.S. involvement for years to come. After the terror attacks on September 11, 2001, the second Bush administration came to view that involvement as an acceptable risk.

Powell opens his *Foreign Affairs* article by quoting one of his heroes, Abraham Lincoln, who, in his annual message to Congress in 1862, described America as "the last best hope of Earth." Lincoln's words became even more prescient following the collapse of the Soviet Union, the fall of the Berlin Wall, and the end of the cold war. America found itself the world's only superpower, and Powell found himself in charge of a reduced military force. He shaped a new national military strategy based on a "change from a focus on global war-fighting to a focus on regional contingencies." He could not foresee where U.S. forces would be needed next, but he notes hot spots and disputes, including the contentious relations of different ethnic groups on the borders of the old Soviet empire and the civil war in Somalia. This view of warfare was in part a result of an altered geopolitical landscape. Throughout most of the twentieth century, war planning was based on the use of massive armies, armed with heavy equipment and supported by air cover, to seize and hold territory. Later, nuclear weapons gave new meaning to the phrase "total war." Powell recognized that in a nuclear age it was highly unlikely that military planners would be called on to engage in the kind of war fought during World War II, particularly with the recent breakup of the Soviet Union and the collapse of the Soviet empire in Eastern Europe. Rather, the U.S. military would more likely be asked to fight limited wars in regional conflicts, requiring the use of more agile, quick-response forces.

Powell lays out the heart of his doctrine, which is based on questions that must be answered before the nation resorts to military force. "Relevant questions include: Is the political objective we seek to achieve important, clearly defined and understood? Have all other nonviolent policy means failed? Will military force achieve the objective? At what cost? Have the gains and risks been analyzed?" And then, crucially, Powell raises the question of an exit strategy: "How might the situation that we seek to alter, once it is altered by force, develop further and what might be the consequences?" If the political objective is sufficiently justified, risks are deemed acceptable, and if diplomatic and economic policies are insufficient alone, he writes, the decision to use military force must be accompanied by "clear and unambiguous objectives … given to the armed forces." When force is used, it must be overwhelmingly decisive, he adds, denouncing the idea of "surgical bombing or a limited attack."

Powell then turns to a summary of the new structure of a post–cold war military. Its focus, he writes, would be a "new emphasis on capabilities as well as threats." He means that forces should be sufficient to meet obligations around the globe, not one single threat from a superpower. He advocates a "Base Force" focused on the Atlantic and Pacific regions as well as a "contingency force" based in the United States, capable of responding to crises anywhere on the globe at a moment's notice. Nuclear capabilities, while greatly reduced, must remain in order to deter the use of nuclear force by other countries, he adds. Finally, Powell calls America's status in 1992 its "fourth rendezvous with destiny," borrowing a phrase Franklin D. Roosevelt had used in World War II. The first rendezvous was the American Revolution, the second was the Civil War, the third was World War II and the subsequent cold war, and the fourth, according to Powell, was the era of American military and economic leadership following the end of cold war, "a time of immense opportunity—an opportunity never seen in the world before."

◆ Remarks to the United Nations Security Council

Through most of his four-year tenure as U.S. secretary of state, Powell was one of the most highly regarded officials in the administration of President George W. Bush. Following the terror attacks of September 11, 2001, pressure mounted within the administration to target Iraq and its dictator, Saddam Hussein, whom Bush viewed as a supporter of terrorists and a cause of instability in the Middle East. Saddam's repeated defiance of UN weapons inspectors, coupled with intelligence reports suggesting that he was amassing weapons of mass destruction (biological, chemical, and nuclear weapons that kill indiscriminately) for use against the United States and its allies, led the administration to call for a preemptive war—a new form of war not tested in American history.

In December 2002, the National Security Council (the president's council of security advisers, including the vice president, the secretaries of defense, state, and the treasury, the chairman of the Joint Chiefs of Staff, and others) instructed the Central Intelligence Agency to prepare a public response to Iraq's declaration that it had no banned weapons. In late January 2003, intelligence officials learned that their work would form the basis for a speech Powell would give to the United Nations. Powell's high level of public credibility led him to be chosen to make the case for war in a climate where many of the world's leaders opposed the war and were skeptical of U.S. intentions. As Powell pre-

Time Line

2001

- **January 20**
  Powell is sworn in as the sixty-fifth U.S. secretary of state.

2003

- **February 5**
  Powell makes the case for the invasion of Iraq in a speech to the United Nations.

2004

- **September 13**
  Powell testifies before Senate Governmental Affairs Committee.

- **November 15**
  Powell announces his resignation as secretary of state, effective January 26, 2005.

pared to speak, he was aware of internal disagreements about the reliability of some intelligence reports he would use in the speech. He ordered aides to purge the speech of much of the evidence deemed questionable, but he never questioned the speech's basic premises.

Powell's speech outlined reasons the administration believed Saddam's regime was harboring weapons of mass destruction, relying on audiotapes, satellite images, and summaries of eyewitness accounts, all of which he shared with his listeners. In the excerpt reproduced here, he begins with reference to UN Resolution 1441, passed unanimously by the Security Council on November 8, 2002. This resolution gave Saddam Hussein "a final opportunity to comply with its disarmament obligations" under previous UN resolutions. Powell notes that in the months prior to the invasion of Iraq, the United Nations had dispatched weapons inspectors to Iraq either to find Hussein's weapons of mass destruction or to discover what he had done with them. American officials, and indeed the United Nations itself, had grown increasingly impatient with what was perceived as Saddam Hussein's lack of cooperation with the weapons inspectors.

Powell goes on to present evidence, first, that Saddam Hussein had biological weapons such as anthrax. He makes reference to the findings of UNSCOM—the United Nations Special Commission, the agency the United Nations had created to ensure Iraq's compliance with its disarmament obligations after the 1991 Gulf War. On the basis of this and other evidence, he paints a vivid picture of Iraq's biological weapons capabilities. He then turns to chemical weapons, pointing out that Saddam Hussein had used such weapons against his neighbors (principally Iran during the 1980s) and his own people. Finally, he takes up the issue of nuclear weapons, again putting forward evi-

U.S. forces examine a suspected mobile biological weapons facility in northern Iraq in late April 2003. No weapons of mass destruction were ever found in Iraq. (AP/Wide World Photos)

dence that the Iraqi dictator maintained a program to develop a nuclear capability.

Powell then remarks on the links between the Iraqi regime and terrorism. In particular, he traces alleged links between Iraq and al Qaeda, the terrorist organization led by Osama bin Laden that was responsible for the terrorist attacks against the United States on September 11, 2001. He notes that al Qaeda operated out of Afghanistan under the protection of the repressive Islamic Taliban regime in that country and that when al Qaeda was shopping for weapons of mass destruction, it turned to Iraq. Powell repeatedly asserts that the findings in the speech were based on "solid sources," which he had been convinced were true. Based on the intelligence accounts he had received, Powell was persuaded that one aspect of his own doctrine had been met: The use of diplomatic and economic sanctions had not been sufficient, and Saddam's defiance had escalated to a point where military force was justified. "Leaving Saddam Hussein in possession of weapons of mass destruction for a few more months or years is not an option, not in a post–September 11th world," he says in the speech's concluding paragraphs.

◆ **Opening Remarks on Intelligence Reform before the Senate Governmental Affairs Committee**

By September 2004 the Bush administration was proposing an overhaul of U.S. intelligence gathering to prevent the type of failures cited in an investigation of Powell's

2003 UN speech. As a result of that investigation, in July 2004 the Senate Select Committee on Intelligence released its "Report on the U.S. Intelligence Community's Prewar Assessments on Iraq," which devoted an entire section to discrediting many of the assertions Powell had made in his UN speech. On September 13, 2004, Powell appeared before the Senate Governmental Affairs Committee, chaired by Senator Susan Collins of Maine (referred to as "Madame Chairman"), to support the Bush administration's efforts to reform the intelligence community. He begins by joining Bush's call to appoint a national intelligence director (called "NID") and give the person in that role authority to determine the budgets for agencies included in the National Foreign Intelligence Program. This program, now called the National Intelligence Program, was not an agency, but the title referred collectively to the activities of the U.S. intelligence community. He also echoes aspects of his Powell doctrine as he explains his role as secretary of state, calling diplomacy—not military force—the "spear point for advancing America's interests around the globe" and the "first line of defense against threats from abroad." Serving diplomacy, he adds, must be the first priority of the intelligence community.

Powell goes on to try to give the committee a picture of the kinds of intelligence needs the secretary of state and other agencies have, arguing that it is crucial that intelligence units be "attuned to the specific requirements of the agencies they serve." He places considerable emphasis on objectivity and "competitive" analysis, in this way making a glancing reference to the intelligence failures associated with the Iraq War, often the result of excessive enthusiasm on the part of intelligence agencies to "prove" a foregone conclusion. He makes reference to "INR," or the Bureau of Intelligence and Research, an intelligence agency that is part of the U.S. State Department. He goes on to point out that while the agencies of the U.S. intelligence community do many things right, they are not very good at "critical self-examination." Again, Powell is suggesting that if the agencies had been better at objectively analyzing their findings, the United States could have avoided some of the mistakes it made in the invasion of Iraq. Overall, Powell expresses his support for an overhauled U.S. intelligence capability in which agencies work cooperatively, share information with one another, and coordinate their efforts. Indeed, many analysts believe that the terror attacks of September 11, 2001, might have been avoided had there been greater cooperation and coordination among intelligence agencies. Because of walls separating the agencies, with each agency pursuing its own investigations, vital pieces of information were not assembled; had they been assembled, the attacks might have been prevented.

During questioning from senators following his prepared remarks, Powell noted that no stockpiles of banned weapons had been found in Iraq, contrary to previous intelligence judgments. He went on to say that over the previous year he had found "some of the sourcing that was used to give me the basis upon which to bring that judgment to the United Nations were flawed, were wrong." He went on to say that "the sourcing had not been vetted widely enough across the intelligence community." What "distressed" him, he said, was that some members of the intelligence community "had knowledge that the sourcing was suspect and that was not known to me" (Pincus, p. A4).

Impact and Legacy

Colin Powell was a trailblazer as the first African American to hold many of the positions he occupied. But Powell did not want to be known for his accomplishments in the context of his race. He will be remembered as an architect of Operation Desert Storm and for helping to shape the post–cold war U.S. military. His article in *Foreign Affairs* was influential in helping move military thinking away from the wars of the past to focus on new threats that required a different kind of military response. But under the administration of George W. Bush, the Powell doctrine was no longer a driving force behind U.S. policy. His view of force as a last resort gave way to a view held by Bush, Vice President Dick Cheney, and others that military force should be used preemptively against foreign threats.

Powell's 2003 UN briefing on the Iraq threat overshadowed many of his other accomplishments. Following the speech's delivery, foreign ministers from the rest of the world reacted tepidly. The speech did not create a groundswell of international support for an invasion of Iraq. But it had a powerful domestic impact, playing a major role in winning support for the war among the American public. The invasion of Iraq succeeded in deposing Saddam Hussein, who was executed in 2006 after a tribunal convicted him of crimes against humanity. But after years of searching and thousands of American casualties, U.S. forces found no weapons of mass destruction. Worse for Powell, the intelligence reports he relied upon in preparing his speech quickly unraveled as being based on faulty information. And public revelations established that analysts had already raised objections to most of the data prior to Powell's speech. Some of those objections had never reached Powell. Powell, despite this setback, enjoyed numerous successes. As secretary of state, he was a key figure in persuading Pakistan to cooperate with U.S. counterterrorism actions in Afghanistan. He attained the largest increase in U.S. foreign aid since the Marshall Plan, the program that helped Europe get back on its feet after the destruction wrought by World War II. He focused attention on the global HIV/AIDs epidemic. Many world leaders hailed him as a moderate with a reputation for honesty and integrity.

Having been victimized by faulty intelligence, Powell was determined that future secretaries of state would not be. In part because of his efforts, Congress approved the Intelligence Reform and Terrorism Prevention Act in December 2004. The legislation created the position of director of national intelligence, who oversees the director of the Central Intelligence Agency. In addition, it renamed the Terrorist Threat Integration Center as the National Counterterrorism Center and placed it under the intelligence director's command. It also created the Privacy and Civil Liberties Oversight Board, which advises the executive branch on the effects of counterterrorism measures on American civil liberties.

Overall, assessments of Powell's career in Washington are mixed. His harshest critics accuse him of allowing himself to be a pawn in the Bush administration. They argue that he was not forceful enough as secretary of state, playing the part of good soldier and frequently acquiescing in his own marginalization by allowing himself to be outflanked by more hawkish figures, such as Vice President Dick Cheney and Defense Secretary Donald Rumsfeld. His supporters, however, contend that he was a moderating force in the Bush administration, frequently taking positions that were opposed to those of administration officials, including Bush himself. Although administration officials often rejected his views, those views became part of the debate and the national discussion about significant events.

Key Sources

Powell's autobiography, *My American Journey* (1995), was written with Joseph Persico and excerpted in the September 18, 1995, issue of *Time* (http://www.time.com/time/magazine/article/0,9171,983438,00.html). Other books by Powell include *In His Own Words: Colin Powell*, with Lisa

"When the political objective is important, clearly defined and understood, when the risks are acceptable, and when the use of force can be effectively combined with diplomatic and economic policies, then clear and unambiguous objectives must be given to the armed forces. These objectives must be firmly linked with the political objectives."

("U.S. Forces: Challenges Ahead")

"The gravity of this moment is matched by the gravity of the threat that Iraq's weapons of mass destruction pose to the world."

(Remarks to the United Nations Security Council)

"None of this should come as a surprise to any of us. Terrorism has been a tool used by Saddam for decades. Saddam was a supporter of terrorism long before these terrorist networks had a name, and this support continues. The nexus of poisons and terror is new. The nexus of Iraq and terror is old. The combination is lethal."

(Remarks to the United Nations Security Council)

"At the State Department, we are the spear point for advancing America's interests around the globe. We are also our first line of defense against threats from abroad. As such, our efforts constitute a critical component of national security."

(Opening Remarks on Intelligence Reform before the Senate Governmental Affairs Committee)

"The intelligence community does many things well, but critical self-examination of its performance, particularly the quality and utility of its analytical products is too often not one of them. Thousands of judgments are made every year, but we've got to do a better job of subjecting all of those judgments to rigorous post-mortem analysis to find out what we did right, as well as what we did wrong."

(Opening Remarks on Intelligence Reform before the Senate Governmental Affairs Committee)

Rogak (1995), and, with Joseph Persico, *A Soldier's Way: An Autobiography* (1995). Powell discussed the 2003 Iraq War in a 2007 interview with Jim Lehrer at the Aspen Institute, "Conversation with Colin Powell," which can be found at http://www.aifestival.org/library/transcript/Powell-Lehrer_transcript.pdf.

Further Reading

■ Articles

Cohen, Richard. "Powell's Flawed Exit Strategy." *Washington Post*, November 16, 2004.

Miller, Greg. "Flaws Cited in Powell's U.N. Speech on Iraq." *Los Angeles Times*, July 15, 2004.

Pincus, Walter. "Support for Intelligence Plan." *Washington Post*, September 14, 2004.

Wilson, Scott. "Reaction Mixed around the World; Some Disappointed by Powell's Departure, Others Welcome It." *Washington Post*, November 16, 2004.

■ Books

DeYoung, Karen. *Soldier: The Life of Colin Powell*. New York: Knopf, 2006.

Harari, Oren. *The Leadership Secrets of Colin Powell*. New York: McGraw-Hill, 2002.

Means, Howard B. *Colin Powell: Soldier/Statesman—Statesman/Soldier*. New York: D. I. Fine, 1992.

Roth, David. *Sacred Honor: A Biography of Colin Powell*. San Francisco, Calif.: HarperSan Francisco, 1993.

Steins, Richard. *Colin Powell: A Biography*. Westport, Conn.: Greenwood Press, 2003.

Weinberger, Caspar. *Fighting for Peace: Seven Critical Years in the Pentagon*. New York: Warner Books, 1990.

■ Web Sites

"Colin Powell's Legend." Consortium for Independent Journalism Web site.

http://ww`w.consortiumnews.com/archive/colin.html.

"Report of the Select Committee on Intelligence on the U.S. Intelligence Community's Prewar Intelligence Assessments on Iraq." GPO Access Web site.

http://www.gpoaccess.gov/serialset/creports/iraq.html.

—Leigh Dyer and Michael J. O'Neal

Questions for Further Study

1. In the late 1930s and through the 1940s, General George Marshall spoke publicly about the nation's needs to prepare for war in his speech to the American Historical Association on the National Organization for War, his speech to the Graduating Class of the U.S. Military Academy (1942), and his Washington's birthday remarks at Princeton University. Compare the nature of his recommendations with those of Colin Powell in his article "U.S. Forces: Challenges Ahead." How had the nature and threat of warfare changed in the decades between Marshall and Powell, and how did those changes require different responses?

2. In "U.S. Forces: Challenges Ahead," Powell outlines criteria that would validate the decision for the nation to go to war. In his remarks to the United Nations Security Council, he lays out a case against the regime of Saddam Hussein in Iraq, providing justification for the U.S.-led war against that regime. Which of the criteria for going to war, if any, do you believe Powell satisfied in his UN address?

3. In his remarks to the United Nations Security Council, Powell justifies going to war with Iraq not because Iraq's armed forces are directly threatening the United States or its allies but because Iraq, in his view, is governed by a regime that supports terrorism. Based on Powell's UN speech, discuss the extent to which fighting terrorism is a "war." Do justifications for fighting terrorism differ from those that might justify a more conventional war?

4. Traditionally the word *hawk* is used to refer to a person who is eager to go to war, while *dove* refers to one who is reluctant to go to war. Based on all three documents, would you classify Powell as a hawk or a dove? Or does his thinking fall somewhere between these two poles? Justify your response with passages from each of the documents.

"U.S. Forces: Challenges Ahead" (1992/1993)

America is a remarkable nation. We are, as Abraham Lincoln told Congress in December 1862, a nation that "cannot escape history" because we are "the last best hope of earth." The president said that his administration and Congress held the "power and...responsibility" to ensure that the hope America promised would be fulfilled. Today, 130 years later, Lincoln's America is the sole superpower left on earth....

In 1989, because of dramatic changes looming over the horizon, we began looking at how to restructure these high-quality armed forces without doing harm to their excellence; in fact, we wanted to improve them even further. Only a fortune-teller could have predicted the specific changes that occurred—the fall of the Berlin Wall, the demise of the Warsaw Pact, the failed coup in the Soviet Union and the eventual disappearance of that empire. But in the Pentagon we did recognize the unmistakable signs of change—the kind that leaves in history's dust those who cling to the past.

President Bush saw this historic change. Working together with his advisers, the president and the secretary of defense outlined a new national security strategy. In the Pentagon we took the new national security strategy and built a military strategy to support it. Then, in August 1990, as President Bush made the first public announcement of America's new approach to national security, Saddam Hussein attacked Kuwait. His brutal aggression caused us to implement our new strategy even as we began publicizing it. Every American was able to see our strategy validated in war.

Today there are other Saddam Husseins in the world. There is one in North Korea, and there is the original still in the Middle East—and no reason to believe his successor would be any different. Moreover, the instability and uncertainty that always accompany the fall of empires are growing rather than diminishing. In the Pentagon we believe our military strategy fits the world we see developing like a tight leather glove.

In the fall of 1992 we are fine-tuning that strategy, restructuring our armed forces so that they are ideally suited to executing it, and proposing a much-reduced multiyear defense budget to pay for it all....

The new national military strategy is an unclassified document. Anyone can read it. It is short, to the point and unambiguous. The central idea in the strategy is the change from a focus on global warfighting to a focus on regional contingencies. No communist hordes threaten western Europe today and, by extension, the rest of the free world. So our new strategy emphasizes being able to deal with individual crises without their escalating to global or thermonuclear war.

Two and a half years ago, as we developed the new strategy, we saw the possibility of a major regional conflict in the Persian Gulf—and it turned out we were right—and a major regional conflict in the Pacific, perhaps on the Korean peninsula, where the Cold War lingers on. We knew then, and we know now, that prudent planning requires that we be able to deal simultaneously with two major crises of this type, however unlikely that might be. In our judgment, the best way to make sure their coincidence remained unlikely was to be ready to react to both, so that if we were involved in one, no one would tempt us into the other.

Moreover we can see more clearly today that danger has not disappeared from the world. All along the southeastern and southern borders of the old Soviet empire, from Moldova to Tajikistan, smoldering disputes and ethnic hatreds disrupt our post–Cold War reverie. In the Balkans such hatreds and centuries-old antagonisms have burst forth into a heart-wrenching civil war. The scenes from Sarajevo defy our idea of justice and human rights and give new meaning to the word "senseless." In Somalia, relief operations are underway amid the chaos and anarchy of another civil war that wracks our idea of justice, human rights and the rule of law. Ruthless warlords make money from donated food and medical supplies. Relief workers are threatened if they do not comply with a local dictator's whims....

To help with the complex issue of the use of "violent" force, some have turned to a set of principles or a when-to-go-to-war doctrine. "Follow these directions and you can't go wrong." There is, however, no fixed set of rules for the use of military force. To set one up is dangerous. First, it destroys the ambiguity we might want to exist in our enemy's mind regarding our intentions. Unless part of our strategy is to destroy that ambiguity, it is usually helpful to keep it intact....

When a "fire" starts that might require committing armed forces, we need to evaluate the circumstances. Relevant questions include: Is the political objective we seek to achieve important, clearly defined and understood? Have all other nonviolent policy means failed? Will military force achieve the objective? At what cost? Have the gains and risks been analyzed? How might the situation that we seek to alter, once it is altered by force, develop further and what might be the consequences?

As an example of this logical process, we can examine the assertions of those who have asked why President Bush did not order our forces on to Baghdad after we had driven the Iraqi army out of Kuwait. We must assume that the political objective of such an order would have been capturing Saddam Hussein. Even if Hussein had waited for us to enter Baghdad, and even if we had been able to capture him, what purpose would it have served? And would serving that purpose have been worth the many more casualties that would have occurred? Would it have been worth the inevitable follow-up: major occupation forces in Iraq for years to come and a very expensive and complex American proconsulship in Baghdad? Fortunately for America, reasonable people at the time thought not. They still do.

When the political objective is important, clearly defined and understood, when the risks are acceptable, and when the use of force can be effectively combined with diplomatic and economic policies, then clear and unambiguous objectives must be given to the armed forces. These objectives must be firmly linked with the political objectives. We must not, for example, send military forces into a crisis with an unclear mission they cannot accomplish—such as we did when we sent the U.S. Marines into Lebanon in 1983. We inserted those proud warriors into the middle of a five-faction civil war complete with terrorists, hostage-takers and a dozen spies in every camp, and said, "Gentlemen, be a buffer." The results were 241 dead Marines and Navy personnel and a U.S. withdrawal from the troubled area.

When force is used deftly—in smooth coordination with diplomatic and economic policy—bullets may never have to fly. Pulling triggers should always be toward the end of the plan, and when those triggers are pulled all of the sound analysis I have just described should back them up.

Over the past three years the U.S. armed forces have been used repeatedly to defend our interests and to achieve our political objectives....

The reason for our success is that in every instance we have carefully matched the use of military force to our political objectives. We owe it to the men and women who go in harm's way to make sure that this is always the case and that their lives are not squandered for unclear purposes.

Military men and women recognize more than most people that not every situation will be crystal clear. We can and do operate in murky, unpredictable circumstances. But we also recognize that military force is not always the right answer. If force is used imprecisely or out of frustration rather than clear analysis, the situation can be made worse.

Decisive means and results are always to be preferred, even if they are not always possible. We should always be skeptical when so-called experts suggest that all a particular crisis calls for is a little surgical bombing or a limited attack. When the "surgery" is over and the desired result is not obtained, a new set of experts then comes forward with talk of just a little escalation—more bombs, more men and women, more force. History has not been kind to this approach to war-making....

Because of the need to accomplish a wide range of missions, our new armed forces will be capabilities oriented as well as threat oriented. When we were confronted by an all-defining, single, overwhelming threat—the Soviet Union—we could focus on that threat as the yardstick of our strategy, tactics, weapons and budget. The Soviet Union is gone. Replacing it is a world of promise and hope—exemplified by the former Soviets themselves as they struggle mightily to make a transformation that the world has never witnessed before. But the U.S.-Soviet standoff imposed a sort of bipolar lock on the world and, in many ways, held the world together. That lock has been removed. Now tectonic plates shift beneath us, causing instability in a dozen different places.

In a few cases, such as Korea and southwest Asia, we can point to particular threats with some degree of certainty; otherwise, we cannot be exact. Most of us anticipated very few of the more than a dozen crises our armed forces have confronted in the past three years. That will not change. We must be ready to meet whatever threats to our interests may arise. We must concentrate on the capabilities of our armed forces to meet a host of threats and not on a single threat. This is a very different orientation. It is so different that some of us have trouble adapting to it; we are so accustomed to the past. Indeed most of our lives were dedicated to the old way of thinking. But in the Department of Defense I believe we have made great progress in changing to this new emphasis on capabilities as well as threats.

Conceptually we refer to our new capabilities-oriented armed forces as "the Base Force." This concept provides for military forces focused on the Atlantic region, the Pacific region, contingencies in other regions and on continued nuclear deterrence.

Across the Atlantic—in Europe, the Mediterranean and the Middle East—America continues to have vital interests. We belong to the most effective alliance in history, NATO. In light of the changes that have taken place in Europe, NATO has revamped its strategic outlook and restructured its forces as dramatically as we have our own....

In 1990 we deployed massive U.S. forces to the Persian Gulf. Using those forces in 1991 we fought an overwhelmingly decisive war. We did this to liberate Kuwait and to strip a regional tyrant of his capacity to wage offensive war and thus destabilize the region. With two-thirds of the world's oil reserves in the region, this action was certainly in our vital interest.

Nothing has changed about the importance of the Middle East. What has changed is that Kuwait is free, oil is flowing and Saddam Hussein threatens no one outside his own borders. A U.S. military presence is crucial to ensuring that this stability continues.

American forces in the Atlantic region—on land and at sea—are part of our conceptual package of Atlantic forces. Also part of that package are forces based in the United States whose orientation is

Glossary

Baghdad	the capital city of Iraq
Balkans	a mountainous geographical region of southeastern Europe and the site of numerous modern conflicts
Cold War	term used to denote the ideological struggle and threat of war between the Western powers, including the United States, and the Communist nations led by the Soviet Union
demise of the Warsaw Pact	end of the military alliance of Central and Eastern European Communist states in July 1991
failed coup in the Soviet Union	reference to the efforts of hard-liners in the government of the Soviet Union to seize power from President Mikhail Gorbachev in August 1991
fall of the Berlin Wall	reference to the opening of the wall separating West Berlin from Communist East Berlin in November 1989; symbol of the end of Communism
hegemony	dominance
NATO	North Atlantic Treaty Organization, a defense pact whose members at the time included the United States and the nations of Western Europe
one in North Korea	reference to Kim Il-sung, the president at the time of North Korea
Pentagon	U.S. Department of Defense headquarters in Virginia, often used as a figure of speech to refer to the nation's defense establishment
post–Cold War reverie	the "dream" of world peace after the collapse of the Soviet Union and the apparent end of the cold war
President Bush	President George H. W. Bush, the forty-first U.S. president
proconsulship	governorship
Saddam Hussein	president of Iraq who ordered the invasion of Kuwait in 1990, leading to the First Gulf War
Somalia	a nation in East Africa torn by civil war in the 1990s
surgical bombing	limited bombing designed to destroy precisely defined targets
tectonic plates	reference to the earth's landmasses, which move over time, suggesting the notion of the ground shifting

toward the Atlantic; should a crisis in the region demand more forces than we have forward-deployed, these forces would reinforce then as rapidly as possible.

In our Base Force we have provided for the same sort of conceptual force package focused on the Pacific region. There too America continues to have vital interests, our security relationships with Japan and the Republic of Korea being at the top of the list.

We have also provided for what we call a "contingency force package." Troops and units in this conceptual package will be located in the United States and be ready to go at a moment's notice. The time from their alert to their movement will be measured in hours and minutes, not in days.

Finally, we provided for a conceptual package of strategic nuclear forces. Notwithstanding the historic reductions proposed for the world's strategic nuclear stockpile, when and if these reductions are complete, we will still have nuclear weapons in the world. We must continue to deter the use of these weapons against America or its friends and allies. This can only be done with a modern, capable and ready nuclear force. We will rely heavily on the most secure leg of our nuclear triad, the ballistic missile submarines. But we will maintain a resilient and capable triad with forces in the other two legs as well, manned bombers and land-based ballistic missiles....

Today, unlike that December day in 1862 when President Lincoln spoke to Congress, the prospects for America are anything but bleak. It is true we have substantial economic challenges facing us, as well as a burning need to reaffirm some of our basic values and beliefs. But if Lincoln were alive today, I do not believe he would trade December 1992 for December 1862.

I believe Mr. Lincoln would be especially excited by the prospects that now lie before his nation. Only three times in our history have we had a "rendezvous with destiny," as President Franklin D. Roosevelt called our challenge in World War II. The American Revolution was one such historical moment because it gave birth to America. The Civil War was another because it made our revolution complete; it made America what it is today. World War II, as Roosevelt so clearly recognized, and the Cold War that followed—which he could not see—combined to provide us the third such occasion. These two wars cleansed the world of tyrannies bent on hegemony and began the spread of democracy and free markets and, as the Soviet Union finally disappeared, accelerated their spread at a dizzying rate.

The summons to leadership that we face at present is our fourth rendezvous with destiny. Answering this summons does not mean peace, prosperity, justice for all and no more wars in the world—any more than the American Revolution meant all people were free, the Civil War meant an end to racial inequality, or World War II and our great victory in the Cold War meant the triumph of democracy and free markets. What our leadership in the world does mean is that these things have a chance. We can have peace. We can continue moving toward greater prosperity for all. We can strive for justice in the world. We can seek to limit the destruction and the casualties of war. We can help enslaved people find their freedom. This is our fourth rendezvous with destiny: to lead the world at a time of immense opportunity—an opportunity never seen in the world before. As Lincoln said in 1862, America could not escape history. In 1992, we must not let history escape us.

REMARKS TO THE UNITED NATIONS SECURITY COUNCIL (2003)

Iraq has now placed itself in danger of the serious consequences called for in UN Resolution 1441. And this body places itself in danger of irrelevance if it allows Iraq to continue to defy its will without responding effectively and immediately.

This issue before us is not how much time we are willing to give the inspectors to be frustrated by Iraqi obstruction. But how much longer are we willing to put up with Iraq's non-compliance before we as a Council, we as the United Nations say, "Enough. Enough."

The gravity of this moment is matched by the gravity of the threat that Iraq's weapons of mass destruction pose to the world. Let me now turn to those deadly weapons programs and describe why they are real and present dangers to the region and to the world.

First, biological weapons. We have talked frequently here about biological weapons. By way of introduction in history, I think there are just three quick points I need to make. First, you will recall that it took UNSCOM four long and frustrating years to pry, to pry an admission out of Iraq that it had biological weapons. Second, when Iraq finally admitted having these weapons in 1995, the quantities were vast. Less than a teaspoon of dry anthrax, a little bit—about this amount. This is just about the amount of a teaspoon. Less than a teaspoon full of dry anthrax in an envelope shut down the United States Senate in the fall of 2001.

This forced several hundred people to undergo emergency medical treatment and killed two postal workers just from an amount, just about this quantity that was inside of an envelope.

Iraq declared 8,500 liters of anthrax. But UNSCOM estimates that Saddam Hussein could have produced 25,000 liters. If concentrated into this dry form, this amount would be enough to fill tens upon tens upon tens of thousands of teaspoons. And Saddam Hussein has not verifiably accounted for even one teaspoonful of this deadly material. And that is my third point. And it is key. The Iraqis have never accounted for all of the biological weapons they admitted they had and we know they had.

They have never accounted for all the organic material used to make them. And they have not accounted for many of the weapons filled with these agents such as there are 400 bombs. This is evi-

dence, not conjecture. This is true. This is all well documented....

There can be no doubt that Saddam Hussein has biological weapons and the capability to rapidly produce more, many more. And he has the ability to dispense these lethal poisons and diseases in ways that can cause massive death and destruction.

If biological weapons seem too terrible to contemplate, chemical weapons are equally chilling....

Saddam Hussein has chemical weapons. Saddam Hussein has used such weapons. And Saddam Hussein has no compunction about using them again—against his neighbors and against his own people. And we have sources who tell us that he recently has authorized his field commanders to use them. He wouldn't be passing out the orders if he didn't have the weapons or the intent to use them....

Let me turn now to nuclear weapons. We have no indication that Saddam Hussein has ever abandoned his nuclear weapons program. On the contrary, we have more than a decade of proof that he remains determined to acquire nuclear weapons.

To fully appreciate the challenge that we face today, remember that in 1991 the inspectors searched Iraq's primary nuclear weapons facilities for the first time, and they found nothing to conclude that Iraq had a nuclear weapons program. But, based on defector information, in May of 1991, Saddam Hussein's lie was exposed. In truth, Saddam Hussein had a massive clandestine nuclear weapons program that covered several different techniques to enrich uranium, including electromagnetic isotope separation, gas centrifuge and gas diffusion....

My friends, the information I have presented to you about these terrible weapons and about Iraq's continued flaunting of its obligations under Security Council Resolution 1441 links to a subject I now want to spend a little bit of time on, and that has to do with terrorism.

Our concern is not just about these illicit weapons; it's the way that these illicit weapons can be connected to terrorists and terrorist organizations that have no compunction about using such devices against innocent people around the world.

Iraq and terrorism go back decades. Baghdad trains Palestine Liberation Front members in small arms and explosives. Saddam uses the Arab Liberation Front to funnel money to the families of Palestinian suicide bombers in order to prolong the Intifadah. And it's no secret that Saddam's own intelligence service was involved in dozens of attacks or attempted assassinations in the 1990s....

And the record of Saddam Hussein's cooperation with other Islamist terrorist organizations is clear. Hamas, for example, opened an office in Baghdad in 1999 and Iraq has hosted conferences attended by Palestine Islamic Jihad. These groups are at the forefront of sponsoring suicide attacks against Israel.

Al-Qaida continues to have a deep interest in acquiring weapons of mass destruction....I can trace the story of a senior terrorist operative telling how Iraq provided training in these weapons to al-Qaida.

Fortunately, this operative is now detained and he has told his story. I will relate it to you now as he, himself, described it.

This senior al-Qaida terrorist was responsible for one of al-Qaida's training camps in Afghanistan. His information comes firsthand from his personal involvement at senior levels of al-Qaida. He says bin Laden and his top deputy in Afghanistan, deceased al-Qaida leader Mohammed Atef, did not believe that al-Qaida labs in Afghanistan were capable enough to manufacture these chemical or biological agents. They needed to go somewhere else. They had to look outside of Afghanistan for help.

Where did they go? Where did they look? They went to Iraq. The support that this detainee describes

Glossary

al-Qaida	an Arabic name that means literally "the base"; an Islamic terrorist group responsible for the terrorist attacks on the United States of September 11, 2001
Arab Liberation Front	a faction of the Palestinian Liberation Organization, a militant group based in Palestine
Baghdad	the capital city of Iraq
bin Laden	Osama bin Laden, the founder and leader of al Qaeda
clandestine	secret, hidden
conjecture	speculation, guesswork
electromagnetic isotope separation	a process that uses magnets to enrich uranium
enrich uranium	the process of extracting from the element uranium the isotopes that are fissionable, that is, useful for atomic energy or nuclear weapons
gas centrifuge	a method of enriching uranium that relies on centripetal force
gas diffusion	often called gaseous diffusion, a method of enriching uranium that forces isotopes of uranium through membranes to separate atoms
Hamas	a militant Islamist Palestinian group, part political party and part military organization
Intifadah	an Arabic word that literally means "shaking off" but is usually translated as "uprising" or "rebellion" and most commonly used to refer to Palestinian resistance to Israeli rule
liters	metric units of measurement equal to approximately a quart
Palestine Islamic Jihad	a Palestinian militant organization, more formally, the Islamic Jihad Movement in Palestine
Palestine Liberation Front	a Palestinian militant group
post–September 11 world	changes in Western defense and security postures after the terrorist attacks on the United States of September 11, 2001
Saddam Hussein	president of Iraq

included Iraq offering chemical or biological weapons training for two al-Qaida associates beginning in December 2000. He says that a militant known as Abdullah al-Araqi had been sent to Iraq several times between 1997 and 2000 for help in acquiring poisons and gasses. Abdullah al-Araqi characterized the relationship he forged with Iraqi officials as successful.

As I said at the outset, none of this should come as a surprise to any of us. Terrorism has been a tool used by Saddam for decades. Saddam was a supporter of terrorism long before these terrorist networks had a name, and this support continues. The nexus of poisons and terror is new. The nexus of Iraq and terror is old. The combination is lethal.

With this track record, Iraqi denials of supporting terrorism take their place alongside the other Iraqi denials of weapons of mass destruction. It is all a web of lies.

When we confront a regime that harbors ambitions for regional domination, hides weapons of mass destruction, and provides haven and active support for terrorists, we are not confronting the past; we are confronting the present. And unless we act, we are confronting an even more frightening future....

We know that Saddam Hussein is determined to keep his weapons of mass destruction, is determined to make more. Given Saddam Hussein's history of aggression, given what we know of his grandiose plans, given what we know of his terrorist associations, and given his determination to exact revenge on those who oppose him, should we take the risk that he will not someday use these weapons at a time and a place and in a manner of his choosing, at a time when the world is in a much weaker position to respond?

The United States will not and cannot run that risk for the American people. Leaving Saddam Hussein in possession of weapons of mass destruction for a few more months or years is not an option, not in a post–September 11 world.

Opening Remarks on Intelligence Reform before the Senate Governmental Affairs Committee (2004)

I am pleased to have this opportunity to share with you my thoughts on the reform of the intelligence community. I have been a consumer of intelligence in one way or another throughout my 40 plus years of public service: From the tactical level on the battlefield as a second lieutenant, to the highest levels of the military, as Chairman of the Joint Chiefs of Staff, National Security Advisor, and now, as Secretary of State. And I hope that I can offer some helpful insights from the perspective of the conduct of America's foreign policy....

Madam Chairman, let me say at the outset that I fully support President Bush's proposals on intelligence reform. A strong national intelligence director is essential. That strength is gained primarily by giving the NID real budget authority. In that regard, the President's proposal will give the NID authority to determine the budgets for agencies that are part of the National Foreign Intelligence Program....

The President's proposal will require important changes to the 1947 National Security Act, changes I know that members of this committee will be looking at carefully. An example of such a change would be the plan to establish the new position of the Director of CIA and to define the possibilities of that agency, responsibilities that will continue to include the authority for covert action and the need to lead in the area of HUMINT collection....

As you and the other members of this committee in the Congress are reviewing the President's proposal, and as you are considering what final product of your very important deliberations will actually be, I would ask that you take into account the unique requirements of the Secretary of State and the Department of State and of the conduct of foreign policy for which I am responsible to the President and to the American people.

Let me give you some insights, if I may, on why the Secretary of State's needs are somewhat unique, but why they, too, would be well served by such reform as President Bush has proposed.

Diplomacy is both offensive and defensive in its application. At the State Department, we are the spear point for advancing America's interests around the globe. We are also our first line of defense against threats from abroad. As such, our efforts constitute a critical component of national security....

The needs of diplomacy require more than a good ability to imagine the worst. They require real expertise, close attention and careful analysis of all source information. To be helpful to me and my colleagues in the Department of State, many of whom are extremely knowledgeable about the countries and issues they cover, the intelligence community must provide insights and add value to the information that we already collect through diplomatic channels. When the intelligence community weighs in with less than this level of expertise, it is a distraction rather than an asset....

To do my job, I need both tailored intelligence support responsive to, indeed, able to anticipate my needs, and I need informed, competitive analysis. Precisely because my intelligence needs differ from those of the Secretary of Defense or the Secretary of Homeland Security or the Secretary of Energy, not to mention the unique requirement of our military services, I'm not well served, nor are they, by collectors and analysts who do not understand my unique needs, or who attempt to provide a one-size-fits-all assessment....

Any reorganization of the intelligence community must preserve and promote intelligence units that are attuned to the specific requirements of the agencies they serve. Such units should be designed to ensure their independence and objectivity, but at the same time be sufficiently integrated into the parent organization to ensure intimate understanding of what is needed, when it is needed, and how it can most effectively be presented to policy makers. That's the relationship that I have with INR.

My INR must be able to recruit and retain genuine experts able to provide real value to the policy making process. This requires appropriate and different career paths and training opportunities. We need specialists in INR, not generalists: Late-evening relief pitchers and designated hitters, not just utility infielders. For example, INR is in close touch with all of our embassies, in close touch with the regional bureau chiefs of the Department of State....

What I need, as Secretary of State, is the best judgment of those most knowledgeable about the problem. INR and the Department of State, more broadly, are home to many specialists who are experts on topics of greatest concern to those charged with implementing the President's foreign policy agenda.

But INR is too small to have a critical mass of expertise on almost anything. INR and the Secretary of State need comparable and complimentary expertise elsewhere in the intelligence community....

Let me make one other point, Madame Chairman, the intelligence community does many things well, but critical self-examination of its performance, particularly the quality and utility of its analytical products is too often not one of them. Thousands of judgments are made every year, but we've got to do a better job of subjecting all of those judgments to rigorous post-mortem analysis to find out what we did right, as well as what we did wrong. When we did something wrong, why did we do it wrong, to make sure we don't do it wrong again. We have to have alternative judgments in order to make sure that we are getting it right....

As you know, President Bush has issued an Executive Order to improve the sharing of information on terrorism. We need to extend its provisions to intelligence on all subjects. In this regard, simple but critical guidelines would include separation of information on sources and methods from content so that content can be shared widely, easily and at minimal levels of classification. For this to work, collectors must have clear ways to indicate the degree of confidence that the information is reliable and user friendly procedures for providing additional information for those who need it....

Similarly, decisions on who needs information should be made by agency heads or their designees not collectors. Every day I am sent information that can be seen only by a small number of senior policymakers who often cannot put the reports in the proper context or fully comprehend their significance. Intelligence is another name for information, and information isn't useful if it does not get to the right people in a timely fashion.

Glossary

1947 National Security Act	the act signed by President Harry S. Truman that, among other things, established the National Security Council to oversee and coordinate U.S. intelligence gathering
CIA	the Central Intelligence Agency, the chief U.S. organization responsible for gathering overseas intelligence
HUMINT	abbreviation for human intelligence, or intelligence gathering through contact with people rather than through technology
INR	the Bureau of Intelligence Research, a component of the U.S. State Department that analyzes intelligence information
post-mortem	literally, "after death," used here to mean "afterward," that is, following an event or operation
President Bush	George W. Bush, the forty-third U.S. president

Ronald Reagan (Library of Congress)

RONALD REAGAN

1911–2004

Fortieth President of the United States

Featured Documents
- ◆ "A Time for Choosing" Speech (1964)
- ◆ Remarks at the Republican National Convention (1976)
- ◆ First Inaugural Address (1981)
- ◆ "Evil Empire" Speech (1983)
- ◆ Letter to the American People about Alzheimer's Disease (1994)

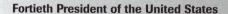

Reagan, Ronald

Overview

As president, Ronald Reagan earned a reputation as the "Great Communicator" because he conveyed ideas in striking, vivid, and memorable ways. While he was president from 1981 until 1989 and for several years afterward, many people attributed his success as a speaker mainly to his experience as an actor in films and on television. There was another important reason, however, why Reagan became the "Great Communicator": He often wrote the words that he read so effectively. The release of his personal and presidential papers beginning in the late 1990s revealed that Reagan wrote extensively. He was an avid correspondent, kept a diary during his White House years, and penned some of the most memorable speeches that he gave as private citizen, governor of California, and president. He often revised speeches that staff assistants prepared, replacing their drafts with pages he wrote in longhand on yellow legal pads. Reagan preferred to use his own words when he could because, as he said soon after leaving the White House, "I came with a script" (Cannon, p. 771). He meant that he brought to the presidency a set of core convictions—opposition to high taxes, mistrust of big government, abhorrence of Communism, and an abiding faith in the goodness of the American people—that shaped his outlook throughout his years in politics. His ideas resonated with so many of his fellow citizens because he expressed them with a simplicity and sincerity that made people believe the best about themselves and their nation.

Reagan was born on February 6, 1911, in Tampico, Illinois, into a poor family that moved several times before settling in Dixon, Illinois. Despite the hardships of his youth, Reagan developed a strong sense of optimism that he carried with him throughout his life. His mother, a member of the Christian Church (Disciples of Christ), taught him that everything occurred according to God's plan. Reagan graduated from Eureka College in 1932, when the Great Depression was most severe, yet he still found a job as a sports announcer at a radio station in Davenport, Iowa. Sports announcing soon allowed Reagan to embark on a movie career. In 1937 he signed a contract with Warner Bros. Pictures, and he gave solid performances mainly in what were then called B movies, low-budget films that were the second halves of the double features that commonly played in the-

aters. Between April 1942 and December 1945, Reagan served in the Army Air Forces and made official films connected to the U.S. war effort during World War II.

After the war, as his film career declined, Reagan became involved in politics. Between 1947 and 1952 he was president of the Screen Actors Guild, a union that represented performers in film and television. As the cold war emerged and fears about Communist influence in the motion picture industry rose, Reagan testified before the House Un-American Activities Committee in 1947 and provided names of alleged Communists to the Federal Bureau of Investigation. Although he had been a liberal Democrat, his politics became more conservative, especially after he began working for General Electric (GE) in 1954. He was the host of the weekly television drama series *General Electric Theater*, and he also spoke at GE plants around the country. His talks became increasingly political, as he developed those core convictions that shaped his thinking on public issues. In 1962 he registered as a Republican. Four years later he made his first run for office, winning the governorship of California; he gained a second term in 1970. Reagan left the governor's mansion in 1975 and challenged President Gerald R. Ford for the Republican nomination for president in 1976. Ford won a narrow victory over Reagan but lost the election to Jimmy Carter. In 1980 Reagan easily secured his party's nomination and overwhelmed Carter in November.

As president, Reagan proposed sweeping changes in both domestic and foreign policy. Reagan's first priority when he took office on January 20, 1981, was to lift the nation's economy out of stagflation, a severe and persistent combination of high inflation and unemployment. Reagan secured cuts in income tax rates, reductions in federal economic regulations, and decreases in the rate of spending on social welfare programs. Although the economy fell into a severe recession during 1981–1982, it recovered the following year, with inflation falling to its lowest level in more than a decade. Reagan also made drastic changes in national security policies. He persuaded Congress to approve sharp increases in defense spending, which he said were necessary to protect against Soviet efforts to gain power and influence around the world. Reagan easily won reelection in 1984, and during his second term there was a remarkable improvement in Soviet-American relations after Mikhail

Time Line

1911
- **February 6**
  Ronald Reagan is born in Tampico, Illinois.

1932
- **June 7**
  Reagan graduates from Eureka College.

1942
- **April 19**
  Reagan begins active duty in the Army Air Forces with the First Motion Picture Unit at Culver City, California, serving until December 9, 1945.

1964
- **October 27**
  Reagan's campaign speech for the presidential candidate Barry Goldwater, "A Time for Choosing," is broadcast on national television.

1966
- **November 8**
  Reagan is elected governor of California.

1976
- **August 19**
  Reagan addresses the Republican National Convention in Kansas City, Missouri.

1981
- **January 20**
  Reagan is sworn in as president and delivers his first inaugural address.

1983
- **March 8**
  In Orlando, Florida, Reagan gives his "evil empire" address to a meeting of the National Association of Evangelicals.

1984
- **November 6**
  Reagan wins a second term as president by defeating the Democratic candidate, Walter Mondale.

Gorbachev came to power in Moscow in 1985. Reagan and Gorbachev held several meetings, established a cooperative relationship, negotiated important treaties, and made progress in ending the cold war. Despite the Iran-Contra scandal over the provision of arms to secure the release of U.S. hostages in Middle East and the illegal support of counterrevolutionaries in Nicaragua, Reagan left office a popular president in January 1989. He died of complications related to Alzheimer's disease on June 5, 2004.

Explanation and Analysis of Documents

Important documents spanning Reagan's three decades as a prominent figure in national politics reveal his abiding convictions and the reasons he became known as the "Great Communicator." His campaign speech for Barry Goldwater marked Reagan's debut in national politics in 1964 and made him a leader of the conservative movement, and his remarks at the Republican National Convention in 1976 inspired supporters, at a moment of defeat, to hope for eventual victory. After Reagan achieved that triumph in the election of 1980, his first inaugural address outlined many of the principles and policies that would guide his presidency in domestic affairs. His "evil empire" speech of 1983 emphasized the importance of moral values, especially in the cold war struggle between the United States and the Soviet Union. In 1994, almost six years after leaving the presidency, Reagan retired from public life in a simple and moving letter and reminded the American people one last time that their country's best days were still ahead.

◆ "A Time for Choosing" Speech

On October 27, 1964, millions of viewers saw a familiar figure in an unfamiliar role when Reagan appeared that evening on the National Broadcasting Company television network urging voters to support the Republican nominee for president, Senator Barry Goldwater of Arizona. Most Americans who knew Reagan as an actor did not realize that he had become increasingly involved in politics during the previous decade as he toured the country as a corporate spokesperson for GE. In speeches at meetings of business associations and civic organizations on what he called "the mashed potato circuit," Reagan extolled the success of big business and warned of the dangers of big government (Reagan, 1965, p. 263). His speeches reflected GE's corporate philosophy, but the views were Reagan's own as he moved away from the liberal Democratic positions he had embraced when he arrived in Hollywood. In 1964, after Reagan had given a speech at a Goldwater fund-raising event in Los Angeles, a group of wealthy Republican campaign contributors asked whether he would be willing to repeat his remarks on national television. Reagan agreed, and he gave the speech once more before an audience of Republicans who gathered in the network's studio.

Reagan begins by telling his audience that the Goldwater campaign has not provided him with a text; his words and ideas are his own. Reagan had actually given a version of this speech dozens of times before as he toured the country for GE. Because he disliked flying, Reagan often traveled by train to his speaking engagements and used that time to read extensively, refine his ideas, and incorporate new arguments and anecdotes into his talks. By 1964 "the Speech," as he called it, was polished, his delivery poised, and his message persuasive to conservative audiences. "A Time for Choosing" explains why voters should support Goldwater for president, but it makes that case by summarizing the main political principles that Reagan adopted as he became a conservative.

Reagan tries to encourage voters to back Goldwater by using himself as an example of a lifelong Democrat who had recently switched parties. He tells his audience that Democratic policies had created an illusory peace and a false prosperity. He insists that high taxes, budget deficits, and the eroding value of the dollar threaten the health of the economy. Reagan also maintains that because of the cold war struggle with the Soviet Union and its allies, "we're at war with the most dangerous enemy that has ever faced mankind in his long climb from the swamp to the stars." He asserts that the United States is a beacon of hope to people around the world who yearn for liberty and a refuge for those who seek to escape the oppression of Communist dictatorships.

As he often did in his speeches or writings, Reagan connects these specific issues to a fundamental principle. The most important question that the American people face in the election of 1964, Reagan declares, was not whom they should support for president—Goldwater or the Democratic nominee, President Lyndon B. Johnson. At issue was whether Americans could preserve "the freedoms that were intended for us by the Founding Fathers." The alternatives Reagan poses are stark: either up to the dream of "the ultimate in individual freedom consistent with law and order, or down to the ant heap of totalitarianism." There is no middle ground. Reagan was calling attention to what he believed were the dangers of liberal reform programs, which had become common in American life since the New Deal of President Franklin D. Roosevelt during the Great Depression of the 1930s. Many Americans supported the New Deal and its successors, such as Johnson's Great Society, because these programs protected them against economic hardships or improved their quality of life. Yet Reagan maintains that liberals, however well intentioned, were trading liberty for security and following the "downward course" toward totalitarianism. Their programs required a powerful "centralized government,... the very thing the Founding Fathers sought to minimize." Reagan thinks it is time for choosing. Either "we believe in our capacity for self-government or...we abandon the American revolution and confess that a little intellectual elite in a far-distant capitol can plan our lives for us better than we can plan them ourselves."

Reagan then offers a variety of examples of government regulatory and reform programs that had gone awry. He had learned from his years on the "mashed potato circuit" that such vivid examples helped persuade listeners to accept his arguments. The examples and statistics support-

Time Line

1987
- **December 8**
  Reagan and Mikhail Gorbachev sign the Intermediate-Range Nuclear Forces Treaty in Washington, D.C.

1994
- **November 5**
  Reagan informs the American people that he has been diagnosed with Alzheimer's disease.

2004
- **June 5**
  Reagan dies from complications of Alzheimer's disease in Los Angeles, California.

ed his contention that big government is inefficient, wasteful, and dangerous. Reagan maintains that the architects of many federal programs had forgotten something that the Founders keenly understood—"that outside of its legitimate functions, government does nothing as well or as efficiently as the private sector of the economy." He discusses programs that grow ever larger, such as those to aid foreign nations, to illustrate what he claims are the difficulties of controlling big government. "A government bureau," he declares, "is the nearest thing to eternal life we'll ever see on this earth." Reagan also believed that new government powers came at the expense of personal liberties, and claims here that "proliferating bureaus and ... regulations" have endangered constitutional safeguards and threatened private property. Once more he returns to his main theme that liberal proponents of government regulation had started the country down the road to Socialism. "Freedom has never been so fragile, so close to slipping from our grasp as it is at this moment," he asserts.

Reagan next charges that the advocates of big government at home threatened American security abroad. Just as liberal domestic policies were leading the United States toward Socialism, liberal international policies were increasing the danger of "surrender" in the cold war. In the final paragraphs of his address, Reagan tries to turn the tables on critics of Goldwater and other hardline anti-Communists who insisted that the United States should take strong action, including the use of nuclear weapons, to defeat Communist foes. Reagan instead maintains that the real threat to national security comes from liberal advocates of social welfare programs who desired an accommodation with the Soviet Union that was tantamount to appeasement. That charge was inflammatory, since *appeasement* is a word that evokes memories of Western leaders who tried to limit the expansion of Nazi Germany in the 1930s by meeting some of Adolf Hitler's demands for the territory of neighboring countries. Reagan refused to

President Gerald Ford, First Lady Betty Ford, Senator Bob Dole, and Elizabeth Dole celebrate winning the nomination amidst floating balloons at the Republican National Convention, Kansas City, Missouri. (Library of Congress)

accept the legitimacy of Communist rule, and he insists that there must not be any agreement aimed at reducing cold war tensions that compromises the chances for freedom of those people "enslaved behind the Iron Curtain." Once more he connects current policy issues to the principles of the Founders when he approvingly quotes Alexander Hamilton: "A nation which can prefer disgrace to danger is prepared for a master, and deserves one."

Even though he raises gloomy and even frightening prospects, Reagan, as he usually did, ends his speech on a note of optimism. What set him apart from many other conservatives of the 1960s was his faith that the American people would make the right choices and that their strength and wisdom would ultimately prevail. Reagan looked to the past to provide hope for the future. He closes by borrowing from the famous phrases of two presidents. The first is from Franklin D. Roosevelt, who told the American people during the grim days of the depression, in 1936, that they had "a rendezvous with destiny." The second is from Abraham Lincoln, who wrote in 1862 that during the Civil War, the Union was "the last best hope of earth."

Reagan's speech was a hit. It produced a flood of contributions to the Goldwater campaign in the week before the election. Those donations and Reagan's spirited appeal for votes, however, could not keep Goldwater from losing in a landslide to President Johnson. Because Goldwater carried only six states and just 39 percent of the popular vote, many observers thought the conservative movement had suffered a disastrous defeat. Yet because he had demonstrated that he was thoughtful, articulate, personable, and engaging, Reagan attracted the attention of some wealthy Republicans in California who were certain that he could carry his conservative message to victory. In 1966 Reagan made his first run for public office, winning election as governor of California. Many of the proposals that made him popular with California voters, such as reducing taxes, cutting welfare costs, and protecting private property, were the same ones he had emphasized in his 1964 speech. Overall, then, "A Time for Choosing," turned out to be a remarkably successful speech not for Goldwater, but for Reagan.

◆ Remarks at the Republican National Convention

Although Reagan usually delivered his best speeches when relying on a written text, he gave one of his most inspiring talks when he spoke extemporaneously at the Republican National Convention in Kansas City, Missouri. Reagan addressed the convention on August 19, 1976, just a day after he had narrowly lost his party's presidential nomination to President Gerald R. Ford. Reagan decided to challenge Ford for the nomination in 1976 because he doubted the strength of Ford's conservative convictions. Reagan and Ford waged a vigorous battle in the primaries and at state conventions, and the victor was uncertain until the delegates voted in Kansas City. After accepting the nomination, Ford invited Reagan to address the convention. Some observers thought that the speech would be Reagan's valedictory—a farewell to presidential politics, since, at age sixty-five, he would be too old to make another bid for his party's presidential nomination.

Reagan begins with a call for Republicans as well as Democrats and independents to rally behind the platform his party had adopted. He praises the platform for its "bold, unmistakable colors, with no pastel shades." The colors appealed to him because his campaign staff had chosen many of them. In order to promote party unity, the Ford forces had made concessions on many issues, or platform planks, that were important to Reagan. In this speech, Reagan asserts that these positions provide a clear alternative to the liberal views that Democrats had embraced since the 1930s.

Reagan next uses his experience of writing a letter for a time capsule as a way of discussing two issues that were vital to him and many of his conservative supporters. The first is individual freedom, which he maintains—as he had in "A Time for Choosing"—had eroded while Democrats controlled Congress and the White House. The second is the danger of nuclear war. Reagan warns of the risks to "the civilized world" that arise from the nuclear missiles that "the great powers have poised and aimed at each other." Implicit in his discussion is his concern about the threat to

U.S. security that the Soviets posed, as well as his uneasiness with the doctrine of mutual assured destruction that protected Americans from nuclear war. According to this doctrine, neither Soviets nor Americans would launch a nuclear attack because each one knew that its adversary would have sufficient strength to retaliate. Reagan thought that there should be a more reliable way of preventing all-out war than the vulnerability of millions of people to nuclear devastation.

He explains the importance of the issues of freedom and defense by connecting the decisions that Americans were making in 1976 to future generations. He often said that Americans were custodians of values that they had inherited from the Founders of their republic. In this speech, he reminds his fellow citizens that their choices will have consequences a century later. He wonders whether the Americans who will open the time capsule will "look back with appreciation" because "we met our challenge" by preserving individual liberty and averting "nuclear destruction."

In closing, Reagan appeals to Republicans to carry their message to the American people. On the surface, he seems to be urging Republicans to elect their candidates, including Ford, in November. Yet conservatives who supported Reagan heard a very different message, one that Reagan surely intended. They believed he was calling on them to carry their principles to victory within the Republican Party. His final quotation, from General Douglas MacArthur, the commander of U.S. forces during most of the Korean War, implies that conservatives should not be content with compromises. Reagan's remarks inspired conservatives to work even harder to secure the nomination and election of candidates who embraced their ideas. Reagan's stirring presentation also suggested that he had not closed the door to one more campaign for the Republican presidential nomination. Before he left Kansas City, Reagan told some convention delegates that he and his wife, Nancy, were not going back to California to "sit on our rocking chairs and say, 'That's all for us'" (Reagan, 1990, p. 203). This speech, then, provided hope for a conservative movement that was gaining power in the Republican Party and to those who wanted Reagan to lead it to victory.

◆ First Inaugural Address

In his first speech as president, Reagan combined a long-term vision with a plan for immediate action. Reagan wanted to explain the convictions that shaped his political thinking—the ideas that he had embraced even before his speech for Goldwater in 1964—and that would guide his presidency. He also wanted to tell the American people that his top priority was restoring the health of the economy. When Reagan became president, the "misery index"—the total of the unemployment rate and the rate of inflation—exceeded 20 percent. Reagan wanted to show how his most basic political principles could offer solutions to the nation's economic ills, and he asked his aide Kenneth Khachigian to write a first draft of his address. While he retained some of Khachigian's ideas and words, Reagan made many changes in the original draft. What Reagan

said to the American people after he took the oath of office on January 20, 1981, was thoroughly his own.

In this speech, Reagan wastes little time addressing what he calls "an economic affliction of great proportions." He describes the corrosive effects of high inflation and unemployment, explains that their causes reach back several decades, and calls for action "today in order to preserve tomorrow." His most important, and most memorable, assertion is that "in this present crisis, government is not the solution to our problem; government is the problem." Reagan had been saying something very similar for decades. He asserts once more that government often serves its own interests rather than those of the people who grant its powers.

Although he provides no details about the economic policies his administration will follow, Reagan promises to "curb the size and influence of the Federal establishment" in order to remove "the roadblocks that have slowed our economy and reduced productivity." The main problem with the economy, in his view, is that government has stifled the productivity of workers and has impeded the innovation of entrepreneurs. Reagan, in short, says that his abiding belief in a maximum of individual freedom and a minimum of government regulation would be the key to reopening the door to prosperity.

The depth and duration of the country's economic problems had demoralized many people, but Reagan, as usual, predicts a bright future. Americans, he says, control their own destiny, and it was time "to begin an era of national renewal." He encourages his fellow citizens to "dream heroic dreams," and he lauds the everyday heroes in factories, on farms, and in businesses. The courage, strength, and determination of the American people would eventually triumph, and he pledges that "your dreams, your hopes, your goals are going to be the dreams, the hopes, and the goals of this administration."

Reagan also counted on the courage and commitment of the American people to protect their nation from foreign adversaries. He predicts that reform at home would strengthen America's reputation "as a beacon of hope for those who do not now have freedom." Once more he repeats that peace is precious, but freedom is even dearer.

Reagan closes by using a keen sense of place to surmount the barriers of time and to connect past and present—the sacrifices of yesterday with the challenges of today. He notes that the inauguration ceremony was occurring for the first time on the West Front of the Capitol, which faces the monuments to George Washington, Thomas Jefferson, and Abraham Lincoln, and, in the distance, the markers where fallen heroes rest at Arlington National Cemetery. Reagan tells the story of one veteran, Martin Treptow, whose wartime diary recorded his determination to sacrifice and endure. He used that story even though he knew that Treptow was buried in Wisconsin, not at Arlington. Reagan thought the story was too good to eliminate or to alter by mentioning the location of Treptow's grave. It provided a moving, theatrical conclusion to a speech in which Reagan asks his fellow Americans "to believe in ourselves and to believe in our capacity to perform great deeds." Reagan thought that on the political stage, just as on the movie set, writers and performers were entitled to some artistic license.

The inaugural address and additional efforts to mobilize public support helped persuade Congress to pass Reagan's economic program, which reduced individual income tax rates and cut the budgets of some social programs. Reagan maintained that the tax cuts would stimulate the economy, but within weeks of their passage a steep recession began, and the president's popularity plunged. In 1983 the economy recovered, inflation declined, and when Reagan ran for reelection in 1984, his campaign commercials proclaimed that it was "morning again" in America. Economists still debate how much Reagan's tax and budget cuts contributed to the recovery and how much the monetary policies of the Federal Reserve System and the chair of its board of governors, Paul A. Volcker, were responsible for squeezing inflation out of the economy. Reagan, however, was convinced that the tax cuts were the key to the economic expansion that continued until after he left the White House. Throughout his presidency Reagan firmly held to the ideas about individual freedom, government power, and economic policy that he had expressed in his first inaugural address.

◆ "Evil Empire" Speech

When Reagan spoke to the National Association of Evangelicals (NAE) in Orlando, Florida, on March 8, 1983, he used the memorable term *evil empire* to describe the Soviet Union. It was powerful language that in Reagan's view explained why the United States had been locked in a cold war with the Soviets since the end of World War II. Those words were not Reagan's but White House speechwriter Anthony Dolan's. Reagan, however, extensively revised Dolan's draft, and the final version of this speech reflected his outlook and included many of his own words.

Despite that memorable phrase, this speech was not mainly about the cold war, the Soviet Union, or international affairs. It was an address about moral values, how they underlay American democracy, and how many political disagreements were at bottom moral conflicts. Reagan spoke at a time when his defense and foreign policies divided the American people. His hard-line policies won considerable praise, but they also produced anxiety and even alarm, especially as arms control negotiations stalled and international tensions rose. The president hoped to persuade the members of the NAE and other Christian conservatives to support his national security policies, as they had his social policies.

Reagan began by trying to establish a rapport with his audience, members of the NAE, an organization that had been founded in 1942 and, four decades later, had 3.5 million members with strong religious views. He tells them that he often prayed and was grateful for all the prayers for success. He then uses humor, as he frequently did in his talks, to win over his audience. In this case, the humor is partly at his own expense, as the joke is about a politician

who is trying to reach heaven. "You have to understand how things are up here," Saint Peter declares. "We've got thousands and thousands of clergy. You're the first politician who ever made it." But after the laughter, Reagan asserts that many political leaders, himself included, based their political thinking on religious conviction. At the end of this opening section, Reagan introduces the speech's major idea, explaining that American democracy thrived because of widespread faith in God.

In the next section of his address, Reagan warns that the traditional values that he and the members of the NAE cherish are facing formidable challenges. The president concentrates on three controversies to make his point. The first involves the provision of contraceptives to young women at federally funded clinics. Reagan presents this issue as one of federal "bureaucrats and social engineers" depriving parents of control of their children and, in so doing, turning sexual activity into a "purely physical" matter rather than a moral choice. Once more, as he had in previous speeches, the president asserts that government officials harmed rather than helped ordinary Americans.

The president next discusses the controversy over the exclusion of prayer from public schools. The Supreme Court had ruled in 1962 that mandatory school prayer was unconstitutional. The president and many evangelical Christians who supported him, including members of the NAE, favored a constitutional amendment that would give students the opportunity to participate in voluntary prayer during the school day. Reagan's third example of declining morality concerns the volatile issue of abortion. In 1973, in the case of *Roe v. Wade*, the Supreme Court had ruled that a woman had a right to abortion during her first three months of pregnancy and that states could restrict access to abortion at later stages of pregnancy. For millions of Americans, abortion was a moral issue. Many insisted that abortion was a private choice for a woman, her family, and her physician that involved her health and well-being and control of her body. Many others, including the president and the NAE, maintained that abortion involved the taking of human life. The issues of birth control for young women, school prayer, and abortion could be discouraging, Reagan tells his audience, because they suggested a decline in the nation's morality.

Still Reagan sees reason for hope. In the next section of his address, the president cites evidence of "a great spiritual awakening." He declares that American history is a "story of hopes fulfilled and dreams made into reality." This idea was central to Reagan's understanding of the American nation and what it represented. He thought that the United States was a unique experiment in freedom, a beacon of hope to people around the world, and a society that allowed people to achieve their potential. As usual, when Reagan looked to the future, he was an optimist.

Reagan next shifts from domestic to international affairs, as he concentrates on the cold war struggle with the Soviet Union. He contends that the U.S.-Soviet struggle was not only a conflict over power or security or a competition between different economic or social systems. He declares that it was primarily a moral contest between two nations with fundamentally different values. Reagan explains that the United States sought cooperation with the Soviets, but not at the cost of "our principles and standards" or "our freedom." He was replying to critics who complained that his defense buildup and strong condemnations of Communism during his first two years in the White House had worsened Soviet-American relations. Reagan suggests that those who disagree with his Soviet policies are like the appeasers of the 1930s, who did not understand that Nazi Germany was a totalitarian nation with unlimited ambitions for aggressive expansion.

The proposal for a freeze of U.S. and Soviet nuclear arsenals jeopardized national security, according to the president. The nuclear freeze movement gathered momentum in the early 1980s, drawing support from concerned citizens who thought that the U.S. and Soviet governments should stop adding to their nuclear arsenals as a first step toward controlling the arms race. In this speech Reagan asserts that the freeze proposal, while simple and appealing, is deceptive and dangerous. In the president's view, a freeze would allow the Soviets to retain superiority in some categories of nuclear weapons. In addition, a freeze could lead only to an illusory peace, since it would not change Soviet values, ideology, or ambitions. Reagan told his audience in Orlando something that he had said in "A Time for Choosing" and that he repeated often during his presidency: Peace would come only through strength.

Reagan next shifts back to a comparison of U.S. and Soviet morality. Those who enforced totalitarian dominance in the Soviet Union and Eastern Europe by denying individual rights such as the freedom to worship are "the focus of evil in the modern world." This discussion of evil culminates in the famous phrase that gave this address its popular title.

Reagan then calls the members of the NAE, as people of the church, to a moral crusade. Just as they fought evils at home—such as the exclusion of prayer from public schools and the corrupting effects of abortion—so they should rally against international evil by supporting administration efforts to defeat a nuclear freeze proposal that could benefit only the Soviet Union and the totalitarianism it sought to extend. He urges his listeners to place the debate about a nuclear freeze in the context of the cold war "struggle between right and wrong and good and evil." One nation, as Reagan previously explained, was an inspiration for freedom-loving people the world over or, as the president often said, "a shining city upon a hill." The other was "an evil empire."

Reagan, as usual, ends his address on a hopeful note. He reiterates that the real battle in the United States and the world is a moral conflict. The victor will not be the side with superior military strength but the one with greater spiritual resolve. Reagan predicts that the forces of freedom will prevail, as he declares, "I believe that communism is another sad, bizarre chapter in human history whose last pages even now are being written." Ultimately, religious conviction, cooperation, and common purpose, in the words of Thomas Paine, the famous writer from the era of the American Revolution, will enable Americans "to begin the world over again."

"Evil empire" became a convenient way of summarizing Reagan's views about the Soviet Union, but it did not explain the improvement in Soviet-American relations that occurred during Reagan's second term as president. Reagan never changed his views about the evils of Communism, but he did alter his thinking about the possibilities of reaching agreements with the Soviets that could slow the arms race, strengthen international security, and advance human rights. Reagan found a partner in Mikhail Gorbachev, who became the Soviet leader in March 1985. Reagan sensed that Gorbachev was "a different sort" of Soviet leader, partly because of his willingness to negotiate agreements to reduce each country's arsenal of nuclear missiles and warheads and not just to limit the size of future increases in nuclear armament (Reagan, 1990, p. 12). When Gorbachev visited the United States in December 1987, the two leaders signed a treaty to eliminate their intermediate-range nuclear forces. The agreement symbolized the rapid, and unexpected, improvement in Soviet-American relations during Reagan's last years in office. When Reagan journeyed to the Soviet Union in May 1988, he told reporters who asked about the memorable phrase that he had used five years earlier, that "evil empire" was part of another era.

◆ **Letter to the American People about Alzheimer's Disease**

Reagan's last public statement was surely his most poignant and perhaps his most eloquent. On November 5, 1994, Reagan released a handwritten letter in which he told the American people that he had been diagnosed with Alzheimer's disease. In this letter he explains that he and his wife, Nancy, had decided to share this news with their fellow citizens, as they had done with information about their previous illnesses, in the hope of promoting greater awareness of the disease and its effects on those who suffer from it and their families.

Reagan uses what could have been a sad and somber occasion to give thanks for the joy he has experienced throughout his life. He looks forward in his last years to the simple pleasures that have provided so much satisfaction. As usual, he expresses his "eternal optimism," seeing "a bright dawn ahead" for America even as he contemplates "the sunset" of his life. On this final, public occasion, Reagan says goodbye in the same way he had spoken for so many years to the American people—with conviction, directness, simplicity, and hope.

Impact and Legacy

Reagan's reputation among historians has improved as they have learned more about his writings. During his presidency and for awhile afterward, some people thought that Reagan was an "acting president," a leader who had few ideas of his own and whose strength was using his performing skills to read the lines that others wrote for him. As his personal and official papers have opened for research, it has become clear that Reagan did indeed have his own ideas and that he knew how to express them powerfully and persuasively. His ideas were simple, and they changed little from the time he entered politics until he retired from the presidency. He thought government's powers should be limited, he deplored high taxes, he believed Communist adversaries posed the greatest dangers to American freedom and security, and he trusted the American people to make the right choices. The power of his ideas came not from their originality or subtlety but from their simplicity and their timelessness. What would make America great, Reagan said, was what had made America great.

Historians continue to disagree about the wisdom or effectiveness of Reagan's policies. Some emphasize that his actions sometimes failed to match his rhetoric. For example, while he criticized federal budget deficits in his first inaugural address for "mortgaging our future and our children's future," he added more to the national debt than all the presidents before him combined. During his eight years in the White House, the national debt almost tripled, growing from $994 billion to a staggering $2.9 trillion. Yet whatever their judgments about the president's policies, historians usually agree that Reagan had important ideas about public issues and knew how to win wide and enthusiastic support for them.

Reagan often said that there were no easy solutions to the nation's problems, only simple ones, and he explained them with simple eloquence. Reagan wrote his speeches with an ear for his audience. His experience in Hollywood and on the "mashed potato circuit" made him a master at engaging audiences and keeping their attention. He told stories that made listeners smile or shed a tear. The stories or the statistics often illustrated a fundamental conviction about freedom, responsibility, power, or morality, the themes to which Reagan returned time and again when he spoke. When he discussed those themes, he usually made one of his familiar arguments—that big government threatened individual liberty, that Communism was an abhorrent and dangerous social system, or that the creativity, courage, and common sense of the American people could meet any challenge. Whatever he discussed, whatever the circumstances, his optimism always prevailed. People liked Reagan and believed what he said because he always glimpsed a better future and inspired them to achieve it by remaining faithful to the values of their past.

Reagan's most important legacy is that he played a major role in making conservatism a powerful political force during the 1980s and long afterward. He helped shift the political center to the right, and he changed the national conversation about some issues that were especially important to him. His emphasis on lowering taxes helped make it difficult, if not impossible, for political leaders to propose tax increases, except in dire circumstances. He made *big government* a common term of opprobrium. He helped turn liberalism into the "L-word" during the 1980s with his attacks on what he said were expensive social programs that eroded individual responsibility or deprived families and communities of control over their own affairs.

He ensured that long after he left the White House the Republican Party would stand for his essential goals: low taxes, strong defense, and social conservatism. Reagan's presidency even influenced the Democratic Party. President Bill Clinton, a moderate Democrat, almost sounded like a Reagan Republican when he declared in his State of the Union address in 1996 that "the era of big government is over" (Brownlee and Graham, p. 57). What Reagan called "the Speech" became one of the most important documents of twentieth-century American politics. It defined American conservatism, and it framed the issues that dominated national politics during the last decades of the twentieth century and even beyond.

Key Sources

The records from Reagan's presidency and governorship are in the Ronald Reagan Presidential Library in Simi Valley, California. The library also has Reagan's personal papers, but permission from the Reagan family is required to consult them. Reagan's public statements, proclamations, speeches, and news conferences are in *Public Papers of the Presidents of the United States: Ronald Reagan*, 8 vols. in 15 parts (1982–1991). An online version is available on the Web page of the American Presidency Project at the University of California, Santa Barbara (http://www.presidency.ucsb.edu/). Reagan wrote his first autobiography, *Where's the Rest of Me?* (1965), with Richard G. Hubler just before his first campaign for governor. His second autobiography, *An American Life* (1990), includes his account of his presidency. Samples of his correspondence can be found in Kiron K. Skinner, Annelise Graebner Anderson, and Martin Anderson, eds., *Reagan: A Life in Letters* (2003). Many of the scripts he wrote for his syndicated radio program in the 1970s are in Kiron K. Skinner, Annelise Anderson, and Martin Anderson, eds., *Reagan, in His Own Hand* (2001), and selections from his presidential diaries are contained in Douglas Brinkley, ed., *The Reagan Diaries* (2007).

Further Reading

■ Books

Brownlee, W. Elliot, and Hugh Davis Graham. *The Reagan Presidency: Pragmatic Conservatism and Its Legacies*. Lawrence: University Press of Kansas, 2003.

Cannon, Lou. *President Reagan: The Role of a Lifetime*. New York: PublicAffairs, 2000.

Diggins, John Patrick. *Ronald Reagan: Fate, Freedom, and the Making of History*. New York: W. W. Norton, 2007.

FitzGerald, Frances R. *Way Out There in the Blue: Reagan, Star Wars, and the End of the Cold War*. New York: Simon and Schuster, 2000.

Reagan, Ronald

"No government ever voluntarily reduces itself in size. So governments' programs, once launched, never disappear. Actually, a government bureau is the nearest thing to eternal life we'll ever see on this earth."

("A Time for Choosing" Speech)

"And suddenly it dawned on me; those who would read this letter a hundred years from now will know whether those missiles were fired. They will know whether we met our challenge. Whether they have the freedoms that we have known up until now will depend on what we do here."

(Remarks at the Republican National Convention)

"In this present crisis, government is not the solution to our problem; government is the problem."

(First Inaugural Address)

"I do not believe in a fate that will fall on us no matter what we do. I do believe in a fate that will fall on us if we do nothing. So, with all the creative energy at our command, let us begin an era of national renewal."

(First Inaugural Address)

"Yes, let us pray for the salvation of all of those who live in that totalitarian darkness—pray they will discover the joy of knowing God. But until they do, let us be aware that while they preach the supremacy of the state, declare its omnipotence over individual man, and predict its eventual domination of all peoples on the Earth, they are the focus of evil in the modern world."

("Evil Empire" Speech)

"I believe that communism is another sad, bizarre chapter in human history whose last pages even now are being written."

("Evil Empire" Speech)

"I now begin the journey that will lead me into the sunset of my life. I know that for America there will always be a bright dawn ahead."

(Letter to the American People about Alzheimer's Disease)

Pemberton, William E. *Exit with Honor: The Life and Presidency of Ronald Reagan*. Armonk, N.Y.: M. E. Sharpe, 1997.

Reeves, Richard. *President Reagan: The Triumph of Imagination*. New York: Simon and Schuster, 2005.

—Chester Pach

Questions for Further Study

1. Although he became the leading figure in a conservative revolution within the Republican Party, Reagan began his political career as a Democrat. When asked about this shift in allegiance, he often said that it was not he who had changed but rather the party itself. Use his speech "A Time for Choosing" as a guide to discuss the reasons why he chose to leave the Democratic Party. Do you agree or disagree with his statement that the party had changed? Why or why not?

2. In his 1976 address to the Republican National Convention, Reagan builds on the idea of a time capsule and what he would say to people a hundred years hence. Try this idea for yourself: What would you say to people a century after your own time about America and its place in the world? What, in your opinion, would have been the long-term results for the nation if it had followed the course Reagan recommended in the four political addresses included here, including (for instance) a strong defense, unbending opposition to totalitarianism and terrorism, and reduced government control?

3. Although he was often attacked for his alleged lack of concern for the poor, Reagan had his own vision of how to achieve social justice, which he expressed in two speeches separated by nearly two decades, his 1964 television speech and his inaugural address. On what bases did he disagree with Democratic solutions to problems of poverty, crime, and racism? Evaluate the relative merits of Reagan's conservative approach and that of his opposition on the left. Which do you think has proved more effective?

4. Discuss the two central themes of Reagan's "evil empire" speech: first, the fundamental opposition between American freedom and totalitarian repression and, second, the importance of a religiously based morality as an underpinning to a free society. How well does he make these two points? With regard to the first, research the facts of Soviet history that might have brought him to the conclusion that the Soviet Union was an "evil empire" and discuss whether he was right in his evaluation. As for the second argument, do you agree with his underlying principle that religious faith is necessary to guarantee freedom?

5. Compare and contrast appraisals of Reagan written during the time of his presidency with those following his death. How much change do you see, and what do you think explains this shift?

"A Time for Choosing" Speech (1964)

I have spent most of my life as a Democrat. I recently have seen fit to follow another course. I believe that the issues confronting us cross party lines. Now, one side in this campaign has been telling us that the issues of this election are the maintenance of peace and prosperity. The line has been used, "We've never had it so good."

But I have an uncomfortable feeling that this prosperity isn't something on which we can base our hopes for the future. No nation in history has ever survived a tax burden that reached a third of its national income. Today, 37 cents out of every dollar earned in this country is the tax collector's share, and yet our government continues to spend 17 million dollars a day more than the government takes in. We haven't balanced our budget 28 out of the last 34 years. We've raised our debt limit three times in the last twelve months, and now our national debt is one and a half times bigger than all the combined debts of all the nations of the world. We have 15 billion dollars in gold in our treasury; we don't own an ounce. Foreign dollar claims are 27.3 billion dollars. And we've just had announced that the dollar of 1939 will now purchase 45 cents in its total value.

As for the peace that we would preserve, I wonder who among us would like to approach the wife or mother whose husband or son has died in South Vietnam and ask them if they think this is a peace that should be maintained indefinitely. Do they mean peace, or do they mean we just want to be left in peace? There can be no real peace while one American is dying some place in the world for the rest of us. We're at war with the most dangerous enemy that has ever faced mankind in his long climb from the swamp to the stars, and it's been said if we lose that war, and in so doing lose this way of freedom of ours, history will record with the greatest astonishment that those who had the most to lose did the least to prevent its happening. Well I think it's time we ask ourselves if we still know the freedoms that were intended for us by the Founding Fathers.

Not too long ago, two friends of mine were talking to a Cuban refugee, a businessman who had escaped from Castro, and in the midst of his story one of my friends turned to the other and said, "We don't know how lucky we are." And the Cuban stopped and said, "How lucky you are? I had some-place to escape to." And in that sentence he told us the entire story. If we lose freedom here, there's no place to escape to. This is the last stand on earth....

This is the issue of this election: Whether we believe in our capacity for self-government or whether we abandon the American Revolution and confess that a little intellectual elite in a far-distant capital can plan our lives for us better than we can plan them ourselves.

You and I are told increasingly we have to choose between a left or right. Well I'd like to suggest there is no such thing as a left or right. There's only an up or down—[up] man's old—old-aged dream, the ultimate in individual freedom consistent with law and order, or down to the ant heap of totalitarianism. And regardless of their sincerity, their humanitarian motives, those who would trade our freedom for security have embarked on this downward course.

In this vote-harvesting time, they use terms like the "Great Society," or as we were told a few days ago by the President, we must accept a greater government activity in the affairs of the people....Another voice says, "The profit motive has become outmoded. It must be replaced by the incentives of the welfare state."...

"The full power of centralized government"—this was the very thing the Founding Fathers sought to minimize. They knew that governments don't control things. A government can't control the economy without controlling people. And they knew when a government sets out to do that, it must use force and coercion to achieve its purpose. They also knew, those Founding Fathers, that outside of its legitimate functions, government does nothing as well or as economically as the private sector of the economy.

Now, we have no better example of this than government's involvement in the farm economy over the last 30 years. Since 1955, the cost of this program has nearly doubled. One-fourth of farming in America is responsible for 85 percent of the farm surplus. Three-fourths of farming is out on the free market and has known a 21 percent increase in the per capita consumption of all its produce. You see, that one-fourth of farming—that's regulated and controlled by the federal government. In the last three years we've spent 43 dollars in the feed grain program for every dollar bushel of corn we don't grow....

Meanwhile, back in the city, under urban renewal the assault on freedom carries on. Private property rights [are] so diluted that public interest is almost anything a few government planners decide it should be. In a program that takes from the needy and gives to the greedy, we see such spectacles as in Cleveland, Ohio, a million-and-a-half-dollar building completed only three years ago must be destroyed to make way for what government officials call a "more compatible use of the land." The President tells us he's now going to start building public housing units in the thousands, where heretofore we've only built them in the hundreds. But FHA and the Veterans Administration tell us they have 120,000 housing units they've taken back through mortgage foreclosure. For three decades, we've sought to solve the problems of unemployment through government planning, and the more the plans fail, the more the planners plan....

We have so many people who can't see a fat man standing beside a thin one without coming to the conclusion the fat man got that way by taking advantage of the thin one. So they're going to solve all the problems of human misery through government and government planning. Well, now, if government planning and welfare had the answer—and they've had almost 30 years of it—shouldn't we expect government to read the score to us once in a while? Shouldn't they be telling us about the decline each year in the number of people needing help? The reduction in the need for public housing?...

Now—we're for a provision that destitution should not follow unemployment by reason of old age, and to that end we've accepted Social Security as a step toward meeting the problem.

But we're against those entrusted with this program when they practice deception regarding its fiscal shortcomings, when they charge that any criticism of the program means that we want to end payments to those people who depend on them for a livelihood. They've called it "insurance" to us in a hundred million pieces of literature. But then they appeared before the Supreme Court and they testified it was a welfare program. They only use the term "insurance" to sell it to the people....

I think we're against forcing all citizens, regardless of need, into a compulsory government program, especially when we have such examples, as was announced last week, when France admitted that their Medicare program is now bankrupt. They've come to the end of the road....

No government ever voluntarily reduces itself in size. So governments' programs, once launched, never disappear.

Actually, a government bureau is the nearest thing to eternal life we'll ever see on this earth.

Federal employees—federal employees number two and a half million; and federal, state, and local, one out of six of the nation's work force employed by government. These proliferating bureaus with their thousands of regulations have cost us many of our constitutional safeguards. How many of us realize that today federal agents can invade a man's property without a warrant? They can impose a fine without a formal hearing, let alone a trial by jury? And they can seize and sell his property at auction to enforce the payment of that fine....

Now it doesn't require expropriation or confiscation of private property or business to impose socialism on a people. What does it mean whether you hold the deed to the—or the title to your business or property if the government holds the power of life and death over that business or property? And such machinery already exists. The government can find some charge to bring against any concern it chooses to prosecute. Every businessman has his own tale of harassment. Somewhere a perversion has taken place. Our natural, unalienable rights are now considered to be a dispensation of government, and freedom has never been so fragile, so close to slipping from our grasp as it is at this moment.

Our Democratic opponents seem unwilling to debate these issues. They want to make you and I believe that this is a contest between two men—that we're to choose just between two personalities....

Those who would trade our freedom for the soup kitchen of the welfare state have told us they have a utopian solution of peace without victory. They call their policy "accommodation." And they say if we'll only avoid any direct confrontation with the enemy, he'll forget his evil ways and learn to love us. All who oppose them are indicted as warmongers. They say we offer simple answers to complex problems. Well, perhaps there is a simple answer—not an easy answer—but simple: If you and I have the courage to tell our elected officials that we want our national policy based on what we know in our hearts is morally right.

We cannot buy our security, our freedom from the threat of the bomb, by committing an immorality so great as saying to a billion human beings now enslaved behind the Iron Curtain, "Give up your dreams of freedom because to save our own skins, we're willing to make a deal with your slave masters." Alexander Hamilton said, "A nation which can prefer disgrace to danger is prepared for a master, and deserves one." Now let's set the record straight. There's no argument over the choice between peace and war, but there's only one guaranteed way you can have peace—and you can have it in the next second—surrender.

Admittedly, there's a risk in any course we follow other than this, but every lesson of history tells us that the greater risk lies in appeasement, and this is the specter our well-meaning liberal friends refuse to face—that their policy of accommodation is appeasement, and it gives no choice between peace and war, only between fight or surrender....

You and I know and do not believe that life is so dear and peace so sweet as to be purchased at the price of chains and slavery. If nothing in life is worth dying for, when did this begin—just in the face of this enemy? Or should Moses have told the children of Israel to live in slavery under the pharaohs? Should Christ have refused the cross? Should the patriots at Concord Bridge have thrown down their guns and refused to fire the shot heard 'round the world? The

martyrs of history were not fools, and our honored dead who gave their lives to stop the advance of the Nazis didn't die in vain. Where, then, is the road to peace? Well, it's a simple answer after all.

You and I have the courage to say to our enemies, "There is a price we will not pay." "There is a point beyond which they must not advance." And this— this is the meaning in the phrase of Barry Goldwater's "peace through strength." Winston Churchill said, "The destiny of man is not measured by material computations. When great forces are on the move in the world, we learn we're spirits—not animals." And he said, "There's something going on in time and space, and beyond time and space, which, whether we like it or not, spells duty."

You and I have a rendezvous with destiny.

We'll preserve for our children this, the last best hope of man on earth, or we'll sentence them to take the last step into a thousand years of darkness.

Glossary

bomb	nuclear warfare in general
concern	business, firm, or enterprise
dispensation	something that is granted or given, usually from a higher- to a lower-ranking entity
expropriation	the act of taking property, particularly for public use
Iron Curtain	a metaphorical barrier between the totalitarian Communist nations and the liberal democratic world
perversion	deviation from established norms or goals
urban renewal	a controversial program, which reached its peak in the period from the late 1950s to the mid-1970s, that involved reclamation of allegedly blighted urban neighborhoods by replacement of old buildings and environments with new ones

REMARKS AT THE REPUBLICAN NATIONAL CONVENTION (1976)

Thank you very much. Mr. President, Mrs. Ford, Mr. Vice President, Mr. Vice President to be, the distinguished guests here, and you, ladies and gentlemen: I am going to say fellow Republicans here, but also those who are watching from a distance, all of those millions of Democrats and Independents who I know are looking for a cause around which to rally and which I believe we can give them.

Mr. President, before you arrived tonight, these wonderful people here, when we came in, gave Nancy and myself a welcome. That, plus this, and plus your kindness and generosity in honoring us by bringing us down here will give us a memory that will live in our hearts forever.

Watching on television these last few nights, and I have seen you also with the warmth that you greeted Nancy, and you also filled my heart with joy when you did that.

May I just say some words. There are cynics who say that a party platform is something that no one bothers to read and it doesn't very often amount to much.

Whether it is different this time than it has ever been before, I believe the Republican Party has a platform that is a banner of bold, unmistakable colors, with no pastel shades.

We have just heard a call to arms based on that platform, and a call to us to really be successful in communicating and reveal to the American people the difference between this platform and the platform of the opposing party, which is nothing but a revamp and a reissue and a running of a late, late show of the thing that we have been hearing from them for the last 40 years.

If I could just take a moment; I had an assignment the other day. Someone asked me to write a letter for a time capsule that is going to be opened in Los Angeles a hundred years from now, on our Tricentennial.

It sounded like an easy assignment. They suggested I write something about the problems and the issues today. I set out to do so, riding down the coast in an automobile, looking at the blue Pacific out on one side and the Santa Ynez Mountains on the other, and I couldn't help but wonder if it was going to be that beautiful a hundred years from now as it was on that summer day.

Then, as I tried to write—let your own minds turn to that task. You are going to write for people a hundred years from now, who know all about us. We know nothing about them. We don't know what kind of a world they will be living in.

And suddenly I thought to myself, if I write of the problems, they will be the domestic problems the President spoke of here tonight; the challenges confronting us, the erosion of freedom that has taken place under Democratic rule in this country, the invasion of private rights, the controls and restrictions on the vitality of the great free economy that we enjoy. These are our challenges that we must meet.

And then again, there is that challenge of which he spoke, that we live in a world in which the great powers have poised and aimed at each other horrible missiles of destruction, nuclear weapons that can in

Glossary

great general	General Douglas MacArthur, who led U.S. troops in the Pacific in World War II, and commanded U.S. forces in the Korean War
late, late show	in the pre-cable era, one of the few late-night television-viewing options was the so-called late-late show, usually featuring old movies
party platform	a series of statements representing the official views of a political party on various issues of concern to the electorate
pastel shades	soft, gentle colors—an idea used metaphorically by Reagan here to suggest principles that have been watered down

a matter of minutes arrive at each other's country and destroy, virtually, the civilized world we live in.

And suddenly it dawned on me, those who would read this letter a hundred years from now will know whether those missiles were fired. They will know whether we met our challenge. Whether they have the freedoms that we have known up until now will depend on what we do here.

Will they look back with appreciation and say, "Thank God for those people in 1976 who headed off that loss of freedom, who kept us now 100 years later free, who kept our world from nuclear destruction"?

And if we failed, they probably won't get to read the letter at all because it spoke of individual freedom, and they won't be allowed to talk of that or read of it.

This is our challenge; and this is why here in this hall tonight, better than we have ever done before, we have got to quit talking to each other and about each other and go out and communicate to the world that we may be fewer in numbers than we have ever been, but we carry the message they are waiting for.

We must go forth from here united, determined that what a great general said a few years ago is true: There is no substitute for victory, Mr. President.

First Inaugural Address (1981)

The business of our nation goes forward. These United States are confronted with an economic affliction of great proportions. We suffer from the longest and one of the worst sustained inflations in our national history. It distorts our economic decisions, penalizes thrift, and crushes the struggling young and the fixed-income elderly alike. It threatens to shatter the lives of millions of our people.

Idle industries have cast workers into unemployment, human misery, and personal indignity. Those who do work are denied a fair return for their labor by a tax system which penalizes successful achievement and keeps us from maintaining full productivity.

But great as our tax burden is, it has not kept pace with public spending. For decades we have piled deficit upon deficit, mortgaging our future and our children's future for the temporary convenience of the present. To continue this long trend is to guarantee tremendous social, cultural, political, and economic upheavals....

We must act today in order to preserve tomorrow. And let there be no misunderstanding: We are going to begin to act, beginning today....

In this present crisis, government is not the solution to our problem; government is the problem. From time to time we've been tempted to believe that society has become too complex to be managed by self-rule, that government by an elite group is superior to government for, by, and of the people. Well, if no one among us is capable of governing himself, then who among us has the capacity to govern someone else? All of us together, in and out of government, must bear the burden. The solutions we seek must be equitable, with no one group singled out to pay a higher price....

This administration's objective will be a healthy, vigorous, growing economy that provides equal opportunities for all Americans, with no barriers born of bigotry or discrimination....All must share in the productive work of this "new beginning," and all must share in the bounty of a revived economy....

It is my intention to curb the size and influence of the Federal establishment and to demand recognition of the distinction between the powers granted to the Federal Government and those reserved to the States or to the people. All of us need to be reminded that the Federal Government did not create the States; the States created the Federal Government....

It's not my intention to do away with government. It is rather to make it work—work with us, not over us; to stand by our side, not ride on our back. Government can and must provide opportunity, not smother it; foster productivity, not stifle it.

It is no coincidence that our present troubles parallel and are proportionate to the intervention and intrusion in our lives that result from unnecessary and excessive growth of government.... With all the creative energy at our command, let us begin an era of national renewal. Let us renew our determination, our courage, and our strength. And let us renew our faith and our hope.

We have every right to dream heroic dreams. Those who say that we're in a time when there are no heroes, they just don't know where to look. You can see heroes every day going in and out of factory gates....There are entrepreneurs with faith in themselves and faith in an idea who create new jobs, new wealth and opportunity....

Now, I have used the words "they" and "their" in speaking of these heroes. I could say "you" and "your," because I'm addressing the heroes of whom I speak—you, the citizens of this blessed land. Your dreams, your hopes, your goals are going to be the dreams, the hopes, and the goals of this administration, so help me God.

We shall reflect the compassion that is so much a part of your makeup. How can we love our country and not love our countrymen; and loving them, reach out a hand when they fall, heal them when they're sick, and provide opportunity to make them self-sufficient so they will be equal in fact and not just in theory?...

In the days ahead I will propose removing the roadblocks that have slowed our economy and reduced productivity. Steps will be taken aimed at restoring the balance between the various levels of government. Progress may be slow, measured in inches and feet, not miles, but we will progress....

As we renew ourselves here in our own land, we will be seen as having greater strength throughout the world. We will again be the exemplar of freedom and a beacon of hope for those who do not now have freedom.

To those neighbors and allies who share our freedom, we will strengthen our historic ties and assure them of our support and firm commitment. We will match loyalty with loyalty. We will strive for mutually beneficial relations....

As for the enemies of freedom, those who are potential adversaries, they will be reminded that peace is the highest aspiration of the American people. We will negotiate for it, sacrifice for it; we will not surrender for it, now or ever.

Our forbearance should never be misunderstood. Our reluctance for conflict should not be misjudged as a failure of will. When action is required to preserve our national security, we will act....

Above all, we must realize that no arsenal or no weapon in the arsenals of the world is so formidable as the will and moral courage of free men and women. It is a weapon our adversaries in today's world do not have. It is a weapon that we as Americans do have....

Directly in front of me, the monument to a monumental man, George Washington, father of our country. A man of humility who came to greatness reluctantly. He led America out of revolutionary victory into infant nationhood. Off to one side, the stately memorial to Thomas Jefferson. The Declaration of Independence flames with his eloquence. And then, beyond the Reflecting Pool, the dignified columns of the Lincoln Memorial. Whoever would understand in his heart the meaning of America will find it in the life of Abraham Lincoln.

Beyond those monuments to heroism is the Potomac River, and on the far shore the sloping hills of Arlington National Cemetery, with its row upon row of simple white markers bearing crosses or Stars of David. They add up to only a tiny fraction of the price that has been paid for our freedom....

Under one such marker lies a young man, Martin Treptow, who left his job in a small town barbershop in 1917 to go to France with the famed Rainbow Division. There, on the western front, he was killed trying to carry a message between battalions under heavy artillery fire.

We're told that on his body was found a diary. On the flyleaf under the heading, "My Pledge," he had written these words: "America must win this war. Therefore I will work, I will save, I will sacrifice, I will endure, I will fight cheerfully and do my utmost, as if the issue of the whole struggle depended on me alone."

The crisis we are facing today does not require of us the kind of sacrifice that Martin Treptow and so many thousands of others were called upon to make. It does require, however, our best effort and our willingness to believe in ourselves and to believe in our capacity to perform great deeds, to believe that together with God's help we can and will resolve the problems which now confront us.

And after all, why shouldn't we believe that? We are Americans.

Glossary

deficit	a shortfall in a government budget brought about when expenses exceed income
inflation	an economic situation characterized by rising prices and a corresponding decline in purchasing power
Martin Treptow	A U.S. Army private who, after volunteering for the mission, was killed while delivering an important message during the Second Battle of the Marne in July 1918
Rainbow Division	the 42nd Infantry Division (Mechanized) of the U.S. Army, nicknamed for the rainbow in its insignia
Stars of David	symbols of Judaism traditionally used on the graves of Jewish soldiers

"Evil Empire" Speech (1983)

The other day in the East Room of the White House at a meeting there, someone asked me whether I was aware of all the people out there who were praying for the President. And I had to say, "Yes, I am. I've felt it. I believe in intercessionary prayer." But I couldn't help but say to that questioner after he'd asked the question that... if sometimes when he was praying he got a busy signal, it was just me in there ahead of him. I think I understand how Abraham Lincoln felt when he said, "I have been driven many times to my knees by the overwhelming conviction that I had nowhere else to go." From the joy and the good feeling of this conference, I go to a political reception. Now, I don't know why, but that bit of scheduling reminds me of a story—which I'll share with you.

An evangelical minister and a politician arrived at Heaven's gate one day together. And St. Peter, after doing all the necessary formalities, took them in hand to show them where their quarters would be. And he took them to a small, single room with a bed, a chair, and a table and said this was for the clergyman. And the politician was a little worried about what might be in store for him. And he couldn't believe it then when St. Peter stopped in front of a beautiful mansion with lovely grounds, many servants, and told him that these would be his quarters.

And he couldn't help but ask, ... "There's something wrong—how do I get this mansion while that good and holy man only gets a single room?" And St. Peter said, "You have to understand how things are up here. We've got thousands and thousands of clergy. You're the first politician who ever made it."

But I don't want to contribute to a stereotype. So, I tell you there are a great many God-fearing, dedicated, noble men and women in public life, present company included. And, yes, we need your help to keep us ever mindful of the ideas and the principles that brought us into the public arena in the first place. The basis of those ideals and principles is a commitment to freedom and personal liberty that, itself, is grounded in the much deeper realization that freedom prospers only where the blessings of God are avidly sought and humbly accepted.

The American experiment in democracy rests on this insight. Its discovery was the great triumph of our Founding Fathers, voiced by William Penn when he said: "If we will not be governed by God, we must be governed by tyrants." Explaining the inalienable rights of men, Jefferson said, "The God who gave us life, gave us liberty at the same time." And it was George Washington who said that "of all the dispositions and habits which lead to political prosperity, religion and morality are indispensable supports."...

I want you to know that this administration is motivated by a political philosophy that sees the greatness of America in you, her people, and in your families, churches, neighborhoods, communities—the institutions that foster and nourish values like concern for others and respect for the rule of law under God.

Now, I don't have to tell you that this puts us in opposition to, or at least out of step with, a prevailing attitude of many who have turned to a modern-day secularism, discarding the tried and time-tested values upon which our very civilization is based. No matter how well intentioned, their value system is radically different from that of most Americans. And while they proclaim that they're freeing us from superstitions of the past, they've taken upon themselves the job of superintending us by government rule and regulation. Sometimes their voices are louder than ours, but they are not yet a majority.

An example of that vocal superiority is evident in a controversy now going on in Washington....

An organization of citizens, sincerely motivated and deeply concerned about the increase in illegitimate births and abortions involving girls well below the age of consent, some time ago established a nationwide network of clinics to offer help to these girls and, hopefully, alleviate this situation.... However, in their well-intentioned effort, these clinics have decided to provide advice and birth control drugs and devices to underage girls without the knowledge of their parents.

For some years now, the federal government has helped with funds to subsidize these clinics. In providing for this, the Congress decreed that every effort would be made to maximize parental participation. Nevertheless, the drugs and devices are prescribed without getting parental consent or giving notification after they've done so. Girls termed "sexually active"—and that has replaced the word "promiscuous"—are given this help in order to prevent illegitimate birth or abortion.

Well, we have ordered clinics receiving federal funds to notify the parents such help has been given.

One of the nation's leading newspapers has created the term "squeal rule" in editorializing against us for doing this, and we're being criticized for violating the privacy of young people....But no one seems to mention morality as playing a part in the subject of sex.

Is all of Judeo-Christian tradition wrong? Are we to believe that something so sacred can be looked upon as a purely physical thing with no potential for emotional and psychological harm? And isn't it the parents' right to give counsel and advice to keep their children from making mistakes that may affect their entire lives?

Many of us in government would like to know what parents think about this intrusion in their family by government. We're going to fight in the courts. The right of parents and the rights of family take precedence over those of Washington-based bureaucrats and social engineers.

But the fight against parental notification is really only one example of many attempts to water down traditional values and even abrogate the original terms of American democracy. Freedom prospers when religion is vibrant and the rule of law under God is acknowledged. When our Founding Fathers passed the first amendment, they sought to protect churches from government interference. They never intended to construct a wall of hostility between government and the concept of religious belief itself....

The evidence of this permeates our history and our government. The Declaration of Independence mentions the Supreme Being no less than four times. "In God We Trust" is engraved on our coinage. The Supreme Court opens its proceedings with a religious invocation. And the members of Congress open their sessions with a prayer. I just happen to believe the schoolchildren of the United States are entitled to the same privileges as Supreme Court justices and congressmen....

More than a decade ago, a Supreme Court decision literally wiped off the books of 50 states statutes protecting the rights of unborn children. Abortion on demand now takes the lives of up to one and a half million unborn children a year. Human life legislation ending this tragedy will someday pass the Congress, and you and I must never rest until it does. Unless and until it can be proven that the unborn child is not a living entity, then its right to life, liberty, and the pursuit of happiness must be protected....

I have directed the Health and Human Services Department to make clear to every health care facility in the United States that the Rehabilitation Act of 1973 protects all handicapped persons against discrimination based on handicaps, including infants....

There's a great spiritual awakening in America, a renewal of the traditional values that have been the bedrock of America's goodness and greatness....

I think the items that we've discussed here today must be a key part of the nation's political agenda. For the first time the Congress is openly and seriously debating and dealing with the prayer and abortion issues—and that's enormous progress right there. I repeat: America is in the midst of a spiritual awakening and a moral renewal....

I know that you've been horrified, as have I, by the resurgence of some hate groups preaching bigotry and prejudice. Use the mighty voice of your pulpits and the powerful standing of your churches to denounce and isolate these hate groups in our midst. The commandment given us is clear and simple: "Thou shalt love thy neighbor as thyself."

But whatever sad episodes exist in our past, any objective observer must hold a positive view of American history, a history that has been the story of hopes fulfilled and dreams made into reality. Especially in this century, America has kept alight the torch of freedom, but not just for ourselves but for millions of others around the world.

And this brings me to my final point today. During my first press conference as president, in answer to a direct question, I pointed out that, as good Marxist-Leninists, the Soviet leaders have openly and publicly declared that the only morality they recognize is that which will further their cause, which is world revolution. I think I should point out I was only quoting Lenin, their guiding spirit, who said in 1920 that they repudiate all morality that proceeds from supernatural ideas—that's their name for religion—or ideas that are outside class conceptions. Morality is entirely subordinate to the interests of class war. And everything is moral that is necessary for the annihilation of the old, exploiting social order and for uniting the proletariat.

Well, I think the refusal of many influential people to accept this elementary fact of Soviet doctrine illustrates an historical reluctance to see totalitarian powers for what they are. We saw this phenomenon in the 1930's. We see it too often today.

This doesn't mean we should isolate ourselves and refuse to seek an understanding with them. I intend to do everything I can to persuade them of our peaceful intent....

At the same time, however, they must be made to understand we will never compromise our principles and standards. We will never give away our freedom. We will never abandon our belief in God. And we will never stop searching for a genuine peace. But we can assure none of these things America stands for through the so-called nuclear freeze solutions proposed by some....

Yes, let us pray for the salvation of all of those who live in that totalitarian darkness—pray they will discover the joy of knowing God. But until they do, let us be aware that while they preach the supremacy of the state, declare its omnipotence over individual man, and predict its eventual domination of all peoples on the Earth, they are the focus of evil in the modern world....

I urge you to speak out against those who would place the United States in a position of military and moral inferiority....In your discussions of the nuclear freeze proposals, I urge you to beware the temptation of pride—the temptation of blithely declaring yourselves above it all and label both sides equally at fault, to ignore the facts of history and the aggressive impulses of an evil empire, to simply call the arms race a giant misunderstanding and thereby remove yourself from the struggle between right and wrong and good and evil....

While America's military strength is important, let me add here that I've always maintained that the struggle now going on for the world will never be decided by bombs or rockets, by armies or military might. The real crisis we face today is a spiritual one; at root, it is a test of moral will and faith....

I believe we shall rise to the challenge. I believe that communism is another sad, bizarre chapter in human history whose last pages even now are being written. I believe this because the source of our strength in the quest for human freedom is not material, but spiritual. And because it knows no limitation, it must terrify and ultimately triumph over those who would enslave their fellow man. For in the words of Isaiah: "He giveth power to the faint; and to them that have no might He increased strength.... But they that wait upon the Lord shall renew their strength; they shall mount up with wings as eagles; they shall run, and not be weary."

Yes, change your world. One of our Founding Fathers, Thomas Paine, said, "We have it within our power to begin the world over again." We can do it, doing together what no one church could do by itself.

Glossary

abrogate	abolish or annul
class conceptions	a reference to the idea of "class consciousness," a foundational principle in Marxism that holds that history is a series of struggles between economic classes
evangelical	characterizing a religious group (primarily Protestant) whose adherents strongly advocate preaching the Christian Gospel to non-Christians and who tend to take a conservative, fundamentalist approach to biblical interpretation
intercessionary prayer	also called *intercessory prayer*, the act of praying on behalf of someone else
Marxist-Leninists	adherents of a totalitarian political system based on the theories of the German economist Karl Marx and the Russian revolutionary Vladimir Lenin
nuclear freeze	a proposed "freeze," or complete stop, on the building of nuclear armaments by the United States
proletariat	industrial workers, in Marxist class theory
secularism	a general principle of strict separation between religious and nonreligious sectors of public life, particularly government, law, science, and education
social engineers	advocates of applying, to society as a whole, theories of group organization based on principles of social science; generally a pejorative term suggestive of totalitarianism in one form or another
totalitarian	referring to a political system characterized by total control over every aspect of life and society

LETTER TO THE AMERICAN PEOPLE ABOUT ALZHEIMER'S DISEASE (1994)

My Fellow Americans,

I have recently been told that I am one of the millions of Americans who will be afflicted with Alzheimer's Disease.

Upon learning this news, Nancy and I had to decide whether as private citizens we would keep this a private matter or whether we would make this news known in a public way.

In the past Nancy suffered from breast cancer and I had my cancer surgeries. We found through our open disclosures we were able to raise public awareness. We were happy that as a result many more people underwent testing.

They were treated in early stages and able to return to normal, healthy lives.

So now, we feel it is important to share it with you. In opening our hearts, we hope this might promote greater awareness of this condition. Perhaps it will encourage a clearer understanding of the individuals and families who are affected by it.

At the moment I feel just fine. I intend to live the remainder of the years God gives me on this earth doing the things I have always done. I will continue to share life's journey with my beloved Nancy and my family. I plan to enjoy the great outdoors and stay in touch with my friends and supporters.

Unfortunately, as Alzheimer's Disease progresses, the family often bears a heavy burden. I only wish there was some way I could spare Nancy from this painful experience. When the time comes I am confident that with your help she will face it with faith and courage.

In closing let me thank you, the American people for giving me the great honor of allowing me to serve as your President. When the Lord calls me home, whenever that may be, I will leave with the greatest love for this country of ours and eternal optimism for its future.

I now begin the journey that will lead me into the sunset of my life. I know that for America there will always be a bright dawn ahead.

Thank you, my friends. May God always bless you.

Sincerely,

Ronald Reagan

Glossary

Alzheimer's Disease	a degenerative condition, first identified by German psychiatrist Alois Alzheimer in 1906, involving a gradual but irreversible (and ultimately fatal) loss of brain functioning

William Rehnquist (Library of Congress)

WILLIAM REHNQUIST

1924–2005

Sixteenth Chief Justice of the United States

Featured Documents
- ◆ *Roe v. Wade* (1973)
- ◆ *United States v. Lopez* (1995)
- ◆ *George W. Bush et al. v. Albert Gore, Jr., et al.* (2000)

Overview

As chief justice of the United States, William Hubbs Rehnquist oversaw the Court's profound shift in a conservative direction after the more liberal leadership of his predecessor, Warren Burger. Rehnquist was born on October 1, 1924, in Milwaukee, Wisconsin. After serving in the U.S. Army Air Forces from 1943 to 1946, he attended Stanford University in California, earning bachelor's and master's degrees in political science. After two years at Harvard University, where he earned a second master's degree in government in 1950, he returned to Stanford to attend law school. There he graduated first in his class in 1952; one of his classmates was his future Supreme Court colleague Sandra Day O'Connor.

After serving as a judicial clerk for Supreme Court Justice Robert Jackson during the Court's 1952–1953 term, Rehnquist settled in Phoenix, Arizona, where he worked at a law firm and became active in Republican Party politics. From 1969 to 1971 he was assistant attorney general in the U.S. Justice Department's Office of Legal Counsel. In 1971 President Richard Nixon nominated him for a seat on the Supreme Court; after confirmation by the Senate, Rehnquist assumed his seat in 1972. In 1986 President Ronald Reagan nominated him to the position of chief justice, a position he held, despite ill health in his later years, until his death on September 3, 2005.

As a member of the nation's highest court, Rehnquist wrote primarily decisions in which he explained the legal principles and reasoning that had led to the decision. This type of legal writing requires the justice to outline the facts of the case, cite statutes and legal precedents (previous court decisions) that have a bearing on the case, and then demonstrate how those statutes and precedents should be used to decide the case at hand. Typically, when the Supreme Court arrives at a decision, the chief justice assigns the task of writing the Court's decision to one of the justices who joined the majority, though the chief justice has often reserved that task for himself. In the case of such key Court decisions as *United States v. Lopez* and *George W. Bush et al. v. Albert Gore, Jr., et al.*, Rehnquist himself wrote the decisions. Often, however, justices who do not join with the majority and disagree with the Court's decision file a dissent outlining the basis of their disagreement. In the landmark *Roe v. Wade* abortion decision, Rehnquist disagreed with the majority and wrote such a dissent.

Explanation and Analysis of Documents

As a new conservative justice on the liberal Court presided over by Chief Justice Warren Burger, Rehnquist was often the Court's lone voice of dissent. This willingness to disagree with the majority was nowhere more in evidence than in *Roe v. Wade*, the landmark 1973 case that struck down state laws outlawing abortion. Throughout his career, Rehnquist resisted efforts of the Court to expand federal powers—as he did in *United States v. Lopez*—and when he could, he defended the rights of the states against the imposition of federal power. It was in part for this reason that the Rehnquist Court declined to interfere with Florida election procedures in *George W. Bush et al. v. Albert Gore, Jr., et al.* He differed from the Court in maintaining that the Fourteenth Amendment to the Constitution, passed in the wake of the Civil War and designed to extend equal rights to newly freed slaves, did not extend to such issues as the rights of women and children. Although his opinions in his early years failed to persuade the Court majority, they laid the groundwork for the Court's shift in a more conservative direction after he rose to the position of chief justice.

◆ *Roe v. Wade*

Roe v. Wade has arguably been one of the Supreme Court's most controversial decisions. In its seven-to-two majority opinion, the Court struck down a Texas law—and by implication similar laws in other states—restricting the right of a woman to have an abortion. Rehnquist and Justice Byron White both dissented from the majority opinion.

The case was that of a Texas woman, Norma McCorvey ("Jane Roe"), who wanted to end a pregnancy she attributed to rape (a claim she later recanted). Under Texas law, however, abortion was illegal. On McCorvey's behalf, two attorneys filed suit in the U.S. District Court in Texas, naming Roe as plaintiff and Dallas County District Attorney Henry Wade, representing the state of Texas, as defendant. The suit asked the district court to invalidate the Texas statute making abortion illegal so that Roe could have an abortion. The district court ruled in Roe's favor but turned down her request for an injunction blocking enforcement of the state's antiabortion laws. Because neither side obtained the full ruling each wished, both filed appeals. The case reached the Supreme Court, where it was argued on December 13, 1971. However, before the Court issued its decision, Rehnquist and Lewis Powell, Jr., joined the Court, so the case was

Time Line

1924
- **October 1**
  William Rehnquist is born in Milwaukee, Wisconsin.

1943–1946
- Rehnquist serves as an enlistee in U.S. Army Air Forces.

1952
- Rehnquist graduates from Stanford University Law School.

1969
- **January**
  Rehnquist is appointed assistant U.S. attorney general in the Justice Department's Office of Legal Counsel, a post he holds until 1971.

1971
- **October 21**
  President Richard Nixon appoints Rehnquist associate justice of the U.S. Supreme Court.

1973
- **January 22**
  Rehnquist writes a dissent from the majority in *Roe v. Wade.*

1986
- **June 20**
  President Ronald Reagan appoints Rehnquist chief justice of the United States.

1995
- **April 26**
  Rehnquist writes the majority opinion in *United States v. Lopez.*

2000
- **December 12**
  Rehnquist writes the Supreme Court's opinion in *George W. Bush et al. v. Albert Gore, Jr., et al.*, settling the disputed presidential election.

2005
- **September 3**
  Rehnquist dies in Arlington, Virginia.

reargued on October 11, 1972. The Court issued its decision on January 22, 1973.

The Court's majority based its decision principally on a "right to privacy" that they argued was implicit in the due process clause of the Constitution's Fourteenth Amendment. This amendment states that no state "shall deprive any person of life, liberty, or property, without due process of law." They argued that abortion was a "fundamental right" guaranteed by the Constitution and that therefore the state could restrict it only if it had a compelling interest in doing so (the so-called strict scrutiny standard for examining whether a law is constitutional). The majority concluded that the state had no compelling interest, and therefore laws restricting the right of abortion were unconstitutional.

Rehnquist (and White) vigorously dissented from this view. In the two paragraphs of section I of his dissent, Rehnquist first argues that, in effect, the Court should not have even heard the case. The Supreme Court does not hear theoretical cases. There has to be an actual plaintiff and an actual set of facts—a case—on which the Court can base its decision. Rehnquist notes that the record failed to show that "Jane Roe" was, in fact, such a plaintiff. Rehnquist goes on, however, to state that even if Roe did have a case properly before the Court, he disagreed with the Court's conclusion that the Constitution prohibits the states from regulating abortions in the first trimester of pregnancy.

When the Court reviews a law, or statute, for constitutionality, it balances the interest that the state has in regulating certain behavior against the interest a citizen has in pursuing the behavior. This attempt to find balance is made because every law takes away, even if only slightly, a citizen's right to do something and infringes on freedom to some degree. Thus, the Court is always weighing the interests of the state to maintain order, health, safety, and so on along with the interests of the individual to be free from unnecessary and overly intrusive regulation. The Court must determine whether a statute takes away too much freedom for the sake of public interests. In order to review whether a statute has gone too far in restricting individual behavior, the Court first identifies how important the citizen's interest in the regulated behavior is and then determines how important the state's interest in regulating the behavior is. Only then can a decision be made.

Rehnquist calls the act of having an abortion a "transaction resulting in an operation." Thus he takes the position that a citizen's interest in engaging in this behavior is not as important in the equation as some other behaviors, such as saving one's own life. He notes that if the statute prevented women from having abortions even to save their own lives, it would be unconstitutional because the regulation would be outweighed by the citizen's interest in life, a fundamental right protected by the Constitution.

By contrast, the majority opinion identifies the act of having an abortion as part of a fundamental right to privacy that arises out of rights specifically protected by the Fourteenth Amendment of the Constitution. When a right is defined as fundamental, it is the most important kind of interest a citizen can have and is difficult for a state to overcome. But Justice Rehnquist calls the citizen's interest at issue not a general right to privacy but, more narrowly, the right to an abortion, which is not fundamental because it has been regulated throughout history. Indeed, Rehnquist notes, abortion was regulated before the Fourteenth Amendment was even added to the Constitution, and he states this historical fact as support for the view that the drafters of the Fourteenth Amendment must not have thought abortion was a fundamental right. Therefore, he concludes, they did not intend to take away from the states the power to regulate it.

Rehnquist also disagrees with the Court's decision to parse a pregnancy into parts, prohibiting states from regulating first-trimester abortions while permitting them to regulate abortions after the end of the first trimester. This, he believes, was not within the power of the judiciary but is instead a matter appropriate for the legislature because it goes beyond simply interpreting the Constitution, which is the Court's role. Finally, he disagrees with the Court's decision to strike down the entire Texas statute, as parts of it regulated abortions after the first trimester, which the Court found were permissible regulations. Therefore, Rehnquist states, the Court should have struck down only the impermissible portions of the statute.

Although Rehnquist was not on the prevailing side of the issue raised by *Roe v. Wade*, his fundamental argument—that the Constitution, and specifically the Fourteenth Amendment, is silent on any presumed "right" to privacy—continues to be debated in other contexts, such as gay rights, and abortion opponents continue to make a similar argument.

◆ *United States v. Lopez*

The U.S. Supreme Court is the nation's highest court of appeal. As a court of appeal, it does not retry cases but instead reviews cases from lower courts to ensure that the constitutional rights of parties are protected and that the law was applied correctly. In this case, the Supreme Court was asked to review the constitutionality of the Gun-Free School Zones Act of 1990, which made it a federal offense for anyone, including a student, to carry a gun onto school property or the area surrounding it. The respondent in this case—that is, the party who "responds" to the appeal filed by the "petitioner"—was Alfonso Lopez, a student who was charged with carrying a gun to school. Lopez asked a lower district court, which initially heard the case, to dismiss the charge. The district court denied his request. The case was appealed to a U.S. appeals court, which found the 1990 act unconstitutional. In *United States v. Lopez*, the Supreme Court affirmed the ruling of the appeals court.

At issue in this case was the reach of the U.S. Congress under the commerce clause, Article I, Section 8, Clause 3 of the U.S. Constitution. This clause gives Congress the power to regulate interstate commerce, or commerce that crosses state lines; commerce conducted solely within a state (intrastate commerce) falls under the authority of that state, not the federal government. In modern life, there are few forms of commerce that do not take place

Norma McCorvey, the "Jane Roe" of Supreme Court's **Roe v. Wade** *decision* (AP/Wide World Photos)

over state lines; products are sold in more than one state, suppliers of raw materials come from other states, and so on. Accordingly, there are few types of commerce that the federal government cannot regulate.

The larger question becomes, what is "commerce"? Normally, the word applies to the buying and selling of goods and services. But during the twentieth century, Congress began to regard as commerce any activity that might have a bearing on the economic fortunes of a community. Thus, even though a school would not normally be thought of as a business, its activities can have economic effects that extend across state lines. The level of education of a workforce, for example, can have an impact on whether or not businesses outside the state will do business in the community served by the school. In the case of guns and schools, Congress essentially decided that because schools can have an impact on interstate commerce, it had the authority to regulate guns in and around school property.

In the view of some legal scholars, Congress has extended its understanding of interstate commerce in ways that the Constitution does not support and never intended. This belief is the essence of Rehnquist's holding in *United States v. Lopez*. In the first sentence, he states explicitly, "The [Gun-Free School Zones] Act exceeds Congress' Commerce Clause authority." He notes that although the Court has sometimes upheld state laws regulating intrastate commerce because they have an impact on interstate commerce, the act in question, as a criminal statute, has nothing to do with economic activity. He goes on to elaborate that sometimes such a statute can be part of a broader set of regulations that can, in fact, affect interstate commerce and that failure to uphold the one regulation would make it difficult for the broader set of laws to succeed in their intent. Rehnquist rejects the view that the Gun-Free School Zones Act is such a law. He continues by noting that the act of carrying a gun to school has nothing to do with interstate commerce or any kind of economic activity that would affect interstate commerce. He concludes that a law such as the one in question turns the commerce clause into a general police power on the part of the federal government, thus usurping the power of the states. It should be noted that Rehnquist was not in any way defending guns in schools. Rather, his view was that the federal government has no authority to regulate guns in schools, at least not on the basis of the commerce clause.

United States v. Lopez was a landmark case. Normally, the Supreme Court is more likely to overturn a law that bears on fundamental rights. The Court will apply the strict scrutiny standard it applied in *Roe v. Wade* to determine whether the state has a compelling interest in regulating the behavior in question. The Court, though, has another test, usually called the "rational basis standard." This standard is less strict and applies in cases that do not involve fundamental rights. In applying the standard, the Court asks whether the state has an important or "rational" interest in controlling the behavior, and most of the time it concludes that it does, so relatively few such laws are declared unconstitutional. Further, because such cases do not involve fundamental rights, the Court will rarely overturn laws that it examines using the rational basis standard. *United States v. Lopez* was just such a case, so the Court's willingness to overturn the law and rein in Congress in its interpretation of the commerce clause was noteworthy. With the cases as a precedent, other congressional acts that are justified on the basis of the commerce clause are susceptible to increased scrutiny by the courts.

◆ *George W. Bush et al. v. Albert Gore, Jr., et al.*

For more than a month after Election Day in November 2000, the outcome of the presidential race between Republican George W. Bush and Democrat Al Gore remained in doubt. Results on election night gave Gore 254 electoral votes to Bush's 246. Neither had the requisite 270 electoral votes. However, Florida, New Mexico, and Oregon were too close to call. New Mexico and Oregon had a total of twelve electoral votes. At that point, though, the outcome of the election would hinge on the much larger state of Florida and its twenty-five electoral votes. Whoever won Florida would win the election.

What followed was a period of contention and confusion. Because of the razor-thin margin separating Bush and Gore, state law required a recount. Additionally, Gore demanded a manual recount of ballots in three counties. No irregularities were found, and Bush won the recount by a minuscule margin. Immediately, though, suspicions of irregularities arose. In one liberal county, conservative Pat Buchanan, running as a third-party candidate, received an unaccountably high number of votes, leading to concerns that the layout of the ballot was confusing to voters who had intended to vote for Gore but voted for Buchanan instead—a point that Buchanan himself conceded. Other charges began to fly: that African Americans had been prevented from going to the polls; that absentee ballots, particularly those from military personnel overseas, were improperly counted; that voters in the Republican panhandle of Florida (which is in the central time zone) were, in effect, disenfranchised because some national news networks prematurely called the election for Gore based on results from the rest of the state (which is in the eastern time zone), causing people to not vote because they believed that the election was, for all intents and purposes, over.

In light of these considerations, legal wrangling began. The Gore team demanded a manual recount of votes in four counties based on the belief that some votes for Gore had not been counted. State law required all counties to submit their returns within one week, and it soon became clear that the counties could not complete the time-consuming manual recount process in that time. When two of the counties petitioned the courts for an extension, the Bush team went to federal court to oppose the granting of an extension. Moreover, there were disputes about how to conduct the manual recounts, and American television viewers became familiar with images of state officials examining punch ballots in an effort to determine whether they were valid.

Matters came to a head when the Gore campaign appealed to the Florida Supreme Court, which ordered that the recount should go forward despite the deadlines. The Bush team appealed to the U.S. Supreme Court, which vacated the Florida Supreme Court's decision and sent the case back for further consideration. Once again the Florida court ordered the recount to proceed. Again the Bush team opposed this move, and the U.S. Supreme Court ordered the recount to stop. Then, on December 12, 2000, the Supreme Court ruled by a seven-to-two vote that the method of recounting ballots ordered by the Florida court was unconstitutional. The Court's ruling in *Bush v. Gore* effectively stopped all recounts, allowing the state board of elections to declare Bush the winner. The decision was issued "per curiam," meaning by the court as a whole rather than by individual justices. A per curiam decision is usually a brief decision that includes little or no elaboration or explanation. In addition, Rehnquist, with the concurrence of Justices Antonin Scalia and Clarence Thomas, wrote an opinion in which they detailed the reasons for the Court's decision.

In section I, Rehnquist outlines the Court's rationale for intervening. He notes that while in general the federal courts defer to the states on matters of state law—in this case, statutes governing elections—the election of the nation's president is not an "ordinary" matter. He notes, in particular, that Article II, Section 1, Clause 2 of the U.S. Constitution confers a duty on state governments with regard to conducting a presidential election in each state. Specifically, it imposes this duty on the state legislatures. Accordingly, state courts lack the authority to intervene in or modify federal election procedures as outlined in a state's statutes. In Florida the legislature by law had delegated the conduct of elections to the state's secretary of state. In a case where a state court, such as the Florida Supreme Court, is attempting to interfere with the constitutional duties of the legislature, the U.S. Supreme Court is obligated to intervene.

In section II, Rehnquist outlines the provisions of Florida law governing elections and the counting of election returns. In particular, Rehnquist notes that under Florida law the state's secretary of state is the "chief election officer" and as such has the responsibility to "obtain and maintain uniformity in the application, operation, and interpretation of the election laws." The question of uniformity was crucial, for the Court concluded that the state had no uniform procedure for conducting the kind of manual recount that the Gore team was requesting. Rehnquist goes on to describe the state's process for "certification." After all ballots have been cast and counted, the secretary of state then *certifies* the election winner; state law required such certification to take place by a certain deadline. The problem, of course, is that if one of the candidates disputes the election results, the amount of time necessary for contesting the results and then for the state to investigate the matter is necessarily limited in the case of a presidential election. Rehnquist makes clear that in its ruling to allow recounts to proceed, the Florida Supreme Court was essentially ignoring state law and usurping the authority of the state election authorities.

To this point, Rehnquist is addressing primarily procedural issues. He then turns to the substance of the dispute—the claim by Gore that some people who voted for him had their ballots declared invalid. In examining punch ballots, officials discovered numerous cases where the voter had apparently tried to vote for Gore but the "chad," the bit of paper punched out in a punch ballot, was still hanging on to the ballot; the caution to voters on the ballot itself refers to these as "chips." Additionally, there were instances of the so-called pregnant chad, where it appeared that the voter had tried to punch the ballot but succeeded only in making an indentation. Although these ballots by statute were invalid, many Gore supporters wanted them to be counted as reflecting the will of the voters; throughout, these are referred to as "undervotes." Rehnquist rejects this view. He notes that the ballots in question clearly instruct voters to make sure their ballots are clearly and cleanly marked and that "THERE ARE NO CHIPS LEFT HANGING ON THE BACK OF THE CARD." He states explicitly, "There is no basis for reading the Florida statutes as requiring the counting of improperly marked ballots."

Essential Quotes

"*I have difficulty in concluding, as the Court does, that the right of 'privacy' is involved in this case.*"

(*Roe v. Wade*)

"*To reach its result, the Court necessarily has had to find within the scope of the Fourteenth Amendment a right that was apparently completely unknown to the drafters of the Amendment.*"

(*Roe v. Wade*)

"*The possession of a gun in a local school zone is in no sense an economic activity that might, through repetition elsewhere, have such a substantial effect on interstate commerce.*"

(*United States v. Lopez*)

"*The scheme that the Florida Supreme Court's opinion attributes to the legislature is one in which machines are required to be 'capable of correctly counting votes,' but which nonetheless regularly produces elections in which legal votes are predictably not tabulated, so that in close elections manual recounts are regularly required. This is of course absurd.*"

(*Bush v. Gore*)

In section III, Rehnquist returns to procedural issues, particularly the issue of the limited amount of time available to conduct a recount. He notes that just four days before the time when certification was required, the Florida Supreme Court ordered the manual recounting of tens of thousands of ballots—a clear impossibility. He notes that these ballots had all been counted, then counted again in the mandatory recount. There was no allegation of any kind of fraud. Therefore, ordering a further recount in a "delusive" effort to arrive at a 100 percent accurate vote total was impossible. Rehnquist concludes that the Florida Supreme Court overstepped its authority and contravened the will of the state legislature. Therefore, the Supreme Court reversed the Florida court's decision, effectively putting an end to the dispute.

Rehnquist's argument did little to appease Gore's supporters. Throughout the administration of the winner, George W. Bush, Gore supporters continued to believe that the election had been stolen, particularly in light of the fact that Gore won the overall popular vote (but not the crucial electoral vote). Charges continued to be made that somehow Bush's brother, Jeb, who at the time was governor of Florida, rigged the election; that the state secretary of state, a Bush supporter, was complicit in rigging the election; and that the Supreme Court was stacked with justices appointed by Bush's father, George H. W. Bush.

Impact and Legacy

William Rehnquist was appointed to the Supreme Court and then appointed chief justice with a mandate to shift the Court in a more conservative direction in the wake of the more liberal Court presided over by his predecessor, Warren Burger. During his early years on the Court, he was often the only dissenter in eight-to-one decisions, earning him the nickname "the Lone Ranger." Although his colleagues on the Burger Court usually outvoted him, he began to lay the groundwork for a more conservative jurisprudence that would take hold during his years as chief justice.

In particular, Rehnquist was the architect of a jurisprudence often called the New Federalism. This term refers to the belief that one of the chief goals of the Court was to protect states from intrusion by the federal government, a principle Rehnquist and many others believed is enshrined in Article I of the Constitution, which expressly limits the powers of Congress. Consistently throughout his career, he attempted to rein in the power of the federal government and allow states, where possible, to follow their own legal course. His decision in *United States v. Lopez* is a clear example; in his view, Congress exceeded its authority when it attempted to use the Constitution's commerce clause to impose a regulation on what should be a state matter. He applied this principle consistently in other cases. For exam-

Questions for Further Study

1. Discuss the issues of importance and the reasoning behind Rehnquist's dissent in *Roe v. Wade*, starting with his argument that the case itself should never have come before the Supreme Court because it involved a "theoretical" issue rather than a matter of constitutional law. Most important of the issues is the matter of a "right to privacy," which his fellow justices found in the Constitution, specifically the Fourteenth Amendment, but which Rehnquist did not. Do you believe that a right to privacy is guaranteed in the Constitution? If so, should it extend to abortion rights? Is abortion a "fundamental" right? Finally, regardless of your position on abortion, do you believe that *Roe* was the right case to address the issue?

2. What is unusual about *United States v. Lopez* as a case involving nonfundamental rights? Put another way, why is it significant that the Court reviewed and ultimately overturned a ruling that did not involve fundamental rights? Begin by defining the difference between fundamental and nonfundamental rights and then examine the facts of the case. What is a reasonable limit to congressional power under the commerce clause of the Constitution? What is the "rational basis standard," and how was it applied in this case?

3. Few recent Supreme Court decisions have been as controversial as *George W. Bush et al. v. Albert Gore, Jr., et al.*. Numerous books have been written on the subject, most arguing that the Court acted wrongly in striking down the lower court's ruling and ordering that the Florida recount cease. Do you agree? Discuss the history and facts of the case, including the problems with the physical ballots themselves and the resulting controversy over counting votes. Was Gore justified in disputing the election outcome, or should he have dropped his case in the interest of national unity? Compare his actions to those of Richard Nixon, who lost in 1960 by a narrow margin in the popular vote but refused to dispute the outcome, despite allegations that Chicago Democrats had engaged in ballot stuffing.

ple, in 2000 he struck down a provision of the 1994 Violence against Women Act. This act made "gender motivated violence" a federal cause of action. Rehnquist did not think that violence against women was not a serious problem. His belief was that it was a local matter, beyond the reach of the federal government. As he put it, "The Constitution requires a distinction between what is truly national and what is truly local" (*U.S. v. Morrison*, 120 S. Ct. 1754 [2000]).

Rehnquist also opposed the expansion of judicial interpretation of the Fourteenth Amendment. As demonstrated in his dissent in *Roe v. Wade*, he disagreed with the Burger Court's view that the Fourteenth Amendment grants a right to privacy, a right that is not enumerated in the Constitution. In such matters as civil rights, he argued that the Fourteenth Amendment did not give an individual the right to seek redress in the courts on the basis of "disparate impact"—the notion that a policy, while not explicitly discriminatory, has a disproportionately negative impact on a racial group.

Many members of the legal community maintain that Rehnquist was not a particularly elegant writer. He provided few ringing phrases and sentences, in contrast to some of his predecessors on the Court. His arguments were often somewhat obscure and tortuous. Nevertheless, even his opponents agreed that he had a keen legal mind and that the impact of his views would influence the Court and national policy for years to come.

Key Sources

Rehnquist wrote four books: *The Supreme Court: How It Was, How It Is* (1987), which was revised as *The Supreme Court* (2002); *Grand Inquests: The Historic Impeachments of Justice Samuel Chase and President Andrew Johnson* (1992); *All the Laws but One: Civil Liber-*

ties in Wartime (1998); and *The Centennial Crisis: The Disputed Election of 1876* (2004).

Further Reading

■ Books

Belsky, Martin H., ed. *The Rehnquist Court: A Retrospective*. New York: Oxford University Press, 2002.

Bradley, Craig, ed. *The Rehnquist Legacy*. New York: Cambridge University Press, 2006.

Hensley, Thomas R. *The Rehnquist Court Justices, Rulings, and Legacy*. Santa Barbara, Calif.: ABC-CLIO, 2006.

Hudson, David L. *The Rehnquist Court: Understanding Its Impact and Legacy*. Westport, Conn.: Praeger Publishers, 2007.

Maltz, Earl M. *Rehnquist Justice: Understanding the Court Dynamic*. Lawrence: University Press of Kansas, 2003.

Savage, David G. *Turning Right: The Making of the Rehnquist Supreme Court*. New York: Wiley, 1993.

Schwartz, Herman, ed. *The Rehnquist Court: Judicial Activism on the Right*. New York: Hill and Wang, 2002.

Tushnet, Mark. *A Court Divided: The Rehnquist Court and the Future of Constitutional Law*. New York: W. W. Norton, 2005.

Woodward, Robert, and Scott Armstrong. *The Brethren: Inside the Supreme Court*. New York: Simon and Schuster, 1979.

—Michael J. O'Neal

Roe v. Wade (1973)

Rehnquist dissent

The Court's opinion brings to the decision of this troubling question both extensive historical fact and a wealth of legal scholarship. While the opinion thus commands my respect, I find myself nonetheless in fundamental disagreement with those parts of it that invalidate the Texas statute in question, and therefore dissent.

◆ I

The Court's opinion decides that a State may impose virtually no restriction on the performance of abortions during the first trimester of pregnancy. Our previous decisions indicate that a necessary predicate for such an opinion is a plaintiff who was in her first trimester of pregnancy at some time during the pendency of her lawsuit. While a party may vindicate his own constitutional rights, he may not seek vindication for the rights of others. The Court's statement of facts in this case makes clear, however, that the record in no way indicates the presence of such a plaintiff. We know only that plaintiff Roe at the time of filing her complaint was a pregnant woman; for aught that appears in this record, she may have been in her last trimester of pregnancy as of the date the complaint was filed.

Nothing in the Court's opinion indicates that Texas might not constitutionally apply its proscription of abortion as written to a woman in that stage of pregnancy. Nonetheless, the Court uses her complaint against the Texas statute as a fulcrum for deciding that States may impose virtually no restrictions on medical abortions performed during the first trimester of pregnancy. In deciding such a hypothetical lawsuit, the Court departs from the longstanding admonition that it should never "formulate a rule of constitutional law broader than is required by the precise facts to which it is to be applied."

◆ II

Even if there were a plaintiff in this case capable of litigating the issue which the Court decides, I would reach a conclusion opposite to that reached by the Court. I have difficulty in concluding, as the Court does, that the right of "privacy" is involved in this case. Texas, by the statute here challenged, bars the performance of a medical abortion by a licensed physician on a plaintiff such as Roe. A transaction resulting in an operation such as this is not "private" in the ordinary usage of that word. Nor is the "privacy" that the Court finds here even a distant relative of the freedom from searches and seizures protected by the Fourth Amendment to the Constitution, which the Court has referred to as embodying a right to privacy.

If the Court means by the term "privacy" no more than that the claim of a person to be free from unwanted state regulation of consensual transactions may be a form of "liberty" protected by the Fourteenth Amendment, there is no doubt that similar claims have been upheld in our earlier decisions on the basis of that liberty. I agree with the statement of MR. JUSTICE STEWART in his concurring opinion that the "liberty," against deprivation of which without due process the Fourteenth Amendment protects, embraces more than the rights found in the Bill of Rights. But that liberty is not guaranteed absolutely against deprivation, only against deprivation without due process of law. The test traditionally applied in the area of social and economic legislation is whether or not a law such as that challenged has a rational relation to a valid state objective. The Due Process Clause of the Fourteenth Amendment undoubtedly does place a limit, albeit a broad one, on legislative power to enact laws such as this. If the Texas statute were to prohibit an abortion even where the mother's life is in jeopardy, I have little doubt that such a statute would lack a rational relation to a valid state objective.... But the Court's sweeping invalidation of any restrictions on abortion during the first trimester is impossible to justify under that standard, and the conscious weighing of competing factors that the Court's opinion apparently substitutes for the established test is far more appropriate to a legislative judgment than to a judicial one.

The Court eschews the history of the Fourteenth Amendment in its reliance on the "compelling state interest" test. But the Court adds a new wrinkle to this test by transposing it from the legal considerations associated with the Equal Protection Clause of the Fourteenth Amendment to this case arising under the Due Process Clause of the Fourteenth Amendment. Unless I misapprehend the consequences of this transplanting of the "compelling state interest test," the Court's opinion will accomplish the seemingly impossible feat of leaving this area of the law more confused than it found it.

While the Court's opinion quotes from the dissent of Mr. Justice Holmes in *Lochner v. New York*, the result it reaches is more closely attuned to the majority opinion of Mr. Justice Peckham in that case. As in Lochner and similar cases applying substantive due process standards to economic and social welfare legislation, the adoption of the compelling state interest standard will inevitably require this Court to examine the legislative policies and pass on the wisdom of these policies in the very process of deciding whether a particular state interest put forward may or may not be "compelling." The decision here to break pregnancy into three distinct terms and to outline the permissible restrictions the State may impose in each one, for example, partakes more of judicial legislation than it does of a determination of the intent of the drafters of the Fourteenth Amendment.

The fact that a majority of the States reflecting, after all, the majority sentiment in those States, have had restrictions on abortions for at least a century is a strong indication, it seems to me, that the asserted right to an abortion is not "so rooted in the traditions and conscience of our people as to be ranked as fundamental." Even today, when society's views on abortion are changing, the very existence of the debate is evidence that the "right" to an abortion is not so universally accepted as the appellant would have us believe.

To reach its result, the Court necessarily has had to find within the scope of the Fourteenth Amendment a right that was apparently completely unknown to the drafters of the Amendment. As early as 1821, the first state law dealing directly with abortion was enacted by the Connecticut Legislature. By the time of the adoption of the Fourteenth Amendment in 1868, there were at least 36 laws enacted by state or territorial legislatures limiting abortion. While many States have amended or updated their laws, 21 of the laws on the books in 1868 remain in effect today. Indeed, the Texas statute struck down today was, as the majority notes, first enacted in 1857 and "has remained substantially unchanged to the present time."

There apparently was no question concerning the validity of this provision or of any of the other state statutes when the Fourteenth Amendment was adopted. The only conclusion possible from this history is that the drafters did not intend to have the Fourteenth Amendment withdraw from the States the power to legislate with respect to this matter.

◆ III

Even if one were to agree that the case that the Court decides were here, and that the enunciation of the substantive constitutional law in the Court's opinion were proper, the actual disposition of the case by the Court is still difficult to justify. The Texas statute is struck down in toto, even though the Court apparently concedes that at later periods of pregnancy Texas might impose these selfsame statutory limitations on abortion. My understanding of past practice is that a statute found to be invalid as applied to a particular plaintiff, but not unconstitutional as a whole, is not simply "'struck down'" but is, instead, declared unconstitutional as applied to the fact situation before the Court.

For all of the foregoing reasons, I respectfully dissent.

Glossary

eschews	avoids, rejects
"formulate a rule of constitutional law ..."	quotation from Justice Oliver Wendell Holmes in *Chastleton Corporation et al. v. Sinclair et al.* (1924)
in toto	entirely, in total
Mr. Justice Holmes	Oliver Wendell Holmes, associate justice of the Supreme Court
Mr. Justice Peckham	Rufus Wheeler Peckham, associate justice of the Supreme Court
pendency	the state of being pending or in process
predicate	precondition, requirement
"so rooted in the traditions ..."	quotation from Supreme Court justice Benjamin Cardozo in *Snyder v. Massachusetts* (1934)

UNITED STATES V. LOPEZ (1995)

After respondent, then a 12th-grade student, carried a concealed handgun into his high school, he was charged with violating the Gun-Free School Zones Act of 1990, which forbids "any individual knowingly to possess a firearm at a place that [he] knows…is a school zone," 18 U. S. C. 922(q)(1)(A). The District Court denied his motion to dismiss the indictment, concluding that 922(q) is a constitutional exercise of Congress' power to regulate activities in and affecting commerce. In reversing, the Court of Appeals held that, in light of what it characterized as insufficient congressional findings and legislative history, 922(q) is invalid as beyond Congress' power under the Commerce Clause.

Held:

The Act exceeds Congress' Commerce Clause authority. First, although this Court has upheld a wide variety of congressional Acts regulating intrastate economic activity that substantially affected interstate commerce, the possession of a gun in a local school zone is in no sense an economic activity that might, through repetition elsewhere, have such a substantial effect on interstate commerce. Section 922(q) is a criminal statute that by its terms has nothing to do with "commerce" or any sort of economic enterprise, however broadly those terms are defined. Nor is it an essential part of a larger regulation of economic activity, in which the regulatory scheme could be undercut unless the intrastate activity were regulated. It cannot, therefore, be sustained under the Court's cases upholding regulations of activities that arise out of or are connected with a commercial transaction, which viewed in the aggregate, substantially affects interstate commerce. Second, 922(q) contains no jurisdictional element which would ensure, through case-by-case inquiry, that the firearms possession in question has the requisite nexus with interstate commerce. Respondent was a local student at a local school; there is no indication that he had recently moved in interstate commerce, and there is no requirement that his possession of the firearm have any concrete tie to interstate commerce. To uphold the Government's contention that 922(q) is justified because firearms possession in a local school zone does indeed substantially affect interstate commerce would require this Court to pile inference upon inference in a manner that would bid fair to convert congressional Commerce Clause authority to a general police power of the sort held only by the States.

Glossary

nexus	connection

GEORGE W. BUSH ET AL. V. ALBERT GORE, JR., ET AL. (2000)

Rehnquist concurrence

We join the per curiam opinion. We write separately because we believe there are additional grounds that require us to reverse the Florida Supreme Court's decision.

◆ I

We deal here not with an ordinary election, but with an election for the President of the United States. In *Burroughs v. United States*, we said: "While presidential electors are not officers or agents of the federal government, they exercise federal functions under, and discharge duties in virtue of authority conferred by, the Constitution of the United States. The President is vested with the executive power of the nation. The importance of his election and the vital character of its relationship to and effect upon the welfare and safety of the whole people cannot be too strongly stated."

Likewise, in *Anderson v. Celebrezze*, we said: "[I]n the context of a Presidential election, state-imposed restrictions implicate a uniquely important national interest. For the President and the Vice President of the United States are the only elected officials who represent all the voters in the Nation."

In most cases, comity and respect for federalism compel us to defer to the decisions of state courts on issues of state law. That practice reflects our understanding that the decisions of state courts are definitive pronouncements of the will of the States as sovereigns. Of course, in ordinary cases, the distribution of powers among the branches of a State's government raises no questions of federal constitutional law, subject to the requirement that the government be republican in character. But there are a few exceptional cases in which the Constitution imposes a duty or confers a power on a particular branch of a State's government. This is one of them. Article II, §1, cl. 2, provides that "[e]ach State shall appoint, in such Manner as the Legislature thereof may direct," electors for President and Vice President. Thus, the text of the election law itself, and not just its interpretation by the courts of the States, takes on independent significance.

In *McPherson v. Blacker*, we explained that Art. II, §1, cl. 2, "convey[s] the broadest power of deter-mination" and "leaves it to the legislature exclusively to define the method" of appointment. A significant departure from the legislative scheme for appointing Presidential electors presents a federal constitutional question.

3 U.S.C. §5 informs our application of Art. II, §1, cl. 2, to the Florida statutory scheme, which, as the Florida Supreme Court acknowledged, took that statute into account. Section 5 provides that the State's selection of electors "shall be conclusive, and shall govern in the counting of the electoral votes" if the electors are chosen under laws enacted prior to election day, and if the selection process is completed six days prior to the meeting of the electoral college. As we noted in *Bush v. Palm Beach County Canvassing Bd.*, "Since §5 contains a principle of federal law that would assure finality of the State's determination if made pursuant to a state law in effect before the election, a legislative wish to take advantage of the 'safe harbor' would counsel against any construction of the Election Code that Congress might deem to be a change in the law."

If we are to respect the legislature's Article II powers, therefore, we must ensure that postelection state-court actions do not frustrate the legislative desire to attain the "safe harbor" provided by §5.

In Florida, the legislature has chosen to hold statewide elections to appoint the State's 25 electors. Importantly, the legislature has delegated the authority to run the elections and to oversee election disputes to the Secretary of State (Secretary), and to state circuit courts. Isolated sections of the code may well admit of more than one interpretation, but the general coherence of the legislative scheme may not be altered by judicial interpretation so as to wholly change the statutorily provided apportionment of responsibility among these various bodies. In any election but a Presidential election, the Florida Supreme Court can give as little or as much deference to Florida's executives as it chooses, so far as Article II is concerned, and this Court will have no cause to question the court's actions. But, with respect to a Presidential election, the court must be both mindful of the legislature's role under Article II in choosing the manner of appointing electors and deferential to those bodies expressly empowered by the legislature to carry out its constitutional mandate.

In order to determine whether a state court has infringed upon the legislature's authority, we necessarily must examine the law of the State as it existed prior to the action of the court. Though we generally defer to state courts on the interpretation of state law there are of course areas in which the Constitution requires this Court to undertake an independent, if still deferential, analysis of state law....

This inquiry does not imply a disrespect for state courts but rather a respect for the constitutionally prescribed role of state legislatures. To attach definitive weight to the pronouncement of a state court, when the very question at issue is whether the court has actually departed from the statutory meaning, would be to abdicate our responsibility to enforce the explicit requirements of Article II.

◆ **II**

Acting pursuant to its constitutional grant of authority, the Florida Legislature has created a detailed, if not perfectly crafted, statutory scheme that provides for appointment of Presidential electors by direct election. Under the statute, "[v]otes cast for the actual candidates for President and Vice President shall be counted as votes cast for the presidential electors supporting such candidates." The legislature has designated the Secretary of State as the "chief election officer," with the responsibility to "[o]btain and maintain uniformity in the application, operation, and interpretation of the election laws." The state legislature has delegated to county canvassing boards the duties of administering elections. Those boards are responsible for providing results to the state Elections Canvassing Commission, comprising the Governor, the Secretary of State, and the Director of the Division of Elections....

After the election has taken place, the canvassing boards receive returns from precincts, count the votes, and in the event that a candidate was defeated by .5% or less, conduct a mandatory recount. The county canvassing boards must file certified election returns with the Department of State by 5 p.m. on the seventh day following the election. The Elections Canvassing Commission must then certify the results of the election.

The state legislature has also provided mechanisms both for protesting election returns and for contesting certified election results. Section 102.166 governs protests. Any protest must be filed prior to the certification of election results by the county canvassing board. Once a protest has been filed, "the county canvassing board may authorize a manual recount." If a sample recount conducted pursuant to §102.166(5) "indicates an error in the vote tabulation which could affect the outcome of the election," the county canvassing board is instructed to: "(a) Correct the error and recount the remaining precincts with the vote tabulation system; (b) Request the Department of State to verify the tabulation software; or (c) Manually recount all ballots," In the event a canvassing board chooses to conduct a manual recount of all ballots, §102.166(7) prescribes procedures for such a recount.

Contests to the certification of an election, on the other hand, are controlled by §102.168. The grounds for contesting an election include "[r]eceipt of a number of illegal votes or rejection of a number of legal votes sufficient to change or place in doubt the result of the election." Any contest must be filed in the appropriate Florida circuit court, and the canvassing board or election board is the proper party defendant. Section 102.168(8) provides that "[t]he circuit judge to whom the contest is presented may fashion such orders as he or she deems necessary to ensure that each allegation in the complaint is investigated, examined, or checked, to prevent or correct any alleged wrong, and to provide any relief appropriate under such circumstances." In Presidential elections, the contest period necessarily terminates on the date set by 3 U.S.C. §5 for concluding the State's "final determination" of election controversies.

In its first decision, *Palm Beach Canvassing Bd. v. Harris (Harris I)*, the Florida Supreme Court extended the 7-day statutory certification deadline established by the legislature. This modification of the code, by lengthening the protest period, necessarily shortened the contest period for Presidential elections. Underlying the extension of the certification deadline and the shortchanging of the contest period was, presumably, the clear implication that certification was a matter of significance: The certified winner would enjoy presumptive validity, making a contest proceeding by the losing candidate an uphill battle. In its latest opinion, however, the court empties certification of virtually all legal consequence during the contest, and in doing so departs from the provisions enacted by the Florida Legislature.

The court determined that canvassing boards' decisions regarding whether to recount ballots past the certification deadline (even the certification deadline established by Harris I) are to be reviewed de novo, although the election code clearly vests discretion whether to recount in the boards, and sets strict deadlines subject to the Secretary's rejection of late tallies and monetary fines for tardiness. Moreover, the Florida court held that all late vote tallies arriving during the contest period should be automatically included in the certification regardless of the certification deadline (even the certification deadline established by Harris I), thus virtually eliminating both the deadline and the Secretary's discretion to disregard recounts that violate it.

Moreover, the court's interpretation of "legal vote," and hence its decision to order a contest-period recount, plainly departed from the legislative scheme. Florida statutory law cannot reasonably be thought to require the counting of improperly marked ballots. Each Florida precinct before election day provides instructions on how properly to cast a vote, §101.46; each polling place on election day contains a working model of the voting machine it uses, §101.5611; and each voting booth contains a sample ballot, §101.46. In precincts using punch-card ballots, voters are instructed to punch out the ballot cleanly:

AFTER VOTING, CHECK YOUR BALLOT CARD TO BE SURE YOUR VOTING SELECTIONS ARE CLEARLY AND CLEANLY PUNCHED AND THERE ARE NO CHIPS LEFT HANGING ON THE BACK OF THE CARD.

No reasonable person would call it "an error in the vote tabulation," or a "rejection of legal votes," when electronic or electromechanical equipment performs precisely in the manner designed, and fails to count those ballots that are not marked in the manner that these voting instructions explicitly and prominently specify. The scheme that the Florida Supreme Court's opinion attributes to the legislature is one in which machines are required to be "capable of correctly counting votes," but which nonetheless regularly produces elections in which legal votes are predictably not tabulated, so that in close elections manual recounts are regularly required. This is of course absurd. The Secretary of State, who is authorized by law to issue binding interpretations of the election code, rejected this peculiar reading of the statutes. The Florida Supreme Court, although it must defer to the Secretary's interpretations, rejected her reasonable interpretation and embraced the peculiar one. (Harris III).

But as we indicated in our remand of the earlier case, in a Presidential election the clearly expressed intent of the legislature must prevail. And there is no basis for reading the Florida statutes as requiring the counting of improperly marked ballots, as an examination of the Florida Supreme Court's textual analysis shows. We will not parse that analysis here, except to note that the principal provision of the election code on which it relied, §101.5614(5), was, as the Chief Justice pointed out in his dissent from Harris II, entirely irrelevant. The State's Attorney General

(who was supporting the Gore challenge) confirmed in oral argument here that never before the present election had a manual recount been conducted on the basis of the contention that "undervotes" should have been examined to determine voter intent. For the court to step away from this established practice, prescribed by the Secretary of State, the state official charged by the legislature with "responsibility to ... [o]btain and maintain uniformity in the application, operation, and interpretation of the election laws," was to depart from the legislative scheme.

◆ **III**

The scope and nature of the remedy ordered by the Florida Supreme Court jeopardizes the "legislative wish" to take advantage of the safe harbor provided by 3 U.S.C. §5. December 12, 2000, is the last date for a final determination of the Florida electors that will satisfy §5. Yet in the late afternoon of December 8th—four days before this deadline—the Supreme Court of Florida ordered recounts of tens of thousands of so-called "undervotes" spread through 64 of the State's 67 counties. This was done in a search for elusive—perhaps delusive—certainty as to the exact count of 6 million votes. But no one claims that these ballots have not previously been tabulated; they were initially read by voting machines at the time of the election, and thereafter reread by virtue of Florida's automatic recount provision. No one claims there was any fraud in the election. The Supreme Court of Florida ordered this additional recount under the provision of the election code giving the circuit judge the authority to provide relief that is "appropriate under such circumstances."

Surely when the Florida Legislature empowered the courts of the State to grant "appropriate" relief, it must have meant relief that would have become final by the cutoff date of 3 U.S.C. §5. In light of the inevitable legal challenges and ensuing appeals to the Supreme Court of Florida and petitions for certiorari to this Court, the entire recounting process could not possibly be completed by that date. Whereas the majority in the Supreme Court of Florida stated its confidence that "the remaining undervotes in these counties can be [counted] within the required time frame," it made no assertion that the seemingly inevitable appeals could be disposed of in that time. Although the Florida Supreme Court has on occasion taken over a year to resolve disputes over local elections, it has heard and decided the appeals in the present case with great promptness. But the federal deadlines for the Presidential election simply do not permit even such a shortened process....

Given all these factors, and in light of the legislative intent identified by the Florida Supreme Court to bring Florida within the "safe harbor" provision of 3 U.S.C. §5, the remedy prescribed by the Supreme Court of Florida cannot be deemed an "appropriate" one as of December 8. It significantly departed from the statutory framework in place on November 7, and authorized open-ended further proceedings which could not be completed by December 12, thereby preventing a final determination by that date.

For these reasons, in addition to those given in the per curiam, we would reverse.

certiorari	a writ issued by a higher court ordering a lower court to deliver a case record for review; more generally, the granting of a right to appeal a case
comity	the principle of legal reciprocity, meaning that a jurisdiction respects the validity and effects of judicial, legislative, and executive acts of another jurisdiction
de novo	a legal term for "anew" or "from the beginning," meaning that a court of appeals is not required to defer to the rulings of a lower court
pursuant to	according to
remand	the act of a higher court of sending a case back to a lower court for reconsideration
safe harbor	any set of regulations that, if followed, guarantee compliance with the law

Walter Reuther (AP/Wide World Photos)

WALTER REUTHER   1907–1970

Labor Movement Leader

Reuther, Walter

Featured Documents
- ◆ "500 Planes a Day" Speech (1940)
- ◆ National Hour Radio Address on Inflation (1946)
- ◆ "The Guaranteed Annual Wage" Address (1955)
- ◆ Address before the Annual Convention of the National Association for the Advancement of Colored People (1957)
- ◆ Address before the Berlin Freedom Rally (1959)

Overview

Walter Reuther was a leading figure in the American labor movement, serving as president of the United Automobile Workers (UAW) from 1946 to 1970. He was born in Wheeling, West Virginia, on September 1, 1907. His father, Valentine, worked as a brewer and taught his sons, Walter and Victor, the importance of union membership and social activism. At the age of nineteen, Reuther moved to Detroit and joined Ford Motor Company as a tool and die maker. Fired by Ford because of his campaign work for the Socialist Party, he traveled to the Soviet Union with his brother, where they trained employees at the Ford-Soviet joint venture facility in Gorky and observed Stalin's rule firsthand.

When the brothers returned to the United States in 1935, Walter became active in Detroit union politics and was elected to the UAW's executive board in 1936. He was instrumental in unionizing Detroit's automobile industry, gaining notoriety in May 1937 when Ford company policemen attacked a group of UAW representatives who were distributing union flyers outside the Ford complex in Dearborn, Michigan. The incident became known as the Battle of the Overpass. Publicity photos of a battered Reuther made him a celebrity, and in 1939 the UAW named him head of the General Motors (GM) department.

In 1940 Reuther devised a proposal to capitalize on underutilized capacity in the nation's automobile manufacturing plants. In his "500 Planes a Day" plan, which he outlined to the public in a series of articles and speeches, he proposed that idle production facilities be used to manufacture five hundred military planes a day to aid Britain and its allies. Reuther enhanced his national reputation when he argued that GM could raise its workers' wages without raising the price of its cars. In his 1946 National Hour radio address on inflation, Reuther called for the automobile manufacturer to reveal its financial status to the public and to act in the interests of society, not just its shareholders. In 1948 GM agreed to a contract tying wage increases to increases in the cost of living and in productivity.

As president of the UAW, Reuther fought to increase benefits for union workers, claiming that job security and dignity for manufacturing employees would benefit the entire country, not just union labor. He campaigned for such ideas as a cost-of-living wage increase, unemployment benefits, health

and life insurance, bereavement pay, and pension plans. Reuther called for a guaranteed annual wage and delivered a key address to the 1955 UAW convention outlining his ideas.

Reuther traveled widely outside the United States; he believed that the labor movement had to be international in order to truly achieve its objectives. He helped found the International Confederation of Free Trade Unions. Once a supporter of Communism, Reuther turned against the Soviet Union and in 1959 addressed the May Day Freedom Rally in West Berlin.

Reuther was also engaged in a wide variety of social issues in his day. An ardent supporter of the civil rights movement, he was one of the few white people honored with a place on the podium at the March on Washington in 1963. Reuther was a friend of Martin Luther King, Jr.; he contributed to the Southern Christian Leadership Conference and delivered a speech before the 1957 convention of the National Association for the Advancement of Colored People (NAACP) in Detroit. He worked to develop low-cost housing in Detroit and built a worker education center near Black Lake in northern Michigan. On their way to visit the Black Lake facility, Reuther and his wife, May, were killed when their plane crashed on May 9, 1970.

Explanation and Analysis of Documents

As head of the UAW, Reuther was one of the most important figures in the history of American labor. Not only did he win significant benefits for manufacturing workers, he also had a revolutionary vision for a society involving a partnership between management, business, and workers in decision making. In his many public addresses, Reuther sought to depict the American laborer as part of the middle class, placing blue-collar and white-collar workers on the same level. Five key documents reflect Reuther's concept for a new society: the "500 planes a day" speech, a radio address on inflation, and his addresses before the 1955 UAW convention, the 1957 NAACP convention, and the Berlin Freedom Rally in 1959.

◆ "500 Planes a Day" Speech
In 1940 Hitler brazenly invaded nation after nation in Western Europe and launched the Battle of Britain on July

Time Line

1907
- **September 1**
  Walter Reuther is born in Wheeling, West Virginia.

1927
- **April**
  Reuther is hired by Ford as a tool and die worker in Detroit.

1932
- **September 30**
  Ford fires Reuther for his activities in support of the Socialist Party.

1933
- **February 16**
  Victor and Walter Reuther leave for Germany and Russia.

1937
- **May 26**
  Reuther and three other workers are beaten by Ford company police in the Battle of the Overpass.

1939
- **May**
  Reuther heads the United Automobile Workers' General Motors department.

1940
- **June 24**
  The United Automobile Workers and General Motors sign a contract.
- **December 28**
  Reuther delivers his "500 planes a day" speech.

1945
- **November 21**
  A General Motors strike begins.

1946
- **February 10**
  Reuther delivers his National Hour radio address on inflation.
- **March 27**
  Reuther becomes president of the United Automobile Workers.

---

10. Although the United States remained neutral in the growing conflict, the Neutrality Act of 1939 allowed America to sell France and England weapons and other matériel. By mid-1940 public fears about entering the war began to be overshadowed by the desire to help the struggling British cause. In May, President Franklin Delano Roosevelt asked Congress to triple the military budget and called for the production of fifty thousand military airplanes a year— more warplanes than existed in the world at that time.

However, the nation lacked the capacity to manufacture planes on such a large scale. Building new plants in which the planes could be designed and manufactured would take years, and Hitler's acceleration of hostilities added to the urgency of the military buildup. One possible solution was to use existing plant capacity in the automobile industry, to cease production of cars and devote those resources to building aircraft. But Detroit's manufacturers were less than enthusiastic about losing business in what was then a growing and profitable consumer market.

In his "500 planes" speech Reuther outlined his plan for meeting the nation's war production needs by using under-utilized or idle factory capacity in the automobile industry. Draped in patriotic language, the speech lays out a program that benefits not just the war effort but the automobile industry as well. It is a prime example of Reuther illustrating the leadership role of labor in American society. In his emotional introduction Reuther invokes the code of chivalry to convey the technological realities of modern warfare and also to emphasize that America is honor-bound to come to Britain's aid. He juxtaposes the image of Londoners "huddled in the subways" for safety with that of Americans "huddled over blueprints"; this imagery makes it clear that while Americans have the luxury of pondering over plans, the British people do not.

Reuther establishes labor's ownership of the plan to build five hundred planes a day using idle automobile manufacturing capacity. He notes that workers in Detroit developed the plan, and attributes their motivation to patriotism and defense of freedom. However, Reuther's plan also served to bolster organized labor's position in American politics and society. At a time when corporate executives wielded enormous influence in the Roosevelt administration (they were called "dollar a year men" for their willingness to work for little or no pay), Reuther's plan highlighted the ineffectiveness of top-down managerial approaches to manufacturing problems. Reducing idle capacity also meant increasing work hours for union laborers, which translated into higher wages. Finally, producing aircraft components in Detroit instead of southern California, where many of the new aerospace manufacturing plants were being built, would strengthen the power of organized labor. In California unions were not well established, and many of the newer factories would be "open shops," or nonunion facilities. Reuther's plan would move much of the production, and thus the labor, to Detroit, shoring up union representation in the aircraft industry.

Reuther then turns to the details of his plan. Even during periods of high consumer demand, like 1940, American automobile plants operated at only a portion of their total capacity. Reuther gives specific examples of how automobile factories could be used to manufacture warplanes, including the Hupmobile plant; the Hupmobile was a car built by the Hupp Motor Company. Most important, Reuther calls for a joint production board to oversee the plan's implementation. Comprising government, management, and labor representatives, this board would put unionized labor on the same level as government and management, allowing it equal participation in decision making. This was a revolutionary idea for the time.

Reuther makes a very brief reference to an ongoing labor dispute between the UAW and Ford Motor Company. In June 1940, as head of UAW's GM department, Reuther successfully negotiated a contract with GM that standardized wages across plants and job categories and created mechanisms for redressing cases of wage discrimination. Ford, however, continued to fight union representation in its factories. Reuther mentions the Wagner Act, which was also known as the National Labor Relations Act. Passed in 1935, the act provided a number of protections for organized labor, including the right of workers to join a union of their choice without interference from their employer. Nevertheless, in the years following, Reuther and other UAW representatives had met with considerable company opposition when attempting to sign up union members at Ford plants.

Reuther closes by invoking the authority of the president of the United States; Roosevelt's interest in labor's plan gave it considerable credibility. Reuther ends with two memorable phrases that return the listener to the urgency of war and British honor. Here, Reuther mentions Eton, a famous and prestigious boys' school and one of England's oldest institutions, referring to a quotation that emphasizes the school's order and discipline. Thus, Reuther posits the American automobile factory as the equivalent of Eton: a respected institution that instills the same values. His final line is particularly important because Americans were supportive of the British war effort but fearful about sending their own men into battle. Reuther astutely ends his speech with the reassurance that because of labor's efforts, such a sacrifice will not be needed.

Automobile executives, aircraft manufacturers, and the military criticized Reuther's plan, and thus it never materialized. However, it caused a national sensation, and positioned the UAW and American labor in general as a positive force in a patriotic effort. Following the Japanese attack on Pearl Harbor just a year later, American manufacturers did, in fact, shift their production to the war effort; by June 1942, 66 percent of the automobile industry's machine tools were producing military supplies. Although the speech was motivated by the desire to enhance union labor's power, it also illustrates his larger vision for a society in which the average worker would have a voice in how to organize and employ the nation's productive resources.

◆ National Hour Radio Address on Inflation

The postwar years ushered in an era of unprecedented consumer confidence and consumption, including an

Time Line

1952	■ Reuther is elected president of the Congress of Industrial Organizations.
1955	■ **June 8** Ford and the United Automobile Workers reach agreement on a contract.
	■ **March 27** Reuther gives the opening address, "The Guaranteed Annual Wage," to the fifteenth constitutional convention of the United Automobile Workers.
1957	■ **June 26** Reuther addresses the annual convention of the National Association for the Advancement of Colored People in Detroit.
1959	■ **May 1** Reuther gives the Berlin Freedom Rally address in West Berlin.
1970	■ **May 9** Reuther is killed in a plane crash.

upsurge in automobile sales. From 69,500 in 1945, new car sales rose to 2.1 million in 1946. In the midst of this prosperity, automobile workers experienced a decline in real wages. Reuther led a UAW campaign to win GM workers a 30 percent pay increase, claiming that the company could meet this demand without raising the price of its cars. At an impasse with the company, GM workers went on strike in November 1945.

The strike was unpopular with the public, although there was some sympathy with the workers' demand for a pay increase. GM took out regular newspaper advertisements to influence public opinion; Reuther took to the airwaves with a radio address in February 1946. In this speech Reuther portrays the striking workers as American consumers, linking them with his listening audience. In language characteristic of many of his addresses, he presents union labor as united with the American people in a fight for a greater cause: in this case, the battle against inflation.

Reuther employs many of the same tactics in this address that he did in other speeches to the American public. He presents the UAW as being on the same side as the president of the United States; GM is thus portrayed as being on the opposite side of the nation's best interests. Reuther claims that corporate management "squeeze[s]"

British Royal Air Force patrol planes in flight on June 18, 1940, during the Battle of Britain. (AP/Wide World Photos)

the consumer and prevents American workers from providing for their wives and children. His antimanagement rhetoric places government, union labor, and the American public on the same side in the labor dispute; GM becomes the villain, seeking "the most outrageous profits in history."

GM initially agreed only to an 18 percent wage increase, but later strikes resulted in historic gains by the UAW. Under Reuther's leadership, the UAW negotiated a contract with GM in 1948 that provided for cost-of-living wage increases and tied raises to productivity. Future contract negotiations included improved health and safety measures as well as health, retirement, and unemployment benefits. A determined negotiator, Reuther was also a savvy public relations man. His National Hour address illustrates his ability to position organized labor as part of middle-class American society.

◆ **"The Guaranteed Annual Wage" Address**

On March 27, 1955, Reuther gave the opening address to the fifteenth convention of the UAW, held in Cleveland, Ohio. As president of the UAW, in 1950 Reuther had negotiated a landmark agreement between the union and the "Big Three" automobile manufacturers. Known as the Treaty of Detroit, this contract provided some collective bargaining rights for workers as well as strike protection for management. Next on the UAW's agenda was the fight for a guaranteed annual wage, which was a concept developed during the Great Depression to guarantee some kind of job security during economic downturns. In his 1955 address Reuther describes his plan for the guaranteed annual wage, As in his other speeches, Reuther seeks to position unionized labor as a key decision maker in American politics and society. The guaranteed annual wage is part of Reuther's larger agenda to establish the UAW, and labor in general, as players rather than pawns in the American economy. Although he spoke on the floor of the union convention, Reuther knew his address would reach a wider audience through media coverage; thus, his speech is directed at business and the public as well as his fellow union members.

Reuther defines the guaranteed annual wage in terms of larger societal values; the idea must be "economically sound," "morally right," and "socially responsible." He then explains why the campaign meets those three requirements. A guaranteed annual wage makes economic sense because it restores purchasing power to American families and evens out the negative impacts of the business cycle (unemployment). Reuther devotes much of his speech to defending the morality of a guaranteed wage; this was characteristic of many of his speeches, in which he tied the causes of the UAW to the broader American public using patriotic examples or by setting labor and the general public on the side of virtue in a battle against management. In this case, Reuther points to the role of costs in business, highlighting the difference between management and labor in the process. If it is moral to pay executive salaries every year, why is it not moral to pay laborers their wages every year? asks Reuther. He highlights the disparity between executive salaries and workers' wages to further emphasize the chasm between the public and management and to gain sympathy for the idea of a guaranteed annual wage. He then uses one of his characteristic techniques, portraying union workers as consumers. By emphasizing the class difference between labor and management, Reuther further distances corporate executives from the average American and reinforces the bond between the UAW and the public.

Reuther closes with one of his signature endings, enlisting the American public in a cause greater than just the well-being of the UAW. The guaranteed annual wage becomes not just a union campaign but a program for an improved American economy. In the 1950s most Americans approved giving union workers reasonable pay increases that would bring them into the fold of middle-class society as well as avoid disruptive strikes. Reuther's speech reflects these attitudes but also reveals his own revolutionary concept for labor-management relations. In essentially calling for a salary instead of an hourly wage for autoworkers, Reuther seeks to erode the boundaries between labor and management, allowing labor to have more control and authority in the workplace. As a planning tool, the guaranteed annual wage was criticized as a form of Socialism, yet Reuther carefully frames it in terms of American consumerism and a capitalist economy, distancing himself and the labor movement from their past Communist and Socialist affiliations. Although the UAW never won a guaranteed annual wage, it did achieve supplemental unemployment benefits, which provided a cushion for workers in the event of layoffs. In addition, Reuther's concept engendered a larger debate about management-labor relations and the impact of business cycles.

◆ **Address before the Annual Convention of the National Association for the Advancement of Colored People**

Reuther is best known for his role as a labor leader. However, he actively participated in the civil rights movement and spoke at the 1963 March on Washington. Reuther was a member of the board of directors of the

NAACP and advocated the creation of a fair employment practices commission in Michigan. This excerpt from Reuther's speech at the 1957 convention of the NAACP illustrates his oft-used technique of highlighting the common ground between American labor and his audience, casting whatever obstacles his listeners face as broader challenges that they and the UAW together can overcome. Reuther liberally uses references to the morality and patriotism of the UAW and the NAACP, depicting black Americans and American laborers as agents of social change.

Reuther invokes a religious tone early in the speech, describing the NAACP's cause as a "crusade" in which all are "blessed" to participate. He then notes the war effort of the automobile industry, describing it as a fight against totalitarianism. Reuther mentions the Detroit race riot of 1943, one of several violent racial disturbances that took place in industrial areas during World War II. Job opportunities in areas such as Detroit encouraged southern blacks to migrate north, and the resulting influx of large numbers of African Americans led to growing conflict in what was then a segregated society. The Detroit riot lasted three days, causing hundreds of injuries, thirty-four deaths, and substantial property damage. Reuther contrasts this racial violence with the camaraderie inside the factory, although racial tension existed in the workplace as well. Black workers were among the strongest supporters of the UAW, particularly in Detroit, and there were often disputes among old-line white union workers and the newer black members.

Reuther emphasizes the "solidarity of human brotherhood" in organized labor but does not ignore the reality of discrimination in the factory. He blames not racial tension between workers, however, but the employers. He refers to contract language prohibiting discrimination on the basis of race; in 1941 President Franklin Roosevelt had created the Fair Employment Practices Committee, which outlawed racial discrimination in the defense industry. After Roosevelt's death in 1945, the committee had less support in Congress; despite President Harry S. Truman's backing, in 1950 southern senators blocked legislation that would have continued the committee. Thus, employment discrimination was a major issue for the NAACP and the UAW in 1957, when Reuther gave this address; he calls for the matter to be taken up in "the halls of Congress."

Reuther mentions George Meany as the head of the AFL-CIO. In 1952 Reuther was elected president of the Congress of Industrial Organizations (CIO), which was initially part of the American Federation of Labor (AFL). The CIO was an umbrella organization representing workers employed in mass production. In 1937 the CIO split from the more conservative AFL, primarily over differences in tactics. As cold war politics moved most labor representatives away from Socialism, the differences between the AFL and the CIO diminished, and Reuther engineered a reunion of the two groups in 1955, with Meany as head of the new AFL-CIO. Later, Reuther grew critical of Meany's ineffective leadership and in 1968 withdrew the UAW from the AFL-CIO's umbrella.

Labor leaders George Meany (left) and Walter Reuther (right) symbolically share control of a kingsize gavel as they pronounce the merger of the American Federation of Labor (AFL) and the Congress of Industrial Organizations (CIO) in 1955. (AP/Wide World Photos)

Reuther closes his speech with a discussion of more general civil rights, stating that union labor stands behind the broader goals of the movement, including voting rights, fair housing, equal education, and desegregation of public facilities. Once again, Reuther links the cause of the American worker to greater society, placing organized labor and the NAACP in a moral battle for the soul of America.

◆ **Address before the Berlin Freedom Rally**

Reuther's life, tragically cut short by a plane crash, spanned the politically charged years of the cold war. After World War II, the city of Berlin was divided into four sectors occupied, respectively, by the British, the Americans, and the French (West Berlin) and the Soviet Union (East Berlin). As conditions in the Soviet-controlled portion of the city deteriorated, German citizens flocked to West Berlin by the thousands. To stem what was fast becoming a hemorrhage of skilled professional workers, the Soviet premier Nikita Khrushchev demanded in 1959 that all Western powers vacate Berlin, stating that the city would be turned over entirely to the East German government. The Western powers refused to leave, setting the stage for one of many cold war crises in Berlin.

In his youth, Reuther had allied himself with the Communist Party but, like many Americans who had been leftists in the 1930s, denounced any such affiliations following the Hitler-Stalin pact of 1939. In the political debates of the 1950s cold war, Reuther advocated a dialogue between the United States and the Soviet Union, a position that rankled many conservatives who were staunchly opposed to any hint of rapprochement with the Soviets. In 1959 the mayor of Berlin, Willy Brandt, invited Reuther to speak at a freedom rally organized by West Germany's trade unions. Speaking in German, Reuther addressed a crowd of six hundred thousand at the Brandenburg Gate, where John F. Kennedy would deliver a famous address in 1963 and Ronald Reagan would in 1987 call on the Soviets to tear down the wall separating East and West Germany.

Reuther begins characteristically by linking his audience with the American labor movement. As corporations began to organize globally, Reuther believed that workers would need to also organize internationally to achieve their objectives. A founding member of the International Confederation of Free Trade Unions, Reuther envisioned a worldwide labor movement that rejected Communism. This speech to the West German trade unions thus emphasizes the common interest of American and German workers in freedom.

Reuther refers to the earlier Berlin blockade. In 1948 the Soviets restricted access to the city in reaction against Western efforts to integrate the city's quadrants, including the introduction of currency reform measures. With ground transportation halted, no food or other supplies could get into the city. President Truman ordered planes to deliver needed materials to West Berlin in what is now known as the Berlin airlift, one of the earliest showdowns between the United States and the Soviet Union in the cold war. The airlift became a symbol of Soviet tyranny and American freedom during the cold war, and Reuther invokes that history early in his speech to reinforce the tie between Berlin and the United States.

Reuther uses the term *iron curtain*, made famous by British prime minister Winston Churchill in a speech given in 1946 at an American college. In this part of his address, Reuther extends the community of those who cherish "freedom and human dignity" to Poland, Hungary, and China. Poznan, a city in Poland, was the site of a massive anti-Communist demonstration in 1956 in which more than fifty people were killed. That same year, Soviet troops entered Budapest, Hungary, to quell student demonstrations. Finally, in March 1959, Tibetans rebelled unsuccessfully against the Communist Chinese in Lhasa; as a consequence, the Tibetan spiritual leader, the Dalai Lama, went into exile in India. Similarly to the way in which he sets management in opposition to labor and the American public, Reuther joins several nations with America in opposition to Communist aggression.

American labor unions, particularly the industrial organizations, had a history of engaging in leftist political activities. In the heart of the cold war years, Reuther's speech to the May Day rally in West Germany sent a strong message that organized labor stood against Communism and Soviet aggression. Distancing himself personally from his past political affiliations, Reuther nevertheless signaled his own rather liberal position of favoring détente with the USSR. This document shows Reuther's political savvy as well as his belief in a broader, international cause for organized labor.

Impact and Legacy

George Romney of the Automobile Manufacturers Association called Walter Reuther "the most dangerous man in Detroit," commenting on the UAW leader's ability to effect real change in labor's status in society. Historians generally agree; the biographer Nelson Lichtenstein used Romney's quote for the title of his book on Reuther. Guided by his vision of a society in which labor shared decision making with government and business, Reuther fought not just for workers' benefits but also for broader issues of social justice. For Reuther, a just society was one in which industrial organizations reflected the American values of freedom and equality.

Reuther's emphasis on social justice led to tangible gains for UAW workers as well as a visible role for labor in larger political matters. Arguing that better-paid and more secure workers could more effectively participate in the American economy, Reuther won improvements in benefits for autoworkers, including unemployment compensation, pension income, and health insurance. He traveled overseas, involving himself not only in international labor organizations but also in cold war politics. Although it was initially shunned, his plan for converting peacetime manufacturing capacity to military production was eventually implemented during World War II. Finally, his insistence on a nation reflective of its own values placed him to the fore of the civil rights movement.

Reuther's speeches and writings exhibit distinctive qualities. He was a master of the use of slogans, such as the memorable title of his plan, "500 Planes a Day." Reuther often follows a format that involves establishing two sides in a moral battle in which labor is on the side of justice. Although his rhetoric can appear to be self-serving on behalf of his organization, he employed his powers of persuasive speech to advance a larger mission, which was to change the nature of work in America by giving dignity and social meaning to the mass-production worker. Reuther left a legacy as one of the most influential labor leaders in history, but his documents reflect the larger vision behind that legacy.

Key Sources

Wayne State University's Walter P. Reuther Library holds Reuther's papers from his term as president of the UAW. These include correspondence and scrapbooks as well as memos and other business documents. Original copies of Reuther's speeches are contained in the archives, and some are available electronically on the library's Web site (http://reuther100.wayne.edu/). Henry M. Christman collected and edited many of Reuther's speeches in one volume, *Walter P. Reuther: Selected Papers* (1961).

Further Reading

■ Books

Carew, Anthony. *Walter Reuther*. Manchester, U.K.: Manchester University Press, 1993.

Dayton, Eldorous L. *Walter Reuther: The Autocrat of the Bargaining Table*. New York: Devin-Adair, 1958.

Howe, Irving, and B. J. Widick. *The UAW and Walter Reuther*. New York: Random House, 1949.

Lichtenstein, Nelson. *The Most Dangerous Man in Detroit: Walter Reuther and the Fate of American Labor*. New York: Basic Books, 1995.

Essential Quotes

"England's battles, it used to be said, were won on the playing fields of Eton. America's can be won on the assembly lines of Detroit."

("500 Planes a Day" Speech)

"American labor does not want a ten cent wage increase in one pocket, with a fifteen cent price increase taken out of the other pocket."

(National Hour Radio Address on Inflation)

"I say, based upon the standards of human decency and human morality, no one can say that any man is worth 150 times another man working for the same company. No one is that much better than the other fellow. And no one needs that much more."

("The Guaranteed Annual Wage" Address)

"When the people of Detroit were rioting and destroying and killing each other on the streets, white and Negro workers worked side by side in brotherhood in the plants under our contracts. Because they had learned to know the meaning of human solidarity, of brotherhood, because they had learned through the hard experience of struggle that when the employer can divide you and pit white against black, American-born against foreign-born, he can divide and rule and exploit everyone."

(Address before the Annual Convention of the National Association for the Advancement of Colored People)

"The free labor movement is in the vanguard of the struggle for peace and freedom because we have understood that the struggle for peace and freedom is inseparably tied together with the struggle for social justice."

(Address before the Berlin Freedom Rally)

Reuther, Victor. *The Brothers Reuther and the Story of the UAW: A Memoir*. New York: Houghton Mifflin, 1976.

■ **Web Sites**

"Walter Reuther (1907–1970)." AFL-CIO Web site. http://www.aflcio.org/aboutus/history/history/reuther.cfm.

"No Greater Calling: The Life of Walter P. Reuther." Wayne State University's Walter P. Reuther Library Web site. http://reuther100.wayne.edu/.

—Karen Linkletter

Questions for Further Study

1. Like many idealistic young Westerners in the period between the world wars, Reuther initially admired Soviet Communism. A trip to the alleged workers' paradise—actually a gruesome dictatorship whose people endured calamities vastly greater than those visited on America in the Great Depression—changed his mind completely, and thereafter he rejected all association with Communism or Communists. Research and discuss his experiences in Russia and how they affected him. How was his anti-Communism reflected in later speeches, particularly the one given before the Berlin Freedom Rally? How do these same principles tie in with his opposition to racist policies in the United States, as discussed in his NAACP address?

2. How did Reuther, through his words and ideas, attempt to raise the standing of the labor movement and particularly the UAW? Consider, for instance, his "500 planes" speech, in which he associates the American worker with traditions of bravery and nobility, or his 1955 address on the guaranteed annual wage, wherein he attempts to place labor and management on the same level in terms of importance and corresponding benefits. How effective was he in bringing about the erosion of class distinctions that he promoted in his speeches? And how beneficial did these efforts prove for American labor as a whole?

3. In his 1946 radio address on inflation, Reuther calls for wage increases as a means of helping workers adjust to inflation, even if these raises would result in increased prices for automobiles. Yet a counterargument could be made that raising the price tags on cars, which are among the central elements in the U.S. economy, would itself spur inflation. What do you think? Is his position here inconsistent with his claim in the "500 planes" speech that wages could be raised without changing the cost of the finished product? If there is an apparent inconsistency, can this be attributed to the enormous changes that took place during the 1940s rather than to any shortcoming in Reuther's logic?

4. Examine and evaluate Reuther's argument for a guaranteed annual wage, including his use of statistics. What is his three-part standard for evaluating the guaranteed annual wage in terms of larger societal values, and how well does he present his position on this? Discuss the relative pros and cons, both in general terms and with regard to auto industry employees in particular, of working on a traditional hourly wage system or a yearly salary system (as the annual wage program, in essence, was).

"500 Planes a Day" Speech (1940)

Good evening, Fellow Americans.

When knighthood was in flower, it was considered a blot on one's honor to attack an opponent before he was ready. Unfortunately these gentlemanly rules have long since been abandoned. Were Herr Hitler a knight of old he would no doubt be content to call off his Luftwaffe and wait two or three years until British and American plane production were sufficient to enable the R.A.F. to meet him in fair and equal combat.

But there is no chivalry wasted on the present battle between a well-prepared Reich and a frantically preparing Britain. When I picked up this morning's paper I read that the three-day Christmas truce was over and huge fires were again lighting the London night skies. Britain's need is planes and that need is fierce and urgent. We must supply them, and Hitler will not wait while we pursue the normal leisurely methods of production.

In London they are huddled in the subways praying for aid from America. In America we are huddled over blueprints praying that Hitler will be obliging enough to postpone an "all out" attack on England for another two years until new plants finally begin to turn out engines and aircraft.

Packard has just finished pouring the concrete for its new engine factory and Ford may soon be ready to begin digging the ditches in which to sink the foundations for his. Not until the Fall of 1942, almost two years hence, will these bright shiny new factories actually begin to turn out the engines. This is snail's pace production in the age of lightning war.

Conventional methods will never bring results in unconventional warfare, and the workers of the automotive and aircraft industries for whom we speak propose a bold alternative, quickly applied.

We believe that without disturbing present aircraft plant production schedules we can supplement them by turning out 500 planes a day of a single standard fighting model by the use of idle automotive capacity. We believe that this can be done after six months of preparation as compared to the 18 months or two years required to get new plane and engine factories into production.

This is Labor's Plan, as worked out by the automotive workers of Detroit and presented to President Roosevelt by Philip Murray, President of the Congress of Industrial Organizations.

Why should labor concern itself, some may ask, with speeding plane production? Labor is concerned because it believes a strengthened defense essential to our country's safety in this era of axis aggression. Labor is concerned because it believes that our country's main defense is the little fortress isle holding off the bombing planes of Nazism on the other side of the Atlantic. Labor is concerned because wherever Nazism is victorious, the precious liberties that differentiate free men and free workers form slaves are destroyed....

If it were true that our productive machinery and our productive man power were working at capacity, the task of speeding aid to Britain and quickening our own defense beyond the present pace would be hopeless. Fortunately, despite the headlines which tell us of unfillable orders and labor shortages, we have a huge reservoir of unused machinery, unused plants, unused skill and unused labor to fall back upon.

The automotive industry, the mass production marvel of the world, over a year's period works at 50 percent of its total maximum capacity. We believe the other 50 percent can be adapted to the manufacture of planes.

The tool and die workers of the automobile industry, the most skillful machinists in the world, the men who turn the production engineering blueprints into the realities of the machine, are also partially idle. A third of them are either totally unemployed, on part time or working temporarily on ordinary production jobs.

Thus we have idle machinery and idle skilled labor. We propose to bring them together for the mass production of defense planes....

Why wait for entirely new plants to be built which cannot go into production until almost two years have passed. We believe we can do the job of adapting idle automotive machinery to plane production in six months. The capacity of this idle machinery is greater than the over-all capacity of the motor construction industries of Germany, Italy and Japan combined.

Labor proposes the establishment of a joint aircraft production board representing government, management and labor. It proposes that this board make a survey of the entire automotive industry, determining exactly what unused capacity is available in each plant. It proposes that this board then take the engineering blueprints for a fighter plane, break these blueprints down into its component parts and assign the manufacture of these parts to the various plants in accordance with their idle capacity.

Labor proposes to mobilize all the unused capacity of the great automotive tool and die shops and their workers to the job of making the necessary tools, dies, jigs and fixtures to adapt this automotive machinery to plane production.

The automotive industry contains idle plants as well as idle machinery and idle men. Outstanding among the great idle plants in Detroit is the Hupmobile plant now completely unused. We propose that it be used to assemble the parts of the engine and that other plants be used to assemble the parts for the wings and the fuselage. Huge, cheaply and easily constructed hangars around the Wayne County, Michigan, and Cleveland airports could be used for final assembly and the complete planes could be flown out of them.

Labor's plan springs from the pooled experience and knowledge of skilled workers in all the automotive plants, the same skilled workers who are called upon year by year in the industry to produce new machine marvels. Each manufacturer has the benefit of his skilled workers. We of the United Automobile Workers, CIO, have the benefit of the skilled man power in all the automotive plants, not just in one of them.

Labor asks only in return that its hard-won rights be preserved. Labor asks only that manufacturers like Ford be forced to obey the Wagner Act, as have his competitors, General Motors and the smaller companies. Labor asks only that it be allowed to contribute its own creative experience and knowledge and that it be given a voice in the education of its program.

The President of the United States yesterday expressed great interest in our plan, and said that he had asked his new Office of Production Management to investigate it.

No question of policy needs to be settled. The President has laid down the policy. We must have more planes. Postponement of tooling of new automobile models would make available the necessary

England's battles… were won on the playing fields of Eton	reference to words often attributed to Britain's Duke of Wellington upon remembering his defeat of Napoleon in 1815: "the battle of Waterloo was won on the playing fields of Eton"—meaning that those who won that battle had learned the qualities they needed for military victory as student athletes at prestigious Eton College
Hupmobile	a car produced between 1909 and 1940 by Detroit's Hupp Motor Company
jigs	tools used for controlling the direction, location, and movement of other tools used in metalworking, woodworking, and related industries
lightning war	a translation of the German term *blitzkrieg*, by which the Nazis referred to the style of military tactics that won them control over vast areas of land in Europe and North Africa during the period 1939–1942
little fortress isle	Britain
Luftwaffe	the air force of Nazi Germany
Packard	the Packard Motor Company, which produced luxury automobiles from 1899 to 1958
R.A.F.	Royal Air Force
Reich	a term the Nazis used to identify the Holy Roman Empire of medieval times and the modern Imperial Germany (1871–1918), calling their own state the Third Reich.
tool and die workers	highly skilled machinists
tooling	manufacturing
Wagner Act	the 1935 National Labor Relations Act, which provided broad protections to union members and their activities

skilled help for the tooling for mass production of defense planes. No private considerations must interfere. When men are being drafted this is little enough to ask of the automotive industry.

Quantity production was achieved in the Reich and is being achieved in England by the methods labor now proposes to apply to the automotive industry.

The difference and our opportunity is that we have in the automotive industry the greatest mass production machine the world has ever seen. Treated as one great production unit, it can in half a year's time turn out planes in unheard of numbers and swamp the Luftwaffe. This is labor's answer to Hitler aggression, American labor's reply to the cries of its enslaved brothers under the Nazi yoke in Europe.

England's battles, it used to be said, were won on the playing fields of Eton. America's can be won on the assembly lines of Detroit.

Give England planes and there will be no need to give her men.

Reuther, Walter

NATIONAL HOUR RADIO ADDRESS ON INFLATION (1946)

The major threat of inflation today comes from the pressure campaign of big business for unjustified price increases.

Wage increases are no longer the major issue in the dispute which is holding up our progress toward the goals of full employment, full production and full consumption. The major issue now is prices.

From the beginning of the GM controversy, the GM workers and their union have conducted an all-out fight against price increases. The Union has consistently stated that we did not want a *wage* increase that would necessitate one red cent in higher prices. The recommendations of the President's Fact Finding Board supported our contention—that General Motors could grant the wage increase without a price increase.

Despite this fact, the General Motors Corporation continues to defy the President's recommendation. GM, the Steel industry and other large corporations are hell-bent on destroying price control. They are determined to squeeze out of the American consumer unnecessary and unjustified price increase.

American labor does not want a ten cent wage increase in one pocket, with a fifteen cent price increase taken out of the other pocket. We do not want to be paid off in the wooden nickels of inflation. We want, and we are fighting for, an increase in *real wages*—an increase in purchasing power. We want wages that will buy more food, more clothes, better housing—more of the good things of life that we need for ourselves, our wives and our children.

The picket lines of the GM workers are the front line defenses against industry's attempt to wreck price control. We are determined that the government and the American people shall not be hi-jacked into permitting higher prices that would provide industry with the most outrageous profits in history.

We call upon President Truman to stand firm against price increases, and to mobilize the support of the people who in overwhelming majority favor rigid price control. That is the way inflation can be defeated. That is the way it must be defeated.

Glossary

inflation	an economic situation characterized by rising prices and a corresponding decline in purchasing power

"THE GUARANTEED ANNUAL WAGE" ADDRESS (1955)

The guaranteed annual wage is an important move in achieving full production and full employment in peacetime.... We don't say, we never have said—all the reactionary propagandists, notwithstanding—we have never claimed that a worker in the United States or a worker in Canada, is automatically entitled to economic security. We have no sympathy for a fellow who can get a job and doesn't want to work.

What we say is that while the worker is not entitled to automatic economic security, he is entitled to an opportunity for a good job at decent wages to earn that economic security.

When we fight for the guaranteed wage, we are not asking to be paid for not working. We just don't want our people to be penalized when they don't have a job through no fault of their own.

We have said at conferences in the past, and we have tried to formulate our economic demands in the light of three essential conditions.

First, our demands must be economically sound. They can't be based upon wishful thinking. They have to be based upon solid and sound economic facts.

Second, they have to be morally right. We have to fight for righteousness and justice.

Third, they can't be selfish demands that make progress at the expense of our neighbor. They have to be socially responsible. They have to reflect the basic needs of all people.

Our demands in 1955 meet those conditions. They meet those conditions on the basis of a careful and objective study. No one can deny the fact that economically we are in trouble in America. Nobody can deny the fact that economically Canada is in trouble because there is unemployment in these countries. In the United States we still have the equivalent of 5,000,000 unemployed. In Canada, their unemployment is even higher in proportion to the working force....

Now, why the unemployment? We all know. We have said it many times. Everyone ought to understand it. We are in trouble in the United States, Canada is in trouble, because of the growing and serious imbalance between our ability to create wealth with our tremendous productive power and the inability of millions of families to consume that abundance because they lack adequate purchasing power....

They say to us, "Is the guaranteed annual wage morally right?" I say that no demand in the history of collective bargaining has ever been more morally right than the guaranteed annual wage. Just look at industry. They pay their taxes by the year. They pay the interest on their loans by the year. They pay their executives by the year. If they rent a building, they pay the rent by the year. If they have six months' production, they don't call the landlord and say, "Well, we just shut the plant down, we won't pay the rent for the rest of the year." They pay the rent twelve months every year. The only element of production that gets paid by the hour or by the piece and not by the year is the human equation—the most important equation in production.

If it is morally right to meet the cost of modern industry, pay your taxes by the year and your interest on these investments by the year, your executive salaries by the year, then we say it is morally right to pay the workers by the year, and in 1955 we intend to make it possible in our industry....

We don't begrudge one penny that these corporation executives are paid. We know that when corporation management makes a contribution to the economic well-being of the country and to the economic progress of our country they are entitled to a just reward for their economic contribution. But we say that when workers make their contribution they, too, are entitled to just compensation for their contribution....

Take Mr. Curtice, the President of the General Motors Corporation. He probably is a very efficient executive. No one begrudges him a penny he gets. But in 1954 the General Motors Corporation paid him very well. We don't object to that. What we object to is Mr. Curtice denying our right, the GM workers' right, to be paid well....

We analyzed his salary on an hourly basis so we could understand it. Based upon fifty-two weeks a year, 40 hours a week, Mr. Curtice got $329 an hour. It would have taken the average GM worker 50 years to earn what Mr. Curtice got in one year....

I say, based upon the standards of human decency and human morality, no one can say that any man is worth 150 times another man working for the same company. No one is that much better than the other fellow. And no one needs that much more.

When they gave 60 General Motors executives last year in salary and bonuses $12,600,000 divided up among 60 people, do you think that when those executives got that money, they bought one more quart of milk? Do you think that they bought one more pair of shoes for their kids? Do you think they called the doctor one more time? Of course not.

But you give the GM workers the guaranteed annual wage, you give the retired GM workers higher pensions, you give all workers higher purchasing power and they buy more milk and shoes and clothing and call the doctor when they need him.

That is why we say that the guaranteed annual wage and that your economic program is more than a matter of justice to the worker. It is a matter of necessity for the whole economy.

Glossary

collective bargaining	organized negotiation between workers and employers
Mr. Curtice	Harlow H. Curtice, president of General Motors throughout most of the 1950s
reactionary	one who reacts against progressive social ideas by calling for extreme conservatism and a return to the past

Address before the Annual Convention of the National Association for the Advancement of Colored People (1957)

I'm proud to belong to the NAACP, because it is made up of people who are dedicated in a great crusade to make America true to itself. This is what this is about. Make America live up to its highest hopes and aspirations and translate those hopes and aspirations into practical, tangible reality in the lives of all people, whether they are white or black, whether they live in the North or in the South. I say that each of us is blessed that we can be engaged in this crusade, in this struggle for justice for human dignity—in this struggle to wipe out in every phase of our national life, every ugly and immoral kind of discrimination....

Since you meet in the city in which the headquarters of the UAW is located, I am sure you will permit me to bring to you the fraternal greetings and the best wishes from the one and a half million members of the UAW, and I would like to say for them that we are with you all the way until victory is ours in this fight for civil rights.

You have come back. You were here in 1943. Detroit was the great arsenal of democracy. We were turning out more weapons of war with which to fight Hitlerism, totalitarianism, than was any other city in the world. But unfortunately, this city went wrong and we had tragic, ugly race riots back in that period. But one of the things that we have always been proud of about the UAW is that when the people of Detroit were rioting and destroying and killing each other on the streets, white and Negro workers worked side by side in brotherhood in the plants under our contracts. Because they had learned to know the meaning of human solidarity, of brotherhood, because they had learned through the hard experience of struggle that when the employer can divide you and pit white against black, American-born against foreign-born, he can divide and rule and exploit everyone. And we learned a lesson that only in the solidarity of human brotherhood, only as you stand together with your fellow man can you solve your basic problems....

I think we all realize that the world is troubled—that we live with crisis in America and the people of every nation are living with crisis in the world. I have been saying for a long time that the crisis in the world is not economic or political or military. Essentially, the crisis in the world is a moral crisis. It's a reflection of man's growing immorality to himself. Of man's growing inhumanity to man. The H-bomb is the highest and most terrible destructive expression of that growing inhumanity.

And in a sense our crisis in America, the crises in education, the crisis in civil rights is not political, it is moral. We've got all that it takes to solve these problems. But we haven't demonstrated the moral courage to step up to solving these problems, and this is our basic problem. America is in crisis, not because it lacks economic resources, not because it lacks the political know-how, not because we don't know how to do the job of squaring democracy's practices with its noble promises. We just haven't demonstrated the moral courage. And until we do, we will not meet this basic crisis in civil rights and in education....

We're proud in the Auto Worker's Union of the progress we've made. Other unions have made progress in breaking down discrimination in the factories. But we haven't got one single major contract, although we've got one and a half million workers under contract, and although we try and try and try at the bargaining table in which the employer has agreed to a clause prohibiting discrimination because of race or creed or color at the hiring gate. They say to us, "Oh, you don't represent the workers until we employ them. We aren't going to let you say anything about who we hire. After we hire them, then you can talk about their work, their conditions of employment, their wages." Well, we believe that the question of the policy at the hiring gate is important, and if we can't do it at the bargaining table, then we have to do it in the halls of Congress.

Now there are many other things we need to be thinking about. I want to say to this Convention of the NAACP, the American labor movement is not a fair weather friend of yours in the fight for civil rights. I want to say for the AFL-CIO, its leadership, George Meany, and the people involved in directing that organization: "We are with you all the way, and we are going to stay with you all the way until we get on the statute books of America effective civil rights legislation in all of these fields, not only in FEPC, but in every other aspect of our national life."

We want an America in which every citizen is equal when he walks into the polling place to cast his ballot. We want an America in which every child has educational opportunity, an America in which every citizen has equal job opportunity, equal rights to the use of all public facilities, the right to live in a decent neighborhood, in a decent house.

It's about time we look at this problem of clearing the slums in our major cities. We're not clearing the slums. We're just modernizing them. We're just creating new ghettoes. I say it's about time we had some courage to build decent communities in which all Americans can live on an integrated basis as decent citizens living together in a wholesome community.

Now these are not matters of special privileges. These are basic rights to which every American is entitled. And no American should be satisfied with less.

The task is difficult. The struggle will be hard, but let us always remember that human progress has never been served to mankind on a silver platter. The history of the world shows chapter after chapter that men of faith and courage have had to fight to bring to fulfillment their dreams and their hopes and their aspirations. What we need to do is to keep the faith. Keep the faith in ourselves. And when the going is rough, as it will be, let us remember that the test of one's convictions is not how did you behave, how did you stand up when it was convenient and comfortable. The test of one's convictions is do you stand up for the things that you believe when it takes courage? Do you stand up in the face of adversity, in the face of great controversy? This is the kind of fight we are engaged in. That's why when the going is rough, always remember that there are millions of us, and that together we can move mountains, and that together we can solve this problem and make America in the image of what it really stands for.

Glossary

ghettoes	districts or sections of a city occupied almost exclusively by members of a particular ethnic group—usually as a result of laws preventing them from living among the general population; a term often associated with poor areas
H-bomb	the so-called hydrogen bomb, first successfully tested in 1952, which was considerably more lethal than the atomic bombs dropped on Japan in 1945
man's ... inhumanity to man	a phrase coined by the Scottish poet Robert Burns in 1785 and widely used in the 1950s and 1960s
Negro	at the time, the most common and "politically correct" term for African Americans
totalitarianism	a political system characterized by total government control over every aspect of life and society
We're not clearing the slums ...	a reference to urban renewal, a controversial program involving reclamation of allegedly blighted urban neighborhoods by replacement of old buildings and environments with new ones

ADDRESS BEFORE THE BERLIN FREEDOM RALLY (1959)

It is a great joy for me to be in Berlin once again. I greet you and extend to you the hand of friendship and solidarity in behalf of the 16 million members of the American trade union movement.

Berlin is once again the testing ground for freedom. It is not your freedom alone that is being challenged by Soviet tyranny. It is our freedom as well as your freedom, for freedom is an indivisible value and when the freedom of one is threatened, the freedom of all is in jeopardy. No man and no people live as an island unto themselves. We all live in one world—a world which grows smaller and smaller every day as science and technology move forward. You do not stand alone. Your American trade union colleagues stand firmly with you. The people of America and the people of the free world stand firmly with you in defense of our common freedom.

As you know, I am no newcomer to your city. I first came here during the dark days of 1933 when the shadow of Hitlerism fell across your city. I was with you again at the war's end as you struggled to reestablish the basis of normal economic life and when blind prejudice tried to prevent the restoration of essential industry. I was with you speaking out against the evil policy of dismantlement. But the new despotism of the East was not content to dismantle factories. It was soon obvious they were determined to dismantle freedom and life itself. Their effort to starve you into submission through the blockade failed because of your courage and determination. The blockade failed because the entire free world stood firmly with you....

Today, as I stand facing the Brandenberg Gate, I think not only of the threats to our mutual freedom but also of the millions who live on the other side of this gate and on the other side of the Iron Curtain which locks out freedom and human dignity. I hope that our voices from this great rally of free men might carry through and beyond the Brandenburg Gate, penetrating the Iron Curtain, not only to East Berliners but likewise to the heroes of Poznan and Budapest and, yes, to the latest victims of Communist aggression in remote Tibet....

The free labor movement is in the vanguard of the struggle for peace and freedom because we have understood that the struggle for peace and freedom is inseparably tied together with the struggle for social justice. Peace and freedom cannot be made secure in a vacuum. They must be made secure in a world in which pressing human problems cry for a solution.

I can say in truthfulness that the only war in which the American people wish to engage is this war against poverty, hunger, against ignorance and disease. In such a war all mankind will be victors. The promise of such a world at peace, dedicating its combined resources to the fulfillment of human needs everywhere, will kindle the same hopes and warm response in the hearts of Russian people as among the people in the free world....

Glossary

blockade	an effort by one nation or power to prevent the transport of people or supplies to and from another enemy nation or power
Brandenburg Gate	a massive structure, completed in 1791, that has served as a symbol of Berlin—especially during the cold war, when the gate stood just inside the Communist-controlled sector
dark days of 1933	reference to the Nazi takeover of Germany, which began with Hitler's appointment as the nation's chancellor on January 30, 1933
Iron Curtain	a term for the metaphorical barrier between the totalitarian Communist nations and the liberal democratic world
vanguard	leaders or forerunners, a term often employed by Communists in reference to themselves

In this hour of tension and uncertainty keep strong your faith in freedom's cause—keep strong your faith in yourselves. Your freedom and the freedom of the whole world is being put to the test in Berlin. Stand fast, for you do not stand alone. The people of America—the people of the free world—stand firmly with you in friendship and solidarity. Together we shall keep the door to freedom open in Berlin. Together we shall build a world of peace, freedom, security, social justice, and brotherhood.

Condoleezza Rice (AP/Wide World Photos)

CONDOLEEZZA RICE
1954–
U.S. Secretary of State

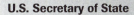

Featured Documents
- ◆ Address to the Republican National Convention (2000)
- ◆ "International Support for Iraqi Democracy" (2005)
- ◆ "Transformational Diplomacy" (2006)
- ◆ Keynote Address at the Annual Meeting of the World Economic Forum (2008)

Overview

In 2005, during the second term of President George W. Bush, Condoleezza Rice became the first African American woman to serve as secretary of state. In this role, as well as in her capacity as national security adviser from 2001 to 2005, Rice was one of the most influential architects of the foreign policy of the Bush administration and its war on terror in the aftermath of the 9/11 terrorist attacks on the United States. She was a staunch supporter of military interventions in Afghanistan and Iraq. She also favored moves to stabilize the Middle East; in particular, she encouraged the Israeli government to withdraw from the Gaza Strip in 2005 and supported democratic elections in Palestine. Rice has described her policy as "transformational diplomacy," a form of diplomacy that does not simply take into account the world as it is but actively seeks to change it by expanding democracy and the principles of a free-market economy—beliefs that she outlined in such documents as her "Transformational Diplomacy" speech at Georgetown University and her address to the World Economic Forum. Rice's influential role in the foreign policy of the Bush administration, as well as her repeatedly stated loyalty to the president, made her a target of censure from critics of the military interventions that she so forcefully championed. As national security adviser she was also harshly criticized for the lack of effective measures to prevent the 9/11 terrorist attacks. However, she has also been praised as an inspirational model for overcoming racial discrimination and forging a successful career first as an academic and then as a politician and diplomat.

Rice was born November 14, 1954, in Birmingham, Alabama, and grew up near Titusville. Throughout Rice's childhood years, Alabama strictly enforced its racial segregation laws. Growing up in a segregated state strengthened her determination to overcome a hostile context and to be considered as an individual and not merely part of a group. Rice often paid homage to those lessons of American individualism that illustrate the primacy of personal interest and self-determination. Her individualism has both an economic and a political significance. It identifies with the tenets of capitalism, such as a free market, competition, and private property, and with the concepts of consensual government and the right of citizens to choose who governs them. However, critics have pointed out that this stance seems to clash with U.S. support of authoritarian regimes in such countries as Saudi Arabia and Egypt as well as with U.S. disapproval of the democratic victory of Hamas in the January 2006 Palestinian elections.

In 1967 Rice and her family moved to Denver, Colorado. She attended a private Catholic girls' school and earned a bachelor's degree in political science from the University of Denver in 1974. The following year she received a master's degree from the University of Notre Dame. She returned to Denver for her PhD, which she obtained from the Graduate School of International Studies in 1981. That same year she joined the Stanford University faculty as a professor of political science. From 1989 to 1991 she served in the administration of President George H. W. Bush as director and then senior director of Soviet and East European affairs on the National Security Council and as a special assistant to the president for national security affairs. Early on, Rice's main interest was the Soviet Union and the Eastern European Communist bloc. In 1993 she was appointed provost at Stanford, a position she held for six years. During her tenure she worked resolutely to balance the university budget, a stance that earned her praise from the board of trustees and criticism from some of the faculty, who deemed Rice's plan to cut millions of dollars from the budget more suitable to a corporation than to a university community.

Explanation and Analysis of the Documents

Condoleezza Rice played an important part on the American diplomatic scene at crucial times of change in foreign relations. Rice first arrived at the White House in 1989 as the expert on the Eastern European Communist bloc for then national security adviser Brent Scowcroft. These were the final years of the cold war, and Rice had a key role in shaping the policy of President George H. W. Bush's administration toward the process of German reunification. But it was in the administration of Bush's son George W. Bush that Rice acquired national and international visibility as a politician and public figure. The relationship that Rice developed with the elder Bush would later help her to be appointed national security adviser and then secretary of state in the administration of the younger Bush. The four documents that follow are all from this second part of Rice's political career and highlight her diplo-

Time Line

1954

■ **November 14**
Condoleezza Rice is born
in Birmingham, Alabama.

1974

■ Rice earns her bachelor's
degree in political science
from the University of
Denver.

1975

■ Rice receives a master's
degree from the University
of Notre Dame.

1981

■ Rice obtains a PhD from
the Graduate School of
International Studies at the
University of Denver and
becomes a member of the
faculty of Stanford
University.

1989

■ Rice is selected to serve as
a Soviet expert for the
National Security Council
in the administration of
President George H. W.
Bush; she remains in this
post until 1991.

1993

■ Rice is appointed provost
of Stanford University.

2000

■ **August 1**
Rice addresses the
Republican National
Convention, publicly
endorsing the ticket of
George W. Bush and Dick
Cheney.

■ **December 17**
President-elect George W.
Bush names Rice as his
national security adviser.

2004

■ **April 8**
Rice testifies before the
National Commission on
Terrorist Attacks upon the
United States, after having
declined to do so in
March.

■ **November 16**
Rice is appointed secretary
of state by President
George W. Bush for his
second term and replaces
Colin Powell.

matic agenda for American foreign policy: her passionate endorsement of George W. Bush as a presidential candidate at the Republican National Convention in 2000, her speech outlining the successes of American military intervention in Iraq just before the first parliamentary elections, her definition of "transformational diplomacy," and her keynote address at the World Economic Forum.

◆ **Speech at the Republican National Convention**

In August 2000, Rice addressed the Republican National Convention with a speech that strongly supported George W. Bush's bid for presidency in the name of peace, democracy, and equality of opportunity within the economic framework of free-market capitalism. Rice begins with a traditional theme explored in countless American speeches, from the sermons of the Pilgrims to Bill Clinton's 1993 inaugural address: America has a mission to accomplish, serving as a model for the entire world, and every American can take part in this process. In Rice's words, America has a "unique opportunity to lead the forward march of freedom and to fortify the peace."

After stating America's mission, Rice pays homage to all the American soldiers who "served over the decades" to ensure that "tyranny would not stand" and to "those great Republican Presidents who sustained American leadership through the decades, ended the Cold War and lifted our nuclear nightmare." She thanks three by name: Gerald Ford, Ronald Reagan, and George Herbert Walker Bush. Rice goes on to say that liberty and democracy are sustained by a free-market economy. The state's intervention in economic matters should be kept to a minimum as "prosperity flows to those who can tap the genius of their people." George W. Bush, she says, is the right president to lead America in the new century because he is committed to "America's principled leadership in the world." She calls this kind of leadership the "legacy and tradition" of the Republican Party. Rice then interweaves this political legacy with her family history, relating that it was the Republicans' commitment to equality, particularly racial equality, that drew her father to the party in 1952 after Democrats refused to register him to vote. She makes it clear, however, that her allegiance to the Republican Party did not simply follow family tradition. She joined the party, she says, because it "sees me as an individual, not as part of a group." She also espouses the party's stress on family values, on liberty, and on the fact that "peace begins with strength."

In a clear reference to the sexual and political scandals and the charges of perjury that besieged Bill Clinton, the Democrat who had held the presidency for the past two terms, Rice extols Bush and his running mate, Dick Cheney, for their understanding of the importance of "integrity in the Oval Office." She calls Bush "a man of his word," who would always tells the truth. Rice further praises the nominee for his awareness that "America's armed forces are not a global police force" but assures her audience that if compelled to deploy military force, Bush "will do so to win." While Rice is careful to state that the priority of foreign policy is "the maintenance of peace," she also emphasizes the need for a president who will not allow the nation to be blackmailed by "outlaw states" and who understands the new world balance after the end of the cold war. Rice then pays tribute to Bush's ability in foreign policy and to his diplomatic skills, which she says would earn new allies for the United States, as well as to his understanding that free trade can extend democracy abroad. This tribute became problematic, given the outcry and criticism that Bush's military intervention in Iraq caused throughout the world. Critics decried the idea that democracy can simply be exported to countries that have been ruled by dictatorships for decades.

At the end of her speech Rice returns to her initial rhetorical strategy of interweaving family history with the national mythology, in this case the American dream of upward mobility. Rice describes America as a nation made up of different ethnic groups. She notes that the coexistence of different ethnic groups in America had not always been "easy" but adds that the country had constantly been a destination for those people who were fleeing tyranny in search of hope and opportunity and to "pursue happiness in this great land" (a phrase that directly echoes the Declaration of Independence). Where people came from, Rice says, did not matter in America as long as they wanted to improve themselves and worked hard at it. Rice then illustrates this belief through the family parable of her grandfather, who rose from his humble origins in Alabama to become a college-educated Presbyterian minister. This was not simply a family story, she asserts, but "an American story." Rice concludes by referring to the George W. Bush's expressed policy of "compassionate" conservatism, defining him as the candidate who could "affirm the American dream for us all" and expand it beyond the nation's borders. American ideals thus become universal and timeless.

◆ "International Support for Iraqi Democracy"

Rice's speech at the Heritage Foundation in Washington, D.C., was an important statement of the progress made in Iraq since the beginning of the American military intervention. Rice proudly outlines the international support for the intervention and emphasizes the central role of the United States in the liberation of Iraq. Speaking two days before the first Iraqi parliamentary elections since the fall of the dictator Saddam Hussein, she answers critics of the American mission in Iraq, linking the establishment of democracy in the country to the democratic hopes of the entire Middle East and, in turn, to American and world security. Rice argues that if the international military coalition were to "desert Iraq's democrats at their time of greatest need," it would "embolden every enemy of liberty across the Middle East" and "destroy any chance that the people of this region have of building a future of hope and decency." If Iraq fell into the hands of the "small but deadly group" of al Qaeda terrorists, she says, it would become "the heart of a totalitarian empire that encompasses the Islamic world." The terrorists' triumph in the Middle East would put them in a position to threaten the security of the United States. Rice vows (quoting President Bush) that "America will not retreat from a fight that we can and must win."

<table>

Time Line		
2005	■ **January 26**	The Senate confirms Rice as secretary of state.
	■ **December 13**	Rice delivers her speech "International Support for Iraqi Democracy" to the Heritage Foundation in Washington, D.C.
2006	■ **January 18**	Rice outlines her strategy of "transformational diplomacy" before the School of Foreign Service at Georgetown University.
2008	■ **January 23**	Rice gives the keynote address at the annual meeting of the World Economic Forum in Davos, Switzerland.

</table>

Two years after the United States entered Baghdad, bringing the first phase of the war to an end, Rice concedes that victory in that country was a goal that could not be achieved overnight. Yet amid growing talk of fabrication of evidence on Iraqi possession of weapons of mass destruction to justify the invasion, and in the face of increasing national and international protests, Rice asserts that support for the mission had grown. She offers Iraqi citizens as an inspirational example to the world for having freely chosen democracy over tyranny. The development of a democratic system in Iraq, she says, had won international support for the military coalition that was helping in this process. Rice is also careful to dispel suspicions of American imperialism, stating that the ultimate goal of the mission is to make Iraqis able to defend their own country, allowing American soldiers to "return home to their families with the honor that they deserve." The international support was not limited to the military sphere only but also included economic help "to liberate the entrepreneurial spirit of the Iraqi people." Here, as in many other of her speeches, Rice links democracy and free-market capitalism as mutually essential.

International support for the Iraqi mission was clearly shown, Rice asserts, by the UN endorsement that coalition forces had received and by growing approval in the Arab world. In the face of this rising endorsement, Rice expresses disappointment that the international community was boycotting Saddam's trial (a trial that would end in November 2006 with a death sentence, carried out in December of that year) and that neighboring Arab countries such as Syria and Iran were still supporting the violence that besieged Iraqi society. Yet the enemies of Iraqi democracy,

A Palestinian police officer carries a flag outside the Jewish settlement of Netzarim, in the Gaza Strip, during the Israeli withdrawal from the region. (AP/Wide World Photos)

enemies that Rice identifies with those opposing military intervention in the country, were considerably fewer than at the beginning of armed operations. She attributes this to the leadership of President Bush. The concluding remarks of her speech affirm the central role that the United States had played in restoring democracy to Iraq. She depicts America as a world leader in the advancement of freedom. Iraq thus becomes a universal and timeless example and, tellingly, Rice links Bush's "promise of a free Iraq" to President Ronald Reagan's support of freedom in Latin America and in the Soviet Union at the time of the cold war.

♦ **"Transformational Diplomacy"**

This speech, delivered at Georgetown University, gives a clear outline of how Rice envisioned the mission of diplomacy in the twenty-first century. According to her, an effective type of diplomacy "not only reports about the world as it is, but seeks to change the world itself." That was why she used the adjective *transformational* to describe such diplomacy. The challenges of globalization, she says, required a new model of international relations, one that took into account changes occurring worldwide in the concept of national sovereignty. In the past, Rice explains, individual states were thought to be responsible for threats emerging from their own territories. In the twenty-first century, however, we could no longer assume that individual states were able to control such threats, which because of the power of technology to collapse distances, could easily become global rather than local dangers. To avoid these security risks, American diplomacy must work with U.S. allies to advance security interests, development interests, and democratic ideals. Although Rice is careful to stress that "transformational diplomacy is rooted in partnership; not in paternalism," she makes clear her belief that the United States should play a leading role in helping "foreign citizens" to "better their own lives and to build their own nations and to transform their own futures."

To meet the challenges of the new century, Rice says, the United States needed to transform its diplomatic corps in a sweeping reorganization comparable to those undergone in the aftermath of World War II and after the end of the cold war. Rice emphasizes that America had to reposition its diplomatic forces around the world in order to be better represented in countries in Latin America, Africa, and the Middle East that were in transition toward more democratic institutions. According to Rice, American diplomacy must counter the global threat of terrorism with local and regional policies, deploying "small, agile transnational networks of our diplomats." The United States should have an adequate diplomatic presence not only in foreign capitals but also spread "more widely across countries."

A central element of transformational diplomacy, in Rice's view, was cooperation between diplomats and the military. She describes as an embodiment of this partnership the State Department's new Office of Reconstruction and Stabilization, with its goal of preventing failed states from becoming global security threats. Rice adds that the role of the military was no longer limited to traditional armed interventions but involved assistance efforts on "the tsunami-wrecked coasts of Indonesia" or "in disaster relief in Pakistan." Both American diplomats and soldiers needed to do more than interact with important foreign officials; they also needed to "be active in the field" and "engage with private citizens in emerging regional centers."

Again quoting President Bush, Rice claims America's leading role among the nations "on the right side of freedom's divide." The United States, she says, stood as an example for "all people who finds themselves on the wrong side of that divide." Because America was made up of people of diverse backgrounds, ethnic groups, and religions, it could function as a paradigm of tolerance for those countries where "difference is a license to kill," encouraging them to adopt more inclusive solutions. What mattered in the United States, Rice claims, was not a person's ethnicity or religion but that one was an American and "devoted to an ideal and to a set of beliefs that unites us." Here again she suggests that American identity is timeless and free from ideological and historical constraints. But in expressing her hope for a diplomatic corps whose composition reflected this racial and ethnic diversity, Rice acknowledges the difficulties of creating an inclusive American democracy. She mentions the portrait of Thomas Jefferson that hangs in her office. She sometimes wondered, she says, what Jefferson would have thought of the fact that "my ancestors, who were three-fifths of a man in his constitution," would produce a secretary of state charged with carrying out America's democratic mission in the world.

♦ **Keynote Address at the Annual Meeting of the World Economic Forum**

Rice's keynote address at the World Economic Forum exemplifies her belief that democracy and social justice could be effective only when supported by free-market economic policies. She asserts that the values and ideas that have guided the United States since its foundation—"political and eco-

"We acknowledge together this remarkable truth: the future belongs to liberty—fueled by markets and trade, protected by the rule of law and propelled by the fundamental rights of the individual. Information and knowledge can no longer be bottled up by the state. Prosperity flows to those who can tap the genius of their people."

(Speech at the National Republican Convention)

"[George W. Bush] realizes that we are a nation that has been forged not from common blood but from common purpose—that the faces of America are the faces of the world. It has not been easy for our country to make 'We, the people' mean all the people. Democracy in America is a work in progress—not a finished masterpiece."

(Speech at the National Republican Convention)

"As the Iraqi people have inspired the world by freely embracing democracy, an international consensus has emerged that securing democracy in Iraq is strategically essential. This new consensus is generating international support that, quite frankly, was not fully present in the earliest days of Iraq's liberation."

("International Support for Iraqi Democracy")

"I would define the objective of transformational diplomacy this way: to work with our many partners around the world, to build and sustain democratic, well-governed states that will respond to the needs of their people and conduct themselves responsibly in the international system. Let me be clear, transformational diplomacy is rooted in partnership; not in paternalism."

("Transformational Diplomacy")

"I would submit to you this evening that there is not one challenge in the world today that will get better if we approach it without confidence in the appeal and effectiveness of our ideals—political and economic freedom, open markets and free trade, human dignity and human rights, equal opportunity and the rule of law. Without these principles, backed by all forms of national power, we may be able to manage global problems for awhile, but we will not lay a foundation to solve them."

(Keynote Address at the Annual Meeting of the World Economic Forum) nomic freedom, open markets and free trade, human dignity and human rights, equal opportunity and the rule of law"— are universal. She sees American interests and ideals as being almost synonymous, mutually advancing each other and working together for a more developed, freer, and safer world.

On the matter of economic development, despite the "extraordinary opportunities of the global economy," Rice admits that the present level of worldwide deprivation is still not acceptable. Yet she is careful not to charge the capitalist system for the unbalanced distribution of wealth. On the contrary, her solution would be to enhance free markets and free trade, as these, coupled with a fair government that invests in people, would lead to the creation of prosperity and a fair social structure. As in the speech on transformational diplomacy, Rice states that developing nations should not be treated with paternalism but as equal partners and should be supported as long as their governments endorse "economic reform, investment in health and education, the rule of law and a fight against corruption." The establishment of a more just economic system should go hand in hand with the promotion of democracy, which Rice says is the best guarantee of peace among nations. On the matter of diplomatic relations, the secretary of state challenges the claim by Lord Palmerston (prime minister of Britain in the mid-nineteenth century) that "nations have no permanent enemies and no permanent allies, only permanent interests." While she agrees that nations such as the United States have no permanent enemies because they "harbor no permanent hatreds," she disagrees with the idea that nations have no permanent allies. She asserts that over the years America had established a firm network of such allies. Rice was attempting here to dispel the criticism that, because of the interventionist policy of the Bush administration, America's international reputation had steadily declined.

Rice concedes that America made mistakes throughout its history. But owing to its historical progress toward making its democratic institutions more inclusive for groups who were initially excluded from them (such as African Americans), the United States still stood as an example for countries in transition. Although their inherent optimism and confidence in their ideals sometimes made Americans impatient with the slow pace of change in other nations, the lessons of their own long democratic improvement make them aware of "how long and difficult the path to democracy" could be for those countries. In accordance with her belief in transformational diplomacy, Rice concludes that, although economists, politicians, and diplomats had to confront the world as it is, it did not mean that they should not struggle to make it better.

Impact and Legacy

First as a national security adviser and then as secretary of state, Condoleezza Rice had a key role in devising American foreign policy at a time when the threats of the cold

Questions for Further Study

1. Whereas a large percentage of African Americans identify with the Democratic Party, Rice is a Republican. What are the reasons she gives, in her speech before the Republican National Convention, for her party affiliation? Why, in your opinion, have Republicans—despite being the party who freed the slaves and supported the election of African American leaders in the South during Reconstruction—failed to maintain their influence in the African American community? Has the party changed in the ensuing years? How do you think the party could attract more black voters?

2. One of the persistent themes in Rice's speeches included here, particularly those from 2005 and 2008, is the idea that free markets are essential to democracy. Do you agree? How has capitalism served to increase freedom in nations such as South Korea, and how might it affect the future of other nations—most notably China—in which markets are growing but freedom is still limited? In your argument, be sure to cite Rice's own words and address her points as they relate to the nation of principal concern in her two speeches: Iraq.

3. Discuss Rice's "transformational diplomacy" as she presents it both in the speech by that name and in her address to the World Economic Forum. What exactly does it mean, and how would she apply it in the international environment of the early twenty-first century? How, according to Rice, have foreign policy concerns shifted in modern times, and how would she adjust the diplomatic corps to deal with these concerns more effectively? Do you agree with her idea of envisioning the world as it could be, rather than merely accepting the way it is? Are her ideas the best vision of that future?

war were replaced by the new menace of international terrorism. Rice favored a more interventionist style for American diplomacy, one that justified preemptive strikes against nations thought to be hostile to democracy and supportive of terrorism and totalitarianism. This belief led the United States into two long and uncertain conflicts, first against the Taliban in Afghanistan and then against Saddam Hussein's dictatorship in Iraq. The Bush administration and Rice, as one of its longest-lasting members, were accused of fabricating evidence and violating human rights in justifying and carrying out these interventions. Former secretary of state Madeleine Albright, whose father, the professor of international politics Josef Korbel, was Rice's mentor at the University of Denver and attracted her to the study of political science, has argued that under the policy of the Bush administration the term *democracy* became militarized. Some critics also blamed Rice, as national security adviser, for failing to forestall the 9/11 terrorist attacks.

More sympathetic commentators have emphasized Rice's achievements while in office. She swayed the Bush administration to reopen negotiations with North Korea regarding the latter's nuclear weapons program, to back similar negotiations that European countries had opened with Iran. Additionally, she persuaded the United Nations to investigate war crimes taking place in Sudan. She was also able on at least two occasions to curb violence in the ongoing conflict between the Israelis and Palestinians. Further, her personal achievements are not to be denied. She rose from the segregated Alabama of her youth to a key position in the White House. According to one of her biographers, Marcus Mabry, Rice's roles on the stage of American diplomacy demonstrate her determination to overcome unfavorable circumstances. Her attainment of prominent political positions has cast her as a role model for many African Americans and for members of other minority groups.

Key Sources

With Philip D. Zeliko, Rice wrote *Germany Unified and Europe Transformed: A Study in Statecraft* (1995). Kiron Skinner, Serhiy Kudelia, Bruce Bueno de Mesquita, and Rice wrote *The Strategy of Campaigning: Lessons from Ronald Reagan and Boris Yeltsin* (2008). Her article "Campaign 2000: Promoting the National Interest" appeared in *Foreign Affairs* (January/February 2000).

Further Reading

■ Books

Bumiller, Elisabeth. *Condoleezza Rice: An American Life*. New York: Random House, 2007.

Draper, Robert. *Dead Certain: The Presidency of George W. Bush*. New York: Free Press, 2007.

Kessler, Glenn. *The Confidante: Condoleezza Rice and the Creation of the Bush Legacy*. New York: St. Martin's Press, 2007.

Mabry, Marcus. *Twice as Good: Condoleezza Rice and Her Path to Power*. New York: Modern Times/Rodale, 2007.

—Luca Prono

ADDRESS TO THE REPUBLICAN NATIONAL CONVENTION (2000)

Tonight, we gather to reflect on America's unique opportunity to lead the forward march of freedom and to fortify the peace.

We offer special thanks to all those Private Ryans who served over the decades—so that tyranny would not stand.

We remember those great Republican Presidents who sustained American leadership through the decades, ended the Cold War and lifted our nuclear nightmare. Thank you—Gerald Ford, Ronald Reagan and George Herbert Walker Bush.

And we acknowledge together this remarkable truth: the future belongs to liberty—fueled by markets and trade, protected by the rule of law and propelled by the fundamental rights of the individual. Information and knowledge can no longer be bottled up by the state. Prosperity flows to those who can tap the genius of their people.

We have a presidential nominee who knows what America must do to fulfill the promise of this new century. We have a nominee who knows the power of truth and honor. We have a nominee who will be the next great President of the United States—Texas Governor George W. Bush.

It is fitting that I stand before you to talk about Governor Bush's commitment to America's principled leadership in the world, because that is the legacy and tradition of our Party—because our Party's principles made me a Republican.

The first Republican I knew was my father and he is still the Republican I most admire. He joined our party because the Democrats in Jim Crow Alabama of 1952 would not register him to vote. The Republicans did....

I joined for different reasons. I found a party that sees me as an individual, not as part of a group. I found a party that puts family first. I found a party that has love of liberty at its core. And I found a party that believes that peace begins with strength.

George W. Bush and Dick Cheney live and breathe these Republican principles. They understand what is required for our time, and what is timeless. It all begins with integrity in the Oval Office. George W. Bush is a man of his word. Friend and foe will know that he tells the truth.

He believes that America has a special responsibility to keep the peace—that the fair cause of freedom depends on our strength and purpose. He recognizes that the magnificent men and women of America's armed forces are not a global police force....

They are the strongest shield and surest sword in the maintenance of peace. If the time ever comes to use military force, President George W. Bush will do so to win—because for him, victory is not a dirty word.

George W. Bush will never allow America and our allies to be blackmailed. And make no mistake; blackmail is what the outlaw states seeking long-range ballistic missiles have in mind. It is time to move beyond the Cold War. It is time to have a President devoted to a new nuclear strategy and to the deployment of effective missile defenses at the earliest possible date. George W. Bush knows that America has allies and friends who share our values. As he has said, the President should call our allies when they are not needed, so that he can call upon them when they are needed....

The George W. Bush I know is a man of uncommonly good judgment. He is focused and consistent. He believes that we Americans are at our best when we exercise power without fanfare or arrogance. He speaks plainly and with a positive spirit. In the past year, I have had a glimpse of what kind of President he will be....

George W. Bush will work with Congress so that America speaks with one voice. He has demonstrated in this campaign that he will never use foreign policy for narrow partisan purposes.

The United States cannot lead unless the President inspires the American people to accept their international responsibilities. George W. Bush will inspire us, because he understands who we are....

He realizes that we are a nation that has been forged not from common blood but from common purpose—that the faces of America are the faces of the world. It has not been easy for our country to make "We, the people" mean all the people. Democracy in America is a work in progress—not a finished masterpiece.

But even with its flaws, this unique American experience provides a shining beacon to peoples who still suffer in places where ethnic difference is a license to kill.

And George W. Bush understands that America is special among nations. That throughout our history, people everywhere have been inspired to flee tyranny and the constraints of class to gain liberty and pursue happiness in this great land.

In America, with education and hard work, it really does not matter where you came from—it matters where you are going. But that truth cannot be sustained if it is not renewed in each generation—as it was with my grandfather.

George W. Bush would have liked Granddaddy Rice. He was a poor farmer's son in rural Alabama—but he recognized the importance of education. Around 1918, he decided it was time to get book learning, so he asked, in the language of the day, where a colored man could go to college. He was told about little Stillman College, a school about 50 miles away. So Granddaddy saved his cotton for tuition and went off to Tuscaloosa....

My family has been Presbyterian and college-educated ever since. This is not just my grandfather's story—it is an American story.

My friends, George W. Bush challenges us to call upon our better selves—to be compassionate toward those who are less fortunate; to cherish and educate every child, descendants of slaves and immigrants alike, and to thereby affirm the American dream for us all.

On that foundation, confident of who we are, we will extend peace, prosperity and liberty beyond our shores.

Elect George W. Bush and Dick Cheney! God bless you and God bless America.

Glossary

Cold War	the atmosphere of suspicion and tension surrounding relations between the United States and its allies and the Soviet Union and its allies during the post–World War II period
Dick Cheney	U.S. vice president under George W. Bush
George Herbert Walker Bush	forty-first U.S. president and the father of George W. Bush
Gerald Ford	thirty-eighth U.S. president
Jim Crow	the informal name given to the system of laws and customs that kept African Americans in a subservient position in the nineteenth and early twentieth centuries
Private Ryans	reference to a character in the Academy Award–winning 1998 movie *Saving Private Ryan* about the search, during World War II, for a missing soldier whose brothers had all been killed in action
Ronald Reagan	fortieth U.S. president

"INTERNATIONAL SUPPORT FOR IRAQI DEMOCRACY" (2005)

I have come to Heritage today on the cusp of an historic event. Two days from now, the Iraqi people will go to the polls for the third time since January. And they will elect a parliament to govern their nation for the next four years. All across Iraq today, representatives from some 300 political parties are staging rallies, they're holding televised debates, they're hanging campaign posters, and they're taking their case to the Iraqi people. They are asking for the consent of the governed....

The...enemy we face, the terrorists, are a small but deadly group, motivated by the global ideology of hatred that fuels al-Qaida, and they will stop at nothing to make Iraq the heart of a totalitarian empire that encompasses the entire Islamic world. If we quit now, we will give the terrorists exactly what they want. We will desert Iraq's democrats at their time of greatest need. We will embolden every enemy of liberty across the Middle East. We will destroy any chance that the people of this region have of building a future of hope and decency. And most of all, we will make America more vulnerable.

In abandoning future generations in the Middle East to despair and terror, we also condemn future generations in the United States to insecurity and fear. And President Bush has made clear that on his watch, America will not retreat from a fight that we can and must win.

The American people also want to know what victory means in Iraq. And President Bush has answered, defining victory as the establishment of a free and democratic Iraq that can guarantee the freedom, meet the needs and defend the rights of all its citizens. As the President has said, victory in this struggle will not be a singular event....Rather, victory, like democracy itself, will be a steady but definable process that will not be won overnight....

What is the international community doing to advance the cause of victory in Iraq?

To answer simply: As the Iraqi people have inspired the world by freely embracing democracy, an international consensus has emerged that securing democracy in Iraq is strategically essential. This new consensus is generating international support that, quite frankly, was not fully present in the earliest days of Iraq's liberation....

On the security front, our coalition today remains strong and active. Some 30 nations are contributing over 22,000 soldiers, who are risking their lives alongside brave Iraqi and brave American troops. Like generations of Americans before them, our men and women in uniform are distinguishing themselves today through selfless service. They are heroically defending the freedom of others against a determined enemy. And we in America mourn the loss and honor the sacrifice of our many sons and daughters who have fallen in Iraq and around the world to protect our way of life....

Over time, the role of our coalition will also evolve, as Iraqis assume greater responsibility for their own security. With every passing day, Iraqis become better able to defend their nation and themselves and this enables us to shift more of our forces to helping Iraqis build the institutions of their new democracy. In the coming months and years, this will enable America's men and women in uniform, as well as those of our coalition, to return home to their families with the honor that they deserve....

On the political front, the international community is increasingly overcoming old divisions and supporting Iraq's transition to democracy. We have now passed four major Security Council resolutions on Iraq, most of them unanimously, pledging the UN's support for everything from an international mandate for our coalition forces, to an international rejection of terrorism in Iraq, to the goal of advancing Iraq's democratic process.

Yet, as welcome as this broad support is, I'm sad to say that the international community has barely done anything to help Iraq prosecute Saddam Hussein. All who expressed their devotion to human rights and the rule of law have a special obligation to help the Iraqis bring to justice one of the world's most murderous tyrants. The international community's effective boycott of Saddam's trial is only harming the Iraqi people, who are now working to secure the hope of justice and freedom that Saddam long denied them.

The Iraqi people clearly voiced their desire for freedom through democratic elections this January. And the sight of eight million free Iraqis, proudly displaying their ink-stained fingers, inspired new levels of international support for the goal of democracy in Iraq. In June, the United States and the European

Union co-hosted an international conference in Brussels, at which more than 80 countries agreed to a new international partnership to support Iraq's freely elected government....

Finally, a new and hopeful change has been the growing support that Iraq now receives from its neighbors....And Iraq's neighbors have welcomed it back into the Arab League. Many Arab governments now recognize the legitimacy of Iraq's democratically elected leaders.... Now, some of Iraq's neighbors are showing themselves to be no friends of the Iraqi people. Syria has still not taken sufficient action to stop the terrorists who cross into Iraq from its territory. And Iran continues to meddle in Iraqi affairs and to support violence in Iraqi society.

Nevertheless, the enemies of Iraq are increasingly fewer and isolating themselves from the international community, because today, the world is more united than ever in support of a new Iraq. In just two days, when Iraqis make history by electing the most democratic leaders in the entire Middle East, they will do so with the moral and financial and diplomatic backing of an overwhelming majority of the world.

This is remarkable when you consider how sharply divided the world was only three years ago. President Bush's vision of an Iraqi democracy, standing as a tribute to its citizens and serving as an inspiration to its neighbors, was neither grasped nor supported by many in the international community. Many believed that despotism was the permanent political condition of the Middle East. And they were prepared to countenance the false stability of undemocratic governments....

The lesson, my friends, is clear: When America leads with principle in the world, freedom's cause grows stronger. We saw this when Ronald Reagan spurned friendly dictators and supported freedom's cause in Latin America. We saw this as well when Reagan called out the true character of the Soviet Union and liberated a democratic longing that ended the Cold War. And we are seeing this today, as the world awakens to the promise of a free Iraq.

Glossary

al-Qaida	an Arabic term (often rendered al Qaeda) that means literally "the base"; an Islamic terrorist group responsible for the 9/11 terrorist attacks on the United States
Arab League	informal name for the League of Arab States, a regional organization of Arabic states formed in 1945
Cold War	the atmosphere of suspicion and tension surrounding relations between the United States and its allies and the Soviet Union and its allies during the post–World War II period
Ronald Reagan	fortieth U.S. president
Saddam Hussein	became president of Iraq in 1979; at the time of this speech, on trial in Iraq for crimes against humanity
Security Council	an organ of the United Nations responsible for international peace and security

"TRANSFORMATIONAL DIPLOMACY" (2006)

Almost a year ago today in his second Inaugural Address, President Bush laid out a vision that now leads America into the world. "It is the policy of the United States," the President said, "to seek and support the growth of democratic movements and institutions in every nation and culture with the ultimate goal of ending tyranny in our world." To achieve this bold mission, America needs equally bold diplomacy, a diplomacy that not only reports about the world as it is, but seeks to change the world itself. I and others have called this mission "transformational diplomacy." And today I want to explain what it is in principle and how we are advancing it in practice....

At the same time, other challenges have assumed a new urgency. Since its creation more than 350 years ago, the modern state system has rested on the concept of sovereignty. It was always assumed that every state could control and direct the threats emerging from its territory. It was also assumed that weak and poorly governed states were merely a burden to their people, or at most, an international humanitarian concern but never a true security threat.

Today, however, these old assumptions no longer hold. Technology is collapsing the distance that once clearly separated right here from over there. And the greatest threats now emerge more within states than between them. The fundamental character of regimes now matters more than the international distribution of power. In this world it is impossible to draw neat, clear lines between our security interests, our development efforts and our democratic ideals. American diplomacy must integrate and advance all of these goals together.

So, I would define the objective of transformational diplomacy this way: to work with our many partners around the world, to build and sustain democratic, well-governed states that will respond to the needs of their people and conduct themselves responsibly in the international system. Let me be clear, transformational diplomacy is rooted in partnership, not in paternalism. In doing things with people, not for them; we seek to use America's diplomatic power to help foreign citizens better their own lives and to build their own nations and to transform their own futures.

In extraordinary times like those of today, when the very terrain of history is shifting beneath our feet, we must transform old diplomatic institutions to serve new diplomatic purposes. This kind of challenge is sweeping and difficult but it is not unprecedented; America has done this kind of work before. In the aftermath of World War II, as the Cold War hardened into place, we turned our diplomatic focus to Europe and parts of Asia....

To advance transformational diplomacy, ... we must change our diplomatic posture. In the 21st century, emerging nations like India and China and Brazil and Egypt and Indonesia and South Africa are increasingly shaping the course of history. At the same time, the new front lines of our diplomacy are appearing more clearly, in transitional countries of Africa and of Latin America and of the Middle East. Our current global posture does not really reflect that fact....It is clear today that America must begin to reposition our diplomatic forces around the world, so over the next few years the United States will begin to shift several hundred of our diplomatic positions to new critical posts for the 21st century....

We will also put new emphasis on our regional and transnational strategies. In the 21st century, geographic regions are growing ever more integrated economically, politically and culturally. This creates new opportunities but it also presents new challenges, especially from transnational threats like terrorism and weapons proliferation and drug smuggling and trafficking in persons and disease.

Building regional partnerships is one foundation today of our counterterrorism strategy. We are empowering countries that have the will to fight terror but need help with the means. And we are joining with key regional countries like Indonesia and Nigeria and Morocco and Pakistan, working together not only to take the fight to the enemy but also to combat the ideology of hatred that uses terror as a weapon....

Rather than station many experts in every embassy, we will now deploy small, agile transnational networks of our diplomats. These rapid response teams will monitor and combat the spread of pandemics across entire continents. We are adopting a more regional strategy in our public diplomacy as well.

Transformational diplomacy requires us to move our diplomatic presence out of foreign capitals and to spread it more widely across countries. We must work on the front lines of domestic reform as well as in the back rooms of foreign ministries. There are nearly 200 cities worldwide with over one million people in which the United States has no formal diplomatic presence. This is where the action is today and this is where we must be. To reach citizens in bustling new population centers, we cannot always build new consulates beyond a nation's capital....

In today's world, our diplomats will not only work in different places, they will work in different communities and they will serve in different kinds of conditions, like reconstruction and stabilization missions, where they must partner more directly with the military. So to advance transformational diplomacy we are empowering our diplomats to work more jointly with our men and women in uniform.

Over the past 15 years, as violent state failure has become a greater global threat, our military has borne a disproportionate share of post-conflict responsibilities because we have not had the standing civilian capability to play our part fully. This was true in Somalia and Haiti, in Bosnia, in Kosovo, and it is still partially true in Iraq and Afghanistan.

These experiences have shown us the need to enhance our ability to work more effectively at the critical intersections of diplomacy, democracy promotion, economic reconstruction and military security. That is why President Bush created within the State Department the Office of Reconstruction and Stabilization. Recently, President Bush broadened the authority and mandate for this office and Congress authorized the Pentagon to transfer up to $100 million to State in the event of a post-conflict operation, funds that would empower our reconstruction and stabilization efforts. We have an expansive vision for this new office, and let there be no doubt, we are committed to realizing it....

We for decades have [had] positions in our Foreign Service called Political Advisors to Military Forces....

We station these diplomats where the world of diplomacy intersects the world of military force, but increasingly this intersection is seen in the dusty streets of Fallujah or the tsunami-wrecked coasts of Indonesia. I want American diplomats to eagerly seek our assignments working side-by-side with our men and women in uniform, whether it is in disaster relief in Pakistan or in stabilization missions in Liberia or fighting the illegal drug trade in Latin America.

Finally, to advance transformational diplomacy, we are preparing our people with new expertise and challenging them with new expectations....Over the course of this new century, we will ask the men and women of the State Department to be active in the field. We will need them to engage with private citizens in emerging regional centers, not just with government officials in their nations' capitals. We must train record numbers of people to master difficult languages like Arabic and Chinese and Farsi and Urdu....

President Bush has outlined the historic calling of our time. We on the right side of freedom's divide have a responsibility to help all people who find themselves on the wrong side of that divide. The men and women of American diplomacy are being summoned to advance an exciting new mission. But there is one other great asset that America will bring to this challenge....America stands as a tremendous example of what can happen when people of diverse backgrounds, ethnic groups, religions all call themselves American. Because it does not matter whether you are Italian American or African American or Korean American. It does not matter whether you are Muslim or Presbyterian or Jewish or Catholic. What matters is that you are American and you are devoted to an ideal and to a set of beliefs that unites us....

In order for America to fully play its role in the world, it must send out into the world a diplomatic

Glossary

Cold War	the atmosphere of suspicion and tension surrounding relations between the United States and its allies and the Soviet Union and its allies during the post–World War II period
Fallujah	city in Iraq
Farsi	often called Persian, the principal language of Iran, Afghanistan, and Tajikistan
Somalia and Haiti, in Bosnia, in Kosovo	scenes of U.S. military presence in the late twentieth century
Urdu	the official language of Pakistan and one of the official languages of India

force, a diplomatic corps that reflects that great diversity....

I sit in an office when I meet with foreign secretaries and foreign ministers from around the world that is a grand office that looks like it's actually out of the 19th century although it was actually built in 1947, but that's very American, too. And there's a portrait of Thomas Jefferson that looks direct at me when I am speaking to those foreign ministers, and I wonder sometimes, "What would Mr. Jefferson have thought?" What would he have thought about America's reach and influence in the world? What would he have thought about America's pursuit of the democratic enterprise on behalf of the peoples of the world? What would he have thought that an ancestor—that my ancestors, who were three-fifths of a man in his constitution, would produce a Secretary of State who would carry out that mission?...

America has come a long way and America stands as a symbol but also a reality for all of those who have a long way to go, that democracy is hard and democracy takes time, but democracy is always worth it.

KEYNOTE ADDRESS AT THE ANNUAL MEETING OF THE WORLD ECONOMIC FORUM (2008)

I want to talk about the importance of ideals and …the need for optimism.…

I recognize that there is a climate of anxiety in our world today. And it is tempting for many people to turn inward, to secure what they have, and to shut others out. Some want to go it alone. And there is certainly cynicism about the salience of our ideals when it seems that it's just hard enough to protect our interests.

I know that many are worried by the recent fluctuations in U.S. financial markets, and by concerns about the U.S. economy.…

The U.S. economy is resilient, its structure is sound, and its long-term economic fundamentals are healthy. The United States continues to welcome foreign investment and free trade. And the economy, our economy, will remain a leading engine of global economic growth. So we should have confidence in the underlying strength of the global economy—and act with confidence on the basis of principles that lead to success in this world.

And on that note, I would submit to you this evening that there is not one challenge in the world today that will get better if we approach it without confidence in the appeal and effectiveness of our ideals—political and economic freedom, open markets and free trade, human dignity and human rights, equal opportunity and the rule of law. Without these principles, backed by all forms of national power, we may be able to manage global problems for awhile, but we will not lay a foundation to solve them.

This is the core of America's approach to the world. We do not accept a firm distinction between our national interests and our universal ideals, and we seek to marry our power and our principles together to achieve great and enduring progress. This American approach to the world did not begin with President Bush. Indeed, it is as old as America itself. I have referred to this tradition as American Realism.

It was American Realism that enabled the United States to come into being in the first place. It was American Realism that led us to rally our allies to build a balance of power that favored freedom in the last century. And in this century, it is this American Realism that shapes our global leadership in three critical areas that I'd like to talk about tonight: the promotion of a just economic model of development;

the promotion of a freer, more democratic world; and the role of diplomacy in overcoming differences between nations.

First, let us take development. Amidst the extraordinary opportunities of the global economy, … the amount of deprivation in our world still remains unacceptable. Half of our fellow human beings live on less than $2 a day.…But as we approach the challenges of development, let us remember that we know what works: We know that when states embrace free markets and free trade, govern justly and invest in their people, they can create prosperity and then translate it into social justice for all their citizens.

Yes, some states are growing economically through a kind of "authoritarian capitalism." But it is at least an open question whether it is sustainable for a government to respect people s talents but not their rights. In the long run, democracy, development, and social justice must go hand in hand.

We must treat developing nations not as objects of our policy, but as equal partners in a shared endeavor of dignity. We must support leaders and citizens in developing nations who are transforming the character of their countries—through good governance and economic reform, investment in health and education, the rule of law and a fight against corruption.…

As we work for a more just economic order, we must also work to promote a freer and more democratic world.…

Democracy is the most realistic way for diverse peoples to resolve their differences, and share power, and heal social divisions without violence or repression.

Democracy is the most likely way to ensure that women have an equal place in society and an equal right to make the basic choices that define their lives.

And democracy is the most realistic path to lasting peace among nations. In the short run, there will surely be struggles and setbacks.…But delaying the start of the democratic enterprise will only mask tensions and breed frustrations that will not be suppressed forever.

Now this brings us, finally, to the matter of diplomacy. Do optimism and idealism play a role in this endeavor, which is by its very nature the art of the possible? Is it as Lord Palmerston said—that "nations have no permanent enemies and no permanent allies, only permanent interests"?

Well, I can assure you that America has no permanent enemies, because we harbor no permanent hatreds. The United States is sometimes thought of as a nation that perhaps does not dwell enough on its own history. To that, I say: Good for us. Because too much focus on history can become a prison for nations.

Diplomacy, if properly practiced, is not just talking for the sake of talking. It requires incentives and disincentives to make the choice clear to those with whom you are dealing that you will change your behavior if they are willing to change theirs. Diplomacy can make possible a world in which old enemies can become, if not friends, then no longer adversaries....

All conflicts must end, and nations need not have permanent enemies. But Lord Palmerston was wrong on the other part of his quote—that nations have no permanent allies. The United States has permanent allies: They are the allies with whom we share values—allies like Japan, and South Korea, and Australia, the allies we have in our own hemisphere, and of course, the allies we have across this continent—within NATO and the European Union....

It is true...that optimism and confidence in our ideals are perhaps a part of the American character, and I admit that this can make us a somewhat impatient nation. Though we realize that our ideals and our interests may be in tension in the short term, and

that they are surely tested by the complexities of the real world, we know that they tend to be in harmony when we take the long view.

Like any nation, we have made mistakes throughout our history, and we are going to make them again. But our confidence in our principles, and our impatience with the pace of change, is also a source of our greatest successes—and this will ensure that the United States remains a strong, confident, and capable global leader in the 21st century.

Yes, our ideals and our optimism make Americans impatient, but our history, our experience, should make us patient at the same time. We, of all people, realize how long and difficult the path of democracy really is. After all, when our Founding Fathers said "We the People," they did not mean me. It took the Great Emancipator, Abraham Lincoln, to overcome the compromise in our Constitution that made the founding of the United States of America possible, but that made my ancestors three-fifths of a man.

So we Americans have no reason for false pride and every reason for humility. And we believe that human imperfection makes democracy more important, and all who are striving for it more deserving of patience and support. History provides so many affirming examples of this....

That ultimately is the role of confidence in the eventual triumph of our ideals: to face the world everyday as it is, but to know that it does not have to be that way—and to keep in sight the better, not perfect, but better world that it can be.

Glossary

"nations have no permanent enemies..."	common misquotation of Lord Palmerston's statement to the British House of Commons in 1848; in fact, he said, "We have no eternal allies, and we have no perpetual enemies. Our interests are eternal and perpetual, and those interests it is our duty to follow."
European Union	an economic and political union of twenty-seven member countries, primarily in Europe
Lord Palmerston	Henry John Temple, 3rd Viscount Palmerston, twice prime minister of England
NATO	the North Atlantic Treaty Organization, a defense pact whose members include the United States and numerous European nations

Eleanor Roosevelt (Library of Congress)

ELEANOR ROOSEVELT   1884–1962

First Lady and Human Rights Activist

Featured Documents
♦ **"Women Must Learn to Play the Game as Men Do" (1928)**
♦ **Resignation from the Daughters of the American Revolution (1939)**
♦ **"The Struggle for Human Rights" (1948)**
♦ **Remarks at the United Nations concerning Human Rights (1958)**

Overview

Eleanor Roosevelt cast a long shadow over the American political landscape. Her life spanned the crises the nation faced as it confronted two world wars, the Great Depression, the cold war, the birth of the United Nations and the human rights movement, and the resurgence of intense debates over civil rights, civil liberties, and feminism. Her transition from progressive reformer to New Dealer to human rights activist put a human face on the policies promoted by her husband, President Franklin Roosevelt, and on the United Nations, the Democratic and Republican parties, and liberalism and its critics.

In late 1936 Roosevelt moved beyond writing books and a monthly newspaper column for *Pictorial Review* to writing "My Day," a syndicated column distributed six days a week to more than forty newspapers across the nation until 1962, when illness forced her to reduce her output to three days a week. In 1941 she embarked on her own radio career, interviewing noted political leaders, average citizens, and authors on issues of current interest. From 1948 through 1961 she hosted more than three hundred radio broadcasts featuring interviews with many of the world's major leaders and commentary on the most pressing issues of the day, and she appeared as a guest on more than seventy news programs. As television became a feature of the American landscape, Roosevelt embraced the new medium, and from 1959 until early fall 1962 she anchored *Prospects of Mankind*, a news-hour program for Education Television (the forerunner of public television) usually broadcast from Brandeis University. Roosevelt used her program to call Americans to embrace their responsibilities as citizens of a democratic nation and a world shattered by crises, both domestic and foreign.

As a child, Roosevelt never envisioned a political career, even though her uncle Theodore became president of the United States. Born on October 11, 1884, to aristocratic lineage and privilege, raised by a mother who mocked her looks and timidity, and orphaned by the age of ten, Anna Eleanor Roosevelt spent her childhood combating fear and disappointment. Her confidence developed when she sailed to London to attend the Allenswood Academy, whose bold, outspoken headmistress, Marie Souvestre, was devoted to Roosevelt and gave her the encouragement she needed to overcome the rejection that had dominated her early life.

Roosevelt returned to New York upon graduation, made her debut in society, and threw herself into settlement work and other progressive reforms. In 1905 she married Franklin D. Roosevelt, her fifth cousin once removed, and over eleven years gave birth to six children. Child rearing replaced progressive politics until the Roosevelts moved to Washington when Franklin joined the administration of Woodrow Wilson as secretary of the navy in 1913. With children in school and the world at war, Roosevelt threw herself into wartime relief efforts and began to find her own voice. She translated for international women's labor meetings and developed close friendships with the reformers who would spur her activism. By 1920, as she accompanied Franklin, then the Democratic vice presidential nominee, on the campaign trail, she knew that politics would define her life. Ironically, she thought it would be her husband's work rather than her own that would shape her future.

When James Cox and Franklin Roosevelt lost in the 1920 presidential election and polio temporarily sidelined Franklin's public career, Eleanor reentered the political arena in new ways—as a spokesperson and organizer. By 1928, when New Yorkers elected Franklin as governor, Eleanor had become a significant political player in her own right. She had helped manage the women's divisions of the state and national Democratic Party, edited their newsletters, chaired legislative committees of national reform organizations, testified before Congress on an international peace plan, and designed grassroots campaigns for Democratic candidates across the state. She urged women to become actively engaged in policy and politics, championed housing reform, supported the right to organize, and learned "to play the game as men do," a phrase she used in the title of a 1928 article.

In 1933, when Roosevelt returned to Washington, D.C., as first lady, she had to adjust her public profile and craft a role that supported her husband. After negotiating with her husband and his aides, she assumed the role of the president's eyes and ears, traveling around the country to investigate New Deal programs (the president's sweeping economic plans to lead the nation out of the Great Depression), and then reporting her findings upon her return. Her unprecedented travel and outreach to citizens generated widespread public support. A record-shattering four hundred thousand Americans wrote to her in the first six months of the Roosevelt administration.

1884

■ **October 11**
Anna Eleanor Roosevelt is born in New York City.

1905

■ **March 17**
Roosevelt marries Franklin Delano Roosevelt in New York City.

1923

■ **July 2**
With Esther Lape, Roosevelt becomes co-chair of the Bok Peace Prize Committee, organized to select a model international organization Congress could embrace; she holds the position until 1924.

1924

■ Democratic National Committee appoints Roosevelt chair of its platform committee on women's issues, a position she holds until 1928.

1925

■ **May**
Roosevelt assumes editorial duties for the *Women's Democratic News* and remains as editor until March 1933.

1928

■ **April**
"Women Must Learn to Play the Game as Men Do" is published in *Red Book Magazine*.

■ **Spring**
Roosevelt assumes leadership of the Women's Division of the New York State Democratic Committee, serving until March 1932.

1933

■ **March 6**
Roosevelt holds the first of her regular press conferences, becoming the first first lady to meet regularly with the press.

1936

■ **January 1**
Roosevelt writes her first nationally syndicated column, "My Day," which she continues to publish until September 1962.

This support gave Roosevelt a platform to address the issues to which she devoted her life—housing reform, education, labor, and the living wage—and the recovery, relief, and reform policies the New Deal promoted. She championed the inclusion of women and young people in emergency programs and played a key role in the formation of the National Youth Administration, the Federal Project Number One programs (to put artists and writers to work), and the construction of the so-called She-She-She camps to provide work for unemployed women. Working closely with Mary McLeod Bethune (an adviser to the president and the founder of what is now Bethune-Cookman College) and Walter White (executive director of the National Association for the Advancement of Colored People, or NAACP), she became the administration's face for civil rights and minority concerns and played a lead role in securing the Lincoln Memorial as the venue for a concert by the renowned black contralto Marian Anderson. She also urged her husband to sign the executive order banning discrimination in wartime defense industries. As the nation prepared for war, she promoted civil defense plans, tried to prepare women and young people for the sacrifices war would inflict, and spoke out in defense of civil liberties. Again defying precedent, she flew to London in 1941 to examine the damage German bombs had inflicted, and in 1943 she spent five weeks visiting seventeen war-torn islands in the Pacific. These actions generated intense passion from both her supporters and detractors, making her one of the most beloved and most despised first ladies in American history.

Franklin's sudden death on April 12, 1945, presented Roosevelt with different challenges. She confided to Lorena Hickok, a reporter with whom she had a close personal relationship, that her husband's death marked the end of a historical period, leaving her wondering what she could achieve on her own. Rejecting pressure to run for office, lead a college, or administer a political action committee, Roosevelt remained focused on "My Day," reassuring friends and colleagues that she would not be silenced. In December 1945, despite her early misgivings, she accepted President Harry Truman's request that she join the first U.S. delegation to the United Nations. For the next seven years, Roosevelt devoted the majority of her time to the UN, where she shepherded the drafting and adoption of the Universal Declaration of Human Rights, helped develop UN refugee and humanitarian relief policies, and spoke out forcefully in support of the creation of Israel. Although her tenure ended at the close of the Truman administration, Roosevelt remained devoted to the UN, volunteering to help organize the United Nations Association and to defend the UN against conservative attacks.

Roosevelt also remained politically active, campaigning for liberal Democrats and serving on the boards of civil rights, labor, and education associations. She spoke out against Senator Joseph McCarthy, notorious for sensational accusations of Communism in government in the early 1950s, and had a very public dispute with Francis Cardinal Spellman, the archbishop of the New York diocese and a cardinal in the Catholic Church, over federal aid to parochial schools. In 1956 she chaired the civil rights division of the Democratic Platform Committee and traveled widely in support of Adlai Stevenson's presidential campaign. She also traveled the world, circling the globe three times and chronicling her observations for readers. In 1961 she pressured President John Kennedy to appoint more women in upper levels of his administration. The president responded by appointing her chair of his Presidential Commission on the Status of Women. Roosevelt died on November 7, 1962, in New York City.

Explanation and Analysis of Documents

Eleanor Roosevelt was arguably the most active and outspoken of the nation's first ladies, one who hurled herself into the national political arena and into international issues such as human rights. The more she observed the welter of events through which she lived, the more roles she assumed and the more articulate, more public, and more insistent her voice became. In the process, she used a wide variety of media, including print, radio, film, and television, to make her case, generating twenty-seven books, more than eight thousand columns, over 550 articles, and an average of seventy-five lectures a year. Four documents—just a smattering of her prolific output—give readers insight into some of her major concerns: the role of women in politics, racial inequality in the United States, and international human rights. In these and other documents, she showed an uncanny ability to speak directly to the people whom she most wished to reach in simple yet colorful and concrete language.

◆ **"Women Must Learn to Play the Game as Men Do"**

In 1920 ratification of the Nineteenth Amendment to the U.S. Constitution granted American women the right to vote. The attainment of voting rights brought to a climax the efforts of several generations of women political figures who had labored for decades to build a powerful grassroots movement behind female suffrage and then leveraged it to force the amendment's enactment. At the time, many believed that the enfranchisement of women would empower the movement's leaders to assume commanding positions within the hierarchy of the nation's major political parties and to gain real concessions for the nation's women in doing so. This goal proved short-lived, however, as women leaders instead found themselves marginalized within Democratic and Republican institutions dominated by men and lacking the support of an energized women's network, which had declined in intensity and fractured into opposing camps once the unifying goal of suffrage had been attained. Some, like Carrie Chapman Catt, all but abandoned electoral politics to focus on different pursuits, while others, like Alice Paul, sought to re-create the women's movement under the auspices of a National Woman's Party. A fellow organizer in her own right, Eleanor Roosevelt disagreed with both directions and sought to point the way toward a third in a 1928 article titled "Women Must Learn to Play the Game as Men Do."

Time Line

1939

■ **February 26**
Roosevelt resigns from the Daughters of the American Revolution in protest of its refusal to allow Marian Anderson to perform in Constitution Hall; she publishes her views on the matter in a "My Day" column the next day.

1940

■ **December 10**
Roosevelt testifies before Congress in support of aid to migrant farmworkers, becoming the first first lady to appear before Congress.

1945

■ **December 21**
Roosevelt joins U.S. delegation to the United Nations and serves until the end of 1952, representing the United States on the Social, Humanitarian and Cultural Commission.

1946

■ **April 29**
Roosevelt is elected chair of the United Nations Commission on Human Rights and leads the drafting and adoption of the Universal Declaration of Human Rights.

1948

■ **September 28**
Roosevelt delivers a speech about the future of human rights to the United Nations General Assembly.

1958

■ **March 27**
Roosevelt delivers remarks at the United Nations and presents to the Human Right Commission the booklet "In Your Hands."

1961

■ **December 14**
Roosevelt assumes the chairmanship of the President's Commission on the Status of Women; she remains in the post until August 1962.

Time Line

1962

■ **May 26**
Roosevelt chairs a commission of inquiry into attacks on civil rights workers.

■ **November 7**
Roosevelt dies in New York City.

At the time, Roosevelt was actively organizing women in New York State behind Al Smith's presidential campaign, and her husband was running for governor. Both experiences confirmed Roosevelt's sense that women had not yet achieved political equality with men. She writes:

> In those circles which decide the affairs of national politics, women have no voice or power whatever.... They are called upon to produce votes, but they are kept in ignorance of noteworthy plans and affairs.... Beneath the veneer of courtesy and outward show of consideration universally accorded women, there is a widespread male hostility—age-old, perhaps—against sharing with them any actual control.

One solution that Roosevelt rejected was the formation of a separate party for women. With her reference to a "Woman's Party," she alludes to the work primarily of Alice Paul, a leading suffragist of the early twentieth century. Paul and her associates gained notoriety by picketing the White House for two and half years in an effort to persuade President Woodrow Wilson to support a constitutional amendment granting women the right to vote. After the passage of the Nineteenth Amendment in 1920, Paul turned her attention to the larger issue of equal rights for women and wrote the earliest version of the Equal Rights Amendment in 1921. She and other members of the National Woman's Party, which Paul had helped found in 1916, remained active in trying to nominate women for office and in securing passage of an equal rights amendment. Rather than following Paul's lead, however, Roosevelt instead advocated intense party-based organization at the local, state, and national levels, culminating in the designation of female "bosses" with enough clout to field and elect candidates, press legislation, and dispense patronage, just as men did. "Our means is to elect, accept and back women political bosses," she wrote. "If women believe they have a right and duty in political life today, they must learn to talk the language of men. They must not only master the phraseology, but also understand the machinery which men have built up through years of practical experience."

Roosevelt knew that her call for direct engagement in the most rudimentary, unglamorous, and even unsavory political work on the part of women would strike many of her contemporaries as unladylike, but she insisted upon its necessity in order to make women's equality a reality. As she puts it,

Certain women profess to be horrified at the thought of women bosses bartering and dickering in the hard game of politics with men. But many more women realize that we are living in a material world, and that politics cannot be played from the clouds. To sum up, women must learn to play the game as men do.

Interestingly, Roosevelt did not necessarily blame men for this state of affairs, at least not entirely. She notes that women had had the vote for only ten years and that their participation in political affairs was something completely new. Both men and women conformed to the prejudices of the past, so she raises the question of whether men can be blamed for finding it difficult to adapt to modern life as the old prejudices were being thrown off. She was also critical of women for not being more politically engaged. Although many resisted her call at first, Roosevelt applied this reasoning to her own public career, which for thirty years sustained her as the most powerful woman in the Democratic Party—a "boss" of tremendous capacity, enduring influence, and an outsize historical legacy.

◆ **Resignation from the Daughters of the American Revolution**

On Easter Sunday, April 9, 1939, seventy-five thousand people gathered at the steps of the Lincoln Memorial to hear Marian Anderson, the world's greatest contralto, perform. She had entertained crowned heads and elected officials in Europe, had won the highest awards her profession could bestow, and had entertained the Roosevelts in the White House. Her previous performances in the District of Columbia before sold-out racially mixed audiences received rave reviews. Yet Anderson struggled to find an auditorium suitable for a benefit concert for the Howard School of Music after the Daughters of the American Revolution (DAR) refused to rent its facility, Constitution Hall, to Anderson because she was African American. The DAR is an organization based on lineage; membership is open to any woman who can trace her lineage back to the Revolutionary War era and whose ancestor signed the Declaration of Independence, fought in the war, took part in the Boston Tea Party, attended the Continental Congress, or otherwise served the fledgling nation. The organization was first founded at the state level in 1890 and was incorporated nationally by congressional charter in 1896. The purposes of the DAR remain the same as they were over a century ago: preserving historic sites and artifacts, funding educational endeavors, and promoting patriotism. Throughout the early decades of its existence, the DAR quietly held to discriminatory practices; in recent decades, however, the organization has rid itself of those practices, recognizing that numerous African Americans aided their country in various capacities at the time of its founding.

At first, the DAR denied that race was the reason for turning down the request to use Constitution Hall for the concert, but soon the truth emerged. When the DAR refused to reverse its decision, renowned Washingtonians organized and petitioned the District of Columbia School

Contralto Marian Anderson performs below the steps of Washington's Lincoln Memorial on April 9, 1939, after she had been refused permission to perform in Washington's Constitution Hall. (AP/Wide World Photos)

Board for permission to use the Armstrong High School auditorium for the concert, only to have their petition quickly rejected. Roosevelt debated what action to take on Anderson's behalf. By early January she had already agreed to present the Spingarn Medal for outstanding achievement by a black American to Anderson at the national NAACP convention and had met with the NAACP secretary Walter White and conference chair Dr. Elizabeth Yates Webb to discuss the broadcast of the awards ceremony. She had further invited Anderson to perform for Britain's king and queen at the White House in June and had telegraphed her support to Howard University. Although initially she thought she should not attack the DAR's decision, she changed her mind and resigned from the organization on February 26. Her resignation letter is simple and self-effacing, yet her statement to the DAR's president, Mrs. Henry M. Robert, Jr., was direct: "You had an opportunity to lead in an enlightened way and it seems to me that your organization has failed."

The power of understatement displayed in her "My Day" column of February 27, 1939, revealed Roosevelt's finger on the pulse of the nation. Carefully portraying the situation in impersonal, nonthreatening terms with which the majority of her readers would identify, she refrains from naming the issue or the organization that had caused her distress. Roosevelt introduces the dilemma simply: "The question is, if you belong to an organization and disapprove of an action which is typical of a policy, should you resign or is it better to work for a changed point of view within the organization?" Telling her readers that she preferred to work for change, she goes on to say that she "usually stayed in until I had at least made a fight and had been defeated." When she lost, she accepted defeat and "decided I was wrong or, perhaps, a little too far ahead of the thinking of the majority at that time." But this case did not fit that pattern because this organization was one "in which I can do no active work" and "to remain as a member implies approval of that action." Resignation was the best option. The next day, the column was splashed across the front pages of American newspapers from San Francisco to New York City. Although others had resigned from the DAR over this issue, Roosevelt's action effectively placed Anderson, the DAR, and Jim Crow (the name given to the system of laws and customs that kept African Americans segregated) on a national stage.

After the concert, Roosevelt worked to keep the issue before the public. That year she presented the NAACP's Spingarn Medal to Anderson at the organization's national convention in Richmond, Virginia. The symbolism of the nation's first lady presenting this noted civil rights honor to Anderson in the capital of the Civil War Confederacy on Independence Day weekend was dramatic. The demand for seats was so overwhelming that tickets for the event were unavailable a week after the announcement was made. On the day of the ceremony, the crowd overflowed the five-thousand-seat capacity of the Richmond "Mosque" (the name given to the exotic theater building now called the Landmark) and spilled out into the streets to hear Roosevelt praise Anderson's poise and courage and urge others to put aside their comfort and complacency to help those whom society discounted.

This incident made Roosevelt recognize the impact she had when she employed her column for political persuasion. In 1939 she was just beginning to use "My Day" as a political forum. The response the column generated showed her the impact she had when she spoke out on a political event. Major public opinion polls revealed that her support for Anderson increased her popularity in all areas of the country, except the Deep South. Roosevelt's distributor, United Features Syndicate, recognized the appeal of "My Day" and in April 1940 awarded her a five-year renewal contract for the column.

◆ **"The Struggle for Human Rights"**

In the fall of 1948 Roosevelt journeyed to Paris to attend the UN General Assembly's third session and to introduce for discussion and final approval the text of an "International Declaration of Human Rights" written by the UN's Human Rights Commission, which she chaired. At the time, the growing estrangement of the United States from the Soviet Union had already emerged as the defining feature of international politics in the postwar world and the most serious threat to the long-term maintenance of international peace and security. This state of affairs extended especially to the United Nations, established three years earlier to promote peaceful relations among its signatories though now a central battleground in the tense standoff between its two most powerful member states. Having already witnessed many American priorities falter in this fractious diplomatic environment, Roosevelt undertook a full-blown political campaign to build support for the declaration's passage, the broad rationale for which she unveiled in a major policy address at the Sorbonne (the common name at the time for the University of Paris and various of its successor institutions) on September 28, 1948.

Rather than evade or paper over the ideological conflict at the heart of Soviet-American tensions, Roosevelt used her speech to position the declaration as a challenge to the totalitarian state model favored by the Soviet Union and a successor to the signature documents and events of democratic transformation in North America and western Europe. "I have chosen to discuss it here in France, at the Sorbonne, because here in this soil the roots of human freedom have long ago struck deep and here they have been richly nourished," she tells the assembly. "We are fighting this battle again today as it was fought at the time of the French Revolution and at the time of the American Revolution." In this context she makes reference to the Declaration of the Rights of Man (which also included the words "and Citizen" as part of the full title). This was a 1789 document promulgated by the National Assembly of France during the French Revolution. Roosevelt goes on to describe the process by which the Declaration of Human Rights was created, noting that the work of the UN's Human Rights Commission was incomplete; while the commission had completed the declaration per se, it had not yet finished the binding treaty that would accompany the declaration and that, presumably, the UN's member nations would sign.

The advent of World War II coupled with the postwar reckoning of its greatest atrocity, the Holocaust, had given new urgency to the need to renew these values and update them for an international community twice plunged into global war in the previous thirty years. At the heart of this renewal lay the principle that universal human rights protect "the full development of individual personality" whenever and wherever it exists, without distinction as to race, sex, language, or religion and within parameters that acknowledge the basic human rights of "freedom of speech and a free press; freedom of religion and worship; freedom of assembly and the right of petition; the right of men to be secure in their homes and free from unreasonable search and seizure and from arbitrary arrest and punishment." Of utmost concern to Roosevelt was the integrity of these principles in the face of totalitarian attempts to undermine them by changing their definition. "We must not be deluded by the efforts of the forces of reaction to prostitute the great words of our free tradition and thereby to confuse the struggle," she declares. "Democracy, freedom, human rights have come to have a definite meaning to the people of the world which we must not allow any nation to so change that they are made synonymous with suppression and dictatorship."

Roosevelt notes that only four member states of the Human Rights Commission abstained from voting to approve the document. These states were the Soviet Union, Ukraine, Byelorussia, and Yugoslavia, all Communist led. The Soviet Union, she hastens to point out, had not met this standard in its own affairs; yet, uncharacteristically for an American diplomat at the time, she concedes later that the United States had not done so either. She uses the issue of race relations to illustrate her point. "We recognize that we have some problems of discrimination.... Through normal democratic processes we are coming to understand our needs and how we can attain full equality for all our people. Free discussion on the subject is permitted."

By contrast, Roosevelt takes note of the Soviet government's claim that "it has reached a point where all races within her borders are officially considered equal … and they insist they have no discrimination where minorities are concerned." But she reminds her audience of "other aspects of the development of freedom," such as the ability to speak one's mind freely, "which are essential before the mere absence of discrimination is worth much, and these are lacking in the Soviet Union." She goes on to point out fundamental differences in the meaning of the very word *freedom* and how those differences translate into differences in the meaning of such expressions as "freedom of the press." In the Soviet Union, she notes, "freedom of the press" means that the state provides the machinery and salaries that allow newspapers to be published; in the West, such freedom pertains to the unfettered ability to question and criticize the government.

By establishing a standard that the world's population might look to as the rightful guarantees of civil society, Roosevelt hoped to foreclose any possibility that their meaning could change at the behest of despotism or the will of future dictators, as they had in Nazi Germany when Hitler rose to power. In closing, she tells her audience:

> The propaganda we have witnessed in the recent past, like that we perceive in these days, seeks to impugn, to undermine, and to destroy the liberty and independence of peoples. Such propaganda poses to all peoples the issue whether to doubt their heritage of rights and therefore to compromise the principles by which they live, or try to accept the challenge, redouble their vigilance, and stand steadfast in the struggle to maintain and enlarge human freedoms.

Animated by the desire to make her own contribution in this regard, Roosevelt continued to campaign on behalf of the Declaration of Human Rights through the fall of 1948. On December 10, at midnight, she saw her efforts rewarded with its final adoption by the UN General Assembly. She considered the declaration's adoption her life's greatest accomplishment.

♦ **Remarks at the United Nations concerning Human Rights**

Throughout the drafting process, Roosevelt insisted that the Universal Declaration of Human Rights be as clear as it was thorough. If people could not understand it, it could not move them to action, and its powerful vision would be compromised. Roosevelt considered the adoption of the declaration her finest accomplishment and dedicated the rest of her life to activities tied to it. This was not a simple or safe task. As the cold war escalated, the declaration's critics alleged, incorrectly, that the declaration deprived nations of sovereign power, made citizens wards of the state, mandated Socialism, and so on.

Roosevelt dedicated enormous energy to combating these attacks. As the declaration's passage neared its tenth anniversary, she addressed the UN in support of a publication insisting that the fate of human rights lay "in your hands," the title she gave to the booklet she wanted to see published and distributed. Whereas in Paris in 1948, Roosevelt had addressed the international diplomatic community charged with negotiating international law and approving the declaration, she directed her remarks of March 27, 1958, to the citizens of the world—the "your" of the title. She spoke simply and without fanfare, determined to present the scope and power of human rights. Human rights are universal, domestic as well as international ("in small places, close to home") and require "concerted citizen action" for their recognition and protection.

Impact and Legacy

For decades after her death, historians treated Roosevelt as her husband's "missus," who, through selfless devotion and reconciliation with personal unhappiness, became her husband's eyes and ears and the nation's conscience. Roosevelt encouraged this portrayal, concerned that any attention she received would undercut her husband's legacy. Although Joseph Lash, Roosevelt's friend and chosen biographer, struggles to transcend this image, his depiction of her focuses more on the reach of her heart than the scope of her political influence.

In later years, however, historians uncovered the impact Roosevelt had on domestic and international politics and policy. Susan Ware outlines the extensive network of women reformers Roosevelt developed in the 1920s and 1930s and its impact on New Deal labor, health, and unemployment policies. Blanche Cook reconstructs Roosevelt's influence on the Subsistence Homestead program and the Employment Act of 1937 and her struggle to make New Deal policies more racially inclusive. Allida Black traces Roosevelt's civil rights efforts and focuses on her post–White House career at home, when she often argued with Harry Truman, Dwight Eisenhower, and John F. Kennedy—insisting that America was on trial before the world to demonstrate what democracy meant and claiming that the way to defeat Communism was to show the world that democratic nations provided housing, education, health care, and safe employment to all their citizens. Mary Ann Glendon chronicles Roosevelt's skill in drafting the Universal Declaration of Human Rights.

As scholars and policy makers began to review Roosevelt's life, a powerful legacy emerged. She redefined the role of first lady. Not content to be silent on issues that concerned her, Roosevelt spoke out through her newspaper column, national lecture tours, and press conferences. She became Washington's most noted spokesperson for civil rights, quality low-income housing, women's employment, and labor. In the process, her stature grew, as did criticism of her actions. Yet Roosevelt exerted the most influence on politics and policy after she left the White House. As the guiding force behind the Universal Declaration of Human Rights and its unstinting advocate, she played a key role in organizing the modern human rights movement. Further-

"If women believe they have a right and duty in political life today, they must learn to talk the language of men. They must…understand the machinery which men have built up through years of practical experience. Against the men bosses there must be women bosses who can talk as equals, with the backing of a coherent organization of women voters behind them."

("Women Must Learn to Play the Game as Men Do")

"Women must learn to play the game as men do….They can keep their ideals; but they must face facts and deal with them practically."

("Women Must Learn to Play the Game as Men Do")

"You had an opportunity to lead in an enlightened way and it seems to me that your organization has failed."

(Resignation from the Daughters of the American Revolution)

"Human rights are a fundamental object of law and government in a just society."

("The Struggle for Human Rights")

"People who continue to be denied the respect to which they are entitled as human beings will not acquiesce forever in such denial."

("The Struggle for Human Rights")

"We must not be confused about what freedom is. Basic human rights are simple and easily understood: freedom of speech and a free press; freedom of religion and worship; freedom of assembly and the right of petition; the right of men to be secure in their homes and free from unreasonable search and seizure and from arbitrary arrest and punishment."

("The Struggle for Human Rights")

"Where, after all, do universal human rights begin? In small places, close to home—so close and so small that they cannot be seen on any map of the world."

(Remarks to the United Nations concerning Human Rights)

more, she convinced the U.S. State Department that human rights included political and civil rights as well as economic, social, and cultural rights. In doing so, she helped define the most pressing issues of our time—who are considered citizens, what rights they have, how those rights are protected, and what responsibilities the world has when those rights are abused by individual nations.

As one of the nation's most widely syndicated journalists and most popular lecturers, Roosevelt helped define postwar liberalism. Her opposition to loyalty oaths, censorship, and the politics of fear showed those who followed her that one could be opposed to Communism without succumbing to politics governed by panic. Roosevelt's legacy increases with time. Her tireless efforts on behalf of civil rights, federal aid to education, the Peace Corps, women's rights, and the right of labor to organize have influenced several subsequent generations of American diplomats, human rights leaders, women elected officials, and others. Not seen simply as the wife of a great president, Roosevelt is recognized as having been an important leader in her own right.

Questions for Further Study

1. Discuss the interaction between Eleanor Roosevelt and her husband, President Franklin D. Roosevelt. How was she unusual as a first lady, and how did she defy precedent by her actions, particularly during World War II? Do you think that her work served to complement that of her husband, or did it cause conflict? If so, was that conflict justified, for instance, in the case of her outspoken support for Marian Anderson? What effect, if any, did the Roosevelts' personal and marital relationship have on their political interactions?

2. Critique Roosevelt's arguments in "Women Must Learn to Play the Game as Men Do." How does she offer a "third way," distinct from the solutions presented by the feminists Carrie Chapman Catt and Alice Paul? How does she respond to those who might claim it is "unladylike" for women to be involved in political campaigns, and how do her ideas about political organization subtly prove her point that women can be just as effective in politics as men? Also notable is the fact that she does not blame men for the state of affairs, noting instead that old prejudices are slow to die. Do you agree with her? How might feminists of her time or later have regarded her position on this issue?

3. Discuss events leading up to Roosevelt's resignation from the Daughters of the American Revolution and the "My Day" column in which she announced her resignation. How does Roosevelt use understatement to make her point? How effective is she in doing so? How would you answer the question she raises: "If you belong to an organization and disapprove of an action which is typical of a policy, shall you resign or is it better to work for a changed point of view within the organization?" Give reasons for your answer, and consider various situations in which you might be forced to make the same kind of choice Roosevelt had to make.

4. In her 1948 speech on human rights, Roosevelt harshly critiques totalitarianism, particularly as represented by the Soviet Union; yet the United States, with its continuing racial problems, is not exempt from her criticism. Discuss her approach to the problems of segregation and racism in America as they relate to the world context and compare her consideration of this subject with that of another female diplomat six decades later: Condoleezza Rice. The latter, in her "Transformational Diplomacy" speech and her address to the World Economic Forum, noted that as an African American woman, she had not always been represented by the U.S. Constitution. What differences do Roosevelt and Rice see between the U.S. system and that of more repressive regimes, and how do these distinctions offer hope of continued progress on civil rights in the United States?

5. Critics of Roosevelt's actions as a diplomat maintained that she failed to recognize the threat posed by Soviet totalitarianism and the ways in which dictatorial regimes might cynically exploit the ideals underlying the United Nations. What does her 1948 speech say about her views on these subjects? Despite her strong stance in the 1948 speech, how might her critics have been justified in calling her naive about the harsh realities of world politics? How did her views change between the earlier address and her 1958 remarks before the United Nations?

Key Sources

Eleanor Roosevelt's personal papers are housed at the Franklin D. Roosevelt Library in Hyde Park, New York. The Eleanor Roosevelt Papers Project at George Washington University (www.gwu.edu/~erpapers) has additional archival material relevant to Roosevelt's post–White House career and offers a complete electronic edition of "My Day." David Emblidge assembled a collection of "My Day" columns titled *My Day: The Best of Eleanor Roosevelt's Acclaimed Newspaper Columns, 1936–1962* (2001). Susan Ware and others compiled *The Papers of Eleanor Roosevelt: 1933–1945* (1986). Allida Black edited *The Eleanor Roosevelt Papers*, Vol. 1: *The Human Rights Years, 1945–1948* (2007). *The Autobiography of Eleanor Roosevelt* was published in 1961. An earlier autobiography is *This Is My Story* (1937). Roosevelt also authored *You Learn by Living* (1960).

Further Reading

■ Articles

Lachman, Seymour P. "The Cardinal, the Congressmen, and the First Lady." *Journal of Church and State* (winter, 1965): 35–66.

Pfeffer, Paula F. "Eleanor Roosevelt and the National and World Women's Parties." *Historian* (Fall 1996): 39–58.

■ Books

Black, Allida M. *Casting Her Own Shadow: Eleanor Roosevelt and the Shaping of Postwar Liberalism* . New York: Columbia University Press, 1995.

———. *Courage in a Dangerous World: The Political Writings of Eleanor Roosevelt*. New York: Columbia University Press, 2000.

Cook, Blanche Wiesen. *Eleanor Roosevelt*. Vol. 1: *1884–1933*. New York: Penguin, 1992; Vol. 2: *1933–1938*. New York: Penguin, 1999.

Glendon, Mary Ann. *A World Made New: Eleanor Roosevelt and the Universal Declaration of Human Rights*. New York: Random House, 2001.

Lash, Joseph P. *Eleanor and Franklin*. New York: W. W. Norton, 1971.

———. *Eleanor: The Years Alone*. New York: W. W. Norton, 1972.

Ware, Susan. *Beyond Suffrage: Women in the New Deal*. Cambridge, Mass.: Harvard University Press, 1981.

Youngs, J. William T., and Oscar Handlin. *Eleanor Roosevelt: A Personal and Public Life*. Boston: Little, Brown, 1985.

■ Web Sites

"Anna Eleanor Roosevelt." The White House Web site. http://www.whitehouse.gov/history/firstladies/ar32.html.

—Allida Black

"Women Must Learn to Play the Game as Men Do" (1928)

Women have been voting for ten years. But have they achieved actual political equality with men? No. They go through the gesture of going to the polls; their votes are solicited by politicians; and they possess the external aspect of equal rights. But it is mostly a gesture without real power. With some outstanding exceptions, women who have gone into politics are refused serious consideration by the men leaders. Generally they are treated most courteously, to be sure, but what they want, what they have to say, is regarded as of little weight. In fact, they have no actual influence or say at all in the consequential councils of their parties.

In small things they are listened to; but when it comes to asking for important things they generally find they are up against a blank wall. This is true of local committees, State committees, and the national organizations of both major political parties.

From all over the United States, women of both camps have come to me, and their experiences are practically the same. When meetings are to be held at which momentous matters are to be decided, the women members often are not asked. When they are notified of formal meetings where important matters are to be ratified, they generally find all these things have been planned and prepared, without consultation with them, in secret confabs of the men beforehand. If they have objections to proposed policies or candidates, they are adroitly overruled. They are not allowed to run for office to any appreciable extent and if they propose candidates of their own sex, reasons are usually found for their elimination which, while diplomatic and polite, are just pretexts nevertheless.

In those circles which decide the affairs of national politics, women have no voice or power whatever. On the national committee of each party there is a woman representative from every State, and a woman appears as vice-chairman. Before national elections they will be told to organize the women throughout the United States, and asked to help in minor ways in raising funds. But when it comes to those grave councils at which possible candidates are discussed, as well as party policies, they are rarely invited in. At the national conventions no woman has ever been asked to serve on the platform committee.

Politically, as a sex, women are generally "frozen out" from any intrinsic share of influence in their parties.

The machinery of party politics has always been in the hands of men, and still is. Our statesmen and legislators are still keeping in form as the successors of the early warriors gathering around the campfire plotting the next day's attack. Yes, they have made feints indicating they are willing to let the women into the high councils of the parties. But, in fact, the women who have gone into the political game will tell you they are excluded from any actual kind of important participation. They are called upon to produce votes, but they are kept in ignorance of noteworthy plans and affairs. Their requests are seldom refused outright, but they are put off with a technique that is an art in itself. The fact is that generally women are not taken seriously. With certain exceptions, men still as a class dismiss their consequence and value in politics, cherishing the old-fashioned concept that their place is in the home. While women's votes are a factor to be counted upon, and figure largely in any impending campaign, the individual women who figure in party councils are regarded by their male confrères as having no real power back of them. And they haven't....

Beneath the veneer of courtesy and outward show of consideration universally accorded women, there is a widespread male hostility—age-old, perhaps—against sharing with them any actual control.

How many excuses haven't I heard for not giving nominations to women! "Oh, she wouldn't like the kind of work she'd have to do!" Or, "You know she wouldn't like the people she'd have to associate with—that's not a job for a nice, refined woman." Or more usually: "You see, there is so little patronage nowadays. We must give every appointment the most careful consideration. We've got to consider the good of the party." "The good of the party" eliminates women!

When no women are present at the meetings, the leaders are more outspoken. "No, we're not going to have any woman on the ticket," declared one leader according to a report once made to me. "Those fool women are always making trouble, anyway. We won't have any we don't have to have, and if we have none, let's get one we understand."

It is a strong and liberal man, indeed, who speaks on behalf of the women at those secret conclaves, and endeavors to have them fairly treated.

To many women who fought so long and so valiantly for suffrage, what has happened has been most discouraging. For one reason or another, most of the leaders who carried the early fight to success have dropped out of politics. This has been in many ways unfortunate. Among them were women with gifts of real leadership. They were exceptional and high types of women, idealists concerned in carrying a cause to victory, with no idea of personal advancement or gain. In fact, attaining the vote was only part of a program for equal rights—an external gesture toward economic independence, and social and spiritual equality with men.

When the franchise was finally achieved, their interest was not held by any ambition for political preferment or honors. To learn the intricate machinery of politics and play the men's game left them cold. The routine of political office held no appeal. One of the most prominent of those early crusaders today gives her energies to campaigning for world peace. By nature a propagandist, it would be impossible to interest her in either of the major parties. Another woman, who donated hundreds of thousands of dollars to the cause, frankly admits she has never even cast a vote. She considers the situation, with women coping with men in the leading parties, utterly hopeless. Like many others, she regards suffrage as an empty victory, equal rights a travesty, and the vote a gesture without power.

An extreme point of view, in my opinion. There is a method—and not the one advocated by certain militants who hold aloof from party politics—by which, I believe, the end of a fair representation and share in control may be attained.

Personally, I do not believe in a Woman's Party. A woman's ticket could never possibly succeed. And to crystallize the issues on the basis of sex-opposition would only further antagonize men, congeal their age-old prejudices, and widen the chasm of existing differences.

How, then, can we bring the men leaders to concede participation in party affairs, adequate representation and real political equality?

Our means is to elect, accept and back women political bosses....

If women believe they have a right and duty in political life today, they must learn to talk the language of men. They must not only master the phraseology, but also understand the machinery which men have built up through years of practical experience. Against the men bosses there must be women bosses who can talk as equals, with the backing of a coherent organization of women voters behind them....

I should not want the average woman, or the exceptional woman for that matter, who for one reason or another could not do a public job well, to take one at present. For just now a woman must do better than a man, for whatever she does in the public eye reflects on the whole cause of women. There are women in the United States I would gladly see run for any office. But if we cannot have the best I should prefer to wait and prepare a little longer until women are more ready to make a fine contribution to public life in any office they might hold.

An old politician once objected, "Don't you think these women lose their allure, that the bloom is just a little gone? Men are no longer interested?"

Frankly, I don't know. I imagine the answer is individual. It was once said that men did not marry women who showed too much intelligence. In my youth I knew women who hid their college degrees as if they were one of the seven deadly sins. But all that is passing, and so will pass many other prejudices that have their origin in the ancient tradition that women are a by-product of creation.

Remember, women have voted just ten years. They have held responsible positions in big business enterprises only since the war, to any great extent. The men at the head of big business or controlling politics are for the most part middle-aged men. Their wives grew up in an era when no public question was discussed in

Glossary

conclaves	secret meetings
confabs	shortened form of "confabulations," or discussions, chats, or meetings
franchise	right to vote
veneer	a facing or ornamental coating, usually a thin layer of more valuable wood over inferior wood

a popular manner, when men talked politics over their wine or cigars, and pulled their waistcoats down, on joining the ladies, to talk music, or the play or the latest scandal. Can you blame them if the adjustment to modern conditions is somewhat difficult?

Certain women profess to be horrified at the thought of women bosses bartering and dickering in the hard game of politics with men. But many more women realize that we are living in a material world, and that politics cannot be played from the clouds. To sum up, women must learn to play the game as men do. If they go into politics, they must stick to their jobs, respect the time and work of others, master a knowledge of history and human nature, learn diplomacy, subordinate their likes and dislikes of the moment and choose leaders to act for them and to whom they will be loyal. They can keep their ideals; but they must face facts and deal with them practically.

RESIGNATION FROM THE DAUGHTERS OF THE AMERICAN REVOLUTION (1939)

Resignation Letter

February 26, 1939.

My dear Mrs. Henry M. Robert, Jr.:

I am afraid that I have never been a very useful member of the Daughters of the American Revolution, so I know it will make very little difference to you whether I resign, or whether I continue to be a member of your organization.

However, I am in complete disagreement with the attitude taken in refusing Constitution Hall to a great artist. You have set an example which seems to me unfortunate, and I feel obliged to send in to you my resignation. You had an opportunity to lead in an enlightened way and it seems to me that your organization has failed.

I realize that many people will not agree with me, but feeling as I do this seems to me the only proper procedure to follow.

Very sincerely yours,

Eleanor Roosevelt

"My Day"

WASHINGTON, Sunday—Here we are back in Washington. I woke this morning to what sounded like a real spring rain. The grass outside my window looks green and, though I suppose we will probably have a blizzard next week, at the moment I feel as though spring had really arrived.

I am having a very peaceful day. I drove my car a short distance out of the city this morning to pilot some friends of mine who are starting off for a vacation in Florida. I think this will be my only excursion out of the White House today, for I have plenty of work to do on an accumulation of mail and I hope to get through in time to enjoy an evening of uninterrupted reading.

I have been debating in my mind for some time, a question which I have had to debate with myself once or twice before in my life. Usually I have decided differently from the way in which I am deciding now. The question is, if you belong to an organization and disapprove of an action which is typical of a policy, should you resign or is it better to work for a changed point of view within the organization? In the past, when I was able to work actively in any organization to which I belonged, I have usually stayed in until I had at least made a fight and had been defeated.

Even then, I have, as a rule, accepted my defeat and decided I was wrong or, perhaps, a little too far ahead of the thinking of the majority at that time. I have often found that the thing in which I was interested was done some years later. But, in this case, I belong to an organization in which I can do no active work. They have taken an action which has been widely talked of in the press. To remain as a member implies approval of that action, and therefore I am resigning.

Glossary

Constitution Hall	the largest concert hall in Washington, D.C., built in 1929 and owned by the Daughters of the American Revolution
Sunday	February 27, 1939

"THE STRUGGLE FOR HUMAN RIGHTS" (1948)

I have come this evening to talk with you on one of the greatest issues of our time—that is the preservation of human freedom. I have chosen to discuss it here in France, at the Sorbonne, because here in this soil the roots of human freedom have long ago struck deep and here they have been richly nourished. It was here the Declaration of the Rights of Man was proclaimed, and the great slogans of the French Revolution—liberty, equality, fraternity—fired the imagination of men. I have chosen to discuss this issue in Europe because this has been the scene of the greatest historic battles between freedom and tyranny. I have chosen to discuss it in the early days of the General Assembly because the issue of human liberty is decisive for the settlement of outstanding political differences and for the future of the United Nations.

The decisive importance of this issue was fully recognized by the founders of the United Nations at San Francisco. Concern for the preservation and promotion of human rights and fundamental freedoms stands at the heart of the United Nations. Its Charter is distinguished by its preoccupation with the rights and welfare of individual men and women. The United Nations has made it clear that it intends to uphold human rights and to protect the dignity of the human personality. In the preamble to the Charter the keynote is set when it declares: "We the people of the United Nations determined … to reaffirm faith in fundamental human rights, in the dignity and worth of the human person, in the equal rights of men and women and of nations large and small, and … to promote social progress and better standards of life in larger freedom." This reflects the basic premise of the Charter that the peace and security of mankind are dependent on mutual respect for the rights and freedoms of all.…

The Human Rights Commission was given as its first and most important task the preparation of an International Bill of Rights. The General Assembly which opened its third session here in Paris a few days ago will have before it the first fruit of the Commission's labors in this task, that is the International Declaration of Human Rights.…

This Declaration was finally completed after much work during the last session of the Human Rights Commission in New York in the spring of 1948. The Economic and Social Council has sent it without recommendation to the General Assembly, together with other documents transmitted by the Human Rights Commission.

It was decided in our Commission that a Bill of Rights should contain two parts:

1. A Declaration which could be approved through action of the Member States of the United Nations in the General Assembly. This Declaration would have great moral force, and would say to the peoples of the world "this is what we hope human rights may mean to all people in the years to come." We have put down here the rights that we consider basic for individual human beings the world over to have. Without them, we feel that the full development of individual personality is impossible.

2. The second part of the bill, which the Human Rights Commission has not yet completed because of the lack of time, is a covenant which would be in the form of a treaty to be presented to the nations of the world. Each nation, as it is prepared to do so, would ratify this covenant and the covenant would then become binding on the nations which adhere to it. Each nation ratifying would then be obligated to change its laws wherever they did not conform to the points contained in the covenant.

This covenant, of course, would have to be a simpler document. It could not state aspirations, which we feel to be permissible in the Declaration. It could only state rights which could be assured by law and it must contain methods of implementation, and no state ratifying the covenant could be allowed to disregard it. The methods of implementation have not yet been agreed upon, nor have they been given adequate consideration by the Commission at any of its meetings. There certainly should be discussion on the entire question of this world Bill of Human Rights and there may be acceptance by this Assembly of the Declaration if they come to agreement on it. The acceptance of the Declaration, I think, should encourage every nation in the coming months to discuss its meaning with its people so that they will be better prepared to accept the covenant with a deeper understanding of the problems involved when that is presented, we hope, a year from now and, we hope, accepted.

The Declaration has come from the Human Rights Commission with unanimous acceptance except for four abstentions—the U.S.S.R., Yugoslavia, Ukraine, and Byelorussia. The reason for this is a fundamental difference in the conception of human rights as they exist in these states and in certain other Member States in the United Nations.

In the discussion before the Assembly, I think it should be made crystal clear what these differences are and tonight I want to spend a little time making them clear to you. It seems to me there is a valid reason for taking the time today to think carefully and clearly on the subject of human rights, because in the acceptance and observance of these rights lies the root, I believe, of our chance for peace in the future, and for the strengthening of the United Nations organization to the point where it can maintain peace in the future.

We must not be confused about what freedom is. Basic human rights are simple and easily understood: freedom of speech and a free press; freedom of religion and worship; freedom of assembly and the right of petition; the right of men to be secure in their homes and free from unreasonable search and seizure and from arbitrary arrest and punishment.

We must not be deluded by the efforts of the forces of reaction to prostitute the great words of our free tradition and thereby to confuse the struggle. Democracy, freedom, human rights have come to have a definite meaning to the people of the world which we must not allow any nation to so change that they are made synonymous with suppression and dictatorship.

There are basic differences that show up even in the use of words between a democratic and a totalitarian country. For instance "democracy" means one thing to the U.S.S.R. and another to the U.S.A. and, I know, in France. I have served since the first meeting of the nuclear commission on the Human Rights Commission, and I think this point stands out clearly.

The U.S.S.R. Representatives assert that they already have achieved many things which we, in what they call the "bourgeois democracies" cannot achieve because their government controls the accomplishment of these things. Our government seems powerless to them because, in the last analysis, it is controlled by the people. They would not put it that way—they would say that the people in the U.S.S.R. control their government by allowing their government to have certain absolute rights. We, on the other hand, feel that certain rights can never be granted to the government, but must be kept in the hands of the people.

For instance, the U.S.S.R. will assert that their press is free because the state makes it free by providing the machinery, the paper, and even the money for salaries for the people who work on the paper. They state that there is no control over what is printed in the various papers that they subsidize in this manner, such, for instance, as a trade-union paper. But what would happen if a paper were to print ideas which were critical of the basic policies and beliefs of the Communist government? I am sure some good reason would be found for abolishing the paper.

It is true that there have been many cases where newspapers in the U.S.S.R. have criticized officials and their actions and have been responsible for the removal of those officials, but in doing so they did not criticize anything which was fundamental to Communist beliefs. They simply criticized methods of doing things, so one must differentiate between things which are permissible, such as criticism of any individual or of the manner of doing things, and the criticism of a belief which would be considered vital to the acceptance of Communism....

I have great sympathy with the Russian people. They love their country and have always defended it valiantly against invaders. They have been through a period of revolution, as a result of which they were for a time cut off from outside contact. They have not lost their resulting suspicion of other countries and the great difficulty is today that their government encourages this suspicion and seems to believe that force alone will bring them respect.

We, in the democracies, believe in a kind of international respect and action which is reciprocal. We do not think others should treat us differently from the way they wish to be treated. It is interference in other countries that especially stirs up antagonism against the Soviet Government. If it wishes to feel secure in developing its economic and political theories within its territory, then it should grant to others that same security. We believe in the freedom of people to make their own mistakes. We do not interfere with them and they should not interfere with others.

The basic problem confronting the world today, as I said in the beginning, is the preservation of human freedom for the individual and consequently for the society of which he is a part. We are fighting this battle again today as it was fought at the time of the French Revolution and at the time of the American Revolution. The issue of human liberty is as decisive now as it was then. I want to give you my conception of what is meant in my country by freedom of the individual.

Long ago in London during a discussion with Mr. Vyshinsky, he told me there was no such thing as freedom for the individual in the world. All freedom of the individual was conditioned by the rights of other individuals. That, of course, I granted. I said: "We approach the question from a different point of view; we here in the United Nations are trying to develop ideals which will be broader in outlook, which will consider first the rights of man, which will consider what makes man more free: not governments, but man."

The totalitarian state typically places the will of the people second to decrees promulgated by a few men at the top.

Naturally there must always be consideration of the rights of others; but in a democracy this is not a restriction. Indeed, in our democracies we make our freedoms secure because each of us is expected to respect the rights of others and we are free to make our own laws.

Freedom for our peoples is not only a right, but also a tool. Freedom of speech, freedom of the press, freedom of information, freedom of assembly—these are not just abstract ideals to us; they are tools with which we create a way of life, a way of life in which we can enjoy freedom.

Sometimes the processes of democracy are slow, and I have known some of our leaders to say that a benevolent dictatorship would accomplish the ends desired in a much shorter time than it takes to go through the democratic processes of discussion and the slow formation of public opinion. But there is no way of insuring that a dictatorship will remain benevolent or that power once in the hands of a few will be returned to the people without struggle or revolution. This we have learned by experience and we accept the slow processes of democracy because we know that short-cuts compromise principles on which no compromise is possible.

The final expression of the opinion of the people with us is through free and honest elections, with valid choices on basic issues and candidates. The secret ballot is an essential to free elections but you must have a choice before you. I have heard my husband say many times that a people need never lose their freedom if they kept their right to a secret ballot and if they used that secret ballot to the full.

Basic decisions of our society are made through the expressed will of the people. That is why when we see these liberties threatened, instead of falling apart, our nation becomes unified and our democracies come together as a unified group in spite of our varied backgrounds and many racial strains.

In the United States we have a capitalistic economy. That is because public opinion favors that type of economy under the conditions in which we live. But we have imposed certain restraints; for instance, we have anti-trust laws. These are the legal evidence of the determination of the American people to maintain an economy of free competition and not to allow monopolies to take away the people's freedom.

Our trade-unions grow stronger because the people come to believe that this is the proper way to guarantee the rights of the workers and that the right to organize and to bargain collectively keeps the balance between the actual producer and the investor of money and the manager in industry who watches over the man who works with his hands and who produces the materials which are our tangible wealth.

In the United States we are old enough not to claim perfection. We recognize that we have some problems of discrimination, but we find steady progress being made in the solution of these problems. Through normal democratic processes we are coming to understand our needs and how we can attain full equality for all our people. Free discussion on the subject is permitted. Our Supreme Court has recently rendered decisions to clarify a number of our laws to guarantee the rights of all.

The U.S.S.R. claims it has reached a point where all races within her borders are officially considered equal and have equal rights and they insist they have no discrimination where minorities are concerned.

This is a laudable objective but there are other aspects of the development of freedom for the individual which are essential before the mere absence of discrimination is worth much, and these are lacking in the Soviet Union. Unless they are being denied freedoms which they want and which they see other people have, people do not usually complain of discrimination. It is these other freedoms—the basic freedoms of speech, of the press, of religion and conscience, of assembly, of fair trial and freedom from arbitrary arrest and punishment, which a totalitarian government cannot safely give its people and which give meaning to freedom from discrimination.

It is my belief, and I am sure it is also yours, that the struggle for democracy and freedom is a critical struggle, for their preservation is essential to the great objective of the United Nations to maintain international peace and security.

Among free men the end cannot justify the means. We know the patterns of totalitarianism—the single political party, the control of schools, press, radio, the arts, the sciences, and the church to support autocratic authority; these are the age-old patterns against which men have struggled for three thousand years. These are the signs of reaction, retreat, and retrogression.

The United Nations must hold fast to the heritage of freedom won by the struggle of its peoples; it must help us to pass it on to generations to come.

The development of the ideal of freedom and its translation into the everyday life of the people in great areas of the earth is the product of the efforts of many peoples. It is the fruit of a long tradition of vigorous thinking and courageous action. No one race and no one people can claim to have done all the work to achieve greater dignity for human beings and greater freedom to develop human personality. In each generation and in each country there must be a continuation of the struggle and new steps forward must be taken since this is preeminently a field in which to stand still is to retreat.

The field of human rights is not one in which compromise on fundamental principles are possible. The work of the Commission on Human Rights is illustrative. The Declaration of Human Rights provides: "Everyone has the right to leave any country, including his own." The Soviet Representative said he would agree to this right if a single phrase was added to it—"in accordance with the procedure laid down in the laws of that country." It is obvious that to accept this would be not only to compromise but to nullify the right stated. This case forcefully illustrates the importance of the proposition that we must ever be alert not to compromise fundamental human rights merely for the sake of reaching unanimity and thus lose them.

As I see it, it is not going to be easy to attain unanimity with respect to our different concepts of government and human rights. The struggle is bound to be difficult and one in which we must be firm but patient. If we adhere faithfully to our principles I think it is possible for us to maintain freedom and to do so peacefully and without recourse to force.

The future must see the broadening of human rights throughout the world. People who have glimpsed freedom will never be content until they have secured it for themselves. In a true sense, human rights are a fundamental object of law and government in a just society. Human rights exist to the degree that they are respected by people in relations with each other and by governments in relations with their citizens.

Glossary

anti-trust laws	laws designed to prevent or break up trusts, or business combinations that monopolize an industry and drive out competition
benevolent dictatorship	a system of authoritarian government that attempts to exert total control for the good of the people
bourgeois democracies	a term used by Communist economists and political theorists to refer to Western democracies run by and for the bourgeoisie, or the middle-class owners of capital and the means of production
capitalistic economy	an economic system in which private citizens rather than the government own the means of production (capital) and economic decisions are guided by free-market forces
Hitler	Adolf Hitler, dictator of Nazi Germany before and during World War II
Mr. Vyshinsky	Andrey Vyshinsky, Soviet diplomat, jurist, and foreign minister
nullify	render invalid
Sorbonne	the common name for the University of Paris, derived from one of the university's first colleges, the Collège de Sorbonne
totalitarian	describing a system of government in which the state maintains absolute control over virtually all aspects of citizens' lives
U.S.S.R.	the Union of Soviet Socialist Republics, or Soviet Union, which has since broken apart into its constituent republics, including Russia

The world at large is aware of the tragic consequences for human beings ruled by totalitarian systems. If we examine Hitler's rise to power, we see how the chains are forged which keep the individual a slave and we can see many similarities in the way things are accomplished in other countries. Politically men must be free to discuss and to arrive at as many facts as possible and there must be at least a two-party system in a country because when there is only one political party, too many things can be subordinated to the interests of that one party and it becomes a tyrant and not an instrument of democratic government.

The propaganda we have witnessed in the recent past, like that we perceive in these days, seeks to impugn, to undermine, and to destroy the liberty and independence of peoples. Such propaganda poses to all peoples the issue whether to doubt their heritage of rights and therefore to compromise the principles by which they live, or try to accept the challenge, redouble their vigilance, and stand steadfast in the struggle to maintain and enlarge human freedoms.

People who continue to be denied the respect to which they are entitled as human beings will not acquiesce forever in such denial.

The Charter of the United Nations is a guiding beacon along the way to the achievement of human rights and fundamental freedoms throughout the world. The immediate test is not only the extent to which human rights and freedoms have already been achieved, but the direction in which the world is moving. Is there a faithful compliance with the objectives of the Charter if some countries continue to curtail human rights and freedoms instead of to promote the universal respect for an observance of human rights and freedoms for all as called for by the Charter?

The place to discuss the issue of human rights is in the forum of the United Nations. The United Nations has been set up as the common meeting ground for nations, where we can consider together our mutual problems and take advantage of our differences in experience. It is inherent in our firm attachment to democracy and freedom that we stand always ready to use the fundamental democratic procedures of honest discussion and negotiation. It is now as always our hope that despite the wide differences in approach we face in the world today, we can with mutual good faith in the principles of the United Nations Charter, arrive at a common basis of understanding. We are here to join the meetings of this great international Assembly which meets in your beautiful capital city of Paris. Freedom for the individual is an inseparable part of the cherished traditions of France. As one of the Delegates from the United States I pray Almighty God that we may win another victory here for the rights and freedoms of all men.

REMARKS AT THE UNITED NATIONS CONCERNING HUMAN RIGHTS (1958)

I am here in behalf of thirty-two national organizations representing millions of citizens—of all faiths; of every complexion; in all parts of the United States. The devotion of so many Americans to human rights is symbolized by this booklet, IN YOUR HANDS. It is a guide to community action. It is a spontaneous and resounding answer to the United Nations' call for world-wide, year-long observances of the Tenth Anniversary of the Universal Declaration of Human Rights.

Where, after all, do universal human rights begin? In small places, close to home—so close and so small that they cannot be seen on any map of the world. Yet they *are* the world of the individual person: the neighborhood he lives in; the school or college he attends; the factory, farm or office where he works. Such are the places where every man, woman, and child seeks equal justice, equal opportunity, equal dignity without discrimination. Unless these rights have meaning there, they have little meaning anywhere. Without concerted citizen action to uphold them close to home, we shall look in vain for progress in the larger world.

Thus we believe that the destiny of human rights is in the hands of all our citizens in all our communities. That is why we have called this guidebook IN YOUR HANDS. We shall do our utmost, in the coming months, to put it in the hands of individuals and groups across the land.

It is our hope that this book may inspire them to strengthen their relations with one another; to acquaint themselves with the Universal Declaration of Human Rights; to discuss it with their neighbors; to examine their own practices in the light of the standard it has raised; and to improve these practices wherever improvement is needed. In so doing, all of us together can make a vital and enduring contribution to this Tenth Anniversary observance.

I now have the honor, as spokesman for the organization joined in this effort, to present to you and your colleagues in the Commission on Human Rights these 18 copies of IN YOUR HANDS, one for each commission member—a token of our faith that, under your leadership, the communities of every country will bring human rights to full reality in the community of the world.

Franklin Delano Roosevelt (Library of Congress)

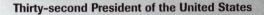

FRANKLIN DELANO ROOSEVELT 1882–1945

Thirty-second President of the United States

Featured Documents
- ◆ First Inaugural Address (1933)
- ◆ "Four Freedoms" Message to Congress (1941)
- ◆ "Second Bill of Rights" Message to Congress (1944)

Overview

Franklin Delano Roosevelt was the thirty-second and longest-serving president of the United States, leading the nation from the depths of the Great Depression in 1933 until the final months of World War II. An inspiring personality, innovative policy maker, and exceptionally skillful politician, he brought the country through two of its most formidable challenges and left a legacy of hope and progress. Roosevelt was born in 1882 into a family of Dutch and French ancestry at the ancestral home in Hyde Park, New York, with every privilege that the Gilded Age could offer. While he was attending Harvard College, his fifth cousin Theodore Roosevelt became president, through his policies reinforcing the notion of service in the pursuit of a better society. In 1902 Franklin Roosevelt encountered Theodore's niece Eleanor during a visit to the White House; the two married three years later while Franklin was attending Columbia Law School. Roosevelt left Columbia in 1907 to take the bar exam and entered private practice at the Wall Street firm of Carter, Ledyard & Milburn the following year. He and Eleanor remained married until his death forty years later, but over time they came to live somewhat separate personal lives.

The call to public service came quickly to the well-connected and convivial Roosevelt, who was elected as a reform Democrat to the New York State Senate in 1910. He proved popular in Albany and among his fellow party members. He was reelected in 1912 but resigned shortly thereafter to serve as assistant secretary of the navy in the administration of President Woodrow Wilson. With the opening of World War I in 1914, Roosevelt overhauled the navy into a force capable of protecting the transatlantic shipping lanes and bringing 2 million Americans and countless tons of supplies to Europe. As the war ended in late 1918, Roosevelt oversaw the massive efforts to bring American troops home and then to demobilize the navy. He resigned in July 1920 in order to pursue an unsuccessful bid for the vice presidency.

In August 1921, while vacationing in New Brunswick, Canada, Roosevelt contracted an illness that resulted in lifelong paralysis from the waist down. In his struggle to overcome the paralysis, he developed determination and a sense of humanity that aptly shaped his character for the coming challenges. Elected New York's governor in the fall of 1928, Roosevelt returned to Albany to be a well-regard-

ed reformer; he was easily reelected in 1930. Roosevelt's popularity and achievements running the nation's most populous state were compared favorably to President Herbert Hoover's early record in Washington, D.C. In 1932, running against Hoover, Roosevelt was elected president by a wide margin. His inspiring inaugural address offered the nation an ambitious reform agenda referred to as the New Deal, and he would tackle the economic crisis by creating an "alphabet soup" of programs. During his first term, unemployment dropped, and the gross national product inched toward recovery. The nation rewarded Roosevelt with reelection in 1936 and even larger majorities in both houses of Congress. Emboldened by success, Roosevelt grew more ambitious in his second term. However, the conservative Supreme Court thwarted him, most notably by finding unconstitutional the National Industrial Recovery Act, in which Congress had delegated to the president extraordinary economic powers. Piqued and perhaps overconfident, Roosevelt proposed adding new justices to the Court in a scheme to overwhelm the conservatives. In attempting to dictate terms to another sovereign branch of government, Roosevelt went too far; Democrats threatened open rebellion, and he backed down. But the Supreme Court took heed and subsequently found that other New Deal acts did indeed pass constitutional muster.

By 1937 Germany had remilitarized, Italy had conquered Ethiopia, and Japan was engaged in the conquest of China. Recognizing the growing threat and Americans' unwillingness to fight, Roosevelt called for a quarantine of aggressor nations. Over the next four years, Roosevelt publicly supported the embargo policy even while he secretly supported China and the democracies concerned and prepared the nation's armed forces for war. By January 1941, Roosevelt was walking a fine line between the isolationist views held by many Americans and the need to prevent a cataclysm. His annual message to Congress of that month announced bolstered material support through the new Lend-Lease program, while establishing "four essential human freedoms" as a common vision for America and the rest of the free world.

Eleven months later, a massive Japanese air assault on the U.S. naval base at Pearl Harbor, Hawaii, brought the United States into the conflict; declaring war on Japan, Roosevelt informed the nation the following day that December 7, 1941, would be "a date which will live in infamy." Days later, Germany and Italy declared war on the

1882

- **January 30**
  Franklin Delano Roosevelt is born in Hyde Park, New York.

1903

- **June 24**
  Roosevelt graduates from Harvard College.

1907

- Roosevelt leaves Columbia Law School and passes the New York bar exam.

1908

- Roosevelt joins the law firm of Carter, Ledyard & Milburn.

1910

- Roosevelt is elected a New York State senator.

1913

- **April**
  Roosevelt is named assistant secretary of the navy in the administration of Woodrow Wilson.

1920

- Roosevelt is the Democratic nominee for vice president of the United States on a ticket with James N. Cox.

1921

- **August**
  Roosevelt contracts an illness, believed to be polio, resulting in paralysis.

1928

- **November 4**
  Roosevelt is elected governor of New York; he is reelected two years later.

1932

- **November 8**
  Roosevelt is elected president of the United States, a post he retains through three reelections, serving until his death.

1933

- **March 4**
  Roosevelt delivers his first inaugural address.

United States. Suddenly, Roosevelt became a wartime leader facing lethal enemies in both Europe and the Pacific. The first years of war were horrible, as U.S. forces retreated in the Pacific while mobilizing for ultimate offensives. The diplomatic, political, military, strategic, intelligence, and logistical challenges were all extraordinary. Roosevelt built an alliance with Britain, the Soviet Union, and other remaining Allied powers and oversaw the greatest mobilization of materiel and personnel in history. The entire U.S. economy was placed on a wartime footing, as every American was called upon to make sacrifices for the war effort. Indeed, the lingering depression ended almost instantly as every able-bodied hand went to work on farms, in factories and shipyards, or in the armed services.

By the summer of 1944 the war's tide had clearly turned. The Allies had taken Rome. In the wake of the D-day invasion of Normandy in June, Allied troops were crawling across northern France, while the Soviet Union's Red Army was pushing the Germans back into Poland. But victory was not a foregone conclusion, such that Roosevelt could not allow himself to retire despite his rapidly failing health; he wanted to ensure the success of the "second Bill of Rights" that he had promoted in his annual message to Congress of January. Under pressure from Democratic Party leaders, Roosevelt selected Harry S. Truman, a centrist senator from Missouri, as his new vice presidential running mate. That November the new team handily defeated the Republican ticket headed by governors Thomas Dewey and John Bricker. On April 12, 1945, while visiting his retreat in Warm Springs, Georgia, Roosevelt suffered a cerebral hemorrhage and died. Truman served only eighty-two days as vice president, and little was done to prepare him for the challenges that would follow.

Explanation and Analysis of Documents

Roosevelt regularly broadcast his speeches to the American public, explaining his ambitious plans and conveying his infectious optimism to a nation that needed both. Delivered live from the Capitol and broadcast nationally by radio on March 4, 1933, his first inaugural address ranks among the most famous, important, and inspiring of all presidential speeches. His annual message to Congress of January 6, 1941, introduced both Lend-Lease and the "four freedoms," forever altering America's relationship with the outside world. In contrast to these first two speeches, Roosevelt's 1944 annual message to Congress failed to spark the nation's imagination; the ambitious "second Bill of Rights" agenda he proposed in it has not been achieved.

◆ First Inaugural Address

Roosevelt's first inaugural address immediately and clearly signaled the nature of his "New Deal" for the country and its government. In March 1933, the once-robust American economy was suffering grievously. Banks were closed in thirty-two of forty-eight states. Industrial production had fallen by more than half. Food prices had dropped by 60 percent, which, when added to the dust bowl conditions afflicting the Great Plains, devastated farmers and communities around the country. One-quarter of the workforce was unemployed, and 2 million people were homeless. During the fall electoral campaign, Roosevelt promised a recovery program that he would call the New Deal, seeking more equitable distribution of resources.

Roosevelt's 1933 inaugural address opens with a candid admission that Americans are suffering and a call to transcend the widespread and unjustified terror gripping much of the nation. Roosevelt confronts the despair, famously claiming "the only thing we have to fear is fear itself." With his dramatic and memorable opening, Roosevelt signals a fresh start and a vigorous new vision for the leadership role of a government that would inspire people to strive together, as one nation, to rebuild the shattered economy. He goes on to describe the circumstances not with statistics but from the perspectives of individuals struggling to pay taxes, to sell their produce, to pay for necessities, and to finance retirement. Roosevelt emphasizes the idea that people wanted to work and needed the government's support for the creation of decent jobs. The crisis, as he diagnoses it, is a product of failures of vision, determination, and leadership—all of which he offers in abundance.

The vision Roosevelt offers is one of a united and prosperous nation. Unity had given way to the selfish, mindless, and joyless pursuit of evanescent profits. Greedy people had taken over the temple of civilization, seeking short-term gains at the expense of their fellow men. Echoing the Gospels, Roosevelt declares that the money changers have fled from the temple in failure. Following the theme, he claims that the nation's destiny will be fulfilled when its people minister to themselves and to their fellow men. This ministry is to be one of good work—of good jobs that pay enough and contribute to the building of a stronger nation.

Roosevelt outlines how he intends to establish more careful regulation of the economy to safeguard against excessive greed. He distills the necessary safeguards down to the strict governmental supervision of financial institutions to end speculation and the assurance of a sound currency. He calls on Congress to pass a broad range of laws to create the new regulatory state—and if Congress would not launch such an ambitious recovery program, he would assume emergency authority to "wage a war against the emergency." During his first one hundred days and the months that followed, Roosevelt indeed introduced the programs he described in his inaugural address. Fortunately for the constitutional order, he worked with an eager Congress. Together they crafted and passed the breathtaking array of measures intended to provide emergency relief, stimulate recovery, and ensure structural reforms. To provide quick assistance, they channeled unemployment benefits through a new Federal Emergency Relief Administration and put a quarter million men to work on rural projects in the Civilian Conservation Corps. They established and expanded various financial programs, stabilizing agricultural commodity prices to assist farmers, providing mortgage relief for farmers and homeowners, and extend-

Time Line

1941

■ **January 6**
Roosevelt delivers his annual message to Congress, proposing the Lend-Lease program and articulating "four essential human freedoms."

■ **December 7**
The Japanese attack Pearl Harbor, bringing the United States into World War II.

1944

■ **January 11**
Roosevelt delivers his annual message to Congress as the tide of the war is turning, a speech in which he calls for a "second Bill of Rights."

1945

■ **February 4–11**
Roosevelt attends the Yalta Conference with Soviet leader Joseph Stalin and Britain's prime minister, Winston Churchill.

■ **April 12**
Roosevelt dies at Warm Springs, Georgia.

ing credit to industry to put people back to work. And they repealed the decade-long prohibition on the manufacture and sale of alcoholic beverages, lifting the spirits of millions while at the same time generating new tax revenues.

Throughout the national emergency—and despite the obvious need to increase spending—Roosevelt respected the traditional concern for living within one's means. In an effort to balance the budget against ballooning relief and recovery measures, Roosevelt cut government salaries and reduced spending on the military (including veterans' benefits), research, and education. Throughout the Great Depression, Roosevelt managed to balance the regular budget, although he doubled the debt-funded emergency budget. In addition to the relief and stimulus programs, the Roosevelt administration launched bold reforms to restore the economy and protect the well-being of individuals. The Glass-Steagall Act reformed the banking industry and protected depositors, principally by insuring deposits and prohibiting certain arrangements that created conflicts of interest among the financial institutions. The National Industrial Recovery Act promoted unionization, reduced destructive competition, and established minimum prices. The new Securities and Exchange Commission regulated the sale and resale of securities, mostly by requiring extensive disclosure and punishing deception.

As well as articulating his vision of the New Deal he believed the nation needed, Roosevelt used his inaugural address to promulgate a new foreign policy, that of a "good neighbor." In contrast to the recent admixture of isolationism from Europe and overt interventionism in the Western Hemisphere, the new policy was to be based on respect for international obligations and sanctity of agreements. It would not eschew formal relationships with other countries but would call for much more hesitancy regarding interference with internal affairs. The good-neighbor policy became a catchphrase for the normalization of U.S. foreign relations following the years of relative diplomatic isolation punctuated by a series of military interventions in the Caribbean. In recent years, the United States had sent troops to several Latin American countries, including Nicaragua, the Dominican Republic, and Haiti. As it turned out, the United States did continue to dominate the region, but during the Roosevelt years it was far more reluctant to conduct military interventions. Later, the United States would help develop regional security arrangements such as the North Atlantic Treaty Organization.

In the end, Roosevelt's first inaugural address reflected his realistic assessment of the grim reality faced by Americans in March 1933 as well as hope for a brighter and more secure future. He called on the nation to pull together, prioritize the dignity and value of work, and create and seize opportunities for the pursuit of a common good. This vision infused the next twelve years of Roosevelt's administration and his life.

◆ "Four Freedoms" Message to Congress

President Roosevelt pointedly opened his annual message to Congress of January 6, 1941, by noting that he was speaking at an unprecedented moment in history. For the first time in over a century, and, as he believed, to a greater extent than ever before, a foreign war threatened the fundamental security of the United States. The collapse of France in the summer of 1940 had evinced an expanding geopolitical crisis that could no longer be ignored. The Axis powers had conquered or otherwise come to dominate significant portions of Europe and Asia, including Austria, Czechoslovakia, the Low Countries, Greece, Norway, Yugoslavia, Korea, and much of China and Southeast Asia. By late 1940 America's entry into the war seemed inevitable to many, including possibly Roosevelt. By January 1941 the Axis war machine clearly endangered freedom everywhere. The oceans could no longer sustain Americans' long-standing sense of invulnerability.

In the face of these grim facts, Roosevelt had been reelected in November 1940 for an unprecedented third term, campaigning on a promise that "your boys are not going to be sent into any foreign wars." Roosevelt may not have believed his own campaign promise, but tendering it appears to have been necessary for his reelection; in retrospect, his apparent deceit seems both obvious and excusable. Facing isolationist sentiment at home and a fast-spreading war that threatened to engulf the United States, he had no easy choices. Speaking for the only

major Western European power holding out against the Axis, Prime Minister Winston Churchill had convinced Roosevelt of the need to support England in its hour of need. The prolonged Battle of Britain was taking a terrible toll, and Churchill warned America's president that without cash and supplies, the United Kingdom would also succumb.

In his annual message to Congress and the nation of January 1941, Roosevelt forthrightly informs the American people that they could not expect any generosity from the Axis dictators and that Americans' freedoms were in jeopardy. He also warns of saboteurs who would corrode the United States from within in order to lay the groundwork for an inevitable invasion. He thus argues that the vulnerability of the nation and its political system dictated increased defense measures and the assuming of a greater role in events outside America's borders. Accordingly, he calls for a more aggressive buildup of the nation's arms and armaments. He had already established ambitious production goals, and now he sought to meet and even exceed them. The United States would become the arsenal of democracy. Roosevelt also calls for greater public and political resolve to defend the nation and its democratic cause, asking for bipartisan support for all measures intended to ensure peace. Alluding to the British failure to secure peace through the 1938 Munich agreement, Roosevelt adds that such a peace would not endure if it were "bought at the cost of other people's freedom."

To avoid a greater calamity in Europe, as indicated in this address, Roosevelt offers to lend or lease war equipment and supplies to the British. To minimize the impression that he was taking the country to war through indirect means, Roosevelt frames the program in a soothing metaphor. In his typically elliptical fashion, Roosevelt likens the deal to lending a garden hose to a neighbor whose house was on fire. Suppressing the fire would end the threat of its spread, and then the neighbor would return the hose. During the winter of 1940–1941, Roosevelt's new appeal to the American people took shape in two tacks, addressing the material and the moral. Lending the British a proverbial fire hose through the Lend-Lease Act, Roosevelt claimed, would reduce the likelihood that the United States would have to join the war. Meanwhile, he articulated to the public America's shared destiny with Britain and her free allies.

At the close of his 1941 annual message, Roosevelt lays out a vision statement of a world in which the United States could find common cause with states such as Great Britain and also with individuals around the world regardless of nationality. Roosevelt's vision for a secure postwar world rested upon four freedoms. He declares, "The first is freedom of speech and expression—everywhere in the world. The second is freedom of every person to worship God in his own way—everywhere in the world." Clearly, Roosevelt adopted these first two freedoms from the U.S. Constitution's First Amendment. For the third freedom, he drew on his own New Deal economic programs and signaled the need for international cooperation in order to

The battleship USS Arizona *belches smoke as it topples over into the sea during the Japanese surprise attack on Pearl Harbor, Hawaii, December 7, 1941.* (AP/Wide World Photos)

achieve their objectives globally: "The third is freedom from want—which, translated into world terms, means economic understandings which will secure to every nation a healthy peacetime life for its inhabitants—everywhere in the world." Finally, and most famously, Roosevelt addresses what he viewed as the circumstances necessitating his new policy and how to avoid war in the future. "The fourth is freedom from fear—which, translated into world terms, means a world-wide reduction in armaments to such a point and in such a thorough fashion that no nation will be in a position to commit an act of physical aggression against any neighbor—anywhere in the world."

With his four freedoms, Roosevelt clearly articulated a common vision for those opposing Axis aggression and seeking to establish a more secure future. For ten months Roosevelt pursued that vision by lending and leasing much-needed equipment and supplies to those directly engaged in the fighting. Then, on December 7, 1941, the Japanese attack on Pearl Harbor finally resolved the issues of if, how, and when the United States would join the war. The isolationist movement quickly folded, and Americans generally

rallied to Roosevelt's vision for a fair and secure postwar world. Over the next few years, the four freedoms were incorporated part and parcel into the foundational documents of modern international law. The 1945 Charter of the United Nations included them as basic principles; the 1948 Universal Declaration of Human Rights incorporated them as inherent to human dignity and inalienable; and numerous international conventions have sought to promote them ever since.

◆ "Second Bill of Rights" Message to Congress

By January 1944 the tide of World War II was starting to turn in favor of the United States and the Allies. After years of terrible losses, they had finally prevailed over the German submarine threat to shipping in the North Atlantic and had taken over North Africa on the way to Sicily. The Soviets had blunted the German invasion at the massive Battle of Stalingrad, while in the Pacific the Japanese had been pushed onto the defensive, mostly by American forces. Although he was suffering from a bout of influenza that prevented him from delivering his annual message to

Congress in person, Roosevelt was reasonably buoyant. His address reprised the themes of security about which he had spoken so fervently in the past. He continued to maintain that lasting peace required not only an end to Axis aggression but also economic, social, and moral security.

The address opens with a concise statement of the war's purposes and moves quickly to a vision for stability and prosperity in the postwar world. While the language is tough-minded, it also evinces some naïveté about the nature of the Soviet regime. He refers to the United States and the Allies as "like-minded people" before characterizing the Axis powers as gangsters seeking to enslave humanity. While historians today might agree with the assessment of the German, Italian, and Japanese regimes as "gangster" states, the same label would likely be applied to Stalin's Union of Soviet Socialist Republics, with its gulags, genocidal collectivization and resettlement programs, and murderous show trials. Nor did Chiang Kai-shek's Republic of China share many democratic values with Britain or the United States. Rather than saying that the Allies were "like-minded," Roosevelt would have been more accurate to say that they shared a common interest in seeing the Axis powers defeated. Yet, as Roosevelt insists, the Allies also shared a desire to develop their nations' intellectual, economic, and social capital in peace.

Thus, Roosevelt returns to the themes of his annual message to Congress of 1941. His vision for a postwar world required both an end to hostilities and the restoration of stable economies providing justice and opportunity. He asserts, "Freedom from fear is eternally linked with freedom from want." He goes on to explain his view that international development is not what would now be called a zero-sum game. In contrast to the mercantilists who had preceded him, Roosevelt firmly believed that the rising tide would raise all boats—that widespread economic development would lead to better standards of living for people in the United States and around the world. He cautions, however, that greedy people seeking preferments threatened this paradigm. Roosevelt speaks of his intent to remain vigilant against self-centered war profiteers, including those who sought unfair government contracts, those who charged exorbitant prices, and those who collectively withheld their much-needed labor for better pay. He strongly urges restraint against greed and explains that the nation would be wealthier for it. Moreover, with the nation deeply engaged in a global war, greed or even distracted attention might mean more dead American soldiers.

Having iterated the importance of supporting the war effort with selflessness and determination, Roosevelt proceeds to dedicate most of the address to his vision for a postwar America. As it had been since he first assumed office in 1933, much of Roosevelt's attention was focused on the restoration of a fair, stable, and prosperous economy. He speaks of principally seeking to achieve fairness by eliminating war profiteering. He calls for—and indeed elicited from Congress—high individual and corporate taxes to recover "unreasonable" profits. He proposes renegotiating war contracts to ensure that they did not excessively reward the companies that had manufactured, provisioned, and serviced the enormous war machine. In these efforts, Roosevelt appears to have been motivated more by a concern for relative fairness than by the idea of financing the war as efficiently and inexpensively as possible. His notions of fairness also brought him to call for greater price-stabilization programs to ensure that people could eat and that farmers could make decent livings. Besides supporting the idea that everyone participate in and benefit from the wartime economy, Roosevelt here proposes a national service program to provide employment for all able-bodied men and women. Soldiers, sailors, airmen, and marines were being asked to risk everything, he notes, so other Americans should be expected to make similar sacrifices for the common good. While this proposal did not bear fruit, statesmen continue to revisit it with each passing generation.

In the most important—and widely overlooked—passages of this address, Roosevelt supports a "second Bill of Rights" for all Americans as a basis for postwar security and prosperity. If the original Bill of Rights reflected Enlightenment views about civil and political rights, Roosevelt intended the successor to assure opportunity and a decent life for all "regardless of station, race, or creed." To this end, Roosevelt suggests formal recognition of a new package of rights that had sadly gone unmet for many poor and disadvantaged Americans throughout the nation's history. These included, most notably, rights to education, a decent job, a home, and health care, as well as adequate protection against the economic fears engendered by old age, sickness, accidents, and unemployment. Taken together, this cluster of rights resembles the modern social contracts that some postwar Western European nations have guaranteed their citizens. In 1944 Roosevelt's proposal failed to gain sufficient momentum in the United States; like his plan for national service, the idea of a second Bill of Rights quickly died. On the other hand, many of the individual rights outlined by Roosevelt remain aspirations that have been pursued in fits and starts by national and local governments with some successes.

Roosevelt's enlightened vision for American security contributed significantly to the defeat of the Axis powers and the collective articulation of a more fair and prosperous country. In the end, however, some of his more sweeping proposals for economic security failed. In the absence of a national service obligation and a comprehensive agenda for ensuring economic rights, Roosevelt's vision remains unfulfilled today.

Impact and Legacy

The Great Depression and World War II wrought suffering on a previously unimaginable scale. As president, Franklin Roosevelt strove tirelessly for more than twelve years to restore and then draw upon America's courage and strength through this tragic era. His policy track record was mixed. For every success, such as the Civilian Conservation Corps, there was a failure, like the Court-packing debacle.

"Let me assert my firm belief that the only thing we have to fear is fear itself—nameless, unreasoning, unjustified terror which paralyzes needed efforts to convert retreat into advance."

(First Inaugural Address)

"Finally, in our progress toward a resumption of work we require two safeguards against a return of the evils of the old order; there must be a strict supervision of all banking and credits and investments; there must be an end to speculation with other people's money, and there must be provision for an adequate but sound currency."

(First Inaugural Address)

"In the future days, which we seek to make secure, we look forward to a world founded upon four essential human freedoms. The first is freedom of speech and expression.... The second is freedom of every person to worship God in his own way.... The third is freedom from want.... The fourth is freedom from fear."

("Four Freedoms" Message to Congress)

"The one supreme objective for the future,...for each Nation individually, and for all the United Nations, can be summed up in one word: Security. And that means not only physical security which provides safety from attacks by aggressors. It means also economic security, social security, moral security—in a family of Nations."

("Second Bill of Rights" Message to Congress)

"People who are hungry and out of a job are the stuff of which dictatorships are made. In our day these economic truths have become accepted as self-evident. We have accepted, so to speak, a second Bill of Rights under which a new basis of security and prosperity can be established for all regardless of station, race, or creed."

("Second Bill of Rights" Message to Congress)

His management skills were often inscrutable, and he failed to train his vice presidents to assume the office if necessary. Thus, the burden of office fell on Harry Truman after only a few weeks of service. Overall, Roosevelt left a domestic legacy of a strong central government empowered to act to ensure the security, health, and prosperity of its citizens. To achieve this formidable goal, he expanded the power and resources of the federal government, particularly the size and authority of the executive branch.

Roosevelt's greatest contributions, however, lay in his remarkable use of the spoken word to inspire the nation—and eventually much of the world. While he had many domestic opponents who disliked him so much that they would not even speak his name, everyone agreed that he was an exceptionally talented communicator. Roosevelt exploited every available medium to speak with his constituents. He was a pioneer of the use of frequent radio broadcasts—the famous "fireside chats"—as an informal way to explain his perspectives and programs to the citizens of the nation. He spoke often with newspaper and radio reporters, and he excelled at delivering formal addresses. His first inaugural address is widely credited as turning a new page in American history. His 1941 annual message to Congress, with its four freedoms, provided a vision statement for a more peaceful and secure postwar world. And his 1944 annual message to Congress offered another vision, of a more just and prosperous nation with real opportunity for all. These speeches continue to inspire his-

Questions for Further Study

1. How did Roosevelt change the very nature of the presidency and the role of the U.S. government, and how does his first inaugural address set the stage for those changes? Discuss and evaluate the programs of the New Deal. How well did they deal with the economic and social problems of the nation at that time, and what was their long-term effect?

2. Evaluate the concept of rights presented in Roosevelt's 1941 and 1944 messages to Congress. What, in your view, is a *right*? Be sure to address the question of "negative" rights as enumerated in the Constitution compared with the "positive" rights presented by Roosevelt: Whereas negative rights involve freedom from limitations, positive rights require action on the part of a government. Do you think positive rights, such as "freedom from want," are justified? Is it fair to say that when a government promises to provide materially for its citizens as a matter of right—by guaranteeing them housing or education or health care—that it is limiting the rights of other citizens by requiring them to pay for these programs through their taxes? Why or why not?

3. Compare and contrast the situations confronted by Roosevelt when he gave his "four freedoms" speech in 1941 and George W. Bush at the time of his "axis of evil" speech in 2002. What points does Roosevelt make about defense and national security? How do these apply in the twenty-first-century war on terror? How are the views of the two presidents similar? How are they different? What role does the U.S. relationship with the United Kingdom play in both men's global strategies?

4. Among the many proposals outlined in Roosevelt's "Second Bill of Rights" is a program of national service. Discuss the idea of national service and argue for or against it. What would be the benefits and the drawbacks, and how might these stack up against one another? Benefits might include increased career opportunities and a rise in patriotic sentiment and community spirit. Furthermore, bringing together young people from around the nation might help reduce racism and prejudice, while increasing the prospects for education and social mobility among individuals from disadvantaged environments. On the other hand, drawbacks would include the cost, the increased power of the federal government, and the loss of freedom involved in a mandatory program of national service.

5. Consider Roosevelt as a communicator. What were his greatest strengths, and how do his speeches—not only the ones included here but others from his long presidency—display those strengths? Compare and contrast the way he used radio as a medium with the approach to television taken by John F. Kennedy and Richard Nixon or the use of the Internet by Barack Obama.

torians and statesmen with their wisdom and practicality—not to mention the generous spirit of the ideas and the élan of Roosevelt's delivery. Through his policies and speeches alike, Roosevelt left a progressive framework and a vision of greatness for a government that he championed as being, above all, for and by the people.

Key Sources

Franklin Roosevelt's prolific output is available in books, at his library, and online. Many of Roosevelt's papers are widely accessible through such published works as Edgar B. Nixon, ed., *Franklin D. Roosevelt and Foreign Affairs*, 3 vols. (1969); Samuel Irving Rosenman, ed., *The Public Papers and Addresses of Franklin D. Roosevelt*, 13 vols. (1938–1950); B. D. Zevin, ed., *Nothing to Fear: The Selected Addresses of Franklin Delano Roosevelt, 1932–1945* (1970); and George McJimsey, ed., *Documentary History of the Franklin D. Roosevelt Presidency* (2001). The National Archives and Records Administration runs the Franklin D. Roosevelt Presidential Library and Museum in Hyde Park, New York, which provides access to many original documents online (http://www.fdrlibrary.marist.edu/research.html).

Further Reading

■ Articles

Shulman, Mark R. "The Four Freedoms as Good Law and Grand Strategy." *National Security Law Report* 30, no. 3 (October 2008): 20–21.

———. "The Four Freedoms: Good Neighbors Make Good Law and Good Policy in a Time of Insecurity." *Fordham Law Review* 77 (November 2008): 555–581.

■ Books

Divine, Robert A. *Roosevelt and World War II*. Baltimore: Johns Hopkins University Press, 1969.

Kennedy, David M. *Freedom from Fear: The American People in Depression and War, 1929–1945*. New York: Oxford University Press, 1999.

Larrabee, Eric. *Commander in Chief: Franklin Delano Roosevelt, His Lieutenants, and Their War*. New York: Simon & Schuster, 1988.

Leuchtenburg, William E. *Franklin D. Roosevelt and the New Deal, 1932–1940*. New York: Harper & Row, 1963.

Maney, Patrick J. *The Roosevelt Presence: The Life and Legacy of FDR*. Berkeley: University of California Press, 1998.

Sunstein, Cass R. *The Second Bill of Rights: FDR's Unfinished Revolution and Why We Need It More than Ever*. New York: Basic Books, 2004.

■ Web Sites

"FDR Biography." Franklin and Eleanor Roosevelt Institute Web site. http://www.feri.org/common/news/info_detail.cfm?QID=2044 &ClientID=11005.

—Mark R. Shulman

FIRST INAUGURAL ADDRESS (1933)

I am certain that my fellow Americans expect that on my induction into the Presidency I will address them with a candor and a decision which the present situation of our Nation impels. This is preeminently the time to speak the truth, the whole truth, frankly and boldly. Nor need we shrink from honestly facing conditions in our country today. This great Nation will endure as it has endured, will revive and will prosper. So, first of all, let me assert my firm belief that the only thing we have to fear is fear itself—nameless, unreasoning, unjustified terror which paralyzes needed efforts to convert retreat into advance. In every dark hour of our national life a leadership of frankness and vigor has met with that understanding and support of the people themselves which is essential to victory. I am convinced that you will again give that support to leadership in these critical days.

In such a spirit on my part and on yours we face our common difficulties. They concern, thank God, only material things. Values have shrunken to fantastic levels; taxes have risen; our ability to pay has fallen; government of all kinds is faced by serious curtailment of income; the means of exchange are frozen in the currents of trade; the withered leaves of industrial enterprise lie on every side; farmers find no markets for their produce; the savings of many years in thousands of families are gone.

More important, a host of unemployed citizens face the grim problem of existence, and an equally great number toil with little return. Only a foolish optimist can deny the dark realities of the moment.

Yet our distress comes from no failure of substance. We are stricken by no plague of locusts. Compared with the perils which our forefathers conquered because they believed and were not afraid, we have still much to be thankful for. Nature still offers her bounty and human efforts have multiplied it. Plenty is at our doorstep, but a generous use of it languishes in the very sight of the supply. Primarily this is because the rulers of the exchange of mankind's goods have failed, through their own stubbornness and their own incompetence, have admitted their failure, and abdicated. Practices of the unscrupulous money changers stand indicted in the court of public opinion, rejected by the hearts and minds of men.

True they have tried, but their efforts have been cast in the pattern of an outworn tradition. Faced by failure of credit they have proposed only the lending of more money. Stripped of the lure of profit by which to induce our people to follow their false leadership, they have resorted to exhortations, pleading tearfully for restored confidence. They know only the rules of a generation of self-seekers. They have no vision, and when there is no vision the people perish.

The money changers have fled from their high seats in the temple of our civilization. We may now restore that temple to the ancient truths. The measure of the restoration lies in the extent to which we apply social values more noble than mere monetary profit.

Happiness lies not in the mere possession of money; it lies in the joy of achievement, in the thrill of creative effort. The joy and moral stimulation of work no longer must be forgotten in the mad chase of evanescent profits. These dark days will be worth all they cost us if they teach us that our true destiny is not to be ministered unto but to minister to ourselves and to our fellow men....

Restoration calls, however, not for changes in ethics alone. This Nation asks for action, and action now.

Our greatest primary task is to put people to work. This is no unsolvable problem if we face it wisely and courageously. It can be accomplished in part by direct recruiting by the Government itself, treating the task as we would treat the emergency of a war, but at the same time, through this employment, accomplishing greatly needed projects to stimulate and reorganize the use of our natural resources....

Finally, in our progress toward a resumption of work we require two safeguards against a return of the evils of the old order; there must be a strict supervision of all banking and credits and investments; there must be an end to speculation with other people's money, and there must be provision for an adequate but sound currency.

There are the lines of attack. I shall presently urge upon a new Congress in special session detailed measures for their fulfillment, and I shall seek the immediate assistance of the several States.

Through this program of action we address ourselves to putting our own national house in order and making income balance outgo. Our international trade relations, though vastly important, are in point of time and necessity secondary to the establishment of a sound national economy. I favor as a practical policy the putting of first things first. I shall spare no effort to restore world trade by international economic readjustment, but the emergency at home cannot wait on that accomplishment.

The basic thought that guides these specific means of national recovery is not narrowly nationalistic. It is the insistence, as a first consideration, upon the interdependence of the various elements in all parts of the United States—a recognition of the old and permanently important manifestation of the American spirit of the pioneer. It is the way to recovery. It is the immediate way. It is the strongest assurance that the recovery will endure.

In the field of world policy I would dedicate this Nation to the policy of the good neighbor—the neighbor who resolutely respects himself and, because he does so, respects the rights of others—the neighbor who respects his obligations and respects the sanctity of his agreements in and with a world of neighbors.

If I read the temper of our people correctly, we now realize as we have never realized before our interdependence on each other; that we can not merely take but we must give as well; that if we are to go forward, we must move as a trained and loyal army willing to sacrifice for the good of a common discipline, because without such discipline no progress is made, no leadership becomes effective. We are, I know, ready and willing to submit our lives and property to such discipline, because it makes possible a leadership which aims at a larger good. This I propose to offer, pledging that the larger purposes will bind upon us all as a sacred obligation with a unity of duty hitherto evoked only in time of armed strife....

It is to be hoped that the normal balance of executive and legislative authority may be wholly adequate to meet the unprecedented task before us. But it may be that an unprecedented demand and need for undelayed action may call for temporary departure from that normal balance of public procedure.

I am prepared under my constitutional duty to recommend the measures that a stricken nation in the midst of a stricken world may require. These measures, or such other measures as the Congress may build out of its experience and wisdom, I shall seek, within my constitutional authority, to bring to speedy adoption.

But in the event that the Congress shall fail to take one of these two courses, and in the event that the national emergency is still critical, I shall not evade the clear course of duty that will then confront me. I shall ask the Congress for the one remaining instrument to meet the crisis—broad Executive power to wage a war against the emergency, as great as the power that would be given to me if we were in fact invaded by a foreign foe....

We face the arduous days that lie before us in the warm courage of the national unity; with the clear consciousness of seeking old and precious moral values; with the clean satisfaction that comes from the stem performance of duty by old and young alike. We aim at the assurance of a rounded and permanent national life.

We do not distrust the future of essential democracy. The people of the United States have not failed. In their need they have registered a mandate that they want direct, vigorous action. They have asked for discipline and direction under leadership. They have made me the present instrument of their wishes. In the spirit of the gift I take it.

In this dedication of a Nation we humbly ask the blessing of God. May He protect each and every one of us. May He guide me in the days to come.

Glossary

money changers	members of the financial industry, such as bankers and investment brokers

"Four Freedoms" Message to Congress (1941)

I address you, the Members of the Seventy-seventh Congress, at a moment unprecedented in the history of the Union. I use the word "unprecedented," because at no previous time has American security been as seriously threatened from without as it is today.

Since the permanent formation of our Government under the Constitution, in 1789, most of the periods of crisis in our history have related to our domestic affairs. Fortunately, only one of these—the four-year War Between the States—ever threatened our national unity. Today, thank God, one hundred and thirty million Americans, in forty-eight States, have forgotten points of the compass in our national unity....

Every realist knows that the democratic way of life is at this moment being directly assailed in every part of the world—assailed either by arms, or by secret spreading of poisonous propaganda by those who seek to destroy unity and promote discord in nations that are still at peace.

During sixteen long months this assault has blotted out the whole pattern of democratic life in an appalling number of independent nations, great and small. The assailants are still on the march, threatening other nations, great and small.

Therefore, as your President, performing my constitutional duty to "give to the Congress information of the state of the Union," I find it, unhappily, necessary to report that the future and the safety of our country and of our democracy are overwhelmingly involved in events far beyond our borders.

Armed defense of democratic existence is now being gallantly waged in four continents. If that defense fails, all the population and all the resources of Europe, Asia, Africa and Australasia will be dominated by the conquerors. Let us remember that the total of those populations and their resources in those four continents greatly exceeds the sum total of the population and the resources of the whole of the Western Hemisphere—many times over....

No realistic American can expect from a dictator's peace international generosity, or return of true independence, or world disarmament, or freedom of expression, or freedom of religion—or even good business.

Such a peace would bring no security for us or for our neighbors. "Those, who would give up essential liberty to purchase a little temporary safety, deserve neither liberty nor safety."

As a nation, we may take pride in the fact that we are softhearted; but we cannot afford to be softheaded.

We must always be wary of those who with sounding brass and a tinkling cymbal preach the "ism" of appeasement.

We must especially beware of that small group of selfish men who would clip the wings of the American eagle in order to feather their own nests.

I have recently pointed out how quickly the tempo of modern warfare could bring into our very midst the physical attack which we must eventually expect if the dictator nations win this war.

There is much loose talk of our immunity from immediate and direct invasion from across the seas. Obviously, as long as the British Navy retains its power, no such danger exists. Even if there were no British Navy, it is not probable that any enemy would be stupid enough to attack us by landing troops in the United States from across thousands of miles of ocean, until it had acquired strategic bases from which to operate.

But we learn much from the lessons of the past years in Europe—particularly the lesson of Norway, whose essential seaports were captured by treachery and surprise built up over a series of years.

The first phase of the invasion of this Hemisphere would not be the landing of regular troops. The necessary strategic points would be occupied by secret agents and their dupes—and great numbers of them are already here, and in Latin America.

As long as the aggressor nations maintain the offensive, they—not we—will choose the time and the place and the method of their attack.

That is why the future of all the American Republics is today in serious danger.

That is why this Annual Message to the Congress is unique in our history.

That is why every member of the Executive Branch of the Government and every member of the Congress faces great responsibility and great accountability.

The need of the moment is that our actions and our policy should be devoted primarily—almost exclusively—to meeting this foreign peril. For all our domestic problems are now a part of the great emergency.

Just as our national policy in internal affairs has been based upon a decent respect for the rights and the dignity of all our fellow men within our gates, so our national policy in foreign affairs has been based on a decent respect for the rights and dignity of all nations, large and small. And the justice of morality must and will win in the end.

Our national policy is this:

First, by an impressive expression of the public will and without regard to partisanship, we are committed to all-inclusive national defense.

Second, by an impressive expression of the public will and without regard to partisanship, we are committed to full support of all those resolute peoples, everywhere, who are resisting aggression and are thereby keeping war away from our Hemisphere. By this support, we express our determination that the democratic cause shall prevail; and we strengthen the defense and the security of our own nation.

Third, by an impressive expression of the public will and without regard to partisanship, we are committed to the proposition that principles of morality and considerations for our own security will never permit us to acquiesce in a peace dictated by aggressors and sponsored by appeasers. We know that enduring peace cannot be bought at the cost of other people's freedom.

In the recent national election there was no substantial difference between the two great parties in respect to that national policy. No issue was fought out on this line before the American electorate. Today it is abundantly evident that American citizens everywhere are demanding and supporting speedy and complete action in recognition of obvious danger.

Therefore, the immediate need is a swift and driving increase in our armament production....

I am not satisfied with the progress thus far made. The men in charge of the program represent the best in training, in ability, and in patriotism. They are not satisfied with the progress thus far made. None of us will be satisfied until the job is done....

To change a whole nation from a basis of peacetime production of implements of peace to a basis of wartime production of implements of war is no small task. And the greatest difficulty comes at the beginning of the program, when new tools, new plant facilities, new assembly lines, and new ship ways must first be constructed before the actual materiel begins to flow steadily and speedily from them.

The Congress, of course, must rightly keep itself informed at all times of the progress of the program. However, there is certain information, as the Congress itself will readily recognize, which, in the interests of our own security and those of the nations that we are supporting, must of needs be kept in confidence.

New circumstances are constantly begetting new needs for our safety. I shall ask this Congress for greatly increased new appropriations and authorizations to carry on what we have begun.

I also ask this Congress for authority and for funds sufficient to manufacture additional munitions and war supplies of many kinds, to be turned over to those nations which are now in actual war with aggressor nations.

Our most useful and immediate role is to act as an arsenal for them as well as for ourselves. They do not need man power, but they do need billions of dollars worth of the weapons of defense.

The time is near when they will not be able to pay for them all in ready cash. We cannot, and we will not, tell them that they must surrender, merely because of present inability to pay for the weapons which we know they must have.

I do not recommend that we make them a loan of dollars with which to pay for these weapons—a loan to be repaid in dollars.

I recommend that we make it possible for those nations to continue to obtain war materials in the United States, fitting their orders into our own program. Nearly all their materiel would, if the time ever came, be useful for our own defense....

Let us say to the democracies: "We Americans are vitally concerned in your defense of freedom. We are putting forth our energies, our resources and our organizing powers to give you the strength to regain and maintain a free world. We shall send you, in ever-increasing numbers, ships, planes, tanks, guns. This is our purpose and our pledge."

In fulfillment of this purpose we will not be intimidated by the threats of dictators that they will regard as a breach of international law or as an act of war our aid to the democracies which dare to resist their aggression. Such aid is not an act of war, even if a dictator should unilaterally proclaim it so to be....

Their only interest is in a new one-way international law, which lacks mutuality in its observance, and, therefore, becomes an instrument of oppression.

The happiness of future generations of Americans may well depend upon how effective and how immediate we can make our aid felt. No one can tell the exact character of the emergency situations that we may be called upon to meet. The Nation's hands must not be tied when the Nation's life is in danger.

We must all prepare to make the sacrifices that the emergency—almost as serious as war itself—

demands. Whatever stands in the way of speed and efficiency in defense preparations must give way to the national need....

As men do not live by bread alone, they do not fight by armaments alone. Those who man our defenses, and those behind them who build our defenses, must have the stamina and the courage which come from unshakable belief in the manner of life which they are defending. The mighty action that we are calling for cannot be based on a disregard of all things worth fighting for.

The Nation takes great satisfaction and much strength from the things which have been done to make its people conscious of their individual stake in the preservation of democratic life in America. Those things have toughened the fibre of our people, have renewed their faith and strengthened their devotion to the institutions we make ready to protect.

Certainly this is no time for any of us to stop thinking about the social and economic problems which are the root cause of the social revolution which is today a supreme factor in the world.

For there is nothing mysterious about the foundations of a healthy and strong democracy. The basic things expected by our people of their political and economic systems are simple. They are:

Equality of opportunity for youth and for others.

Jobs for those who can work.

Security for those who need it.

The ending of special privilege for the few.

The preservation of civil liberties for all.

The enjoyment of the fruits of scientific progress in a wider and constantly rising standard of living.

These are the simple, basic things that must never be lost sight of in the turmoil and unbelievable complexity of our modern world. The inner and abiding strength of our economic and political systems is dependent upon the degree to which they fulfill these expectations.

Many subjects connected with our social economy call for immediate improvement.

As examples:

We should bring more citizens under the coverage of old-age pensions and unemployment insurance.

We should widen the opportunities for adequate medical care.

We should plan a better system by which persons deserving or needing gainful employment may obtain it.

I have called for personal sacrifice. I am assured of the willingness of almost all Americans to respond to that call.

A part of the sacrifice means the payment of more money in taxes. In my Budget Message I shall recommend that a greater portion of this great defense program be paid for from taxation than we are paying today. No person should try, or be allowed, to get rich out of this program; and the principle of tax payments in accordance with ability to pay should be constantly before our eyes to guide our legislation....

Glossary

acquiesce in	agree to
antithesis	opposite
Australasia	Australia, New Zealand, and the South Pacific islands
materiel	munitions, military supplies
sounding brass and a tinkling cymbal	an allusion to 1 Corinthians 13:1
"Those, who would give up essential liberty...	quotation from Benjamin Franklin in *An Historical Review of the Constitution and Government of Pennsylvania* (1759)

In the future days, which we seek to make secure, we look forward to a world founded upon four essential human freedoms.

The first is freedom of speech and expression—everywhere in the world.

The second is freedom of every person to worship God in his own way—everywhere in the world.

The third is freedom from want—which, translated into world terms, means economic understandings which will secure to every nation a healthy peacetime life for its inhabitants—everywhere in the world.

The fourth is freedom from fear—which, translated into world terms, means a world-wide reduction of armaments to such a point and in such a thorough fashion that no nation will be in a position to commit an act of physical aggression against any neighbor—anywhere in the world.

That is no vision of a distant millennium. It is a definite basis for a kind of world attainable in our own time and generation. That kind of world is the very antithesis of the so-called new order of tyranny which the dictators seek to create with the crash of a bomb.

To that new order we oppose the greater conception—the moral order. A good society is able to face schemes of world domination and foreign revolutions alike without fear.

Since the beginning of our American history, we have been engaged in change—in a perpetual peaceful revolution—a revolution which goes on steadily, quietly adjusting itself to changing conditions—without the concentration camp or the quick-lime in the ditch. The world order which we seek is the cooperation of free countries, working together in a friendly, civilized society.

This nation has placed its destiny in the hands and heads and hearts of its millions of free men and women; and its faith in freedom under the guidance of God. Freedom means the supremacy of human rights everywhere. Our support goes to those who struggle to gain those rights or keep them. Our strength is our unity of purpose. To that high concept there can be no end save victory.

"Second Bill of Rights" Message to Congress (1944)

This Nation in the past two years has become an active partner in the world's greatest war against human slavery.

We have joined with like-minded people in order to defend ourselves in a world that has been gravely threatened with gangster rule.

But I do not think that any of us Americans can be content with mere survival. Sacrifices that we and our allies are making impose upon us all a sacred obligation to see to it that out of this war we and our children will gain something better than mere survival.

We are united in determination that this war shall not be followed by another interim which leads to new disaster—that we shall not repeat the tragic errors of ostrich isolationism—that we shall not repeat the excesses of the wild twenties when this Nation went for a joy ride on a roller coaster which ended in a tragic crash....

The one supreme objective for the future, which we discussed for each Nation individually, and for all the United Nations, can be summed up in one word: Security.

And that means not only physical security which provides safety from attacks by aggressors. It means also economic security, social security, moral security—in a family of Nations.

In the plain down-to-earth talks that I had with the Generalissimo and Marshal Stalin and Prime Minister Churchill, it was abundantly clear that they are all most deeply interested in the resumption of peaceful progress by their own peoples—progress toward a better life. All our allies want freedom to develop their lands and resources, to build up industry, to increase education and individual opportunity, and to raise standards of living.

All our allies have learned by bitter experience that real development will not be possible if they are to be diverted from their purpose by repeated wars—or even threats of war.

China and Russia are truly united with Britain and America in recognition of this essential fact:

The best interests of each Nation, large and small, demand that all freedom-loving Nations shall join together in a just and durable system of peace. In the present world situation, evidenced by the actions of Germany, Italy, and Japan, unquestioned military control over disturbers of the peace is as necessary among Nations as it is among citizens in a community. And an equally basic essential to peace is a decent standard of living for all individual men and women and children in all Nations. Freedom from fear is eternally linked with freedom from want.

There are people who burrow through our Nation like unseeing moles, and attempt to spread the suspicion that if other Nations are encouraged to raise their standards of living, our own American standard of living must of necessity be depressed.

The fact is the very contrary. It has been shown time and again that if the standard of living of any country goes up, so does its purchasing power—and that such a rise encourages a better standard of living in neighboring countries with whom it trades. That is just plain common sense—and it is the kind of plain common sense that provided the basis for our discussions at Moscow, Cairo, and Teheran....

The overwhelming majority of our people have met the demands of this war with magnificent courage and understanding. They have accepted inconveniences; they have accepted hardships; they have accepted tragic sacrifices. And they are ready and eager to make whatever further contributions are needed to win the war as quickly as possible—if only they are given the chance to know what is required of them.

However, while the majority goes on about its great work without complaint, a noisy minority maintains an uproar of demands for special favors for special groups. There are pests who swarm through the lobbies of the Congress and the cocktail bars of Washington, representing these special groups as opposed to the basic interests of the Nation as a whole. They have come to look upon the war primarily as a chance to make profits for themselves at the expense of their neighbors—profits in money or in terms of political or social preferment.

Such selfish agitation can be highly dangerous in wartime. It creates confusion. It damages morale. It hampers our national effort. It muddies the waters and therefore prolongs the war....

Increased food costs, for example, will bring new demands for wage increases from all war workers, which will in turn raise all prices of all things including those things which the farmers themselves have to buy. Increased wages or prices will each in turn produce the same results. They all have a particularly disastrous result on all fixed income groups.

And I hope you will remember that all of us in this Government represent the fixed income group just as much as we represent business owners, workers, and farmers. This group of fixed income people includes: teachers, clergy, policemen, firemen, widows and minors on fixed incomes, wives and dependents of our soldiers and sailors, and old-age pensioners. They and their families add up to one-quarter of our one hundred and thirty million people. They have few or no high pressure representatives at the Capitol. In a period of gross inflation they would be the worst sufferers.

If ever there was a time to subordinate individual or group selfishness to the national good, that time is now. Disunity at home—bickerings, self-seeking partisanship, stoppages of work, inflation, business as usual, politics as usual, luxury as usual—these are the influences which can undermine the morale of the brave men ready to die at the front for us here....

Overconfidence and complacency are among our deadliest enemies. Last spring—after notable victories at Stalingrad and in Tunisia and against the U-boats on the high seas—overconfidence became so pronounced that war production fell off. In two months, June and July, 1943, more than a thousand airplanes that could have been made and should have been made were not made. Those who failed to make them were not on strike. They were merely saying, "The war's in the bag—so let's relax."

That attitude on the part of anyone—Government or management or labor—can lengthen this war. It can kill American boys....

Therefore, in order to concentrate all our energies and resources on winning the war, and to maintain a fair and stable economy at home, I recommend that the Congress adopt:

(1) A realistic tax law—which will tax all unreasonable profits, both individual and corporate, and reduce the ultimate cost of the war to our sons and daughters. The tax bill now under consideration by the Congress does not begin to meet this test.

(2) A continuation of the law for the renegotiation of war contracts—which will prevent exorbitant profits and assure fair prices to the Government. For two long years I have pleaded with the Congress to take undue profits out of war.

(3) A cost of food law—which will enable the Government (a) to place a reasonable floor under the prices the farmer may expect for his production; and (b) to place a ceiling on the prices a consumer will have to pay for the food he buys. This should apply to necessities only; and will require public funds to carry out. It will cost in appropriations about one percent of the present annual cost of the war.

(4) Early reenactment of the stabilization statute of October, 1942. This expires June 30, 1944, and if it is not extended well in advance, the country might just as well expect price chaos by summer. We cannot have stabilization by wishful thinking. We must take positive action to maintain the integrity of the American dollar.

(5) A national service law—which, for the duration of the war, will prevent strikes, and, with certain appropriate exceptions, will make available for war production or for any other essential services every able-bodied adult in this Nation. These five measures together form a just and equitable whole. I would not recommend a national service law unless the other laws were passed to keep down the cost of living, to share equitably the burdens of taxation, to hold the stabilization line, and to prevent undue profits....

As you know, I have for three years hesitated to recommend a national service act. Today, however, I am convinced of its necessity. Although I believe that we and our allies can win the war without such a measure, I am certain that nothing less than total mobilization of all our resources of manpower and capital will guarantee an earlier victory, and reduce the toll of suffering and sorrow and blood.

I have received a joint recommendation for this law from the heads of the War Department, the Navy Department, and the Maritime Commission. These are the men who bear responsibility for the procurement of the necessary arms and equipment, and for the successful prosecution of the war in the field. They say:

When the very life of the Nation is in peril the responsibility for service is common to all men and women. In such a time there can be no discrimination between the men and women who are assigned by the Government to its defense at the battlefront and the men and women assigned to producing the vital materials essential to successful military operations. A prompt enactment of a National Service

Law would be merely an expression of the universality of this responsibility.

I believe the country will agree that those statements are the solemn truth.

National service is the most democratic way to wage a war. Like selective service for the armed forces, it rests on the obligation of each citizen to serve his Nation to his utmost where he is best qualified....

There are millions of American men and women who are not in this war at all. It is not because they do not want to be in it. But they want to know where they can best do their share. National service provides that direction. It will be a means by which every man and woman can find that inner satisfaction which comes from making the fullest possible contribution to victory.

I know that all civilian war workers will be glad to be able to say many years hence to their grandchildren: "Yes, I, too, was in service in the great war. I was on duty in an airplane factory, and I helped make hundreds of fighting planes. The Government told me that in doing that I was performing my most useful work in the service of my country."...

It will give our people at home the assurance that they are standing four-square behind our soldiers and sailors. And it will give our enemies demoralizing assurance that we mean business—that we, 130,000,000 Americans, are on the march to Rome, Berlin, and Tokyo.

I hope that the Congress will recognize that, although this is a political year, national service is an issue which transcends politics. Great power must be used for great purposes....

It is our duty now to begin to lay the plans and determine the strategy for the winning of a lasting peace and the establishment of an American standard of living higher than ever before known. We cannot be content, no matter how high that general standard of living may be, if some fraction of our people—whether it be one-third or one-fifth or one-tenth- is ill-fed, ill-clothed, ill-housed, and insecure.

This Republic had its beginning, and grew to its present strength, under the protection of certain inalienable political rights—among them the rights of free speech, free press, free worship, trial by jury, freedom from unreasonable searches and seizures. They were our rights to life and liberty.

As our Nation has grown in size and stature, however—as our industrial economy expanded—these political rights proved inadequate to assure us equality in the pursuit of happiness.

Glossary

Cairo	the capital city of Egypt
Marshall Stalin	Joseph Stalin, as general secretary of the Communist Party, the ruler of the Soviet Union
Moscow	the capital city of the Soviet Union
"Necessitous men are not free men"	loose quotation from a 1762 British legal decision
ostrich isolationism	withdrawal from the world's affairs by "sticking one's head in the sand," as ostriches are mistakenly believed to do when faced with danger
Prime Minister Churchill	Winston Churchill, British prime minister during most of World War II
remunerative	offering compensation, or pay
Stalingrad	city in Russia, now Volgograd
Teheran	the capital city of Iran
The Generaliss'imo	Francisco Franco, unelected leader of Spain
Tunisia	country in North Africa
twenties	the 1920s, a period of social, economic, and cultural excess
U-boats	German submarines: underwater boats

We have come to a clear realization of the fact that true individual freedom cannot exist without economic security and independence. "Necessitous men are not free men." People who are hungry and out of a job are the stuff of which dictatorships are made.

In our day these economic truths have become accepted as self-evident. We have accepted, so to speak, a second Bill of Rights under which a new basis of security and prosperity can be established for all regardless of station, race, or creed.

Among these are:

The right to a useful and remunerative job in the industries or shops or farms or mines of the Nation;

The right to earn enough to provide adequate food and clothing and recreation;

The right of every farmer to raise and sell his products at a return which will give him and his family a decent living;

The right of every businessman, large and small, to trade in an atmosphere of freedom from unfair competition and domination by monopolies at home or abroad;

The right of every family to a decent home;

The right to adequate medical care and the opportunity to achieve and enjoy good health;

The right to adequate protection from the economic fears of old age, sickness, accident, and unemployment;

The right to a good education.

All of these rights spell security. And after this war is won we must be prepared to move forward, in the implementation of these rights, to new goals of human happiness and well-being.

America's own rightful place in the world depends in large part upon how fully these and similar rights have been carried into practice for our citizens. For unless there is security here at home there cannot be lasting peace in the world....

I ask the Congress to explore the means for implementing this economic bill of rights—for it is definitely the responsibility of the Congress so to do. Many of these problems are already before committees of the Congress in the form of proposed legislation. I shall from time to time communicate with the Congress with respect to these and further proposals. In the event that no adequate program of progress is evolved, I am certain that the Nation will be conscious of the fact.

Our fighting men abroad—and their families at home—expect such a program and have the right to insist upon it. It is to their demands that this Government should pay heed rather than to the whining demands of selfish pressure groups who seek to feather their nests while young Americans are dying....

I have often said that there are no two fronts for America in this war. There is only one front. There is one line of unity which extends from the hearts of the people at home to the men of our attacking forces in our farthest outposts. When we speak of our total effort, we speak of the factory and the field, and the mine as well as of the battleground—we speak of the soldier and the civilian, the citizen and his Government.

Each and every one of us has a solemn obligation under God to serve this Nation in its most critical hour—to keep this Nation great—to make this Nation greater in a better world.

Theodore Roosevelt (Library of Congress)

THEODORE ROOSEVELT

1858–1919

Twenty-sixth President of the United States

Featured Documents
- ◆ Letter to Oliver Wendell Holmes (1903)
- ◆ Special Message to Congress (1908)
- ◆ *Theodore Roosevelt: An Autobiography* (1913)
- ◆ Statements Pertaining to Conservation (1903–1916)
- ◆ Speech to the New York Republican State Convention (1918)

Overview

In style and in substance, Theodore Roosevelt, who occupied the White House from 1901 to 1909, was the first modern American president. A gifted and courageous politician and a natural leader with an intuitive grasp of the value of public relations, Roosevelt employed the "bully pulpit" of the presidency to great effect as he pursued path-breaking, transformative programs in both domestic and foreign affairs. Roosevelt's various initiatives pertaining to workers' rights, consumer protection, and restrictions on corporate behavior in the public interest were labeled the Square Deal, and they launched the process of progressive reform that was to become a central feature of American life in the twentieth century. Roosevelt also was the first—and remains the most ambitious and the most significant—environmentalist president in U.S. history. Regarding foreign policy, Roosevelt determinedly built up the U.S. Navy (particularly its battleship fleet) and brought America into the center of global diplomacy by establishing U.S. hegemony in the Caribbean, upholding U.S. interests in the western Pacific, constructing a strong partnership between the United States and Great Britain, and employing personal mediation to end one great power war and to prevent another. In the process, Roosevelt greatly enhanced the international image and stature of the United States.

The second of four children and the older of two sons, Roosevelt was born into the comfort of a prosperous, close-knit family in New York City on October 27, 1858. The young Roosevelt was educated at home by tutors. His two extended sojourns abroad and frequent visits to the countryside facilitated the development of a cosmopolitan spirit and a passionate, lifelong interest in nature that would lead him to become one of the United States' foremost authorities on natural history. Graduating from Harvard College in 1880, Roosevelt embarked on a career that over the next two decades proved varied and productive. After serving in the New York State Assembly as a Republican reformer, he spent substantial portions of 1884–1886 as a rancher and hunter in the Badlands of the Dakota Territory. From 1889 to 1895 Roosevelt held an appointment on the U.S. Civil Service Commission, following which he became president of New York City's Board of Police Commissioners. Then, from 1897 to 1900, he served, respectively, as a highly influential assistant secretary of the navy, as the heroic (and fortunate) colonel of the "Rough Riders" during the Spanish-American War, and as a dynamic governor of New York. Throughout these twenty years, Roosevelt wrote prolifically on a wide range of subjects, including U.S. history and life in the American West. *The Naval War of 1812* (1882) revealed Roosevelt as a budding strategic thinker, while *The Winning of the West* (1889–1896), a four-volume history of the frontier from 1769 to 1807, was his most formidable and important scholarly undertaking.

Displeased with the independent conduct and reformist policies of Governor Roosevelt, New York's Republican Party boss Thomas Platt maneuvered to secure the nomination of his state's popular chief executive as President William McKinley's running mate in 1900, hoping that vice presidential obscurity would befall Roosevelt. Instead, when McKinley succumbed to an assassin's bullet on September 14, 1901, the forty-two-year-old Roosevelt became the youngest ever president in U.S. history.

President Roosevelt was a broad constructionist, believing that the president possesses a wide range of powers that are not expressly withheld from him by the U.S. Constitution. By skillfully acting in accord with this theory and also by working effectively with Congress, Roosevelt was able to build an extraordinary record of achievement in domestic and foreign policy. He immensely enjoyed his seven and one-half years as president and almost certainly would have won decisively if he had sought another term in 1908. But on the heels of his landslide victory in 1904, Roosevelt had issued an ill-considered public pledge to relinquish his office in March 1909, and he stood by that pledge.

Roosevelt's postpresidential decade was filled with adventures, political battles, and literary output. In June 1910 Roosevelt returned from a long trip to Africa, Great Britain, and continental Europe unhappy with the work of his hand-picked successor, President William Howard Taft. Eventually Roosevelt challenged Taft, unsuccessfully, for the 1912 Republican nomination. Attributing the failure of this endeavor to unscrupulous behavior by conservative Republican operatives, Roosevelt then bolted the Republicans and formed the Progressive ("Bull Moose") Party. As the Progressive nominee, although he outpolled Taft by a wide margin and won the electoral votes of six states, Roosevelt still came in a distant second to the Democrat

1858
■ **October 27**
Theodore Roosevelt is born in New York City.

1880
■ **June 30**
Roosevelt graduates magna cum laude from Harvard College.

1881
■ **November 8**
Roosevelt is elected as a Republican to the New York State Assembly, marking the beginning of his career in public service.

1897
■ **April 6**
Roosevelt is appointed assistant secretary of the navy.

1898
■ **July 1**
Roosevelt leads the Rough Riders (the First U.S. Volunteer Cavalry) in a successful attack on entrenched Spanish forces in Cuba in the Battle of San Juan Hill.

■ **November 8**
Roosevelt is elected governor of New York.

1900
■ **November 6**
Roosevelt is elected vice president of the United States.

1901
■ **September 14**
President William McKinley dies, and Roosevelt is sworn in as president of the United States.

1903
■ **March 14**
By executive order Roosevelt establishes, on Pelican Island, Florida, the first federal bird reservation.

■ **July 25**
Roosevelt writes a letter to Supreme Court Justice Oliver Wendell Holmes on the Alaskan boundary dispute.

Woodrow Wilson, who assumed the presidency in 1913. As a detractor of Wilson and an outspoken proponent of preparedness and a pro-Allies policy during World War I, Roosevelt inexorably drifted back into the Republican Party. When the United States entered the war in April 1917, Roosevelt requested but was denied the opportunity to fight at the front. His four sons did take part, and Quentin, the youngest, was killed in aerial combat over France. During these postpresidential years, Roosevelt wrote several books—most notably *Theodore Roosevelt: An Autobiography* (1913) and *Through the Brazilian Wilderness* (1914)—and innumerable magazine and newspaper articles. Notwithstanding a multitude of grand accomplishments in the realm of public service, a very active family life, a variety of recreational passions, and truly voluminous reading, Roosevelt astonishingly managed over a relatively short lifespan to write approximately thirty books, many hundreds of articles and speeches, and more than one hundred thousand letters. Roosevelt was considered a leading contender for the 1920 Republican presidential nomination at the time of his death on January 6, 1919.

Explanation and Analysis of Documents

Countless available documents illustrate important aspects of Theodore Roosevelt's career. Four of the five documents presented here illuminate the significance of Roosevelt's presidency. The first and third shed light on the sophistication and the effectiveness of his foreign policy; the second centers on his agenda for far-reaching domestic reform; the fourth brings into sharp focus the well-considered purposes and the extraordinary accomplishments of his conservation program. The fifth document demonstrates the vibrancy of Roosevelt's ideas about domestic and foreign policy questions during his postpresidential decade and his continuing prominence in American politics, even during the final year of his life.

◆ Letter to Oliver Wendell Holmes

Although it is not well known, Roosevelt's letter of July 25, 1903, to Supreme Court Justice Oliver Wendell Holmes reveals much about the style and the substance of his foreign policy. Roosevelt was a sophisticated thinker who had a firm grasp of the complexities of the world of the early twentieth century and who devised his initiatives accordingly. While he charted the broad course of U.S. foreign relations, Roosevelt was also a hands-on diplomatist who often attended personally to the significant details of important foreign policy problems. He adhered to the maxim "Speak softly and carry a big stick." His usual preference was to conduct diplomacy informally via private communications dispatched outside the established channels. As for substance, the president believed that morality and national honor must be major considerations in the foreign policy arena. And the cornerstone of Rooseveltian statecraft was a determined, ongoing, and highly successful effort to build a strong partnership between Great

Britain and the United States. Roosevelt's letter to Holmes illustrates all of these aspects of his diplomacy.

The Alaskan boundary dispute grew out of Canadian claims—sparked by a gold rush in the region of Canada's Klondike River in the late 1890s—to territory that the United States, Britain, and Canada had considered American since the U.S. acquisition of Alaska from Russia in 1867. Britain felt obliged to uphold Canada's contention out of loyalty to a self-governing colony that had contributed substantially to Britain's recent difficult war against the Boers in southern Africa. But for his part, Roosevelt perceived "the Canadian contention" as "an outrage pure and simple" (qtd. in Tilchin, p. 38).

Roosevelt's view of the Alaskan boundary dispute as a question of international morality and national honor was, however, far from the whole of the matter. From the outset of his presidency, Roosevelt had been striving with commitment to forge a special relationship between Britain and America. He looked upon Germany, Russia, and Japan as potential enemies of the United States, whereas, in sharp contrast, he saw Britain as a natural and essential U.S. friend. Roosevelt viewed Britain and the United States as sharing not only a language but also a common political and cultural heritage and destiny. Moreover, the two countries' international interests tended to coincide. Especially, Roosevelt anticipated that an unofficial Anglo-American alliance would bring together Britain's unparalleled Royal Navy and the increasingly formidable U.S. Navy to form a potent deterrent to aggression by any rival powers. Thus, concerning the Alaskan border dispute, Roosevelt intended to do his best not to undermine his pursuit of U.S.-British solidarity while still upholding the rights and honor of the United States.

Rooseveltian "big stick" diplomacy typically featured demonstrations of U.S. naval power, most dramatically toward Germany during the Venezuelan crisis of 1902–1903 and, several years later, toward Japan. But Britain, too, was confronted with a big stick—in this case forces of the U.S. Army—during the Alaskan quarrel. Big stick diplomacy was grounded in a series of principles, one of which was to avoid humiliating the targeted country. Therefore, the U.S. troops dispatched by Roosevelt to the disputed area in March 1902 were to be transferred there "as quietly and unostentatiously as possible" (qtd. in Tilchin, p. 38).

Having consented in January 1903 to the establishment of a boundary commission of three Americans (who together could prevent an unacceptable decision), two Canadians, and one Briton, and having studied and mastered all the intricacies of the disagreement, Roosevelt proceeded over the next nine months to engage personally and intensively in the quest for a satisfactory resolution. He utilized a number of agents, including Holmes, to relay his ideas and his bottom-line positions privately to the British government. In his letter to Holmes, while expressing his adamancy on the core issue—the "indefensible ... claim of the Canadians for access to deep water along any part of the Canadian coast"—Roosevelt extends himself in an effort to signal the aspects of the question on which he

Roosevelt, Theodore

Time Line

1903

■ **October 20**
The Alaskan boundary dispute is formally resolved, ending a months-long effort by Roosevelt that included his letter to Holmes.

■ **November 18**
About two weeks after Panama's successful uprising against Colombian rule, tacitly supported by Roosevelt, Panama signs a treaty granting permanent sovereignty over the Panama Canal Zone to the United States.

1904

■ **November 8**
Roosevelt wins a decisive victory over Alton Parker in the presidential election.

1905

■ **March 4**
Roosevelt is inaugurated for a new term as president.

■ **September 5**
The signing of the Treaty of Portsmouth, engineered by Roosevelt, ends the Russo-Japanese War.

1906

■ **June**
Roosevelt signs the Antiquities Act, the Hepburn Act, the Pure Food and Drug Act, and the Meat Inspection Act.

1907

■ **December 16**
Roosevelt's Great White Fleet begins its fourteen-month world cruise.

1908

■ **January 31**
Roosevelt presents to Congress his most radical presidential message.

1909

■ **March 4**
William Howard Taft, Roosevelt's hand-picked successor, is inaugurated.

1912

- **August 5–7**
  The new Progressive ("Bull Moose") Party holds its convention in Chicago and nominates Roosevelt as its presidential candidate.

- **October 14**
  Roosevelt is wounded by a would-be assassin in Milwaukee.

- **November 5**
  Woodrow Wilson wins the presidential election, with Roosevelt finishing second and Taft third.

1913

- Roosevelt writes and publishes *Theodore Roosevelt: An Autobiography*.

1914

- **February 27– April 26**
  Roosevelt and about twenty others explore the perilous River of Doubt (renamed the Rio Roosevelt during their journey) in Brazil.

1917

- **April 6**
  The United States enters World War I by declaring war on Germany.

1918

- **July 18**
  Roosevelt delivers a speech to the New York Republican State Convention in Saratoga.

1919

- **January 6**
  Roosevelt dies in his sleep from a coronary embolism at his home in Oyster Bay, New York.

would be willing to yield and thereby to limit the awkwardness of a British retreat. Thus, he states, "there is room for argument about the islands in the mouth of the Portland Channel." (Canada would end up with the two largest of those four islands.) Roosevelt's many agents would make sure that "the English understand my purpose." If it became necessary, Roosevelt planned "to run the line as we claim it," but first he wished "to exhaust every effort to have the affair settled peacefully and with due regard to

England's dignity." The president's adept hands-on diplomacy accomplished its objective. Despite Canadian protests, Britain accepted the concessions offered by Roosevelt and settled the Alaskan dispute. A satisfied Roosevelt would always believe—correctly—that this settlement had removed the last major obstacle impeding his drive for Anglo-American unity.

One broader observation might be added. Throughout his presidency, Roosevelt was almost uniformly successful both in his dealings with specific foreign policy problems and in conceiving and implementing an overall strategy. His Alaskan diplomacy—of which his letter to Holmes was one important part—helps illuminate why "in the foreign policy arena Roosevelt was probably the greatest of all U.S. presidents" (Tilchin, pp. ix–x).

◆ Special Message to Congress

The presidency of Theodore Roosevelt coincided closely with the first half of what is often referred to as the Progressive era in U.S. history. In response to political and economic systems that catered to the rich and powerful, that disregarded the legitimate grievances of common citizens, and that were rife with corruption, concerned Americans fought for reforms on the local, state, and national levels. In Roosevelt, these progressives found a president who shared many of their ideas and who strove to achieve many of their aims.

Roosevelt called his domestic reform agenda, which emphasized corporate accountability and protections for laborers and consumers, the Square Deal. Himself a product of the upper class, Roosevelt was highly skeptical about the morality and public-spiritedness of most large corporations and most wealthy individuals. While his reputation as a trustbuster was well deserved—for his administration initiated many successful antitrust cases, most famously against J. P. Morgan's Northern Securities Company, the Standard Oil Company, and the American Tobacco Company—his primary objective with regard to big business was not to dismantle corporations but rather to establish the federal government's authority to supervise and regulate them. The supervisory and regulatory structure built by Roosevelt was embodied in his creation in 1903 of the Department of Commerce and Labor (which included a Bureau of Corporations) and in the Hepburn Act (which won for the Interstate Commerce Commission substantial and workable regulatory power over the nation's railroads), the Meat Inspection Act, and the Pure Food and Drug Act, all passed in 1906. As a check on corporate dominance, labor unions, he believed, had become a necessity. Roosevelt's goals encompassed laws to curb child labor, to provide workmen's compensation, and to punish corporate criminals. In addition, during his second term, the president began forcefully advocating graduated income and inheritance taxes.

From 1906 on, Roosevelt's domestic reform objectives were more far-reaching and his language more strident than they had been earlier in his presidency. His annual message to Congress of December 1906 signaled a more frontal assault on corporate misconduct. Charges and countercharges by Roosevelt and his corporate foes came in rapid succession during the months that followed, especially during the economic downturn and eventual panic of 1907. In December 1907 he boldly called for federal supervision of all interstate business. Earlier that year, William Allen White, an astute and articulate friend and admirer of Roosevelt, had written an article for *McClure's* titled "Roosevelt: A Force for Righteousness."

The culmination of the president's radicalization was his stunning special message to Congress of January 31, 1908. Here Roosevelt lashes out sharply at "certain wealthy men …whose conduct should be abhorrent to every man of ordinarily decent conscience" and at the politicians and newspapers who carried their banner. "From the Railroad Rate Law to the Pure Food Law," Roosevelt charges, "every measure for honesty in business has been opposed by these men … with every resource that bitter and unscrupulous craft could suggest and the command of almost unlimited money secure." In his call for "a just employers' liability law," Roosevelt condemns "the special pleaders for business dishonesty, [who], in denouncing the present Administration for enforcing the law against the huge and corrupt corporations which have defied the law, also denounce it for endeavoring to secure sadly needed labor legislation." He contends that uncontrolled "law-defying wealth" not only would bring "dire evil to the Republic" but also would be certain to generate in reaction "a vindictive and dreadful radicalism." Thus, "decent citizens" must not allow "those rich men whose lives are corrupt and evil to domineer in swollen pride, unchecked and unhindered, over the destinies of this country." Roosevelt is confident that the struggle in which he and his supporters are engaged on behalf of the American people will be won, and that the future will be bright for the people of the United States. He declares, "No misdeeds done in the present must be permitted to shroud from our eyes the glorious future of the Nation….There is no nation so absolutely sure of ultimate success as ours."

Roosevelt's message of January 31 "evoked an extraordinary reaction." Many congressional Democrats "punctuated its reading with round after round of spontaneous applause," whereas "the great body of Republicans sat glumly." Newspapers labeled by Roosevelt as dutiful mouthpieces for unsavory corporate masters fired back at the president, with the *New York Times* recommending that Roosevelt seek "the attention of a psychiatrist" (Harbaugh, p. 326).

Roosevelt did not relent even slightly in the face of his critics' withering disparagement of his speech and his policies. On the contrary, he vigorously carried forward the fight for social and economic justice for the remainder of his presidency and throughout the following decade as well. Still, Roosevelt's departure from the presidency in March 1909 proved to be a historical watershed. In his raging battle with the Republican Party's conservative "old guard," he had greatly advanced the project of transforming the Republicans into a progressive organization; minus Roosevelt's executive leadership, that effort rapidly faltered. In

the tumultuous political year of 1912, Roosevelt actually bolted the Republicans and accepted the presidential nomination of the new Progressive Party. While the cause of progressivism still had a bright future, Republican progressivism would be marginalized for at least the next century.

◆ Theodore Roosevelt: An Autobiography

Shortly after his defeat in the presidential election of 1912, Roosevelt undertook to write an autobiography, which he completed in the early fall of 1913. Even the best memoirs tend to be self-serving, and *Theodore Roosevelt: An Autobiography* is no exception. Nevertheless, Roosevelt brought to bear on this project his fine literary talents, his extensive experience as a writer of history, his profound understanding of many current issues, and his desire to share a life story of which he was justifiably very proud. The end product was a very readable, reputable, and revealing volume, which continues to be looked upon by historians as a valuable primary resource.

Roosevelt's extraordinarily successful foreign policy presents the student of history with a sizable roster of major accomplishments. Particularly notable among them were the development of a deep-rooted friendship between Great Britain and the United States and two adroit mediations that ended one great power war and forestalled another. Roosevelt brought Russian and Japanese representatives to the United States in August 1905 and proceeded to engineer the Treaty of Portsmouth, which ended the Russo-Japanese War of 1904–1905 and won for the president a Nobel Peace Prize. Roosevelt's diplomacy also was instrumental in resolving the Franco-German Moroccan crisis of 1905–1906, which very conceivably could have resulted in a world war. As proud as he was of his service to peace as a mediator par excellence, Roosevelt appears to have been even prouder of his attainments pertaining to the Panama Canal and the U.S. Navy. Such an interpretation is supported by plentiful evidence, including Roosevelt's claim, put forward in his autobiography, that "the two American achievements that really impressed foreign peoples during the first dozen years of this century were the digging of the Panama Canal and the cruise of the battle fleet round the world."

Having secured an agreement with Great Britain in November 1901 permitting U.S. control and fortification of a future canal across the Central American isthmus, Roosevelt became frustrated in 1903 when he determined that Colombia, then sovereign in Panama, was negotiating with the United States in bad faith. Well aware of the strong and rising secessionist ferment in Panama, Roosevelt encouraged the secessionists—though only privately and even then only by indirection. The president soon transferred U.S. naval vessels to the waters near Panama to prevent Colombia from landing troops to suppress an uprising. Panama's revolution against Colombian rule was swift, successful, and practically bloodless. Shortly afterward, the Hay-Bunau-Varilla Treaty of November 18, 1903, granted the United States sovereignty "in perpetuity" over a ten-mile-wide canal zone and made Panama a virtual U.S. protectorate. For the remainder of his presidency, Roosevelt was heavily (and very usefully) involved in the building of the Panama Canal, a mammoth and enormously complex project that would take about a decade to complete.

As for the navy, Roosevelt, the author of *The Naval War of 1812* and former assistant secretary of the navy, came into the presidency as a big-navy advocate possessing a high level of expertise on naval issues. Focusing his efforts primarily on the construction of modern battleships, Roosevelt elevated the U.S. Navy from the world's sixth largest in 1901 to the second in size by 1907. He also dramatically upgraded the navy's readiness and efficiency.

Relations between the United States and Japan were tense in 1907 owing to anti-Japanese agitation and violence on the American West Coast and the continuing arrival in America of large numbers of Japanese laborers. A U.S.-Japan war, while not likely, was becoming an increasing possibility. At the same time, Roosevelt was worried about the parsimony of Congress and the apathy of the American public regarding naval matters. So, in his single most illustrious act of big stick diplomacy, in December 1907 Roosevelt dispatched his "Great White Fleet" of sixteen battleships on a fourteen-month world cruise. Not a threatening word was written or spoken—indeed, the fleet visited Japan in October 1908 and was met there with a grand welcome—but the message that America was powerful and prepared to uphold its interests was unmistakable. Back home, public enthusiasm for the highly publicized cruise had the intended effect of loosening congressional purse strings with regard to funding the president's naval building proposals. "No single thing in the history of the new United States Navy," Roosevelt asserts in his autobiography, "has done as much to stimulate popular interest and belief in it as the world cruise."

The circumnavigation of the globe by the Great White Fleet actually contributed to a marked improvement in U.S.-Japanese relations in 1908. The Root-Takahira Agreement of November 1908—in which Japan pledged to respect U.S. control of the Philippines in exchange for U.S. assurances concerning Japan's priorities on the East Asian mainland—demonstrated to the world the establishment of a respectful and amicable U.S.-Japan relationship and signaled a climactic triumph for Roosevelt's Japanese policy. Therefore, Roosevelt could declare five years later with some justification, "The most important service that I rendered to peace was the voyage of the battle fleet round the world."

◆ **Statements Pertaining to Conservation**

In his Square Deal reforms, in his foreign policy, and perhaps most of all in his conservation program, Roosevelt believed firmly that he was fulfilling the president's duty to serve as the "steward" of the American people—future generations pointedly included. In his view, the federal government was obligated to promote justice and the common good, and the president had a vital role to play in this process. Consistent with his broad constructionist principles, Roosevelt operated on the theory that the president can and should exercise stewardship by taking action on behalf of the public, except in cases where a law or the Constitution expressly forbids him to take such action. In the area of conservation, Roosevelt pursued a pathbreaking and enormously ambitious policy embodying the two concepts of controlled utilization and preservation.

Controlled utilization was the guiding principle behind the establishment by Roosevelt, empowered by congressional legislation, of forest reserves and irrigation projects in the western states. He created 150 new forest reserves on approximately 150 million acres of land, and he launched the first twenty-four federal irrigation projects. Regarding his thinking on this matter, in 1907 he declared, "Unless we maintain an adequate material basis for our civilization, we can not maintain the institutions in which we take so great and so just a pride; and to waste and destroy our natural resources means to undermine this material basis." In 1909 he remarked, "If we allow great industrial organizations to exercise unregulated control of the means of production and the necessaries of life, we deprive the Americans of today and of the future of industrial liberty, a right no less precious and vital than political freedom."

Roosevelt's rapid and extensive creation of forest reserves occurred as a response to what the president perceived as the greed and recklessness of lumber syndicates. These entities reacted by persuading members of Congress over whom they had influence to enact disabling legislation. Early in 1907 an amendment was attached to an agricultural appropriations bill prohibiting the establishment of any additional forest reserves in the six states of Colorado, Wyoming, Idaho, Montana, Washington, and Oregon. While supporters of the amendment calculated correctly that Roosevelt would have difficulty vetoing this important appropriations bill, he nonetheless outmaneuvered (and infuriated) them. The Constitution stipulates that the president has ten days to sign or veto an act of Congress. Under the management of Chief Forester Gifford Pinchot, Roosevelt's knowledgeable and dedicated right-hand man in the realm of conservation policy, government employees worked long days behind the scenes to produce comprehensive lists of areas in the affected states that should be designated as forest reserves. On March 2, just before he signed the amended agricultural appropriations bill, Roosevelt shocked his foes by proclaiming the establishment in the six states in question of twenty-one new forest reserves totaling 16 million acres.

Preservation was the other half of Roosevelt's conservation policy. The protection of birds and other wildlife (Roosevelt was among the country's leading wildlife experts) and the permanent safeguarding of the nation's greatest natural wonders were the two primary purposes of his preservation initiatives. Roosevelt inherited congressional authority to create national parks and gained similar authority to create national monuments through the Antiquities Act of 1906, and he was very active on both fronts. For the creation of four national game preserves, Roosevelt was empowered in each instance by a separate act of Congress. Somewhat differently, the president's declarations establishing federal

Pelican Island, the first reservation in what became the National Wildlife Refuge System (AP/Wide World Photos)

bird reservations, actions not authorized by Congress, manifested his broad constructionist philosophy. Discovering in 1903 that no law prevented such declarations, Roosevelt designated Pelican Island, Florida, the first of these reservations and then proceeded to designate fifty more over the remaining years of his presidency.

Roosevelt's outlook on preservation is well represented in his observations in 1903 on the Grand Canyon, established as both a national monument and a national game preserve in 1908:

> In the Grand Canyon, Arizona has a natural wonder which, so far as I know, is in kind absolutely unparalleled throughout the rest of the world.... You can not improve on it. The ages have been at work on it, and man can only mar it. What you can do is keep it for your children, your children's children, and for all who come after you.

In 1916 he declared,

> With the great majority of our most interesting and important wild birds and beasts the prime need is to protect them,... especially by the creation of sanctuaries and refuges.... The progress made in the United States, of recent years, in creating and policing bird refuges, has been of capital importance.

Conservation was a matter of the highest priority for Roosevelt. In addition to all the forest reserves, irrigation projects, national parks and monuments, and bird and wildlife sanctuaries for which he was responsible, he appointed four commissions to investigate issues pertinent to his conservation policy and, during the final year of his presidency, convened three major conservation conferences—altogether constituting a truly breathtaking record. Roosevelt stands without question as the foremost environmentalist president in American history. Just as he had intended, his farsighted stewardship of the nation's environment has benefited and will continue to benefit multiple generations of Americans.

◆ **Speech to the New York Republican State Convention**

Roosevelt's speech to the New York Republican State Convention was among the most significant addresses delivered by the former president during the final year of his life. Roosevelt's remarks reveal much about his outlook on the war leadership provided by President Woodrow Wilson; about Roosevelt's perspectives on World War I, America's role in the war, and the proper shape of the eventual peace; and about the persistence of Roosevelt's progressive prescriptions for confronting the nation's domestic policy challenges.

Roosevelt had advocated U.S. intervention on the side of the Allies long before the United States declared war on Germany in April 1917. In addition, he had repeatedly criticized Wilson for what Roosevelt perceived to be an insufficient preparedness program. In this speech, he chastises the current chief executive by expressing the hope "that never again shall we be caught in such humiliating inability to defend ourselves and assert our rights as has been the case during the last four years.... Nine-tenths of wisdom consists in being wise in time." Roosevelt also laments what he views as the incompetence of the Wilson administration's conduct of the war since U.S. entry: "A very small degree of efficiency in handling the War Department would have meant that our army in France on January 1st would have far surpassed in size and equipment the army we have over there now in July." But "at last we have begun to send over enough soldiers to count for something real in the struggle. We have begun to give them some airplanes." (The preceding sentence incidentally illuminates the extremely difficult timing of this speech for Roosevelt and his family. The characteristically stoic Roosevelt spoke in Saratoga as scheduled on July 18 despite the knowledge that fighter pilot Quentin Roosevelt, his beloved youngest son, had only days earlier been shot down over France, his condition still unknown. The Roosevelts' worst fears would be realized on July 20, when the news came to them that Quentin had been killed in action.)

Regretting that for four years other nations "have fought our battles, and we have only just begun to fight for ourselves," Roosevelt urges his countrymen to "make the finishing of the war an American task." Moreover, the finish to which he is referring must be decisive, for Germany had proved itself to be a barbaric, outlaw power: "There must be no peace until Germany is beaten to her knees.... We must refuse any peace except the peace of overwhelming victory, a peace which will guarantee us against the threat of German world dominion by securing to every well-behaved civilized power its real and complete freedom." Roosevelt did not live to weigh in on the Treaty of Versailles, but it seems very likely that he would have rejected the view—widely held by several generations of historians—that the treaty was excessively punitive toward Germany. It is probable, rather, that Roosevelt would have assumed the opposite stance—that he would have considered the treaty too lenient. Extending this analysis, it is reasonable to speculate that had he lived through the 1930s, Roosevelt would have attributed the rise of the Nazi menace in large measure to a treaty that had inadequately subdued Germany and had thereby left the door open for a renewed German drive for "world dominion."

Roosevelt's speech at Saratoga was a reflection of his reconciliation with and restored stature within the Republican Party, which he had abandoned in 1912 and to which he had returned in 1916. Indeed, in the months preceding his death in January 1919, Roosevelt was looked upon by many as the front-runner for the 1920 Republican presidential nomination. Undoubtedly attracted by the prospect of such an affirmation and opportunity, Roosevelt nonetheless adhered firmly to his progressive principles. Thus, women "should be given [the vote] at once in the nation at large." Businessmen should be "subject to such regulation and control by the Government as will prevent injustice and sharp dealing among themselves or toward their employees, or as regards outsiders and the general public." And "labor should be treated...as a partner in the enterprises in which it is associated; housing and living conditions must be favorable; ... there must be insurance against old age, sickness and involuntary unemployment; and a share in the money reward for increased business success." One might reflect that positions of this nature either would ultimately have blocked the nomination of Roosevelt by a predominantly conservative party or would have led to the reinvigoration of Republican progressivism—in the latter event profoundly altering the direction of American political history.

Impact and Legacy

Throughout his career and especially as president of the United States, Theodore Roosevelt measured up to his own high standards for morality and public-spiritedness. He labored consistently to overcome injustices and build a more equitable and decent society (although he did determine gradually—and grudgingly—that southern racial injustice was a problem beyond any president's capacity to rectify during the first decade of the twentieth century). Roosevelt fulfilled his ideal of presidential stewardship through his Square Deal policies, through his bold and unprecedented environmental initiatives, and through an equally bold, well-conceived, and well-executed foreign policy that strengthened and protected the United States while advancing the cause of international stability and peace.

A farsighted leader with a long-range view, Roosevelt left a durable legacy that has benefited the people of the United States and the world ever since his White House years. He launched the process of extensive progressive reform in twentieth-century America—a process that would be carried forward primarily by Democratic presidents, most spectacularly by Roosevelt's distant cousin Franklin D. Roosevelt. Theodore Roosevelt's actions in the realm of conservation likewise conferred enormous benefits on future generations of Americans; moreover, the Republican Roosevelt provided the model for the conservationist presidents—again Democrats—who have come after him. As a foreign policy thinker and leader, Roosevelt was ahead of his time; unlike his first several successors, Republican and Democratic, he clearly recognized the importance of a militarily formidable United States acting in concert with Great Britain to deter and, when necessary, to defeat aggressors. It would take the disastrous failure of isolationism and appeasement and the terrible experience of World War II to revive Roosevelt's outlook on U.S. foreign relations and to bring his guiding precepts—a powerful and credible American military apparatus, broadly conceived U.S. interests, and Anglo-American solidarity and preeminence—into the mainstream, where they have been ever since.

Theodore Roosevelt's legacy encompasses more than the enduring nature of his internal and external policies. From 1909 to the present—and especially since the 1950s—Roosevelt has been widely viewed as the prototype of the activist, ethically upright chief executive moving the United States forward with wisdom, a steady hand, and a long-term perspective. Unlike those twentieth-century

"I wish to exhaust every effort to have the affair settled peacefully and with due regard to England's dignity."

(Letter to Oliver Wendell Holmes)

"The attacks by these great corporations on the Administration's actions have been given a wide circulation throughout the country, in the newspapers and otherwise, by those writers and speakers who, consciously or unconsciously, act as the representatives of predatory wealth—of the wealth accumulated on a giant scale by all forms of iniquity."

(Special Message to Congress)

"Throughout the seven and a half years that I was President, I pursued without faltering one consistent foreign policy, a policy of genuine international good will and of consideration for the rights of others, and at the same time of steady preparedness."

(Theodore Roosevelt: An Autobiography)

"The two American achievements that really impressed foreign peoples during the first dozen years of this century were the digging of the Panama Canal and the cruise of the battle fleet round the world."

(Theodore Roosevelt: An Autobiography)

"We have gotten past the stage, my fellow-citizens, when we are to be pardoned if we treat any part of our country as something to be skinned for two or three years for the use of the present generation, whether it is the forest, the water, the scenery. Whatever it is, handle it so that your children's children will get the benefit of it."

(Statements Pertaining to Conservation)

"When we have closed the giant war we must then prepare for the giant tasks of peace. First and foremost we should act on Washington's advice, and in time of peace prepare against war, so that never again shall we be caught in such humiliating inability to defend ourselves and assert our rights as has been the case during the last four years."

(Speech to the New York Republican State Convention)

presents for whom retrospective reverence tends to be partisan—most notably the Democrat Franklin Roosevelt and the Republican Ronald Reagan—Theodore Roosevelt's historical image has transcended partisan politics, and he has become an iconic figure for Republicans and Democrats alike. (Harry Truman also falls into this category.) Books, articles, and films on Roosevelt have poured forth at a rapid clip over the past sixty years, and the cumulative impact of all this scholarly and popular writing and filmmaking has been to enhance ever more the historical reputation of the United States' twenty-sixth president. Like his hero Abraham Lincoln, Theodore Roosevelt is a president whose eminent stature almost assuredly will continue to stand the test of time.

Key Sources

The most important primary resource on Theodore Roosevelt's career and presidency is the Theodore Roosevelt Papers. This enormous collection is available on 485 well-indexed rolls of microfilm, most of which contain letters written by or to Roosevelt. These papers are located at the Library of Congress in Washington, D.C. (their original repository) and at the Harvard College Library, which also houses the very large and rich (particularly with regard to Roosevelt's family life) Theodore Roosevelt Collection. The greater part of Roosevelt's own voluminous writings (including his autobiography) were gathered together shortly after his death in *The Works of Theodore Roosevelt*, published in a Memorial Edition, 24 vols. (1923–1926), and a National Edition, 20 vols. (1926), both edited by Hermann Hagedorn. The bulky *Theodore Roosevelt Cyclopedia*, edited by Albert B. Hart and Herbert R. Ferleger, first published in 1941 and reissued in 1989, presents well-selected excerpts from Roosevelt's speeches and writings on a wide variety of topics. Even more valuable are the eight published volumes of *The Letters of Theodore Roosevelt* (1951–1954), selected by Elting E. Morison and his associates. A number of films about Roosevelt have been produced, the most enlightening

Questions for Further Study

1. Compare and contrast the two Roosevelts—Theodore and Franklin—as presidents and leaders. Consider, for instance, the similarities in their backgrounds, not only in terms of their obvious family connection but also with regard to their involvement in the Department of the Navy. How much linkage do you see between the two presidents' administrations, their views on the role of the federal government and the role of the president, and their influence on the creation of the modern federal state? What differences, if any, do you see in their approaches? To what extent can those differences be attributed to the fact that the first Roosevelt was a Republican and the second a Democrat?

2. Discuss and evaluate Roosevelt's achievements in foreign policy as referenced in his 1903 letter to Oliver Wendell Holmes and the excerpt from his autobiography. Be sure to include Roosevelt's role in settling the Russo-Japanese War, for which he received the Nobel Peace Prize, as well as his handling of matters that included the Alaska border dispute, the Moroccan crisis, and heightened tensions between the United States and Japan. What aspects of his approach to foreign relations explain his remarkable record of success in that area? How are these ideas and principles presented in the Holmes letter?

3. Examine Roosevelt's "Square Deal" and his overall domestic reform agenda, which introduced a supervisory and regulatory structure designed to counteract business monopolies, or "trusts." How did his progressivism fit within the context of the Republican Party at that time? Why did he split from the Republicans, and why did he eventually rejoin the fold? What similarities do you see between Roosevelt and another liberal Republican who won at least as much support from Democrats as from his own party, 2008 presidential candidate Senator John McCain?

4. What ideas did Roosevelt have about the environment, as demonstrated by his statements on conservation? Discuss the principles of controlled utilization and protection and the way in which Roosevelt dealt with the lumber syndicates. To what extent were his ideas ahead of their time, and how might he fit within the modern environmental movement if he were alive today?

of which are *The Indomitable Teddy Roosevelt* (1983) and *TR: The Story of Theodore Roosevelt* (1996). The Theodore Roosevelt Association Web site (http://www.theodoreroosevelt.org) offers a wealth of information and interpretation pertaining to Roosevelt and includes the entire *Theodore Roosevelt Cyclopedia*.

Further Reading

■ Articles

Tilchin, William N. "Morality and the Presidency of Theodore Roosevelt," *Long Term View* 3, no. 3 (Fall 1996): 56–65. Reprinted in *Theodore Roosevelt Association Journal* 28, no. 1 (Winter 2007): 4–11.

■ Books

Brands, H. W. *TR: The Last Romantic*. New York: Basic Books, 1997.

Dalton, Kathleen. *Theodore Roosevelt: A Strenuous Life*. New York: Knopf, 2002.

Gould, Lewis L. *The Presidency of Theodore Roosevelt*. Lawrence: University Press of Kansas, 1991.

Harbaugh, William H. *Power and Responsibility: The Life and Times of Theodore Roosevelt*. 1961. Reprint. Newton, Conn.: American Political Biography Press, 1997.

Morris, Edmund. *Theodore Rex*. New York: Random House, 2001.

Tilchin, William N. *Theodore Roosevelt and the British Empire: A Study in Presidential Statecraft*. New York: St. Martin's Press, 1997.

—William N. Tilchin

LETTER TO OLIVER WENDELL HOLMES (1903)

I thank you very much for your letter, which I thoroughly enjoyed. There is one point on which I think I ought to give you full information, in view of [Joseph] Chamberlain's remark to you. This is about the Alaska Boundary matter and if you happen to meet Chamberlain again you are entirely at liberty to tell him what I say, although of course it must be privately and unofficially. Nothing but my very earnest desire to get on well with England and my reluctance to come to a break made me consent to the appointment of a Joint Commission in this case; for I regard the attitude of Canada, which England has backed, as having the scantest possible warrant in justice. However, there were but two alternatives. Either I could appoint a commission and give a chance for agreement; or I could do as I shall of course do in case this commission fails, and request Congress to make an appropriation which will enable me to run the boundary on my own hook. As regards most of Great Britain's claim, there is not, in my judgment, enough to warrant so much as a consideration by the United States; and if it were not that there are two or three lesser points on which there is doubt, I could not, even for the object I have mentioned, have consented to appoint a commission. The claim of the Canadians for access to deep water along any part of the Canadian coast is just exactly as indefensible as if they should now suddenly claim the island of Nantucket. There is not a man fit to go on the commission in all the United States who would treat this claim any more respectfully than he would treat a claim to Nantucket. In the same way the preposterous claim once advanced, but I think now aban-

doned by the Canadians, that the Portland Channel was not the Portland Channel but something else unknown, is no more worth discussing than the claim that the 49th Parallel meant the 50th Parallel or else the 48th.

But there are points which the commission can genuinely consider. There is room for argument about the islands in the mouth of the Portland Channel. I think on this the American case much the stronger of the two. Still, the British have a case. Again, it may well be that there are places in which there is room for doubt as to whether there actually is a chain of mountains parallel to the coast within the ten-league limit. Here again there is a chance for honest difference and honest final agreement. I believe that no three men in the United States could be found who would be more anxious than our own delegates to do justice to the British claim on all points where there is even a color of right on the British side. But the objection raised by certain Canadian authorities to Lodge, Root and Turner, and especially to Lodge and Root, was that they had committed themselves on the general proposition. No man in public life in any position of prominence could have possibly avoided committing himself on the proposition, any more than Mr. Chamberlain could avoid committing himself on the question of the ownership of the Orkneys if some Scandinavian country suddenly claimed them. If this claim embodied points as to which there was legitimate doubt, I believe Mr. Chamberlain would act fairly and squarely in deciding the matter; but if he appointed a commission to settle up all those questions, I certainly

Glossary

Chamberlain	Joseph Chamberlain, British politician and statesman who served as Britain's colonial secretary
Lodge, Root and Turner	Senator Henry Cabot Lodge, Secretary of War Elihu Root, and former senator George Turner, Roosevelt's appointees to the Alaska Boundary Commission
Nantucket	an island off the coast of Massachusetts
Orkneys	the Orkney Islands, a chain of islands running north from Scotland
Portland Channel	a channel in the vicinity of Vancouver, British Columbia, in Canada

should not expect him to appoint three men, if he could find them, who believed that as to the Orkneys the question was an open one. Similarly I wish to repeat that no three men fit for the position could be found in all the United States who would not already have come to some conclusion as to certain features of the Canadian claim—not as to all of them.

Let me add that I earnestly hope the English understand my purpose. I wish to make one last effort to bring about an agreement through the commission, which will enable the people of both countries to say that the result represents the feeling of the representatives of both countries. But if there is a disagreement I wish it distinctly understood, not only that there will be no arbitration of the matter, but that in my message to Congress I shall take a position which will prevent any possibility of arbitration hereafter; a position, I am inclined to believe, which will render it necessary for Congress to give me the authority to run the line as we claim it, by our own people, without any further regard to the attitude of England and Canada. If I paid attention to mere abstract right, that is the position I ought to take anyhow. I have not taken it because I wish to exhaust every effort to have the affair settled peacefully and with due regard to England's dignity.

SPECIAL MESSAGE TO CONGRESS (1908)

The attacks by these great corporations on the Administration's actions have been given a wide circulation throughout the country, in the newspapers and otherwise, by those writers and speakers who, consciously or unconsciously, act as the representatives of predatory wealth—of the wealth accumulated on a giant scale by all forms of iniquity, ranging from the oppression of wage-workers to unfair and unwholesome methods of crushing out competition, and to defrauding the public by stock-jobbing and the manipulation of securities. Certain wealthy men of this stamp, whose conduct should be abhorrent to every man of ordinarily decent conscience, and who commit the hideous wrong of teaching our young men that phenomenal business success must ordinarily be based on dishonesty, have during the last few months made it apparent that they have banded together to work for a reaction. Their endeavor is to overthrow and discredit all who honestly administer the law, to prevent any additional legislation which would check and restrain them, and to secure if possible a freedom from all restraint which will permit every unscrupulous wrong-doer to do what he wishes unchecked provided he has enough money. The only way to counteract the movement in which these men are engaged is to make clear to the public just what they have done in the past and just what they are seeking to accomplish in the present....

Under no circumstances would we countenance attacks upon law-abiding property, or do aught but condemn those who hold up rich men as being evil men because of their riches. On the contrary, our whole effort is to insist upon conduct, and neither wealth nor property nor any other class distinction, as being the proper standard by which to judge the actions of men. For the honest man of great wealth we have a hearty regard, just as we have a hearty regard for the honest politician and honest newspaper. But part of the movement to uphold honesty must be a movement to frown on dishonesty. We attack only the corrupt men of wealth, who find in the purchased politician and in the purchased newspaper the most efficient defender of corruption. Our main quarrel is not with these agents and representatives of the interests....They are but puppets, who move as the strings are pulled. It is not the puppets, but the strong, cunning men and the mighty forces working for evil behind and through the puppets, with whom we have to deal. We seek to control law-defying wealth; in the first place to prevent its doing dire evil to the Republic, and in the next place to avoid the vindictive and dreadful radicalism which, if left uncontrolled, it is certain in the end to arouse. Sweeping attacks upon all property, upon all men of means, without regard to whether they do well or ill would sound the death-knell of the Republic; and such attacks become inevitable if decent citizens permit those rich men whose lives are corrupt and evil to domineer in swollen pride, unchecked and unhindered, over the destinies of this country....

The books and pamphlets, the controlled newspapers, the speeches by public or private men, to which I refer, are usually and especially in the interest of the Standard Oil Trust and of certain notorious railroad combinations, but they also defend other individuals and corporations of great wealth that have been guilty of wrong-doing. It is only rarely that the men responsible for the wrong-doing themselves speak or write. Normally they hire others to do their bidding, or find others who will do it without hire. From the Railroad Rate Law to the Pure Food Law, every measure for honesty in business has been opposed by these men on its passage and its administration with every resource that bitter and unscrupulous craft could suggest and the command of almost unlimited money secure....The extraordinary violence of the assaults upon our policy contained in these speeches, editorials, articles, advertisements, and pamphlets, and the enormous sums of money spent in these various ways, give a fairly accurate measure of the anger and terror which our public actions have caused the corrupt men of vast wealth to feel in the very marrow of their being....

Much is said, in these attacks upon the policy of the present Administration, about the rights of "innocent stockholders."...There has been in the past grave wrong done innocent stockholders by overcapitalization, stock-watering, stock-jobbing, stock-manipulation. This we have sought to prevent, first, by exposing the thing done and punishing the offender when any existing law had been violated; second, by recommending the passage of laws which would make unlawful similar practices for the future. The public men, lawyers, and editors who loudly proclaim their sympathy for the "innocent stockholders" when a great law-defying corporation is punished are the first to protest with frantic vehemence against all efforts by law to put a stop to the practices which are the real and ultimate sources of the damage alike to the stockholders and the public. The apologists of successful dishonesty always declaim against any effort to punish or prevent it, on the ground that any such effort will "unsettle business." It is they who by their acts have unsettled business; and the very men raising this cry spend hundreds of thousands of dollars in securing, by speech, editorial, book, or pamphlet, the defence by misstatements of what they have done; and yet when public servants correct their misstatements by telling the truth they declaim against them for breaking silence, lest "values be depreciated." They have hurt honest business men, honest working men, honest farmers; and now they clamor against the truth being told....

The "business" which is hurt by the movement for honesty is the kind of business which, in the long run, it pays the country to have hurt. It is the kind of business which has tended to make the very name "high finance" a term of scandal to which all honest American men of business should join in putting an end. The special pleaders for business dishonesty, in denouncing the present Administration for enforcing the law against the huge and corrupt corporations which have defied the law, also denounce it for endeavoring to secure sadly needed labor legislation, such as a far-reaching law making employers liable for injuries to their employees. It is meet and fit that the apologists for corrupt wealth should oppose every effort to relieve weak and helpless people from crushing misfortune brought upon them by injury in the business from which they gain a bare livelihood. The burden should be distributed. It is hypocritical baseness to speak of a girl who works in a factory where the dangerous machinery is unprotected as having the "right" freely to contract to expose herself

to dangers to life and limb. She has no alternative but to suffer want or else to expose herself to such dangers, and when she loses a hand or is otherwise maimed or disfigured for life, it is a moral wrong that the whole burden of the risk necessarily incidental to the business should be placed with crushing weight upon her weak shoulders, and all who profit by her work escape scot-free. This is what opponents of a just employers' liability law advocate; and it is consistent that they should usually also advocate immunity for those most dangerous members of the criminal class—the criminals of great wealth....

We have just passed through two months of acute financial stress. ...At such a time there is a natural tendency on the part of many men to feel gloomy and frightened at the outlook; but there is no justification for this feeling. There is no nation so absolutely sure of ultimate success as ours. Of course we shall succeed. Ours is a Nation of masterful energy, with a continent for its domain, and it feels within its veins the thrill which comes to those who know that they possess the future. We are not cast down by the fear of failure. We are upheld by the confident hope of ultimate triumph. The wrongs that exist are to be corrected; but they in no way justify doubt as to the final outcome, doubt as to the great material prosperity of the future, or of the lofty spiritual life which is to be built upon that prosperity as a foundation. No misdeeds done in the present must be permitted to shroud from our eyes the glorious future of the Nation; but because of this very fact it behooves us never to swerve from our resolute purpose to cut out wrong-doing and uphold what is right.

I do not for a moment believe that the actions of this Administration have brought on business distress; so far as this is due to local and not world-wide causes, and to the actions of any particular individuals, it is due to the speculative folly and flagrant dishonesty of a few men of great wealth, who seek to shield themselves from the effects of their own

Glossary

overcapitalization	attaching a higher value to a corporation than the corporation's assets warrant, with the purpose of misleading investors
Pure Food Law	the Pure Food and Drug Act of 1906
Railroad Rate Law	a generic reference to laws regulating railroad rates, including the Hepburn Act of 1906
stock-jobbing	stock market speculation, with the intent of making quick rather than long-term profits
stock-watering	artificially inflating the value of stocks

wrong-doing by ascribing its results to the actions of those who have sought to put a stop to the wrong-doing. But if it were true that to cut out rottenness from the body politic meant a momentary check to an unhealthy seeming prosperity, I should not for one moment hesitate to put the knife to the corruption. On behalf of all our people, on behalf no less of the honest man of means than of the honest man who earns each day's livelihood by that day's sweat of his brow, it is necessary to insist upon honesty in business and politics alike, in all walks of life, in big things and in little things; upon just and fair dealing as between man and man.

THEODORE ROOSEVELT: AN AUTOBIOGRAPHY (1913)

Throughout the seven and a half years that I was President, I pursued without faltering one consistent foreign policy, a policy of genuine international good will and of consideration for the rights of others, and at the same time of steady preparedness. The weakest nations knew that they, no less than the strongest, were safe from insult and injury at our hands; and the strong and the weak alike also knew that we possessed both the will and the ability to guard ourselves from wrong or insult at the hands of any one....

In my own judgment the most important service that I rendered to peace was the voyage of the battle fleet round the world. I had become convinced that for many reasons it was essential that we should have it clearly understood, by our own people especially, but also by other peoples, that the Pacific was as much our home waters as the Atlantic, and that our fleet could and would at will pass from one to the other of the two great oceans. It seemed to me evident that such a voyage would greatly benefit the navy itself; would arouse popular interest in and enthusiasm for the navy; and would make foreign nations accept as a matter of course that our fleet should from time to time be gathered in the Pacific, just as from time to time it was gathered in the Atlantic, and that its presence in one ocean was no more to be accepted as a mark of hostility to any Asiatic power than its presence in the Atlantic was to be accepted as a mark of hostility to any European power....

My prime purpose was to impress the American people; and this purpose was fully achieved. The cruise did make a very deep impression abroad; boasting about what we have done does not impress foreign nations at all, except unfavorably, but positive achievement does; and the two American achievements that really impressed foreign peoples during the first dozen years of this century were the digging of the Panama Canal and the cruise of the battle fleet round the world. But the impression made on our own people was of far greater consequence. No single thing in the history of the new United States Navy has done as much to stimulate popular interest and belief in it as the world cruise....

I first directed the fleet, of sixteen battleships, to go round through the Straits of Magellan to San Francisco. From thence I ordered them to New Zealand and Australia, then to the Philippines, China and Japan, and home through Suez—they stopped in the Mediterranean to help the sufferers from the earthquake in Messina, by the way, and did this work as effectively as they had done all their other work....The coaling and other preparations were made in such excellent shape by the Department [of the Navy] that there was never a hitch, not so much as the delay of an hour, in keeping every appointment made.... The fleet practiced incessantly during the voyage, both with the guns and in battle tactics, and came home [in February 1909] a much more efficient fighting instrument than when it started [in December 1907].

Glossary

Messina	a city and province on Sicily, a large island south of Italy in the Mediterranean Sea, the site of a massive earthquake and tsunami on December 28, 1908
Straits of Magellan	a navigable sea route around the southern tip of South America

STATEMENTS PERTAINING TO CONSERVATION (1903–1916)

1903

First and foremost, you can never afford to forget for one moment what is the object of the forest policy. Primarily that object is not to preserve forests because they are beautiful—though that is good in itself—not to preserve them because they are refuges for the wild creatures of the wilderness—though that too is good in itself—but the primary object of the forest policy as of the land policy of the United States, is the making of prosperous homes, is part of the traditional policy of home-making of our country. Every other consideration comes as secondary. The whole effort of the government in dealing with the forests must be directed to this end, keeping in view the fact that it is not only necessary to start the homes as prosperous, but to keep them so. That is the way the forests have need to be kept. You can start a prosperous home by destroying the forest, but you do not keep it.

1903

In the Grand Canyon, Arizona has a natural wonder which, so far as I know, is in kind absolutely unparalleled throughout the rest of the world. I want to ask you to do one thing in connection with it in your own interest and in the interest of the country—to keep this great wonder of nature as it now is. …You can not improve on it. The ages have been at work on it, and man can only mar it. What you can do is to keep it for your children, your children's children, and for all who come after you, as one of the great sights which every American if he can travel at all should see. We have gotten past the stage, my fellow-citizens, when we are to be pardoned if we treat any part of our country as something to be skinned for two or three years for the use of the present generation, whether it is the forest, the water, the scenery. Whatever it is, handle it so that your children's children will get the benefit of it.

1907

The conservation of our natural resources and their proper use constitute the fundamental problem which underlies almost every other problem of our national life. Unless we maintain an adequate material basis for our civilization, we can not maintain the institutions in which we take so great and so just a pride; and to waste and destroy our natural resources means to undermine this material basis.

1908

We have become great because of the lavish use of our resources and we have just reason to be proud of our growth. But the time has come to inquire seriously what will happen when our forests are gone, when the coal, the iron, the oil, and the gas are exhausted, when the soils have been still further impoverished and washed into the streams, polluting the rivers, denuding the fields, and obstructing navigation….It is time for us now as a nation to exercise the same reasonable foresight in dealing with our great natural resources that would be shown by any prudent man in conserving and wisely using the property which contains the assurance of well-being for himself and his children.

1909

I desire to make grateful acknowledgment to the men, both in and out of the Government service, who have prepared the first inventory of our natural resources. They have made it possible for this Nation to take a great step forward. Their work is helping us to see that the greatest questions before us are not partisan questions, but questions upon which men of all parties and all shades of opinion may be united for the common good. Among such questions, on the material side, the conservation of natural resources stands first. It is the bottom round of the ladder on our upward progress toward a condition in which the Nation as a whole, and its citizens as individuals, will set national efficiency and the public welfare before personal profit.

The policy of conservation is perhaps the most typical example of the general policies which this Government has made peculiarly its own during the opening years of the present century. The function of our Government is to insure to all its citizens, now and hereafter, their rights to life, liberty and the pursuit of happiness. If we of this generation destroy the resources from which our children would otherwise derive their livelihood, we reduce the capacity of our land to support a population, and so either degrade the standard of living or deprive the coming generations of their right to life on this continent. If we allow great industrial organizations to exercise unregulated control of the means of production and the necessaries of life, we deprive the Americans of today and of the future of industrial liberty, a right no less precious and vital than political freedom. Industrial liberty was a fruit of political liberty, and in turn has become one of its chief supports, and exactly as we stand for political democracy so we must stand for industrial democracy.

1910

Of all the questions which can come before this nation, short of the actual preservation of its existence in a great war, there is none which compares in importance with the great central task of leaving this land even a better land for our descendants than it is for us, and training them into a better race to inhabit the land and pass it on. Conservation is a great moral issue, for it involves the patriotic duty of insuring the safety and continuance of the nation.

1916

As yet with the great majority of our most interesting and important wild birds and beasts the prime need is to protect them, not only by laws limiting the open season and the size of the individual bag, but especially by the creation of sanctuaries and refuges. And, while the work of the collector is still necessary, the work of the trained faunal naturalist, who is primarily an observer of the life histories of the wild things, is even more necessary. The progress made in the United States, of recent years, in creating and policing bird refuges, has been of capital importance.

SPEECH TO THE NEW YORK REPUBLICAN STATE CONVENTION (1918)

Americanism means that we are a nation. But it is no use to be a nation if the nation cannot defend itself, if its sons cannot and will not fight for its existence. The one task to which at this time we must all of us devote all our energies is to win this war and to win it now. We must speed up the war. We must insist upon absolute efficiency in our war activities. We must insist upon a peace conditioned upon the complete overthrow of Germany and the removal of all threat of German world dominion. We have across the seas a most gallant American army. The man is a poor American whose veins do not thrill with pride as he reads of the feats of our fighting men in France. Moreover, at last we have begun to send over enough soldiers to count for something real in the struggle. We have begun to give them some airplanes. As yet they only have what cannon we can get from the French, and we could get the army across at all only by the lavish use of British ships. But we have seemingly made a real start in ship production and airplane production at home, and we actually have several hundred thousand soldiers at the fighting front....

A very small degree of efficiency in handling the War Department would have meant that our army in France on January 1st would have far surpassed in size and equipment the army we have over there now in July. In such event the German drive would probably have been beaten back at once; exactly as if we had done our duty since the sinking of the *Lusitania* (which was the "Firing on Fort Sumter" of this war), and had prepared in advance, we would have put a couple of million men in the field a year ago; in which event Russia would never have broken, and the war would unquestionably have been over before this. Nine-tenths of wisdom consists in being wise in time.

It is too late to remedy the past. It is a case of spilled milk. But let us avoid spilling the milk in the same fashion in the future. Let us begin to prepare now so that we shall not next year be again apologizing for a shortage of troops, guns, ships and airplanes. For four years the English and French, and for over three years the Italians, have fought our battles, and we have only just begun to fight for ourselves. This is not right. We have a larger population and greater resources than Germany or than France and Great Britain taken together. We have played a poor part in the early stages of the world war. Let us make the finishing of the war an American task....

There must be no peace until Germany is beaten to her knees. To leave her with a strangle-hold on Russia, and, through her vassal allies, Austria, Bulgaria and Turkey, dominant in Central Europe and Asia Minor, would mean that she had won the war and taken a giant stride towards world dominion. Belgium must be reinstated and reimbursed; France must receive back Alsace and Lorraine; Turkey must be driven from Europe, Armenia made free, the Syrian Christians protected, and the Jews given Palestine. Italian-Austria must go to Italy and Roumanian-Hungary to Roumania. Moreover, we must raise against the German menace the sleeping sword of the Slavs of Central Europe; we must establish the great free commonwealth of the Poles, the Czecho-Slovaks and the Jugo-Slavs, and save the other submerged peoples who are their neighbors. Unless we do all this, unless we stand by all our Allies who have stood by us, we shall have failed in making the liberty of well-behaved civilized peoples secure, and we shall have shown that our announcement about making the world safe for democracy was an empty boast....

When we have closed the giant war we must then prepare for the giant tasks of peace. First and foremost we should act on Washington's advice, and in time of peace prepare against war, so that never again shall we be caught in such humiliating inability to defend ourselves and assert our rights as has been the case during the last four years....

The preparation for the tasks of peace must be in the interest of all our people, of those who dwell in the open country and of those who dwell in the cities; of all men who live honestly and toil with head or hand, and of all women just as much as of all men. Often there can be identity of function between men and women, generally there cannot be, but always there must be full equality of right. Women have the vote in this state. They should be given it at once in the nation at large. And in the councils of this state, and in the councils of our party, women should be admitted to their share of the direction on an exact equality with the men, and whenever it is wisely possible their judgment and directive power should be utilized in association with men rather than separately.

In our industrial activities, alike of farmer, wage worker and business man, our aim should be cooperation among ourselves, and control by the state to the degree necessary, but not beyond the degree necessary, in order to prevent tyranny and yet to encourage and reward individual excellence. Business men should be permitted to cooperate and combine, subject to such regulation and control by the Government as will prevent injustice and sharp dealing among themselves or towards their employees, or as regards outsiders and the general public. There should be no penalizing of business merely because of its size, although, of course, there is peculiar need of supervision of big business. Government ownership should be avoided wherever possible; our purpose should be to steer between the anarchy of unregulated individualism and the deadening formalism and inefficiency of widespread state ownership. From time to time it has been found and will be found necessary for the Government to own and run certain businesses, the uninterrupted prosecution of which is necessary to the public welfare and which cannot be adequately controlled in any other way, but normally this is as inadvisable as to permit such business concerns to be free from all Government supervision and direction.... Profiteering out of the war should be stopped, but it is mere common sense to say that proper profit making should be encouraged, for unless there is a profit the business cannot run, labor cannot be paid, and neither the public nor the Government can be served. And the misery in which this country was plunged before our business was artificially stimulated by the outbreak of the world war shows the need of a protective tariff.

Labor likewise should have full right to cooperate and combine, full right to collective bargaining and collective action; subject always, as in the case of capital, to the paramount general interest of the public, of the commonwealth; and the prime feature of this paramount general interest is that each man shall do justice and shall receive justice. Hereafter in a very real sense labor should be treated, both as regards conditions of work and conditions of reward, as a partner in the enterprises in which it is associated; housing and living conditions must be favorable; effort must be made to see that the work is interesting, there must be insurance against old age, sickness and involuntary unemployment; and a share in the money reward for increased business success, whether it comes from efficiency shown in speeding up or from labor-saving machinery or from any other cause. And on the other side there must be no restriction of output, no levelling down, no failure by the man to exert his full powers, and to receive the full reward to which his individual excellence entitles him; and no failure to recognize that unless there is a proper reward for the capital invested and for the management provided, absolute industrial disaster will result to every human being in this country.

The welfare of the farmer stands as the bedrock welfare of the entire commonwealth. Hitherto he has not received the full share of industrial reward and benefit to which he is entitled. He can receive it only as the result of organization and cooperation.... The state can wisely supplement such work of cooperation, but most of such work it cannot with wisdom itself undertake.

These, in brief outline, are the tasks of rebuilding and upbuilding which are before us when peace comes. But the prime needs now are the needs of war. We must insist that this whole country be unified, nationalized, Americanized, and that no division of our American loyalty and American citizenship along the lines of national origin or of adherence to an alien flag be for one instant tolerated. We must insist upon speeding up the war, so that our giant strength may be fully utilized, and next year our armies overseas at least equal in the aggregate to the German armies. We must refuse any peace except the peace of overwhelming victory, a peace which will guarantee us against the threat of German world dominion by securing to every well-behaved civilized power its real and complete freedom.

Glossary

Alsace and Lorraine	regions along the border of France and Germany
Asia Minor	a region in western Asia made up primarily of modern-day Turkey
Firing on Fort Sumter	the first hostilities of the U.S. Civil War, when Confederate ships fired on the Union fort in South Carolina
Lusitania	a British ocean liner sunk by a German submarine in May 1915

JOHN ROSS.

A CHEROKEE CHIEF.

PUBLISHED BY DANIEL RICE & JAMES G. CLARK, PHILAD.ᵃ
Drawn, Printed & Coloured at the Lithographic & Print Colouring Establishment, 94 Walnut St.
Entered according to act of Congress in the Year 1843 by James G. Clark in the Clerks office of the District Court of the Eastern District of Pennsyᵃ

John Ross (Library of Congress)

JOHN ROSS   1790–1866

Chief of the Cherokee Nation

Featured Documents
◆ Memorial to Congress (1829)
◆ Letter to David Crockett (1831)
◆ Annual Message to the Cherokee Nation (1832)
◆ Letter to Martin Van Buren (1837)
◆ Address to the Cherokee Nation (1838)
◆ Address to a General Council of the Cherokee Nation (1839)

Overview

John Ross was born along the Coosa River in present-day Alabama on October 3, 1790. Ross was a Cherokee by virtue of his descent from his Cherokee grandmother. His maternal side of the family introduced him to Cherokee culture, and his father, a trader from Scotland, ensured that he received a formal education. By the time he was a young man, John Ross was comfortable in both the Cherokee and Anglo-American worlds and was prepared to assume a leadership role in his tribe. He became a successful planter and businessman, establishing a trading post and ferry service with his brother, Lewis. After fighting on the side of Andrew Jackson's army in the Creek Civil War (1813–1814)—a conflict between traditionalist Creek who resisted American encroachment into their territory and more accomodationist Creek who wanted to adopt aspects of Anglo-American culture and maintain peaceful relations—Ross assumed the responsibilities of clerk to the Cherokee chief Pathkiller. He was elected to the Cherokee national council in 1817 and from 1818 to 1827 presided over the committee that handled the nation's day-to-day affairs. Ross became principal chief pro tem upon Pathkiller's death in 1827. That same year he was elected to the committee that drafted the Cherokee national constitution. In 1828 the Cherokee elected Ross as their first principal chief under the new constitution, a position he held until his death in 1866.

Ross held the Cherokee Nation together through its greatest crisis, the expulsion of the tribe from its homeland in the Southeast. In the 1820s politicians in Georgia began demanding that the Cherokee leave the state. For the next ten years Ross fiercely opposed the United States' efforts to appease Georgia and remove the Cherokee. In the early 1830s he supervised a legal challenge to Georgia's trespasses on Cherokee sovereignty. In December 1835 the leaders of a dissident faction (often called the Treaty Party) negotiated the Treaty of New Echota, which required the Cherokee to depart for the West in two years. Ross unsuccessfully lobbied Congress and the president to reject the treaty, which was signed by only a small minority of the tribe and without the consent of the Cherokee government. Ross was never able to persuade the U.S. government to change its

course on removal, and in 1838 he left with his nation for new Cherokee lands in the Indian Territory, in what is now northeastern Oklahoma. A quarter to a half of the Cherokee population, including Ross's first wife, died as a direct consequence of their removal. The relocation was so devastating to the Cherokee that in the latter years of the nineteenth century it came to be known as the Trail of Tears.

Once in Indian Territory, Ross was reelected chief of the reconstituted Cherokee Nation and oversaw the enactment of a new constitution. In the 1840s and 1850s he led them through a political reunification of competing factions and an economic and social renascence, as they rebuilt schools, churches, and businesses. The American Civil War, however, ended the brief period of prosperity. At the war's outbreak in 1861, the Cherokee Nation signed a treaty of alliance with the Confederacy. Ross had tried to keep the Cherokee neutral in the conflict, but he was unable to persuade the rest of the government to his side. The war brought a Union invasion into the Cherokee Nation, which again prompted civil conflict among the Cherokee and produced widespread death and property destruction. In 1862 Ross abandoned the Confederate alliance, affiliated with the Union, and traveled to Washington, D.C., to try to protect Cherokee interests with the U.S. government. He remained in Washington for the duration of the war and died there on August 1, 1866.

Explanation and Analysis of Documents

The documents chosen for inclusion here represent a series of speeches and personal communications that Chief John Ross authored as he guided the Cherokee Nation through the removal crisis. They reveal much about Ross's personality and political tactics, showing him to have been an optimistic pragmatist and a skilled politician. He was an ardent advocate for his nation and a reassuring but candid communicator to his citizens.

His memorial to the U.S. Congress and a letter to Congressman David ("Davy") Crockett demonstrate how Ross used his rhetorical and political skills to try to forestall the removal of the Cherokee. His 1832 annual message to the Cherokee reveals how Ross kept his constituents informed

Time Line

1790
- **October 3**
  John Ross is born along the Coosa River in present-day Alabama.

1813–1814
- Ross fights with Andrew Jackson's forces during the Creek Civil War.

1817
- Ross is elected to the newly formed Cherokee national council, the nation's legislature.

1827
- Ross becomes principal chief pro tem of the Cherokee Nation and presides over its first constitutional convention.

1828
- Ross is elected principal chief of the Cherokee Nation.

1829
- **February 27**
  Ross delivers a memorial to Congress, pleading that the federal government intervene in the attempts of the Georgia legislature to extend its jurisdiction over the Cherokee Nation.

1830–1832
- Ross supervises legal proceedings for the nation against the state of Georgia.

1831
- **January 13**
  Ross writes an impassioned letter of appreciation to David Crockett, who had voted against the 1830 Indian Removal Act.

1832
- In *Worcester v. Georgia* the U.S. Supreme Court declares that the Cherokee Nation is a distinct political and sovereign community and that Georgia's extension laws are illegal and unconstitutional.

of national developments during the crisis. In the fourth document, a letter to the new president, Martin Van Buren, Ross tries once more to turn the United States away from its plans to remove the Cherokee. In his 1838 address to the Cherokee, Ross consoles his citizens after most of them had been rounded up by federal troops and placed in internment camps in preparation for their relocation to the West. In his 1839 address to the general council, Ross calls on the Cherokee people to reunify in their new home in the Indian Territory and rebuild their nation.

◆ **Memorial to Congress**

In the late 1780s the U.S. government developed a national Indian relations policy that was designed to bring order to the nation's frontier, promote peace with the Indian tribes, and provide for an orderly expansion into the West. George Washington, the first president, and Henry Knox, his secretary of war, decided to treat the Indian tribes as sovereign nations, deal with them through the mechanism of diplomatic treaties, and pay them for their lands. The two leaders also offered a plan to prepare Native Americans for integration into American society. Under the plan, the United States would teach Native Americans how to farm, speak, live, and worship like Anglo-Americans. Once converted to the Anglo-American life of yeoman farming, Knox theorized, Indians would no longer need all of the lands that they had heretofore used as hunting grounds. The United States could then buy these lands and distribute them to American citizens. As the frontier moved west and as the United States acquired Indian land, American Indians would be engulfed, assimilated, and disappear into the fabric of white society.

Washington and Knox, however, underestimated how fast the U.S. population would grow, how desperate individual Americans would become for their own lands in the west, and how uninterested citizens would be in living with and among Native Americans. The two leaders also failed to understand that most Indians would have little interest in abandoning their traditional culture. Sensing that the plan for Indian assimilation was going to take much longer than originally expected, around 1803 President Thomas Jefferson developed another plan: The government would persuade tribes to move across the Mississippi River to the Louisiana Territory that his administration had just purchased from France. In the distant west, Jefferson surmised, Indians would have more time to prepare for their eventual assimilation. The year before the Lousiana Purchase, Jefferson's government had negotiated the Compact of 1802. In the compact, Georgia surrendered its claims to its western lands (territory that eventually comprised Alabama and Mississippi) in exchange for a promise from the federal government that it would extinguish the land titles of the Cherokee and Creek as soon as it could be managed peacefully and on a reasonable basis. In the 1820s Georgia began demanding that the federal government complete the compact and remove the two tribes from the state. Presidents James Monroe and John Quincy Adams agreed with the general idea of removing the tribes to the Louisiana Territory but insisted that the Indians consent to any relocation. The Creek relented in 1826 in the Treaty of Washington and departed from the state, but the Cherokee refused to submit.

The Cherokee, for their part, believed that they had satisfied the U.S. government's call to become "civilized." They had adopted a constitutional form of republican government that included a bicameral legislature, a chief executive (the principal chief), a judicial system with an appellate court, and a written code of laws. They had developed their own syllabary, which they used to write and publish a newspaper, and had established schools and Christian churches. Many Cherokee had developed prosperous businesses and farms. The Cherokee, however, refused to accede to Georgia's demands that they surrender their land and leave the state. Cherokee leaders consistently maintained that the Cherokee people were a sovereign nation. In the eighteenth century they had relinquished much of their once-vast territory to Great Britain. After the American Revolutionary War, they had ceded a number of large parcels to the United States. By the early 1820s the Cherokee government was adamant that it would never again give up any of its territory. By this time, young John Ross had emerged as an influential force in Cherokee politics and a vocal leader for the nation in its opposition to land cessions and removal.

The Cherokee's insistence that they were a sovereign nation holding complete title to their national territory antagonized pro-removal advocates in Georgia. The Georgia legislature, frustrated with federal inaction, took matters into its own hands when, in 1827, it passed a law annexing Cherokee territory into existing Georgian counties. In 1828 it passed another law that extended its legal jurisdiction over the Cherokee people and purported to abolish the Cherokee's government, laws, and courts. That same year, John Ross was elected principal chief of the Cherokee Nation. In an 1829 memorial, Ross, writing on behalf of the Cherokee leadership, appealed to Congress to protect his nation from Georgia's attacks.

Ross was an artful debater, and he used several tactics to try to persuade congressmen to his view. First, he appeals to the legislators' sense of justice. Ross describes Georgia's extension legislation, explains how it encroaches upon the sovereignty of the Cherokee Nation, and pleads for Congress to intervene on behalf of the Cherokee. Ross states that their nation had always respected the provisions of the treaties it had signed with the United States and had met American demands with "repeated cession of lands, until no more can be reasonably spared." He criticizes Georgia for trying to impose its will on a "weak, defenceless, and innocent nation of people" and for requiring the Cherokee to call upon the United States to come to its aid. Later in the memorial, he thanks the Congress for encouraging the Cherokee to become a civilized people, notes how much progress they had made on the road to civilization, and then suggests how unfair it would be for the United States to remove them after they had been so successful in their transformation. He points out that the Cherokee had

Time Line

1832
■ **October 10**
Ross delivers his annual message to the Cherokee people, exhorting them to remain unified in the face of increasing encroachments on the sovereignty of their nation.

1835
■ **December 29**
A dissident faction of Cherokee signs the Treaty of New Echota, which commits the Cherokee to remove from their homeland within two years.

1836
■ Ross bitterly opposes the Treaty of New Echota, which is ratified by the U.S. Senate on May 23.

1836–1838
■ Ross lobbies the U.S. government to overturn the Treaty of New Echota.

1837
■ **March 16**
Ross pleads in a letter to the new president, Martin Van Buren, to cancel the government's plan for the removal of the Cherokee.

1838
■ **Summer**
U.S. troops round up the Cherokee and march them to internment stockades.

■ **July 21**
In an address to the Cherokee Nation, Ross attempts to console his people and ready them for the coming journey to Oklahoma.

■ **Fall**
Detachments of Cherokee, supervised by the Cherokee government, begin departing on the approximately eight-hundred-mile journey to the Indian Territory; along the way four thousand to eight thousand Cherokee die.

1839
■ **June 10**
After arriving in Oklahoma, Ross addresses the disparate factions of Cherokee and pleads for unity.

Time Line

1861
- While Ross believes that the Cherokee should remain unaligned in the Civil War, support for the South by many members of the nation leads to an alliance with the Confederacy.

1862
- Union forces invade the Cherokee Nation, leading Ross to flee first to Philadelphia and then to Washington, D.C. He formally denounces the Confederacy.

1866
- Ross attempts to negotiate a treaty with the United States to solidify relations following the Civil War.

- **August 1**
  Ross dies in Washington, D.C., days after the treaty is ratified.

not been a party to the Compact of 1802 and contends that they should not be forced to suffer the consequences of an agreement to which they were not a party.

Ross's memorial is also defiant. He asserts that the Cherokee rejected the plans for removal and ridicules the claim that a relocation west of the Mississippi would benefit the Indians. The Cherokee, Ross writes, wanted to remain where they were, in a place where they were prosperous and happy. The chief declares that "the right of regulating our own internal affairs is a right which we have inherited from the Author of our existence, which we have always exercised, and have never surrendered." Ross understood that antagonistic feelings on the part of the Cherokee would undermine any chance of compromise, and he typically put the best light on the Cherokee's adversaries and publicly gave them the benefit of the doubt in their intentions. Despite all that the Georgia leadership had done to the Cherokee up to this point, Ross said that he did not doubt "the virtue and magnanimity of the People of Georgia."

◆ Letter to David Crockett

By 1829 Andrew Jackson, who had been a proponent of Indian removal for over a decade, had been elected president of the United States. During his campaign, Jackson had spoken forcefully for the removal of the Cherokee. With this powerful ally now established in the White House, emboldened Georgia legislators continued their efforts to drive the Cherokee out of the state by ordering a survey of Cherokee lands that would be used to distribute them by lottery to white Georgians. In May 1830, Jackson's allies in the U.S. Congress passed the Indian Removal Act, which gave the president the authority to negotiate treaties in which a tribe would surrender its homeland in the east for new territory west of the Mississippi River. Congress also appropriated $500,000 to fund the removal of all of the eastern tribes. John Ross had lobbied vigorously against the Indian Removal Act of 1830; in an 1831 letter he thanked Tennessee Congressman David Crockett for his opposition to the bill.

Ross's private letter to Crockett was quite distinct from his public statements, for it was filled with Christian apocalyptic references, language that perhaps offers insight into the chief's spiritual views. After praising Crockett's courage in voting against the removal bill, Ross condemns the proponents of removal and declares that "the day of retributive justice must and will come." He then tells Crockett, "This Nation owes a debt of gratitude which the pages of history will bear record of until time shall be no more—and for which they will receive a just reward in the Courts of Heaven." Whether the Cherokee would be saved from removal, Ross writes, "is for the wisdom, magnanimity, & justice of the United States to determine." At the end of his letter, Ross expresses his incredulity that President Jackson would abandon the Cherokee and ignore the treaties that required the United States to protect them from Georgia's trespasses. The chief reminds Crockett that he knew Jackson from their joint service in the Creek Civil War. Perhaps, aware that Crockett and Jackson knew each other, Ross may have hoped that his last defiant words in the letter—"And whatever may be the final result of our present difficulties and troubles, we are prepared to meet it—but never to remove West of the Mississippi"—would reach Jackson.

◆ Annual Message to the Cherokee Nation

When Ross's lobbying efforts failed to prevent the Indian Removal Act from becoming law, he turned his attention to repelling Georgia's encroachments on Cherokee sovereignty. After attempts at negotiation were unsuccessful, he engineered a Cherokee suit against the state of Georgia, alleging that its extension laws violated Cherokee rights as a sovereign nation and unconstitutionally interfered with the treaty relationship between the Cherokee Nation and the United States. After the U.S. Supreme Court refused to accept jurisdiction over the issue in *Cherokee Nation v. Georgia* (1831), Ross searched for a way to get a case before the Court.

Georgia provided them with the opportunity when it arrested Samuel Worcester and several other missionaries in the fall of 1831. A year earlier the state had passed a law prohibiting white people from entering the Cherokee Nation without the permission of the governor. The law, which required non-Indians to swear allegiance to the state, was designed to keep white missionaries from assisting the Cherokee in their resistance campaign. In September, Georgia arrested several missionaries for unlawfully living in Cherokee territory. Among them was Worcester, a missionary from New England who had been advising Cherokee leaders on their opposition to removal. The state convicted Worcester and sentenced him to four years of hard labor in the state prison. Worcester appealed the conviction, and in the resulting case, *Worcester v. Georgia* (1832), the Supreme Court ruled that the Cherokee were a sovereign nation and that Georgia's extension laws were unconstitutional.

The decision, however revolutionary, was without effect. Georgia refused to recognize it, and President Jackson and Congress did nothing to see it enforced. Georgia's surveying of Cherokee land continued in earnest, and in the fall of 1832 the governor of Georgia initiated the lottery to distribute Cherokee land lots to white people. Since Georgia had abolished the Cherokee Nation's government, the nation had been required to move its operations and meetings outside the state's putative borders. On October 10, 1832, the Cherokee people convened in council in the small community of Red Clay. In his address to the Cherokee Nation, Ross first reviews what the Cherokee government had done in the preceding months. The government had moved to keep operating, despite the fact that Georgia was preventing the Cherokee from holding elections, and had achieved a stunning legal triumph in *Worcester*. Ross then describes how conditions for the Cherokee had changed since Andrew Jackson came into office as president. He recalls how President James Monroe had contemplated the conundrum raised by the Compact of 1802 and had declared that there was no obligation in that agreement to require the United States to remove the Cherokee without their consent. Ross notes sadly that with Jackson's election the United States had abandoned its responsibility to recognize and protect the treaty rights of the Cherokee and that Congress had passed legislation, the Indian Removal Act of 1830, to bring about their relocation.

Ross then attempts to maintain a unified opposition to relocation, even though he knew that other Cherokee leaders were contemplating signing a removal treaty. He warns his nation that relocation would destroy their right to exist as a free and sovereign nation and predicts that its relations with the United States would be "dissolved." The chief also attempts to alert the Cherokee to the conditions that they would face if they removed to the West. The Cherokee would not be secure in their own territory, he says, which was "badly watered and only skirted on the margin of water courses." Ross also notes that the United States would force some fifteen to twenty different tribes, speaking distinct languages, to integrate into one nation. They would be governed, he adds, "by no doubt, white rulers." Ross adds that the Cherokee would not feel at home among these peoples who were "cherishing a variety of habits and customs, a portion civilized, another half civilized and others uncivilized." He declares that the United States had not been forthcoming on its plans for the tribes in the Indian Territory and says that he fears that "there is no safety for this nation" if it abandons its homeland and relocates.

In his conclusion Ross calls for the Cherokee to "remain united in the support of our common interests & national rights," resting their confidence in "the justice of our cause and the righteous decision of the Supreme Court of the

U.S. upon it." He tells the Cherokee to trust "in the constitutional power of the government" to execute the Court's decision. Ross closes by encouraging the Cherokee people to place their faith in the "virtue of the people of the U. States" and "the guidance of a Benignant Providence" to see that the U.S. government would find the will to respect the treaties it had signed with the Cherokee Nation.

◆ Letter to Martin Van Buren

The pressures brought to bear by the Jackson administration to sign a removal treaty prompted internal stress in the Cherokee Nation. The refusal of Georgia to follow the *Worcester* edict and the unwillingness of Jackson or Congress to come to their aid ultimately factionalized the Cherokee. Bitter divisions formed between those, such as Ross, who wanted to continue the opposition to removal and those who were beginning to argue that only relocation to the West would ensure the survival of the nation. Ross remained a powerful advocate against removal despite the fact that Georgia seized his plantation and turned it over to whites in its land lottery.

Almost all of the Cherokee had opposed removal until 1832. However, the federal government's refusal to enforce *Worcester* persuaded a small but influential group that continued resistance was futile. Those favoring removal, who became known as the "Treaty Party," met in the Cherokee capital of New Echota. They were led by Major Ridge, an elder statesman of the Cherokee; his son John Ridge; and his nephew, Elias Boudinot, the editor of the *Cherokee Phoenix*. Major Ridge had long been an advocate of remaining in Georgia, but he shifted his position following a meeting with President Jackson, who told him that the Cherokee people had no choice but to leave. On December 29, 1835, Major Ridge and his followers signed the Treaty of New Echota with the federal agent John Schermerhorn. The agreement required the Cherokee to surrender their homeland in the Southeast in exchange for new lands in the western Indian Territory. The federal government also promised to pay the Cherokee $5 million and to reimburse them for the improvements they lost as a result of their relocation. The government also agreed to pay the costs of immigration and one year's provisions to lay in crops and acclimate to their new home.

On March 16, 1837, Ross wrote a letter on behalf of the Cherokee leadership vigorously pressing the new president, Martin Van Buren, to overturn the treaty. He congratulates Van Buren on his election and then astutely appeals, as he often did in his official correspondence, to the president's sense of honor. He writes that he knew that the United States, a Christian nation once led by men such as Washington and Jefferson, would never intentionally harm the Cherokee. The chief then moves directly to his request to have the new president reconsider the Treaty of New Echota. He reports that those who signed the agreement at New Echota did not represent the Cherokee Nation and asserts that nine-tenths of the Cherokee people opposed the treaty. (The following year he supported his claim by presenting a petition protesting the treaty signed by sixteen thousand

Cherokee.) At the most, Ross argues, only seven hundred Cherokee had attended the New Echota council; of those, only seventy-nine had agreed with the treaty. The United States had ignored the will of the vast majority of the Cherokee people and its recognized representatives and had completed an agreement with a dissident minority.

Ross also points out that the Cherokee government never authorized the agreement or the delegation that negotiated it. Ross explains how the treaty had been drafted while the formal representatives of the Cherokee Nation were in Washington trying to meet with President Andrew Jackson. In the letter, Ross strongly implies that Jackson and other government officials participated in a subterfuge to avoid dealing with the true representatives of the Cherokee Nation. The Cherokee government "never authorized the formation of this spurious Compact," he writes, and he calls on Van Buren to investigate the conditions under which the treaty was negotiated.

The federal commissioners who had negotiated the treaty, Ross adds, had also violated the instructions given to them by the secretary of war, Lewis Cass. According to Ross, the federal government had ordered the treaty commissioners to secure the agreement of a *majority* of "headmen and warriors" and that the final decision on the treaty was to be considered "by the people themselves in open Council." Ross asks rhetorically if the United States would acknowledge a treaty signed by "any twenty citizens of the United States, holding no public station, authorized by no national act," which had the effect of "stripping every citizen of his home and of his property."

Ross explains that the Cherokee government had not ratified the agreement, nor had they even considered it as a nation, for "a large body of troops has been stationed in the Cherokee Nation, prepared to put down any meeting convened to deliberate upon the subject." Cherokee citizens who opposed the treaty had been arrested, Ross reports, and John Wool, the commander of the American forces sent into the Cherokee Nation, had threatened the leaders if they tried to determine how many of their people opposed the treaty. In his closing paragraphs, Ross makes a promise to Van Buren. He tells him that if a federal investigation fails to agree with the facts regarding the treaty as he had presented them, then "we shall no longer ask you to delay exercising your power in the enforcement of your rights." "Our fate is in your hands," Ross concludes. "May the God of truth tear away every disguise and concealment from our case—may the God of justice guide your determination and the God of mercy stay the hand of our brother uplifted for our destruction."

◆ Address to the Cherokee Nation

The Treaty of New Echota had provided that the Cherokee would have two years from the date of its ratification by the U.S. Senate to remove to Indian Territory. During that time Ross begged, pleaded, and lobbied the U.S. government to reconsider the treaty and to delay or cancel the relocation. By the spring of 1838 the time had passed for the Cherokee to remove, and the United States had lost its

patience. While Ross was in Washington advocating for delay, President Van Buren sent the U.S. Army into the Cherokee Nation with orders to round up the Cherokee and prepare them for relocation. The army, supported by volunteers from the neighboring southern states, combed the southern countryside gathering up people; soldiers took by force those who refused to go and marched them to the internment camps. Almost all of the Cherokee, perhaps as many as sixteen hundred, were housed in squalid, hastily built stockades. Over a brutally hot summer, hundreds died from exposure and from dysentery, cholera, and other diseases. Hundreds more died as they were being transported by boat to the West.

Deeply disheartened by these events, Ross returned to the Cherokee Nation in July and addressed his people from Camp Aquohee, one of the internment stockades. He tells them that the Cherokee government had done all within its power to change the United States' course of action but that "when the strong arm of power is raised against the weak and defenseless, the force of argument must fail." He reports that he has persuaded General Winfield Scott, who was ordered by Van Buren to complete the removal of the Cherokee, to postpone their departure until fall, when the weather would be "more propitious." In the address, Ross tries to calm his people, who have been angered and demoralized by their capture and internment. He praises them for the way they have accepted their fate, calls upon them to comply with the removal peacefully, and attempts to reassure them that they will be provided for on their journey to the West. He empathizes with the plight in which the Cherokee found themselves, "encamped in the forests along the sylvan brooks where you once gathered your flock of sheep and herds of cattle." "Here," Ross laments, "homeless and outcasts, we are only for a short space to be permitted to taking a passing view of the houses and farms we once inhabited & cultivated & the places in which we happily worshiped Almighty God."

◆ Address to a General Council of the Cherokee Nation

Early detachments of Cherokee suffered horrible losses as they were forced onto boats by the army for their journey to the West. Ross went to Scott and begged him to allow the Cherokee to supervise their own removal. Scott agreed. The Cherokee thus migrated to the West as a nation; they were not, as some histories declare, forcibly marched by the U.S. Army to the Indian Territory. Clearly, Scott's decision to allow the Cherokee to superintend their own removal reduced the loss of life brought on by the exodus. Still, their incarceration in the stockades and their journey to the Indian Territory through the brutal winter of 1838–1839 resulted in the deaths of an estimated one-quarter to one-half of the Cherokee population.

The end of the journey did not bring peace for the Cherokee. First, Ross had to try to heal the divisions created by the Treaty of New Echota and the removal. In addition, he had to find some way to unite the newly arrived Cherokee with the "Old Setters," the Cherokee and their descendants who had relocated to the West in the early years of the nineteenth century. In this address to the Cherokee people, Ross declares their community to be strong and intact. He also reaches out to the Old Settlers, who were concerned that their political voice would be overwhelmed by those of the nationally famous chief and the thousands of Cherokee who had just arrived. Ross promised that although the new arrivals vastly outnumbered the Old Settlers, all Cherokee would be treated equally and would possess the same rights and privileges. In closing, Ross refers to the words of Jesus that Abraham Lincoln would adopt so effectively in his "House Divided" speech some twenty years later: "A House divided against itself cannot stand."

Just twelve days after his address, assailants brutally killed Major Ridge, John Ridge, and Elias Boudinot. When Major Ridge had signed the Treaty of New Echota, he reportedly commented that he was signing his death warrant. In fact, the Cherokee Nation had in the 1820s passed a law providing for death for any Cherokee who sold land without the consent of the Cherokee government. Members of the Treaty Party accused Ross's supporters of murdering the three men; Ross's followers contended that the victims were only receiving their just punishment under Cherokee law. The attacks on the Treaty Party leaders set off a long period of vendetta killings between the two factions that ended only after the United States brokered a peace in 1846. After the settlement of this internal strife, Ross led the Cherokee Nation into a period of renewal and prosperity. Unfortunately for the Cherokee, however, this renaissance ended when they were pulled into the Civil War.

Impact and Legacy

The fact that John Ross was reelected time and time again and served as principal chief for almost forty years is a testament to his political sagacity. Ross led his people through a national calamity with determination and a sense of reassuring grace. It is difficult to imagine anything short of declaring outright war that Ross could have done to forestall removal any longer. His exertions in Washington—lobbying federal officials to come to the aid of the Cherokee, preparing memorials of protest, and drafting letters to such congressmen as Davy Crockett—almost achieved his purpose of persuading the United States to reconsider its treaty commitments to the Cherokee. The House of Representatives approved the Indian Removal Act of 1830 by a mere five votes. Certainly, Ross's arguments against removal and his pronouncements praising the progress of the Cherokee people had a role in fomenting the congressional opposition that almost defeated the bill.

Although he fought removal to the bitter end, when the inevitable time for departure for the West drew near, Ross was able to transform his rhetoric. After years of combative jousting with Congress, presidents Jackson and Van Buren, and the state of Georgia, Ross understood that he had to reassure the Cherokee people in the face of the catastrophe that was upon them. When U.S. troops came to the doors

of Cherokee households and took them away to internment stockades, Ross came home to the nation to fortify his people in their time of greatest distress. When he persuaded Winfield Scott to allow the Cherokee Nation to supervise its own relocation, he transformed removal from an unmitigated catastrophe into a moment of national pride. Still today, Cherokee in Oklahoma comment on the fact that their ancestors were able to relocate as a united nation and not as individuals walking at the point of a federal bayonet. Once in Indian Territory, Ross was, to use a word that he favored, magnanimous in dealing with the Old Settlers and the Treaty Party. He wanted to be chief of all of the Cherokee, not just the majority that admired him and elected him over and over again, and his conscientious choice of unifying language certainly helped heal the bitter wounds caused by the removal.

Looking back at Ross's work and language during the removal crisis, one cannot help but note the chief's deep well of respect for the republican values of the United States, his self-effacing style, and his ability to flatter his opponents, all in the face of one of the worst tragedies an Indian leader can imagine—the sundering of the precious relationship between people and land. That he almost single-handedly forestalled the removal of the Cherokee, that he led them through the crisis without the nation splintering apart, and that he resurrected a unified nation in the West, are all testament to the remarkable leadership of John Ross.

Key Sources

The Papers of Chief John Ross were edited by Gary E. Moulton and published in a two-volume set in 1985. Volume 1 covers the period 1807–1839. Volume 2 includes papers from 1840 until Ross's death in 1866. Other Ross papers can be found at the Gilcrease Institute in Tulsa, Oklahoma; among the John Howard Payne Papers at the Newberry Library; among the William Wirt Papers at the Maryland Historical Society; and in the Georgia Department of Archives and the Tennessee State Library and Archives. Finally, Ross documents appear on microfilm in the records of the War Department maintained by the National Archives.

Further Reading

■ **Books**

Garrison, Tim Alan. *The Legal Ideology of Removal: The Southern Judiciary and the Sovereignty of Native American Nations.* Athens: University of Georgia Press, 2002.

McLoughlin, William G. *Cherokee Renascence in the New Republic.* Princeton, N.J.: Princeton University Press, 1992.

———. *After the Trail of Tears: The Cherokees' Struggle for Sovereignty, 1839–1880.* Chapel Hill: University of North Carolina Press, 1993.

"The right of regulating our own internal affairs is a right which we have inherited from the Author of our existence, which we have always exercised, and have never surrendered."

(Memorial to Congress)

"Cupidity and avarice by sophistry intrigue and corruption may for a while prevail—but, the day of retributive justice must and will come, when, integrity and moral worth will predominate and make the shameless monster hide its head. Whether this day will come in time to save the suffering Cherokees from violence and fraud, it is for the wisdom, magnanimity & justice of the United States to determine."

(Letter to David Crockett)

"By this act, every Indian tribe who may exchange for any of the districts of land set apart by the President under this law and who shall remove upon it, that moment its national character as a distinct community will cease, and its relations with the United States under former treaties as such, dissolved."

(Annual Message to the Cherokee Nation)

"In short the whole weight and influence of the government have been exerted, to aid the small faction which has usurped the right to bind us, to alarm the timid, to overpower the resolute, to persuade the confiding, to compel the weak among us, to give their sanction to this instrument."

(Letter to Martin Van Buren)

"Here, homeless and outcasts, we are only for a short space to be permitted to take a passing view of the houses and farms we once inhabited & cultivated & the places in which we happily worshiped Almighty God."

(Address to the Cherokee Nation)

"Let us kindle our social fire and take measures for cementing our reunion as a nation, by establishing the basis for a government suited to the condition and wants of the whole people; whereby, wholesome laws may be enacted and administered for the security and protection of property, life and other sacred rights, of the community."

(Address to a General Council of the Cherokee Nation)

Moulton, Gary E. *John Ross: Cherokee Chief.* Athens: University of Georgia Press, 1978.

Perdue, Theda, and Michael D. Green. *The Cherokee Nation and the Trail of Tears.* New York: Viking Adult, 2007.

Wilkins, Thurman. *Cherokee Tragedy: The Story of the Ridge Family and the Decimation of a People.* New York: Macmillan Press, 1970.

—Tim Alan Garrison and Kristin Teigen

Questions for Further Study

1. Discuss the broad outlines of U.S. government policy toward Native Americans, beginning with George Washington's generally tolerant attitude and continuing through the shift in position with the Jefferson administration and the Louisiana Purchase. Explain the differences between Washington's and Jefferson's approaches, along with the flaws in each. How did these changes in policy affect Ross, and how did he attempt to protect the sovereignty of the Cherokee nation with his 1829 memorial to Congress?

2. Examine the structure and history of the Cherokee nation as well as Ross's impact on its creation and survival. In what ways are the organization and government of the nation similar to that of the United States, and in what ways were they different? How does Ross, through the documents included here, make the case for the rights of the Cherokee to possess their own nation? How justified are the claims he and others made on behalf of the nation?

3. Compare and contrast Ross and another prominent Native American leader of the nineteenth century, Eli Parker. Consider, for instance, the ways in which both were heavily influenced by—indeed, one could say, products of—the culture and civilization established by white descendants of Europeans in America. How did this affect their language and their approach to dealing with the federal government? What successes did each enjoy in attempting to protect his people's rights, and how did each man deal with his inability to significantly sway American policy?

4. Discuss the subject of Indian removal as presented, on the one hand, by President Andrew Jackson in his 1830 annual message to Congress and, on the other hand, by Ross in his letters to David Crockett and Martin Van Buren. What justifications does each man use for his position? Who argues his case more convincingly? What did Ross do to minimize the hardships associated with removal once it came, and what more could he have done?

MEMORIAL TO CONGRESS (1829)

We, the undersigned, Representatives of the Cherokee nation, beg leave to present before your honorable bodies a subject of the deepest interest to our nation, as involving the most sacred rights and privileges of the Cherokee People. The Legislature of Georgia, during its late session, passed an act to add a large portion of our Territory to that State, and to extend her jurisdiction over the same, and declaring "all laws and usages, made and enforced in said Territory by the Indians, to be null and void after the first of June, 1830. No Indian, or descendent of an Indian, to be a competent witness, or a party to any suit to which a white man is a party." This act involves a question of great magnitude and of serious import, and which calls for the deliberation and decision of Congress. It is a question upon which the salvation and happiness or the misery and destruction of *a nation* depends, therefore it should not be trifled with. The anxious solicitude of Georgia to obtain our lands through the United States by treaty was known to us, and after having accommodated her desires (with that of other States bordering on our territory) by repeated cession of lands, until no more can be reasonably spared, it was not conceived, much less believed, that *a State*, proud of *Liberty*, and tenacious of the *rights of man*, would condescend to have placed herself before the world, in the imposing attitude of a usurper of the most sacred rights and privileges of a weak, defenceless, and innocent nation of people, who are in perfect peace with the United States, and to whom the faith of the United States is solemnly pledged to protect and defend them against the encroachments of their citizens.

In acknowledgment for the protection of the United States and the consideration of guaranteeing to our nation forever the security of our lands &c., the Cherokee nation ceded by treaty a large tract of country to the United States, and stipulated that the said Cherokee nation "will not hold any treaty with any *foreign power, individual State*, or with *individuals of any State*." These stipulations on our part have been faithfully observed, and ever shall be.

The right of regulating our own internal affairs is a right which we have inherited from the Author of our existence, which we have always exercised, and have never surrendered. Our nation had no voice in the formation of the Federal compact between the States; and if the United States have involved themselves by an agreement with Georgia relative to the purchase of our lands, and have failed to comply with it in the strictest letter of their compact, it is a matter to be adjusted between themselves; and on no principle of justice can an innocent people, who were in no way a party to that compact, be held responsible for its fulfilment; consequently they should not be oppressed, in direct violation of the solemn obligations pledged by treaties for their protection.

It is with pain and deep regret we have witnessed the various plans which have been advised within a few years past by some of the officers of the General Government, and the measures adopted by Congress in conformity to those plans, with the view of effecting the removal of our nation beyond the Mississippi, for the purpose, as has been expressed to promote our interest and permanent happiness, and save us from the impending fate which has swept others into oblivion....

We cannot but believe, that, if the same zeal and exertion were to be used by the General Government and the State of Georgia, to effect a mutual compromise in the adjustment of their compact, as [it] has been, and is now, using to effect our removal, it could be done to the satisfaction of the people of Georgia, and without any sacrifice to the United States. We should be wanting in liberal and charitable feelings were we to doubt the virtue and magnanimity of the People of Georgia, and we do believe that there are men in that State whose moral and religious worth stands forth inferior to none within the United States. Why, then, should the power that framed the Constitution of Georgia and made the compact with the United States be not exercised for the honor of the country and the peace, happiness, and preservation of a people, who were the original proprietors of a large portion of the country now in the possession of that State? And whose title to the soil they now occupy, is lost in the ages of antiquity, whose interests are becoming identified with those of the United States, and at whose call they are ever ready to obey in the hour of danger....

We cannot admit that Georgia has the right to extend her jurisdiction over our territory, nor are the Cherokee people prepared to submit to her persecuting edict. We would therefore respectfully and solemnly protest, in behalf of the Cherokee nation, before your honorable bodies, against the extension of the laws of Georgia over any part of our Territory, and appeal to the United States' Government for justice and protection. The great Washington advised a plan and afforded aid for the general improvement of our nation, in agriculture, science, and government. President Jefferson followed the noble example....

This kind and generous policy to meliorate our condition, has been blessed with the happiest results: our improvement has been without a parallel in the history of all Indian nations. Agriculture is every where pursued, and the interests of our citizens are permanent in the soil. We have enjoyed the blessings of Christian instruction; the advantages of education and merit are justly appreciated, a Government of regular law has been adopted, and the nation, under a continuance of the fostering care of the United States, will stand forth as a living testimony, that all Indian nations are not doomed to the fate which has swept many from the face of the earth. Under the parental protection of the United States, we have arrived at the present degree of improvement, and they are now to decide whether we shall continue as a people or be abandoned to destruction.

LETTER TO DAVID CROCKETT (1831)

It is gratifying to hear that your vote on the Indian Bill has given general satisfaction to your constituents—that it has or will produce for you among the friends of humanity & justice a just respect and admiration, I cannot doubt. Cupidity and avarice by sophistry intrigue and corruption may for a while prevail—but, the day of retributive justice must and will come, when, integrity and moral worth will predominate and make the shameless monster hide its head. Whether this day will come in time to save the suffering Cherokees from violence and fraud, it is for the wisdom, magnanimity & justice of the United States to determine. To those Gentlemen who have so honorably and ably vindicated the rights of the poor Indians in Congress at the last session, this Nation owes a debt of gratitude which the pages of history will bear record of until time shall be no more—and for which they will receive a just reward in the Courts of Heaven.... The Cherokees have borne with untiring fortitude and forbearance all those oppressive acts which Georgia have ungraciously heaped upon them, and they have escaped the serpentine movements made against them by her coadjutors. Still entertaining confidence in the justice and good faith of the United States, the Cherokees flatter themselves that the present Congress will do something definitively for the relief of their sufferings.... How the President of the U States [Andrew Jackson] can reconcile it to his feelings to withdraw from us the protection pledged by treaty, and to allow the state of Georgia to usurp from us the rights and liberties of freemen and to keep up a standing military force in our country and in time of profound peace too, I cannot understand. Such a manoeuvre under state authority exhibits a warlike movement and is calculated to distroy the peace and tranquility of our citizens, as there can be no doubt that it is repugnant to the Constitution, statutes and treaties of the United States. I have known Genl. Jackson from my boyhood—my earliest and warmest friends in Tennessee are generally his advocates—during the late war [1813–1814] I held a rank [lieutenant] in the Cherokee regiment & fought by his side—and so far as common sense will dictate to me that his measures are correct & just I should be among the last to oppose them—but it is with deep regret, I say, that his policy towards the aborigines, in my opinion, has been unrelenting and in effect ruinous to their best interests and happiness. And whatever may be the final result of our present difficulties and troubles, we are prepared to meet it—but never to remove West of the Mississippi upon lands within the limits of the U States. May health and happiness attend you. I am Sir very respectfully your obt. Servt.

Glossary

coadjutors	assistants or confederates
sophistry	ingenious but deceptive form of argument

ANNUAL MESSAGE TO THE CHEROKEE NATION (1832)

At your late extra session [in August] you deemed it impossible, for the people to hold the General elections in peace, agreeably to the mode prescribed by the Constitution, because, Georgia had placed her military in array against that system; consequently the subject was referred to a committee of the people from the several Districts, who devised and reported a plan, for keeping up the Government of the Nation, during the continuance of our present difficulties with that state, & which plan was accepted, and then referred to the people and by them adopted—so far, as I am informed, the necessity which dictated this scheme of expediency has been duly appreciated, and the measure will be received by the people, through out the several districts.

Wherever we scrutinize the acts of the United States Government towards Indians generally, and especially in reference to the nation, we cannot fail to see that those acts have been directed by systematic course of policy, adopted solely to promote the views, wishes and interests of the General or State governments—and, that these few acts of benevolence on the part of the United States for Indian improvement and civilization, have been adopted, only, from secondary considerations, and more, with the view to advance their own glory and national aggrandizement, than, to promote the true interest and permanent happiness of our race. I wish not to be misunderstood. I make no insinuation that such feeling has always existed in the controlment of the actions of the General Government towards Indians. There was a day, when better feeling directed the helm of Government—and in that day, justice stalked abroad in the land. The features of the numerous existing treaties between the United States and this nation plainly exhibits the ligament of our political connexion, and the stipulations contained in them, unequivocally recognize and acknowledge all the rights for which we have been contending, and by virtue of which, the Supreme Court has finally decided them in our favor. The time was, when the intellectual capacity and habitual propensities of the Indian to receive civil and religious instructions and to conform to the habits of civilized life, were openly repudiated as problematical and visionary—this formed the basis of argument for those who opposed the encouragement of Indian improvement. But no sooner than the surrounding States becoming coterminous with the locality of our nation, the intercourse between their citizens and ours increased with such rapidity as to produce a change in the habits of our people, which finally led to the establishment of schools in our country by individuals and benevolent societies; the great progress made in the improvement of the youth both in a moral and religious point of view soon dispelled all doubts in regard to the practibility of Indian civilization.

Thus by experimental demonstration the argument of the sceptic, has been prostrated, and the insinuating dissembler continued and brought to silence on this head. By the Treaty of 1819, Georgia discovered that the United States had so firmly acknowledged the rights of this nation, and so fully provided for its permanent security, and the final civilization of its citizens, and being moved by the spirit of cupidity and avarice she became extremely pressing in her applications to the Government of the United States, for the negotiations of a new treaty with this nation, for an additional cession of land for her benefit: and the Executive of the Union [James Monroe] being disposed and ever ready to meet the wishes of the State on this subject, commissioners were soon appointed for that object; but finding all overtures unavailing, Georgia became more restless and clamorous in her importunity and openly charged the General Government with the crime of having encouraged and facilitated the progress of Indian civilization, and thereby teaching this nation how to appreciate the value of our country and the consequent inability of the Government ever to purchase more lands from us. To this illiberal charge, Mr. Monroe the then President of the United States, in a message submitting the whole subject before Congress, very correctly responded, thus—"I have full confidence that my predecessors exerted their best endeavors to execute this compact (between the United States and the State of Georgia) in all its parts....I have also been animated, since I came into the office, with the same zeal. I have no hesitation, however, to declare it as my opinion, that the Indian title was not effected in the slightest circumstance by the compact with Georgia, and there is no obligation on the United States to remove the Indians by force. The express stipulation of the compact that their title should be extinguished at the expense of the United States, when it may be done *peaceable* and on *peaceable* conditions, is a full proof that it was the clear and distinct understanding of both parties to it, that the

Indians had a right to the territory, in the disposal of which they were to be regarded as free agents.... In the proceedings of the Executive branch of the General Government in reference to us since that period, it will be seen that they have run counter to their former treaty engagements with this nation, having for its object the general welfare and happiness of the Cherokee people in the permanent enjoyment of their national rights. And with the view of giving effect to this new fangled system of policy, for changing the existing relations established between the United States and the Indian nations under former treaties; and to make the system a general one, Congress under the auspices of President [Andrew] Jackson's administration passed a law entitled, *an act* "To provide for an exchange of lands with the Indians residing in any of the States or Territories, and for their removal west of the Mississippi."...

It will at once be seen that by this act, every Indian tribe who may exchange for any of the districts of land set apart by the President under this law and who shall remove upon it, that moment its national character as a distinct community will cease, and its relations with the United States under former treaties as such, dissolved. Here then is a country, in extent, agreeable to the report of the surveyor, six hundred miles long and two hundred miles wide, bordering on the States of Missouri and Territory of Arkansas spreading over an extensive prairie badly watered and only skirted on the margin of water courses and poor ridges with copses of wood, to be laid off into districts of various dimensions according to the contracts to be made with the several Tribes of Indians and to be assigned to and occupied by some fifteen or twenty different tribes, and all speaking different languages, and cherishing a variety of habits and customs, a portion civilized, another half civilized and others uncivilized, and these congregated tribes of Indians to be regulated under one General Government; by no doubt, white rulers—but whether Congress is to be employed in digesting a municipal code of laws for them, and in mending it from session to session or whether the President of the U. States, is to be sole legislator or whether the business is to be delegated to civil or military prefect, or placed under the diocess of "*the Indian Board*," we are not told. But of this it is certain, that the sovereign jurisdiction over the country is exclusively vested in the U. States and that Congress has not given the President any power to relinquish it, to the Indian Tribes or Nations—and should any tribe who have been located, ever become dissatisfied with its situation and remove therefrom, Congress can authorize it to be settled by citizens of any states— & by a late act of Congress three Commissioners have been appointed to locate the emigrants and to adjust the boundaries of the several tribes and other difficulties that exist between them, and the said Commissioners are also requited *to report to the War Department a plan for the government of the Indians*. ... I have thought proper ... to show that in the prosecution of the emigrating scheme the policy of the United States has never been fully developed by three agents to our people, and that there is no safety for this nation to change the relation it sustains towards the United States, under existing treaties and to adopt the new one by emigration. In the present state of things, you can do little more by legislation than to adopt such measures as will be calculated to keep our citizens correctly informed of the true posture of the public affairs, that they may remain united in the support of our common interests & national rights—also securing the administration of justice between individuals in their private transactions so far as it may be practicable to do so. Confiding in the justice of our cause and the righteous decision of the Supreme Court of the U.S. upon it, and also in the constitutional power of the Federal Government to have it executed—we cannot but hope that the virtue of the people of the U. States will ultimately controul the faithful execution of their treaty, obligations for our national protection and under this reliance let us still patiently endure our oppressions and place our trust under the guidance of a Benignant Providence.

Glossary

benignant	benign, kind
coterminous	equal in extent
diocess	variant spelling of *diocese*, here meaning territorial jurisdiction
Treaty of 1819	treaty between the United States and the Cherokee Nation signed on February 27 of that year

LETTER TO MARTIN VAN BUREN (1837)

Washington City March l6th 1837

Sir

The people constituting the Cherokee Nation beg leave to congratulate you on your accession to the lofty and dignified situation which you have been called upon by your Countrymen to fill. That this event may prove under the blessing of Providence equally beneficial to those over whom you now preside, as honorable to the Individual upon whom so valued a trust has been reposed, is our most earnest and sincere prayer.

Among those who have been placed under your protecting influences may we not be permitted to number ourselves, and may we not be allowed after the manner of our fathers to address the President of the Union as their guardian and their friend, as holding in his hands the equal scales of justice and the power to enforce his decisions?

It is in this character that the Cherokee Nation venture to approach the Executive to ask for a hearing, that their claims be investigated and that such measure of justice be meted to them as shall appear to be due. Beyond this they have nothing to ask, within these limits they will not indulge an apprehension that they shall meet with a refusal....

The government has been apprized in part of the insuperable objections to the acknowledgment by the Nation of the so called treaty [1835] submitted to the Senate for its ratification in 1836.

If you will listen to us we will briefly refer to some of them, and we beg your Excellency to understand us, in this matter, as speaking what we believe to be the feeling and language of more than nine tenths of our nation....

Our reception was kind and we were acknowledged to be entitled to the character which we claimed to possess. Our credentials were exhibited, and in an official interview with the President [Andrew Jackson] we were informed by him that whenever we should present any proposition for the consideration of the government, through the War Department, it should be immediately attended to.

While engaged in preparing our communications in pursuance of this proffer, we learned that intelligence had been received that a treaty had in fact been entered into at New Echota. It was from this period that our troubles began to assume a more positive character. To this instrument subsequently received, and, after many most material changes in its substantial provisions, submitted to the Senate for its ratification are we to attribute the distress under which our nation now labors, and the dangers which impend over us.

The Cherokee Nation never authorized the formation of this spurious Compact. They never conferred upon the individuals who signed it any authority to give it their assent. They have never recognised its validity and never can. They have protested against it as a fraud upon themselves and upon the United States. They have proffered themselves able to establish all these allegations by the most abundant proof. They ask of you Sir that these allegations be examined, fully and by impartial individuals, enjoying your entire confidence. By the results of such an investigation, by your own judgment upon the fairness, the justice, the legality of this act and the proceedings connected with it they must necessarily abide. Will the Government of the United States claim the right to enforce a contract thus assailed by the other nominal party to it? Will they refuse to examine into charges of such grave import?...

I. We aver that the Cherokee nation never authorized its formation.

In all negotiations with ourselves and we believe every other Indian Nation, the government of the United States have conducted them with the regularly authorized agents of the other party. The internal arrangements of our nation, by which certain persons are clothed with powers to represent and act for the whole, have been long known and constantly recognised. No government has ever claimed the right to pass the regular representatives of another people, to carry on negotiations with any who may claim, without exhibiting, full authority from those whom they profess to represent, and whom they undertake to bind....

[Moreover,] the meeting at New Echota did not fully represent the Cherokee Nation. Statements have been made from different sources showing the number there present. The largest number, including men women and children Indians and negroes does not exceed seven hundred—while highly respectable witnesses positively aver that not more than three hundred were assembled and only seventy nine approved of what was done. In determining whether such an instrument imposes on the Cherokee Nation the obligation of performing its stipulations, surely it is important to understand by how many it was sanctioned, and by what authority they undertook to bind others who were not professed parties. The very manner in which these proceedings purport to be verified is so singular to our eyes—so different from what has been customary on similar occasions, that this circumstance alone is calculated to awaken suspicion and to strengthen our statements.

Sustained however, as we are, we unhesitatingly assert the fact that less than one hundred individuals of the Cherokee Nation, irregularly convened and acting irregularly, ever sanctioned this instrument, so far as even to assent to the appointment of the individuals by whom it was signed. This we consider as not only unjust to us, but equally so to the United States. In the instructions given to the Commissioners it is expressly stated that "although there can be no objection to a free interchange of opinion and a conditional arrangement on all disputed points between them and a committee fairly and publicly chosen, should the Cherokees think it proper to commit the details, in the first instance, to such a committee; but the *final action* upon the subject must be had by the people themselves in open Council." "If there is any dispute as to the decision of the majority, an actual census will be taken of the persons present exhibiting their names, and they will pass before the commissioners and state whether they are in favor of or against the arrangement proposed; and this census, together with the result, will be certified by the Commissioners and Transmitted with their other proceedings to the seat of Govt." In a previous communication made by these same commissioners to one of the undersigned, as the *Principal Chief Cherokee Nation*, it was distinctly asserted, that "the Commissioners, in their instructions, *are required to obtain the consent of a majority of your headmen and warriors to a treaty to make it valid*, and for this purpose, it is necessary to have an accurate census of the Nation taken now." In the address of the President of the 16th March 1835 to the Nation, we were given to understand that with the Nation at large rested the power of ultimately acceding to or not the proposed terms. It was the understanding of this delegation and of the Nation that this course should be pursued, and the very notice under which the Council at New Echota was convened called upon the individuals of the nation to act for themselves in the business, and implied the right of the

nation collectively to assent to or dissent from the terms proposed.

If after all this public and mutual understanding, an instrument, which originated in a meeting where not only one twentieth part of the nation was convened, most essentially varied after having been submitted to their inspection, and ultimately approved only by the small number who actually affixed their signatures to it, can be considered obligatory upon the whole Cherokee nation, upon the same principle another compact which we may choose to sign with any twenty citizens of the United States, holding no public station, authorized by no national act, might, had we the power, be enforced against you to the extent of stripping every citizen of his home and of his property.

II. Nor can there be any foundation for the belief that the Cherokee Nation have ever assented to the instrument in question by any subsequent act which could be considered as a ratification. The whole nation had been led to believe from the official language addressed to them that, whatever might be done by any of their agents, would not be held obligatory until it had received the approbation of the Nation. Not only has no such sanction ever been obtained, but it has never been asked at their hands. So far from this being the case every means has been resorted to to stifle the expression of public opinion among them. A large body of troops has been stationed in the Cherokee Nation prepared to put down any meeting convened to deliberate upon the subject. The Commanding General [John E. Wool], whose high character is a guaranty that he is acting in obedience to precise instructions, in his general order of November 3rd 1836, has, in terms too plain and significant to be misunderstood, apprized us of the consequences which will follow any attempt to ascertain and concentrate the opinions of our people. Several instances have already occurred in which arrests have been made of individuals supposed to be inimical to the treaty as it is called. In short the whole weight and influence of the government have been exerted, to aid the small faction which has usurped the right to bind us, to alarm the timid, to overpower the resolute, to persuade the confiding, to compel the weak among us, to give their sanction to this instrument....

These are, we submit to your Excellency, manifestations not to be misunderstood of the state of opinion and of feeling among us. We are aware that efforts have been made to injure us in the estimation of this government. As individuals our characters have been assailed—our motives misrepresented—

our conduct and our acts distorted. We cannot however but believe that among the many high minded and honorable men who know us and who enjoy your confidence, some may be found who have done and will do us justice.

We do not arrogate to ourselves so high a standing in your estimation, as to authorize us to ask that you will reply implicitly upon our statements; but we have deceived ourselves most egregiously if we have not presented to the consideration of the government sufficient grounds to induce hesitation and enquiry. You have at your command hundreds of individuals to whom you may confide the duty of making the investigation which we solicit. Select such as you can implicitly believe associate with them but a single individual to be appointed by us to direct to the sources of information, and if we fail to establish the truth of our allegations we shall no longer ask you to delay exercising your power in the enforcement of your rights. Should it however appear from such investigation that this instrument has been made without authority, that it meets with the almost unanimous reprobation of our nation, that you have been deceived by false information, we cannot and we will not believe that under its color, and under the sanction of those principles of justice which impose an obligation faithfully to perform our compacts and our promises, we shall be forced to submit to its iniquitous provisions. Sooner would we ask you to make no investigation, institute no inquiry. Satisfy yourselves, endeavor to satisfy mankind and your God that all is right—assert the imperative duty of conforming to treaty stipulations—stand upon the high ground of power, employ your strength and drive to desperation to exile and to death those whom you have called your children, and who have placed themselves under your protection. Our fate is in your hands—may the God of truth tear away every disguise and concealment from our case—may the God of justice guide your determination and the God of mercy stay the hand of our brother uplifted for our destruction.

Glossary

arrogate	to claim, usually unjustly

ADDRESS TO THE CHEROKEE NATION (1838)

Your delegation have in the discharge of the duties imposed upon them, most scrupulously observed to the best of their full abilities the known wishes and sentiments of the whole Nation, in the support of our common rights and interests. But, when the strong arm of power is raised against the weak and defenseless, the force of argument must fail. Our Nation have been besieged by a powerful Army and you have been captured in peace from your various domestic pursuits. And your wives & children placed in forts under a military guard for the purpose of being immediately transported to the West of the Mississippi— and a portion of them have actually been sent off!! Your leading men feeling for your distress, respectfully appealed to the magnanimity of the gallant and generous Commanding General [Winfield Scott] for a suspension of your removal until autumn, a season more propitious for a healthful and comfortable removal from a salubrious clime to a sickly one. As you all well know, this petition has been favourably received and kindly granted. These things transpired in the absence of your Delegation and whilst they were at Washington City in actual Negotiation and under a hopeful prospect of success, for concluding an arrangement with the United States through the Secry. of War [Joel R. Poinsett], and thereby alleviating our Nation from the embarrassing difficulties with which we have for years past been troubled. But, alas! the Negotiation was unexpectedly and suddenly terminated by the Secry. of War and the subject matter submitted to Congress by the President of the United States [Martin Van Buren] in a manner wholly inexplicable to the Delegation. Congress, has made an appropriation to meet the expenses for transportation, subsistence &c amounting to One Million forty seven thousand and sixty seven Dollars. Also an additional sum of One hundred thousand Dollars for arrearages of Annuities, for blankets clothing for the poor, medical aid &c. The Delegation have been advised by the Secretary of War that Major Genl. Winfield Scott has been instructed to close an arrangement with them for the control and management of our own emigration; thus has the Mission to Washington terminated; and the Delegation have found you under a Military duress, encamped in the forests along the sylvan brooks where you once gathered your flock of sheep and herds of cattle. Here, homeless and outcasts, we are only for a short space to be permitted to taking a passing view of the houses and farms we once inhabited & cultivated & the places in which we happily worshiped Almighty God. Amid these our afflictions, I rejoice, however, to find that you have so wisely and with Christian firmness maintained your peaceful and respectful relations toward our white brethren, as well as in the discharge of the solemn duties we owe one to the other, among ourselves. It is especially gratifying to me to be informed verbally by the Commanding Genl. who is charged with the painful duty of removing us from the land of our Nativity, that, he has found you faithful and honorable in the fulfilment of every promise or engagement which you have made with him, and that in no instance have you ever told him a lie. This distinguished officer has been pleased further to assure me, that, so far as it may be within his power to grant our request in reference to our comfortable removal, that the interests and wishes of the Nation shall be consulted and adopted.

ADDRESS TO A GENERAL COUNCIL OF THE CHEROKEE NATION (1839)

Thro. the misterious dispensations of providence we have been permitted to meet in General Council on the border of the great plains of the West. Altho, many of us have for a series of years past been separated, yet, we have not and cannot lose sight of the fact, that we are all of the household of the Cherokee family and of one blood. We have already met, shook hands and conversed together. In recognising and embracing each other as Countrymen, friends and relations, Let us kindle our social fire and take measures for cementing our reunion as a nation, by establishing the basis for a government suited to the condition and wants of the whole people; whereby, wholesome laws may be enacted and administered for the security and protection of property, life and other sacred rights, of the community. Our meeting on this occasion is full of interest and is of peculiar importance to the welfare of our people. I trust therefore that harmony and good understanding will continue to prevail and that the questions which may come up for consideration will be maturely weighed previous to a final decision....

And, altho, being compelled by the strong arm of power to come here, yet in doing so, they have not trespassed or infringed upon any of the rights and privileges of those who were here previous to themselves—because it is evident, from the facts of the case that the rights and privileges of the people are equal. Notwithstanding the late emigrants removed in their National Capacity and constitute a large majority, yet, there is no intention nor desire on the part of their representatives to propose or require any thing, but what may be strictly equitable & just and sattisfactory to the people. Being persuaded that these feelings will be fully reciprocated, I trust that the subject-matter of this Council will be referred to the respective representatives of the Eastern and Western people—and that, in their joint deliberations, we may speedily come to some sattisfactory conclusion for the permanent reunion and welfare of our Nation. Without referring in detail to our acknowledged Treaties and other documentary facts to show, I will conclude by remarking that there are great interests of a public and private character yet to be adjusted with the Govt. of the U. States and which can only be secured by a just and amicable course on the part of our Nation. The injuries and losses sustained by the Nation from the whites in violation of treaty stipulations, holds a strong claim on the justice of the people and Govt. of the U. States which it is to be hoped will in the end be remunerated. The tenure of the soil on which we now stand and the relations which shall hereafter exist between our Nation and the United States are questions of the first magnitude, and necessary to be understood and clearly defined by a General Compact, for the security and protection of the permanent welfare and happiness of our Nation. Let us never forget this self evident truth—that a House divided against itself cannot stand—or "united we stand and divided we fall."

Margaret Sanger (Library of Congress)

MARGARET SANGER

1879–1966

Woman's Rights Activist

Featured Documents
- "Sexual Impulse—Part II" (1912)
- "The Prevention of Conception" (1914)
- Hotel Brevoort Speech (1916)
- "Birth Control and Racial Betterment" (1919)

Overview

Margaret Higgins was born into a working-class family on September 14, 1879, in Corning, New York, the sixth of eleven children. Her father, a stonecutter, was an activist for woman suffrage and Socialism. Sanger was educated at St. Mary's School in Corning, New York, and then attended Claverack College in Claverack and the Hudson River Institute in Hudson. She left school in 1899, owing to the financial constraints of her family. After caring for her mother in her final illness, Sanger enrolled at the White Plains Hospital Nursing School. In 1902 she married the architect William Sanger, with whom she had three children. In 1912, having settled in New York City, Sanger started work in the slums of the Lower East Side, where she saw the devastating effects of unplanned pregnancies on mothers and their children. That year she began writing a column, "What Every Girl Should Know," for the Socialist newspaper the *New York Call*, in which "Sexual Impulse" appeared in two parts.

Leading the movement to make birth control legal, safe, and accessible, Sanger devoted herself to educating the public about sexuality and a woman's need to be in control of her childbearing decisions. For Sanger, birth control was both a basic human right and the means for women to achieve sexual autonomy. In March 1914 she published the first issue of the *Woman Rebel*, featuring the article "The Prevention of Conception." For this, she was indicted on federal charges of violating the Comstock Act of 1873, which prohibited distributing "obscene" literature and material (including contraceptive materials and information) through the mails. Many of Sanger's early documents served the dual purpose of educating her audience and attracting official suppression, which gave her the opportunity to make legal challenges and to create publicity for the cause. Sanger went to Europe rather than appearing in court to face charges. She returned to the United States in 1915 and continued her crusade by lecturing nationwide. On the eve of her trial in January of 1916 she addressed her supporters at the Hotel Brevoort in Manhattan, defending her methods in rallying support for birth control. The charges against her were eventually dismissed.

Later that year Sanger and her associates opened a birth control clinic in a poor New York City neighborhood, handing out contraceptive information and materials. This time she was arrested under state law and was sentenced to a month in prison. Upon her release she only intensified her activities. Sanger's article "Birth Control and Racial Betterment," in which she discussed the controversial topic of eugenics as it related to birth control, was published in 1919 in the *Birth Control Review*, a monthly periodical she had started two years earlier. In 1921 she founded the American Birth Control League, a group that later became Planned Parenthood. Her continued advocacy of birth control won widespread public support for its legalization and brought about the creation of contraceptive clinics across the country, along with the development of new birth control methods. Sanger died on September 6, 1966, in Tucson, Arizona.

Explanation and Analysis of Documents

Margaret Sanger was a New York City nurse in 1912, when she wrote "Sexual Impulse—Part II," but by the time she wrote "Birth Control and Racial Betterment" in 1919, she had launched a new movement for birth control and women's empowerment. The documents discussed here represent her early activism, beginning with her goal of promoting sex education and then focusing specifically on birth control. They reflect a rhetoric that changed as she grew more experienced and was exposed to different kinds of activism. She sought to reach broader and broader segments of the population, first speaking to working-class women, then to middle-class and society women, and finally to an audience that included physicians, legislators, and eugenicists (scientists who dealt with control of hereditary characteristics). Three of these documents were published as articles, while a fourth was delivered as a speech. Individually they capture specific moments in Sanger's life, but collectively they tell a story of changing tactics, audiences, and goals. Until the end of her active and long life Sanger continued to refine her arguments and address new and different audiences on behalf of birth control, but she always maintained that birth control was fundamentally both the right and the responsibility of each woman.

"Sexual Impulse—Part II"

In 1912 Sanger reworked some of the informal talks on sex hygiene she had given to small groups of Socialist women into a series of articles for the *New York Call*, the

Socialist Party's daily newspaper. "Sexual Impulse—Part II" was the seventh article in a twelve-part series published between November 17, 1912, and March 2, 1913. Sanger's frank approach to sexual issues drew the attention of the U.S. postal authorities, who suppressed the final article in the series, prompting the *Call* to run a blank column with the heading, "What Every Girl Should Know; NOTHING! By Order of the Post Office Department." The censored article was published in its entirety a month later.

With "Sexual Impulse—Part II," Sanger put forth a new brand of feminism that equated women's autonomy with sexual knowledge and freedom. She argues that women have sexual needs and desires every bit as powerful as men's, something that many authors denied. Sanger calls the sexual urge a "creative instinct" not to be used entirely for procreation but also not to be wasted in youth. And, she says, "instead of allowing it to remain dormant and make her odd and whimsical, the modern Woman turns her sexual impulse into a big directing force." She further makes the distinction between sex and love, saying, "Let us not confuse the sexual impulse with love, for it alone is not love, but merely a necessary quality for the growth of love." Sanger borrows from the writings of the social purity reformers and sex radicals of the late nineteenth century who implored men and women to practice self-restraint and conserve sexual energy in order to build character and strength and to learn the difference between love and desire. Here Sanger adds a feminist component to the argument by advising young women to strive for political and economic independence. As she put it, "When women gain their economic freedom they will cease being playthings and utilities for men, but will assert themselves and choose the father of their offspring." Naturally, they would choose their mates based on eugenic principles of heredity, health, and intelligence rather than settling for the first eligible caretaker. Indeed, borrowing from George Bernard Shaw, Sanger claims that such a woman would "hunt down her ideal in order to produce the Superman." The article, and the series in general, established a theme that Sanger carried through her sex education writings over the next several decades—that women can achieve sexual freedom only if they attain sexual knowledge.

◆ "The Prevention of Conception"

In March 1914 Sanger published the first issue of her radical feminist monthly, the *Woman Rebel*. In the first issue, she dedicated the paper to building a "conscious fighting character" in women and included the Industrial Workers of the World slogan "No Gods, No Masters" on its masthead. The short article "The Prevention of Conception" represents Sanger's first public declaration in favor of legalizing birth control, a phrase that she and her fellow activists coined. In this article, one of the shaping documents of the U.S. birth control movement, Sanger establishes the goals of the birth control campaign: to defy the Comstock Act, which had labeled birth control obscene and banned the circulation of contraceptives and contraceptive information; to increase access to safe and effective contraceptives and thereby reduce the numbers of dangerous and illegal abortions; and to give working-class women the knowledge and means of controlling their fertility.

"The Prevention of Conception" was aimed directly at working-class women and offers frank descriptions of the predicament they found themselves in: With little access to knowledge, health care, or sanitary living conditions, they had large, unhealthy families, without hope for betterment. Sanger points out the double standard that allowed middle-class moralists to condemn and outlaw birth control, while in their own clean homes they practiced birth control and had small, healthy, and well-educated families. Sanger also claims that birth control could serve a revolutionary function. If the working classes could bring down their family size through birth control, they would command higher wages as a result of the shortage of available workers.

Sanger's ideas on birth control's use as a tool of class warfare reflected those of the anarchist feminist Emma Goldman and must be understood as a response to the distrust that many Socialists had for birth control. Earlier adherents of Socialism, calling themselves neo-Malthusians and operating in Europe, had argued that that if the working classes used birth control, it would reduce the chances of social revolt. (The ideas of the neo-Malthusians drew on a set of doctrines taken from Thomas Malthus, specifically his theory that limited resources keep populations in check and reduce economic growth.) If families had fewer children, workers would not be driven to labor organizing or demanding more equitable economic distributions. Thus, many Socialists opposed birth control as a palliative that distracted workers from real inequities. In Sanger's view, "no plagues, famines or wars could ever frighten the capitalist class so much as the universal practice of the prevention of conception. On the other hand no better method could be utilized for increasing the wages of the workers." Her claim in "The Prevention of Conception" that workers could use birth control to "frighten" capitalists turned neo-Malthusian theory on its head.

The first issue of the *Woman Rebel* was one of seven issues suppressed by the postal service. In August 1914 the federal government indicted Sanger for publishing and disseminating obscene material, including "The Prevention of Conception." According to the government, she had violated nine counts of the Comstock Act. Sanger published one more issue of the *Woman Rebel* in September; released copies of *Family Limitation*, her how-to pamphlet on birth control; and fled the country to avoid prosecution. Her bold defiance of the law generated publicity about an issue that seldom received coverage in the press and set in motion a series of events that led to the formation of the birth control movement.

◆ **The Hotel Brevoort Speech**

While Sanger was in exile in Europe, her estranged husband, William Sanger, had been arrested for giving an undercover postal agent a copy of his wife's contraceptive guide *Family Limitation*. William Sanger's trial and imprisonment in September 1915 galvanized support for the legalization of

Time Line	
1916	■ **February** The charges against Sanger are dropped. ■ **October 16** Sanger opens the Brownsville birth control clinic in Brooklyn, New York, and is arrested ten days later; her conviction results in a thirty-day prison term.
1917	■ **February** Sanger publishes the first issue of the *Birth Control Review*.
1919	■ **February** Sanger's article "Birth Control and Racial Betterment" is published in the *Birth Control Review*.
1921	■ **October** Sanger founds the American Birth Control League.
1923	■ **January 1** Sanger opens the Birth Control Clinical Research Bureau, the first legal birth control clinic in the nation.
1928	■ **June 8** Sanger resigns from the American Birth Control League.
1929	■ **April** Sanger forms the National Committee on Federal Legislation for Birth Control.
1939	■ **January** The Birth Control Federation of America is formed by the merger of the American Birth Control League and Sanger's clinic (renamed Planned Parenthood Federation of America in 1942).

1951
- Sanger procures a grant for Gregory Pincus to begin hormonal contraceptive research.

1952
- Sanger helps found the International Planned Parenthood Federation and is elected its first president.

1960
- The first birth control pill, Enovid, is approved as a contraceptive by the Food and Drug Administration.

1966
- **September 6**
  Sanger dies in Tucson, Arizona.

birth control and led to the formation of the National Birth Control League, the first such organization in the country. In early October, Margaret Sanger returned to the United States to face trial. While Sanger was preparing for her defense, her daughter, Peggy, died of pneumonia at the age of five. On the eve of her criminal trial, in a charged atmosphere following her husband's imprisonment and their daughter's death, Sanger addressed nearly two hundred supporters at the Hotel Brevoort on the lower end of Fifth Avenue in Manhattan. They had come to hear her and other speakers discuss the nascent movement for birth control.

Sanger used the Brevoort speech to defend the law-defying tactics she had employed to rouse public opinion about the need for accessible and effective birth control. She does not present birth control as a revolutionary idea but instead an enlightened one, advocated by the greatest minds in history but suppressed by an obsolete law. "There is nothing new, nothing radical in birth control," she claims. "Aristotle advocated it; Plato advocated it; all our great and modern thinkers have advocated it!" She speaks of the urgency of the situation—both her own circumstance and the plight of working-class women forced to rely on dangerous abortion procedures or else bring unwanted children into the world. Sanger referred to this night as her "maiden speech" and with it announced her leadership of the birth control movement. In the Hotel Brevoort speech Sanger personalizes her relationship with the movement—the first of many times that she depicted it as a cause to which she had devoted her life. "I felt myself in the position of one who has discovered that a house is on fire; and I found it was up to me to shout out the warning!" She stakes out a unique position as figurehead, personification of the movement, and its only American leader, and she maintained that position until her death sixty years later.

One can sense a shift of Sanger's direction in the Brevoort speech as she targets the middle class, social

workers "so much better fitted to carry on this work," and wealthy women and physicians. The meeting was not held in a Socialist Party hall, and Sanger aims her words at a far broader audience than she ever had before. She was beginning to build a movement, centered on her unique view of birth control. Following the dismissal of charges against her, she set out on a cross-country speaking tour, elaborating on the themes she had laid out at the Brevoort Hotel.

◆ **"Birth Control and Racial Betterment"**

In the late 1910s Sanger worked to expand the birth control movement beyond its radical base and draw support from academics, scientists, and physicians in an effort to win greater public acceptance and pave the way for the establishment of legal clinics. A court ruling in 1919 on the appeal of her conviction for having opened the first birth control clinic in America in 1916 had allowed for the setting up of doctor-run clinics. But the scientific and medical establishments still questioned the legitimacy of birth control, distrusted Sanger's lay leadership, and resisted affiliations with a movement perceived to be both feminist and too extreme.

Among these establishment figures were eugenicists—scientists, academics, and laypeople who believed that heredity was responsible for the mental and physical traits of individuals. They argued that scientifically directed breeding could encourage good characteristics and prevent defects from being transmitted to future generations. They believed that the mentally deficient were more prone to procreate and in procreating put a burden on society that the educated and more "fit" had to bear. Some went further and argued that entire races or nations were inferior. These eugenicists sought to limit the fertility of the poor, of nonwhites, and of recent immigrants who, they thought, were more likely to pass on inferior character traits such as shiftlessness, intemperance, sexual immorality, and criminality as well as mental retardation. By holding out the promise of resolving social problems and relieving society of the burden of supporting the poor, the insane, criminals, and the so-called feeble-minded, eugenics attracted Progressives, reactionaries, Socialists, and National Socialists (Nazis)—all convinced, at least for a time, that a better society could be built through scientific breeding.

"Birth Control and Racial Betterment" was Sanger's first extended discussion of eugenics. It was published in the *Birth Control Review*, a monthly journal meant to unite birth control activists across the country. In the article, Sanger attempts to align eugenics and birth control by emphasizing their shared goals. Her aim was both to capitalize on the popularity of eugenics, a reputable branch of social science in the immediate post–World War I period, and to make birth control respectable—more a health and economic matter and less a campaign for reproductive rights. Sanger believed that birth control must work in concert with eugenics to produce a stronger and healthier human race. She argues in this article that the two movements must together help reduce the reproduction of both the physically and economically "unfit"—those who would pass on debilitating illness or disability as well as those who

A family of eight in their New York City tenement home ca. 1911 (Library of Congress)

could not provide proper care for their children. However, she disagrees vehemently with the majority of eugenicists, who called for increased fertility from the wealthier and more educated classes. As she put it, "We hold that the world is already over-populated. Eugenists [her term] imply or insist that a woman's first duty is to the state; we contend that her duty to herself is her first duty to the state."

Sanger insists that all women be given contraceptive information and access to safe birth control so that each woman could make her own childbearing decisions. Sanger also addresses sterilization, heredity, and spacing of births, topics she would expand upon in *Pivot of Civilization* (1922), her most sustained work on eugenics and the intellectual foundation of the birth control movement. Sanger's early writings on eugenics defended women and the working class against the assumptions of eugenicists. The eugenicists believed that normal, healthy women ought to have as many children as possible, while those judged unfit should have their right to make childbearing decisions taken away. Sanger, trusting that a woman knew her own home conditions and health best, argued that any woman, wealthy or poor, was the best arbiter of when she should have a child. For Sanger *poor* was not a synonym for "unfit," and birth control was a tool that families would adopt themselves rather than having it imposed upon them—a tactic the eugenicists advocated.

Impact and Legacy

Margaret Sanger's experiences as a nurse, Socialist, labor organizer, and working-class woman persuaded her that reproductive choice was critical to securing women's freedom and economic advancement. She saw birth control as the tool whereby women would take command of their lives and believed those who barred women access to this information were actively doing so to keep women poor and powerless. Her writings reproduced here show Sanger's commitment to providing women with information about sex and birth control in the belief that they would benefit from that information.

Sanger's sex education writings helped advance women's knowledge of health, discarding the views of nineteenth-century medical literature that tended to treat women's bodies as delicate, fragile reproductive machines, without sexuality. Along with others in the early-twentieth-century sex hygiene movement, Sanger promoted education as a means of liberating sex from Victorian-era prudery. Her particular contribution was to extend the discussion to girls and women who had little access to instructional or educational literature of any value. Sanger helped make women's sexuality—its repression, potential, and liberation—the central theme for most of the important sex education literature of the pre– and post–World War I eras.

"Society, too, condemns the natural expression of Woman's emotion, save under certain prescribed conditions. In consequence of this, women suppress their maternal desires and today direct this great force into other channels, participating in the bigger and broader movements and activities in which they are active today."

("Sexual Impulse—Part II")

"When women gain their economic freedom they will cease being playthings and utilities for men, but will assert themselves and choose the father of their offspring."

("Sexual Impulse—Part II")

"No plagues, famines or wars could ever frighten the capitalist class so much as the universal practice of the prevention of conception. On the other hand no better method could be utilized for increasing the wages of the workers."

("The Prevention of Conception")

"I realize keenly that many of those who understand and would support the birth control propaganda if it were carried out in a safe and sane manner, cannot sympathize with nor countenance the methods I have followed in my attempt to arouse the working women to the fact that bringing a child into the world is the greatest responsibility."

(Hotel Brevoort Speech)

"We maintain that a woman possessing an adequate knowledge of her reproductive functions is the best judge of the time and conditions under which her child should be brought into the world. We further maintain it is her right, regardless of all other considerations, to determine whether she shall bear children or not."

("Birth Control and Racial Betterment")

"Only upon a free, self-determining motherhood can rest any unshakable structure of racial betterment."

("Birth Control and Racial Betterment")

Sanger's eugenic writings continued to evolve as she sought the support of more liberal eugenicists, championing birth control for those with genetically transmitted mental or physical defects. She even went so far as to advocate forced sterilization for the mentally incompetent. Throughout the 1920s she tried to win over the support of major eugenicists, most of whom were wary of associating with radical birth controllers like Sanger. In the 1930s she adopted eugenic arguments for birth control that stressed that those receiving public charity during the depression ought to restrict their birthrate. In some cases Sanger's eugenic writings are troubling, but overall she remains true to the arguments she made in 1919. While she did not back efforts to limit population growth solely on the basis of class, ethnicity, or race and refused to encourage the white, native-born middle and upper classes to have more children, Sanger's reputation was permanently tainted by her association with race-based eugenics.

Sanger's early speeches and publications changed the public debate about birth control. She wrote angry essays that accused society of keeping necessary information from women in order to control them. This single-minded focus on woman's rights and responsibilities made her an impor-tant national figure. While she is also known for other efforts—the creation of birth control organizations and clinics, sponsorship of the development of the birth control pill, and the legalization of medically controlled birth control—Sanger is best known as the "Woman Rebel," the angry feminist who challenged society to provide women with the means of securing their own liberation.

Key Sources

Margaret Sanger's voluminous papers are located at the Sophia Smith Collection at Smith College and also at the Library of Congress. Esther Katz edited *The Selected Papers of Margaret Sanger*, Vol. 1: *The Woman Rebel, 1900–1928* (2002) and Vol. 2: *Birth Control Comes of Age, 1928–1939* (2007). Selected writings are available at the Margaret Sanger Papers Project, New York University (http://www.nyu.edu/projects/sanger). For details on Sanger's life see *My Fight for Birth Control* (1931) and *Autobiography* (1938); for her views on women, birth control, and eugenics see *Woman and the New Race* (1920), *Pivot of Civilization* (1922), *Happiness in Marriage* (1926), and *Motherhood in Bondage* (1928).

Questions for Further Study

1. What were Sanger's greatest achievements with regard to woman's rights, social recognition of female sexuality, and birth control? To what extent were her positions influenced by her early involvement in Socialism? Do you agree that contraception and abortion are inseparable, as Sanger would have said? In other words, is it possible to support contraception while opposing abortion, and should Sanger have attempted to establish a greater distinction between the two methods of birth control?

2. Research and discuss the ideas and influence of Thomas Malthus, the English theorist who maintained that population growth would always be limited by scarcity of resources. How did Socialists of Sanger's time and earlier interpret Malthus? How did she take issue with both the other Socialists and Malthus himself in her 1914 piece on preventing conception?

3. How did Sanger set about reaching increasingly larger audiences in her career, and how is this reflected in the documents included here, most notably the Hotel Brevoort speech? Discuss the challenges she faced first in winning over women and then other groups, particularly medical and scientific professionals. To what extent was she successful?

4. Examine the growth and influence of the eugenics movement in the late nineteenth and early twentieth centuries, culminating with its use to justify racist social engineering as advocated by the Nazis and other extremist political groups. To what degree did Sanger embrace the racism and classism inherent in eugenic theory? On the other hand, can some or all of her views on the issue be excused on the basis of the fact that in the 1910s eugenics had yet to be discredited and enjoyed the support of many otherwise admirable leaders? To what extent has her association with the eugenics movement hurt Sanger's reputation, and how justifiable is that?

Further Reading

■ Books

Chesler, Ellen. *Woman of Valor: Margaret Sanger and the Birth Control Movement in America*. New York: Simon & Schuster, 1992.

Gordon, Linda. *The Moral Property of Women: A History of Birth Control Politics in America*. Urbana: University of Illinois Press, 2002.

Kennedy, David. *Birth Control in America: The Career of Margaret Sanger*. New Haven, Conn.: Yale University Press, 1970.

Lader, Lawrence. *The Margaret Sanger Story and the Fight for Birth Control*. New York: Doubleday, 1975.

McCann, Carol. *Birth Control Politics in the United States, 1916–1945*. Ithaca, N.Y.: Cornell University Press, 1999.

Reed, James. *The Birth Control Movement in American Society: From Private Vice to Public Virtue*. Princeton, N.J.: Princeton University Press, 1984.

—Esther Katz and Cathy Moran Hajo

"SEXUAL IMPULSE—PART II" (1912)

In the first part of this article we learned that the sexual impulse is a combination of the two impulses, the one which impels the discharge of ripe sex cells, strongest in the boy, and the other which impels the individual to touch or caress an individual of the opposite sex, strongest in the girl.

Every girl has in mind an ideal man. This ideal begins to form sometime in the early adolescent age. He is usually distinct in her mind as to his physical qualities, such as dark or light hair, or brown or blue eyes. He is always a certain physical type, and often remains an ideal to her through life. At the forming period of the type she will be attracted toward many men who seem to answer the ideal type, but as she reads and develops through the various stages of the adolescent period, the ideal changes and grows with her. As she reaches the romantic stage the ideal must be brave, daring, courteous. If she is inclined toward out-door sports he must be athletic. And so it goes on until the twenty-third year, when the average girl has a fairly settled idea of the man who would suit her as a mate through life.

When the sexual impulse makes itself felt strongly in the adolescent boy or girl, they, feeling satisfied with the physical beauty and perfection of the other, marry, they are unconscious that the incentive to love when based on physical attraction alone is soon destroyed. For sickness, poverty or disease will affect even the most seemingly perfect physical attraction.

Let us not confuse the sexual impulse with love, for it alone is not love, but merely a necessary quality for the growth of love.

No sexual attraction or impulse is the foundation of the beautiful emotion of love. Upon this is built respect, self-control, sympathy, unity of purpose, many common tastes and desires, building up and up until this real love unites two individuals as one being, one life. Then it becomes the strongest and purest emotion of which the human soul is capable.

There is no doubt that the natural aim of the sexual impulse is the sexual act, yet when the impulse is strongest and followed by the sexual act without love or any of the relative instincts which go to make up love, the relations are invariably followed by a feeling of disgust. Respect for each other and for one's self is a primary essential to this intimate relation.

In plant and animal life the reproductive cell of the male is the active seeker of the passive female cell, imbued with the instinct to chase and bodily capture the female cell for the purpose of reproduction.

This instinct man, as he is today, has inherited, and, as with the lower forms of life, the senses are intensely involved. It is kept alive by the sense of sight, sound and smell, and reaches its highest development through the sense of touch. It is heightened by touching smooth and soft surfaces—which is said to account for the pleasure of kissing.

In the early part of this article I spoke of the desire to touch being stronger in girls than in boys. This desire leads a girl to kiss and fondle a man without any conscious desire for the sexual act; whereas in the man, to be touched and caressed by the girl for whom he has a sexual attraction, stimulates the accumulation of sex cells, and the desire for the sexual act becomes paramount in his mind. Many a young girl bubbling over with the joy of living, innocent of any serious consequences, is oft-times misjudged by men on account of these natural actions. But she soon puts on her armor of defense, and stifles and represses any outbursts of affection.

Society, too, condemns the natural expression of Woman's emotion, save under certain prescribed conditions. In consequence of this, women suppress their maternal desires and today direct this great force into other channels, participating in the bigger and broader movements and activities in which they are active today.

This is one reason why the type of the so-called "old maid," so characteristic of the generation past, has disappeared. These great maternal powers are being used up in the activities of modern life. Instead of allowing it to remain dormant and make her odd and whimsical, the modern Woman turns her sexual impulse into a big directing force.

That the male creature is the pursuer of the female in all forms of life, there is no question, but that the female has the choice of selection and uses fine discrimination in her choice, cannot be denied either. This instinct of selection seems to lie dormant in women of today, for at puberty nature calls to every girl to make a selection suitable to her nature. Yet few girls follow this instinct on account of the specter of economic insecurity which looms up before them. Instead of asking themselves: "Are we matable and sympathetic?" they ask: "Shall we have enough food, clothing and shelter?"

Indeed, girls, this system increases our degradation, and places us in ideals lower than the animals. All over the civilized world today girls are being given and taken in marriage with but one purpose in view; to be well-supported by the man who takes her. She does not concern herself with the man's physical condition: his hereditary taints, the cleanliness of his mind or past life, nor with the future race.

There will no doubt be a great change in Woman's attitude on this subject in the next few years. When women gain their economic freedom they will cease being playthings and utilities for men, but will assert themselves and choose the father of their offspring. As Bernard Shaw tells of her in one of his greatest plays, she will hunt down her ideal in order to produce the Superman.

There seems to be a general tendency on the part of the Woman who is demanding political freedom, to demand sexual freedom also. When a girl reaches the age nearing thirty her natural development tends toward sexual freedom. It seems as though nature, knowing the time of reproduction is drawing to a close, calls with all the fury of her strength to complete its development and procreate.

It is at this age where physicians claim a Woman awakens to the sexual desire, and it is at this age that women seek affection, or gratification with a "lover." To her there is nothing to say; she is mature, developed and can judge for herself where best her happiness lies.

But to the young girl at the age of say twenty, or even younger, immature, mentally undeveloped, there is something she should know, and that is that every physical impulse, every sensual feeling, every lustful desire will come to her whitewashed with the sacred word LOVE.

Neither the boy nor the girl knows the difference between the sexual impulse and love. A boys meets a girl, he feels a great attraction for her, he feels the sexual impulse throbbing within him, he is full of this life-giving current—he feels it throughout his being, he walks lighter and straighter, he feels it in his voice, in his laughter, he grows tenderer within himself, and to women. He feels all this and is sure it is a love that will never die. If there is an attraction on the girl's part there is no difficulty in persuading her that this feeling IS love.

But it is not love; it is the creative force of sexual impulse scattered through his being and the sexual act brings it to its climax.

If motherhood comes to the girl through this relation, she has developed and the experience has enriched her life. But today the girl has an idea she has escaped the greatest disgrace when she has avoided motherhood. If the relation was based on physical attraction, a few abortions and the monotony of every day life soon remove this, and the man goes elsewhere in search of this wonderful sensation which he felt at first, but did not know how to keep or how to use.

The girl, however, has become a new being, sexually awakened and conscious of it. But ignorant of the use of the forces she possesses, she plunges forth blindly, with social and economic forces against her, and prostitution beckoning at every turn. So she soon passes with the crowd on the road to the Easiest Way. This is the story of thousands of young girls living in prostitution.

Women should know that the creative instinct does not need to be expended entirely on the propagation of the race. Though the sex cells are placed in a part of the anatomy for the essential purpose of easily expelling them into the female for the purpose of reproduction there are other elements in the sexual fluid which are the essence of blood, nerve, brain and muscle. When redirected into the building and strengthening of these we find men or women of the greatest endurance and greatest magnetic power. A girl can waste her creative powers by brooding over a love affair to the extent of exhausting her system, with results not unlike the effects of masturbation and debauchery.

Of course the sexual impulse is natural. It is natural in animals, degenerates, and in normal man. But in man it is mixed with other essentials which, together, are termed love. These essentials are derived from man's power of reasoning by which he is known as a higher species and through which he differs from the animals.

When man emerged from the jungle and stood upright on his hind legs, the shape of his head and his face changed from the long jaw and flat head of the animal to the flat face and high head of the man. All progress from that time forward was made along mental lines. According to the universal law then in existence he should have been limited to a geographical area and killed by the extreme heat or cold or starved for one kind of food if it were not obtained, but against all these he fought, because he became endowed with such attributes as reason, knowledge and will-power. Instead of using his creative powers solely in hunting food and reproducing his species, he used this force in making plans for his self-preservation. He built rafts and boats to cross rivers and streams, he devised methods of clothing himself against extreme heat and cold and discovered various ways of preparing food for different climates suitable for his various needs. In other words he conserved his creative force and redirected it into channels which have resulted in giving him precedence over all other living creatures. For man has developed a CONSCIOUS MIND which asserts itself by reasoning, which in turn has developed his brain-power.

It is said a fish as large as a man has a brain no larger than the kernel of an almond. In all fish and reptiles where there is no great brain development, there is also no conscious sexual control. The lower down in the scale of human development we go the less sexual control we find. It is said that the aboriginal Australian, the lowest known species of the human family, just a step higher than the chimpanzee in brain development, has so little sexual control that police authority alone prevents him from obtaining sexual satisfaction on the streets. According to one writer, the rapist has just enough brain development to raise him above the animal, but like the animal, when in heat knows no law except nature

which impels him to procreate whatever the result. Every normal man and Woman has the power to control and direct his sexual impulse. Men and women who have it in control and constantly use their brain cells in thinking deeply, are never sensual.

It is well to understand that the natural aim of the sexual impulse is the sexual act and the natural aim of the sexual act is reproduction, though it does not always result in this. It is possible for conception to take place without love, it is even possible that there is no conscious knowledge to procreate before or during the act, yet this does not disprove the fact that nature has designed it for the purpose of reproduction, no matter what uses man has put it to today....

Every girl should know that to hold in check the sexual impulse; to absorb this power into the system until there is a freely conscious sympathy, a confidence and respect between her and her ideal; that this will go toward building up the sexual impulse and will make the purest, strongest and most sacred passion of adult life, compared to which all other passions pale into insignificance.

Glossary

Bernard Shaw	George Bernard Shaw, Irish playwright, author of the play *Man and Superman* (1903)

"THE PREVENTION OF CONCEPTION" (1914)

Is there any reason why women should not receive clean, harmless, scientific knowledge on how to prevent conception? Everybody is aware that the old, stupid fallacy that such knowledge will cause a girl to enter into prostitution has long been shattered. Seldom does a prostitute become pregnant. Seldom does the girl practicing promiscuity become pregnant. The women of the upper middle class have all available knowledge and implements to prevent conception. The woman of the lower middle class is struggling for this knowledge. She tries various methods of prevention, and after a few years of experience plus medical advice succeeds in discovering some method suitable to her individual self. The woman of the people is the only one left in ignorance of this information. Her neighbors, relatives and friends tell her stories of special devices and the success of them all. They tell her also of the blood-sucking men with M.D. after their names who perform operations for the price of so-and-

so. But the working woman's purse is thin. It's far cheaper to have a baby, though God knows what it will do after it gets here. Then, too, all other classes of women live in places where there is at least a semblance of privacy and sanitation. It is easier for them to care for themselves whereas the large majority of the women of the people have no bathing or sanitary conveniences. This accounts too for the fact that the higher the standard of living, the more care can be taken and fewer children result. No plagues, famines or wars could ever frighten the capitalist class so much as the universal practice of the prevention of conception. On the other hand no better method could be utilized for increasing the wages of the workers.

As is well known, a law exists forbidding the imparting of information on this subject, the penalty being several years' imprisonment. Is it not the time to defy this law? And what fitter place could be found than in the pages of the WOMAN REBEL?

HOTEL BREVOORT SPEECH (1916)

It seems to me that this evening and this gathering are significant and important, not only because the idea of birth control has brought together all of us workers of such diverse outlooks and temperaments, but especially because of the time chosen for it—the eve of my trial…and because of the dignified and representative intelligence which has supported me in this battle.

For I realize keenly that many of those who understand and would support the birth control propaganda if it were carried out in a safe and sane manner, cannot sympathize with nor countenance the methods I have followed in my attempt to arouse the working women to the fact that bringing a child into the world is the greatest responsibility.

They tell me that The Woman Rebel was badly written; that it was crude; that it was emotional, and hysterical; that it mixed issues; that is was defiant, and too radical.

Well, to all of these indictments I plead guilty! I know that any, and perhaps all of you are better able to cope with the subject than I am. I know that physicians and scientists have a great technical fund of information—greater than I had on the subject of family limitation.

There is nothing new, nothing radical in birth control. Aristotle advocated it; Plato advocated it; all our great and modern thinkers have advocated it!

It is an idea that must appeal to any mature intelligence.

But yet all this scientific and technical discussion has only had the effect of producing more technical and scientific discussion—all very necessary and very stimulating to that very small group of men and women who could understand it.

But, all during the long years while this matter was being…discussed, advocated, refuted, the people themselves—the poor people especially—were blindly, desperately practicing family limitation—just as they are practicing it today.

But to them birth control does not mean what it does to us.

To them it has meant the most barbaric methods. It has meant the killing of babies—infanticide,—abortions,—in one crude way or another.

Women, from time immemorial, have tried to avoid unwanted motherhood.

We all know the tribe of professional abortionists which has sprung up and profited by this terrible misfortune.

We know, too, that when the practice of abortion was put under the ban by the church, the alternate evil—the foundling asylum, with its horrifying history—sprang up.

There is no need to go into the terrible facts concerning the recklessness, the misery, the filth, with which children have been and still are being brought into the world.

I merely want to point out the situation I found when I entered the battle.

On the one hand, I found the wise men, the sages, the scientists, discussing birth control among themselves.

But their ideas were sterile. They did not influence nor affect the tremendous facts of life among the working classes and the disinherited!

How could I approach [and] bridge this chasm? How could I reach these people? How could I awaken public opinion to this tremendous problem?

I might have taken up the a policy of safety, sanity and conservatism—but would I have got a hearing?

And as I became more and more conscious of the vital importance of this idea, I felt myself in the position of one who has discovered that a house is on fire; and I found that it was up to me to shout out the warning!

Glossary

Aristotle…Plato	Greek philosophers of the fourth century BCE

The tone of the voice may have been indelicate and unladylike, and was not at all the tone than many of us would rather hear.

But this very gathering—this honor you have thrust upon me—is ample proof that intelligent and constructive thought has been aroused.

Some of us may only be fit to dramatize a situation—to focus attention upon obsolete laws, like this one I must face tomorrow morning.

Then, others, more experienced in constructive organization, can gather together all this sympathy and interest which has been aroused, and direct it.

I thank you for your encouragement and support. And my request to you tonight is that all you social workers—so much better fitted to carry on this work than I—that you consider and organize this interest.

This is the most next important step and only in this way can I be vindicated!

Let us put U S. of A upon the map of the civilized world!

"BIRTH CONTROL AND RACIAL BETTERMENT" (1919)

Before eugenists and others who are laboring for racial betterment can succeed, they must first clear the way for Birth Control. Like the advocates of Birth Control, the eugenists, for instance, are seeking to assist the race toward the elimination of the unfit. Both are seeking a single end but they lay emphasis upon different methods.

Eugenists emphasize the mating of healthy couples for the conscious purpose of producing healthy children, the sterilization of the unfit to prevent their populating the world with their kind and they may, perhaps, agree with us that contraception is a necessary measure among the masses of the workers, where wages do not keep pace with the growth of the family and its necessities in the way of food, clothing, housing, medical attention, education and the like.

We who advocate Birth Control, on the other hand, lay all our emphasis upon stopping not only the reproduction of the unfit but upon stopping all reproduction when there is not economic means of providing proper care for those who are born in health. The eugenist also believes that a woman should bear as many healthy children as possible as a duty to the state. We hold that the world is already over-populated. Eugenists imply or insist that a woman's first duty is to the state; we contend that her duty to herself is her first duty to the state.

We maintain that a woman possessing an adequate knowledge of her reproductive functions is the best judge of the time and conditions under which her child should be brought into the world. We further maintain that it is her right, regardless of all other considerations, to determine whether she shall bear children or not, and how many children she shall bear if she chooses to become a mother. To this end we insist that information in regard to scientific contraceptives be made open to all. We believe that if such information is placed within the reach of all, we will have made it possible to take the first, greatest step toward racial betterment and that this step, assisted in no small measure by the educational propaganda of eugenists and members of similar schools, will be taken.

One fundamental fact alone, however, indicates the necessity of Birth Control if eugenics is to accomplish its purpose. Unless contraceptives are used, a child is likely to be born within a year of the last one. Even when the mother is exceptionally robust this frequent child-bearing is a heavy drain upon her system and nine times in ten, it is drain upon the offspring. The mother's system has not had time to replenish itself with those elements which have been so radically diminished in bringing the child to birth, and of course it has not had time to establish that reserve stock of these same elements which are necessary to the strength and well-being of the next child. The mother's health is more than likely to be wrecked and the later children are almost sure to fall short of that nervous and muscular health which might otherwise have been theirs. Thus we hold that the fruits of the most perfect eugenic marriage are likely to be bad health in the mother and in the later children, if Birth Control is not utilized for the purpose of properly spacing the progeny.

This principle asserts itself in all of the economic layers of society but its effects may be modified to a considerable extent by those women who have the means to provide adequate care of themselves during the ante-natal period and adequate care of the child after it is born. With the great masses of the people, however, such care is either exceedingly difficult or impossible. Among the majority of wage-workers, the frequent arrival of children means not only the wrecking of the mother's health and the physical handicapping of the child, but often the disheartening and demoralization of the father, the stunting of the children through bad living conditions and early toil, and in that generation or the next, the contributing of morons, feeble-minded, insane and various criminal types to the already tremendous social burden constituted by these unfit.

While I personally believe in the sterilization of the feeble-minded, the insane and the syphiletic, I have not been able to discover that these measures are more than superficial deterrents when applied to the constantly growing stream of the unfit. They are excellent means of meeting a certain phase of the situation, but I believe in regard to these, as in regard to other eugenic means, that they do not go to the bottom of the matter. Neither the mating of healthy couples nor the sterilization of certain recognized types of the unfit touches the great problem of unlimited reproduction of those whose housing, clothing, and food are all inadequate to physical and mental health. These measures do not touch those great masses, who through economic pressure populate the slums and there produce in their helplessness other helpless, diseased and incompetent masses, who overwhelm all that eugenics can do among those whose economic condition is better.

Birth Control, on the other hand, not only opens the way to the eugenist, but it preserves his work. Furthermore, it not only prepares the ground in a natural fashion for the development of a higher standard of motherhood and of family life, but enables the child to be better born, better cared for in infancy and better educated.

Birth Control of itself, by freeing the reproductive instinct from its present chains, will make a better race. A family subsisting upon a certain wage will naturally give better care to one or two children upon that wage than it would to four or six or eight or ten, and the two children are much less likely have to go into child labor factories and sweat-shops than are the eight or ten. The situation is too plain for argument.

Concrete examples of the eugenic effects of Birth Control are the most convincing evidence. In Holland, where Birth Control is taught in clinics conducted by nurses specially trained for that purpose, military statistics show that the average stature of men has increased four inches in thirty years. Ninety per cent of the men were fit for army service, while in the United States, less than 50 per cent. were.

The fighting qualities of the French *poilu*, his endurance, and his fitness have been the amazement of military authorities in the Great War. The present generation of Frenchmen, as everyone knows who remembers the horror with which "anti-race suicidists" greeted the French tendency to Birth Control, is the product largely of Birth Control methods.

Eugenics without Birth Control seems to us a house [built] upon the sands. It is at the mercy of the rising stream of the unfit. It cannot stand against the furious winds of economic pressure which have buffeted into partial or total helplessness a tremendous proportion of the human race. Only upon a free, self-determining motherhood can rest any unshakable structure of racial betterment.

Glossary

ante-natal period	the period before birth
eugenists	practitioners of eugenics, or efforts to improve the quality of offspring by selective breeding; usually spelled "eugenicists"
Great War	World War I
poilu	"hairy one"; a French infantryman
syphiletic	afflicted with syphilis, a sexually transmitted disease

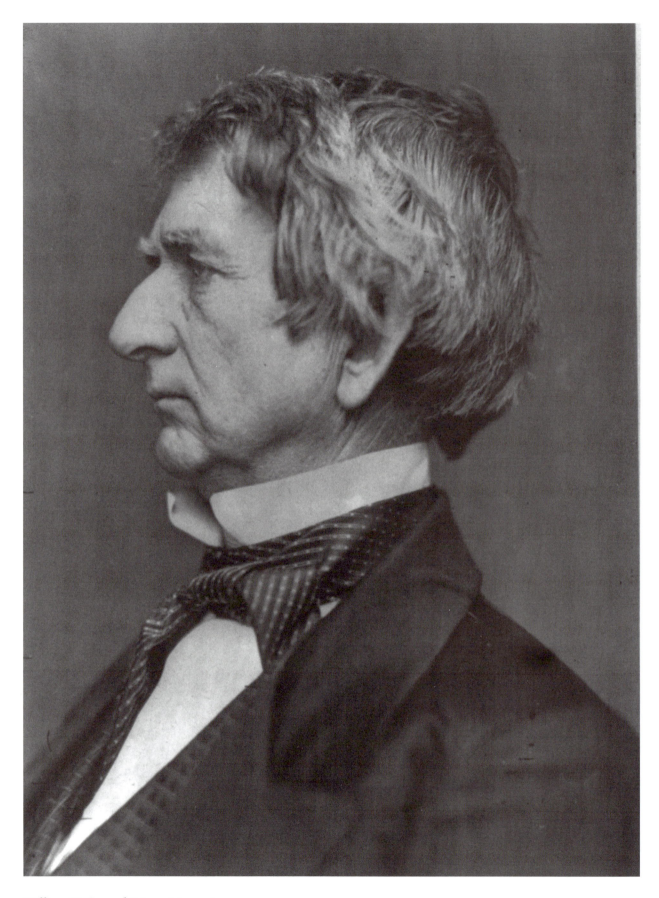

William H. Seward (Library of Congress)

WILLIAM HENRY SEWARD   1801–1872

Governor, U.S. Senator, Presidential Candidate, and Secretary of State

Featured Documents
- ◆ Speech on the Admission of California to Statehood (1850)
- ◆ Speech on the "Irrepressible Conflict" (1858)
- ◆ Memorandum to President Abraham Lincoln (1861)

Overview

William Henry Seward was born in New York in 1801. After graduating from Union College in 1820, he passed the state bar exam in 1822 and began to practice law. He first entered politics by running unsuccessfully for the New York State Senate in 1828. Two years later, he won the office on the Anti-Masonic Party ticket with the help of his political mentor, Thurlow Weed. After an unsuccessful bid for the New York governorship in 1834, he was elected four years later as a Whig and served two terms. Seward compiled a progressive record as governor, supporting prison reform, immigrant rights, and financial aid to parochial schools. His unwillingness to extradite three black fugitives to Virginia won him the support of antislavery advocates across the nation.

After leaving the governorship in 1842, Seward returned to private law practice in Auburn, New York, while remaining active in Whig Party affairs. In 1846 he was heavily criticized for representing the black former convict William Freeman in a murder trial, using an insanity defense. Although Freedman was convicted, Seward's eloquence in attacking racial prejudice during the trial marked him as a man of principle. He campaigned actively for the Whig presidential candidate Zachary Taylor in 1848 and was himself elected to the U.S. Senate early the following year.

Seward entered the Senate in time to participate in debates over Henry Clay's compromise resolutions, which were aimed at resolving the issue of slavery in newly acquired U.S. territories. Seward soon became a leader of the antislavery forces and an opponent to southern domination of the federal government. After the disintegration of the Whigs in 1853–1854, he joined the new Republican Party and was seen as a likely presidential prospect. In 1860, however, he unexpectedly lost his party's nomination to Abraham Lincoln.

Taking the post of secretary of state under Lincoln, Seward guided U.S. foreign policy in the midst of the Civil War. He succeeded in his primary mission of keeping Great Britain and France from recognizing the Confederacy and entering the conflict. A strong believer in the Monroe Doctrine, he helped prevent France from maintaining a puppet state in Mexico under Emperor Maximilian. On April 14, 1865, the night that Lincoln was killed, Seward himself narrowly escaped assassination. He stayed on as secretary of state when Andrew Johnson assumed the presidency. In

1867 he signed a treaty with Russia for the purchase of Alaska, an accomplishment that was ridiculed at the time as "Seward's folly." After leaving office in 1869, he traveled to speaking engagements and took a yearlong trip around the world. He died at his Auburn home in 1872.

Explanation and Analysis of Documents

Seward's years in public life coincided with the struggle between northern and southern political leaders over the issue of slavery. The preservation of the Union and the growth of U.S. power abroad also became pressing concerns during this period. As both a public official and a partisan campaigner, Seward promoted the restriction of slavery and the strengthening of the United States as a nation built upon a free labor system. As secretary of state, he asserted America's rights against foreign encroachment even as he faced the challenge of southern rebellion. Seward's speech on statehood for California, his "irrepressible conflict" speech, and his memorandum to Lincoln on the eve of the Civil War demonstrate his ability to combine careful analysis with high idealism and bold political strategy.

◆ Speech on the Admission of California to Statehood

In mid-1848 the Treaty of Guadalupe Hidalgo transferred thousands of miles of Mexican territory to the United States. Debate over whether the newly acquired land would be opened to slavery began almost immediately. Thanks to the discovery of gold in 1849, California experienced fast population growth and had an immediate need for government. Southern leaders in the U.S. Congress, however, were reluctant to admit California as a free state without guarantees of protection for slavery in other territories. On January 21, 1850, President Zachary Taylor recommended admitting California to the Union under the antislavery constitution drawn up by its citizens. Eight days later, Senator Henry Clay of Kentucky introduced a set of compromise resolutions that combined California statehood with other measures addressing slavery-related issues. On March 11, Seward responded to Clay's proposals in his first major speech as a U.S. senator. Although he offered it primarily in support of Taylor's position on California, the speech dealt at length with larger issues of slavery, constitutional theory, and national sovereignty.

1801 ■ **May 16**
William H. Seward is born in Florida, New York.

1830 ■ Seward is elected to the New York State Senate.

1834 ■ Seward is defeated in his first bid for the New York governorship.

1838 ■ Seward is elected to the first of two terms as New York governor.

1849 ■ Seward is elected to the U.S. Senate.

1850 ■ **March 11**
Seward delivers a speech in favor of the admission of California to statehood, known as the "higher law" speech.

1855 ■ Seward is reelected to the U.S. Senate.

1858 ■ **October 25**
Seward delivers his "irrepressible conflict" speech.

1860 ■ **May 18**
Seward is defeated in his bid for the Republican presidential nomination.

1861 ■ **March 5**
Under President Abraham Lincoln, Seward takes office as secretary of state.

1865 ■ **April 14**
Seward narrowly escapes assassination.

1867 ■ **March 30**
Seward signs the Alaska annexation treaty.

In the excerpt included here, Seward begins by asserting that California can never be anything less than a state. The United States cannot afford to put off California's request, as otherwise the chance to unite the Atlantic and Pacific coasts in common political and economic interests might be lost. The benefits of admitting California were obvious; only a misguided attempt to link its statehood with slavery-related questions stood in the way. In bold, unequivocal terms, Seward declares his opposition to "any and all" compromise measures related to this issue. In his view, legislative compromises were inherently wrong, both in principle and in their practical effect of stifling judgment and closing down debate. In this case, the Clay compromise proposals threatened to have a "paralyzing" effect on those challenging slavery now and in the future.

Seward here challenges the idea advanced by Senator John C. Calhoun and other southern leaders that states can intrinsically be "slave" states. Specifically, he disputes the notion that slavery as an institution can have primacy over the principles of freedom embodied in the U.S. Constitution. In fact, he says, freedom is a "perpetual, organic, universal" institution that protects even the slaveholder as much as any citizen. While a state could continue to exist without slavery, it could not do so without freedom. Seward terms slavery "accidental" and "incongruous," a vestige of England's colonial rule that has been out of step with the expansion of rights since American independence. Thus, it was particularly objectionable to him that this outmoded institution was being allowed to strengthen its dominance of the nation as a whole. Ignoring the inherent right to freedom within the newly acquired territories in the West would only compound the error. The national government had "no arbitrary power" to permit slavery to enter its acquired domains; rather, the principles of the Constitution—"liberty" among them—had to guide federal stewardship of new territories.

In the following paragraph, Seward introduces the phrase that would make this speech famous. He asserts that "there is a higher law than the Constitution," one that regulates the actions of the government. On the surface, Seward essentially states that the moral imperative of God's authority overrules human government. It should be noted that using an outside authority (most often the Bible) to help interpret and justify man-made laws was not uncommon in nineteenth-century America. In advocating his compromise measures, Clay had indicated that a higher authority (specifically, Nature) would ensure that slavery would not take root in the new territories. In another Senate speech on this subject, Jefferson Davis referred to God's role in establishing slavery in the South. In citing a "higher law," Seward underscores moral principles to be used in the interpretation of the Constitution, rather than suggesting that the Constitution should be discarded. Still, the idea that something other than the Constitution should be considered in formulating national policy then aroused a storm of criticism.

Continuing on this theme, Seward quotes the English philosopher Francis Bacon regarding the power of nations to shape future generations. He then affirms that the United States owes its present greatness to the willingness of the Founders to establish wise and just institutions. The Founders were unable to abolish slavery in their own time; nevertheless, it would violate their intentions to allow slavery to spread further. To support this view, Seward refers to the Northwest Ordinance, passed by Congress in 1787, which forbade slavery in the future states of Ohio, Indiana, Michigan, Illinois, and Wisconsin. Seward flatly declares that there would have been no slave states at all in the Union if the Founders "had had the free alternative as we now have"—a direct challenge to the assertion by Calhoun, Davis, and their allies that slavery was "a positive good" for the South. More than an evil in itself, Seward contends, slavery is a threat to the larger welfare of the nation, undermining democracy and carrying the seeds of despotic rule. For these and other reasons, Seward asks how any responsible statesman could even consider extending the reach of slavery. He opposed doing so for the good of both the new western territories and the United States as a whole. In strongly moral terms, he again voices opposition to any compromise on the issue of slavery in order to secure the admission of California.

Seward next turns to the question of whether definite prohibition against slavery was necessary in the new territories. He reaffirms his support for the Wilmot Proviso, an amendment offered by Representative David Wilmot in 1846 forbidding slavery in territory acquired from Mexico. Clay, Senator Daniel Webster, and other pro-compromise leaders claimed that the arid climate of the new western lands made slavery all but impossible there, rendering its prohibition unnecessary. In refuting the idea that slavery could be maintained only in the American South, Seward notes that it once existed across Europe and continued to exist (in the form of serfdom) in Russia. Because slave labor was cheaper than free labor, no area was intrinsically protected from it. He adds that slavery had been legal in his native state of New York during his childhood (though the institution was being phased out over time).

Looking beyond the current controversy, Seward believed that slavery would inevitably be abolished for both moral and economic reasons. He makes clear that he does not favor its overthrow by force, though he adds that "all measures which fortify slavery or extend it" would be likely to provoke violence. (Pro-slavery leaders and compromise advocates saw this comment as a threat against slavery wherever it existed, rather than merely a warning against its further spread.) Carefully walking a narrow line, Seward states that the end of slavery should be hastened by all legal means but emphasizes that no free state was proposing to extend its own laws into a slave state. Still, he was not prepared to offer any further guarantees that slavery would remain untouched in the South. In his view, even the threat of conquest of the North by the South would not change the situation; restricting the debate over slavery, likewise, would not divert the course of history. In prophetic tones, Seward predicts that the slave states would favor emancipation "sooner or later," because any "wise" nation would inevitably do so.

Time Line

1869	■ **March 4** Seward retires from public life.
1870	■ **August 9** Seward begins a yearlong trip around the world.
1872	■ **October 10** Seward dies in Auburn, New York.

As an ardent nationalist, Seward professes to be shocked at any expression of disunionist sentiment by his Senate colleagues. He reaffirms his belief that the American people, in the North and the South, were loyal to the United States. Even as he praises the patriotic spirit of Americans in both sections, Seward declares that he will not compromise his principles to avoid provoking southern extremists. The fear of southern states leaving the Union, he contends, was unwarranted. (In hindsight, Seward clearly underestimated the degree of anger and defiance among extreme southern defenders of slavery. He would continue to downplay the threat of disunion until the outbreak of the Civil War in 1861.) Closing with a visionary flourish, Seward speaks in the voice of future Americans addressing the present generation. More than military power or even national honor, they desire a country "free from the calamities and the sorrows of human bondage." With this grand imagery, Seward aims beyond his fellow senators for a broader national audience.

Seward's speech indeed stirred a great deal of controversy. Taylor disavowed it, despite the defense it offered for his California policy. Clay said it contained "wild, reckless, and abominable theories, which strike at the foundations of all property, and threaten to crush in ruins the fabric of civilized society" (Nevins, vol. 1, p. 301). Southern partisans were even more incensed, with some threatening Seward with violence. However, the idea of a "higher law" condemning slavery appealed to many northern opponents of slavery. Despite Seward's opposition, Clay's measures were passed later that year as the Compromise of 1850, which included the northern concession that the territories of Utah and New Mexico would not be designated free states but would have popular sovereignty with regard to slavery.

◆ Speech on the "Irrepressible Conflict"

By 1858 the debate over slavery had grown increasingly intense and bitter. Four years earlier, the Kansas-Nebraska Act had opened up to slavery those territories north of the 1820 Missouri Compromise line. Northern indignation over this act led to the formation of the Republican Party, dedicated to restricting slavery's expansion. Seward left the disintegrating Whigs to join the Republicans in 1855. Though he did not seek the party's nomination for president the following year, after the election of the Democrat James Buchanan he became the leading candidate for the 1860 Republican nomination. Toward that end, Seward campaigned extensively for his party during the 1858 elections. On October 25 of that year, he delivered a speech in Rochester, New York, on behalf of the gubernatorial candidate Edwin D. Morgan that inspired both praise and outrage far beyond the state.

Seward begins by acknowledging the intensity of Republican Party supporters during the campaign. The apparent pro-southern bias of President Buchanan, along with such events as the warfare over slavery in Kansas and the Supreme Court's controversial *Dred Scott* decision, had boosted Republican fortunes across the North. Seizing on this partisan enthusiasm, Seward quickly takes aim at Buchanan's fellow Democrats and begins his indictment of their failures and misdeeds.

Seward states bluntly that the United States was divided between two opposing political systems, one based on slavery and the other on free labor. The fact that the slaves were of African origin was irrelevant; what was relevant to the case he makes was the debasing effect that slavery had on American society overall. If the principle behind slavery was accepted, white laborers, too, could potentially be reduced to bondage. The antagonism between the slave and free labor systems could be seen in Europe, where a despotic Russia stood in opposition to a largely free Europe. Seward points out that two such incompatible systems could not be expected to coexist in the same country. (This thought is similar to Abraham Lincoln's statement that "a house divided against itself cannot stand," made during his campaign for the Senate in Illinois four months earlier.)

Indeed, these two opposing labor systems threatened to impede America's efforts to achieve "a higher and more perfect social unity" as a nation. Unlike those who continued to preach compromise, Seward states that an "irrepressible conflict" existed between the forces of slavery and free labor, one that would lead to an inevitable "collision." Playing to his partisan audience's worst fears, he raises the possibility that even New York could become a slave market if the pro-slavery Democrats had their way. The *Dred Scott* decision's holding that slaves were private property protected by the Constitution throughout the country made such an unlikely possibility seem plausible. Seward claims that awareness of the prospect of a collision between the two labor systems dated back to the days of the Founding Fathers. Even though they lacked the ability to settle the issue then, the Founders anticipated that slavery would ultimately be abolished in both the North and the South.

According to Seward, collusion between corrupt federal officials and various wealthy interests had helped slavery survive and expand. These forces would not be satisfied with the gains they had made in recent years, he warns. By annexing foreign territories (Cuba, in particular) and repealing the ban on the African slave trade, pro-slavery politicians could further tighten their hold on the Union. A compliant Supreme Court could block any attempts to restrict slavery through constitutional amendment or local statutes. The southern-dominated Democrats, in sum, would not stop until the entire United States was enmeshed in the slavery system. Seward devotes the rest of his speech to driving home his point that the Democratic Party was merely a vehicle for southern slaveholders to control the federal government. Without its southern base, the party would be reduced to "a helpless and hopeless minority" in the rest of the country. The perception that the Democratic presidents Franklin Pierce and James Buchanan displayed pro-southern sympathies added credence to Seward's arguments.

Seward expresses confidence that the Republicans would triumph. In his view, the party daken up the cause of equal rights that belonged to the Democrats before they surrendered to the pro-slavery South. He reminds his audience that his party took its name from the original Democratic-Republican Party, led by Thomas Jefferson in opposition to the aristocratic Federalists. Although the Democratic Party claimed Jefferson as its founder, it was the new Republicans who were his rightful heirs. In conclusion, Seward hails the uprising of antislavery voters as a "revolution" that would "confound and overthrow" the Democrats with "one decisive blow."

Seward's "irrepressible conflict" speech ignited an even more heated debate than had his "higher law" speech eight years earlier. By all indications, he did not intend his speech to be anything more than a reiteration of familiar Republican arguments. But to southern politicians and newspaper editors (as well as some northern ones), the suggestion that conflict was "irrepressible" was nothing less than a call for violence. Republicans generally endorsed his sentiments, though some felt his language was too extreme. For his part, Seward was taken aback by the response and tried to soften his message in subsequent campaign appearances. Ultimately, his prospects for the 1860 Republican presidential nomination were probably damaged by the speech's perceived radicalism.

◆ **Memorandum to President Abraham Lincoln**

Seward's loss of the 1860 Republican presidential nomination to Abraham Lincoln came as a shock to his supporters. After winning the election, Lincoln chose Seward to be his secretary of state. Many expected the new secretary to become the unofficial "premier" of the administration, dominating the less-experienced Lincoln behind the scenes. After taking office, Seward became concerned that the president had no clear plans for dealing with the growing secession crisis and the threat of civil war. The immediate question of whether to reinforce federal forts in the South was especially pressing. With this in mind, Seward expressed his concerns in a memorandum to Lincoln written on April 1, 1861.

Seward begins by asserting that the administration lacks "a policy either domestic or foreign." He indirectly faults the president for spending his time dealing with office seekers rather than "more grave matters." The filling of patronage jobs, he implores, had to be completed quickly or put aside before the dangers to the country grew even

A cartoon titled "The Irrepressible Conflict" shows Seward being heaved overboard from the "Republican" barge, reflecting the bitterness among New York Republicans at the party's failure to nominate William H. Seward for president at its 1860 national convention. (Library of Congress)

worse. The tone here is urgent and not a little condescending toward the president.

Moving on to domestic policy, Seward stresses the need to change the public debate from the topic of slavery to that of preserving the Union. Partisan issues (such as the Republican Party's opposition to slavery's expansion) needed to be put aside in favor of broad-based patriotism. He notes that the argument over defending or evacuating Fort Sumter (located in the harbor of Charleston, South Carolina, the center of southern disunionism) was problematically seen as a partisan question; even Union supporters had doubted the wisdom of holding on to the fort. To focus attention elsewhere, Seward advocates instead reinforcing federal property along the Gulf of Mexico, in particular Fort Pickens, in Florida. In advising Lincoln to abandon Sumter and concentrate on the more easily defensible forts on the Gulf, Seward intended for the administration to maintain a symbolic federal presence in the South while lessening the chance of a military confrontation.

Thus far, Seward's suggestions in this document are moderate and familiar. His proposals dealing with foreign affairs, to the contrary, are startling in their boldness. In blunt language, he suggests demanding explanations from Spain and France regarding their attempts to occupy Santo Domingo in the Caribbean, in violation of the Monroe Doctrine. If these explanations were not "satisfactory," the United States should declare war on these two nations. Seward also favored warning Great Britain and Russia against intervening in American affairs. Behind these sug-

gested threats is the idea of uniting North and South militarily against a common enemy. In December 1860 Seward had said in a speech that if a European power moved against the United States, "all the hills of South Carolina would pour forth their populations for the rescue of New York" (Potter, p. 369). The fact that Seward would propose such risky moves indicates his frustration over Lincoln's apparent inability to deal with the secession crisis.

Finally, Seward asserts that the administration must be energetic in pursuing its policy, whatever it might be. Someone had to take a leadership role—and if Lincoln is unable, "some member of his Cabinet" had to do so. Seward communicates that he is willing to step up and take command, concluding disingenuously, "I neither seek to evade nor assume responsibility."

Lincoln responded to the memorandum by meeting with Seward that same day. In a written (but apparently unsent) reply, he reminded his secretary of state that his inaugural address contained a commitment to maintaining control of federal property. He asked why defending Fort Pickens should be considered essential to upholding the Union, while reinforcing Fort Sumter could be seen as merely a partisan act. Lincoln ignored Seward's idea of launching a foreign war. The president closed by stating that if a policy decision needed to be made, "I must do it" (Taylor, p. 151). Whatever else it may have accomplished, Seward's memorandum, in eliciting a response from the president, established that Lincoln indeed intended to be commander in chief in fact as well as in name.

"The Constitution regulates our stewardship; the Constitution devotes the domain to union, to justice, to defence, to welfare, and to liberty. But there is a higher law than the Constitution, which regulates our authority over the domain, and devotes it to the same noble purposes."

(Speech on the Admission of California to Statehood)

"I feel assured that slavery must give way, and will give way, to the salutary instructions of economy, and to the ripening influences of humanity."

(Speech on the Admission of California to Statehood)

"You must have guaranties; and the first one is for the surrender of fugitives from labor. That guaranty you cannot have, as I have already shown, because you cannot roll back the tide of social progress."

(Speech on the Admission of California to Statehood)

"The free-labor system conforms to the divine law of equality, which is written in the hearts and consciences of man, and therefore is always and everywhere beneficent."

(Speech on the "Irrepressible Conflict")

"Shall I tell you what this collision means?… It is an irrepressible conflict between opposing and enduring forces, and it means that the United States must and will, sooner or later, become either entirely a slaveholding nation, or entirely a free-labor nation."

(Speech on the "Irrepressible Conflict")

"I know, and you know, that a revolution has begun. I know, and all the world knows, that revolutions never go backward."

(Speech on the "Irrepressible Conflict")

"We must change the question before the public from one upon slavery, or about slavery, for a question upon union or disunion."

(Memorandum to President Abraham Lincoln)

Impact and Legacy

As an orator, Seward did not possess the soaring voice or dramatic presence of contemporaries such as Henry Clay or Daniel Webster. But as a writer and thinker, his abilities placed him in the front rank of nineteenth-century American statesmen. His ability to logically present ideas and express them in subtle yet forceful language was recognized even by his political enemies. Seward had the practical mind of a legal scholar, yet he could also coin instantly memorable phrases that resonated with the American public. His peers at times disagreed about the motivations behind his words. His supporters considered him a man of high principle, fighting against slavery and for national unity on moral grounds. Others thought of him as an opportunistic politician playing the role of the radical one minute, then that of the conservative compromiser the next. Yet few disputed Seward's intellectual gifts or his capability as a leader and administrator.

Seward's "higher law" speech articulated the rising opposition in the North to slavery's expansion. By combining an analysis of the constitutional status of slavery with an overall philosophical attack upon the institution, he laid the basis for the Republican Party's program in the 1850s. Recognizing by 1858 that effective compromise between pro- and antislavery forces was no longer possible, he delivered his "irrepressible conflict" speech as a passionate yet well-reasoned argument for free labor. At the time, Seward's opponents charged him with recklessly endangering the stability of the Union with such fiery language. But time justified his view that slavery was ultimately incompatible with free American institutions.

Seward's legacy is based upon more than his powerful speeches. He was a skillful policy craftsman who knew the value of quiet negotiation as well as public confrontation. An expansive view of America's destiny as a great power guided his decision making. Although it is presumptuous and ill advised in places, his April 1861 memorandum to President Lincoln shows his willingness to both consider public opinion and think in bold strokes. These qualities served him well as secretary of state as he successfully maneuvered to keep foreign powers from interfering in the Civil War. His diplomatic skills enabled him to purchase Alaska from Russia in 1867, even as he endured criticism for serving under Lincoln's embattled successor, Andrew Johnson. Seward was a leader who envisioned a United States built upon free labor and equal rights, and his impact upon his country has been a lasting one.

Key Sources

The William H. Seward Papers are available on microfilm from the University of Rochester Library. The Seward House, in Auburn, New York, also has numerous political and personal documents. George E. Baker, ed., *The Works of William H. Seward*, 5 vols. (1853–1884), contains all of the statesman's important speeches. Frederick William Seward, ed., *William H. Seward: An Autobiography from 1801 to 1834; With a Memoir of His Life, and Selections*

Seward, William Henry

Questions for Further Study

1. The most memorable passage in Seward's speech on the admission of California to the Union is his reference to "a higher law than the Constitution," by which he meant God. Judging from this and the later address on the "irrepressible conflict," how much emphasis did Seward place on the idea that the government should abide by divine authority? How justified were his opponents in their fear that he was attempting to involve a power other than the Constitution in matters that should have been governed solely by that document?

2. Discuss the various lines of argument against slavery that Seward employs in the "irrepressible conflict" speech. How does he contrast the economic and political systems of slaveholding states and nations with those of societies built on free labor? What parallels does he draw between the situation in America and that in the Old World? What unintended impact did this speech—which Seward himself considered a mere restatement of Republican Party positions on the issue of slavery—have on the nation as a whole as well as on Seward's career?

3. What does the 1861 memorandum to President Abraham Lincoln say about Seward's views regarding the president on whose cabinet he served? What was the history of the two men's political interactions, and how did these influence their working relationship during the Civil War? How did Lincoln respond to Seward, both in this particular document and in his overall interactions with him? What does his manner of dealing with Seward say about Lincoln's leadership style?

from His Letters, 3 vols. (1891), is worth seeking out for its excepts from Seward's correspondence and journals.

Further Reading

■ Books

Auer, J. Jeffrey, ed. *Antislavery and Disunion, 1858–1861: Studies in the Rhetoric of Compromise and Conflict.* New York: Harper & Row, 1963.

Foner, Eric. *Free Soil, Free Labor, Free Men: The Ideology of the Republican Party before the Civil War.* New York: Oxford University Press, 1970.

Goodwin, Doris Kearns. *Team of Rivals: The Political Genius of Abraham Lincoln.* New York: Simon & Schuster, 2005.

Holt, Michael F. *The Rise and Fall of the American Whig Party: Jacksonian Politics and the Onset of the Civil War.* New York: Oxford University Press, 1999.

Lothrop, Thornton K. *William Henry Seward.* Boston: Houghton, Mifflin, 1899.

Nevins, Allan. *Ordeal of the Union*, Vol. 1: *Fruits of Manifest Destiny, 1847–1852.* New York: Scribner, 1947.

Potter, David M. *Lincoln and His Party in the Secession Crisis.* New Haven, Conn.: Yale University Press, 1942.

Taylor, John M. *William Henry Seward: Lincoln's Right Hand.* New York: HarperCollins, 1991.

Van Deusen, Glyndon G. *William Henry Seward.* New York: Oxford University Press, 1967.

■ Web Sites

"Seward, William Henry." Biographical Directory of the United States Congress Web site. http://bioguide.congress.gov/scripts/bio display.pl?index=S000261.

"William H. Seward's Biography." Seward House Web site. http://www.sewardhouse.org/biography/.

—Barry Alfonso

SPEECH ON THE ADMISSION OF CALIFORNIA TO STATEHOOD (1850)

California is already a State, a complete and fully appointed State. She never again can be less than that. She can never again be a province or a colony; nor can she be made to shrink and shrivel into the proportions of a federal dependent Territory. California, then, henceforth and forever, must be, what she is now, a State.

The question whether she shall be one of the United States of America has depended on her and on us. Her election has been made. Our consent alone remains suspended; and that consent must be pronounced now or never. I say now or never. Nothing prevents it now, but want of agreement among our selves....

Try not the temper and fidelity of California, at least not now, not yet. Cherish her and indulge her until you have extended your settlements to her borders, and bound her fast by railroads, and canals, and telegraphs, to your interests until her affinities of intercourse are established, and her habits of loyalty are fixed and then she can never be disengaged....

But it is insisted that the admission of California shall be attended by a COMPROMISE of questions which have arisen out Of SLAVERY!

I AM OPPOSED TO ANY SUCH COMPROMISE, IN ANY AND ALL THE FORMS IN WHICH IT HAS BEEN PROPOSED; because, while admitting the purity and the patriotism of all from whom it is my misfortune to differ, I think all legislative compromises, not absolutely necessary, radically wrong and essentially vicious. They involve the surrender of the exercise of judgment and conscience on distinct and separate questions, at distinct and separate times, with the indispensable advantages it affords for ascertaining truth. They involve a relinquishment of the right to reconsider in future the decisions of the present, on questions prematurely anticipated. And they are acts of usurpation as to future questions of the province of future legislators.

Sir, it seems to me as if slavery had laid its paralyzing hand upon myself, and the blood were coursing less freely than its wont through my veins, when I endeavor to suppose that such a compromise has been effected, and that my utterance forever is arrested upon all the great questions social, moral, and political arising out of a subject so important, and as yet so incomprehensible....

There is another aspect of the principle of compromise which deserves consideration. It assumes that slavery, if not the only institution in a slave State, is at least a ruling institution, and that this characteristic is recognised by the Constitution. But slavery is only one of many institutions there. Freedom is equally an institution there. Slavery is only a temporary, accidental, partial and incongruous one. Freedom, on the contrary, is a perpetual, organic, universal one, in harmony with the Constitution of the United States. The slaveholder himself stands under the protection of the latter, in common with all the free citizens of the State. But it is, moreover, an indispensable institution. You may separate slavery from South Carolina, and the State will still remain; but if you subvert Freedom there, the State will cease to exist. But the principle of this compromise gives complete ascendency in the slave States, and in the Constitution of the United States, to the subordinate, accidental, and incongruous, institution over its paramount antagonist. To reduce this claim for slavery to an absurdity, it is only necessary to add that there are only two States in which slaves are a majority, and not one in which the slave holders are not a very disproportionate minority.

But there is yet another aspect in which this principle must be examined. It regards the domain only as a possession, to be enjoyed either in common or by partition by the citizens of the old States. It is true, indeed, that the national domain is ours. It is true it was acquired by the valor and with the wealth of the whole nation. But we hold, nevertheless, no arbitrary power over it. We hold no arbitrary authority over anything, whether acquired lawfully or seized by usurpation. The Constitution regulates our stewardship; the Constitution devotes the domain to union, to justice, to defence, to welfare, and to liberty.

But there is a higher law than the Constitution, which regulates our authority over the domain, and devotes it to the same noble purposes. The territory is a part, no inconsiderable part, of the common heritage of mankind, bestowed upon them by the Creator of the Universe. We are his stewards, and must so discharge our trust as to secure in the highest attainable degree their happiness. How momentous that trust is, we may learn from the instructions of the founder of modern philosophy:

"No man," says Bacon, "can by care-taking, as the Scripture saith, add a cubit to his stature in this little model of a man's body; but, in the great frame of kingdoms and commonwealths, it is in the power of princes or estates to add amplitude and greatness to their kingdoms. For, by introducing such ordinances, constitutions, and customs, as are wise, they may sow greatness to their posterity and successors. But these things are commonly not observed, but left to take their chance."

This is a State, and we are deliberating for it, just as our fathers deliberated in establishing the institutions we enjoy. Whatever superiority there is in our condition and hopes over those of any other "kingdom" or "estate" is due to the fortunate circumstance that our ancestors did not leave things to "take their chance," but that they "added amplitude and greatness" to our commonwealth "by introducing such ordinances, constitutions, and customs, as were wise." We in our turn have succeeded to the same responsibilities, and we cannot approach the duty before us wisely or justly, except we raise ourselves to the great consideration of how we can most certainly "sow greatness to our posterity and successors."

And now the simple, bold, and even awful question which presents itself to us is this: Shall we, who are founding institutions, social and political, for countless millions; shall we, who know by experience the wise and the just, and are free to choose them, and to reject the erroneous and unjust; shall we establish human bondage, or permit it by our sufferance to be established? Sir, our forefathers would not have hesitated an hour. They found slavery existing here, and they left it only because they could not remove it. There is not only no free State which would now establish it, but there is no slave State, which, if it had had the free alternative as we now have, would have founded slavery. Indeed, our revolutionary predecessors had precisely the same question before them in establishing an organic law under which the States of Ohio, Indiana, Michigan, Illinois, and Wisconsin, have since come into the Union, and they solemnly repudiated and excluded slavery from those States forever. I confess that the most alarming evidence of our degeneracy which has yet been given is found in the fact that we even debate such a question.

Sir, there is no Christian nation, thus free to choose as we are, which would establish slavery. I speak on due consideration, because Britain, France, and Mexico, have abolished slavery, and all other European States are preparing to abolish it as speedily as they can. We cannot establish slavery, because there are certain elements of the security, welfare, and greatness of nations, which we all admit or ought to admit, and recognise as essential; and these are the security of natural rights, the diffusion of knowledge, and the freedom of industry. Slavery is incompatible with all of these, and just in proportion to the extent that it prevails and controls in any republican State, just to that extent it subverts the principle of democracy, and converts the State into an aristocracy or a despotism....

It remains only to remark that our own experience has proved the dangerous influence and tendency of slavery. All our apprehensions of dangers, present and future, begin and end with slavery. If slavery, limited as it yet is, now threatens to subvert the Constitution, how can we, as wise and prudent statesmen, enlarge its boundaries and increase its influence, and thus increase already impending dangers. Whether, then, I regard merely the welfare of the future inhabitants of the new Territories, or the security and welfare of the whole people of the United States, or the welfare of the whole family of mankind, I cannot consent to introduce slavery into any part of this continent which is now exempt from what seems to me so great an evil. These are my reasons for declining to compromise the question relating to slavery as a condition of the admission of California....

The argument is that the [Wilmot] Proviso is unnecessary. I answer, there, then, can be no error in insisting upon it. But why is it unnecessary? It is said, first, by reason of climate. I answer, if this be so, why do not the representatives of the slave States concede the Proviso? They deny that the climate prevents the introduction of slavery. Then I will leave nothing to a contingency. But, in truth, I think the weight of argument is against the proposition. Is there any climate where slavery has not existed? It has prevailed all over Europe, from sunny Italy to bleak England, and is existing now, stronger than in any other land, in ice-bound Russia....

Sir, there is no climate uncongenial to slavery. It is true it is less productive than free labor in many northern countries. But so it is less productive than free white labor in even tropical climates. Labor is in quick demand in all new countries. Slave labor is cheaper than free labor, and it would go first into new regions; and wherever it goes it brings labor into dishonor, and therefore free white labor avoids competition with it. Sir, I might rely on climate if I had not been born in a land where slavery existed and this land was all of it north of the fortieth parallel of latitude; and if I did not know the struggle it has cost, and which is yet going on, to get complete relief from the institution and its baleful consequences....

I feel assured that slavery must give way, and will give way, to the salutary instructions of economy, and to the ripening influences of humanity; that emancipation is inevitable, and is near; that it may be hastened or hindered; and that whether it be peaceful or violent, depends upon the question whether it be hastened or hindered; that all measures which fortify slavery or extend it, tend to the consummation of violence; all that check its extension and abate its strength, tend to its peaceful extirpation. But I will adopt none but lawful, constitutional, and peaceful means, to secure even that end; and none such can I or will I forego. Nor do I know any important or responsible body that proposes to do more than this. No free State claims to extend its legislation into a slave State.

None claims that Congress shall usurp power to abolish slavery in the slave States. None claims that any violent, unconstitutional, or unlawful measure shall be embraced. And, on the other hand, if we offer no scheme or plan for the adoption of the slave States, with the assent and co-operation of Congress, it is only because the slave States are unwilling as yet to receive such suggestions, or even to entertain the question of emancipation in any form....

I have thus endeavored to show that there is not now, and there is not likely to occur, any adequate cause for revolution in regard to slavery. But you reply that, nevertheless, you must have guaranties; and the first one is for the surrender of fugitives from labor. That guaranty you cannot have, as I have already shown, because you cannot roll back the tide of social progress. You must be content with what you have. If you wage war against us, you can, at most, only conquer us, and then all you can get will be a treaty, and that you have already....

You insist that you cannot submit to the freedom with which slavery is discussed in the free States. Will a war for slavery arrest or even moderate that discussion? No, sir, that discussion will not cease; war would only inflame it to a greater height. It is a part of the eternal conflict between truth arid error between mind and physical force the conflict of man

against the obstacles which oppose his way to an ultimate and glorious destiny. It will go on until you shall terminate it in the only way in which any State or Nation has ever terminated it by yielding to it yielding in your own time, and in your own manner, indeed, but nevertheless yielding to the progress of emancipation. You will do this, sooner or later, whatever may be your opinion now; because nations which were prudent and humane, and wise as you are, have done so already.

I have heard somewhat here, and almost for the first time in my life, of divided allegiance of allegiance to the South and to the Union of allegiance to States severally and to the Union.... I know only one country and one sovereign—the United States of America and the American People. And such as my allegiance is, is the loyalty of every other citizen of the United States. As I speak, he will speak when his time arrives. He knows no other country and no other sovereign. He has life, liberty, property, and precious affections, and hopes for himself and for his posterity, treasured up in the ark of the Union. He knows as well and feels as strongly as I do that this Government is his own Government; that he is a part of it; that it was established for him, and that it is maintained by him; that it is the only truly wise, just, free, and equal Government that has ever existed; that no other Government could be so wise, just, free, and equal; and that it is safer and more beneficent than any which time or change could bring into its place.

You may tell me, sir, that although all this may be true, yet the trial of faction has not yet been made. Sir, if the trial of faction has not been made, it has not been because faction has not always existed, and has not always menaced a trial, but because faction could find no fulcrum on which to place the lever to subvert the Union, as it can find no fulcrum now; and in this is my confidence. I would not rashly provoke the trial; but I will not suffer a fear, which I have not, to make me compromise one sentiment, one principle of truth or justice, to avert a danger that all experience teaches me is purely chimerical.

Glossary

Bacon	Sir Francis Bacon, English philosopher and author of "Of the True Greatness of Kingdoms and Estates," contained in his 1597 volume *Essays*, the source of the quotation
organic law	the fundamental system of laws on which a nation is founded
serried	pressed together, such as columns of soldiers

Let, then, those who distrust the Union make compromises to save it. I shall not impeach their wisdom, as I certainly cannot their patriotism; but indulging no such apprehensions myself, I shall vote for the admission of California directly, without conditions, without qualifications, and without compromise.

For the vindication of that vote I look not to the verdict of the passing hour, disturbed as the public mind now is by conflicting interests and passions, but to that period, happily not far distant, when the vast regions over which we are now legislating shall have received their destined inhabitants.

While looking forward to that day, its countless generations seem to me to be rising up and passing in dim and shadowy review before us; and a voice comes forth from their serried ranks, saying: "Waste your treasures and your armies, if you will; raze your fortifications to the ground; sink your navies into the sea; transmit to us even a dishonored name, if you must; but the soil you hold in trust for us give it to us free. You found it free, and conquered it to extend a better and surer freedom over it. Whatever choice you have made for your selves, let us have no partial freedom; let us all be free; let the reversion of your broad domain descend to us unincumbered, and free from the calamities and the sorrows of human bondage."

Speech on the "Irrepressible Conflict" (1858)

The unmistakable outbreaks of zeal which occur all around me show that you are earnest men—and such a man am I. Let us, therefore, at least for a time, pass all secondary and collateral questions, whether of a personal or of a general nature, and consider the main subject of the present canvass. The Democratic party, or, to speak more accurately, the party which wears that attractive name, is in possession of the federal government. The Republicans propose to dislodge that party, and dismiss it from its high trust.

The main subject, then, is whether the Democratic party deserves to retain the confidence of the American people....

Our country is a theatre, which exhibits, in full operation, two radically different political systems; the one resting on the basis of servile or slave labor, the other on voluntary labor of freemen. The laborers who are enslaved are all negroes, or persons more or less purely of African derivation. But this is only accidental. The principle of the system is, that labor in every society, by whomsoever performed, is necessarily unintellectual, grovelling and base; and that the laborer, equally for his own good and for the welfare of the State, ought to be enslaved. The white laboring man, whether native or foreigner, is not enslaved, only because he cannot, as yet, be reduced to bondage....

The free-labor system conforms to the divine law of equality, which is written in the hearts and consciences of man, and therefore is always and everywhere beneficent....

Russia yet maintains slavery, and is a despotism. Most of the other European states have abolished slavery, and adopted the system of free labor. It was the antagonistic political tendencies of the two systems which the first Napoleon was contemplating when he predicted that Europe would ultimately be either all Cossack or all republican. Never did human sagacity utter a more pregnant truth. The two systems are at once perceived to be incongruous. But they are more than incongruous—they are incompatible. They never have permanently existed together in one country, and they never can....

Hitherto, the two systems have existed in different States, but side by side within the American Union. This has happened because the Union is a confederation of States. But in another aspect the United States constitute only one nation. Increase of population, which is filling the States out to their very borders, together with a new and extended network of railroads and other avenues, and an internal commerce which daily becomes more intimate, is rapidly bringing the States into a higher and more perfect social unity or consolidation. Thus, these antagonistic systems are continually coming into closer contact, and collision results.

Shall I tell you what this collision means? They who think that it is accidental, unnecessary, the work of interested or fanatical agitators, and therefore ephemeral, mistake the case altogether. It is an irrepressible conflict between opposing and enduring forces, and it means that the United States must and will, sooner or later, become either entirely a slaveholding nation, or entirely a free-labor nation. Either the cotton and rice fields of South Carolina and the sugar plantations of Louisiana will ultimately be tilled by free labor, and Charleston and New Orleans become marts of legitimate merchandise alone, or else the rye-fields and wheat-fields of Massachusetts and New York must again be surrendered by their farmers to slave culture and to the production of slaves, and Boston and New York becomes once more markets for trade in the bodies and souls of men. It is the failure to apprehend this great truth that induces so many unsuccessful attempts at final compromises between the slave and free States, and it is the existence of this great fact that renders all such pretended compromises, when made, vain and ephemeral. Startling as this saying may appear to you, fellow-citizens, it is by no means an original or even a modern one. Our forefathers knew it to be true, and unanimously acted upon it when they framed the constitution of the United States. They regarded the existence of the servile system in so many of the States with sorrow and shame, which they openly confessed, and they looked upon the collision between them, which was then just revealing itself, and which we are now accustomed to deplore, with favor and hope. They knew that one or the other system must exclusively prevail....

In the field of federal politics, slavery, deriving unlooked-for advantages from commercial changes, and energies unforeseen from the facilities of combination between members of the slaveholding class and between that class and other property classes, early rallied, and has at length made a stand, not merely to retain its original defensive position, but to extend its sway throughout the whole Union. ... The plan of operation is this: By continued appliances of patronage and threats of disunion, they will keep a majority favorable to these designs in the Senate, where each State has an equal representation. Through that majority they will defeat, as they best can, the admission of free States and secure the admission of slave States. Under the protection of the judiciary, they will, on the principle of the *Dred Scott* case, carry slavery into all the territories of the United States now existing and hereafter to be organized. By the action of the President and Senate, using the treaty-making power, they will annex foreign slaveholding States. In a favorable conjuncture they will induce Congress to repeal the act of 1808 which prohibits the foreign slave trade, and so they will import from Africa, at a cost of only twenty dollars a head, slaves enough to fill up the interior of the continent. Thus relatively increasing the number of slave States, they will allow no amendment to the constitution prejudicial to their interest; and so, having permanently established their power, they expect the federal judiciary to nullify all State laws which shall interfere with internal or foreign commerce in slaves. ...

How, then, and in what way, shall the necessary resistance be made? There is only one way. The Democratic party must be permanently dislodged from the government. The reason is, that the Democratic party is inextricably committed to the designs of the slaveholders, which I have described. ...

The very constitution of the Democratic party commits it to execute all the designs of the slaveholders, whatever they may be. It is not a party of the whole Union, of all the free States and of all the slave States; nor yet is it a party of the free States in the North and in the Northwest; but it is a sectional and local party, having practically its seat within the slave States, and counting its constituency chiefly and almost exclusively there. Of all its representatives in Congress and in the electoral colleges, two-thirds uniformly come from these States. Its great element of strength lies in the vote of the slaveholders, augmented by the representation of three-fifths of the slaves. Deprive the Democratic party of this strength, and it would be a helpless and hopeless minority, incapable of continued organization. The Democratic party, being thus local and sectional, acquires new strength from the admission of every new slave State, and loses relatively by the admission of every new free State into the Union. ...

This dark record shows you, fellow-citizens, what I was unwilling to announce at an earlier stage of this argument, that of the whole nefarious schedule of slaveholding designs which I have submitted to you, the Democratic party has left only one yet to be consummated—the abrogation of the law which forbids the African slave-trade. ...

But, understanding all this, I know that the Democratic party must go down, and that the Republican party must rise into its place. The Democratic party derived its strength, originally, from its adoption of the principles of equal and exact justice to all men. So long as it practised this principle faithfully it was invulnerable. It became vulnerable when it renounced the principle, and since that time it has maintained itself, not by virtue of its own strength, or even of its traditional merits, but because there as yet had appeared in the political field no other party that had the conscience and the courage to take up, and avow, and practise the life-inspiring principle which the Democratic party had surrendered. At last, the Republican party has appeared. It avows, now, as the Republican party of 1800 did, in one word, its faith and its works, "Equal and exact justice to all men." ...

I know, and you know, that a revolution has begun. I know, and all the world knows, that revolutions never go backward. Twenty senators and a hundred representatives proclaim boldly in Congress to-day sentiments and opinions and principles of freedom which hardly so many men, even in this free State, dared to utter in their own homes twenty years ago. While the government of the United States, under the conduct of the Democratic party, has been all that time surrendering one plain and castle after another to slavery, the people of the United States have been no less steadily and perseveringly gathering together the forces with which to recover back again all the fields and all the castles which have been lost, and to confound and overthrow, by one decisive blow, the betrayers of the constitution and freedom forever.

Glossary

"all Cossack or all republican"	all under heavy-handed military rule or all enjoying freedom under elected governments
first Napoleon	Napoleon Bonaparte, emperor of France

Memorandum to President Abraham Lincoln (1861)

Some Thoughts for the President's Consideration

First. We are at the end of a month's administration, and yet without a policy either domestic or foreign.

Second. This, however, is not culpable, and it has even been unavoidable. The presence of the Senate, with the need to meet applications for patronage, have prevented attention to other and more grave matters.

Third. But further delay to adopt and prosecute our policies for both domestic and foreign affairs would not only bring scandal on the administration, but danger upon the country.

Fourth. To do this we must dismiss the applicants for office. But how? I suggest that we make the local appointments forthwith, leaving foreign or general ones for ulterior and occasional action.

Fifth. The policy at home. I am aware that my views are singular, and perhaps not sufficiently explained. My system is built upon this idea as a ruling one, namely, that we must CHANGE THE QUESTION BEFORE THE PUBLIC FROM ONE UPON SLAVERY, OR ABOUT SLAVERY, for a question upon UNION OR DISUNION.

In other words, from what would be regarded as a party question, to one of *patriotism* or *union*.

The occupation or evacuation of Fort Sumter, although not in fact a slavery or a party question, is so regarded. Witness the temper manifested by the Republicans in the free States, and even by the Union men in the South.

I would therefore terminate it as a safe means for changing the issue. I deem it fortunate that the last administration created the necessity.

For the rest, I would simultaneously defend and reinforce all the ports in the gulf, and have the navy recalled from foreign stations to be prepared for a blockade. Put the island of Key West under martial law.

This will raise distinctly the question of union or disunion. I would maintain every fort and possession in the South.

For Foreign Nations

I would demand explanations from Spain and France, categorically, at once.

I would seek explanations from Great Britain and Russia, and send agents into Canada, Mexico, and Central America to rouse a vigorous continental spirit of independence on this continent against European intervention.

And, if satisfactory explanations are not received from Spain and France,

Would convene Congress and declare war against them.

But whatever policy we adopt, there must be an energetic prosecution of it.

For this purpose it must be somebody's business to pursue and direct it incessantly.

Either the President must do it himself, and be all the while active in it, or Devolve it on some member of his Cabinet. Once adopted, debates on it must end, and all agree and abide.

It is not in my especial province; But I neither seek to evade nor assume responsibility.

Glossary

gulf	the Gulf of Mexico
Key West	the island at the southernmost tip of the Florida Keys, a string of islands extending southwest from the Florida mainland
martial law	administration of law by the military, at the request of government

Roger Sherman (Library of Congress)

ROGER SHERMAN   1721–1793

Founding Father and U.S. Senator

Featured Documents
- ◆ "A Caveat against Injustice; or, An Inquiry into the Evils of a Fluctuating Medium of Exchange" (1752)
- ◆ "Letters of a Countryman" (November 14, 1787)
- ◆ "Letters of a Countryman" (November 22, 1787)

Overview

Roger Sherman, one of the Founders of the United States of America, was the only person who signed all four of the nation's major foundational documents: the Articles of Association, which created the Continental Association; the Declaration of Independence; the Articles of Confederation, the country's first governing constitution; and, finally, the Constitution. He was born on April 19, 1721, in Newtown (later Newton), Massachusetts. After his father's death, the family moved to New Milford, Connecticut, where in time Sherman, despite his lack of formal education, became the town's leading citizen and a major figure in state and national politics. He first worked as a shoemaker and then entered public life as a county surveyor. Later, he studied law and eventually became a justice of the peace, then a county judge, and then an associate justice of the state's Superior Court. He also served as a representative in the state's General Assembly and was the first mayor of New Haven, Connecticut. Meanwhile, Sherman and his brother became prominent merchants, and Sherman's business acumen led him to write "A Caveat against Injustice; or, An Inquiry into the Evils of a Fluctuating Medium of Exchange." This document helped put currency in the colonies on a somewhat sounder footing than it had been.

In the 1770s Sherman actively supported the American colonies' opposition to Great Britain. As a signatory to the Articles of Association, he helped organize a boycott of British goods in response to the Intolerable Acts of 1774. He was a member of the so-called Committee of Five that drafted the Declaration of Independence and was an active member of the Continental Congress. As a delegate to the Constitutional Convention, he forged the Connecticut Compromise, sometimes called the Great Compromise, which was crucial in winning support for the new constitution from both small and large states.

After the Constitution was drafted, the campaign began to urge its ratification by the states—or, in some cases, to oppose it. In support of ratification, Sherman wrote a number of "Letters of a Countryman," which were printed in the *New Haven Gazette*. These letters were part of a flurry of letters and pamphlets published in the various states as supporters and opponents debated their views. Sherman's "Letters" played an important role in persuading Connecticut to ratify the Constitution. Sherman's public career ended with two years in the U.S. Senate. He died on July 23, 1793.

Explanation and Analysis of Documents

Roger Sherman was not widely known as a writer. He was, however, a workmanlike businessman early in his career and later a tireless contributor to the founding of a new nation. The documents from his hand reflect his abiding concerns with putting the American colonies on a sound monetary footing. This concern is reflected in his early document, "A Caveat against Injustice," where he takes on the issue of the colonies' currencies and the problems associated with each colony's creating its own money and the further problems that business owners and citizens had with determining the true value of another colony's money. Later, as a delegate to the Constitutional Convention, Sherman played a key role in the production of the Constitution. His "Letters of a Countryman" were an important part of the debate over ratification of the Constitution.

◆ "A Caveat against Injustice; or, An Inquiry into the Evils of a Fluctuating Medium of Exchange"

In modern life, Americans accept paper currency as a medium of exchange. A ten-dollar bill issued by the national treasury has equal value in all the states and can be used uniformly throughout the country to purchase goods and services. The currency situation in the first half of the eighteenth century was more complicated. Each of the colonies, including Connecticut, functioned in many respects as a sovereign "nation," although before the Revolutionary War, the British Crown exercised considerable control over matters of monetary policy, trade, and taxation. The chief medium of exchange with a stable value was the British pound sterling, which was based on the value of silver. All paper money was backed by an equivalent amount of silver in the British treasury.

Further complicating the situation in the colonies, however, was that "money" often existed in the form of credit. As the American economy grew in the early decades of the century, more and more people were engaged in trade of one form or another. In New England, for example, rather than exchanging money, many people exchanged goods and labor. Thus, a person might provide labor on a neighboring farm, and the farmer would "pay" that person not with money but with a promise of so many bushels of wheat. On a larger scale, when merchants exported and imported goods, both to other colonies and to Britain, they were paid by "bills of credit"—which were essentially promissory notes. These

1721

- ■ **April 19**
  Roger Sherman is born in Newtown, Massachusetts.

1752

- ■ Sherman writes "A Caveat against Injustice; or, An Inquiry into the Evils of a Fluctuating Medium of Exchange."

1754

- ■ Sherman is admitted to the Connecticut bar.

1755–1758

- ■ Sherman serves as a representative in Connecticut's General Assembly.

1760–1761

- ■ Once again, Sherman serves as a representative in Connecticut's General Assembly.

1769

- ■ Sherman gains the post of justice of the Superior Court of Connecticut and serves until 1789.

1774

- ■ Sherman is chosen as a delegate to the First Continental Congress, convened to address the Intolerable Acts.

1775–1776

- ■ Sherman is a delegate to the Second Continental Congress, which adopts the Declaration of Independence; as a member of the Committee of Five, Sherman helps draft the Declaration of Independence.

1784

- ■ Sherman is named mayor of New Haven, Connecticut, a post he holds until 1793.

1787

- ■ Sherman serves as a delegate to the U.S. Constitutional Convention and writes a series of "Letters of a Countryman" for the *New Haven Gazette*, urging ratification of the Constitution.

bills of credit often functioned as a kind of currency. The holder of such a note might sign it over to another person to pay a debt, and that person might use it to buy shoes.

Nevertheless, from time to time, colonies printed and issued paper currency. By law, the value of this currency was fixed, pegged to a certain number of pounds, shillings, and pence supplied by the Crown. The bills themselves had no intrinsic value, unlike, say, silver coins, which have value not just as coins but for the metal they are made of. In times of war, for example, colonies found it necessary to issue paper currency to pay militias and meet other expenses. An ongoing problem was that the value of a bill issued by one colony might not be equal to the value of a bill of the same denomination issued by another colony. The value of such bills depended in large part on how many of them were in circulation. This principle is widely accepted in modern economics. The U.S. Treasury controls the amount of money in circulation, knowing that increasing the supply of money without an equivalent increase in the supply of labor and goods only devalues the currency. Two classes of people are put at distinct disadvantage when the currency loses value: those on fixed incomes, since the value of what money they do have drops; and creditors, because the value of the debts owed to them decreases.

These are the problems that Sherman addresses in "A Caveat against Injustice." In the opening three paragraphs, he summarizes the problem. Other colonies issued bills of credit that became a medium of exchange, but in Sherman's view they failed to maintain funds in the form of silver (and gold) that would ensure the value of these bills. Still, the bills were often used to settle debts in Sherman's home state of Connecticut. Because the bills fluctuated in value—and had no intrinsic value—no one could say what they are really worth. And because that fluctuation was usually in a downward direction, Connecticut creditors, along with "Widows and Orphans," lost money when the value of bills from other colonies declined.

In the section "The Case Stated," Sherman develops an example of the injustice created by an unstable medium of exchange. He imagines a Connecticut merchant selling goods to a customer at a certain price. The merchant extends credit to the buyer, obligating the buyer to pay within a certain time but without specifying what form of currency he will accept. The merchant, of course, wants to be paid with a form of currency that reflects the current value of the goods; if he is paid with currency from a neighboring colony, and if that currency has since been devalued, the merchant loses by the transaction. The debtor, on the other hand, argues that the bills he is using to pay the debt have long been accepted as a medium of exchange. Although no law explicitly obligated the merchant to accept these bills, common law had established that they could be used to settle debts and judgments and that therefore the merchant should accept them. The result is a legal dispute over payment.

In the opening paragraphs of "The Case Stated," Sherman refers to "old tenor" money. This expression designates earlier issues of currency that were backed by specie (that is, silver, gold, or sometimes copper) at a fixed rate. (At the time, the issuance, or printing, of bills was called an "emission," and the government was said to "emit" bills.) The problems of dealing with "old tenor" versus more recently "emitted" money can be illustrated by the situation in neighboring Massachusetts. Dating back to the late seventeenth century, the paper bills of Massachusetts were fixed in value at a rate of 6 shillings per Spanish American silver dollar. But over time, as more and more bills were put into circulation, their value fell, so that by 1739 it took 22 shillings and 6 pence to buy one Spanish dollar. The situation continued to worsen. Despite efforts in Massachusetts to stabilize its currency, by 1742 it took 24 shillings and 9 pence to buy a Spanish silver dollar; by 1749 the exchange rate was up to 45 shillings.

Sherman notes a similar problem in Rhode Island. In 1743 old tenor currency was pegged at a value of 27 shillings to one ounce of silver; but in 1751 the value was changed to 54 shillings and then later to 64 shillings. In subsequent paragraphs, Sherman goes on to illustrate the problem. He notes that if bills are issued in another colony and if those bills have no intrinsic value, then their value comes entirely from the faith and credit of the colony. But if the other colony changes the value of bills, there is no reason that people in Connecticut should be obligated to accept them.

Continuing the argument, Sherman makes the parallel case of "clipped" coins. Historically, a problem governments faced was that people would file small amounts of precious metal off the edges of coins; it is for this reason that most coins of such metal are minted with small parallel ridges along the edge, so that any attempt to file off the metal is readily apparent. Sherman argues that devalued bills from neighboring colonies are like clipped coins, although clipped coins at least retain most of their intrinsic value. Bills, on the other hand, can be devalued by a colony's legislature to the point of worthlessness because the paper they are printed on has no intrinsic value.

Sherman's tone then becomes sharper. He argues that obligating the people of Connecticut to accept devalued bills from neighboring states is equivalent to taking away "Men's Estates and wrong[ing] them of their just and righteous Dues without either Law or Reason." He goes on to characterize this as a species of "fraud," "iniquity," and a "Cheat, Vexation and Snare to us." He offers calculations to demonstrate just how much value is lost to Connecticut by its acceptance of Rhode Island bills. Next, he raises the question of what the people of Connecticut should use instead as a medium of exchange. In answer he notes that "we in this Colony are seated on a very "fruitful Soil," "whose products can "procure us all the Necessaries of Life and as good a Medium of Exchange as any People in the World have or can desire." He concludes by urging the General Assembly of Connecticut to take action "to prevent the Bills last emitted by Rhode-Island Colony from obtaining a Currency among us."

◆ "Letters of a Countryman" (November 14, 1787)

From May 25 to September 17, 1787, the Constitutional Convention took place in Philadelphia. The express pur-

Time Line

1791–1793	■ Sherman represents Connecticut in the U.S. Senate.
1793	■ **July 23** Sherman dies in New Haven.

pose of the convention was to amend the Articles of Confederation, the document under which the United States had been operating since independence from Great Britain. The articles, however, were fraught with problems. Considerable conflict was arising among the states—conflict not unlike that to which Sherman alluded in "A Caveat against Injustice"—and it was becoming apparent to the nation's leaders that the Articles of Confederation was a weak document that granted too much power to the individual states and not enough to the federal government. Many delegates to the convention, among them James Madison and Alexander Hamilton, arrived in Philadelphia with the intention not just of amending the articles but of creating an entirely new constitution.

Even before the convention ended, bitter debate began. Some members of the convention left before the closing ceremonies. Three others refused to sign the new document. As the rest returned to their states to urge ratification, they knew that no one was entirely happy with it. Sherman helped lead the fight for ratification in Connecticut, and to that end he wrote a series of five "Letters of a Countryman," which were published that autumn in the *New Haven Gazette*. The first appeared on November 14, 1787.

The principal issue Sherman addresses in the first letter urging ratification of the new constitution is resistance to the notion of uniting the states into a larger entity. Throughout the states, those who opposed a federal constitution expressed the fear that a strong federal government would correspondingly weaken the states, depriving them of their rights. For example, two of New York's delegates to the Constitutional Convention, Robert Yates and John Lansing, Jr., wrote a letter to the governor of New York in which they voiced their opposition to a consolidated federal government. The core of their argument was that a strong federal government would be "productive of the destruction of the civil liberty of such citizens who could be effectually coerced by it, by reason of the extensive territory of the United States" (qtd. in Elliot, ed., vol. 1, p. 481). The governor of New York, George Clinton, opposed ratification, as did no less a figure than Patrick Henry.

In his letter of November 14, Sherman tries to allay such fears. He notes in the opening two paragraphs that citizens are understandably cautious about trading one form of government that already offers certain advantages for another form of government in the hope that it will offer greater advantages in the future. In the third paragraph, he imagines a small ten-mile-square community being asked to subsume itself in a larger state government but resisting because it considered the request a "violent attempt to wrest from them the only security for their persons or property." He then compares the matter to the absorption of Scotland into Great Britain and the evils that many people in Scotland predicted would befall as a result. He concludes that the people of the ten-mile-square community would be no less secure if they were united to the rest of the state. In the final paragraphs, he suggests that people in entirely independent small communities run the risk of being "unsafe, poor and contemptible" and argues that just as states have not crushed the liberties of the communities within them, so the federal government would not crush the liberties of its constituent states.

Sherman was invested personally in the ratification of the Constitution, for he worked tirelessly to help create the document. Much of the convention's debate focused on two related issues. The first was the nature of the legislative branch of the federal government. Various proposals were put forward about the makeup of the legislature. One, called the Virginia Plan, was proposed by Virginia's governor, Edmund Randolph. It called for a bicameral legislature in which the number of representatives in *both* houses would be based on population. The members of the lower house would be elected by the people; members of the upper house would be elected by the lower house. The legislature would select the nation's president. This plan was often referred to as the "large state plan" because it would have allowed the nation's larger states to dominate the smaller ones.

An alternative, called the New Jersey Plan, was proposed by New Jersey governor William Paterson after a caucus with the smaller states, whose delegates threatened to walk out of the convention if the Virginia plan was accepted. The New Jersey Plan proposed a single house in which each state, regardless of size, would have one representative—a structure not unlike that under the Articles of Confederation—but the legislature would be granted additional powers. This plan, however, would have given smaller states influence in the legislature out of proportion to their population. The plan was rejected, but its proposal made clear that the smaller states would not agree to a constitution that reduced them to appendages of the larger states.

Enter Roger Sherman. Sherman drafted an alternative, usually called the Connecticut Compromise or the Great Compromise, that merged some of the features of each plan. It called for a bicameral legislature with each state having equal representation in the upper house (the Senate) and representation based on population in the lower house (the House of Representatives). In this way, the interests of large and small states were balanced.

The other contentious issue was how to count population, specifically, whether slaves should be counted for purposes of congressional representation in the lower house. The southern states, where the majority of slaves were held, would have been happy to have the slave population fully counted. The northern states, where opposition to slavery was already building, wanted to exclude slaves entirely rather than reward the southern states for owning slaves. The outcome of the debate was the so-called Three-fifths Compromise. Under this plan, five slaves were counted as three people for purposes of representation. Among historians, there is some uncertainty as to who proposed the Three-fifths Compromise. Some say that the idea came from James Wilson of Pennsylvania. Others say that Wilson and Roger Sherman jointly developed the compromise. Either way, the proposal was accepted and incorporated into the Constitution because of the widespread belief that otherwise the southern states would not ratify it. It should be noted that sometimes the Three-fifths Compromise is referred to as the Great Compromise, but this is a historical inaccuracy, for the two were entirely different proposals.

Sherman's other major contribution to the Constitution was the wording of Article I, Section 10, which has to do with currency. Harking back to the concerns he expressed in "A Caveat against Injustice," he insisted that the words "nor emit bills of credit, nor make any thing but gold & silver coin a tender in payment of debts" be included in the article, thus eliminating the possibility that the states' governments would print their own paper currency. He continued to insist that giving a state government the power to print paper money was tantamount to giving it the power to print debased and worthless currency to pay its own debts. Although Sherman does not directly address this matter in his "Letters of a Countryman," it suggests his belief that the new document, vesting powers in the federal government, would solve the young nation's currency problems, and for this reason, Sherman was eager to see it ratified.

Supporters of the Constitution mounted a push to see it ratified early by the most influential states, thus making it harder for other states to reject the document. On October 19, 1787, the Connecticut Assembly called for a series of town meetings to elect ratifying delegates. On January 9, 1788, these delegates voted to ratify the Constitution, making Connecticut the fifth state to do so.

◆ "Letters of a Countryman" (November 22, 1787)

One of the key sticking points in the states about the new Constitution was its lack of a bill of rights—provisions that would explicitly protect the freedom of speech, religion, and the press; the right to trial by jury and the right to bear arms; protection against self-incrimination, illegal search and seizures, and cruel and unusual punishment; and other rights. Even during the convention, many delegates argued that the Constitution was incomplete without such provisions. Although some states quickly ratified the Constitution, it was by no means certain that the necessary nine out of thirteen states would do so. Virginia, New York, and Massachusetts, in particular, were the scenes of contentious and bitter debate. Virginia, over the objections of Patrick Henry and others, finally ratified the Constitution on June 25, 1788, but the state submitted with its ratification a series of recommended amendments that were, in effect, a bill of rights. New Hampshire and New York took similar steps, as did Massachusetts, which insisted that the first U.S. Congress immediately pass a bill of rights.

As with the issue of ratification generally, the issue of a bill of rights inspired pamphlets, letters to newspapers, and other documents debating the issue. Following the custom of the time, many of these documents were published under pseudonyms, with many authors choosing the names of ancient Roman statesmen; in his "Letters of a Countryman" from November 22, 1787, Sherman refers to a number of these people in his final paragraph, including "Brutus," who was probably Robert Yates of New York. One of the leading opponents of a bill of rights was Alexander Hamilton. In Federalist 84, Hamilton, writing under the name Publius, argued that under the new Constitution as submitted, the people were not surrendering their rights. He stated that a bill of rights, such as that implied by the Magna Carta, was necessary only to protect citizens from monarchs who could by fiat usurp those rights. He also argued that a bill of rights was dangerous, for it would carve out exceptions to powers that the Constitution did not grant, thereby implying that the Constitution did, in fact, grant such powers. Essentially, Hamilton argued, a bill of rights could backfire on the nation's citizens.

Sherman entered the debate with his "Letters of a Countryman," opposing inclusion of a bill of rights or making it a condition of ratification. He makes his opposition clear in the third paragraph, where he refers to the "sublimity of *nonsense* and *alarm*, that has been thundered against [the Constitution] in every shape of *metaphoric terror*, on the subject of a *bill of rights*." He argues that a bill of rights is nothing but a "paper protection" and that Congress and the president would continue to hold powers that would enable them to deprive citizens of their rights.

Beginning with the fourth paragraph, Sherman makes his argument. He states that the only real protection people have is the nature of their government. He elaborates by noting that "if you are about to trust your liberties with people whom it is necessary to bind by stipulation, that they shall not keep a standing army, your stipulation is not worth even the trouble of writing." He notes that even the Magna Carta, the thirteenth-century progenitor of modern constitutions, was essentially an act of Parliament, not a constitutionally enshrined bill of rights. In the next paragraph, he points out that Connecticut has a bill of rights but that the state legislature could, if it wanted to, deprive the state's citizens of those rights. In the final paragraphs, Sherman concludes that the only way to ensure liberty is by structuring a federal government in such a way that the citizens have control over the legislature, thus ensuring that the legislature does not pass laws that would deny the liberties that a bill of rights would contain.

It should be noted that Sherman, like others who opposed the inclusion of a bill of rights, was not in any way opposed to the rights themselves. Sherman wanted to see

Essential Quotes

"And this I would lay down as a Principle that can't be denied that a Debtor ought not to pay any Debts with less Value than was contracted for, without the Consent or against the Will of the Creditor."

("A Caveat against Injustice")

"We had better die in a good Cause than live in a bad one."

("A Caveat against Injustice")

"Many instances can be quoted, where people have been unsafe, poor and contemptible, because they were governed only in small bodies; but can any instance be found where they were less safe for uniting?"

("Letters of a Countryman," November 14, 1787)

"The only real security that you can have for all your important rights must be in the nature of your government."

("Letters of a Countryman," November 22, 1787)

the new Constitution that he had helped write ratified. His opposition was to those who wanted to make ratification dependent on the inclusion of a bill of rights that he did not think was necessary. The Constitution was ratified without a bill of rights, but on June 8, 1789, James Madison submitted a bill of rights to the first Congress, thereby preempting the need for another constitutional convention that might undo the work of the first. On December 15, 1791, when Virginia ratified ten of the twelve proposed amendments, they became part of the U.S. Constitution.

Impact and Legacy

Most U.S. citizens recognize the names of Thomas Jefferson and James Madison, Benjamin Franklin and Patrick Henry, and other Founders. Indeed, several of the Founders went on to become presidents. The name of Roger Sherman, though, is less familiar, except to historians. He made no particularly eloquent speeches, such as Patrick Henry's "Give me liberty or give me death" speech. He wrote no eloquent documents, such as the stirring Declaration of Independence or the Preamble to the Constitution.

Nevertheless, Sherman was a highly regarded political figure during his time—Thomas Jefferson is reputed to have once said that Sherman was the one man he knew who never said a foolish thing in his life. Sherman's arguments against inflated currency in the states became part of the Constitution. His "Great Compromise" became part of the foundation of the legislative branch of government. Throughout the Continental Congress and the Constitutional Convention, he tirelessly served on various committees, and his views, if not his exact words, became part of the fabric of government under both the Articles of Confederation and the Constitution. Roger Sherman was one of numerous men and women who toiled to forge a new nation. Without their efforts, the nation might never have survived its infancy and indeed could have been stillborn.

Key Sources

Sherman's letters can be found in Edmund C. Burnett, ed., *The Letters of the Members of the Continental Congress*, 8 vols. (1921–1938). His speeches, which are not quoted verbatim, are in various volumes of the *Annals of Congress*, 16 vols. (1857–1861), and in Max Farrand, ed., *The Records of the Federal Convention*, 4 vols. (1937). The complete text of "Letters of a Countryman" can be found in Paul Leicester Ford, ed., *Essays on the Constitution of the United States: Published during Its Discussion by the People 1787–1788* (1892).

Further Reading

■ Articles

Boyd, Julian P. "Roger Sherman: Portrait of a Cordwainer Statesman." *New England Quarterly* 5 (1932): 221–236.

Gerber, Scott D., "Roger Sherman and the Bill of Rights." *Polity* 28 (Summer 1996): 521–540.

■ Books

Boardman, Roger Sherman. *Roger Sherman, Signer and Statesman*. 1938. Reprint. New York: Da Capo Press, 1971.

Boutell, Lewis Henry. *The Life of Roger Sherman*. 1896. Reprint. Whitefish, Mont.: Kessinger Publishing, 2007.

Questions for Further Study

1. Discuss the history behind Sherman's "Caveat against Injustice," which addressed the need for currency reform in the American colonies. How did the system of financial exchange, including barter, bills of credit, and separate currencies for each colony, develop over time? What remedies did Sherman propose?

2. Analyze Sherman's use of what might be called "thought experiments": hypothetical examples used to illustrate particular points. These include the passage on the Connecticut merchant in his "Caveat against Injustice" as well as the imagined ten-square-mile community described in the first of the "Letters of a Countryman" excerpted here. What particular points was he trying to make, and how were the "thought experiments" employed for those purposes?

3. Explain the debate over representation in the national legislature, a controversy in which Sherman played a pivotal role with his Connecticut Compromise. What solutions did the respective proponents of the New Jersey and Virginia Plans offer? What were the strengths and weaknesses of each? How might either plan, if adopted in its entirety, have influenced the course of American history? How did Sherman help to settle the debate with his compromise?

Collier, Christopher. *Roger Sherman's Connecticut: Yankee Politics and the American Revolution*. Middletown, Conn.: Wesleyan University Press, 1971.

———. *Decision in Philadelphia: The Constitutional Convention of 1787*. New York: Ballantine, 1987.

Elliot, Jonathan, ed. *The Debates in the Several State Conventions on the Adoption of the Federal Constitution*, 4 vols., 2nd ed. Philadelphia: J. P. Lippincott, 1861.

Rommel, John G. *Connecticut's Yankee Patriot: Roger Sherman*. Hartford, Conn.: American Revolution Bicentennial Commission of Connecticut, 1980.

—Michael J. O'Neal

"A Caveat against Injustice; or, An Inquiry into the Evils of a Fluctuating Medium of Exchange" (1752)

Forasmuch, as there have many Disputes arisen of late concerning the Medium of Exchange in this Colony, which have been occasioned chiefly by Reason of our having such large Quantities of Paper Bills of Credit on some of the Neighbouring Governments, passing in Payments among us, and some of those Governments having issued much larger sums of Bills than were necessary to supply themselves with a competent Medium of Exchange, and not having supplied their Treasuries with any Fund for the maintaining the Credit of such Bills; they have therefore been continually depreciating and growing less in their Value, and have been the principal Means of the Depreciation of the Bills of Credit emitted by this Colony, by their passing promiscuously with them; and so have been the Occasion of Much Embarrasment and Injustice, in the Trade and Commerce of the Colony, and many People and especially Widows and Orphans have been great Sufferers thereby.

But our Legislature having at length taken effectual Care to prevent further Depreciation of the Bills of this Colony, and the other Governments not having taken the prudent Care, their Bills of Credit are still sinking in their Value, and have in Fackt sunk much below the Value of the Bills of this Colony.

Yet some People among us, by long Custom, are so far prejudiced in Favour of a sinking Medium, and others not being really sensible of the true State of the Case, are inclined to think that Bills of Credit on the neighbouring Governments ought to be a legal Tender in Payments in this Colony for all Debts due by Book and otherwise where there is no special contract expressly mentioning some other Currency, and others being of a different Opinion, the Disputes have been carried on so far, as to occasion some Expence in the Law, and may be likely to occasion much more, unless prevented by those Prejudices being some way removed. And since it is a Cause wherin every one is more or less interested, I have ventured to shew my Opinion, with a sincere Desire to have Peace and Justice maintained and promoted in the Colony. Not desiring any Person to approve of my Observations any farther than he finds them agreeable to the Principles of Justice and right Reason.

THE CASE STATED

Suppose a Man comes to a Trader's Shop in this Colony to buy Goods, and the Trader sells him a certain Quantity of Goods and tells him the Price is so many Pounds, Shillings and Pence, (let it be more or less) to be paid at the Expiration of one Year, from that Time, and the Man receives the Goods but there is nothing said either by Seller or Buyer, what Currency it is to be paid in, but the Goods are charged according to the Value of Bills of Credit Old Tenor on this Colony.

Now I Query what the Creditor has a Right to demand for a Debt so contracted; or what the Debtor can oblige him to accept in Payment?

The Creditor says, that the Debt being contracted in the Colony of Connecticut, he ought to have what is known by the Laws of said Colony to be Money: And that he has no Right to demand any thing else.

The Debtor says, That Bills of Credit on the neighbouring Governments have for many Years passed promiscuously with the Bills of Credit on this Colony as Money in all Payments, (except special Contracts) and that People in general where the Contracts by [and] large have expected, and do still expect, that any of the Bills of Credit on any of the Governments in New-England, that have obtained a Currency in this Colony will answer in Payment, and in as much as the Creditor did not give him any Notice to the contrary, when he bought the Goods, therefore he thinks that such Bills of Credit ought to be accepted in Payment for the aforesaid Debt.

And altho' there is no particular Statute in this Colony, that such Bills of Credit shall be a legal Tender in Payments of Money: Yet the Practice has been so universal for so long a Time, and the Creditor himself has both received and pass'd them as Money constantly without making Exceptions against them 'till this Debt was contracted, and for many Years all Demands on Book Debts have been for Old Tenor Money indifferently, without Distiction of Colonies, and Judgements in all Courts have been given thereon accordingly: And any of the aforesaid Bills of Credit have pass'd in Payment to satisfy all Judgements, so obtain'd and this universal Custom, the Debtor saith, ought to be esteemed as common Law and ought not without some special Reason to be set aside, and that in this Case there is nothing special; and therefore the Creditor ought not to make Demand or obtain Judgement different from the common Custom of the Colony.

In Answer to this the Creditor saith, that altho' Bills of Credit on the neighbouring Governments have for a Number of Years been pass'd and receiv'd in Payments: Yet it has been only by the voluntary Consent of the Persons receiving them, and not because they were under any Obligation to receive them; and that it is no Argument that a Person shall be obliged to receive any Species where it won't answer his End, because in Time past he has receiv'd it when it would answer.

And the Creditor furthur saith, that such Bills of Credit are of no intrinsick Value, and their Extrinsical Value is fluctuating and very uncertain, and therefore it would be unjust that any Person should be obliged to receive them in Payment as Money in this Colony, (since neither the Colony nor any of the Inhabitants thereof are under any Obligation either to Refund said Bills or to maintain the Credit of them) for Money ought to be something of certain Value, it being that whereby other Things are to be valued.

And I think it is a Principle that must be granted that no Government has Right to impose on its Subjects any foreign Currency to be received in Payments as Money which is not of intrinsick Value; unless such Government will assume and undertake to secure and make Good to the Possessor of such Currency the full Value which they oblige him to receive it for. Because in so doing they would oblige Men to part with their Estates for that which is worth nothing in it self and which they don't know will ever procure him any Thing.

And Rhode-Island Bills of Credit have been so far from being of certain Value and securing to the Posessor the Value that they were first stated at, that they have depreciated almost four seventh Parts in nine Years last past, as appears by their own Acts of Assembly.

For in the year 1743, it appears by the Face of the Bills then emitted that Twenty-seven Shillings Old-Tenor was equal to one Ounce of Silver. And by an Act of their General Assembly pass'd in March last, they stated Fifty-four Shilling Old-Tenor Bills equal to one Ounce of Silver, which sunk their Value one half. And by another Act in June last, (viz. 1751) they stated Sixty-four Shillings in their Old-Tenor Bills equal to one Ounce of Silver. And by another Act in August last they gave Order and Direction to the Courts in that Colony to make Allowance to the Creditors in making up Judgement from Time to Time as the Bills shall depreciate for the Future,

which shews that they expect their Bills of Credit to depreciate for the Future.

And since the Value of The Bills of Credit depend wholly on the Rate at which they are stated and on the Credit of the Government by whom they are emitted and that being the only Reason and Foundation upon which they obtained their first Currency and by which the same has been upheld ever since their first being current and therefore when the Publick Faith and Credit of such Government is violated, then the Reason upon which such Bills obtained their Currency ceases and there remains no Reason why they should be any longer current.

And this I would lay down as a Principle that can't be denied that a Debtor ought not to pay any Debts with less Value than was contracted for, without the Consent or against the Will of the Creditor.

And the Creditor further saith, that his accepting Rhode-Island Bills of Credit when they stood stated equal to Silver at Twenty-seven Shillings an Ounce, can be no Reason that he should receive them at the same Value when they are stated equal to Silver at Fifty-four Shillings an Ounce, and still to receive them at the same Rate when they are so reduced down that Sixty-four Shillings is equal to but one Ounce of Silver, and whoever does receive them so must not only act without, but against Reason.

And the Debtor can't possibly plead without any Truth that he expected to pay in Rhode-Island Bills of Credit at their present Value and under their present Circumstances, (any Debts contracted before the aforesaid Acts of Rhode Island were published) because there was no such Thing (as those Bills are under their present Circumstances) existing at the Time of Contract, for as was observ'd before, the Value of such Bills of Credit depend wholly upon the Rate at which they are stated and on the Credit of the Government by whom they are emitted, and a Bill of Credit for the same Sum that is stated equal to Silver at Twenty-seven Shillings an Ounce, must be of more than double the Value of one stated equal to Silver at Sixty-four Shillings an Ounce if the Credit of the Emitter may be depended on: But if the Emitter's Credit can't be depended on then neither of the Bills aforesaid are of any Value, because it is evident that no Bills of Credit have any Value in themselves, but are given to secure something of intrinsick Value, to the Posessor.

So that the Arguments draw from Custom are of no Force, because the Reasons upon which that Custom were grounded do now cease.

I grant that if any Thing whose Value is intrinsical and invariable the same should obtain a Currency as a Medium of Exchange for a great Number of Years in any Colony, it might with some Reason be urg'd that it ought to be accepted in Payments for Debts where there is no special Agreement for any other Species.

But if what is us'd as a Medium of Exchange is fluctuating in its Value it is no better than unjust Weights and Measures, both which are condemn'd by the Laws of GOD and Man, and therefore the longest and most universal Custom could never make the Use of such a Medium either lawful or reasonable.

Now suppose that Gold or Silver Coines that pass current in Payments at a certain Rate by Tale should have a considerable Part of their Weight filed or clipp'd off will any reasonable Man judge that they ought to pass for the same Value as those of full Weight?

But the State of R...I...d Bills of Credit is much worse than that of Coins that are clipp'd, because what is left of those Coins is of intrinsick Value: But the General Assembly of R...I...d having depreciated their Bills of Credit have thereby violated their Promise from Time to Time, and there is just Reason to suspect their Credit for the Future for the small Value which they now promise for said Bills, and they have not only violated their Promise as to the Value, pretended to be secured to the Posessor by said Bills; but also as to the Time of calling them in and paying the same, they have lengthened out the Time Fifteen Years.

So that if the Posessor must be kept out of the Use of his Money until that Term is expired (and the Bills secure nothing to him sooner.) One Ounce of Silver paid down now, would be worth more than Seven pounds Ten Shillings in such Bills of Credit computing the Interest at 6 per Cent per Annum.

These Things considered, can any reasonable Man think that such Bills of Credit (or rather of no Credit) ought to be a legal Tender in Payment of Money in this Colony for Debts, for which the Debtor received Species of much more Value than those Bills provided the Creditor could get the full Value of them in Silver that they are now stated at....

But to impose Rhode-Island Bills of Credit in Payments for Debts in this Colony when the Creditor never agreed to take them, and that without any Allowance for the Depreciation, would be to take away Men's Estates and wrong them of their just and righteous Dues without either Law or Reason.

And instead of having our Properties defended and secured to us by the Protection of the Government under which we live; we should be always exposed to have them taken from us by Fraud at the Pleasure of other Governments, who have no Right of Jurisdiction over us.

And according to this Argument, if Rhode-Island General Assembly has been pleased last June to have stated their Old-Tenor Bills equal to Silver at Forty-eight Pounds Twelve Shillings an Ounce, instead of Sixty-four Shillings, and to have cut off the Value of them Eighteen Shillings on the Pound, instead of Three Shillings, all Creditors in this Colony would thereby have been necessitated to lose Ninety Pounds out of every Hundred Pounds of their Debts which were then out standing, for if they could take away one Sixth Part of their Value and reduce them so much below the Old-Tenor Bills of this Colony and the Creditor be notwithstanding obliged to receive them without Allowance, by the Rule they might have taken away three Quarters of Nine Tenths or indeed the whole, and the Creditor have had no more Remedy than he has now.

And the Estates of poor Widows and Orphans must according to this Principle in the same unjust Manner be taken away from them and given to others that have no Right to them, (for what the Creditor loses in this way the Debtor gains because the more the Bills of Credit depreciate the less Value the Debtor can produce them for) and according to the Debtor's Arguement the Executive Courts in this Colony must give Judgement in Favour of all this Fraud and Iniquity at least, 'till there is some special Act of Assembly to order them to the contrary; but I believe that every honest Man of Common Sense, upon mature Consideration of the Circumstances of the Case, will think that this is an Iniquity not to be countenanced, but rather to be punished by the Judges....

But it may be further objected, that if it were not for the Bills of Credit on the neighbouring Governments, we should have no Money to Trade with, and what should we do for a Medium of Exchange? or how could we live without?

To this I answer, that if that were indeed the Case, we had better die in a good Cause than live in a bad one. But I apprehend that the Case in Fact is quite the reverse, for we in this Colony are seated on a very fruitful Soil, the Product whereof, with our Labour and Industry and the Divine Blessng thereon, would sufficiently furnish us with and procure us all the Necessaries of Life and as good a Medium of Exchange as any People in the World have or can desire.

But so long as we part with our most valuable Commodities for such Bills of Credit as are no Profit; but rather a Cheat, Vexation and Snare to us, and become a Medium whereby we are continually cheating and wronging one another in our Dealings and Commerce....

And with Submission I would humbly beg Leave to propose it to the wise Consideration of the Honourable General Assembly of this Colony; whether it would not be conductive to the welfare of the Colony to pass some act to prevent the Bills last emitted by Rhode-Island Colony from obtaining a Currency among us.

And to appoint some reasonable Time (not exceeding the Term that our Bills of Credit are allowed to pass) after the Expiration of which none of the Bills of Credit on New Hampshire or Rhode-Island, shall be allowed to pass in this Colony, that so

People having previous Notice thereof may order their Affairs so as to get rid of such Bills to the best Advantage that they can before the Expiration of such Term.

And whether it would not be very much for the Publick Good to lay a large Excise upon all Rum imported into this Colony or distilled herein, thereby effectually to restrain the excessive use thereof, which is such a growing Evil among us and is leading to almost all other Vices.

And I doubt not but that if those two great Evils that have been mentioned were restrained we should soon see better Times.

Glossary

Book Debts	money owed to a business for goods that have been supplied or services that have been performed
Estates	property, possessions
Extrinsical Value	value assigned to something such as currency by usage and common consent
foreasmuch	given that, since, because
intrinsick Value	inherent value
legal Tender	any form of currency that cannot be refused as a means of payment for a debt
shew	antique spelling of "show"
shilling	a former unit of British currency worth one-twentieth of a British pound
Tale	a count, tally, or enumeration
viz.	abbreviation of Latin *videlicet*, or "that is to say"

"Letters of a Countryman" (November 14, 1787)

To the People of Connecticut

You are now called on to make important alterations in your government, by ratifying the new federal constitution. There are, undoubtedly, such advantages to be expected from this measure, as will be sufficient inducement to adopt the proposal, provided it can be done without sacrificing more important advantages, which we now do or may possess. By a wise provision in the constitution of man, whenever a proposal is made to change any present habit or practice, he much more minutely considers what he is to *lose* by the alterations, what effect it is to have on what he at present possesses, than what is to be *hoped* for in the proposed expedient.

Thus people are justly cautious how they exchange present advantages for the hope of others in a system not yet experienced.

Hence all large states have dreaded a division into smaller parts, as being nearly the same thing as ruin; and all smaller states have predicted endless embarrassment from every attempt to unite them into larger. It is no more than probable that if any corner of this State of ten miles square, was now, and long had been independent of the residue of the State, that they would consider a proposal to unite them to the other parts of the State, as a violent attempt to wrest from them the only security for their persons or property. They would lament how little security they should derive from sending one or two members to the legislature at Hartford & New Haven, and all the evils that the Scots predicted from the proposed union with England, in the beginning of the present century, would be thundered with all the vehemence of American politics, from the little ten miles district. But surely no man believes that the inhabitants of this district would be less secure when united to the residue of the State, than when independent. Does any person suppose that the people would be more safe, more happy, or more respectable, if every town in this State was independent, and had no State government?

Is it not certain that government would be weak and irregular, and that the people would be poor and contemptible? And still it must be allowed, that each town would entirely surrender its boasted independence if they should unite in State government, and would retain only about one-eightieth part of the administration of their own affairs.

Has it ever been found, that people's property or persons were less regarded and less protected in large states than in small? Have not the Legislature in large states been as careful not to over-burden the people with taxes as in small? But still it must be admitted, that a single town in a small state holds a greater proportion of the authority than in a large.

If the United States were one single government, provided the constitution of this extensive government was as good as the constitution of this State now is, would this part of it be really in greater danger of oppression or tyranny, than at present? It is true that many people who are *great men* because they go to Hartford to make laws for us once or twice in a year, would then be no greater than their neighbours, as much fewer representatives would be chosen. But would not the people be as safe, governed by their representatives assembled in New York or Philadelphia, as by their representatives assembled in Hartford or New Haven? Many instances can be quoted, where people have been unsafe, poor and contemptible, because they were governed only in small bodies; but can any instance be found where they were less safe for uniting? Has not every instance proved somewhat similar to the so much dreaded union between England and Scotland, where the Scots, instead of becoming a poor, despicable, dependent people, have become much more secure, happy, and respectable? If then, the constitution is a good one, why should we be afraid of uniting, even if the Union was to be much more complete and entire than is proposed?

"LETTERS OF A COUNTRYMAN" (NOVEMBER 22, 1787)

To the People of Connecticut

It is fortunate that you have been but little distressed with that torrent of impertinence and folly, with which the newspaper politicians have over whelmed many parts of our country.

It is enough that you should have heard, that one party has seriously urged, that we should adopt the *New Constitution* because it has been approved by *Washington and Franklin*; and the other, with all the solemnity of apostolic address to *Men, Brethren, Fathers, Friends and Countryman*, have urged that we should reject, as dangerous, every clause thereof, because that *Washington* is more used to command as a soldier, than to reason as a politician—*Franklin is old*, others are *young*—and *Wilson is haughty*. You are too well informed to decide by the opinion of others, and too independent to need a caution against undue influence.

Of a very different nature, tho' only one degree better than the other reasoning, is all that sublimity of *nonsense and alarm*, that has been thundered against it in every shape of *metaphoric terror*, on the subject of a *bill of rights*, the *liberty of the press*, *rights of conscience*, *rights of taxation and election*, *trials in the vicinity*, *freedom of speech*, *trial by jury*, and a *standing army*. These last are undoubtedly important points, much too important to depend on mere paper protection. For, guard such privileges by the strongest expressions, still if you leave the legislative and executive power in the hands of those who are or may be disposed to deprive you of them—you are but slaves. Make an absolute monarch—give him the supreme authority, and guard as much as you will by bills of rights, your liberty of the press, and trial by jury;—he will find means either to take them from you, or to render them useless.

The only real security that you can have for all your important rights must be in the nature of your government. If you suffer any man to govern you who is not strongly interested in supporting your privileges, you will certainly lose them. If you are about to trust your liberties with people whom it is necessary to bind by stipulation, that they shall not keep a standing army, your stipulation is not worth even the trouble of writing. No bill of rights ever yet bound the supreme power longer than the *honeymoon* of a new married couple, unless the *rulers were interested* in preserving the rights; and in that case they have always been ready enough to declare the rights, and to preserve them when they were declared.—The famous English *Magna Charta* is but an act of parliament, which every subsequent parliament has had just as much constitutional power to repeal and annul, as the parliament which made it had to pass it at first. But the security of the nation has always been, that their government was so formed, that at least *one branch* of their legislature must be strongly interested to preserve the rights of the nation.

You have a bill of rights in Connecticut (i.e.) your legislature many years since enacted that the subjects of this state should enjoy certain privileges. Every assembly since that time, could, by the same authority, enact that the subjects should enjoy none of those privileges; and the only reason that it has not long since been so enacted, is that your legislature were as strongly interested in preserving those rights as any of the subjects; and this is your only security that it shall not be so enacted at the next session of assembly: and it is security enough.

Your General Assembly under your present constitution are supreme. They may keep troops on foot in the most profound peace, if they think proper. They have heretofore abridged the trial by jury in some cases, and they can again in all. They can restrain the press, and may lay the most burdensome taxes if they please, and who can forbid? But still the people are perfectly safe that not one of these events shall take place so long as the members of the General Assembly are as much interested, and interested in the same manner, as the other subjects.

On examining the new proposed constitution, there can be no question but that there is authority enough lodged in the proposed Federal Congress, if abused, to do the greatest injury. And it is perfectly idle to object to it, that there is no bill of rights, or to propose to add to it a provision that a trial by jury shall in no case be omitted, or to patch it up by adding a stipulation in favor of the press, or to guard it by removing the paltry objection to the right of Congress to regulate the time and manner of elections.

If you cannot prove by the best of all evidence, viz., by the interest of the rulers, that this authority will not be abused, or at least that those powers are not more likely to be abused by the Congress, than by those who now have the same powers, you must by no means adopt the constitution:—No, not with all the bills of rights and with all the stipulations in favor of the people that can be made.

But if the members of Congress are to be interested just as you and I are, and just as the members of our present legislatures are interested, we shall be just as safe, with even supreme power (if that were granted) in Congress, as in the General Assembly. If the members of Congress can take no improper step which will not affect them as much as it does us, we need not apprehend that they will usurp authorities not given them to injure that society of which they are a part.

The sole question, (so far as any apprehension of tyranny and oppression is concerned) ought to be, how are Congress formed? how far have you a control over them? Decide this, and then all the questions about their power may be dismissed for the amusement of those politicians whose business it is to catch flies, or may occasionally furnish subjects for George Bryan's Pomposity, or the declamations of *Cato—An Old Whig—Son of Liberty—Brutus—Brutus junior—An Officer of the Continental Army,*—the more contemptible *Timoleon,* and the residue of that rabble of writers.

Glossary

An Old Whig	the pseudonym of an Antifederalist who has not been identified
apostolic	term evoking the high seriousness associated with the twelve apostles of Christian scriptures
Brutus	the pseudonym of the author of sixteen Antifederalist articles, generally believed to be Robert Yates
Brutus junior	the pseudonym of an unidentified Antifederalist writer
Cato	pseudonym of the Antifederalist George Clinton, governor of New York
Franklin	Benjamin Franklin, author, statesman, diplomat, inventor, scientist, and one of the nation's founders; delegate to the Constitutional Convention from Pennsylvania
George Bryan	author of the Pennsylvania Constitution
Magna Charta	usually Magna Carta; literally the "Great Charter," a document presented by the English barons to King John in 1215, asserting their legal rights and privileges
Officer in the Continental Army	more accurately, Officer in the Late Continental Army, the name used by the Antifederalist writer William Findley, a Pennsylvania politician and farmer
Son of Liberty	a name taken by numerous opponents of the new Constitution
Timoleon	the pseudonym of an unknown Antifederalist writer
viz.	abbreviation of Latin *videlicet,* or "that is to say"
Washington	George Washington, who would serve as first U.S. president under the new Constitution
Wilson	James Wilson, delegate to the Constitutional Convention from Pennsylvania and later a justice of the first U.S. Supreme Court

Al Smith (Library of Congress)

AL SMITH   1873–1944

Governor and Presidential Candidate

Featured Documents
◆ Address of Acceptance of the Democratic Presidential Nomination (1928)

Overview

The colorful Alfred Emanuel Smith, born on December 30, 1873, on the Lower East Side of Manhattan in New York City, was an iconic figure in American politics and ranks among the most famous candidates who lost in their runs for the presidency. He was a gifted amateur actor and public speaker, talents he turned to use when he began his political career in his twenties. He obtained his first political appointment in 1895 as a clerk in the Office of the City Commissioner of Jurors. His job was to serve subpoenas, for which he was paid the princely sum, for a young man of modest means, of $1,000 a year. Then, in 1903, he won election to the New York State Assembly. There he acquired a reputation as a champion of the working class and a backer of Progressive legislation as he rose through the ranks to become chair of the Ways and Means Committee, minority leader, and speaker. He also won election as sheriff of New York County and president of the city board of aldermen. In 1918 he was elected to the first of four terms as New York's governor (1918–1920 and 1922–1928). Smith's published writings consist primarily of addresses he delivered during his career as a politician. Smith, a Roman Catholic, was the target of vicious assaults because of his religion and for his opposition to Prohibition. However, he generally did not respond in kind but gave issues-oriented speeches about tariffs, waterway development, immigration, and similar policy topics that were often rather dry and failed to rouse the people he addressed.

By the 1920s Smith was achieving a national reputation for the Progressive views he would articulate in his nomination acceptance speech at the Democratic National Convention in 1928. In many respects, the legislation he had sponsored as governor anticipated much of the New Deal legislation proposed by President Franklin D. Roosevelt in response to the Great Depression of the 1930s. Not surprisingly, then, Roosevelt placed Smith's name in nomination at the 1920 Democratic convention. In 1924 Roosevelt once again nominated Smith for president, in the process referring to him by a nickname that would stick, "the Happy Warrior." Smith withdrew his name in favor of a compromise candidate, John W. Davis, but at the 1928 convention he could no longer be denied the nomination. He won handily on the first ballot and chose Joseph Taylor Robinson as his running mate. In his address accepting his party's nomination he outlined most of his Progressive views, particularly as they pertained to such issues as Prohibition, foreign relations, and the rights of the laboring

classes. In the general election, however, he lost to the ticket of Herbert Hoover and Charles Curtis.

In 1932 Smith pursued the Democratic nomination but lost to Roosevelt. Throughout Roosevelt's nearly four terms as president, Smith opposed him, believing that the president's New Deal was too liberal and antibusiness and that it cost too much. Smith supported Roosevelt's opponents: Alfred Landon in 1936 and Wendell Wilkie in 1940. Meanwhile, shortly after the 1928 election, Smith became president of the company that constructed the Empire State Building, at the time the world's tallest building. Perhaps reflecting Smith's talent for efficient administration, the building was finished in less than thirteen months. On October 4, 1944, Smith died at the age of seventy.

Explanation and Analysis of Documents

In 1928 Franklin D. Roosevelt placed Smith's name in nomination for the presidency for the third time, as he had in 1920 and 1924, prompting the humorist Will Rogers to remark that Roosevelt had "devoted his life to nominating Al Smith" and that "you could wake him in the middle of the night and he would start to nominate Al" (qtd. in Johnson and Johnson, p. 86). Smith won on the first ballot and delivered his acceptance address on the steps of the state capitol building in Albany, New York.

◆ Address of Acceptance of the Democratic Presidential Nomination

Progressivism
In the first ten paragraphs of his speech, Smith articulates the Progressive ideals for which he had become known as the governor of New York. The Progressive movement in American politics had begun in the late nineteenth century in response to the nation's transformation from a primarily rural, agrarian society to more of an urban, industrialized one. The movement was ill defined, and the very term *Progressive* in this context can refer to a wide range of impulses dominant in American politics from the 1880s through the 1920s; it can also denote the Progressive Party formed by Theodore Roosevelt in 1912 and whose other prominent presidential candidate in 1924 was Robert ("Battling Bob") M. La Follette.

At its core the Progressive movement had a wide range of goals. Progressives wanted to reform local and state governments and to curb the abuses of large corporations

Time Line

1873

- **December 30**
  Albert Emanuel Smith, Jr., is born.

1895

- Smith obtains his first political appointment as a clerk with the Office of the City Commissioner of Jurors.

1903

- Smith is elected to the New York State Assembly.

1911

- Smith is appointed to the Ways and Means Committee of the New York legislature.

1913

- Smith is elected speaker of the New York State Assembly.

1914– 1915

- Smith serves as minority leader in the New York State Assembly.

1916– 1918

- Smith serves as elected sheriff of New York County.

1918

- Smith wins the first of four terms as governor of New York.

1924

- **July 8**
  Smith is a leading candidate for the Democratic presidential nomination but withdraws his name to break a deadlock at the Democratic National Convention.

1928

- **August 22**
  Smith gives his acceptance speech for the Democratic presidential nomination at the state capitol in Albany, New York.

and "robber barons," a goal achieved in part by the passage of the Sherman Antitrust Act in 1890. Many farmers and others distrusted the nation's financial system, including the banks and stock exchanges, so Progressives wanted to reform those institutions through such measures as the establishment of the Federal Reserve System. Overall, Progressives sought a political system that was fundamentally fairer and not stacked against the poor, immigrants, farmers, and the laboring classes, who provided the muscle for American industry. They wanted a government that was accountable to the people, not to the nation's business and financial interests, the "oligarchy" of the monied classes to which Smith refers. This was the political philosophy that informed Smith's tenure as governor of New York, and he wanted to bring it to the federal government.

Smith owed his Progressive views to his upbringing. He grew up virtually in the shadow of the Brooklyn Bridge, which was under construction during his childhood. His father, the popular, easygoing Alfred Emanuel Smith, Sr., made his living as the owner of a trucking firm, although in those days the "trucks" were horse-drawn; his mother, Catherine Mulvihill Smith, did piecework as a seamstress and for a time ran a small grocery store. Smith's multiethnic heritage mirrored that of the Lower East Side Manhattan neighborhood in which he was raised—his grandparents were English, Irish, Italian, and German—but he identified primarily with the city's Irish community and would become its champion as governor of New York in the 1920s. Although the tenement neighborhood where Smith was raised was poor, Smith himself grew up in relative comfort. He attended the St. James Catholic School in New York City, where he was a dutiful but indifferent student, but in his early teens he had to drop out of school to help support his family after the death of his father. Smith later would achieve success in politics despite having never attended high school or college. He took a job at the Fulton Fish Market for $12 a week, often beginning work at 3:00 am, and also earned money delivering newspapers. He was an altar boy at St. James Church, but he ran with tough youngsters from the neighborhood and earned his education on the streets. The roots of Smith's Progressivism lay in these early experiences.

The Republican Party

In paragraphs 11–15, Smith trains his sights on the Republican Party, which had retained a firm hold on the White House since 1921, after Warren G. Harding soundly defeated the colorless James Cox (whose vice presidential running mate was Franklin D. Roosevelt). During the 1920 campaign Americans were still weary from the lingering effects of World War I. The outgoing Woodrow Wilson administration had demanded sacrifice, patriotism, idealism, and a sense of duty from the American people in response to the war. Many Americans had come to regard Wilson as something of a scolding schoolmarm. Harding, though, promised the public a return to "normalcy." He put the promise most famously in a campaign speech on May 14, 1920, in Boston, when he said (in his characteristic overblown way), "America's present need is not heroics, but healing...not surgery, but serenity; not the dramatic, but the dispassionate; not experiment, but equipoise; not submergence in internationality, but sustainment in triumphant nationality." More succinctly, Harding remains famous for having said, "We want less government in business and more business in government" ("Warren G. Harding," http://www.whitehouse.gov/history/presidents/wh29.html).

When Harding died on August 2, 1923, his vice president, Calvin "Silent Cal" Coolidge, assumed office. Coolidge, also committed to building the nation's material prosperity, once famously remarked that "the man who builds a factory builds a temple" (qtd. in Bittinger, http://www.calvin-coolidge.org/html/the_business_of_america_is_bus.html). Coolidge, who won a full term in 1924, continued the policies of the Harding administration, including less federal spending, lower taxes, a balanced federal budget, and high tariffs on foreign-made goods. Most important, he adopted very much of a laissez-faire attitude toward business. Until the collapse of the nation's economy in the 1930s Americans enjoyed an unprecedented level of prosperity. The nation's gross national product, for example, rose from $86.1 billion in 1923 to $98.2 billion in 1928. Further, unemployment was low, just 1.9 percent in 1926, for instance. This level of prosperity was Smith's chief obstacle, and he chose to counter it by pointing to inequitable distribution of wealth, the large amount of economic power in the hands of corporations, and the scandals that had plagued the Harding administration.

Some would regard any reference by Smith to the Harding scandals as slightly ironic, for Smith owed much of his early political success to Tammany Hall and its leader, Charles "Silent Charlie" Murphy. Tammany Hall had been founded in 1789 to serve as a charitable organization for immigrants and the poor. Throughout the nineteenth and early twentieth centuries, though, it became increasingly involved with local politics, and during certain periods it virtually ran New York City. The organization sometimes relied on corruption and bribes, but it always relied on the granting of favors that it expected would be returned. Still in the twenty-first century the name "Tammany Hall" is used as a figure of speech to refer to political bosses, particularly in big cities, who seize and hold power by granting favors to supporters and friends. Although Al Smith owed much to Tammany Hall, he remained untainted by the corruption that sometimes surrounded it and, indeed, gained a reputation for fairness and honesty and for awarding jobs based not on cronyism but on the applicant's ability. The voters who knew Smith trusted his integrity, trust that he appealed to in his nomination speech.

Tariffs

In paragraphs 16–18, Smith addresses the issue of tariffs. He does not state categorically that he wants to lower tariffs; indeed, high tariffs, in the eyes of many Americans, contributed to the nation's prosperity by protecting American goods and workers. Somewhat vaguely, he

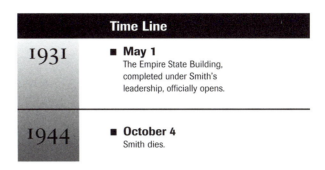

Time Line		
1931	■ **May 1**	The Empire State Building, completed under Smith's leadership, officially opens.
1944	■ **October 4**	Smith dies.

states that his goal is to examine the issue of tariffs on a case-by-case basis.

Foreign Affairs

Beginning with paragraph 19, Smith takes up the issue of America's relationships with foreign nations. During the postwar years the United States had avoided foreign entanglements; Congress, for example, never approved U.S. membership in Wilson's League of Nations. However, Coolidge had been determined to protect American business interests in Central America, including the oil and sugar industries. Coolidge dispatched the U.S. Marines to Nicaragua because he believed that revolutionaries in Mexico were trying to import Communism into Nicaragua and that if Communists assumed power, they would seize American business interests there. These events marked the beginning of a long period of American intervention in Central America, one that lasted into the 1980s. Smith, however, indicates that he would not have invoked the Monroe Doctrine to justify "meddling" in the affairs of Central America.

In paragraph 25, Smith likely alludes indirectly to one of the most significant international matters of the Coolidge administration, the Kellogg-Briand Pact (also referred to as the Pact of Paris). With the shadow of World War I still hanging over Europe, the French foreign minister, Aristide Briand, proposed a joint French-U.S. pact renouncing war. Coolidge's secretary of state, Frank Kellogg, made a counterproposal: that such a pact should include other European nations. Accordingly, on August 27, 1928—just five days after Smith's acceptance speech—the United States, Britain, France, Italy, Japan, Poland, Belgium, and several other nations signed the pact, outlawing war "as an instrument of national policy" (http://www.yale.edu/lawweb/avalon/kbpact/kbpact.htm). Smith expresses his objections to the kind of secret negotiations that gave rise to the pact. Further, he recognizes that an agreement such as the Kellogg-Briand Pact, however well intentioned, was meaningless if the roots causes of war were not eliminated.

Prohibition

Beginning with paragraph 27, Smith takes up the delicate matter of Prohibition. The temperance movement had emerged during the nineteenth century, but in the early years of the twentieth century the effort became more concerted. Individual states passed laws restricting the sale of

Prohibition officers inspecting tanks and vats at the largest distillery ever uncovered in Detroit, on January 5, 1931.
(AP/Wide World Photos)

alcohol and closing down saloons, and by the start of World War I fourteen states had enacted some form of prohibition. The number had risen to twenty-six by 1919. The Anti-Saloon League was particularly active during the war, arguing that Prohibition was necessary to preserve the morals of American troops and to conserve grain for the war effort. By the time the Eighteenth Amendment, banning the "manufacture, sale, or transportation of intoxicating liquors" (but not their consumption), was ratified in 1919, the number of congressional representatives from "dry" states outnumbered those from "wet" states by two to one (http://caselaw.lp.findlaw.com/data/constitution/amendment18/).

Initially, Prohibition and its enabling legislation, the Volstead Act (passed on October 28, 1919, but initially vetoed by Woodrow Wilson), were regarded as a success, for arrests for drunkenness declined and health authorities reported fewer alcohol-related illnesses. But as the Roaring Twenties unfolded, an increasing number of Americans began to see Prohibition as a failure and as a measure that impinged on their personal freedom. For one thing, the act was difficult to enforce. Illegal alcohol entered the country from Canada and Mexico. Moreover, the agents of the U.S. Treasury Department charged with enforcing the act were underpaid, leaving them susceptible to corruption and bribery from bootleggers (so called because people hid slim flasks of liquor in their bootlegs). Drinking remained common in the big cities, particularly at places called speakeasies (the name deriving from the fact that customers were urged to "speak easy," or at a low volume, a measure designed to encourage the police to pass the establishment by, rather than raiding it. Prohibition, as Smith points out, was "insidiously sapping respect for all law," creating a class of criminals and mobsters who grew rich by flouting an unenforceable law. In fact, law-enforcement expenditures quintupled from 1920 to 1930, largely as a result of Prohibition. Such a state of affairs bred cynicism about the rule of law and the efficacy of government in general. Smith's solution to the problem is to amend the Eighteenth Amendment and allow each state to set its own course with regard to alcohol. He also calls for placing the sale of alcohol in public (that is, state) rather than private hands.

Economic Conditions

Smith next turns his attention to economic conditions. A theme of his campaign, and one that he failed to exploit as fully as he might have, was an agricultural depression throughout the 1920s. In the eyes of many voters, the Harding and Coolidge administrations heavily favored industry over agriculture, though the facts might not have supported this belief. For instance, tariffs on foreign farm products remained high during the 1920s. Further, the Capper-Volstead Act of 1922 exempted agricultural cooperatives from antitrust laws, leading to the formation of the Department of Agriculture's Division of Co-operative Marketing. Additionally, the 1923 Agricultural Credits Act gave farmers easier access to loans from the Federal Farm Loan Board. Then, in 1927, Congress passed the McNary-Haugen bill, providing support prices for agricultural products. Although President Coolidge vetoed the bill and it never became law, its initial passage demonstrated that Congress was not indifferent to the plight of farmers. The Federal Farm Board was created in 1929 to help support prices. Despite these measures, farmers faced tough times, mainly as a result of a glut of agricultural products, created in large part by dramatic increases in the use of chemical fertilizers. Smith pledges to take steps to improve the lot of farmers, though he does not specify what measures he would have proposed.

Labor Issues

Smith also addresses labor issues. During the postwar period, organized labor achieved few successes. One reason was that many members of the public associated labor agitation with Communism and foreign agitators. Moreover, the U.S. Supreme Court issued rulings that hurt labor unions. One of the most important was the ruling in *Coronado Coal Co. v. United Mine Workers of America* (1925). In this landmark case the Court turned the nation's antitrust laws against the unions, arguing that strikes and similar actions were a restraint of trade. Under these conditions, the weekly earnings of the average manufacturing worker remained stagnant. In 1924 the figure was $23.93; by 1928 the figure was just $24.97.

Again, Smith appealed to his reputation as state assemblyman and governor as a champion of the working classes. In 1911 the Triangle Shirtwaist Factory fire in New York City, for example, killed 143 workers because the factory's doors were locked to prevent employees from leaving early or stealing materials. In response to the tragedy, Smith sponsored legislation that improved working conditions in factories. He believed that the state, not the political bosses or the church, was responsible for political reform and social welfare. Accordingly, as governor, he favored stronger laws having to do with pensions and workers' compensation. He also introduced a 48-hour workweek for children and women (at a time when laborers routinely worked much longer hours). He also enacted rent controls and extended subsidies for medical care for the poor. Perhaps somewhat ironically, though, he was identified with the more moderate, almost conservative wing of the Democratic Party, for he believed that the state's role was efficient government and that business, where possible, should be allowed to tend to its own concerns. Again, Smith's promise to ameliorate the condition of the laboring classes had teeth, for his record demonstrated his commitment to reform.

Immigration

Finally, Smith takes up the issue of immigration. For at least three decades many Americans of northern European stock had grown to fear immigrants from such places as southern and eastern Europe. These fears had been stoked by World War I, when foreigners were often viewed as dangerous and subversive. Accordingly, there were widespread calls for immigration restriction. These calls were answered by the Johnson-Reed Immigration Act of 1924 (popularly known as the National Origins Act) and other legislation designed to limit the number of immigrants from eastern and southern Europe and from Japan. The National Origins Act accomplished this goal by establishing quotas for each nationality based on the 1890 census, thus favoring immigrants from the "old" immigrant countries of northern Europe and placing at a disadvantage those from the "new" immigrant countries of southern and eastern Europe, whose numbers were lower in 1890. Smith notes that the laws are discriminatory and argues that they must be changed.

Impact and Legacy

Smith's nomination address, as well as his campaign speeches throughout the summer and autumn of 1928, failed to have the desired effect on voters, for Smith was soundly defeated. He and his opponent, Herbert Hoover—who never referred to his opponent by name during the campaign—presented voters with a stark contrast. Smith was a product of an eastern big city; Hoover came from a small town in Iowa. Smith never attended high school and confessed that he virtually never read a book for pleasure; the more scholarly Hoover was educated as an engineer. Smith was easygoing, casual, and flamboyant, and he spoke with sometimes creative grammar and a thick New York accent that many people in the rural Midwest found alien; Hoover's manner was stiff and formal (he wore a tie when he went fishing). Smith was at home in front of immigrants, the poor, and African Americans, though he tended to sound awkward when he spoke into a radio microphone; Hoover had a rich, appealing radio voice, but he had little contact with immigrants and African Americans. Smith was a "wet," meaning he was opposed to Prohibition; Hoover was a "dry," supporting Prohibition (though he occasionally enjoyed a drink in private). Most important, Smith was a Roman Catholic at a time when Protestant America looked with suspicion on Catholics; Hoover, in contrast, was the standard bearer for small-town religious fundamentalism. Perhaps the only thing the two candidates had in common was that both were self-made men and were grateful to the economic system that enabled each to enjoy success. Nevertheless, the contrast between the two candidates mirrored the sharp divisions of the country during the 1920s—divisions between rural conservatives and urban sophisticates, between wets and drys, between Socialists and capitalists, between black and white.

From the start, the Smith candidacy was doomed by what reporters called the "three P's"—Prohibition, Prejudice, and Prosperity. Many conservative fundamentalist voters, who supported Prohibition, believed that a Catholic president's first allegiance would be to the pope in Rome rather than to the American Constitution—the same fear that John F.

Kennedy faced some thirty years later. Indeed, anti-Catholic prejudice ran deep, especially in the South and Midwest. On September 19, 1928, the Smith campaign train crossed into Oklahoma and was met by Ku Klux Klan crosses burning on either side of the tracks. Further, the nation had enjoyed considerable economic prosperity under the Republican administrations of Warren Harding and Calvin Coolidge, allowing Hoover to promise continuing prosperity under the campaign slogan "A chicken in every pot and a car in every garage." During the campaign, Hoover convinced voters that "given a chance to go forward with the policies of the last eight years…poverty will be banished from this nation" (qtd. in *Time*, http://www.time.com/time/magazine/article/0,9171,881167,00.html?iid=chix-sphere). Hoover, along with his running mate, Charles Curtis, won in a landslide, capturing 21.4 million votes to Smith's 15 million. More dramatically, Hoover carried forty states to Smith's eight, including six states in the Deep South and just two—Rhode Island and his native New York—elsewhere.

Although Smith was soundly defeated, his candidacy was a watershed event, for he was the first Irish American and the first Catholic to run for president under the banner of a major political party. Perhaps just as important, his candidacy marked the beginning of a major voter realignment that would affect the fortunes of the Democratic and Republican parties for decades to come. The principles he articulated in his acceptance speech and throughout the campaign reinvigorated the Democratic Party, for Smith won more votes than had any other twentieth-century Democrat, including Woodrow Wilson; many of these votes were cast by women who had gained the right to vote just eight years earlier. In 1924 the vote total was approximately 29 million; in large part because of Smith, the vote total in 1928 increased to more than 36 million. More important, he carried the vote in the nation's large cities; in 1924 the Republican Calvin Coolidge carried the nation's twelve largest cities, but in 1928 those cities all voted for Smith. Four years later, after the collapse of the nation's economy and the onset of the Great Depression, rural voters would join voters in the cities to elect the Democrat Franklin D. Roosevelt. Thus, to the candidacy of Al Smith can be attributed the New Deal coalition of women, Catholics, blue-collar workers, and urban voters that persisted for decades and enabled a Democrat to sit in the White House for twenty-eight of the next thirty-six years.

Key Sources

Smith's own writings, primarily in the form of speeches, can be found in two volumes that were published in the late 1920s. One is *Campaign Addresses of Governor Alfred E. Smith, Democratic Candidate for President, 1928* (1929). The other is *Progressive Democracy: Addresses & State Papers* (1928).

Essential Quotes

"*Government should be constructive, not destructive; progressive, not reactionary.*"

(Address of Acceptance of the Democratic Presidential Nomination)

"*It is a fallacy that there is inconsistency between progressive measures protecting the rights of the people, including the poor and the weak, and a just regard for the rights of legitimate business, great or small.*"

(Address of Acceptance of the Democratic Presidential Nomination)

"*The real outlawry of war must come from a more substantial endeavor to remove the causes of war.*"

(Address of Acceptance of the Democratic Presidential Nomination)

"*Victory, simply for the sake of achieving it, is empty.*"

(Address of Acceptance of the Democratic Presidential Nomination)

Further Reading

■ Articles

Hostetler, Michael J. "Gov. Al Smith Confronts the Catholic Question: The Rhetorical Legacy of the 1928 Campaign." *Communication Quarterly* 46, no. 1 (1998): 12–24.

Neal, Donn C. "What If Al Smith Had Been Elected?" *Presidential Studies Quarterly* 14, no. 2 (1984): 242–248.

Sweeney, James R. "Rum, Romanism, and Virginia Democrats: The Party Leaders and the Campaign of 1928." *Virginia Magazine of History and Biography* 90 (October 1982): 403–431.

■ Books

Eldot, Paula. *Governor Alfred E. Smith: The Politician as Reformer.* New York: Garland, 1983.

Finan, Christopher M. *Alfred E. Smith: The Happy Warrior.* New York: Hill and Wang, 2002.

Johnson, David E., and Johnny R. Johnson. *A Funny Thing Happened on the Way to the White House: Foolhardiness, Folly, and Fraud in Presidential Elections from Andrew Jackson to George W. Bush.* Lanham, Md.: Taylor, 2004.

Josephson, Matthew, and Hannah Josephson. *Al Smith: Hero of the Cities.* Boston: Houghton Mifflin, 1969.

Lichtman, Allan J. *Prejudice and the Old Politics: The Presidential Election of 1928.* Lanham, Md.: Lexington Books, 2000.

Neal, Donn C. *The World beyond the Hudson: Alfred E. Smith and National Politics, 1918–1928.* New York: Garland, 1983.

Slayton, Robert A. *Empire Statesman: The Rise and Redemption of Al Smith.* New York: Free Press, 2007.

■ Web Sites

Cyndy Bittinger, "The Business of America Is Business?" Calvin Coolidge Memorial Foundation Web site. http://www.calvin-coolidge.org/html/the_business_of_america_is_bus.html.

Questions for Further Study

1. Discuss Smith's relationship with his far more well-known contemporary and fellow Democrat, Franklin Delano Roosevelt. The future president supported Smith's own presidential aspirations throughout the 1920s before running in 1932 on a platform that Smith vehemently opposed. What circumstances account for the changes in that relationship? What were the bases for the differences between the two men? Were they entirely political or philosophical, or was there a personal element to it as well? Did Smith himself change his views, shifting gradually toward a more conservative stance, or was the true shift in views on the part of the Democratic Party as it increasingly aligned itself with Rooseveltian liberalism?

2. Although his name could hardly sound more American, Al Smith seemed like a foreigner to the largely white, Protestant, and rural U.S. electorate of the 1920s. Why was this so? Smith's Catholicism, his interactions with and support from members of minority and disadvantaged groups, and Prohibition and its attendant issues are among the topics to consider in addressing this question. How might the presidential elections of the 1920s—particularly in 1928, when Herbert Hoover soundly defeated Smith—have played out differently in the twenty-first century? Pay special attention to the differences between the two men in terms of personality and image, matters that—thanks in large part to television and campaigners' use of it—play an enormously important role in deciding modern-day elections.

3. Smith criticizes the policy of the Harding and Coolidge administrations toward Latin America, particularly Nicaragua. Research and discuss "The situation in Nicaragua" to which he refers, itself a great drama that would exert enormous impact on U.S. foreign policy during the Reagan administration more than half a century later. Pay special attention to the key players in that drama: the revolutionary Augusto Sandino and the great ruling families, most notably, the Chamorros and Somozas, all of whose names continued to reappear in the headlines of the late 1970s and 1980s. What specific actions on the part of the United States did Smith recommend or might he have implemented as president? How does he position his argument in relation to the Monroe Doctrine? Finally, in your opinion, how effective and correct is he, both on the Monroe Doctrine issue specifically and on U.S. foreign policy in general?

"Hoover's Speech." *Time* http://www.time.com/time/magazine/article/0,9171,881167,00.html?iid=chix-sphere.

"Kellogg-Briand Pact 1928." The Avalon Project at Yale Law School Web site. http://www.yale.edu/lawweb/avalon/kbpact/kbpact.htm.

"Warren G. Harding." The White House Web site. http://www.whitehouse.gov/history/presidents/wh29.html.

"U.S. Constitution: Eighteenth Amendment." FindLaw Web site. http://caselaw.lp.findlaw.com/data/constitution/amendment18/.

—Michael J. O'Neal

ADDRESS OF ACCEPTANCE OF THE DEMOCRATIC PRESIDENTIAL NOMINATION (1928)

Upon the steps of this Capitol, where twenty-five years ago I first came into the service of the State, I receive my party's summons to lead it in the nation. Within this building, I learned the principles, the purposes and the functions of government and to know that the greatest privilege that can come to any man is to give himself to a nation which has reared him and raised him from obscurity to be a contender for the highest office in the gift of its people.

Here I confirmed my faith in the principles of the Democratic Party so eloquently defined by Woodrow Wilson: "First, the people as the source and their interests and desires as the text of laws and institutions. Second, individual liberty as the objective of all law." With a gratitude too strong for words and with humble reliance upon the aid of Divine Providence, I accept your summons to the wider field of action.

Government should be constructive, not destructive; progressive, not reactionary. I am entirely unwilling to accept the old order of things as the best unless and until I become convinced that it cannot be made better.

It is our new world theory that government exists for the people as against the old world conception that the people exist for the government. A sharp line separates those who believe that an elect class should be the special object of the government's concern and those who believe that the government is the agent and servant of the people who create it. Dominant in the Republican Party today is the element which proclaims and executes the political theories against which the party liberals like Roosevelt and La Follette and their party insurgents have rebelled. This reactionary element seeks to vindicate the theory of benevolent oligarchy. It assumes that a material prosperity, the very existence of which is challenged, is an excuse for political inequality. It makes the concern of the government, not people, but material things.

I have fought this spirit in my own State. I have had to fight it and to beat it, in order to place upon the statute books every one of the progressive, humane laws for whose enactment I assumed responsibility in my legislative and executive career. I shall know how to fight it in the nation.

It is a fallacy that there is inconsistency between progressive measures protecting the rights of the people, including the poor and the weak, and a just regard for the rights of legitimate business, great or small. Therefore, while I emphasize my belief that legitimate business promotes the national welfare, let me warn the forces of corruption and favoritism, that Democratic victory means that they will be relegated to the rear and the front seats will be occupied by the friends of equal opportunity.

Likewise, government policy should spring from the deliberate action of an informed electorate. Of all men, I have reason to believe that the people can and do grasp the problems of the government. Against the opposition of the self-seeker and the partisan, again and again, I have seen legislation won by the pressure of popular demand, exerted after the people had had an honest, frank and complete explanation of the issues. Great questions of finance, the issuance of millions of dollars of bonds for public projects, the complete reconstruction of the machinery of the State government, the institution of an executive budget, these are but a few of the complicated questions which I, myself, have taken to the electorate. Every citizen has thus learned the nature of the business in hand and appreciated that the State's business is his business.

That direct contact with the people I propose to continue in this campaign and, if I am elected, in the conduct of the nation's affairs. I shall thereby strive to make the nation's policy the true reflection of the nation's ideals. Because I believe in the idealism of the party of Jefferson, Cleveland, and Wilson, my administration will be rooted in liberty under the law; liberty that means freedom to the individual to follow his own will so long as he does not harm his neighbor; the same high moral purpose in our conduct as a nation that actuates the conduct of the God-fearing man and woman; that equality of opportunity which lays the foundation for wholesome family life and opens up the outlook for the betterment of the lives of our children.

In the rugged honesty of Grover Cleveland there originated one of our party's greatest principles: "Public office is a public trust." That principle now takes on new meaning. Political parties are the vehicle for carrying out the popular will. We place responsibility upon the party. The Republican Party today stands responsible for the widespread dishonesty that has honeycombed its administration....

The Democratic Party asks the electorate to withdraw their confidence from the Republican Party and repose it with the Democratic Party pledged to continue those standards of unblemished integrity which characterized every act of the administration of Woodrow Wilson.

But I would not rest our claim for the confidence of the American people alone upon the misdeeds of the opposite party. Ours must be a constructive campaign.

The Republican Party builds its case upon a myth. We are told that only under the benevolent administration of that party can the country enjoy prosperity. When four million men, desirous to work and support their families, are unable to secure employment there is very little in the picture of prosperity to attract them and the millions dependent upon them.

In the year 1926, the latest figures available show that one-twentieth of one per cent of the 430,000 corporations in this country earned 40 per cent of their profits; 40 per cent of the corporations actually lost money; one-fourth of one per cent of these corporations earned two-thirds of the profits of all of them. Specific industries are wholly prostrate and there is widespread business difficulty and discontent among the individual business men of the country.

Prosperity to the extent that we have it is unduly concentrated and has not equitably touched the lives of the farmer, the wage-earner and the individual business man. The claim of governmental economy is as baseless as the claims that general business prosperity exists and that it can exist only under Republican administration.

When the Republican Party came into power in 1921 it definitely promised reorganization of the machinery of government, and abolition or consolidation of unnecessary and overlapping agencies. A Committee was appointed. A representative of the President acted as Chairman. It prepared a plan of reorganization. The plan was filed in the archives. It still remains there. After seven years of Republican control the structure of government is worse than it was in 1921. It is fully as bad as the system which existed in New York State before we secured by constitutional amendment the legislation which consolidated more than one hundred offices, commissions and boards into eighteen coordinated departments, each responsible to the Governor. In contrast with this, the Republican Party in control at Washington when faced with the alternative of loss of patronage for [the] faithful or more efficient and economical management of the government permitted the old order to continue for the benefit of the patronage seekers....

Acting upon the principle of "Equal opportunity for all, special privileges for none," I shall ask Congress to carry out the tariff declaration of our platform. To be sure the Republican Party will attempt in the campaign to misrepresent [the] Democratic attitude to the tariff. The Democratic Party does not and under my leadership will not advocate any sudden or drastic revolution in our economic system which would cause business upheaval and popular distress. This principle was recognized as far back as the passage of the Underwood Tariff Bill. Our platform restates it in unmistakable language. The Democratic Party stands squarely for the maintenance of legitimate business and high standard of wages for American labor. Both can be maintained and at the same time the tariff can be taken out of the realm of politics and treated on a strictly business basis.

A leading Republican writing in criticism of the present tariff law, said: "It stands as one of the most ill drawn pieces of legislation in recent political history. It is probably near the actual truth to say that taking for granted some principle of protection of American business and industry, the country has prospered due to post-war conditions abroad and in spite of, rather than on account of, the Fordney-McCumber tariff." What I have just quoted is no part of a campaign document. It was written a few months ago by Professor William Starr Myers of Princeton University writing the history of his own party.

Against the practice of legislative log-rolling, Woodrow Wilson pointed the way to a remedy. It provided for the creation and maintenance of a non-political, quasi-judicial, fact-finding commission which could investigate and advise the President and Congress as to the tariff duties really required to protect American industry and safeguard the high standard of American wages. In an administration anxious to meet political obligations, the Commission has ceased to function and it has been publicly stated by former members of it that the work of the Commission has been turned over to the advocates of special interests. To bring this about, it is a matter of record that the President demanded the undated resignation of one of its members before he signed his appointment....

The Constitution provides that treaties with foreign powers must be ratified by a vote of two-thirds of the Senate. This is a legal recognition of the truth that in our foreign relations we must rise above party politics and act as a united nation. Any foreign policy must have its roots deep in the approval of a very large majority of our people. Therefore, no greater service was ever rendered by any President than by Woodrow

Wilson when he struck at the methods of secret diplomacy. Today we have close relations, vital to our commercial and world standing, with every other nation. I regard it, therefore, as a paramount duty to keep alive the interest of our people in these questions, and to advise the electorate as to facts and policies.

Through a long line of distinguished Secretaries of State, Republican and Democratic alike, this country had assumed a position of world leadership in the endeavor to outlaw war and substitute reason for force. At the end of President Wilson's administration we enjoyed not only the friendship but the respectful admiration of the peoples of the world. Today we see unmistakable evidences of a widespread distrust of us and unfriendliness to us, particularly among our Latin American neighbors.

I especially stress the necessity for the restoration of cordial relations with Latin America and I take my text from a great Republican Secretary of State, Elihu Root, who said: "We consider that the independence and equal rights of the smallest and weakest member of the family of nations deserve as much respect as those of the great empires. We pretend to no right, privilege or power that we do not freely concede to each one of the American Republics."

The present administration has been false to that declaration of one of its greatest party leaders. The situation in Nicaragua fairly exemplifies our departure from this high standard. The administration has intervened in an election dispute between two conflicting factions, sent our troops into Nicaragua, maintained them there for years, and this without the consent of Congress. To settle this internal dispute, our marines have died and hundreds of Nicaraguans in turn have been killed by our marines. Without consultation with Congress, the administration entered on this long continued occupation of the territory of a supposedly friendly nation by our armed troops.

To no declaration of our platform do I more heartily commit myself than the one for the abolition of the practice of the President of entering into agreements for the settlement of internal disputes in Latin American countries, unless the agreements have been consented to by the Senate as provided for in the Constitution of the United States. I personally declare what the platform declares: "Interference in the purely internal affairs of Latin American countries must cease" and I specifically pledge myself to follow this declaration with regard to Mexico as well as the other Latin American countries.

The Monroe Doctrine must be maintained but not as a pretext for meddling with the purely local concerns of countries which even though they be small are sovereign and entitled to demand and receive respect for their sovereignty. And I shall certainly do all that lies in my power to bring about the fullest concerted action between this country and all the Latin American countries with respect to any step which it may ever be necessary to take to discharge such responsibilities to civilization as may be placed upon us by the Monroe Doctrine.

The evil effect of the administration's policy with respect to Latin America has extended to our relations with the rest of the world. I am not one of those who contend that everything Republican is bad and everything Democratic is good. I approve the effort to renew and extend the arbitration treaties negotiated under the administration of President Wilson. But the usefulness of those treaties as deterrents of war is materially impaired by the reservations asserted by various nations of the right to wage defensive wars as those reservations are interpreted in the light of President Coolidge's record. Defending his policies he announced on April 25, 1927, the doctrine that the person and property of a citizen are a part of the national domain, even when abroad. I do not think the American people would approve a doctrine which would give to Germany, or France, or England, or any other country, the right to regard a citizen of that country or the property of a citizen of that country situated within the borders of the United States a part of the national domain of the foreign country. Our unwarranted intervention in internal affairs in Latin America and this specious reason for it constitute the basis upon which other countries may seek to justify imperialistic policies which threaten world peace and materially lessen the effectiveness which might otherwise lie in the multilateral treaties.

The real outlawry of war must come from a more substantial endeavor to remove the causes of war and in this endeavor the Republican administration has signally failed. I am neither militarist nor jingo. I believe that the people of this country wish to live in peace and amity with the world. Freedom from entangling alliances is a fixed American policy. It does not mean, however, that great nations should not behave to one another with the same decent friendliness and fair play that self-respecting men and women show to one another....

The President of the United States has two constitutional duties with respect to prohibition. The first is embodied in his oath of office. If, with one hand on the Bible and the other hand reaching up to Heaven, I promise the people of this country that "I will faithfully execute the office of President of the

United States and to the best of my ability preserve, protect and defend the Constitution of the United States," you may be sure that I shall live up to that oath to the last degree. I shall to the very limit execute the pledge of our platform "to make an honest endeavor to enforce the 18th Amendment and all other provisions of the Federal Constitution and all laws enacted pursuant thereto."

The President does not make the laws. He does his best to execute them whether he likes them or not. The corruption in enforcement activities which caused a former Republican Prohibition Administrator to state that three-fourths of the dry agents were political ward heelers named by politicians without regard to Civil Service laws and that prohibition is the "new political pork barrel," I will ruthlessly stamp out. Such conditions can not and will not exist under any administration presided over by me.

The second constitutional duty imposed upon the President is "To recommend to the Congress such measures as he shall judge necessary and expedient." Opinion upon prohibition cuts squarely across the two great political parties. There are thousands of so-called "wets" and "drys" in each. The platform of my party is silent upon any question of change in the law. I personally believe that there should be change and I shall advise the Congress in accordance with my constitutional duty of whatever changes I deem "necessary or expedient." It will then be for the people and the representatives in the national and State legislatures to determine whether these changes shall be made.

I will state the reasons for my belief. In a book "Law and its Origin," recently called to my notice, James C. Carter, one of the leaders of the bar of this country, wrote of the conditions which exist "when a law is made declaring conduct widely practiced and widely regarded as innocent to be a crime." He points out that in the enforcement of such a law "trials become scenes of perjury and subornation of perjury; juries find abundant excuses for rendering acquittal or persisting in disagreement contrary to their oaths" and he concludes "Perhaps worst of all is that general regard and reverence for law are impaired, a consequence the mischief of which can scarcely be estimated." These words, written years before the 18th Amendment or the Volstead Act, were prophetic of our situation today.

I believe in temperance. We have not achieved temperance under the present system. The mothers and fathers of young men and women throughout this land know the anxiety and worry which has been brought to them by their children's use of liquor in a way which was unknown before prohibition. I believe in reverence for law. Today disregard of the prohibition laws is insidiously sapping respect for all law. I raise, therefore, what I profoundly believe to be a great moral issue involving the righteousness of our national conduct and the protection of our children's morals.

The remedy, as I have stated, is the fearless application of Jeffersonian principles. Jefferson and his followers foresaw the complex activities of this great, widespread country. They knew that in rural, sparsely settled districts people would develop different desires and customs from those in densely populated sections and that if we were to be a nation united on truly national matters, there had to be a differentiation in local laws to allow for different local habits. It was for this reason that the Democratic platform in 1884 announced "We oppose sumptuary laws which vex the citizens and interfere with individual liberty," and it was for this reason that Woodrow Wilson vetoed the Volstead Act....

I believe moreover that there should be submitted to the people the question of some change in the provisions of the 18th Amendment. Certainly, no one foresaw when the amendment was ratified the conditions which exist today of bootlegging, corruption and open violation of the law in all parts of the country. The people themselves should after this eight years of trial, be permitted to say whether existing conditions should be rectified. I personally believe in an amendment in the 18th Amendment which would give to each individual State itself only after approval by a referendum popular vote of its people the right wholly within its borders to import, manufacture or cause to be manufactured and sell alcoholic beverages, the sale to be made only by the State itself and not for consumption in any public place. We may well learn from the experience of other nations. Our Canadian neighbors have gone far in this manner to solve this problem by the method of sale made by the state itself and not by private individuals.

There is no question here of the return of the saloon. When I stated that the saloon "is and ought to be a defunct institution in this country" I meant it. I mean it today. I will never advocate nor approve any law which directly or indirectly permits the return of the saloon.

Such a change would preserve for the dry states the benefit of a national law that would continue to make interstate shipment of intoxicating beverages a crime. It would preserve for the dry states Federal enforcement of prohibition within their own borders. It would permit to citizens of other states a carefully limited and controlled method of effectuating the popular will wholly within the borders of those states without the old evil of the saloon.

Such a method would re-establish respect for law and terminate the agitation which has injected discord into the ranks of the great political parties which should be standing for the accomplishment of fundamental programs for the nation. I may fairly say even to those who disagree with me that the solution I offer is one based upon the historic policy of the Democratic Party, to assure to each State its complete right of local self-government. I believe it is a solution which would today be offered by Jefferson, or Jackson or Cleveland or Wilson, if those great leaders were with us.

Publicity agents of the Republican administration have written so many articles on our general prosperity, that they have prevented the average man from having a proper appreciation of the degree of distress existing today among farmers and stockraisers. From 1910 to the present time the farm debt has increased by the striking sum of ten billions of dollars, or from four billion to fourteen billion dollars. The value of farm property between 1920 and 1925 decreased by twenty billions of dollars. This depression made itself felt in an enormous increase of bank failures in the agricultural districts. In 1927 there were 830 bank failures, with total liabilities of over 270 millions of dollars, almost entirely in the agricultural sections, as against 49 such failures during the last year of President Wilson's administration....

We have not merely a problem of helping the farmer. While agriculture is one of the most individualized and independent of enterprises, still as the report of the Business Men's Commission points out, "Agriculture is essentially a public function, affected with a clear and unquestionable public interest." The country is an economic whole. If the buying power of agriculture is impaired, the farmer makes fewer trips to Main Street. The shop owner suffers because he has lost a large part of this trade. The manufacturer who supplies him likewise suffers as does the wage earner, because the manufacturer is compelled to curtail his production. And the banker cannot collect his debts or safely extend further credit. This country cannot be a healthy, strong economic body if one of its members, so fundamentally important as agriculture, is sick almost to the point of economic death.

The normal market among the farmers of this country for the products of industry is ten billions of dollars. Our export market according to latest available figures is, exclusive of agricultural products, approximately one billion, six hundred millions of dollars. These large figures furnish striking indica-

tion of the serious blow to national prosperity as a whole which is struck when the buying power of the farmer is paralyzed.

When, therefore, I say that I am in accord with our platform declaration that the solution of this problem must be a prime and immediate concern of the Democratic administration, I make no class appeal. I am stating a proposition as vital to the welfare of business as of agriculture....

The Democratic Party has always recognized this fact and under the administration of Woodrow Wilson, a large body of progressive legislation for the protection of those laboring in industry, was enacted. Our platform continues that tradition of the party. We declare for the principle of collective bargaining which alone can put the laborer upon a basis of fair equality with the employer; for the human principle that labor is not a commodity; for fair treatment to government and Federal employees; and for specific and immediate attention to the serious problems of unemployment.

From these premises it was inevitable that our platform should further recognize grave abuses in the issuance of injunctions in labor disputes which threaten the very principle of collective bargaining. Chief Justice Taft in 1919 stated that government of the relations between capital and labor by injunction was an absurdity. Justice Holmes and Justice Brandeis of the United States Supreme Court unite in an opinion which describes the restraints on labor imposed by a Federal injunction as a reminder of involuntary servitude.

Dissatisfaction and social unrest have grown from these abuses and undoubtedly legislation must be framed to meet just causes for complaint in regard to the unwarranted issuance of injunctions....

I shall continue my sympathetic interest in the advancement of progressive legislation for the protection and advancement of working men and women. Promotion of proper care of maternity, infancy and childhood and the encouragement of those scientific activities of the National Government which advance the safeguards of public health, are so fundamental as to need no expression from me other than my record as legislator and as Governor....

During all of our national life the freedom of entry to the country has been extended to the millions who desired to take advantage of the freedom and the opportunities offered by America. The rugged qualities of our immigrants have helped to develop our country and their children have taken their places high in the annals of American history.

Every race has made its contribution to the betterment of America. While I stand squarely on our platform declaration that the laws which limit immigration must be preserved in full force and effect, I am heartily in favor of removing from the immigration law the harsh provision which separates families, and I am opposed to the principle of restriction based upon the figures of immigrant population contained in a census thirty-eight years old. I believe this is designed to discriminate against certain nationalities, and is an unwise policy. It is in no way essential to a continuance of the restriction advocated in our platform....

Victory, simply for the sake of achieving it, is empty. I am entirely satisfied of our success in November because I am sure we are right and therefore sure that our victory means progress for our nation. I am convinced of the wisdom of our plat-

Glossary

bonds	financial securities sold to investors by a government as a means of financing particular projects or activities
Civil Service	as a group, employees of government other than elected officials
collective bargaining	organized negotiation between workers and employers
Divine Providence	God
duties	taxes or fees
elect class	a group of people supposedly predestined to be leaders and rulers
Elihu Root	U.S. Secretary of War (1899–1904) and Secretary of State (1904–1909), who won the Nobel Peace Prize in 1912
Fordney-McCumber tariff	a protectionist trade bill, named after its sponsors in the House and Senate, respectively, and signed into law in 1922, whose provisions reflected American isolationism following World War I
jingo	one who favors extremely overbearing and virulent nationalism; from the expression "By jingo!" sometimes considered a euphemism for swearing by Jesus
La Follette	Robert La Follette, Wisconsin governor and U.S. senator who split from the left wing of the Democratic Party to form the Progressive Party and ran for president in 1924, garnering over 4 million votes
log-rolling	the practice among legislators of voting for a colleague's bill with the understanding that the favor will be returned
oligarchy	a form of government in which a small group exercises dictatorial control
partisan	someone who strongly favors a particular political party or faction
patronage	the distribution of government jobs and contracts by party bosses and elected officials
platform	a series of statements representing the official views of a political party on various issues of concern to the electorate
pork barrel	appropriation of public funds for special interests, particularly those within a representative's legislative district
protection	an effort to "protect" the industries in one's own nation by putting up trade barriers, such as tariffs and duties, to discourage foreign competition
reactionary	one who reacts against progressive social ideas by calling for extreme conservatism and a return to the past

form. I pledge a complete devotion to the welfare of our country and our people. I place that welfare above every other consideration and I am satisfied that our party is in a position to promote it. To that end I here and now declare to my fellow countrymen from one end of the United States to the other, that I will dedicate myself with all the power and energy that I possess to the service of our great Republic.

Glossary

special interests	groups whose economic clout gives them the power to influence public policy—usually in self-serving ways at odds with the public interest
statute	law; specifically, a law enacted by a legislative body
stockraisers	persons employed in raising livestock
subornation	persuasion of another to commit an illegal act, particularly perjury
sumptuary	referring to laws whose purpose is to curb behavior that, while it may not violate any other laws, is deemed immoral
tariff	a tax or duty on imported goods
temperance	in general, moderation; specifically, opposition to alcohol consumption
Underwood Tariff Bill	the United States Revenue Act of 1913, sponsored by Representative Oscar Underwood (D-AL), which lowered tariffs and imposed the income tax authorized by the Sixteenth Amendment
ward heelers	local political party functionaries
"wets" and "drys"	respectively, opponents and supporters of Prohibition
William Starr Myers	American journalist and educator

Elizabeth Cady Stanton (Library of Congress)

ELIZABETH CADY STANTON   1815–1902

Woman's Rights Activist

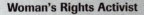

Featured Documents
◆ Declaration of Sentiments (1848)
◆ Address to the New York Legislature (1854)
◆ Speech for the Anniversary of the American Anti-Slavery Society (1860)
◆ "Solitude of Self" (1892)

Overview

Elizabeth Cady was born on November 12, 1815, to Daniel Cady, a judge, and Margaret Livingston Cady, a homemaker, in Johnstown, New York. Raised with four sisters and one brother, she led the life of a privileged miss. When her older brother died, her grieving father told the eleven-year-old Cady that he wished she were a boy. In turn, the girl promised him that she would try to be all her brother had been. She resolved to be manly, becoming good at sports and pursuing the study of Greek and philosophy. She was allowed to read anything she wished in the extensive family library, and her depth of knowledge is evident in her writing. She was also allowed to sit in on her father's discussions of court cases and thus heard firsthand about the legal handicaps of being a woman. Cady learned to debate from her father's law clerks, who liked to tease her with legal riddles. Such challenges honed her analytical skills, also evident in her writing. She attended the Troy Female Seminary (now the Emma Willard School), in Troy, New York.

At the Troy Female Seminary, Cady studied math, philosophy, and the natural sciences in addition to the domestic arts, which she did not like. Following graduation in 1833, she led the life of an upper-class girl, going to parties and traveling to see relatives. During one visit to her cousin Gerrit Smith, she was introduced to the cause of abolition and to ideas concerning individual rights, topics not discussed at home. She also met Henry Brewster Stanton, a renowned abolitionist, and was attracted to his good looks; he, in turn, was attracted to her enthusiasm and assumed she would make abolition her life's work. Despite opposition from her family, they married in 1840 and in June traveled to London for the first international antislavery convention. When a debate concerning the seating of woman delegates developed, Elizabeth Cady Stanton became more concerned about the rights of women than those of slaves. She would equate the positions of women and slaves throughout her life. In London she met the Quaker intellectual and conference delegate Lucretia Mott, beginning a lifelong friendship. Mott encouraged Stanton's independence and developing feminism, and the two resolved to hold a convention once they returned home and to form a society to advocate the rights of women. It took eight years, but in July 1848 the first woman's rights convention, organized principally by Stanton and Mott, was held in Seneca Falls, New York. It was the formal beginning of the woman's rights movement in America. Stanton addressed the convention, delivered the Declaration of Sentiments, and proposed a resolution advocating suffrage for women.

In 1851 she met Susan B. Anthony, whose organizational skills and drive complemented Stanton's abilities in writing and speaking. While Stanton developed strategies for their crusade for woman's rights, Anthony aided her, sometimes in tasks as simple as making dinner for Stanton's family. Together they published the *Revolution*, a national weekly magazine focused on woman's rights. Over the years Stanton was torn between family obligations and her work for woman's rights. She had seven children, all of whom survived into adulthood, an uncommon situation during that time period. In addition to her views on woman's rights, Stanton was outspoken about marriage, divorce, and motherhood. She traveled the lyceum circuit, giving speeches, and was president of the National Woman Suffrage Association, for whom she delivered her address "Solitude of Self." Stanton edited three volumes of the *History of Woman Suffrage* (1881–1886) and published the two-volume *Woman's Bible* (1895–1898), a best-selling, controversial interpretation of the Bible reflecting her lifelong disenchantment with organized religion and its impact on women. She died in New York City from heart failure on October 26, 1902.

Explanation and Analysis of Documents

Stanton's education, unorthodox for a woman of that era, is apparent in her writing. Her articles and speeches are full of classical and biblical references and demonstrate her knowledge of history. In turn, Stanton's early conversations with her father and his law clerks are apparent in the logical development of her arguments. She backs up her positions with engaging examples and uses wit and down-to-earth common sense to capture her audience. Stanton exhibited a womanly demeanor onstage that disarmed many a male audience and made motherhood, normally a private role, a basis for her public career. Unlike some woman's rights activists, she was no "dried up old maid," which gave her arguments more credibility. In her writing and speaking, she focused on enfranchisement for women, marriage and divorce, slavery, and the role of women in society.

Time Line

1815
- **November 12**
  Elizabeth Cady is born in Johnstown, New York.

1840
- **June 12**
  With her husband, Elizabeth Cady Stanton attends the first international antislavery convention, in London.

1848
- **July 19–20**
  Stanton and others hold the first woman's rights convention at Seneca Falls, New York, and present their Declaration of Sentiments.

1851
- **May**
  Stanton meets Susan B. Anthony.

1854
- **February 14**
  Stanton delivers an address to the New York State legislature.

1860
- **May 8**
  Stanton gives a speech to the American Anti-Slavery Society.

1868–1870
- Stanton and Anthony together publish the woman's rights newspaper *Revolution*.

1869
- **May 15**
  Stanton and Anthony form the National Woman Suffrage Association (later combined with the more conservative American Woman Suffrage Association); Stanton serves as its first president.

1892
- **January 18**
  Stanton resigns from the National American Woman Suffrage Association and gives her "Solitude of Self" speech.

1902
- **October 26**
  Stanton dies in New York City.

♦ **Declaration of Sentiments**

Delivered at Seneca Falls, New York, on July 20, 1848, the Declaration of Sentiments, a woman's rights manifesto primarily written by Stanton, was revolutionary and echoed the ideology behind America's own Revolution. By changing the language of the Declaration of Independence, the basic document proclaiming America's independence from tyranny, Stanton brought focus to the failure of that document to provide rights for half of America's citizens: women. The Declaration of Sentiments was presented at the first woman's rights convention, attended by more than one hundred women and men. It was followed by a set of eleven resolutions, including the resolution that women secure the right to vote. Signing the document to support the sentiments and resolutions were sixty-eight women and thirty-two men, including the abolitionist Frederick Douglass, a former slave.

A week before the convention, a group of woman, including Stanton and Mott, decided it was time to speak for the rights of women. The drafting of an advertisement for the convention, to be held at the Wesleyan Chapel in Seneca Falls, prompted the question of what to say there. Stanton hit on the idea of reconstructing Thomas Jefferson's Declaration of Independence to highlight the position of women. In her preface, she amends Jefferson's "one people" to refer to "one portion of the family of man" needing "to assume…a position different from that which they have hitherto occupied." Immediately she is pointing out that Jefferson's "one people" did not include women. The second section of Stanton's declaration adds two words (italicized here) to Jefferson's: "We hold these truths to be self-evident: that all men *and women* are created equal." She continues with women meriting the same rights of "life, liberty, and the pursuit of happiness."

In writing her declaration, Stanton wanted to echo Jefferson's eighteen indictments against the king of England. She remarks, like Jefferson, that "the history of mankind is a history of repeated injuries and usurpation." Rather than accusing the king, she states that these acts have been caused by "man toward woman," resulting in "the establishment of an absolute tyranny over her." Her first indictment is "He has never permitted her to exercise her inalienable right to the elective franchise." Stanton, with her familiarity with the law, believed that women's position would change only through their acquiring the vote. Voting would provide the power to make laws needed for political actions. Another indictment is a reference to a woman's position once married: She became bound to her husband, who had control of her and custody of their children. She was also without property rights, "even to the wages she earns." Although New York State had passed the Married Women's Property Act just months before the convention, the law did not allow a woman to keep the wages she earned, just property inherited. Other states had no such laws. Another indictment is "He has made her, morally, an irresponsible being," since according to the law a woman's husband was her master and was responsible for her actions. Stanton brings up divorce, which she would campaign over throughout her career. Under existing laws and irrespective of the reasons for separation, guardianship of children was awarded to the husband, "regardless of the happiness of women."

Another indictment applied to single women, who could own taxable property but had no voice in government, essentially taxation without representation. In employment, wages were not equal between men and women, and many "avenues to wealth" were closed to women. In addition, few women could attend colleges, since almost all admitted men only; Oberlin College, in Ohio, was the exception. Most damaging to women, according to Stanton, was "a different code of morals for men and women," creating a separate "sphere of action" for women. With this double standard, women were made to be of little account in society.

Following the Declaration of Sentiments were eleven resolutions, framed to redress the indictments. In writing the resolutions, Stanton asked for help from her lawyer husband. When she proposed the ninth resolution—"That it is the duty of the women of this country to secure to themselves their sacred right to the elective franchise"—he declined to support it and refused to attend the conference. Mott also thought the resolution would make the convention look "ridiculous," but she and others signed. Stanton felt that the law played a major role in setting men over women and that by demanding the vote women could work together against their repression and have roles in society beyond those of wife and mother. Concluding her declaration, Stanton calls for further actions, including other woman's rights conventions in different parts of the country, to promote the work of this first convention. Although there was a follow-up convention two weeks later in Rochester, New York, not until 1850 did other states begin to hold such conventions.

◆ **Address to the New York Legislature**

Confusion exists about whether Stanton delivered this speech before the New York State legislature in person. It is agreed that the speech was first given on February 14, 1854, to the New York State Woman's Rights Convention, of which Stanton was president. According to several sources, a few days later Stanton gave the same speech in a packed Senate chamber of the New York State legislature, making it the first address by a woman to a legislative body. Some sources state that Stanton's father threatened to disown her if she spoke to the lawmakers; other sources state that Judge Cady helped in formulating her arguments.

Whatever the truth, the speech is a masterpiece of logical argument, focusing on the fact that since laws deprived women of the right to control their own property and income, women were, as such, unable to define their own needs, a type of self-fulfilling prophecy. In the speech she asks for the vote for women and for the rights for women to sit on juries and to exercise the other rights of citizens. She not only demands changes in the laws affecting relationships between men and women but also clarifies the actual positions of women in society as contrasted with the public's false perceptions. Susan B. Anthony was so impressed by the speech that she published fifty thousand copies of it and put a copy on the

Statue for women's suffrage in the Capitol crypt below the rotunda, featuring (from left) Elizabeth Cady Stanton, Susan B. Anthony, and Lucretia Mott (AP/Wide World Photos)

desk of each legislator. In the speech, Stanton focuses on four principal aspects of women as citizens without rights.

She first addresses the position of women in general who, despite being "free-born citizens," are denied the right to vote. Although women support "the whole machinery of government," they are not represented. Stanton notes that even though women are "moral, virtuous and intelligent," they are thus "classed with idiots, lunatics and negroes." Yet men in these categories, under certain conditions, do have the right to vote. Through the years Stanton saw the legal position of blacks slowly improved while that of women remained unchanged. Using examples of women who accomplished great things, Stanton asks why women are still given no rights. Such examples demonstrate both her style of writing and her background of knowledge. She then wonders why, since it has been declared that "all men were created equal," the nation's government has become "an aristocracy that places the ignorant and vulgar above the educated and refined…an aristocracy that would raise sons above the mothers that bore them." Her implied reference to the British Crown and the inferred reestablishment of aristocracy in this country drives home her point.

In addition to the vote, she demands "trial by a jury of our own peers." She develops her argument by providing background on this basic right, stressing that no man has "ever been satisfied with being tried by jurors higher or lower in the civil or political scale than themselves." She then asks why women should be "dragged before a bar of grim-visaged judges, lawyers and jurors," all men, and questioned on subjects they "scarce breathe in secret to one another." Stanton notes the hundreds of imprisoned women who did not have "that right which you would die to defend for yourselves—trial by a jury of one's peers." Again, she points out the discrepancy between what the country fought for and the reality that not all citizens enjoy the rights gained.

The second part of the speech focuses on the position of married women. She differentiates between marriage under God's law and marriage as a civil contract. If people see marriage as a civil contract, she asks the audience, should marriage not be subject to the same laws that govern other contracts? Stanton asserts that the signing of the marriage contract "is instant civil death to one of the parties." Here she reiterates her position concerning the right of married women to hold property: "The wife who inherits no property holds about the same legal position that does the slave on the southern plantation. She can own nothing, sell nothing." This section also mentions how men have protection of the law from "unruly" wives, but a wife has no rights against a "worthless husband, a confirmed drunkard, a villain or a vagrant." During her own marriage ceremony, Stanton refused to say the word "obey," and as a married woman she preferred to be called Elizabeth Cady Stanton, not Mrs. Henry Stanton. She felt that using her husband's name denoted his ownership of her and that marriage should be between equals.

The third part speaks of the position of a widow, who could keep only one-third of her late husband's "landed estate" and one-half of his personal property. If a wife died first, the husband would keep everything. In some cases a widow became a pauper as a result of the laws. The fourth section focuses on the woman as mother. The law is, according to Stanton, "cruel and ruthless," since the child is the "absolute property of the father," who "may apprentice his son to a gamester or rum-seller...may bind his daughter to the owner of a brothel." If the father were about to die, he could "will away the guardianship of all his children from the mother." In case of separation, the law "gives the children to the father; no matter what his character or condition."

Following her discussion of injustices to classes of women, Stanton addresses those who have wondered "what the wives and daughters could complain of in republican America." Many could not understand what women wanted because, according to Stanton, they could not conceive of the idea that men and women are alike and, therefore, should be accorded the same rights. Stanton states that there should be no special laws for women and concisely answers the question of what women want: "We *ask* no better laws than those you have made for yourself." Anticipating the argument against woman's rights, Stanton states, "You may say that the mass of the women of this state do not make the demand; it comes from a few sour, disappointed old maids and childless women." She shows this as a mistake, detailing how women generally are not content with their lot in life.

This speech made a name for Stanton as a public speaker. Using logic and emotion, humor and flashes of rage, she attacked the subordinate status of women, pounding home her point that women must have the vote to be enabled to effect change.

♦ **Speech for the Anniversary of the American Anti-Slavery Society**

Stanton had been involved in the cause of abolition since before her marriage; friends she made working for abolition included William Lloyd Garrison, who invited her to address the opening session of the annual American Anti-Slavery Society meeting in New York on May 8, 1860. Delivered to an audience of fifteen hundred, her speech is an attack on slavery and an acknowledgment of the work of abolitionists as well as a statement about the chattel-like status of women.

Stanton discusses how black men have been deprived of their rights, using the graphic example of a black man kidnapped from his home in Africa and noting the consequences of slavery for America: "It has corrupted our churches, our politics,... it has gagged our statesmen." Stanton then celebrates the actions of Garrison, who had worked against slavery for thirty years, with others battling "a whole nation, Church and State, law and public sentiment, without the shadow of ever wavering, turning or faltering." Using a biblical reference characteristic of her speeches, Stanton remarks that women are also represented in the fight for abolition as the "Marys and Marthas" who "have gathered round the prophets of our day."

Stanton continues by stating that Garrison's American Anti-Slavery Society is the only one "where the humanity of woman is recognized, and these are the only men who have ever echoed back her cries for justice and equality." She recalls how in 1840, at the World's Anti-Slavery Convention, the British had denied the elected American women delegates a voice since they were not fit, because of their sex, to be delegates. Garrison was to have spoken to the group but refused because the women delegates were not allowed to speak or vote. Stanton's outrage fueled her sense of injustice, which then shifted from the plight of the black slave to that of women. She declares here that the "mission of this Radical Anti-Slavery Movement is not to the African slave alone, but to the slaves of custom, creed and sex, as well." In discussing how men had denounced slavery, she remarks that those (white) men could take only "an objective view," since they had not suffered the torments of slaves; while men as a "privileged class can never conceive the feelings of those who are born to contempt, to inferiority, to degradation," women could. She thus compares the "subjective link" between women and slaves, both being oppressed and victimized.

Stanton shares a conversation she once had with a "reverend gentleman" who did not understand why women felt victimized. In her response to him, she had compared American woman to slaves, "trained up in ignorance of all laws." Speaking of women as living like slaves, her graphic images of women sold "body and soul, to the highest bidder" confused those who could not tell whether she was speaking of black women or white. Her remarks were valid for both and spoke to women's loss of rights in marriage. Stanton's anger at the complacency of the "reverend gentleman" was reflective of her disgust with organized religion, which condoned the lesser role of women in society. She told them that "the condition of woman in republican, Christian America" is no blessing and, recasting Jesus' words in Matthew 25:40, she states that "whatever is done unto one of the least of these my sisters is done also unto me."

Stanton supported the antislavery movement and felt that woman's rights would be granted at the end of the Civil War. However, the abolitionists with whom she worked, including Garrison, turned their backs on woman's rights. Although slaves were freed in 1865 and got the vote in 1870, women were not allowed to vote until 1920.

◆ "Solitude of Self"

Many consider her speech "Solitude of Self" to be Stanton's best work, as did Stanton herself. It was delivered three times in Washington, D.C. First, it was sent in written form, on January 18, 1892, to the congressional Committee of the Judiciary. That afternoon she delivered the speech at the National American Woman Suffrage Association convention, as retiring president of the organization. On January 20 she personally gave the speech to the Senate Committee on Woman Suffrage. The speech proclaims the principles and values underlying the struggle for woman's rights.

She states the main theme of the speech as "the individuality of each human soul." Her first point is that a woman has the right to secure her "own safety and happiness," a phrase echoing the Declaration of Independence. Her allusion to Robinson Crusoe "with her woman Friday" reflects her concern about the individual's essential isolation and the need for self-dependence. Her second point is her usual argument that if a woman is considered a citizen, she must have the same fundamental rights as other citizens. A third point characterizes woman as "an equal factor in civilization"; consequently, her "rights and duties" are the same as a man's. Her fourth point singles out how the specific concerns of woman "as mother, wife, sister, daughter …may involve some special duties and training."

Stanton stresses the importance of higher education in providing woman not only "enlarged freedom of thought and action" but also emancipation from any type of dependency. She again emphasizes the need for woman to have a voice in government and other aspects of her life because she, finally, must depend on herself. Even those women who might "prefer to lean, to be protected and supported" must ultimately "make the voyage of life alone." Extending this metaphor, Stanton declares that a woman, as well as a man, must know "something of the laws of navigation" and be "captain, pilot, engineer," able "to stand at the wheel…and know when to take in the sail." In addition to each individual's essential aloneness, there is an "infinite diversity in human character." With this in mind, Stanton points out the "loss to the nation when any large class of the people is uneducated and unrepresented in the government"—such as with women.

Part of "the complete development of every individual" is education, and "to throw obstacles in the way of a complete education is like putting out the eyes." The woman "with a kind husband to shield her from the adverse winds of life, with wealth, fortune and position," is generally safe. But an "uneducated woman, trained to dependence," has no resources. Although society says a woman does not need education, Stanton disagrees. She asks what an older woman, whose children are grown, can do. Without "companionship in books" or any reason for interest in government reforms,

such women may "soon pass into their dotage." She exhorts the importance of women becoming involved throughout their lives in education, in finance, in community welfare.

Rather than being confined to any gendered sphere, women must be "thoroughly educated for all the positions in life they may be called to fill" and "trained to self-protection by a healthy development of the muscular system and skill in the use of weapons of defense." Some of Stanton's lyceum lectures, particularly "Our Girls," expand upon the necessity for healthy lifestyles, both physical and mental, for young women. She mentions the importance of the knowledge of business for women, not an aspect of the typical woman's sphere. Stanton refutes the common idea that only the domestic arts are suitable studies for women, stating that many men cook, bake, and launder, but they do not have to study such subjects at Harvard or Yale.

Finally, Stanton stresses how "courage, judgment, and the exercise of every faculty of mind and body" should be "strengthened and developed by use" in men and women alike. If confined within a gendered sphere, women cannot fully develop and will not be strengthened by activity. Circling back to the beginning of the speech, Stanton reminds her audience that when each person meets the Angel of Death, each is alone. She closes the speech with a question: "Who, I ask you, can take, dare take, on himself the rights, the duties, the responsibilities of another human soul?" In view of Stanton's preceding logical arguments and examples, it is clear that no human should serve as master to another. She demands equal rights for all individuals, proclaiming that each person must have the tools of survival for his or her voyage through life.

Impact and Legacy

Elizabeth Cady Stanton led the first women's movement in America. She was its founder and philosopher. As its chief writer and speaker, she developed its principles and defined its goals. Although she initially became involved with the rights of black slaves, she shifted her focus to the rights of women and finally to changing the perceived role of women in society. She challenged the concept of separate spheres for men and women in her speeches and lectures, advocating the benefits for women in building physical strength and enhancing self-reliance, campaigning for the rights of women, and educating her audiences about the need for these rights.

The driving force behind the first women's rights convention, Stanton spent more than fifty years working toward getting the vote for women. She was criticized by some as being unwomanly, as not being content to remain in the woman's sphere as wife, mother, and homemaker. Others were angered by her shift from the fight for the rights of black slaves to the fight for woman's rights. Her supporters were often dismayed by her outspoken attitudes against religion and her support of divorce. Stanton did not live to see the fruition of her labors. The Nineteenth Amendment, giving women the right to vote, was passed in 1920.

There is no dearth of primary sources of the writing of Stanton; a problem is that some material has been altered by her children, such as her autobiography *Eighty Years and More* (1898). Her children Harriot Stanton Blatch and Theodore Stanton published *Elizabeth Cady Stanton as Revealed in Her Letters, Diary and Reminiscences* (1922) but destroyed the diary and rewrote some of the letters.

Stanton wrote *Eighty Years and More: Reminiscences, 1815–1897*, with an introduction by Gail Parker in the 1971 edition. Major collections of her work are at the Library of Congress, Douglass College at Rutgers, and Vassar College. Stanton materials can also be found in the papers of the National American Woman Suffrage Association and at the New York Historical Society. An important source is *History of Woman Suffrage* (1881–1902), vols. 1–4, edited by Stanton, Susan B. Anthony, and others.

Essential Quotes

"We hold these truths to be self-evident: that all men and women are created equal."
(Declaration of Sentiments)

"He has made her, if married, in the eye of the law, civilly dead."
(Declaration of Sentiments)

"Now, gentlemen, we would fain know by what authority you have disfranchised one-half the people of this state?"
(Address to the New York Legislature)

"A privileged class can never conceive the feelings of those who are born to contempt, to inferiority, to degradation."
(Speech for the Anniversary of the American Anti-Slavery Society)

"To throw obstacles in the way of a complete education is like putting out the eyes; to deny the rights of property, like cutting off the hands."
("Solitude of Self")

"An uneducated woman, trained to dependence, with no resources in herself must make a failure of any position in life."
("Solitude of Self")

"Nothing strengthens the judgment and quickens the conscience like individual responsibility."
("Solitude of Self")

Further Reading

■ Books

DuBois, Ellen Carol, ed. *The Elizabeth Cady Stanton–Susan B. Anthony Reader: Correspondence, Writings, Speeches.* Boston: Northeastern University Press, 1992.

DuBois, Ellen Carol, and Richard Cándida Smith, eds. *Elizabeth Cady Stanton, Feminist as Thinker: A Reader in Documents and Essays.* New York: New York University Press, 2007.

Griffith, Elisabeth. *In Her Own Right: The Life of Elizabeth Cady Stanton.* New York: Oxford University Press, 1984.

Gurko, Miriam. *The Ladies of Seneca Falls: The Birth of the Woman's Rights Movement.* New York: Macmillan, 1974.

Waggenspack, Beth M. *The Search for Self-Sovereignty: The Oratory of Elizabeth Cady Stanton.* New York: Greenwood Press, 1989.

Wellman, Judith. *The Road to Seneca Falls: Elizabeth Cady Stanton and the First Woman's Rights Convention.* Urbana: University of Illinois Press, 2004.

■ Web Sites

"The Elizabeth Cady Stanton & Susan B. Anthony Papers Project." Rutgers University Web site. http://ecssba.rutgers.edu/docs/documents.html.

"Elizabeth Cady Stanton." Library of Congress "American Memory" Web site. http://memory.loc.gov/ammem/today/nov12.html.

—Marcia B. Dinneen

Questions for Further Study

1. How did Stanton's upbringing influence her later ideas and work? Pay special attention to the role played by her father and the larger world of lawyers and clerks to which he introduced her. What were most positive and negative aspects of Judge Cady's relationship with his daughter, and how did they affect her views as she matured?

2. Discuss the ways in which Stanton used the Declaration of Independence as a model for the Declaration of Sentiments. What parallels was she attempting to draw between her own declaration and the document that announced America's independence from the authority of the British Crown? How did she adapt the indictments against King George III as a means of enumerating the injustices historically visited on women?

3. Evaluate Stanton as a writer. How did she use references to the Bible and the classics? What did this show about the breadth of her education, and how did her wide-ranging knowledge serve to illustrate her larger point that women were equal to men intellectually and in all other regards? How, in her 1854 address to the New York legislature, did she construct her arguments concerning women's rights, and what does this show about her ability to express her ideas?

4. Emancipation, not only for slaves but indeed for women of all races, was among the most important political issues of the nineteenth century, yet there was no small amount of conflict between abolitionists and advocates of women's rights. What was Stanton's view on the subject, and how did her position alienate some—most notably her own husband? How justified were her comparisons between the situations of slaves and women in America?

5. What vision regarding the role of women does Stanton present in her "Solitude of Self" address? How does she make her key points, and how does she call for women to reach their full potential? In what ways were her views—not least her emphasis on physical and self-defense training for females—generations ahead of their time?

DECLARATION OF SENTIMENTS (1848)

When, in the course of human events, it becomes necessary for one portion of the family of man to assume among the people of the earth a position different from that which they have hitherto occupied, but one to which the laws of nature and of nature's God entitle them, a decent respect to the opinions of mankind requires that they should declare the causes that impel them to such a course.

We hold these truths to be self-evident: that all men and women are created equal; that they are endowed by their Creator with certain inalienable rights; that among these are life, liberty, and the pursuit of happiness; that to secure these rights governments are instituted, deriving their just powers from the consent of the governed. Whenever any form of Government becomes destructive of these ends, it is the right of those who suffer from it to refuse allegiance to it, and to insist upon the institution of a new government, laying its foundation on such principles, and organizing its powers in such form as to them shall seem most likely to effect their safety and happiness. Prudence, indeed, will dictate that governments long established should not be changed for light and transient causes; and accordingly, all experience hath shown that mankind are more disposed to suffer, while evils are sufferable, than to right themselves by abolishing the forms to which they are accustomed. But when a long train of abuses and usurpations, pursuing invariably the same object, evinces a design to reduce them under absolute despotism, it is their duty to throw off such government, and to provide new guards for their future security. Such has been the patient sufferance of the women under this government, and such is now the necessity which constrains them to demand the equal station to which they are entitled.

The history of mankind is a history of repeated injuries and usurpations on the part of man toward woman, having in direct object the establishment of an absolute tyranny over her. To prove this, let facts be submitted to a candid world.

He has never permitted her to exercise her inalienable right to the elective franchise.

He has compelled her to submit to laws, in the formation of which she had no voice.

He has withheld from her rights which are given to the most ignorant and degraded men—both natives and foreigners.

Having deprived her of this first right of a citizen, the elective franchise, thereby leaving her without representation in the halls of legislation, he has oppressed her on all sides.

He has made her, if married, in the eye of the law, civilly dead.

He has taken from her all right in property, even to the wages she earns.

He has made her, morally, an irresponsible being, as she can commit many crimes with impunity, provided they be done in the presence of her husband. In the covenant of marriage, she is compelled to promise obedience to her husband, he becoming, to all intents and purposes, her master—the law giving him power to deprive her of her liberty, and to administer chastisement.

He has so framed the laws of divorce, as to what shall be the proper causes of divorce; in case of separation, to whom the guardianship of the children shall be given; as to be wholly regardless of the happiness of women—the law, in all cases, going upon the false supposition of the supremacy of man, and giving all power into his hands.

After depriving her of all rights as a married woman, if single and the owner of property, he has taxed her to support a government which recognizes her only when her property can be made profitable to it.

He has monopolized nearly all the profitable employments, and from those she is permitted to follow, she receives but a scanty remuneration.

He closes against her all the avenues to wealth and distinction, which he considers most honorable to himself. As a teacher of theology, medicine, or law, she is not known.

He has denied her the facilities for obtaining a thorough education—all colleges being closed against her.

He allows her in Church as well as State, but a subordinate position, claiming Apostolic authority for her exclusion from the ministry, and, with some exceptions, from any public participation in the affairs of the Church.

He has created a false public sentiment, by giving to the world a different code of morals for men and women, by which moral delinquencies which exclude women from society, are not only tolerated but deemed of little account in man.

He has usurped the prerogative of Jehovah himself, claiming it as his right to assign for her a sphere of action, when that belongs to her conscience and her God.

He has endeavored, in every way that he could to destroy her confidence in her own powers, to lessen her self-respect, and to make her willing to lead a dependent and abject life.

Now, in view of this entire disfranchisement of one-half the people of this country, their social and religious degradation,—in view of the unjust laws above mentioned, and because women do feel themselves aggrieved, oppressed, and fraudulently deprived of their most sacred rights, we insist that they have immediate admission to all the rights and privileges which belong to them as citizens of these United States.

In entering upon the great work before us, we anticipate no small amount of misconception, misrepresentation, and ridicule; but we shall use every instrumentality within our power to effect our object. We shall employ agents, circulate tracts, petition the State and national Legislatures, and endeavor to enlist the pulpit and the press in our behalf. We hope this Convention will be followed by a series of Conventions, embracing every part of the country.

Firmly relying upon the final triumph of the Right and the True, we do this day affix our signatures to this declaration.

Glossary

claiming Apostolic authority	assuming the rights, conferred by Jesus on the apostle Peter, to make decisions on spiritual matters
elective franchise	the vote
Jehovah	one of the names for God found in Hebrew scriptures

ADDRESS TO THE NEW YORK LEGISLATURE (1854)

Gentlemen, in republican America, in the 19th century, we, the daughters of the revolutionary heroes of '76, demand at your hands the redress of our grievances—a revision of your state constitution—a new code of laws. Permit us then...to call your attention to the legal disabilities under which we labor.

1st. Look at the position of woman as woman. It is not enough for us that by your laws we are permitted to live and breathe, to claim the necessaries of life from our legal protectors...we demand the full recognition of all our rights as citizens of the Empire State. We are ...native, free-born citizens; property-holders, tax-payers; yet are we denied the exercise of our right to the elective franchise. We support ourselves, and, in part, your schools, colleges, churches, your poor-houses, jails, prisons, the army, the navy, the whole machinery of government, and yet we have no voice in your councils. We have every qualification required by the constitution, necessary to the legal voter, but the one of sex. We are moral, virtuous and intelligent, and in all respects quite equal to the proud white man himself, and yet by your laws we are classed with idiots, lunatics and negroes;...in fact, our legal position is lower than that of either; for the negro can be raised to the dignity of a voter if he possess himself of $250; the lunatic can vote in his moments of sanity, and the idiot, too, if he be a male one, and not more than nine-tenths a fool; but we, who have guided great movements of charity, established missions, edited journals, published works on history, economy and statistics; who have governed nations, led armies, filled the professor's chair, taught philosophy and mathematics to the *savans* of our age, discovered planets, piloted ships across the sea, are denied the most sacred rights of citizens, because...we came not into this republic crowned with the dignity of manhood! Woman is theoretically absolved from all allegiance to the laws of the state....

Now, gentlemen, we would fain know by what authority you have disfranchised one-half the people of this state?... Can it be that here, where are acknowledged no royal blood, that you, who have declared that all men were created equal—that governments derive their just powers from the consent of the governed, would willingly build up an aristocracy that places the ignorant and vulgar above the educated and refined—...an aristocracy that would raise sons above the mothers that bore them?...

We demand, in criminal cases, that most sacred of all rights, trial by a jury of our own peers. The...right of trial by a jury of one's own peers is a great, progressive step of advanced civilization. No rank of men have ever been satisfied with being tried by jurors higher or lower in the civil or political scale than themselves.... The nobleman cannot make just laws for the peasant; the slaveholder for the slave; neither can man make and execute just laws for woman, because in each case, the one in power fails to apply the immutable principles of right to any grade but his own. Shall an erring woman be dragged before a bar of grim-visaged judges, lawyers and jurors, there to be grossly questioned in public on subjects which women scarce breathe in secret to one another?...At this moment among the hundreds of women who are shut up in prisons in this state, not one has enjoyed that most sacred of all rights—that right which you would die to defend for yourselves—trial by a jury of one's peers.

2d. Look at the position of woman as wife. Your laws relating to marriage...are in open violation of our enlightened ideas of justice ... If you take the highest view of marriage, as a Divine relation, which love alone can constitute and sanctify, then of course human legislation can only recognize it. Man can neither bind nor loose its ties, for that prerogative belongs to God alone....But if you regard marriage as a civil contract, then let it be subject to the same laws which control all other contracts. Do not make it a kind of half-human, half-divine institution, which you may build up but cannot regulate....

So long as...the parties in all mere civil contracts retain their identity and all the power and independence they had before contracting, with the full right to dissolve all partnerships and contracts for any reason,...upon what principle of civil jurisprudence do you permit the boy of fourteen and the girl of twelve, ...to make a contract more momentous in importance than any other, and then hold them to it,...the whole of their natural lives, in spite of disappointment, deception and misery?...The signing of this contract is instant civil death to one of the parties....The wife who inherits no property holds about the same legal position that does the slave on the southern plantation. She can own nothing, sell nothing. She has no right even to the wages she earns; her person, her time, her services are the property of another....

There is nothing that an unruly wife might do against which the husband has not sufficient protection in the law. But not so with the wife. If she have a worthless husband, a confirmed drunkard, a villain or a vagrant, he has still all the rights of a man, a husband and a father....

3d. Look at the position of woman as widow. ... Behold the magnanimity of the law in allowing the widow to retain a life interest in one-third the landed estate, and one-half the personal property of her husband, and taking the lion's share to itself! Had she died first, the house and land would all have been the husband's....

4th. Look at the position of woman as *mother*.... Behold how cruel and ruthless are your laws touching this most sacred relation.

Nature has clearly made the mother the guardian of the child; but man, in his inordinate love of power, does continually set nature and nature's laws at open defiance. The father may apprentice his child, bind him out to a trade or labor, without the mother's consent—yea, in direct opposition to her most earnest entreaties....

He may apprentice his son to a gamester or rum-seller, and thus cancel his debts of *honor*. By the abuse of this absolute power, he may bind his daughter to the owner of a brothel, and, by the degradation of his child, supply his daily wants. ... Moreover, the father, about to die, may bind out all his children wherever and to whomsoever he may see fit, and thus, in fact, will away the guardianship of all his children from the mother....

Thus, by your laws, the child is the absolute property of the father, wholly at his disposal in life or at death.

In case of separation, the law gives the children to the father; no matter what his character or condition. At this very time we can point you to noble, virtuous, well educated mothers in this state, who have abandoned their husbands for their profligacy and confirmed drunkenness. All these have been robbed of their children, who are in the custody of the husband,...whilst the mothers are permitted to see them but at stated intervals....

By your laws, all these abominable resorts are permitted....But when woman's moral power shall speak through the ballot-box, then shall her influence be seen and felt....

Many have manifested a laudable curiosity to know what the wives and daughters could complain of in republican America, where their sires and sons have so bravely fought for freedom and gloriously secured their independence, trampling all tyranny, bigotry and caste in the dust, and declaring to a waiting world the divine truth that all men are created equal....Here, gentlemen, is our difficulty: When we plead our cause before the law makers ... of the republic, they cannot take in the idea that men and women are alike; and so long as the mass rest in this delusion, the public mind will not be so much startled by the revelation made of the injustice and degradation of woman's position as by the fact that she should at length wake up to a sense of it....

But if, gentlemen, you take the ground that the sexes are alike,...then why all these special laws for woman? Would not one code answer for all of like needs and wants?...We *ask* no better laws than those you have made for yourselves. We need no other protection than that which yourself present law secure to you....

You may say that the mass of the women of this state do not make the demand; it comes from a few sour, disappointed old maids and childless women. You are mistaken; the mass speak through us. ... Do

Glossary

caste	a system of social class or position based on birth
common schools	nineteenth-century American term for public schools
elective franchise	the vote
Empire State	the nickname of New York State, possibly acquired from President George Washington's statement that New York was the "seat of the Empire"
fain	gladly
gamester	gambler
savans	variation of *savants*, or wise and knowing persons

you *candidly* think these wives do not wish to control the wages they earn—to own the land they buy—the houses they build? To have at their disposal their own children, without being subject to the constant interference and tyranny of an idle, worthless profligate?…

For all these, then, we speak. If to this long list you add all the laboring women, who are loudly demanding remuneration for their unending toil—those women who teach in our seminaries, academies and common schools for a miserable pittance; the widows, who are taxed without mercy; the unfortunate ones in our work houses, poor houses and prisons; who are they that we do not now represent? But a small class of fashionable butterflies, who, through the short summer days, seek the sunshine and the flowers; but the cool breezes of autumn and the hoary frosts of winter will soon chase all these away; then, they too will need and seek protection, and through other lips demand, in their turn, justice and equity at your hands.

SPEECH FOR THE ANNIVERSARY OF THE AMERICAN ANTI-SLAVERY SOCIETY (1860)

This is generally known as the platform of one idea—that is negro slavery. In a certain sense this may be true, but the most casual observation of this whole anti-slavery movement…show this one idea to be a great humanitarian one.…In settling the question of the negro's rights, we find out the exact limits of our own, for rights never clash or interfere; and where no individual in a community is denied his rights, the mass are the more perfectly protected in theirs; for whenever any class is subject to fraud or injustice, it shows that the spirit of tyranny is at work, and no one can tell where or how or when the infection will spread.…

It was thought a small matter to kidnap a black man in Africa, and set him to work in the rice swamps of Georgia; but when we look at the panorama of horrors that followed that event, at all the statute laws that were enacted to make that act legal, at the perversion of man's moral sense and innate love of justice in being compelled to defend such laws; … we may, in some measure, appreciate the magnitude of the wrong done to that one, lone, friendless negro, who, under the cover of darkness and the star-spangled banner, was stolen from his African hut and lodged in the hold of the American slaver. … It has corrupted our churches, our politics, our press; … it has gagged our statesmen, and stricken our Northern Senators dumb in their seats; yes, beneath the flag of freedom, Liberty has crouched in fear.

That grand declaration of rights made by WILLIAM LLOYD GARRISON, while yet a printer's boy, was on a higher plane than that of '76. His was uttered with the Christian's view of the dignity of man … the other but from the self-respect of one proud race. But, in spite of noble words, deeds of thirty years of protest, prayers, and preaching, slavery still lives…but in the discussion of this question, in grappling with its foes, how many of us have worked out our salvation; what mountains of superstition have been rolled off the human soul!…

I do not believe that all history affords another such example as the so-called "Garrison Conspiracy"—a body of educated men of decided talent, wealth, rank and position, standing for a quarter of a century battling a whole nation, Church and State, law and public sentiment, without the shadow of ever wavering, turning or faltering, as if chained to the great Gibralter-truth of human freedom and equality. This unheard-of steadfastness can only be accounted for in the fact that woman too is represented in this "conspiracy." Yes, the Marys and Marthas have gathered round the prophets of our day.…

This is the only organization on God's footstool where the humanity of woman is recognized, and these are the only men who have ever echoed back her cries for justice and equality. I shall never forget our champions in the World's Anti-Slavery Convention; how nobly [Wendell] Phillips did speak, and how still more nobly Garrison would not speak, because woman was there denied her rights. Think of a World Convention and one half the world is left out!…

The mission of this Radical Anti-Slavery Movement is not to the African slave alone, but to the slaves of custom, creed and sex, as well; and most faithfully has it done its work.…

Eloquently and earnestly as noble men have denounced slavery on this platform, they have been able to take only an objective view. They can describe the general features of that infernal system—the horrors of the African slave trade…all that is outward they can see; but a privileged class can never conceive the feelings of those who are born to contempt, to inferiority, to degradation. Herein is woman more fully identified with the slave than man can possibly be, for she can take the subjective view. She early learns the misfortune of being born an heir…to martyrdom, to womanhood. For a while the man is born to do whatever he can, for the woman and the negro there is no such privilege.…All mankind stand on the alert to restrain their impulses, check their aspirations, fetter their limbs, lest, in their freedom and strength, in their full development, they should take an even platform with proud man himself. To you, white man, the world throws wide her gates; the way is clear to wealth, to fame, to glory, to renown,…but the black man and the woman are born to shame. The badge of degradation is the skin and sex—the "scarlet letter" so sadly worn upon the breast.…

In conversation with a reverend gentleman, not long ago, I chanced to speak of the injustice done to woman. Ah! said he, so far from complaining, your heart should go out in thankfulness that you are an American woman, for in no country in the world does woman hold so high a position as here. Why, sir, said

I, you must be very ignorant, or very false….Are not nearly two millions of native-born American woman, at this very hour, doomed to the foulest slavery that angels ever wept to witness? Are they not doubly damned as immortal beasts of burden in the field, and sad mothers of a most accursed race? Are not they raised for the express purpose of lust?…Are they not trained up in ignorance of all laws, both human and divine, and denied the right to read the Bible? For them there is no Sabbath, no Jesus, no Heaven, no hope, no holy mission of wife and mother, no privacy of home, nothing sacred to look for, but an eternal sleep in dust and the grave. And these are the daughters and sisters of the first men in the Southern states: think of fathers and brothers selling their own flesh on the auction block, exposing beautiful women of refinement and education in a New Orleans market, and selling them, body and soul, to the highest bidder! And this is the condition of woman in republican, Christian America, and you dare not look me in the face, and tell me that, for blessings such as these, my heart should go out in thankfulness! No, proud priest, you may cover your soul in holy robes, and hide your manhood in a pulpit, and, like the Pharisee of old, turn your face away from the sufferings of your race; but I am a Christian—a follower of Jesus—and "whatever is done unto one of the least of these my sisters is done also unto me."

Glossary

Gibralter	reference to the Rock of Gibraltar in the Strait of Gibraltar off the southern tip of the Iberian Peninsula (Spain and Portugal), often used as a figure of speech for something "rock solid."
Marys and Marthas	sisters who were followers of Jesus, mentioned in the gospels of Luke and John
Pharisee	member of a Jewish sect at the time of Jesus, often a symbol of self-righteousness
Wendell Phillips	American abolitionist
"whatever is done unto one of the least of these…"	a variation of a verse from the biblical book of Matthew, chapter 25, verse 40
William Lloyd Garrison	outspoken American abolitionist and publisher of the antislavery newspaper the *Liberator*

"SOLITUDE OF SELF" (1892)

The point I wish plainly to bring before you on this occasion is the individuality of each human soul; our Protestant idea, the right of individual conscience and judgment—our republican idea, individual citizenship. In discussing the rights of woman, we are to consider, first, what belongs to her as an individual, in a world of her own, the arbiter of her own destiny, an imaginary Robinson Crusoe with her woman Friday on a solitary island. Her rights under such circumstances are to use all her faculties for her own safety and happiness.

Secondly, if we consider her as a citizen, as a member of a great nation, she must have the same rights as all other members, according to the fundamental principles of our Government.

Thirdly, viewed as a woman, an equal factor in civilization, her rights and duties are still the same—individual happiness and development.

Fourthly, it is only the incidental relations of life, such as mother, wife, sister, daughter, that may involve some special duties and training....

The strongest reason for giving woman all the opportunities for higher education, for the full development of her faculties; for giving her the most enlarged freedom of thought and action; a complete emancipation from all forms of bondage, of custom, dependence, superstition;...is the solitude and personal responsibility of her own individual life. The strongest reason why we ask for woman a voice in the government under which she lives; in the religion she is asked to believe; equality in social life, where she is the chief factor; a place in the trades and professions, where she may earn her bread, is because of her birthright to self-sovereignty; because, as an individual, she must rely on herself. No matter how much women prefer to lean, to be protected and supported, nor how much men desire to have them do so, they must make the voyage of life alone, and for safety in an emergency they must know something of the laws of navigation. To guide our own craft, we must be captain, pilot, engineer; with chart and compass to stand at the wheel; to match the wind and waves and know when to take in the sail, and to read the signs in the firmament over all. It matters not whether the solitary voyager is man or woman....

Think for a moment of the immeasurable solitude of self. We come into the world alone...we leave it alone under circumstances peculiar to ourselves.... No one has ever found two blades of ribbon grass alike, and no one will never find two human beings alike. Seeing, then, what must be the infinite diversity in human character, we can in a measure appreciate the loss to a nation when any large class of the people is uneducated and unrepresented in the government. We ask for the complete development of every individual, first, for his own benefit and happiness. ... Again we ask complete individual development for the general good; ... on all questions of national life, and here each man must bear his share of the general burden....

To throw obstacles in the way of a complete education is like putting out the eyes; to deny the rights of property, like cutting off the hands. To deny political equality is to rob the ostracized of all self-respect; of credit in the market place.... [Imagine a woman] Robbed of her natural rights, handicapped by law and custom at every turn, yet compelled to fight her own battles, and in the emergencies of life to fall back on herself for protection....

The young wife and mother...with a kind husband to shield her from the adverse winds of life, with wealth, fortune and position, has a certain harbor of safety.... But to manage a household, have a desirable influence in society, keep her friends and the affections of her husband, train her children and servants well, she must have rare common sense, wisdom, diplomacy, and knowledge of human nature. To do all this she needs the cardinal virtues and the strong points of character that the most successful statesman possesses.

An uneducated woman, trained to dependence, with no resources in herself must make a failure of any position in life. But society says women do not need a knowledge of the world, the liberal training that experience in public life must give, all the advantages of collegiate education; but when for the lack of all this, the woman's happiness is wrecked, alone she bears her humiliation....

In age, when the pleasures of youth are passed, children grown up, married and gone, ... when the hands are weary of active service, ... then men and women alike must fall back on their own resources. If they cannot find companionship in books, if they have no interest in the vital questions of the hour, no interest in watching the consummation of reforms, with which they might have been identified, they soon pass into their dotage. The more fully the faculties of the mind are developed and kept in use, the longer the period of vigor and active interest in all around us continues. If from a lifelong participation in public affairs a woman feels responsible for the laws regulating our system of education, the discipline of our jails and prisons, the sanitary conditions of our private homes, public buildings, and thoroughfares, an interest in commerce, finance, our foreign relations, in any or all of these questions, here solitude will at least be respectable, and she will not be driven to gossip or scandal for entertainment....

Nothing strengthens the judgment and quickens the conscience like individual responsibility. Nothing adds such dignity to character as the recognition of one's self-sovereignty....Seeing, then that the responsibilities of life rests equally on man and woman, that their destiny is the same, they need the same preparation for time and eternity....Rich and poor, intelligent and ignorant, wise and foolish, virtuous and vicious, man and woman, it is ever the same, each soul must depend wholly on itself....

But when...women are recognized as individuals, responsible for their own environments, thoroughly educated for all the positions in life they may be called to fill; with all the resources in themselves that liberal thought and broad culture can give; guided by their own conscience an judgment; trained to self-protection by a healthy development of the muscular system and skill in the use of weapons of defense, and stimu-

lated to self-support by the knowledge of the business world and the pleasure that pecuniary independence must ever give;...they will, in a measure, be fitted for those hours of solitude that come alike to all....

Women are already the equals of men in the whole of realm of thought, in art, science, literature, and government....The poetry and novels of the century are theirs, and they have touched the keynote of reform in religion, politics, and social life....Such is the type of womanhood that an enlightened public sentiment welcomes today, and such the triumph of the facts of life over the false theories of the past.

Is it, then, consistent to hold the developed woman of this day within the same narrow political limits as the dame with the spinning wheel and knitting needle occupied in the past? No! no!...

We see reason sufficient in the outer conditions of human being for individual liberty and development, but when we consider the self dependence of every human soul we see the need of courage, judgment, and the exercise of every faculty of mind and body, strengthened and developed by use, in woman as well as man....

In the supreme moments of danger, alone, woman must ever meet the horrors of the situation; the Angel of Death even makes no royal pathway for her.... In that solemn solitude of self, that links us with the immeasurable and the eternal, each soul lives alone forever....

Such is individual life. Who, I ask you, can take, dare take, on himself the rights, the duties, the responsibilities of another human soul?

Glossary

cardinal virtues	in Christian tradition, the four virtues of justice, prudence, fortitude, and temperance
Robinson Crusoe	the title character of a novel by Daniel Defoe (1719) who was shipwrecked on an island; Friday was the name of his male companion on the island

Joseph Story (Library of Congress)

JOSEPH STORY   1779–1845

Supreme Court Justice

Featured Documents

♦ **Letter to Samuel P. P. Fay as "Matthew Bramble"** (1807)

♦ *United States v. Coolidge* (1813)

♦ **"Privileges of Citizens—Fugitives—Slaves"** (1833)

Overview

Joseph Story dominated the development of American law in the early-nineteenth-century United States. Appointed at age thirty-two, Story spent the rest of his lifetime on the Supreme Court, where he served over twenty years alongside Chief Justice John Marshall and nearly a decade alongside Chief Justice Roger B. Taney. From his position on the bench, Story participated in numerous decisions that established the broad outlines of constitutional jurisprudence, ranging from cases asserting the federal government's supremacy, as in *McCulloch v. Maryland* (1819), to ones defining the meaning of specific provisions such as the commerce clause, as in *Gibbons v. Ogden* (1824), and the fugitive slave clause, as in *Prigg v. Pennsylvania* (1842). In these deliberations, Story advocated nationalist constitutional positions demanding that the states operate under a relative degree of federal restraint.

Story worked diligently to defend and popularize the common law, an unwritten legal code inherited from England that the legal community accessed through the study of imported books and largely unreported court decisions. In the early nineteenth century numerous commentators questioned whether such a legal code was proper for a republic. Story answered with an emphatic yes and even tried, though with limited success, to convince his colleagues that the federal courts possessed an inherent common law authority; he wrote numerous opinions explaining the intricacies of various doctrines. Meanwhile, from his position as Dane Professor of Law at Harvard University, Story worked to educate aspiring lawyers to a proper understanding of legal doctrine. The scholarly Story produced a flood of legal treatises on all manner of legal subjects, which contributed to the growing accessibility of the common law to practicing lawyers. He helped establish the common law as the foundation of American jurisprudence. Story died on September 10, 1845, in Cambridge, Massachusetts.

Explanation and Analysis of Documents

Story, above all, was a scholarly justice devoted to the expansion of national power and the common law. These aspects of his jurisprudence are highlighted in various documents. An 1807 letter to Samuel P. P. Fay, written before he joined the Supreme Court, shows Story's erudition and

his vision of governance. The decision he wrote for *United States v. Coolidge* (1813), written early in his tenure as a Supreme Court justice, demonstrates his commitment to the common law and national authority. In turn, "Privileges of Citizens—Fugitives—Slaves," a chapter from his 1833 treatise on the Constitution, extends those themes in a relatively more scholarly fashion.

♦ Letter to Samuel P. P. Fay as "Matthew Bramble"

In 1807, when he was not yet thirty years old, Story made his first trip to Washington, D.C. He traveled on business, primarily to lobby on behalf of some New England land speculators who had interests in disputed grants in the Old Southwest, but he also made sure to introduce himself to the leading figures in the city. He met President Thomas Jefferson, various members of Congress, and, perhaps most important to Story, the justices of the Supreme Court. At this point Story stood at the beginning of his public career; he had served on his town committee in Salem and was sitting in the Massachusetts House of Representatives. Despite his youth and relative inexperience, however, he already displayed a strong sense of himself as an intellectual and as an advocate of a particular brand of commercially minded republicanism. A letter written to one of his friends during this trip underscores those characteristics.

Story wrote his friend and fellow Harvard graduate Samuel P. P. Fay, describing his travel to and impressions of Washington in a way that was playfully erudite. He bracketed his account with references to English novels, addressing the letter not to Fay but to "Mathew Bramble," a character in Tobias Smollett's comedic work *The Expedition of Humphry Clinker* (1771), and signing the letter under the name of "Jeremy Melford," another character from the novel. In opening, he refers to a second book, James Beresford's *Miseries of Human Life; or, The Last Groans of Timothy Testy and Samuel Sensitive* (1806), to describe his current state: "Take down the *Miseries of Human Life*, and look at the pages of that groaning work for the articles respecting travelling." If Fay sympathized with "the wretch who is soused into a horsepond or bespattered with mud," then he should do the same with Story. Story relates a favorable impression of the unfinished Capitol building—"when the centre is completed the effect will certainly be striking"—but seems less impressed by the city surrounding the yet-to-be completed building. Story also discusses architecture, even though his "curiosity rather

1779

■ **September 18**
Joseph Story is born in Marblehead, Massachusetts.

1798

■ Story graduates from Harvard University and begins reading law under Samuel Sewall.

1801

■ Story begins practicing law in Salem, Massachusetts, and composes "The Power of Solitude," a two-part poem.

1805

■ Story affiliates with Thomas Jefferson's Democratic-Republican Party and wins election to the Massachusetts House of Representatives.

1807

■ **May 29**
During travel in Washington, D.C., Story composes a letter to Samuel P. P. Fay, addressed as "Matthew Bramble."

1808

■ Story wins election to the U.S. House of Representatives.

1812

■ **February 3**
Appointed by President James Madison, Story assumes his seat on the U.S. Supreme Court.

1813

■ **October**
Story writes the circuit court opinion in *United States v. Coolidge*, defending a federal common law of crimes.

1819

■ **February 2**
Story writes a concurrence in *Trustees of Dartmouth College v. Woodward*, which establishes that private corporate charters receive constitutional protection.

respects men than things," because discussing the city's people would result in a "sleepy narrative from a very sleepy pen." Thenceforth, his entire letter rests on what he was "deciding by a first impression, without caring to investigate facts." He closes his letter with a reference to a third novel, Laurence Sterne's *Life and Opinions of Tristram Shandy, Gentleman* (1759–1767), and yet another to *Humphry Clinker*.

This letter underscores two features of Story's personality. First, he considered himself a man of letters. He dropped references to classic and current works of English literature and was at this time a published poet and legal commentator; he later would become the author of numerous judicial opinions and legal treatises. Second, Story ironically portrayed himself as an intellectual sloth. After noting that he was relying on first impressions, he comments that "it is so much easier to loll in one's elbow chair, and decide by speculation, than drudge through matters of fact.... How unfortunate would it be to live in suspense, and at every turn to encounter some stubborn truth, that would overset all our opinions." Yet Story was hardly an armchair commentator; he would devote much of his life to the drudgery of legal research. His judicial opinions and treatises would be meticulously researched, and he would emerge at the center of a group of commentators that would transform the legal landscape of the United States in the early nineteenth century.

Story's description of Washington hinted at an understanding of American political development that would inform his future work. The city held promise: "I confess very few plots of ground are so well adapted for municipal purposes." One day the city might have "a million of inhabitants," but at the moment Washington "seems to demand a century of years before it can become a numerous metropolis." Story attributed the slow growth to two sources. Because the United States was a republic, the capital lacked a despotic government that could "draw its millions to the spot." In addition, Washington showed little sign of becoming a commercial center, and as he notes, "St. Petersburg might be dragged from the fens of the Baltic by a Czar, but among a free people the tide of population follows the mart of commerce more than the residence of power." Over the course of his career, Story would devote himself to articulating what he considered the proper legal foundations for both American republicanism and for commerce. In matters of constitutional law, he believed the nation to be best served by a relatively powerful central government that worked to restrain potentially irresponsible state legislatures. On economic issues, Story favored strict contracts, easy transmission of property, and other policies that generally promoted economic development while providing some security for long-term investors.

Story's letter points to one final feature that would dominate his life: the rigors of travel. The 140 miles between Philadelphia and Washington featured "as execrable roads as can be found in Christendom.... Take my word for it, I am reduced to a mere jelly." Story would make treks to and from Washington many more times over the course of his life. He would return to serve in Congress in 1809 and again to represent his land-speculating clients in *Fletcher v. Peck* (1810), a case that brought him great success. He not only won the case for his clients but also convinced the Supreme Court that, under the Constitution, state governments possessed no authority to rescind grants of property that they had previously made. The Court thus agreed with Story that proper republican governance required that the states be subject to some external restraint.

Story's performance in *Fletcher*, along with his legal work in both state and federal courts in Massachusetts and his continued legal commentary, paid off when the Supreme Court's so-called New England seat opened up in 1811. Story, who despite his growing stature in the New England legal community was still a young and relatively inexperienced lawyer, received the post only after three other nominees declined or were rejected by the Senate. President James Madison offered Story the seat primarily for his decision to affiliate with the Democratic-Republican Party upon entering politics; the list of other qualified candidates in the Federalist bastion of New England had been short to begin with. Story's move to the Supreme Court meant more travel. He logged, according to his best biographer, an estimated one thousand miles a year riding circuit in New England, and he regularly made the five-hundred-mile trek to Washington as well. Such was the life of an early American Supreme Court justice.

◆ **United States v. Coolidge**

Story served on the Supreme Court from 1812 until 1845, and during his long tenure he left an enduring mark on the federal courts. Although he was one of the youngest justices ever appointed to the Court, he arrived with well-developed visions of economic development and constitutional governance. He also brought a penchant for scholarship that synthesized a wide range of legal rules into coherent form and provided the Court, especially when it was under the leadership of Chief Justice John Marshall, with an appearance of intellectual stature. From his position on the bench, Story participated in what many historians identify as a transformation of American law that saw judges taking the lead in making the common law more conducive to rapid capitalist economic growth. His 1829 ruling in *Van Ness v. Pacard* for example, jettisoned a common law rule discouraging lessees from improving the land they rented in favor of a newly created one allowing them do so without penalty, a change that moderately encouraged economic development. In *Swift v. Tyson* (1842), Story articulated a procedural rule in a manner favoring the expanded transferability of the negotiable financial instruments that fueled business investment in nineteenth-century America.

Story's constitutional opinions likewise encouraged economic growth, but he also generally argued that state legislatures needed federal oversight and restraint. One of his first rulings, *Martin v. Hunter's Lessee* (1816), held that the Supreme Court possessed the right to review decisions originating in the state courts. Likewise, his concurring opinion in *Trustees of Dartmouth College v. Woodward* (1819) agreed

Time Line

1829	■ Story becomes the first Dane Professor of Law at Harvard University.
1833	■ Story publishes his *Commentaries on the Constitution of the United States*, with one chapter called "Privileges of Citizens—Fugitives—Slaves."
1837	■ Story issues a defense of the Marshall Court in dissenting opinions in *Charles River Bridge v. Warren Bridge*, *New York v. Miln*, and *Briscoe v. Bank of Kentucky*.
1841	■ **March 9** Story writes an opinion against the slave trade in *Unites States v. The Amistad*.
1842	■ Story writes opinions establishing a federal common law of commerce, in *Swift v. Tyson*, and upholding the Fugitive Slave Law.
1845	■ **September 10** Story dies in Cambridge, Massachusetts.

with Chief Justice John Marshall's majority opinion holding that the Constitution barred the state from altering the charters of private corporations but did so in a manner that both clearly articulated the distinction between public and private corporations and ensured that incorporated business enterprises fell into the latter category. Perhaps the most distinguishing aspect of Story's work on the Court, however, rests in his aggressive judicial nationalism and passionate advocacy for using the common law in the federal courts.

Few decisions demonstrate these features of Story's work more clearly than his relatively early circuit court ruling in *United States v. Coolidge* (1813). In this case, Story's Massachusetts circuit court had before it "an indictment against Cornelius Coolidge and others for forcibly rescuing a prize," but this crime—the act of retaking goods that had been legally seized by another—appeared in no federal statute. The question before the court therefore involved "whether the circuit court of the United States has jurisdiction to punish offences against the United States, which have not been previously defined, and a specific punishment affixed, by some statute of the United States." Story displayed more than a bit of audacity in confronting this issue. For one thing, the Supreme Court had recently ruled in an 1812 decision, *United States v. Hudson and Goodwin*, that the federal courts could not employ a common law of crimes.

In the early 1800s, moreover, federal common law represented a deeply contested matter. Part of the controversy stemmed from the argument that the government created by the Constitution possessed only enumerated powers, such that its courts could access only those powers given to them by statute or by the Constitution itself. This debate had intensified after the election of Jefferson in 1800 because he and his supporters generally advocated a strict construction of constitutional language, and they interpreted use of the common law by the federal judiciary to be an aspect of a Federalist plot to undermine the Republic. Another part of the controversy grew out of arguments that the common law, in whatever jurisdiction, was ill suited to a true republican government because its general impenetrability rendered it inaccessible to lay readers and because its judge-made character provided a potential tool for tyrants. Critics holding this perspective, known to historians as codificationists, contended that a republic needed a written code of laws that any citizen could read and understand. Story's *Coolidge* opinion ran counter to these trends. It rejected *Hudson and Goodwin* and called for a federal common law of crimes, defending this potentially great expansion of federal jurisdiction by portraying the common law as a proper foundation for republican governance.

Story begins his opinion by paying lip service to the enumerated nature of federal powers—"I admit … that the courts of the United States are courts of limited jurisdiction, and cannot exercise any authorities, which are not confided to them by the constitution and laws made in pursuance thereof"—but he insists that the proper exercise of those powers requires the common law. Where the Constitution or a statute grants a power, he contends, "the nature and extent of that authority, and the mode, in which it shall be exercised, must be regulated by the rules of the common law." A proper understanding of the Constitution, Story continues, requires that one draw upon the common law. For example, the document mandates trials by jury for criminal cases (excluding impeachment), and Story supposes "that no person can doubt, that for the explanation of these terms, and for the mode of conducting trials by jury, recourse must be had to the common law." Without reference to the common law, the clause giving the federal courts broad jurisdiction over "all cases in law and equity arising under the constitution" would be "inexplicable." He provides one final example: "The clause providing, that the privilege of the writ of habeas corpus shall not be suspended, unless when in cases of rebellion or invasion the public safety may require it." Only the common law defined this writ and the privileges it conferred. Story concludes that "the existence … of the common law is not only supposed by the constitution, but is appealed to for the construction and interpretation of its powers."

Congress, Story continues, certainly holds the authority to give the circuit courts jurisdiction over all common law crimes. Indeed, it had done so in the Judiciary Act of 1789, which stipulated "that the circuit court 'shall have exclusive cognizance of all crimes and offences cognizable under the authority of the United States, except where that act otherwise provides, or the laws of the United States shall otherwise direct, and concurrent jurisdiction with the district courts of the crimes and offences cognizable therein.'" Congress had not subsequently narrowed that grant of judicial power. Story then departs from the Supreme Court's ruling in *Hudson and Goodwin*, asserting, "The jurisdiction is not …over all crimes and offences specially created and defined by statute. It is of all crimes and offences 'cognizable under the authority of the United States,' that is, of all crimes and offences, to which by the constitution of the United States, the judicial power extends." Congress thus bestowed that jurisdiction in "broad and comprehensive terms."

Having established his circuit court's authority to hear criminal cases, Story then proceeds to define what sort of actions constitute a crime or an offense under the Constitution. He again insists that this step requires "recourse… to the principles of the common law," but he now casts his argument in a manner that responds to codificationist arguments portraying the common law as inherently arbitrary. Congress had passed statutes providing "for the punishment of murder, manslaughter and perjury…but it has no where defined these crimes." One must find the needed definitions in the common law, since "upon any other supposition, the judicial power of the United States would be left … to the mere arbitrary pleasure of the judges, to an uncontrollable and undefined discretion. Whatever may be the dread of the common law,… such a despotic power could hardly be deemed more desirable." Looking across the federal system, Story sees many opportunities for this troublesome discretion. Federal courts could follow state common law in some cases (as the Judiciary Act of 1789, in fact, required of them), but that recourse provided only partial coverage. Massachusetts, for example, recognized no distinction between law and equity; federal courts, rather, did. "How then," Story asks, "shall a suit in equity pending in the circuit court for that district be managed or decided?" Likewise, the United States exclusively exercised admiralty and maritime jurisdiction, the definition of which had to come from the common law. As Story concludes here, "Nothing is more clear, than that the interpretation and exercise of the vested jurisdiction of the courts of the United States must, in the absence of positive law, be governed exclusively by the common law."

Story proceeds to call for a sweeping expansion of federal jurisdiction, of which his understanding embraces "all offences against the sovereignty, the public rights, the public justice, the public peace, the public trade and the public police of the United States." Federal jurisdiction thus included "treasons, and conspiracies to commit treason, embezzlement of the public records, bribery and resistance of the judicial process, riots and misdemeanors on the high seas, frauds and obstructions of the public laws of trade, and robbery and embezzlement of the mail of the United States." The power to punish those committing such offenses must go along with this jurisdiction, as "to suppose a power in a court to try an offence, and not to award any punishment, is to suppose, that the legislature is guilty of the folly of promoting litigation without object, and prohibiting acts, only for the purpose of their being scoffed at in the most solemn manner." Congress, according to Story's reading of the Judiciary Act of 1789, authorized trials of common law crimes, and "it must be deemed to authorize the court to render such a judgment, as the guilt or innocence of the party may require."

Defining a punishment, Story continues, presents no obstacle in these cases, because "the common law affords the proper answer." He writes, "In all cases, where the legislature prohibit any act without annexing any punishment, the common law considers it an indictable offence, and attaches to the breach the penalty of fine and imprisonment." Story is so certain of this rule that he insists that if Congress had not assigned a punishment to treason, "I have no doubt, that the punishment by fine and imprisonment must have attached to the offence." At this point, Story again emphasizes the common law's status as a protector of liberty by returning to his discussion of habeas corpus. He notes that "the privilege of the writ of habeas corpus is so high and interesting, that it has become a prominent article in the constitution," while the Judiciary Act of 1789 authorized circuit courts to grant the writ; "but if nothing more could be done under it, than the legislature have expressly provided, it would be a mere dead letter for its most important purposes." Habeas corpus, Story asserts, "is made the great bulwark of the citizen against the oppressions of the government" only through the reinforcement provided by the common law.

Story thus reaches his conclusions. He holds that the circuit courts possess jurisdiction over the present offense and all other ones against the United States, that the common law provides the definition of these offenses where Congress had not, and that punishments, in the absence of directive statutes, would take the form of fine and imprisonment. In drawing to a close he makes his only mention of *Hudson and Goodwin*, a decision that, though "entitled to the most respectful consideration," needed revisiting. The case actually did not receive a hearing by the full Supreme Court and was not argued before its members; a question of such jurisdictional import deserved a more thorough hearing. Regarding the present case, Story promises to "submit, with the utmost cheerfulness, to the judgment of my brethren," and he takes comfort in the knowledge that, if his opinion proved mistaken, "their superior learning and ability will save the public from an injury by my error." Indeed, his colleagues did not accept his arguments. When the case came before the Supreme Court in 1816, the attorney general William Wirt pronounced his belief that the issue had been settled in *Hudson and Goodwin*; Story voiced his disagreement, while Justice William Johnson, who had written *Hudson and Goodwin*, supported Wirt. Justices Henry Livingston and Bushrod Washington

were receptive to hearing arguments, but no counsel for Coolidge appeared, and no arguments took place. The ruling in *Hudson and Goodwin* thus stood as good law.

Near the end of his career, Story would gain a measure of redemption on the common law issue. In 1842 he convinced his colleagues—on a Court composed, with the exception of Story, of justices appointed after 1816—that the federal courts had a limited common law jurisdiction over certain commercial questions. He did so in *Swift v. Tyson*, which interpreted a provision of the Judiciary Act of 1789 in a manner that permitted the federal courts to approach state court rulings as merely advisory. His approach essentially allowed U.S. courts access to a federal common law of commerce. Yet his *Swift* opinion had none of his *Coolidge* opinion's call for a sweeping common law jurisdiction. Rather, Story's 1842 opinion applied primarily to questions related to negotiable instruments—but through subsequent cases his common law of commerce gradually expanded, first to insurance contracts, then to the construction of wills, and so on. One of *Swift*'s closest students estimates that by 1900, common law principles invoked by later decisions covered more than twenty-five areas of law. Story's common law thinking therefore exerted a powerful influence over the federal courts into the twentieth century.

◆ **"Privileges of Citizens—Fugitives—Slaves"**

By the time he wrote his 1842 *Swift* opinion, Story had largely become an ideological outlier on the Supreme Court. Certainly, he had met with little success in seeking to convince his previous colleagues about the federal courts' recourse to the common law, but in other respects, Story shared broad areas of agreement with the justices who served with him under Chief Justice Marshall. The Marshall Court, which lasted from 1801 to 1835, pursued a nationalist constitutional agenda that in general sought to restrain state legislatures and give federal power a wide range of latitude. In the late 1820s and 1830s this approach fell out of favor with the ascension of Andrew Jackson to the presidency. Jackson and his supporters believed in a sharply limited role for federal power and wanted to give the states a large degree of discretion. Story believed that Jackson's appointees to the Supreme Court, best exemplified by Chief Justice Roger B. Taney, would undermine the achievements of the Marshall Court and perhaps severely damage the Republic. In 1837 Story, who did not normally write separate opinions, wrote a series of dissenting opinions defending his nationalist positions. He remained on the losing end of constitutional questions until his death in 1845, but he had long before shifted his front for the ideological conflict over constitutional interpretation to new ground.

In the 1830s and 1840s Story, in addition to serving as the senior associate justice on the Supreme Court, held the position of Dane Professor of Law at Harvard University, and he worked diligently to build the law school. Story published many of his lectures in a flood of legal treatises, including *Commentaries on the Law of Bailments* (1832), *Commentaries on the Conflict of Laws* (1834), *Commen-*

Watercolor of the Spanish ship La Amistad, *whose crew were overthrown by their cargo of African slaves* (AP/Wide World Photos)

taries on *Equity Jurisprudence* (1836), *Commentaries on Equity Pleadings* (1838), *Commentaries on the Law of Agency* (1839), *Commentaries on the Law of Partnership* (1841), *Commentaries on the Law of Bills of Exchange* (1843), and *Commentaries on the Law of Promissory Notes* (1845). Much of this work focused on bringing a disciplined—Story would have said "scientific"—approach to legal study that took the jumble of common law doctrines and organized them into a coherent whole. But Story also used these treatises to educate young lawyers in what he considered to be the proper legal foundation for a republic and to challenge current political trends. His *Commentaries on the Constitution of the United States* (1833) provides a good example of these aims. Story wrote this work at the time of the nullification crisis, when South Carolina's opposition to a federal tariff led to the state's refusal to collect the tax and to threats of secession. Extreme states' rights theories, especially those of John C. Calhoun, underpinned these arguments, and Story wrote his constitutional commentaries to present a nationalist interpretation. As he did so, however, Story also worked to further his goal of placing federal jurisprudence on a common law foundation.

"Privileges of Citizens—Fugitives—Slaves," a chapter discussing the privileges and immunities clause, the extradition clause, and the fugitive slave clause, underscores Story's efforts to achieve his desired ends. Each of these clauses appears in Article IV of the Constitution. Commentators usually associate this part of the document with issues of federalism, but Story portrays each of these pro-

visions in a nationalist light. According to Story, the privileges and immunities clause, which reads that "the citizens of each state shall be entitled to all privileges and immunities of citizens in the several states," was given this form in the Constitution to clear up some ambiguity from the Articles of Confederation. The articles contained a similar provision, but the text at various points used such terms as "free inhabitants," "free citizens," and "people" to refer to the beneficiaries of the privileges. Such imprecision led to problems. Story, for example, found one construction unavoidable: "It seems … that those, who come under the denomination of free inhabitants of a state, although not citizens of such state, are entitled, in every other state, to all the privileges of free citizens of the latter; that is to greater privileges, than they may be entitled to in their own state." This construction, he argues, requires a state to treat people visiting from other states as citizens even if the state would not recognize such persons as citizens if they resided within its jurisdiction.

The Constitution remedied this problem by streamlining the language and consistently using the word "citizen." The new language ensured not only that states would not treat other states' citizens as aliens but also that citizens enjoyed, as Story notes, "if one may so say, a general citizenship" that entitled them in any state to "all the privileges and immunities, which the citizens of the same state would be entitled to under like circumstances." Such a reading of the clause was anathema to states' rights theorists like Calhoun, who denied that a general American citizenship even existed. Story's discussion of general citizenship segues nicely into his discussion of the extradition clause. Returning alleged criminals from one country to another has been a basic feature of international goodwill. Since this has been true among nations generally, the case for extradition would be even stronger within a Union like that formed by the Constitution. Extradition, Story declares, "is a power most salutary in its general operation, by discouraging crimes, and cutting off the chances of escape from punishment." Moreover, provision for interstate extradition "will promote harmony and good feelings among the states" and "will increase the general sense of the blessings of the national government."

Story moves on to his discussion of the Constitution's fugitive slave clause, which gave masters the right to enter northern states and reclaim alleged fugitives from slavery. Like many New Englanders, Story held misgivings about slavery. He opposed the expansion of slavery and the admission of Texas as a slave state and issued opinions critical of the international slave trade, most notably in the 1841 *Amistad* decision. Even so, in this chapter Story supports the right to reclaim fugitive slaves from the standpoint of national harmony. The clause, he states, "was introduced... solely for the benefit of the slave-holding states," who had expressed concerns that the Articles of Confederation contained no such provision. He then notes that the clause's inclusion came about through "many sacrifices of opinion and feeling...made by the Eastern and Middle states to the peculiar interests of the south." Story sees no reason for complaint here but wishes to "repress the delusive and mischievous notion, that the south has not at all times had its full share of benefits from the Union."

Story closes with a brief discussion of the legal proceedings contemplated by the extradition and fugitive slave clauses. Essentially, they provided for "summary ministerial proceedings, and not the ordinary course of judicial investigations, to ascertain, whether the complaint be well founded, or the claim of ownership be established beyond all legal controversy." Cases of extradition required only that there be prima facie evidence that a person was probably guilty of a crime, and a similar process was appropriate for fugitives from slavery. Story's seemingly neutral reading of this provision in fact challenged the way in which a number of northern states interpreted the Fugitive Slave Law. These states insisted that alleged fugitives from slavery be given more protection than specified in federal statute, and they passed a series of personal liberty laws that provided a variety of due process protections.

Nearly ten years later Story officially incorporated this position into constitutional law with his opinion in *Prigg v. Pennsylvania* (1842). *Prigg* came about in response to state personal liberty laws that imposed various due process requirements on the catching of slaves within the slave states. Story, speaking for a divided Court, held those laws unconstitutional, and in so doing he furthered some of his lifelong goals. *Prigg* continued Story's effort to place the federal courts on a common law foundation by insisting that the fugitive slave clause simply recognized the right of reception, which permitted masters, husbands, and like authority figures to reclaim their charges from wherever they might be unlawfully detained. His ruling also took a nationalist position by stripping from the states all power relating to fugitive slaves. States could neither aid nor hinder the apprehension of fugitives; all of that responsibility rested with the federal government.

Impact and Legacy

When Story died in 1845, he had become a central figure in the development of nineteenth-century American law. His work on the Marshall Court helped establish a high standard for subsequent courts, and the nationalist jurisprudence set out in cases like *Trustees of Dartmouth College v. Woodward* and *Swift v. Tyson* established the starting points for numerous later decisions. Through his duties as Dane Professor of Law, Story likewise exerted a long-term impact, mainly by cementing Harvard's status as a center for legal study in the United States. Finally, although he had only limited success in shifting the federal courts over to a common law footing, Story participated in the establishment of the common law in the United States by tirelessly working to defend, explain, and systematize its doctrines through his writings. Few of Story's contemporaries could boast of such accomplishments.

Key Sources

Joseph Story's papers (some on microfilm) are in archives across the country, including Harvard University, the Library of Congress, and the University of Texas at Austin. Story's numerous Supreme Court and circuit court judicial opinions are contained in the *United States Supreme Court Reports* and the *Federal Reporter*, respectively. Story wrote *Commentaries on the Constitution of the United States*, 3 vols. (1833); *Commentaries on the Conflict of Laws, Foreign and Domestic, in Regard to Contracts, Rights, and Remedies, and Especially in Regard to Marriages, Divorces, Wills, Successions, and Judgments* (1834); and *Commentaries on Equity Jurisprudence, as Administered in England and America* (1836). His letters are available in William Wetmore Story, ed., *Life and Letters of Joseph Story, Associate Justice of the Supreme Court of the United States, and Dane Professor of Law at Harvard University*, 2 vols. (1851), and Charles Warren, ed. *Story-Marshall Correspondence (1819–1831)* (1942).

Further Reading

■ Books

McClellan, James. *Joseph Story and the American Constitution: A Study in Political and Legal Thought with Selected Writings*. Norman: University of Oklahoma Press, 1990.

"*I am now at the seat of government…. Slowly and silently the infant city rises, and seems to demand a century of years before it can become a numerous metropolis. Unfortunately, commerce has not fixed here her abode, and despotism cannot draw its millions to the spot. St. Petersburg might be dragged from the fens of the Baltic by a Czar, but among a free people the tide of population follows the mart of commerce more than the residence of power.*"

(Letter to Samuel P. P. Fay as "Matthew Bramble")

"*Whether the common law of England, in its broadest sense, including equity and admiralty, as well as legal doctrines, be the common law of the United States or not, it can hardly be doubted, that the constitution and laws of the United States are predicated upon the existence of the common law.*"

(*United States v. Coolidge*)

"*I would ask then, what are crimes and offences against the United States, under the construction of its limited sovereignty, by the rules of the common law? Without pretending to enumerate them in detail, I will venture to assert generally, that all offences against the sovereignty, the public rights, the public justice, the public peace, the public trade and the public police of the United States, are crimes and offences against the United States.*"

(*United States v. Coolidge*)

"*It is of vital importance to the public administration of criminal justice, and the security of the respective states, that criminals, who have committed crimes therein, should not find an asylum in other states; but should be surrendered up for trial and punishment. It is a power most salutary in its general operation…. It will promote harmony and good feelings among the states; and it will increase the general sense of the blessings of the national government.*"

("Privileges of Citizens—Fugitives—Slaves")

Newmyer, R. Kent. *Supreme Court Justice Joseph Story: Statesman of the Old Republic*. Chapel Hill: University of North Carolina Press, 1985.

White, G. Edward, with Gerald Gunther. *The Marshall Court and Cultural Change, 1815–35*. New York: Macmillan, 1988.

—Austin Allen

Questions for Further Study

1. Discuss Story as a writer and man of letters, particularly as illustrated in his 1807 letter to Samuel P. P. Fay. Explain the significance of the three English novels referenced, and his purpose in alluding to them. Beyond these literary allusions, what does he say about architecture, travel, and the peculiarities of the nation's capital? How did he seek to portray himself as being intellectually lazy—something he most certainly was not—and what was his purpose in doing so?

2. Define common law, as opposed to statutory law, and explain Story's contribution to establishing its role within the American legal framework. What was his view on the significance of the common law, and how did he work to defend and popularize these concepts? Discuss in particular the controversy over federal common law, the dispute with the codificationists, and the importance of *United States v. Coolidge* to the issue. How successful was Story in promoting and establishing his ideas on common law?

3. Analyze the excerpt from Story's *Commentaries on the Constitution of the United States* (1833), beginning with the three constitutional clauses addressed in this passage: the privileges and immunities, extradition, and fugitive slave clauses found in Article IV. How did his views on these matters place him at odds with Calhoun and other supporters of nullification? How does he confront Calhoun's claim that there is no such thing as citizenship in the United States as a whole? And why did Story, despite his opposition to slavery itself, support the fugitive slave law?

LETTER TO SAMUEL P. P. FAY AS "MATTHEW BRAMBLE" (1807)

My dear Matthew Bramble:

Take down the *Miseries of Human Life*, and look at the pages of that groaning work for the articles respecting travelling. If you have there learned to commiserate the wretch who is soused into a horse-pond or bespattered with mud, I pray you to reserve that compassion for me. Between Philadelphia and Baltimore, one hundred miles, and between Baltimore and Washington, forty miles, are as execrable roads as can be found in Christendom. You would hardly believe yourself in a Christian country, unless every now and then in the intervals of a tremendous jolt you should indulge your fancy. Take my word for it, I am reduced to a mere jelly. No unfortunate wight pounded in a mortar has a less bony claim to consistency. The weather, however, has been delightful, and this with the very pleasant company which I have met at Baltimore, has quite reconciled me to my fate. God help all faint-hearted travellers, for surely they cannot help themselves.

I am now at the seat of government. The capitol is within a stone's throw of me; and the President's house rises in the distance. The capitol is yet unfinished, and the wings only are yet erected. The structure is of freestone, dug from the Potomac, and being strongly impregnated with iron ore, when exposed to the rain its uniformity is tarnished by an ochry appearance. The design appears to be, if not very magnificent, at least very elegant. Between every window pilasters rise in the Corinthian style. The height is three stories, and when the centre is completed the effect will certainly be striking. As I am no architect, it is impossible for me to give any correct detail of the disposition of the internal area. Indeed, as my curiosity rather respects men than things, you would receive a sleepy narrative from a very sleepy pen.

Though Washington is surrounded on all sides by a barren country, yet its local situation is certainly good. It stretches along the northern bank of the very beautiful Potomac, and from an uniform level at the bank, gradually rises into small and gentle elevations. Judging by my eye, and with the beauty which a verdant covering gives it, I confess very few plots of ground are so well adapted for municipal purposes. A million of inhabitants might be enclosed with comfort, within a few miles, and might enjoy a fresh air and lively prospect. It is not, however, as you must have frequently heard, accounted healthy. Whether this be the result of peculiarity of climate, or local causes, is not for me to determine. If you expect to find a considerable town here, you would be greatly disappointed. Brick houses are thinly scattered on the capitol hill; and at the distance of about a mile, a considerable village surrounds the President's house.

Glossary

Corinthian	a style of classical architecture used by the ancient Greeks
Czar	analogous to "king," the title of the Russian monarch
execrable	deplorable, of poor quality
fens	marshes, wetlands
freestone	high-quality, even-grained stone suitable for carving, usually sandstone or limestone
ochry	the color of ochre, used as a pigment and generally a yellowish or yellow-brown color
pilasters	rectangular columns on a building
soused	drenched, dunked
St. Petersburg	at the time, the capital of the Russian Empire
wight	creature, person

Every thing is new, and of course incomplete. Slowly and silently the infant city rises, and seems to demand a century of years before it can become a numerous metropolis. Unfortunately, commerce has not fixed here her abode, and despotism cannot draw its millions to the spot. St. Petersburg might be dragged from the fens of the Baltic by a Czar, but among a free people the tide of population follows the mart of commerce more than the residence of power. You perceive, that with the common fault of travellers, I am already deciding by a first impression, without caring to investigate facts. It is so much easier to loll in one's elbow chair, and decide by speculation, than drudge through matters of fact, that every man consults his comfort by approving or condemning in the mass. How unfortunate would it be to live in suspense, and at every turn to encounter some stubborn truth, that would overset all our opinions.

I will not write a word more on this subject. It is absolutely like Uncle Toby's Siege of Dendermond. The hobby suits me so well, that I cannot resist an eternal inclination to ride....May I reach Brambleton Hall in safety, and enjoy all my whims, dear Matthew, and as ever be,

Thine,

JER. MELFORD.

UNITED STATES V. COOLIDGE (1813)

This was an indictment against Cornelius Coolidge and others for forcibly rescuing a prize....

The simple question is, whether the circuit court of the United States has jurisdiction to punish offences against the United States, which have not been previously defined, and a specific punishment affixed, by some statute of the United States. I do not think it necessary, to consider the more broad question, whether the United States, as a sovereign power, have entirely adopted the common law. This might lead to very elaborate inquiries, and the present question may well be decided, without entering upon the discussion. I admit in the most explicit terms, that the courts of the United States are courts of limited jurisdiction, and cannot exercise any authorities, which are not confided to them by the constitution and laws made in pursuance thereof. But I do contend, that when once an authority is lawfully given, the nature and extent of that authority, and the mode, in which it shall be exercised, must be regulated by the rules of the common law. In my judgment, the whole difficulty and obscurity of the subject has arisen from losing sight of this distinction. Whether the common law of England, in its broadest sense, including equity and admiralty, as well as legal doctrines, be the common law of the United States or not, it can hardly be doubted, that the constitution and laws of the United States are predicated upon the existence of the common law. This has not, as I recollect, been denied by any person, who has maturely weighed the subject, and will abundantly appear upon the slightest examination. The constitution of the United States, for instance, provides that "the trial of all crimes, except in cases of impeachment, shall be by jury." I suppose that no person can doubt, that for the explanation of these terms, and for the mode of conducting trials by jury, recourse must be had to the common law. So the clause, that "the judicial power shall extend to all cases in law and equity arising under the constitution," etc. is inexplicable, without reference to the common law; and the extent of this power must be measured by the powers of courts of law and equity, as exercised and established by that system. Innumerable instances of a like nature may be adduced. I will mention but one more, and that is in the clause providing, that the privilege of the writ of habeas corpus shall not be suspended, unless when in cases of rebellion or invasion the public safety may require it. What is the writ of habeas corpus? What is the privilege which it grants? The common law, and that alone, furnishes the true answer. The existence, therefore, of the common law is not only supposed by the constitution, but is appealed to for the construction and interpretation of its powers.

There can be no doubt, that congress may, under the constitution, confide to the circuit court jurisdiction of all offences against the United States. Has it so done? The judicial act of ... 1789 ... provides, that the circuit court "shall have exclusive cognizance of all crimes and offences cognizable under the authority of the United States, except where that act otherwise provides, or the laws of the United States shall otherwise direct, and concurrent jurisdiction with the district courts of the crimes and offences cognizable therein." No subsequent act has narrowed the jurisdiction; it remains therefore in full operation. The jurisdiction is not, as has sometimes been supposed in argument, over all crimes and offences specially created and defined by statute. It is of all crimes and offences "cognizable under the authority of the United States," that is, of all crimes and offences, to which by the constitution of the United States, the judicial power extends. The jurisdiction could not, therefore, have been given in more broad and comprehensive terms.

The court then having complete jurisdiction, the next point will be to ascertain, what are crimes and offences against the United States. And here I contend, that recourse must be had to the principles of the common law, taken in connexion with the constitution, in order to fix the definition, precisely as in other laws of congress, we resort to the rules of the common law to give them an interpretation. For instance, congress has provided for the punishment of murder, manslaughter and perjury, under certain circumstances; but it has no where defined these crimes. Yet no doubt is ever entertained on trials, that the explanation of them must be sought and exclusively governed by the common law; and upon any other supposition, the judicial power of the United States would be left, in its exercise, to the mere arbitrary pleasure of the judges, to an uncontrollable and undefined discretion. Whatever may be the dread of the common law, I presume, that such a despotic power could hardly be deemed more desirable. The necessity and propriety of this principle will be rendered still more apparent upon a further consideration. There are a great variety of cases arising under the laws of the United States, and particularly those which regard the judicial power, in which the legislative will cannot be effectuated, unless by the adoption of the common law. Many cases may be governed by the laws of the respective states; but still whole classes remain, which cannot be thus disposed of. For example, in Massachusetts no courts of equity exist, and consequently no recognition of the principles or practices of equity, as contradistinguished from law. How then shall a suit in equity pending in the circuit court for that district be managed or decided? There is no law of the United States, which provides for the process, the pleadings, or the principles of adjudication. By what rules then shall the court proceed? Certainly all reasoning and all practice pronounce, by the rules of equity recognised and enforced in the equity courts of England. The illustration is yet more decisive, as to causes of admiralty and maritime jurisdiction; for these exclusively belong to the United States, and nothing in the laws or practice of the respective states can regulate the proceedings or the principles of decision. In my judgment, nothing is more clear, than that the interpretation and exercise of the vested jurisdiction of the courts of the United States must, in the absence of positive law, be governed exclusively by the common law.

I would ask then, what are crimes and offences against the United States, under the construction of its limited sovereignty, by the rules of the common law? Without pretending to enumerate them in detail, I will venture to assert generally, that all offences against the sovereignty, the public rights, the public justice, the public peace, the public trade and the public police of the United States, are crimes and offences against the United States. From the nature of the sovereignty of the United States, which is limited and circumscribed, it is clear that many common law offences, under each of these heads, will still remain cognizable by the states; but whenever the offence is directed against the sovereignty or powers confided to the United States, it is cognizable under its authority. Upon these principles and independent of any statute, I presume that treasons, and conspiracies to commit treason, embezzlement of the public records, bribery and resistance of the judicial process, riots and misdemeanors on the high seas, frauds and obstructions of the public laws of trade, and robbery and embezzlement of the mail

of the United States, would be offences against the United States. At common law, these are clearly public offences, and when directed against the United States, they must upon principle be deemed offences against the United States. If then it be true, that these are offences against the United States, and the circuit court have cognizance thereof, does it not unavoidably follow, that the court must have a right to punish them? In my judgment no proposition of law admits of more perfect demonstration. To suppose a power in a court to try an offence, and not to award any punishment, is to suppose, that the legislature is guilty of the folly of promoting litigation without object, and prohibiting acts, only for the purpose of their being scoffed at in the most solemn manner. If, therefore, it authorize a trial of an offence, it must be deemed to authorize the court to render such a judgment, as the guilt or innocence of the party may require. As to civil actions, the application of the principle has never admitted a doubt; yet in no instance, that I recollect, is the form or the substance of the judgments prescribed by any law. These judgments, however, must unavoidably differ, not only in different actions, but in the same action, according to the nature of the claims and the pleadings of the parties. It is no answer, to say, that the laws of the states will govern in such cases; for these are not always applicable, as suits may be brought in the United States courts, which are not cognizable by state courts; as for instance, equity and admiralty causes. And further, no such general and universal adoption of the practice or laws of the states has been authorized by congress, or sanctioned by the courts of the United States. The invariable usage of these courts has been, in all cases not governed by state laws, to regulate the pleadings and pronounce the judgment of the common law. When I speak here of the common law, I use the word in its largest sense, as including the whole system of English jurisprudence. For the same reason, therefore, that governs in civil causes, I hold that the cognizance of offences includes the power of rendering a judgment of punishment, when the guilt of the party is ascertained by a trial.

But it may be asked, what punishment shall be inflicted? The common law affords the proper answer. It is a settled principle, that where an offence exists, to which no specific punishment is affixed by statute, it is punishable by fine and imprisonment. This is so invariably true, that, in all cases, where the legislature prohibit any act without annexing any punishment, the common law considers it an indictable offence, and attaches to the breach the penalty of fine and imprisonment....I have no diffi-culty in saying, that the same rule must be held to exist here, for the same reason that it is adopted there. If, therefore, treason had been left without punishment by the act of congress, I have no doubt, that the punishment by fine and imprisonment must have attached to the offence.

Upon what ground the common law can be referred to, and made the rule of decision in criminal trials in the courts of the United States, and not in the judgment or punishment, I am at a loss to con-ceive. In criminal cases, the right of trial by jury is preserved, but the proceedings are not specifically regulated. The forms of the indictment and pleadings, the definition and extent of the crime, in some cases the right of challenge, and in all the admission and rejection of evidence, are left unprovided for. Upon what ground then do the courts apply in such cases the rules of the common law? I can perceive no cor-rect ground, unless it be, that the legislature have constantly had in view the rules of the common law, and deemed their application in *casibus omissis* peremptory upon the courts. The privilege of the writ of habeas corpus is so high and interesting, that it has become a prominent article in the constitution; and the judicial act of...1789...has authorized the courts of the United States, and the judges thereof, to issue that writ. But if nothing more could be done under it, than the legislature have expressly provided, it would be a mere dead letter for its most important purpos-es. It is only by engrafting on the authority of the statute the doctrines of the common law, that this writ is made the great bulwark of the citizen against the oppressions of the government. I might enforce

the view, which I have already taken of this subject, by an examination in detail of the organization and exercise of the judicial powers of the courts of the United States, with reference to their equity, admiral-ty, and legal jurisdiction; but it cannot be necessary. If I am right in the positions, which I have already assumed and explained, there is an end of the ques-tion, which has been submitted. If I am wrong, the error is so fundamental, that I cannot hope to reach its source by any merely illustrative process.

The result of my opinion is: 1. That the circuit court has cognizance of all offences against the Unit-ed States. 2. That what those offences are, depends upon the common law applied to the sovereignty and authorities confided to the United States. 3. That the circuit court, having cognizance of all offences against the United States, may punish them by fine and imprisonment, where no punishment is specially pro-vided by statute. I have considered the point, as one open to be discussed, notwithstanding the decision in *U.S. v. Hudson*..., which certainly is entitled to the most respectful consideration; but having been made without argument, and by a majority only of the court, I hope that it is not an improper course to bring the subject again in review for a more solemn decision, as it is not a question of mere ordinary import, but vital-ly affects the jurisdiction of the courts of the United States; a jurisdiction which they cannot lawfully enlarge or diminish. I shall submit, with the utmost cheerfulness, to the judgment of my brethren, and if I have hazarded a rash opinion, I have the consolation to know, that their superior learning and ability will save the public from an injury by my error. That deci-sion, however broad in its language, has not, as I con-

Glossary

adduced	given, cited
cognizable	able to be known or recognized; in legal terms, a cognizable offense is a crime for which the police can make an arrest without a warrant
common law	law established by previous court decisions, as opposed to law established by statute
effectuated	produced, implemented, brought about
equity and admiralty	two forms of law, the first providing fair solutions to legal problems that cannot be solved by fines, monetary judgments, or incarceration and the second covering conflicts on the high seas or related to oceangoing vessels
jurisprudence	theory of law and the legal system
writ of habeas corpus	a legal document ordering that a prisoner be brought before a court to be charged with a crime, issued with the intention of preventing illegal arrests

ceive, settled the question now before the court, so far as it respects offences of admiralty and maritime jurisdiction. The constitution has given to the judicial power of the United States the jurisdiction as "to all cases of admiralty and maritime jurisdiction," and this jurisdiction of course comprehends criminal, as well as civil suits. The admiralty is a court of extensive criminal, as well as civil jurisdiction, and has immemorially exercised both. At least no legal doubt of its criminal authority has ever been successfully urged. By the law of the admiralty, offences, for which no punishment is specially prescribed, are punishable by fine and imprisonment … and as offences of admiralty jurisdiction are exclusively cognizable by the United States, it follows that all such offences are offences against the United States. We have adopted the law of the admiralty in all civil causes cognizable by the admiralty: must it not also be adopted in offences cognizable by the admiralty? It will perhaps be said, that express jurisdiction is given in civil cases of admiralty jurisdiction, but not in criminal cases. This is true in terms; but I contend, that criminal cases are necessarily included in the grant of cognizance of all "crimes and offences cognizable under the authority of the United States"; for crimes and offences within the admiralty jurisdiction are not only cognizable, but cognizable exclusively under the authority of the United States. And congress, in punishing certain offences upon the high seas, which are neither piracies nor felonies, have undoubtedly acted upon the conviction, that such offences were of admiralty and maritime jurisdiction. … Whatever room, therefore, there may be for doubt, as to what common law offences are offences against the United States, there can be none as to admiralty offences. If this be true, then the reasoning, which I have before urged, applies in its full force, and I will not take up time in repeating it. On the whole, my judgment is, that all offences within the admiralty jurisdiction are cognizable by the circuit court, and in the absence of positive law are punishable by fine and imprisonment.

"PRIVILEGES OF CITIZENS—FUGITIVES—SLAVES" (1833)

The fourth article of the constitution contains several important provisions, some of which have been already considered. Among these are, the faith and credit to be given to state acts, records, and judgments, and the mode of proving them, and the effect thereof; the admission of new states into the Union; and the regulation and disposal of the territory, and other property of the United States. We shall now proceed to those, which still remain for examination.

The first is, "The citizens of each state" shall be entitled to all privileges and immunities of "citizens in the several states." There was an article upon the same subject in the confederation, which declared, "that the free inhabitants of each of these states, paupers, vagabonds, and fugitives from justice excepted, shall be entitled to all privileges and immunities of free citizens in the several states; and the people of each state shall, in every other, enjoy all the privileges of trade and commerce, subject to the same duties, impositions, and restrictions, as the inhabitants thereof respectively," etc. It was remarked by the *Federalist*, that there is a strange confusion in this language. Why the terms, free inhabitants, are used in one part of the article, free citizens in another, and people in another; or what is meant by superadding to "all privileges and immunities of free citizens," "all the privileges of trade and commerce," cannot easily be determined. It seems to be a construction, however, scarcely avoidable, that those, who come under the denomination of free inhabitants of a state, although not citizens of such state, are entitled, in every other state, to all the privileges of free citizens of the latter; that is to greater privileges, than they may be entitled to in their own state. So that it was in the power of a particular state, (to which every other state was bound to submit,) not only to confer the rights of citizenship in other states upon any persons, whom it might admit to such rights within itself, but upon any persons, whom it might allow to become inhabitants within its jurisdiction. But even if an exposition could be given to the term, inhabitants, which would confine the stipulated privileges to citizens alone, the difficulty would be diminished only, and not removed. The very improper power was, under the confederation, still retained in each state of naturalizing aliens in every other state.

The provision in the constitution avoids all this ambiguity. It is plain and simple in its language; and its object is not easily to be mistaken. Connected with the exclusive power of naturalization in the national government, it puts at rest many of the difficulties, which affected the construction of the article of the confederation. It is obvious, that, if the citizens of each state were to be deemed aliens to each other, they could not take, or hold real estate, or other privileges, except as other aliens. The intention of this clause was to confer on them, if one may so say, a general citizenship; and to communicate all the privileges and immunities, which the citizens of the same state would be entitled to under the like circumstances.

The next clause is as follows: "A person charged in any state with treason, felony, or other crime, who shall flee from justice, and be found in another state, shall, on demand of the executive authority of the state, from which he fled, be delivered up, to be removed to the state having jurisdiction of the crime." A provision, substantially the same, existed under the confederation.

It has been often made a question, how far any nation is, by the law of nations, and independent of any treaty stipulations, bound to surrender upon demand fugitives from justice, who, having committed crimes in another country, have fled thither for shelter. Mr. Chancellor [James] Kent considers it clear upon principle, as well as authority, that every state is bound to deny an asylum to criminals, and, upon application and due examination of the case, to surrender the fugitive to the foreign state where the crime has been committed. Other distinguished judges and jurists have entertained a different opinion. It is not uncommon for treaties to contain mutual stipulations for the surrender of criminals; and the United States have sometimes been a party to such an arrangement.

But, however the point may be, as to foreign nations, it cannot be questioned, that it is of vital importance to the public administration of criminal justice, and the security of the respective states, that criminals, who have committed crimes therein, should not find an asylum in other states; but should be surrendered up for trial and punishment. It is a power most salutary in its general operation, by discouraging crimes, and cutting off the chances of escape from punishment. It will promote harmony and good feelings among the states; and it will increase the general sense of the blessings of the national government. It will, moreover, give strength to a great moral duty, which neighbouring states especially owe to each other, by elevating the policy of the mutual suppression of crimes into a legal obligation. Hitherto it has proved as useful in practice, as it is unexceptionable in its character.

The next clause is, "No person held to service or labor in one state under the laws thereof, escaping into another, shall in consequence of any law or regulation therein be discharged from such service or labour; but shall be delivered up on the claim of the party, to whom such service or labour may be due."

This clause was introduced into the constitution solely for the benefit of the slave-holding states, to enable them to reclaim their fugitive slaves, who should have escaped into other states, where slavery was not tolerated. The want of such a provision under the confederation was felt, as a grievous inconvenience, by the slave-holding states, since in many states no aid whatsoever would be allowed to the owners; and sometimes indeed they met with open resistance. In fact, it cannot escape the attention of every intelligent reader, that many sacrifices of opinion and feeling are to be found made by the Eastern and Middle states to the peculiar interests of the south. This forms no just subject of complaint; but it should for ever repress the delusive and mischievous notion, that the south has not at all times had its full share of benefits from the Union.

It is obvious, that these provisions for the arrest and removal of fugitives of both classes contemplate summary ministerial proceedings, and not the ordinary course of judicial investigations, to ascertain, whether the complaint be well founded, or the claim of ownership be established beyond all legal controversy. In cases of suspected crimes the guilt or innocence of the party is to be made out at his trial; and not upon the preliminary inquiry, whether he shall be delivered up. All, that would seem in such cases to be necessary, is, that there should be *prima facie* evidence before the executive authority to satisfy its judgment, that there is probable cause to believe the party guilty, such as upon an ordinary warrant would justify his commitment for trial. And in the cases of fugitive slaves there would seem to be the same necessity of requiring only prima facie proofs of ownership, without putting the party to a formal assertion of his rights by a suit at the common law. Congress appear to have acted upon this opinion; and, accordingly, in the statute upon this subject have authorized summary proceedings before a magistrate, upon which he may grant a warrant for a removal.

Glossary

Chancellor [James] Kent	American legal theorist, author of *Commentaries on American Law* (1826–1830)
confederation	here, the United States as it existed under the Articles of Confederation
faith and credit	a legal term referring to the recognition by one state of the acts, records, and judicial proceedings of another, for example, recognition of a marriage that took place in another state
Federalist	a series of eighty-five newspaper articles, written primarily by James Madison and Alexander Hamilton in 1787–1788, urging ratification of the Constitution and outlining a theory of government
prima facie	Latin for "at first sight" or "on the face of it," used in the law to refer to a conclusion that is self-evident based on the facts

Robert A. Taft (AP/Wide World Photos)

ROBERT A. TAFT   1889–1953

U.S. Senator and Presidential Candidate

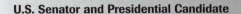

Taft, Robert A.

Overview

Robert A. Taft was born in Cincinnati, Ohio, on September 8, 1889, the eldest child of the future U.S. president William Howard Taft. Educated at Yale College and Harvard Law School, the younger Taft practiced law in Cincinnati for several years, but with his father's substantial political career—as secretary of war, then president, then chief justice—forming the backdrop for his early life, it was perhaps natural that he would also choose politics as a career. Taft served several terms in both houses of the Ohio state legislature in the 1920s and early 1930s. His election to the U.S. Senate in 1938 provided him with the opportunity to become one of the era's most influential spokespersons for the Republican Party and for American conservatism.

Taft's election to the Senate came at a critical time for the Grand Old Party. By the late 1930s Franklin D. Roosevelt's liberal New Deal policies for combating the Great Depression and his efforts to confront the rise of Fascism had centralized power in the national government and especially in the executive branch. Because his policies eased the pains of the hard times, Roosevelt and his Democratic Party were enormously popular with American voters despite the substantial redistribution of government power that his policies promoted. Following Roosevelt's landslide reelection in 1936, the Republicans were left with only sixteen of ninety-eight seats in the Senate, the party's lowest ebb in the modern era, and the voices of most conservatives were effectively silenced. Upon becoming a senator, Taft quickly emerged as one of the most forceful voices of conservative opposition to the liberal Democratic majority. He championed individual liberty, fiscal restraint, and local self-government, the traditional values of American conservatism and the modern Republican Party. After World War II, Taft continued to challenge the expansion of executive authority occasioned by President Harry S. Truman's Fair Deal and the containment policies he employed to counteract the Soviet threat.

As a prominent voice for conservative principles, Taft remained one of the leaders of the Republican Party through the 1940s. He ran unsuccessfully for the Republican presidential nomination in 1940, 1948, and 1952. When his party gained control of the Eighty-third Congress in the 1952 election, Taft became the Senate majority leader, a position he held until his untimely death of a brain hemorrhage on July 31, 1953. Although he failed to

become president as his father had before him, Robert Taft exerted substantial influence on mid-twentieth-century American politics. Taft was a penetrating critic of the positive state, the belief that the federal government had a responsibility to actively promote the general welfare by managing the economy. His criticism of that idea and of American globalism helped shape the modern welfare system and the uses of American military power. He also was essential to the revival of the modern Republican Party. First elected to the Senate only two years after the party's devastating 1936 defeats, Taft lived to see the election in 1952 of a Republican president and Republican majorities in both houses of Congress.

Explanation and Analysis of Documents

Although Taft's career as a Republican senator from Ohio spanned only fourteen years, it was an era of eventful change for the American nation. By the time Taft was sworn in for his first term in January 1939, Franklin D. Roosevelt's efforts to resolve the Great Depression had created an enormous welfare state, forever altering the relationships between individuals and the government and between the states and the national government. Breaking out only two years later, World War II proved to be an event that transformed the United States into an international superpower. Raising, equipping, and financing the armed forces to fight the global war accelerated still further the great expansion of the national government. Throughout the 1940s, Taft was one of the most important critics of these expansionist developments, engaging in a largely rear-guard struggle in defense of limited government and personal responsibility. In his 1946 speech at Kenyon College, in his 1947 speech in Atlantic City, and in a chapter of his 1951 book, Taft articulated his case against the modern welfare state and the national security state.

"Equal Justice under Law: The Heritage of the English-Speaking Peoples and Their Responsibility"

By the time Taft delivered this speech at Kenyon College, in Ohio, in October 1946, a new consensus had emerged among the American people about the role of government. Prior to 1932, most Americans had advocated limited government, belief in which was forged during the American Revolution and premised on the idea that as gov-

1889

■ **September 8**
Robert A. Taft is born in
Cincinnati, Ohio.

1910

■ **June**
Taft graduates from Yale
University.

1913

■ **June**
Taft graduates from
Harvard Law School.

1917

■ **July**
Herbert Hoover hires Taft
to serve as assistant
counsel to the wartime
Food Administration.

1920

■ **November 2**
Taft is elected to the first
of three terms in the Ohio
state legislature.

1930

■ **November 6**
Taft is elected to the Ohio
state senate.

1938

■ **November 8**
Taft is elected to the U.S.
Senate.

1940

■ **June**
Taft loses the Republican
presidential nomination to
Wendell Willkie.

1944

■ **November 7**
Taft is reelected to the U.S.
Senate.

1946

■ **October 5**
Taft speaks on the heritage
of the English-speaking
peoples at Kenyon College,
in Ohio.

1947

■ **March 6**
Taft delivers "The Sound
Basis for Federal Aid to
Education" in Atlantic City,
New Jersey.

ernment power expanded, the liberty of the individual declined. But to combat the Great Depression, Franklin D. Roosevelt rapidly expanded the role of the national government, arguing that in the modern industrial state individuals were necessarily interdependent on one another. By the late 1930s Americans increasingly looked to Washington for jobs, old-age pensions, minimum wages, guarantees for collective bargaining, insurance for their bank accounts, crop subsidies, and a range of additional functions that formerly had been the responsibility of the individual. Similarly, prior to World War II, Americans had been confident that the nation's geographic isolation protected it from all foes and had therefore generally followed George Washington's advice to avoid becoming entangled in foreign alliances. But the weapons of modern war in the hands of the Fascist powers in the 1930s steadily undermined the nation's isolationist tradition; following the Japanese attack on Pearl Harbor, Americans came to understand that in the modern era their national security was deeply entwined with international events.

In this speech, Taft challenges the emerging consensus, arguing that in combating both the Great Depression and Fascism, the United States had undermined the most important principle of the English-speaking peoples' heritage, equal justice under law as a guarantee of individual liberty. The New Deal's creation of numerous government agencies to deal with the economic crisis, he argues, had been the nation's first giant step away from equal justice under law: "Programs for general economic regulation are always inconsistent with justice because the detailed control of millions of individuals can only be carried through by giving arbitrary discretion to administrative boards." World War II expanded still further the grants of arbitrary power to government. Taft acknowledges that the wartime expansion of power was necessary, for if the state failed there could be no individual liberty. Still, he argues vehemently against the Truman administration's claim that the continuation of these powers into the postwar era would be necessary in order to secure the peace. Taft declares, "Unless we desire to weaken for all time the ideals of justice and equality, it is absolutely essential that our program of reconversion and of progress abandon the philosophy of war."

Taft also criticizes actions of American foreign policy at the war's end that he believes similarly threatened the English-speaking peoples' heritage of individual freedom. Although he supported the United Nations in principle, he notes here that because its Security Council had complete power to take whatever action it deemed necessary for international peace, the peacekeeping body as constituted put more emphasis on security than on liberty and justice. He similarly chides the nation for abandoning the ideals of the Atlantic Charter, which proclaimed in August 1941 that the nation would fight Fascism to establish the right of self-determination for people throughout the world. Yet, he notes, in agreements made at the Yalta Conference in February 1945, the United States had accepted the territorial division of the spoils of war. He laments, "Nothing could be further from a rule of law than the making of secret agreements distributing the territory of the earth in accordance with power and expediency." Finally, Taft also finds the recently concluded Nuremberg trials of Nazi leaders to be in violation of the United States' Anglo-Saxon heritage. Because the Nazi leaders were convicted and sentenced to death on the basis of an ex post facto law, Taft maintains that the trials were more concerned with vengeance than justice: "The hanging of the eleven men convicted at Nuremberg will be a blot on the American record which we shall long regret."

This 1946 speech demonstrates all the qualities that made Taft one of the most respected politicians of his day yet one who was not sufficiently popular to ever win the Republican presidential nomination. He first articulates forcefully his conviction that because the United States was founded on the ancient Anglo-Saxon heritage of the rule of law and equal justice under law, these principles are essential for individual liberty. He then argues that both the New Deal and the execution of World War II departed from these principles, thereby undermining America's commitment to individual liberty. By grounding his criticism in these traditional beliefs, Taft provided an intellectual rationale for Republican conservatives to contest the Democrats' advocacy of the positive state and demonstrated even to his opponents that he was a man of sincere conviction, not political expediency. Yet his deep devotion to these bedrock principles often made him appear to be rigid and inflexible. In an era when a majority of Americans had been persuaded that the expansion of the federal government's power had rescued them from economic catastrophe and Fascism, Taft's unrelenting efforts to limit the growth of both the welfare state and the national security state suggested to many that he was wedded too deeply to an outdated political philosophy.

◆ "The Sound Basis for Federal Aid to Education"

Throughout his first term in the Senate, Taft was a consistent critic of the welfare state created by Franklin D. Roosevelt's New Deal. In his view, allowing government bureaucrats in Washington to control such basic aspects of life as employment, housing, health care, and education was the antithesis of the individual's right to life, liberty, and the pursuit of happiness. But Taft's service on a subcommittee of the Senate Labor and Education Committee in 1945 seemed to moderate his views on the role of government. The subcommittee, focused on wartime health and education, investigated why 40 percent of the nation's draft-age men had been ruled unfit for military service because of physical or mental deficiencies. It concluded that the Selective Service System shortfall was largely attributable to widespread variations in state expenditures on education and health care. These findings seemed to persuade Taft that in the modern era the federal government did bear some responsibility for individual welfare, and throughout the late 1940s he offered a series of bills along with New Deal Democrats to provide states with limited federal funds for education and housing.

In his speech to the American Association of School Administrators in Atlantic City, New Jersey, of March

Time Line

1947
- **April 23**
  In the Senate, Taft introduces the Taft-Hartley labor bill, which is later passed as the Labor-Management Relations Act.

1948
- **June**
  Taft loses the Republican presidential nomination to Thomas E. Dewey.

1951
- **November**
  Taft publishes *A Foreign Policy for Americans*, which includes the chapter "The Place of the President and Congress in Foreign Policy."

1952
- **July**
  Taft loses the Republican presidential nomination to Dwight D. Eisenhower.
- **November 4**
  Taft is elected to a third term in the U.S. Senate.

1953
- **January 3**
  Taft is elected Senate majority leader for the Eighty-third Congress.
- **July 31**
  Taft dies in New York City of a brain hemorrhage.

1947, Taft explains why, despite his long-standing opposition to a federal role in education, he is cosponsoring a bill in the Senate (S 472) that provides states with limited federal tax dollars for their public school systems. He argues that in the United States an educated citizenry is essential to maintaining individual liberty and equal justice under law: "We cannot preserve the Republic at all unless the people are taught to read and to think so that they may understand its basic principles themselves and the application of such principles to current problems." Throughout its history, the U.S. government allowed states great freedom to structure their school systems as they saw fit. While this freedom produced wide variations from state to state, overall Taft believed that such localized self-reliance strengthened the Republic. But he acknowledges here that because the wealth of states varies, local control of education also produces wide differences in the amounts of public money spent on education, and "the result is that chil-

Participants in the Big Three Conference are photographed at the Livadia Palace in Yalta on February 12, 1945. Seated (from left) are British Prime Minister Winston Churchill, U.S. President Franklin D. Roosevelt, and Soviet Premier Josef Stalin. (AP/Wide World Photos)

dren in some districts receive a poor education or no education at all." Thus, in these circumstances, he concludes that the federal government has an obligation to ensure that all citizens, regardless of their state, receive a minimum amount of effective schooling. He declares, "It is the concern of the entire nation to see that the principles of the Declaration of Independence and of the Constitution are translated into reality."

In the bill he co-sponsored, Taft took great pains to ensure that federal aid to education would not result in federal domination of education. The bill stipulated that states and local communities would continue to have sole authority to manage their schools and that any federal monies had to supplement, not supplant, efforts made by local authorities to provide for the education of their children. The bill required a state to spend at least 2.2 percent of its annual tax revenues on education in order to be eligible for federal funds. But federal aid would be provided to a state only if one-half of its annual expenditures on education failed to provide at least $40 for each child in public schools. Thus, federal funds would be extended only to poor states that were making good faith efforts but, because of the circumstances of their economies, had insufficient revenues to provide quality education to their children. Although his spon-

sorship of federal aid for education and housing surprised political friends and foes alike, Taft insisted that it was wholly consistent with his long-held political philosophy. His goals remained the same: preserving individual liberty, individual initiative, and equal opportunity. The only modification he had made was in the means used to attain his ends. In this manner, then, Taft struck a balance between the needs of the modern industrial state and his traditional conservative principles. Federal aid to education, he argues, is "a tremendous step forward in assuring to America the means of striving forward constantly toward the ultimate ideal of complete equality and complete liberty."

◆ "The Place of the President and Congress in Foreign Policy"

In late 1951 Taft published *A Foreign Policy for Americans*, in which he addressed the growth of presidential control of foreign policy that had occurred in the 1940s, a development that he believed threatened individual liberty and freedom. During World War II, he accepted the expansion of presidential power related to the war effort as a necessary expedient, but when the peace treaties were signed in 1945, he, like many Americans, expected a speedy demobilization of the military bureaucracy, as had occurred after every previous war in the nation's history. The almost immediate onset of the cold war prevented this demobilization. As the containment of Soviet expansion became the central objective of American foreign policy in the late 1940s, Taft viewed with growing concern the steady rise in the defense budget and the development of a national security state that lodged still more power in the executive branch.

The 1947 National Security Act, for example, added another layer of bureaucracy to the executive branch, including the Department of Defense and the Central Intelligence Agency. The outbreak of the Korean War in June 1950 and President Truman's decision to send American troops without seeking a declaration of war from Congress amplified Taft's worries about the fate of individual liberty. All of his anxieties solidified in early 1951 when President Truman announced in his State of the Union address that he intended to dispatch four divisions of American troops to Europe to shore up the North Atlantic Treaty Organization's defenses; subsequently, Truman stubbornly insisted that the president had absolute authority to send U.S. troops wherever he pleased without congressional assent. The president's position touched off a four-month long "great debate" in the Senate over presidential war-making powers. Taft was a leading critic of the administration's views during the debate and staunchly defended Congress's constitutional role in war making. The issues raised in the debate prompted the Ohio senator to present a lengthy analysis of U.S. foreign policy in the modern era in his 1951 book. Much of the book surveys then-current issues in American foreign policy and served as the opening shot of Taft's third and final campaign to win the Republican presidential nomination. In the excerpted passage from chapter 2, Taft reveals the basis for his beliefs in the limits of American power.

Taft begins his analysis by arguing that although the chief executive could initiate action in foreign policy, the Constitution intended and the American people expected the responsibility to be one shared with Congress. He notes that while the Constitution established the president as commander in chief of the armed forces, it gave Congress certain exclusive powers, such as the power to declare war as well as to raise and maintain an army and a navy. Thus, Taft observes, the president's recent unilateral decisions to dispatch U.S. troops to Korea and to bolster North Atlantic Treaty Organization forces in Europe were clear violations of the Constitution's terms, violations that he believed had grave implications for the nation: "If in the great field of foreign policy the President has the arbitrary and unlimited powers he now claims, then there is an end to freedom in the United States."

Taft extends his criticism by refuting the rationale used by Truman to support his actions. The dispatch of U.S. troops to China during the 1900 Boxer Rebellion was not analogous, Taft contends, because in that instance troops were deployed only to protect American lives and property threatened by the uprising, an action consistent with the president's constitutional role as commander in chief. When U.S. troops were sent to Korea as part of a UN peacekeeping effort, the president claimed that his actions were based on the Charter of the United Nations, which the U.S. Senate had ratified in 1945. Taft states that although the UN charter stipulated that any use of troops could occur only after its Security Council had ratified an agreement with all countries participating in the action (an agreement that specified the exact size and nature of the military mission), no such agreement had been reached with the United States. Nor had the president sought congressional approval for the mission. He observes, "If the President can carry out every recommendation of the Security Council or the General Assembly supported by the vote of the American representative [to the United Nations] whom he can direct, then he has almost unlimited power to do anything in the world in the use of either troops or money."

In the years following World War II, Taft's criticism of the expansion of presidential power over foreign policy was largely at odds with the consensus view then held by most Americans. Because the war had ended with an unconditional victory for the Allied powers, most Americans in the late 1940s and early 1950s believed that the growth in presidential war-making power had been essential to the victory. The advent of the cold war only deepened the trust most Americans placed in the executive branch's management of foreign policy. But when the nation became mired first in the inconclusive Korean War and then in the Vietnam War, revealing how the war-making powers of the executive could be abused, Americans by the late 1960s and early 1970s gained a new appreciation for the warnings Taft had sounded at the dawn of the atomic age.

Impact and Legacy

Throughout his Senate career, Robert Taft brandished speeches, writings, and governmental philosophy that, in general, were all on the dissenting side of American politics. Where earlier generations had been skeptical of government, seeing it mainly as an impediment to individual liberty and freedom, by 1945 a majority of Americans, scarred by the Great Depression, had developed a more positive view of government. Franklin D. Roosevelt's New Deal had aggressively expanded the power of the federal government and especially of the executive branch in response to the economic crisis, and the effects of this approach convinced a majority of Americans by the 1940s that government had both the ability and responsibility to promote the health, welfare, and economic security of its citizens. Similarly, by 1945 the overwhelming victory won largely by the United States over the Axis powers in World War II persuaded most Americans that concentrating control over international relations in the executive branch was essential to national security in the modern era. Taft spoke out against both of these developments and argued consistently that the nation could best secure individual liberty and freedom by limiting the role of government and by allowing individuals to take responsibility for their own lives.

Although Taft's criticisms provided conservatives of his day with arguments that occasionally enabled them to tem-

"The totalitarian idea has spread throughout many nations where, in the nineteenth century, the ideals of liberty and justice were accepted. Even in this country the theory that the state is finally responsible for every condition, and that every problem must be cured by giving the government arbitrary power to act, has been increasingly the philosophy of the twentieth century."

("Equal Justice under Law: The Heritage of the English-Speaking Peoples and Their Responsibility")

"Liberty and equal justice under law must be continuously secured if we are to carry out the purposes of the formation of this Republic; but neither liberty nor justice can be secured without a widely diffused education. We cannot preserve the Republic at all unless the people are taught to read and to think so that they may understand its basic principles themselves and the application of such principles to current problems."

("The Sound Basis for Federal Aid to Education")

"Education is the only defense of liberty against totalitarianism. It may be that intelligent people will be occasionally misled to vest complete power in the state or in a single individual, but without education dictatorships inevitably arise."

("The Sound Basis for Federal Aid to Education")

"There is one very definite limit...on the President's power to send troops abroad: he cannot send troops abroad if the sending of such troops amounts to the making of war. I think that has been frequently asserted; and whenever any broad statements have been made as to the President's power as Commander in Chief to send troops anywhere in the world the point has been made that it is always subject to that particular condition."

("The Place of the President and Congress in Foreign Policy")

"No one can prevent the President continuing to assert his power as President, and it may be that he does have the ability to involve the United States in war, even when he has no right to do so....The President acts at his own peril, if he chooses to usurp authority which the representatives of the people have asserted that he does not possess."

("The Place of the President and Congress in Foreign Policy") per the expansion of state power, most Americans saw in his sometimes strident dissent a hidebound conservative who appeared to be hopelessly out of touch with the needs of modern life. In this way he paid a high political price for his decision to go against the prevailing tides of American public opinion in the 1940s. Though he was elected to three terms in the U.S. Senate, his ambition to become president eluded him despite his three attempts at winning the Republican nomination. Yet even his critics saw his career as a model of courage, one that consistently placed conviction and principle before political expediency.

If in his day Taft often stood outside the political mainstream, the passage of time has cast him in a more favorable light. In the decades after Taft's death, the continued expansion of the welfare state, the intrusion of the federal government into more areas of the citizen's life, and the increased taxation required to sustain the positive state helped to spawn a conservative resurgence that culminated in the election of Ronald Reagan as president in 1980. Reagan's contention that government was not the solution to but the source of the nation's problems echoed Taft's earlier challenges to Roosevelt's New Deal and Truman's Fair Deal. Similarly, to an American people long accustomed to viewing the federal government as a benevolent force in their lives, the Vietnam War and the Watergate scandal of the 1970s demonstrated to many that the expanded power of the positive state could also be a malevolent force that undermined individual freedom and liberty. When Congress finally restricted the president's war-making power through the 1973 War Powers Act, the arguments made by the bill's proponents were strongly reminiscent of those made by Taft in the Senate's "great debate" of 1951. Thus, in the eyes of many Americans today, Robert Taft was not the outdated conservative he seemed to be to his contemporaries but rather a prescient observer of American politics.

Key Sources

The Robert A. Taft Papers at the Library of Congress constitute the essential source for the Ohio senator. A valuable selection of Taft's papers can be found in Clarence E. Wunderlin, Jr., ed., *The Papers of Robert A. Taft*, 4 vols. (1997–2006). Two books written by Taft are important for understanding his political philosophy: *Foundations of Democracy: A Series of Debates* (1939), coauthored by Thomas V. Smith, and *A Foreign Policy for Americans* (1951).

Further Reading

■ Books

Kirk, Russell, and James McClellan. *The Political Principles of Robert A. Taft*. New York: Fleet Press, 1967.

Questions for Further Study

1. Analyze Taft's 1946 speech on equal justice under law. What does he mean when he speaks of a shared English and American tradition of respect for equal justice? How did he believe that the United States had, in responding to the Great Depression and World War II, abandoned its core principles? What does he see as the consequences of this abandonment?

2. What factors led to Taft's support for federal aid to education, as expressed in his 1947 speech on that subject? What was the basis for his critique of the New Deal welfare state, and why did he make an exception where education was concerned?

3. How did Taft's views, as evidenced in the passage from *A Foreign Policy for Americans* (1951), put him at odds with the majority of Americans? Explain how World War II had seen a shift in favor of a strong executive power to make war and why Taft opposed that shift. How does he argue against such executive power in general and, in particular, against President Truman's use of it? What factors brought about yet another shift in public opinion, such that Taft would later seem like a man ahead of his time?

4. To what extent was Taft, as his detractors maintained, a proponent of outmoded ideas, and to what extent was he actually a forerunner of the future conservative movement? What were the foundations of his intellectual conservatism, and what political price did he pay for being out of step with the prevailing national attitude toward big government? To what degree do you believe that history has vindicated him—that is, proved him to have been correct in his analysis?

Patterson, James T. *Mr. Republican: A Biography of Robert A. Taft.* Boston: Houghton Mifflin, 1972.

White, William S. *The Taft Story.* New York: Harper Brothers, 1954.

Wunderlin, Clarence E. *Robert A. Taft: Ideas, Tradition, and Party in U.S. Foreign Policy.* Lanham, Md.: Rowman & Littlefield, 2005.

　—John W. Malsberger

"Equal Justice under Law: The Heritage of the English-Speaking Peoples and Their Responsibility" (1946)

I wish to speak of the heritage of the English-speaking peoples in the field of government, and their responsibility to carry on that heritage, and to extend its tried principles to the entire world as rapidly as that can be done. The very basis of the government of the United States, derived through the Colonies from principles of British government, was the liberty of the individual and the assurance to him of equal treatment and equal justice....

I desire today to speak particularly of equal justice, because it is an essential of individual liberty. Unless there is law, and unless there is an impartial tribunal to administer that law, no man can be really free. Without them only force can determine controversy...and those who have not sufficient force cannot remain free. Without law and an appeal to a just and independent court to interpret that law, every man must be subject to the arbitrary discretion of his ruler or of some subordinate government official.

Over the portal of the great Supreme Court building in Washington are written the words "Equal Justice under Law." The Declaration of Independence, the Constitution of the United States and every pronouncement of the founders of the Government stated the same principle in one form or another....

Unfortunately, the philosophy of equal justice under law, and acceptance of decisions made in accordance with respected institutions, has steadily lost strength during recent years. It is utterly denied in totalitarian states. There the law and the courts are instruments of state policy. It is inconceivable to the people of such a state that a court would concern itself to be fair to those individuals who appear before it when the state has an adverse interest. Nor do they feel any need of being fair between one man and another....The totalitarian idea has spread throughout many nations where, in the nineteenth century, the ideals of liberty and justice were accepted. Even in this country the theory that the state is finally responsible for every condition, and that every problem must be cured by giving the government arbitrary power to act, has been increasingly the philosophy of the twentieth century. It infects men who still profess complete adherence to individual liberty and individual justice, so that we find them willing to sacrifice both to accomplish some economic or social purpose. There is none of the burning devotion to liberty

which characterized Patrick Henry and even the conservative leaders of the American Revolution....

Of course the new philosophy has been promoted by two world wars, for war is a denial both of liberty and of justice. *Inter arma leges silent*. We all of us recognize that justice to the individual, vital as it is, must be subordinate to the tremendous necessity of preserving the nation itself....In this war we have granted arbitrary war powers without appeal to the courts, and now the people have become so accustomed to such powers that the government proposes to continue war powers unimpaired to meet some supposed peace emergency. We hear constantly the fallacious argument, "If you would surrender these rights to win the war, is it not just as necessary to surrender them to win the peace?" Unless we desire to weaken for all time the ideals of justice and equality, it is absolutely essential that our program of reconversion and of progress abandon the philosophy of war, that it be worked out within the principles of justice....

Even before the war we had drifted far from justice at home. Expediency has been the key to the legislation of recent years, and many of the existing bureaus administer the law without any belief in the principle that the government should be fair to every individual according to written law....

When Government undertook to regulate the production of every farmer, telling him what he could sow and what he could reap, it had to set up an administrative machinery far beyond the capacity of any court to control. The enforcement of milk prices, production, and distribution by Federal milk boards has also been pursued without regard to any legal principle. Programs for general economic regulation are always inconsistent with justice because the detailed control of millions of individuals can only be carried through by giving arbitrary discretion to administrative boards. Such boards are always concerned with policy, but not with justice....

I believe more strongly than I can say that if we would maintain progress and liberty in America, it is our responsibility to see not only that laws be rewritten to substitute law for arbitrary discretion, but that the whole attitude of the people be guided from now on by a deep devotion to law, impartiality and equal justice....

Unfortunately, I believe we Americans have also in recent foreign policy been largely affected by principles of expediency and supposed necessity, and abandoned largely the principle of justice. We have drifted into the acceptance of the idea that the world is to be ruled by the power of the great nations and a police force established by them rather than by international law.

I felt very strongly that we should join the United Nations organization, but it was not because I approved the principles established in the Charter. Those who drafted the original Dumbarton Oaks proposals apparently had little knowledge of the heritage of the English-speaking peoples, for in those proposals there was no reference to justice and very little to liberty. At San Francisco a good many declarations were inserted emphasizing the importance of law and justice, but they were not permitted to interfere with the original setup of the Security Council. The Security Council is the very heart of the United Nations, the only body with power to Act. The Charter gives it the power to adopt any measure, economic or military, which it considers necessary to main-

tain or restore international peace and security. The heritage of the English-speaking peoples has always emphasized liberty over peace and justice over security. I believe that liberty and justice offer the only path to permanent peace and security....

Only by pressure against a reluctant Administration did Congress agree to adhere to the decision of an impartial tribunal in the International Court of Justice. Such a willingness on the part of all nations, accepted by the public opinion of the world, is the basic essential of future peace. But the court and international law have been step-children to our government. Force, and a police force, similar to the police force within a nation, have been the keynotes, forgetting that national and local police are only incidental to the enforcement of an underlying law, that force without law is tyranny. This whole policy has been no accident. For years we have been accepting at home the theory that the people are too dumb to understand and that a benevolent executive must be given power to describe policy and administer policy

Anglo-Saxon	reference to two of the Germanic tribes that settled in England during the Middle Ages; more generally, a term used to refer to the British American cultural heritage
Dumbarton Oaks	a mansion in Washington, D.C., where the United Nations was conceived and negotiated during the Dumbarton Oaks Conference, or more formally the Washington Conversations on International Peace and Security Organization
ex post facto	Latin for "after the fact," referring to a law that retroactively makes an act a crime or otherwise changes its legal consequences
Inter arma leges silent	Latin for "in time of war the law is silent"
Kuril Islands	a string of islands that stretches northeast from Japan to Russia
Moscow	the capital of the Soviet Union, now of Russia
Nuremberg	German city where Nazi war criminals were tried after World War II
Patrick Henry	leader of the American Revolution, famous for his statement "Give me liberty or give me death."
reconversion	conversion from a wartime to a peacetime economy
San Francisco	the California city that was the site of the San Francisco Conference, at which the United Nations was formally established
Security Council	the arm of the United Nations that votes on resolutions for maintaining security and peace
Teheran	the capital of Iran
USSR	Union of Soviet Socialist Republics, or the Soviet Union

according to his own prejudices in each individual case. Such a policy, in the world as at home, can lead only to tyranny, or to anarchy.

The Atlantic Charter professed a belief in liberty and justice for all nations, but at Teheran, at Yalta, at Moscow, we forgot law and justice. Nothing could be further from a rule of law than the making of secret agreements distributing the territory of the earth in accordance with power and expediency. We cannot excuse ourselves by declining territorial acquisition ourselves or subjecting ourselves to unreasonable and illogical restriction of our sovereignty over uninhabited Pacific Islands. We are just as much to blame if we acquiesce in unjustified acquisition of territory by others, such as the handing over of the Kuril Islands to Russia without trusteeship of any kind. Without a word of protest, we have agreed to the acquisition of Lithuania, Estonia and Latvia by the USSR against their will. There is little justice to the people of Poland in the boundaries assigned to them. The extending of justice throughout the world may be and is beyond our powers, but certainly we need not join in the principles by which force and national policy is permitted to dominate the world....

I believe that most Americans [also] view with discomfort the war trials which have just been concluded in Germany and are proceeding in Japan. They violate that fundamental principle of American law that a man cannot be tried under an *ex post facto* statute. The hanging of the eleven men convicted at Nuremberg will be a blot on the American record which we shall long regret....

In these trials we have accepted the Russian idea of the purpose of trials, government policy and not justice, having little relation to our Anglo-Saxon heritage. By clothing vengeance in the forms of legal procedure, we may discredit the whole idea of justice in Europe for years to come. In the last analysis, even at the end of a frightful war, we should view the future with more hope if even our enemies believed that we have treated them justly in trials, in the provision of relief and in the final disposal of territory. I pray that we do not repeat the procedure in Japan, where the justification on grounds of vengeance is much less than in Germany....

War has always set back temporarily the ideals of the world. This time because of the tremendous scope of the war, the increased barbarism of its methods and the general prevalence of the doctrine of force and expediency even before the war, the effect today is even worse and the duration of the postwar period of disillusionment may be longer. As I see it, the English-speaking peoples have one great responsibility. That is to restore to the minds of men a devotion to equal justice under law.

"THE SOUND BASIS FOR FEDERAL AID TO EDUCATION" (1947)

It is unnecessary in such a gathering as this to dwell on the importance of education. It lies at the very basis of all intelligent self-government. This nation was founded "to secure the blessings of liberty to ourselves and our posterity." Liberty and equal justice under law must be continuously secured if we are to carry out the purposes of the formation of this Republic; but neither liberty nor justice can be secured without a widely diffused education. We cannot preserve the Republic at all unless the people are taught to read and to think so that they may understand its basic principles themselves and the application of such principles to current problems. No man can be free if he does not understand the opportunities which lie before him. No man can have equality of opportunity if he has not the knowledge to understand how to use the rights which are conferred upon him.

Furthermore, education is essential to economic welfare....Unless men understand to some extent the principles of increased productivity, prosperity can be quickly destroyed. Unless men know what other men have achieved and are educated to a desire for the same improvements, history shows that they remain in perpetual poverty....

Furthermore, education is the only defense of liberty against totalitarianism. It may be that intelligent people will be occasionally misled to vest complete power in the state or in a single individual, but without education dictatorships inevitably arise....

Broadly speaking, this country has done a good job in education. ... Its system was built up on the basis of the control of education by each community, so that the parents in each city, town and county could determine the manner in which their children should be taught. Naturally, the character of education varied throughout the country and was of many different qualities and characters. Experiments in method have been freely made and have failed or succeeded after a fair trial. Men differently taught have developed novel and clashing theories which have finally met in the forum of national debate to be passed upon by the entire people. This variety has promoted a freedom of thought, and consequently a material progress, greater than that of any other country in the world.

This same localization of education has made it in some respects less effective. Some districts have done their job poorly. That is an inevitable incident to local administration....The faults of local administration in some districts cannot be cured, because they are due to the very freedom to make mistakes which is essential to any freedom at all. But in many districts, the failure in education is due to causes which can well be remedied, and in particular if it is due to the poverty of the district, or of the State in which it lies. While money is not the only requirement of a good school system ... it is certainly an essential one. There is a wide variation in the wealth of different States and districts. The income per capita ranges from $484 in Mississippi to $1,452 in Connecticut for the year 1943. The differences between districts in the same State are even wider. The result is that children in some districts receive a poor education or no education at all....

Without question, the primary obligation to educate children under our Constitutional system falls on the States and local districts. But I believe very strongly that the Federal government has a proper function in the field....The Federal government is authorized to levy taxes to provide for the general welfare of the United States, and under that Constitutional grant has the right to dispense money to the States and local districts for purposes not within the Constitutional power of the United States to control or regulate....

My own belief is that the Federal government should assist those States desiring to put a floor under essential services in relief, in medical care, in housing and in education. Apart from the general humanitarian interest in achieving this result, equality of opportunity lies at the basis of this Republic. No child can begin to have equality of opportunity unless he has medical care in his youth, adequate food, decent surroundings and above all, effective schooling. It is the concern of the entire nation to see that the principles of the Declaration of Independence and of the Constitution are translated into reality.

I believe, therefore, that the Federal government should undertake a system of extending financial aid to the States with the objective of enabling the States to provide a basic minimum education to every child, to the end that equal opportunity shall not be interfered with by the financial condition of the State or district of the child's residence. Certain principles, however, seem to me clear.

The administration of education and control of the school system must be completely in the hands of the State and local administrators.... The matter, however, is not quite so simple. ... If Federal aid depends upon the discretion of some Federal officer who has the power to withhold funds, human nature is such that he is apparently under a constant temptation to tell the recipients of the money how they must run their affairs.... Therefore, I believe that the standards should be clearly established in the law, and that the Federal government should interest itself in only one question, whether the statutory standard is complied with and the money used only for the purposes of the Act. If we can reduce the Federal interference to a matter of audit, we may hope to maintain local independence....

The second principle which I believe must underlie any bill for Federal aid is that the Federal contribution shall be auxiliary and shall not become the principal support of education. ... It is not true that the Federal government can levy all the taxes it may like to levy. The present tax burden seems to me a complete discouragement of the very economic activity from which taxes come. The people today on the average are paying nearly one-third of their income in taxation, working one day in three for the government. I believe such a tax system will soon discourage both individual initiative and corporate expansion. The Federal contributions, therefore, to States for matters where States have the primary obligation, like welfare, health, housing and education, must be in a limited amount.

S. 472 provides that, as a necessary condition of Federal aid any State must provide for its primary and secondary educational system at least 2.2 percent of the income of its citizens. This is slightly higher than the national average....

The bill then provides that if 1.1 percent of the State income, which would be one-half the total State and local revenue set aside for primary and secondary education, is insufficient to provide $40 for each child from 5 to 17 years of age in the State, then the Federal government will make up the difference so that one-half of the State revenue plus the Federal contribution will equal $40 for each such child.

It is then required that the State see that every school district in the State receive from Federal, State and local revenues, at least $40 per annum, for each pupil in average daily attendance—excluding interest, debt service and capital outlay. If there are separate colored schools, each colored school must receive such amount. You will note that there will remain to the State to be used in its discretion, one-half of its total school revenues, equal at least to 1.1 percent of the income of its people. Undoubtedly, some districts will get a larger proportion of this surplus fund than others, but it should be entirely possible for a State to provide from such funds a higher minimum base than $40 if it chooses to do so....

In summary, therefore ... if a State after making more than the average effort cannot provide $40 per child from half its revenues, the Federal government will assist the State to see that every child receives at least a $40 education.... S. 472...recognizes the obligation of the national government to see that each child has an adequate education. It recognizes and avoids the dangers of Federal control and leaves to the States the responsibility and the power to work out their own salvation. It would be a tremendous step forward in assuring to America the means of striving forward constantly toward the ultimate ideal of complete equality and complete liberty.

Glossary

"to secure the blessings of liberty to ourselves and our posterity"	quotation from the preamble to the U.S. Constitution

"The Place of the President and Congress in Foreign Policy" (1951)

No one can question the fact that the initiative in American foreign policy lies with the President. But ... the American people certainly do not believe or intend that his power shall be arbitrary and unrestrained. They want a voice in the more important features of that policy, particularly those relating to peace and war. They expect their Senators and Congressmen to be their voice....I shall try to define the place of Congress and the President under our Constitution. The debates in the Senate in early 1951 had even more to do with the question of who shall determine policy than with policy itself....

The fundamental issue in the "great debate" was, and is, whether the President shall decide when the United States shall go to war or whether the people of the United States themselves shall make that decision....

The matter was brought to an issue by the intervention of the President in the Korean War without even telling Congress what he was doing for several weeks. And it was brought still further to the fore by the proposal that we commit troops to an international army under the control of a council of twelve nations. I do not think that the American people have ever faced a more serious constitutional issue or one which in the end may present a greater threat to their freedom....

If in the great field of foreign policy the President has the arbitrary and unlimited powers he now claims, then there is an end to freedom in the United States not only in the foreign field but in the great realm of domestic activity which necessarily follows any foreign commitments....

[A] document was submitted to Congress, entitled *Powers of the President to Send the Armed Forces Outside the United States*, dated February 28, 1951 .... This document contains the most unbridled claims for the authority of the President that I have ever seen written in cold print. In effect, the document asserts that whenever in his opinion American foreign policy requires he may send troops to any point whatsoever in the world, no matter what the war in which the action may involve us. The document also claims that in sending armed forces to carry out a treaty the President does not require any statutory authority whatever, and it does not recognize the difference between a self-executing treaty and one which requires...congressional authority....

Of course, the President has wide powers in foreign policy, but the framers of the Constitution provided expressly that only Congress could do certain things. Those powers are expressed in Section 8 of Article I. Of course, Congress is given the power, and the exclusive power—

To declare war, grant letters of marque and reprisal, and make rules concerning captures on land and water.

To raise and support armies, but no appropriation of money to that use shall be for a longer term than two years....

To provide and maintain a navy.

To make rules for the government and regulation of the land and naval forces....

The Constitution also provides that the President shall have the power to make treaties, but only by and with the advice and consent of the Senate, provided two thirds of the Senators present concur. The President's relationship to the armed forces is stated only in Section 2 of Article II of the Constitution:

The President shall be Commander in Chief of the Army and Navy of the United States....

There is one very definite limit ... on the President's power to send troops abroad: he cannot send troops abroad if the sending of such troops amounts to the making of war. I think that has been frequently asserted; and whenever any broad statements have been made as to the President's power as Commander in Chief to send troops anywhere in the world the point has been made that it is always subject to that particular condition....

Most of the cases which have been cited as authority for the President sending troops abroad are cases where the use of our troops was limited to the protection of American citizens or of American property.

The Boxer Rebellion is frequently cited; but in that case troops were sent into China because the legations in Peking were besieged and the legitimate Chinese Government was unable to defend them against the rebellious Boxers. So the various nations sent their troops there, in order to rescue those who were in the legations. That was a clear effort to protect American lives, to protect American diplomatic lives which were threatened contrary to the law of nations; and certainly it was not an act which would necessarily involve us in war.

The case of the Mexican rebellion is [also] referred to. ... [President Polk's right to dispatch troops] was challenged by a very distinguished American, Abraham Lincoln, who on February 15, 1848, wrote his law partner with reference to Polk's use of the Army against Mexico:

Allow the President to invade a neighboring nation whenever he shall deem it necessary to repel an invasion, and you allow him ... to make war at pleasure. Study to see if you can fix any limit to his power in this respect. If today he should choose to say he thinks it necessary to invade Canada to prevent the British from invading us, how could you stop him? You may say to him, "I see no probability of the British invading us," but he will say to you, "Be silent: I see it if you don't,"

Lincoln said further:

The provision of the Constitution giving the war-making power to Congress was dictated...by the following reasons: Kings had always been involving and impoverishing their people in wars, pretending...that the good of the people was the object. This our convention understood to be the most oppressive of all kingly oppressions, and they resolved to so frame the Constitution that no one man should hold the power of bringing this oppression upon us....

In the case of Korea it was claimed that the intervention could take place under the United Nations Charter on the call of the Security Council. Of course the Security Council never acted under Articles 41 and 42 of the United Nations Charter, and even if it had done so the obligation to send troops is clearly limited by Article 43. That Article provides that troops can only be called for when an agreement has been entered into with the Security Council specifying the number and character of the assistance to be furnished. No such agreement has ever been entered into. The United Nations Participation Act of 1945, approved by President Truman, also made it clear that any agreement which required the providing of military aid must be subsequently approved by Congress, and, of course, it never has been. Not only that, but President Truman sent a cable from Potsdam when the United Nations Charter was under consideration, in which he said: "When any such agreement or agreements are negotiated, it will be my purpose to ask the Congress by appropriate legislation to approve them." The charter was adopted largely on that assurance, but now the President's claims are far beyond what they were then....

If the President can carry out every recommendation of the Security Council or the General Assembly supported by the vote of the American representative

whom he can direct, then he has almost unlimited power to do anything in the world in the use of either troops or money. The Security Council might recommend that the nations should rebuild the canals on the Tigris and Euphrates and establish a vast Garden of Eden in the Kingdom of Iraq. According to the argument made, the President would then have power to use all American forces to establish such an economic project. On the same theory, he could send troops to Tibet to resist Communist aggression or to Indo-China or anywhere else in the world, without the slightest voice of Congress in the matter. If that could be the effect of an international treaty, we had better watch closely the approval of any such treaty in the future....

My conclusion, therefore, is that in the case of Korea, where a war was already under way, we had no right to send troops to a nation, with whom we had no treaty, to defend it against attack by another nation, no matter how unprincipled that aggression might be, unless the whole matter was submitted to Congress and a declaration of war or some other direct authority obtained.

The question of sending troops to Europe is certainly much more complicated. There is no doubt about the President's power to send troops to occupied Germany. There is no question that he can send them if he wants to do so, as Commander in Chief of the Army and Navy....

I think he can [also] station troops in a friendly country if such country asks that the troops be sent and if there is no imminence of attack and if they are stationed there for some possible convenience in repelling a general attack upon the United States itself....

The European Army Project, however ... involves the sending of troops to an international army similar to that which was contemplated under the United Nations Charter. It is an international army, apparently established by twelve nations, with a commander who is appointed by the twelve nations. It seems to me perfectly clear that the President's power as Commander in Chief does not extend to the delegation of that power to a commander who is chosen by any other nation or any other group of nations. I think it is perfectly clear that he cannot enter into an agreement of that kind to set up an international army without submitting the agreement to Congress....

In my opinion, the Senate resolution and the concurrent resolution adopted by the Senate on April 4, 1951, was a clear statement by the Senate that it has the right to pass on any question of sending troops to

Europe to implement the Atlantic Pact [NATO], that it is unconstitutional for the President to send any troops abroad to implement that pact without congressional approval, at least until war comes....

No one can prevent the President continuing to assert his power as President, and it may be that he does have the ability to involve the United States in war, even when he has no right to do so....The President acts at his own peril, if he chooses to usurp authority which the representatives of the people have asserted that he does not possess.

Glossary

Boxer Rebellion	an antiforeign uprising in China from November 1899 to September 1901, so called because it was led by a sect trained in the martial arts
General Assembly	the deliberative body of the United Nations
Indo-China	a region in Southeast Asia that encompasses Vietnam, Laos, and Cambodia
legations	nations' diplomatic representatives in other nations
letters of marque and reprisal	authorizations for the commanders of private ships to detain foreign ships and seize or destroy cargo if the home nations of the foreign ships have committed offenses against the issuing nations
NATO	North Atlantic Treaty Organization, a defense pact that includes the United States, Canada, and various European nations
Polk	James Polk, eleventh U.S. president
Potsdam	a German city southwest of Berlin and the site of a major peace conference among the Allied powers after World War II
Security Council	the arm of the United Nations that votes on resolutions for maintaining security and peace
Tibet	an Asian region north of the Himalayas, currently controlled by the People's Republic of China
Tigris and Euphrates	rivers that flow from Turkey through Iraq

Roger B. Taney (Library of Congress)

ROGER B. TANEY   1777–1864

Fifth Chief Justice of the United States

Featured Documents
◆ *Charles River Bridge v. Warren Bridge* (1837)
◆ *License Cases* (1847)
◆ *Dred Scott v. Sandford* (1857)

Overview

Roger Brooke Taney's legacy on the Supreme Court has been dominated by a bit of judicial overreaching that changed the course of history: his opinion in *Dred Scott v. Sandford*, also known as the Dred Scott Case. Taney served as the United States' fifth chief justice for nearly three decades, for much of that period expanding upon precedents set by his illustrious predecessor, John Marshall. He made important inroads in such areas as federal laws concerning corporations and the application of the Constitution's commerce clause, skillfully balancing the old demands of federalism with the new emphasis on states' rights that characterized the age of Andrew Jackson. Although he wrote more, and not insignificant, opinions after *Dred Scott*, Taney could not outlive the opprobrium that flowed from the decision that declared both that African Americans were not citizens and that the Missouri Compromise—a congressional effort to preserve the balance between slaveholding and non-slaveholding states—was invalid. As the noted Supreme Court historian R. Kent Newmyer has remarked, after *Dred Scott*, "There was nothing left but the grim logic of marching men" (Newmyer, p. 139).

Taney was born into a Catholic family that first settled in the Maryland Tidewater region in the middle of the seventeenth century. Taney's mother had an aristocratic background, but his father was descended from an indentured servant who worked his way up in the world. By the time of Taney's birth in 1777, his father was a wealthy tobacco planter who lavished an excellent education on his second son, who would be obliged to earn his own living. When he was only fifteen, Taney entered Dickinson College in Pennsylvania, from which he graduated as valedictorian in 1795. After three years of reading law in the offices of Judge Jeremiah Chase in Annapolis, Maryland, Taney was admitted to the state bar. That same year he embarked on a political career, serving first as a Federalist member of the Maryland House of Delegates. His career there proved short-lived when the 1800 election brought the Jeffersonian Republicans to power. Taney moved to Frederick, Maryland, where he maintained a successful legal practice. After several defeats he also reentered politics in 1816 as a state senator.

When the Federalist Party disintegrated, Taney joined the Democratic movement led by Andrew Jackson. Taney proved himself a party faithful by serving as state chairman of the committee to elect Jackson as president. In 1831,

while Taney was serving as Maryland's attorney general, Jackson named him to the same position in his cabinet. Taney was also to serve concurrently as Jackson's acting secretary of war. A Jackson stalwart, Taney also played an important role in the president's war on the Bank of the United States in 1832: When Jackson decided to kill the bank by withdrawing federal deposits, it was Taney who fulfilled this mission after two successive secretaries of the treasury refused to comply with the order. A grateful Jackson sought to reward Taney, but the Senate, alienated by the president's unilateral maneuvers, declined to confirm Taney as secretary of the treasury and indefinitely postponed a decision on Taney's nomination to the Supreme Court as an associate justice. Jackson tried again a few months later, nominating Taney as the replacement for Chief Justice John Marshall, who had died on July 6, 1835. The Senate again delayed voting on Taney's nomination, but after a closed executive session, Taney was confirmed.

Following in the wake of the man known as the "Great Chief Justice," Taney had large shoes to fill. He had a reputation as a political hack who was expected to do Jackson's bidding on the Court, just as he had in the cabinet. As if to underscore his political orientation, when making his debut on the Court, Taney broke with tradition by appearing in long trousers—emblematic of radical democracy—rather than the knee breeches sported by his predecessors. But instead of undoing the constitutional nationalism that was the legacy of the Marshall Court, the Taney Court developed what had gone before by expanding it into a more equitable sovereignty shared with the states. The first three cases that came before the Taney Court had been argued during Marshall's tenure, and all three presented questions concerning the balance of powers between federal and state governance. Taney himself wrote the opinion of the Court for the most significant of these cases, *Charles River Bridge v. Warren Bridge*, which departed from Federalist doctrine by allowing that rights vested in states can sometimes override prohibitions memorialized in the Constitution's contracts clause. The Taney Court's gradualism and ability, as demonstrated in the License Cases, to craft compromises between state and federal authority earned the public's respect. Roger Brooke Taney was on course to become one of history's most respected jurists until the Court decided—perhaps unnecessarily—to take on the issue of slavery.

Dred Scott proved to be Taney's undoing—as it nearly did for the nation. Taney lived for another seven years, dur-

1777

■ **March 17**
Roger Brooke Taney is born in Calvert County, Maryland.

1795

■ Taney graduates from Dickinson College in Carlisle, Pennsylvania.

1799

■ **June 19**
Taney is admitted to the Maryland bar.

■ Taney is elected to the Maryland House of Delegates.

1816

■ Taney is elected to the Maryland Senate.

1827

■ **September**
Taney becomes Maryland's state attorney general.

1828

■ Taney serves as chairman of the Andrew Jackson Central Committee of Maryland.

1831

■ President Andrew Jackson appoints Taney to serve concurrently as U.S. attorney general and acting secretary of war.

1833

■ **September 23**
Jackson appoints Taney as secretary of the treasury.

1834

■ **June 24**
Taney resigns as treasury secretary after the Senate votes not to confirm him.

1835

■ **January 15**
Jackson nominates Taney as an associate Supreme Court justice, but the Senate postpones a decision on the appointment.

ing which he wrote a number of laudable opinions, such as his 1861 opinion in *Ex parte Merryman*, a circuit court case condemning President Abraham Lincoln's suspension of the writ of habeas corpus. Lincoln simply ignored the decision; he could do so because *Dred Scott* had thoroughly undermined Taney's authority. Broken, embittered, and impoverished, Taney died while still in office on October 12, 1864—the same day his home state abolished slavery.

Explanation and Analysis of Documents

Roger Taney's career in the U.S. Supreme Court began inauspiciously. A longtime ally of Andrew Jackson, he carried with him a somewhat tarnished reputation as a political hack. In the veto message he had drafted to accompany Jackson's death blow to the national bank, Taney had written: "The opinion of the judges has no more authority over Congress than the opinion of Congress has over the judges, and on that point the President is independent of both. The authority of the Supreme Court must not, therefore, be permitted to control the Congress or the Executive" (http://avalon.law.yale.edu/19th_century/ajveto01.asp). Thus was the power of judicial review, the "invention" of Taney's well-loved predecessor, John Marshall, dismissed out of hand.

It was not long, however, before Taney staked out his own judicial territory, developing a body of law that addressed the public welfare rather than private, individual rights. The three leading cases decided during Taney's first term had all been argued while Marshall was still serving as chief justice, and all would have been decided differently if Marshall had lived. Taney made certain all three were reargued and decided during his first month on the high bench—and he ensured that all three decisions bore his stamp.

Charles River Bridge v. Warren Bridge was the most significant of these decisions and represented a clear departure from the Marshall tradition. Taney would reiterate his emphasis on local authority a decade later in the License Cases, notable for the development of the doctrine of selective exclusiveness, a type of sharing between state and federal governments of the commerce power. The License Cases were also noteworthy for generating nine opinions from six justices, a sign of things to come. In this case the justices were able to agree unanimously on an outcome, but the issue of human commerce prevented them from reaching agreement as to their reasons for doing so. Ten years on, politics—and perhaps the chief justice's hubris—forced the Court to address slavery head on in *Dred Scott v. Sandford*. The result was catastrophic, plunging the nation into civil war and Roger Taney into a purgatory from which he did not escape alive. It would take generations for both the nation and Taney's reputation to recover from the damage wrought by *Dred Scott*.

◆ *Charles River Bridge v. Warren Bridge*

In 1785 the Massachusetts legislature granted a charter to the Charles River Bridge Company to build a bridge connecting Boston with nearby Cambridge. The company was given the right to collect tolls for forty years (later extended to seventy years when another company proposed to build a competing bridge), after which time bridge ownership would revert to the state. The endeavor proved hugely successful, and the profits of the company's shareholders rose with the population of Boston and its environs. In 1828 the state granted a second charter to the Warren Bridge Company to build another bridge nearby the Charles River Bridge, but this contract permitted the Warren Bridge Company to collect only enough tolls to pay for the bridge's construction, or only for a maximum of six years, after which the public would be permitted to use the new bridge free of charge. As might be expected, Charles River Bridge shareholders cried foul and filed suit, declaring that Massachusetts had violated the terms of its original contract, which they said implicitly conferred a monopoly on their company.

The Supreme Court of Massachusetts found against the Charles River Bridge Company, declining to grant an injunction preventing construction of the Warren Bridge. The Charles River Bridge Company then appealed its case to the U.S. Supreme Court, citing the Massachusetts constitutional guarantee of "life, liberty and property" as well as Article I, Section 10, of the Constitution, which reads in pertinent part: "No State shall…pass any Bill of Attainder, ex post facto Law, or Law impairing the Obligation of Contracts." Construction of the Warren Bridge, the appellant claimed, would jeopardize both their property rights and public confidence in government undertakings. Some members of the Marshall Court, which originally heard arguments in the case, agreed with the appellant company, but owing largely to illness and vacancies on the Court, a decision in the case was postponed. When the case was reargued nearly six years later, some of those Marshall Court justices remained, but the new Taney Court was dominated by Jacksonian Democrats, who favored the kind of economic progress represented by the case of the Warren Bridge Company.

Chief Justice Taney wrote an opinion for the four-member majority. The opinion, which Charles River Bridge Company counsel Daniel Webster called both "smooth and plausible" and "cunning and jesuitical" (Newmyer, p. 96), manages to uphold the sanctity of contract while also advancing the interests of the state legislature, itself representing the sovereign power of the people. While asserting that the "rights of private property must be sacredly guarded," Taney also states that "the object and end of all government is to promote the happiness and prosperity of the community." Massachusetts had chartered the first bridge to promote the public good, but a second bridge was needed now for exactly the same reason. Both economic progress and equal opportunity require a ruling favoring the Warren Bridge Company, unless—and here is the heart of the matter—the contract included language expressly granting monopoly rights to the Charles River Bridge Company. It did not.

Conservative observers feared that American corporate law had been forever damaged, but in fact Taney had accomplished something subtle: By warning against the

Time Line

1836

■ **March 28**
Taney is sworn in as the fifth chief justice of the United States.

1837

■ **February 12**
The Supreme Court hands down its opinion in *Charles River Bridge v. Warren Bridge.*

1847

■ **March 6**
The Court hands down its opinion in the License Cases.

1857

■ **March 6–7**
The Court hands down its opinion in *Dred Scott v. Sandford.*

1864

■ **October 12**
Taney dies in Washington, D.C.

dangers of vested economic interests and political power, he made way for technological innovation that would advance both corporate and public welfare. Contrary to what the Marshall Court holdover Justice Joseph Story argued in dissent, the majority's opinion actually increased incentives for economic investment. And although Taney insists that the Court must not engage in nullification of legislation passed to advance the public good, by emphasizing its support for corporate development, his opinion actually increased the Court's influence.

◆ **License Cases**

The collective License Cases consolidated three different cases that had been tried separately in lower courts: *Thurlow v. Massachusetts*, *Fletcher v. Rhode Island*, and *Peirce v. New Hampshire*. Each of these cases concerned the legality of state licensing statutes for imported liquor, which, it was argued, violated constitutionally granted federal control of interstate commerce. The Taney Court unanimously upheld all three state statutes; however, there was no opinion of the Court per se. Six justices wrote nine separate opinions. This multiplicity of views reflected, in part, the composite nature of the License Cases, but it was also a product of national ferment over state control of slavery, the most hotly debated issue of the era.

Chief Justice Taney's opinion is most notable for its elaboration of the police power. In legal terms, *police power* does not refer specifically to the power of police forces, although such power is included in the concept. Rather, *police power* refers to the power of a state or municipality to enact legislation that restricts the activities of others, whether individuals or businesses, to protect public health, safety, and welfare, to prevent fraud, and to promote the economic, social, and moral interests of the citizens within its jurisdiction. The maintenance of a police force is just one of many mechanisms for doing so. The issue that early courts frequently had to deal with was the unclear relationship between state police powers and the power of the federal government. At times, these powers seemed to conflict, and the Tenth Amendment to the Constitution—"The powers not delegated to the United States by the Constitution, nor prohibited by it to the States, are reserved to the States respectively, or to the people"—was not always clear. In the License Cases, Taney dealt with the potential conflict between state and federal law as it pertained to matters of foreign commerce.

Taney had first noted the existence of state police powers in his opinion in the *Charles River Bridge* case, where the Court declined to intrude upon a power so essential to the public well-being and prosperity. For him, police powers and sovereignty were one and the same, and the states retained all powers necessary to internal government that did not conflict with constitutionally granted federal authority. The police power was, in fact, fundamental to the expansion of government during the age of Andrew Jackson, when such power offered the means of enforcing public interest. Taney recognizes the inherent conflict not only between federal and state government but also between community and individual rights. In both contests, he says, public welfare almost invariably trumps other, competing interests—and police powers are the states' basic tool for controlling property for the betterment of society.

Taney begins by outlining the issue at hand:

> whether a state is prohibited by the Constitution of the United States from making any regulations of foreign commerce or of commerce with another state, although such regulation is confined to its own territory and made for its own convenience or interest and does not come in conflict with any law of Congress.

After noting that other members of the Court might disagree, Taney states his view: "The mere grant of power to the general government cannot … be construed to be an absolute prohibition to the exercise of any power over the same subject by the states." He goes on to note that when the U.S. Congress wanted to preserve its exclusive jurisdiction over a matter of law, it typically said so by explicitly prohibiting the states from taking any action in conflict with congressional mandate, which Congress had not done in the matter at hand.

Taney then elaborates his conclusion by summarizing the legal history of two areas of law, that governing "pilots and pilotage" (an area of maritime law) and that governing "health and quarantine laws." These matters were relevant to the case at hand because they each had a bearing on for-

eign commerce. Taney notes that throughout the nation's history, the "maritime states"—that is, seaboard states—had passed various laws regulating maritime activities. These laws had implications for the conduct of foreign commerce, yet the federal government never felt called on to challenge these laws. Taney concludes that if the Court failed to uphold the constitutionality of the challenged laws in the License Cases, the effect would be to render void all such laws passed by the states regulating maritime affairs. Similarly, health and quarantine laws passed in states with ports and harbors had the effect of regulating foreign commerce, yet not only had the federal government not interfered with these laws, it had in fact helped with their enforcement.

After elaborating on the principle that any law, and any Court decision, must be consistent with the Constitution, Taney takes up the matter of the dividing line between Congress's authority to regulate foreign commerce and that of the states. He notes that at some point, imported goods pass into private hands. At that point, those goods are no longer the subject of foreign commerce; they are simply private property, and the federal government has no authority over their disposition. Thus, for example, the Constitution grants Congress the right to levy duties on imported goods, or to regulate the time and place of their importation. But once the goods enter a state, Congress has no constitutional authority to tell the states what to do with them or how to regulate them for the welfare and benefit of their own people.

After the License Cases, the Court would be continually obliged to balance individual rights with the police power. The case also neatly juxtaposed state and federal authority, arriving at a compromise that came to be known as selective exclusiveness, which recognized that the power to control interstate commerce did not belong exclusively to the national government. If the age of Jackson can be said to have advanced states' rights, it did so in large part because the regulation of both commerce and property became, in many instances, the province of police powers. Such would be the state of affairs until the New Deal era of the 1930s, when the balance of power tipped decidedly in favor of the federal government. Long before that, the slavery issue, which brought both property and individual rights into the mix, would prove to be Taney's—and nearly the nation's—undoing.

◆ Dred Scott v. Sandford

In taking on *Dred Scott v. Sandford*, the Taney Court assumed an impossible task. The issues involved—principally, slavery and states' rights—were ones that had bedeviled the nation since its founding. Perhaps understandably, politicians did not want to touch them. Perhaps predictably, it was a politician who forced the issue. In 1856 the Democratic James Buchanan was elected president with the support of every slaveholding state save Maryland, Chief Justice Taney's home state. In his inaugural address, Buchanan informed the country that the Supreme Court would soon decide whether territories would be admitted to the union as slaveholding or non-slaveholding states. In doing so, he revealed—seemingly inadvertently—that he had engaged in illegitimate discussions with the Court about a pending case. His remarks also indicated that *Dred Scott v. Sandford* was every bit as much a political decision as a legal one.

The Taney Court had been obliged to concern itself with slavery on a number of earlier occasions. In *United States v. The Amistad* (1841), Justice Joseph Story wrote an opinion freeing African captives of Spanish slavers from an international squabble over ownership. And in *Prigg v. Pennsylvania* (1842), the Court ruled—once again via an opinion drafted by Justice Story—on the validity of fugitive slave laws. The Court, per Story, upheld the federal law requiring return of escaped slaves, while also striking down a state law encumbering the rendition process. Story added, however, that state officials could not be forced to comply with the federal Fugitive Slave Act. In a concurring opinion, Chief Justice Taney misconstrued Story's ruling, objecting that it would release state judges from any obligation to hear cases concerning fugitive slaves. This mischaracterization helped fuel hostilities between North and South. Taney's personal attitude toward the "peculiar institution" of slavery was ambiguous. He freed his own slaves, going so far as to provide pensions for those too old to earn their own living. But by the time he wrote the opinion of the Court in *Dred Scott v. Sandford*, he had come to view abolitionism as "northern aggression," apparently demonstrating that his Jacksonian bias toward states' rights included endorsement of the right to own slaves. The Dred Scott Case, which presented the "black question" in terms of permitting slavery in the territories—thereby mingling issues of sovereignty with those of southern survival, seemingly would permit him to address his particular concerns about slavery.

It needs to be said, however, that Taney's concerns were far from unique. Until the Thirteenth Amendment abolished it in 1865, the Constitution included a fugitive slave clause. As abolitionists gained in strength and numbers, southern resentment grew against what many viewed as the North's reluctance to fulfill a constitutional obligation. In 1850 slaveholders and non-slaveholders had reached an agreement whereby territorial governments in lands formerly owned by Mexico and surrendered to the United States after the Mexican-American War of 1846 to 1848 would be allowed to determine their own status upon being admitted to the Union. As part of the Compromise of 1850, the federal Fugitive Slave Act was revised, providing harsher penalties against escaped slaves and states that impeded their return. In the North this revised law occasioned riots, rescues, and Harriet Beecher Stowe's influential best-selling novel, *Uncle Tom's Cabin* (1852). The stage was set for war, and it is not much of an exaggeration to say that Taney's opinion in *Dred Scott* set things in motion.

Born into slavery in Virginia in 1797, Dred Scott moved with his master, Peter Blow, to St. Louis. After Blow's death in 1832, Scott was sold to Dr. John Emerson. As an army surgeon, Emerson was posted to a number of locations, including the free state of Illinois and the non-slaveholding Wisconsin Territory. While in Wisconsin with his master, Scott married Harriet Robinson, a slave whose ownership

Front-page article on Dred Scott in Frank Leslie's **Illustrated Newspaper,** *June 27, 1857* (Library of Congress)

was transferred to Emerson in 1836. Two years later Emerson left Wisconsin, leaving the Scotts behind. They had two daughters: Eliza, who was born in 1843, and Lizzie, who was born around 1850. Sometime after 1838 the Scotts had followed Emerson back to St. Louis. When he died in 1843, his widow inherited his slaves. Irene Sanford Emerson followed a common practice of the time, hiring her slaves out to others. In the mid-1840s the widow Emerson moved to New York, leaving the Scotts behind with Henry and Taylor Blow, sons of Dred Scott's original owner.

Henry Blow, an activist in the antislavery Whig Party, agreed to finance a suit in the Missouri courts to secure Dred Scott's freedom. In 1846 a suit was filed against Emerson's estate, asserting that Scott's time in the free state of Illinois and the free Wisconsin Territory rendered him a free man. This first case ended in a mistrial, but a second lawsuit in 1850 resulted in a verdict in Scott's favor. During the two years between trials, the county sheriff hired Scott out for $5 per month. These wages were held in escrow until Scott could secure his freedom. In the meanwhile, the widow Emerson had married a radical antislavery Massachusetts congressman, and she transferred Dred Scott's ownership to her brother, John Sanford, still in St. Louis. When Scott won his freedom in 1850, his new owner stood to lose control of Scott's escrowed wages, so Sanford (his name was misspelled in the official reports) appealed the verdict. In 1852 the Missouri Supreme Court declared that Scott became a slave when he reentered Missouri.

The next year, the entire Scott family sued for their freedom in federal court in St. Louis. One of the ironies of their case was that the circuit court agreed to hear it. In order to file a federal case, Scott's lawyers had to demonstrate that their client had standing based on diversity jurisdiction, that is, that the parties to the case came from different states. The Missouri federal trial court accepted the premise that the defendant, Sanford, was a citizen of New York, while the plaintiff, Scott, was a citizen of Missouri—despite his status as a slave. Scott's third attempt to gain his freedom ended in a declaration that he was still a slave.

By this time, *Dred Scott* had been embraced by the abolitionist movement and was known throughout the land. Sanford's lawyers responded to this national focus by injecting other issues into the case. When the case found its way to the U.S. Supreme Court, the justices found themselves obliged to confront two fundamental questions: Was Scott, an African American, a citizen of the United States who had standing to sue in federal court? Was the Missouri Compromise, which made Wisconsin a free territory, constitutional?

Dred Scott v. Sandford was argued twice before the Supreme Court. After the first argument, which took place February 11–14, 1856, the justices were inclined to sidestep the real issues raised by the case. Instead, the Court intended simply to uphold the Missouri Supreme Court's ruling, reasoning that a state's highest court should have the last word about the state's own laws. Politics intervened, however, and as 1856 was an election year, the Court declined to inflame the atmosphere further just as the nation was about to choose a new president. Furthermore, the justices could not agree on the grounds to use as justification for declaring Dred Scott still a slave: Some wanted to hold that he had no standing in federal court; others wanted to declare that Congress had no power to deprive citizens of their property—their slaves—in the territories. The case was set down for reargument.

The Court listened to oral arguments a second time December 15–18, 1856. The justices did not meet to discuss the case until the following February, when they decided, finally, to tackle the larger issues involved. The chief justice took on the job of writing the opinion for the seven justices who voted against Scott's freedom. Owing in part to Taney's ill health, the decision of the Court was not announced until March 6, 1857. Each of the justices had also written a separate opinion, a sign of the case's significance. Reading a total of 250 pages aloud in open court took two full days.

Taney's opinion for the Court declares Dred Scott still a slave. The reasons behind this decision are many. First, and most damningly, although African Americans could be citizens of a state, they could not be citizens of the United States. As noncitizens, they did not enjoy the privilege of bringing suit in federal court. Second, Scott had never been freed. Third, slaves' status was protected by the Constitution. Taney's next argument builds logically on what he has established, but it leads to an unnecessary—and

fatal—conclusion: Because slavery was protected by the Constitution, the Missouri Compromise, which outlawed the institution in lands, such as the Wisconsin Territory, above the latitude 36° north, was invalid. Taney adds, almost as an afterthought, that whatever status Scott may have had in a free state, as soon as he set foot back in slaveholding Missouri—to which he had returned voluntarily—he reverted to slavery.

Reaction to the decision was swift. While the Buchanan administration and its southern supporters were jubilant, the Court's dismissal of Dred Scott's case convinced others that the federal government was involved in a conspiracy. The decision that was supposed to settle the question of territorial status had, in effect, opened the entire nation to slavery. Northern Democrats quarreled with southern Democrats, splitting the party and creating an opening for the newly reformed Republican Party in the next election. As the historian Charles Warren would later write, "It may fairly be said that Chief Justice Taney elected Abraham Lincoln to the Presidency" (Warren, p. 79).

The newspapers had a field day with *Dred Scott*, whipping up both partisanship and public hysteria. The Democrat-controlled Senate, which supported the Supreme Court's decision, voted to print twenty thousand copies for public circulation. Northern churches, generally supportive of abolition, joined the fray, reading Justice John McLean's dissent (clearly with his cooperation) from the pulpit the day after it was delivered in Court. The other dissenter, Benjamin Curtis, remained so bitter about the majority's decision that he resigned from the Court in September 1857. The nation grew more polarized after *Dred Scott*, which in the end only settled the question of whether a political or legal solution could be found to the controversy over the true nature of the Union. There had been bloodshed before the Supreme Court handed down what has come to be universally considered its most injudicious decision. What followed afterward was a bloodbath.

The Civil War and the later Civil War constitutional amendments overturned *Dred Scott v. Sandford*. While the Thirteenth Amendment, ratified in 1865, abolished slavery, the Fourteenth, ratified in 1868, declared that all persons born in the United States were citizens, regardless of color or previous condition of servitude. Although Taylor Blow emancipated the entire Scott family in 1857, Dred Scott did not live long enough to benefit from the changes wrought by the Civil War amendments. He remained in St. Louis, where he worked as a hotel porter for a decade. Reportedly, he felt that his suit had brought him nothing but trouble. Had he known it would drag on so long, he said, he would never have sued in the first place. Dred Scott died of tuberculosis on September 17, 1858. Taylor Blow's brother paid for Scott's funeral.

Impact and Legacy

The *Dred Scott* decision would haunt Taney for the rest of his days, undermining both his effectiveness and the

Taney, Roger B.

"While the rights of private property are sacredly guarded, we must not forget, that the community also have rights, and that the happiness and well-being of every citizen depends on their faithful preservation."

(*Charles River Bridge v. Warren Bridge*)

"There is no exclusive privilege given to them over the waters of Charles river, above or below their bridge; no right to erect another bridge themselves, nor to prevent other persons from erecting one, no engagement from the state, that another shall not be erected; and no undertaking not to sanction competition, nor to make improvements that may diminish the amount of its income."

(*Charles River Bridge v. Warren Bridge*)

"The controlling and supreme power over commerce with foreign nations and the several states is undoubtedly conferred upon Congress. Yet in my judgment, the state may nevertheless, for the safety or convenience of trade or for the protection of the health of its citizens, make regulations of commerce for its own ports and harbors and for its own territory, and such regulations are valid unless they come in conflict with a law of Congress."

(*License Cases*)

"We think they [people of African ancestry] are not [citizens], and that they are not included, and were not intended to be included, under the word 'citizens' in the Constitution."

(*Dred Scott v. Sandford*)

"It is difficult at this day to realize the state of public opinion in relation to that unfortunate race, which prevailed...at the time of the Declaration of Independence, and when the Constitution of the United States was framed and adopted.... They had for more than a century before been regarded as beings of an inferior order, and altogether unfit to associate with the white race, either in social or political relations; and so far inferior, that they had no rights which the white man was bound to respect; and that the negro might justly and lawfully be reduced to slavery for his benefit."

(*Dred Scott v. Sandford*)

Court's credibility. When Taney wrote a circuit court opinion, *Ex parte Merryman* (1861) condemning the president's revocation of the writ of habeas corpus, Lincoln simply ignored him. Although Taney remained loyal to the Union, throughout the Civil War many in the North blamed him expressly for hastening the conflict that split the nation in two and cost approximately 620,000 American lives. Taney lived for six years after announcing *Dred Scott*, but he died a frustrated, angry man whose tainted legacy outlived him for generations. In 1865, after the House of Representatives passed a bill authorizing erection of a bust of Taney on the Supreme Court grounds, the Senate refused to sign on. It would be another decade before Congress appropriated funds for Taney's Supreme Court memorial.

Modern legal scholarship has generally been kinder to Taney, resurrecting his reputation as one of the most accomplished jurists of his time and indeed of all time. He served on the Court for more than twenty-eight years, the majority of them devoted to a new era of jurisprudence epitomized by such decisions as *Charles River Bridge*, which helped pave the way for a period of economic expansion that would be halted only by the outbreak of civil war. Unfortunately, Taney's democratic impulse also led him

into the morass of *Dred Scott*. Under Taney's leadership, the Court attained an even greater measure of prestige than it had enjoyed during the years it was led by John Marshall. But it would all disappear—almost overnight—when Taney applied his states' rights orientation to the facts of *Dred Scott v. Sandford*. He overplayed his hand by declaring that Congress had erred through interfering with local authority and property rights by signing the Missouri Compromise into law thirty-seven years earlier. This was judicial activism at its worst, and Taney paid a heavy price for what many saw as his arrogance. He was, apparently, incapable of seeing his own faults, and he never truly understood the disgrace others heaped upon him for his miscalculation in thinking he could find the answer to a problem that had evaded all attempts at resolution.

Key Sources

Papers dating from 1770 through 1834 concerning Taney's law practice in Frederick, Maryland, are housed in the Roger Brooke Taney Legal Papers Collection at Dickinson College in Carlisle, Pennsylvania. Documents related to

Questions for Further Study

1. Discuss *Charles River Bridge v. Warren Bridge* in terms of its significance for the Supreme Court and for Taney himself. How did he use this and the two related cases to put his personal stamp on the Court when leadership passed to him from the enormously influential John Marshall? How does his ruling in the case reflect his political and philosophical shift from federalism to Jacksonian democracy? What long-term impact did *Charles River Bridge* exert on the Court and its role within the framework of American government?

2. Examine the issues addressed in the License Cases, including the question of federal control over interstate commerce and the interpretation of the Tenth Amendment. Be sure to explain the principle of police power and Taney's views on that subject. How did the rulings in the License Cases influence the larger public debate over states' rights and slavery?

3. Research and discuss the events, personalities, and issues involved in *Dred Scott v. Sandford*, with a concentration on Taney's pivotal role in the Supreme Court's infamous decision. What were the chief justice's personal views on slavery, and how did these have an effect (or not) on his ruling on the case? What reasoning led him to his conclusion that Scott was still a slave? Although the idea of human slavery is morally repugnant to modern-day people, attempt to explain his thinking from his point of view and to show how Taney's conclusions might logically flow from his premises.

4. How did Taney's reputation change over the years? Consider first his early career, aspects of which led many critics to dismiss him as a mere tool of Andrew Jackson. How did he earn such a reputation, and how did he work to overcome it during his tenure as chief justice? How did his *Dred Scott* decision come to haunt him, and to what extent is Taney himself to blame for this? Finally, how and why have views on Taney's legacy changed in the time since his death?

Taney's legal practice dating from 1805 to 1818 are in the Arthur J. Morris Law Library at the University of Virginia in Charlottesville. Letters between Taney and his executor, David Perine, are among the David M. Perine Papers at the Maryland Historical Society Library Collection in Baltimore. Samuel Tyler's *Memoir of Roger Brooke Taney, LL.D.*, (1872, rept. 2008), contains sketches of Taney's autobiography and an appendix of legal opinions, including that of the *Dred Scott* case. The "Veto Message Regarding the Bank of the United States" can be found at the Avalon Project http://avalon.law.yale.edu/19th_century/ajveto01.asp.

Further Reading

■ Articles
Harris, Robert J. "Chief Justice Taney: Prophet of Reform and Reaction." *Vanderbilt Law Review* 10 (February 1957): 227–257.

Whittington, Keith E. "The Road Not Taken: Dred Scott, Judicial Authority, and Political Questions." *Journal of Politics* 63, no. 2 (2001): 365–391.

■ Books
Allen, Austin. *The Origins of the Dred Scott Case: Jacksonian Jurisprudence and the Supreme Court, 1837–1857*. Athens: University of Georgia Press, 2006.

Fehrenbacher, Don E. *The Dred Scott Case: Its Significance in American Law and Politics*. New York: Oxford University Press, 2001.

Frankfurter, Felix. *The Commerce Clause under Marshall, Taney, and Waite*. Chicago: Quadrangle Books, 1964.

Kutler, Stanley. *Privilege and Creative Destruction: The Charles River Bridge Case*. Baltimore: Johns Hopkins University Press, 1990.

Lewis, Walker. *Without Fear or Favor: A Biography of Chief Justice Roger Brooke Taney*. Boston: Houghton Mifflin, 1965.

Newmyer, R. Kent. *The Supreme Court under Marshall and Taney*. New York: Crowell, 1968.

Schwartz, Bernard. *A History of the Supreme Court*. New York: Oxford University Press, 1993.

Simon, James F. *Lincoln and Chief Justice Taney: Slavery, Secession, and the President's War Powers*. New York: Simon & Schuster, 2006.

Swisher, Carl B. *Roger B. Taney*. Hamden, Conn.: Archon, 1961.

Warren, Charles. *The Supreme Court in United States History* Vol. 3: *1856–1918*. Boston: Little, Brown, 1922.

■ Web Sites
"Dred Scott Decision: The Lawsuit That Started the Civil War." HistoryNet.com Web site. http://www.historynet.com/dred-scott-decision-the-lawsuit-that-started-the-civil-war.htm.

"Roger Brooke Taney (1777–1864)." Encyclopedia Dickinsonia Web site. http://chronicles.dickinson.edu/encyclo/t/ed_taneyR.htm.

"The Revised Dred Scott Case Collection." Washington University Digital Web site. http://digital.wustl.edu/d/dre/index.html.

—Lisa Paddock

CHARLES RIVER BRIDGE V. WARREN BRIDGE (1837)

We are not now left to determine, for the first time, the rules by which public grants are to be construed in this country…the principle recognised, that in grants by the public, nothing passes by implication….

The case now before the court is, in principle, precisely the same. It is a charter from a state; the act of incorporation is silent in relation to the contested power. The argument in favor of the proprietors of the Charles River bridge, is the same, almost in words, with that used by the Providence Bank; that is, that the power claimed by the state, if it exists, may be so used as to destroy the value of the franchise they have granted to the corporation. The argument must receive the same answer; and the fact that the power has been already exercised, so as to destroy the value of the franchise, cannot in any degree affect the principle. The existence of the power does not, and cannot, depend upon the circumstance of its having been exercised or not….

While the rights of private property are sacredly guarded, we must not forget, that the community also have rights, and that the happiness and well-being of every citizen depends on their faithful preservation.

Adopting the rule of construction above stated as the settled one, we proceed to apply it to the charter of 1785, to the proprietors of the Charles River bridge….There is no exclusive privilege given to them over the waters of Charles river, above or below their bridge; no right to erect another bridge themselves, nor to prevent other persons from erecting one, no engagement from the state, that another shall not be erected; and no undertaking not to sanction competition, nor to make improvements that may diminish the amount of its income. Upon all these subjects, the charter is silent; and nothing is said in it about a line of travel, so much insisted on in the argument, in which they are to have exclusive privileges. No words are used, from which an intention to grant any of these rights can be inferred; if the plaintiff is entitled to them, it must be implied, simply, from the nature of the grant; and cannot be inferred, from the words by which the grant is made….

It results from this statement, that the legislature, in the very law extending the charter, asserts its rights to authorize improvements over Charles river which would take off a portion of the travel from this bridge and diminish its profits; and the bridge company accept the renewal thus given, and thus carefully connected with this assertion of the right on the part of the state. Can they, when holding their corporate existence under this law, and deriving their franchises altogether from it, add to the privileges expressed in their charter, an implied agreement, which is in direct conflict with a portion of the law from which they derive their corporate existence? Can the legislature be presumed to have taken upon themselves an implied obligation, contrary to its own acts and declarations contained in the same law? It would be difficult to find a case justifying such an implication, even between individuals; still less will it be found, where sovereign rights are concerned, and where the interests of a whole community would be deeply affected by such an implication. It would, indeed, be a strong exertion of judicial power, acting upon its own views of what justice required, and the parties ought to have done, to raise, by a sort of judicial coercion, an implied contract, and infer it from the nature of the very instrument in which the legislature appear to have taken pains to use words which disavow and repudiate any intention, on the part of the state, to make such a contract….

Amid the multitude of cases which have occurred, and have been daily occurring, for the last forty or fifty years, this is the first instance in which such an implied contract has been contended for, and this court called upon to infer it, from an ordinary act of incorporation, containing nothing more than the usual stipulations and provisions to be found in every such law. The absence of any such controversy, when there must have been so many occasions to give rise to it, .proves, that neither states, nor individuals, nor corporations, ever imagined that such a contract could be implied from such charters. It shows, that the men who voted for these laws, never imagined that they were forming such a contract; and if we maintain that they have made it, we must create it by a legal fiction, in opposition to the truth of the fact, and the obvious intention of the party. We cannot deal thus with the rights reserved to the states; and by legal intendments and mere technical reasoning, take away from them any portion of that power over their own internal police and improvement, which is so necessary to their well-being and prosperity.

And what would be the fruits of this doctrine of implied contracts, on the part of the states, and of property in a line of travel, by a corporation, if it would now be sanctioned by this court? To what results would it lead us?…The millions of property which have been invested in railroads and canals, upon lines of travel which had been before occupied by turnpike corporations, will be put in jeopardy. We shall be thrown back to the improvements of the last century, and obliged to stand still, until the claims of the old turnpike corporations shall be satisfied; and they shall consent to permit these states to avail themselves of the lights of modern science, and to partake of the benefit of those improvements which are now adding to the wealth and prosperity, and the convenience and comfort, of every other part of the civilized world. Nor is this all. This court will find itself compelled to fix, by some arbitrary rule, the width of this new kind of property in a line of travel; for if such a right of property exists, we have no lights to guide us in marking out its extent, unless, indeed, we resort to the old feudal grants, and to the exclusive rights of ferries, by prescription, between towns; and are prepared to decide that when a turnpike road from one town to another, had been made, no railroad or canal, between these two points, could afterwards be established. This Court are not prepared to sanction principles which must lead to such results.

Glossary

franchises	a legal term that generally refers to the rights of an organization to sell its products or services with permission from the local government
implied contract	a legal term referring to a contractual obligation arising out of the actions of the parties rather than from the wording of the written contract
intendments	ways in which the legal system interprets something, in particular the meaning of a law
Providence Bank	reference to an 1830 Supreme Court case, *Providence Bank v. Billings*, in which the Court ruled that the imposition of a state tax on a state-chartered bank was not inconsistent with the contracts clause of the Constitution and was therefore legal

LICENSE CASES (1847)

The question therefore brought up for decision is whether a state is prohibited by the Constitution of the United States from making any regulations of foreign commerce or of commerce with another state, although such regulation is confined to its own territory and made for its own convenience or interest and does not come in conflict with any law of Congress. In other words, whether the grant of power to Congress is of itself a prohibition to the states and renders all state laws upon the subject null and void. This is the question upon which the case turns, and I do not see how it can be decided upon any other ground, provided we adopt the line of division between foreign and domestic commerce as marked out by the court in *Brown v. State of Maryland*....

It is well known that upon this subject a difference of opinion has existed, and still exists, among the members of this Court. But with every respect for the opinion of my brethren with whom I do not agree, it appears to me to be very clear that the mere grant of power to the general government cannot, upon any just principles of construction, be construed to be an absolute prohibition to the exercise of any power over the same subject by the states. The controlling and supreme power over commerce with foreign nations and the several states is undoubtedly conferred upon Congress. Yet in my judgment, the state may nevertheless, for the safety or convenience of trade or for the protection of the health of its citizens, make regulations of commerce for its own ports and harbors and for its own territory, and such regulations are valid unless they come in conflict with a law of Congress. Such evidently I think was the construction which the Constitution universally received at the time of its adoption, as appears from the legislation of Congress and of the several states, and a careful examination of the decisions of this Court will show that so far from sanctioning the opposite doctrine, they recognize and maintain the power of the states.

The language in which the grant of power to the general government is made certainly furnishes no warrant for a different construction, and there is no prohibition to the states. Neither can it be inferred by comparing the provision upon this subject with those that relate to other powers granted by the Constitution to the general government. On the contrary, in many instances, after the grant is made, the Constitution proceeds to prohibit the exercise of the same power by the states in express terms—in some cases absolutely, in others without the consent of Congress. And if it was intended to forbid the states from making any regulations of commerce, it is difficult to account for the omission to prohibit it when that prohibition has been so carefully and distinctly inserted in relation to other powers, where the action of the state over the same subject was intended to be entirely excluded. But if, as I think, the framers of the Constitution ... intended merely to make the power of the federal government supreme upon this subject over that of the states, then the omission of any prohibition is accounted for, and is consistent with the whole instrument. The supremacy of the laws of Congress, in cases of collision with state laws, is secured in the article which declares that the laws of Congress, passed in pursuance of the powers granted, shall be the supreme law; and it is only where both governments may legislate on the same subject that this article can operate. For if the mere grant of power to the general government was in itself a prohibition to the states, there would seem to be no necessity for providing for the supremacy of the laws of Congress, as all state laws upon the subject would be *ipso facto* void, and there could therefore be no such thing as conflicting laws, nor any question about the supremacy of conflicting legislation. It is only where both may legislate on the subject that the question can arise.

I have said that the legislation of Congress and the states has conformed to this construction from the foundation of the government. This is sufficiently exemplified in the laws in relation to pilots and pilotage, and the health and quarantine laws.

In relation to the first, they are admitted on all hands to belong to foreign commerce, and to be subject to the regulations of Congress under the grant of power of which we are speaking. Yet they have been continually regulated by the maritime states as fully and entirely since the adoption of the Constitution as they were before, and there is but one law of Congress making any specific regulation upon the subject, and that passed as late as 1837, and intended... to alter only a single provision of the New York law, leaving the residue of its provisions entirely untouched. It is true that the act of 1789 provides that pilots shall continue to be regulated by the laws of the respective states then in force or which may thereafter be passed until Congress shall make provision on the subject. And undoubtedly Congress had the power, by assenting to the state laws then in force, to make them its own and thus make the previous regulations of the states the regulations of the general government. But it is equally clear that as to all future laws by the states, if the Constitution deprived them of the power of making any regulations on the subject, an act of Congress could not restore it. For it will hardly be contended that an act of Congress can alter the Constitution and confer upon a state a power which the Constitution declares it shall not possess. And if the grant of power to the United States to make regulations of commerce is a prohibition to the states to make any regulation upon the subject, Congress could no more restore to the states the power of which it was thus deprived than it could authorize them to coin money, or make paper money a tender in the payment of debts, or to do any other act forbidden to them by the Constitution. Every pilot law in the commercial states has, it is believed, been either modified or passed since the act of 1789 adopted those then in force, and the provisions since made are all void if the restriction on the power of the states now contended for should be maintained, and the regulations made, the duties imposed, the securities required, and penalties inflicted by these various state laws are mere nullities, and could not be enforced in a court of justice....

So also in regard to health and quarantine laws. They have been continually passed by the states ever since the adoption of the Constitution, and the power to pass them recognized by acts of Congress, and the revenue officers of the general government directed to assist in their execution. Yet all of these health and quarantine laws are necessarily, in some degree, regulations of foreign commerce in the ports and harbors of the state. They subject the ship and cargo and crew to the inspection of a health officer appointed by the state; they prevent the crew and cargo from landing until the inspection is made, and destroy the cargo if deemed dangerous to health. And during all this time, the vessel is detained at the place selected for the quarantine ground by the state authority. The expenses of these precautionary measures are also usually, and I believe universally, charged upon the master, the owner, or the ship, and the amount regulated by the state law, and not by Congress. Now so far as these laws interfere with shipping, navigation, or foreign commerce or impose burdens upon either of them, they are

unquestionably regulations of commerce. Yet, as I have already said, the power has been continually exercised by the states, has been continually recognized by Congress ever since the adoption of the Constitution and constantly affirmed and supported by this Court whenever the subject came before it....

By the 6th article and 2d clause of the Constitution, it is thus declared:

"That this Constitution and the laws of the United States made in pursuance thereof, and treaties made under the authority of the United States, shall be the supreme law of the land."

This provision of the Constitution, it is to be feared, is sometimes applied or expounded without those qualifications which the character of the parties to that instrument and its adaptation to the purposes for which it was created necessarily imply. Every power delegated to the federal government must be expounded in coincidence with a perfect right in the states to all that they have not delegated in coincidence, too, with the possession of every power and right necessary for their existence and preservation, for it is impossible to believe that these ever were, in intention or in fact, ceded to the general government. Laws of the United States, in order to be binding, must be within the legitimate powers vested by the Constitution. Treaties, to be valid, must be made within the scope of the same powers, for there can be no "authority of the United States" save what is derived mediately or immediately, and regularly and legitimately, from the Constitution. A treaty, no more than an ordinary statute, can arbitrarily cede away any one right of a state or of any citizen of a state. In cases of alleged conflict between a law of the United States and the Constitution or between the law of a state and the Constitution or a statute of the United States, this Court must pronounce upon the validity of either law with reference to the Constitution; but whether the decision of the Court in such cases be itself binding or otherwise must depend upon its conformity with, or its warrant from, the Constitution. It cannot be correctly held that a decision, merely because it be by the Supreme Court, is to override alike the Constitution and the laws both of the states and of the United States....By art. 1, §8, clause 4, of the Constitution it is declared "that Congress shall have power to regulate commerce with foreign nations, among the several states, and with the Indian tribes." It is with the first of the grants in this article that we have now to deal. The commerce here spoken of is that traffic between the people of the United States and foreign nations, by which articles are procured by purchase or barter from abroad, or by which the like subjects of traffic are transmitted from the United States to foreign countries, keeping in view always the essential characteristic of this commerce as stamped upon it by the Constitution—namely that it is commerce with foreign nations, or in other words that it is external commerce. ... The power to regulate this commerce may properly comprise the times and places at which, the modes and vehicles in which, and the conditions upon which, it may as foreign commerce be carried on; but precisely at that point of its existence that it is changed from foreign commerce, at that point this power of regulation in the federal government must cease, the subject for the action of this power being gone.

Independently of an express prohibition upon the states to lay duties on imports, this power of regulating foreign commerce may correctly imply a denial to the states of a right to interfere with existing regulations over subjects of foreign commerce; but they must be continuing, and still in reality, subjects of foreign commerce, and such they can no longer be after that commerce with regard to them has terminated, and they are completely vested as property in a citizen of a state....If this were otherwise, then, by the same reasoning, they would remain imports, or subject of foreign commerce, through every possible transmission of title, because they had been once imported.

Imports in a political or fiscal, as well as in common practical acceptation, are properly commodities brought in from abroad which either have not reached their perfect investiture or their alternate destination as property within the jurisdiction of the state, or which still are subject to the power of the government for a fulfillment of the conditions upon which they have been admitted to entrance—as for instance goods on which duties are still unpaid, or which are bonded or in public warehouses. So soon as they are cleared of all control of the government which permits their introduction, and have become the complete and exclusive property of the citizen or resident, they are no longer imports in a political or fiscal or common sense. They are like all other property of the citizen, and should be equally the subjects of domestic regulation and taxation....The objection, that a tax upon an article in bulk (the property of a citizen) is forbidden because it is a burden on foreign commerce, whilst a similar burden is permissible on the very same bulk or on fragments of the same article in the hands of his vendee, it would appear difficult to reconcile with sound reasoning. Every tax is alike a burden, whether it be imposed on larger or smaller subjects, and in either mode must operate on price, and consequently on demand and consumption. If, then, there was any integrity in the objection urged, it should abolish all regulations of retail trade, all taxes on whatever may have been imported.

Glossary

construction	interpretation
investiture	delivery of property or title to that property
ipso facto	Latin for "by the deed itself" or "by the fact itself"; automatically
pilotage	navigation
vendee	the buyer or receiver of sold property

DRED SCOTT V. SANDFORD (1857)

It is difficult at this day to realize the state of public opinion in relation to that unfortunate race, which prevailed in the civilized and enlightened portions of the world at the time of the Declaration of Independence, and when the Constitution of the United States was framed and adopted. But the public history of every European nation displays it in a manner too plain to be mistaken.

They had for more than a century before been regarded as beings of an inferior order, and altogether unfit to associate with the white race, either in social or political relations; and so far inferior, that they had no rights which the white man was bound to respect; and that the negro might justly and lawfully be reduced to slavery for his benefit....

Can a negro, whose ancestors were imported into this country, and sold as slaves, become a member of the political community formed and brought into existence by the Constitution of the United States, and as such become entitled to all the rights, and privileges, and immunities, guarantied by that instrument to the citizen? One of which rights is the privilege of suing in a court of the United States in the cases specified in the Constitution.

We think they [people of African ancestry] are not [citizens], and that they are not included, and were not intended to be included, under the word "citizens" in the Constitution, and can therefore claim none of the rights and privileges which that instrument provides for and secures to citizens of the United States....

The legislation and histories of the times, and the language used in the Declaration of Independence, show, that neither the class of persons who had been imported as slaves, nor their descendants, whether they had become free or not, were then acknowledged as a part of the people, nor intended to be included in the general words used in that memorable instrument.

For if they were so received, and entitled to the privileges and immunities of citizens, it would exempt them from the operation of the special laws and from the police regulations which they considered to be necessary for their own safety. It would give to persons of the negro race, who were recognized as citizens in any one State of the Union, the right to enter every other State whenever they pleased ... to go where they pleased at every hour of the day or night without molestation, unless they committed some violation of law for which a white man would be punished; and it would give them the full liberty of speech in public and in private upon all subjects upon which its own citizens might speak; to hold public meetings upon political affairs, and to keep and carry arms wherever they went. And all of this would be done in the face of the subject race of the same color, both free and slaves, and inevitably producing discontent and insubordination among them, and endangering the peace and safety of the State.

The act of Congress, upon which the plaintiff relies, declares that slavery and involuntary servitude, except as a punishment for crime, shall be forever prohibited in all that part of the territory ceded by France, under the name of Louisiana, which lies north of thirty-six degrees thirty minutes north latitude, and not included within the limits of Missouri. And the difficulty which meets us at the threshold of this part of the inquiry is, whether Congress was authorized to pass this law under any of the powers granted to it by the Constitution; for if the authority is not given by that instrument, it is the duty of this court to declare it void and inoperative, and incapable of conferring freedom upon any one who is held as a slave under the laws of any one of the States.

There is certainly no power given by the Constitution to the Federal Government to establish or maintain colonies bordering on the United States or at a distance, to be ruled and governed at its own pleasure; nor to enlarge its territorial limits in any way, except by the admission of new States. That power is plainly given; and if a new State is admitted, it needs no further legislation by Congress, because the Constitution itself defines the relative rights and powers, and duties of the State, and the citizens of the State, and the Federal Government. But no power is given to acquire a Territory to be held and governed permanently in that character....

It may be safely assumed that citizens of the United States who migrate to a Territory belonging to the people of the United States, cannot be ruled as mere colonists, dependent upon the will of the General Government, and to be governed by any laws it may think proper to impose. The principle upon which our Governments rests is the union of States, sovereign and independent within their own limits in ... their internal and domestic concerns, and bound together as one people by a General Government, possessing certain enumerated and restricted powers, delegated to it by the people of the several States....

But the power of Congress over the person or property of a citizen can never be a mere discretionary power under our Constitution and form of Government. The powers of the Government and the rights and privileges of the citizen are regulated and plainly defined by the Constitution itself. And when the Territory becomes a part of the United States, the Federal Government enters into possession in the character impressed upon it by those who created it. It enters upon it with its powers over the citizen strictly defined, and limited by the Constitution, from which it derives its own existence, and by virtue of which alone it continues to exist and act as a Government and sovereignty. It has no power of any kind beyond it; and it cannot, when it enters a Territory of the United States, put off its character, and assume discretionary or despotic powers which the Constitution has denied to it....

The rights of private property have been guarded with ... care. Thus the rights of property are united with the rights of person, and placed on the same ground by the Fifth Amendment to the Constitution, which provides that no person shall be deprived of life, liberty, and property, without due process of law. And an act of Congress which deprives a citizen of the United States of his liberty or property, merely because he came himself or brought his property into a particular Territory of the United States, and who had committed no offence against the laws, could hardly be dignified with the name of due process of law.

Upon these considerations, it is the opinion of the court that the act of Congress which prohibited a cit-izen from holding and owning property of this kind in the territory of the United States north of the line therein mentioned, is not warranted by the Constitution, and is therefore void; and that neither Dred Scott himself, nor any of his family, were made free by being carried into this territory; even if they had been carried there by the owner, with the intention of becoming a permanent resident.

But there is another point in the case which depends on State power and State law. And it is contended, on the part of the plaintiff, that he is made free by being taken to Rock Island, in the State of Illinois, independently of his residence in the territory of the United States; and being so made free, he was not again reduced to a state of slavery by being brought back to Missouri....

In the case of *Strader et al. v. Graham*...the slaves had been taken from Kentucky to Ohio, with the consent of the owner, and afterwards brought back to Kentucky. And this court held that their status or condition, as free or slave, depended upon the laws of Kentucky, when they were brought back into that State, and not of Ohio....

So in this case. As Scott was a slave when taken into the State of Illinois by his owner, and was there held as such, and brought back in that character, his status, as free or slave, depended on the laws of Missouri, and not of Illinois.

Upon the whole, therefore, it is the judgment of this court, that it appears by the record before us that the plaintiff in error is not a citizen of Missouri, in the sense in which that word is used in the Constitution; and that the Circuit Court of the United States, for that reason, had no jurisdiction in the case, and could give no judgment in it. Its judgment for the defendant must, consequently, be reversed, and a mandate issued, directing the suit to be dismissed for want of jurisdiction.

Glossary

plaintiff in error	a legal term referring to the party who challenges the ruling of a lower court

Tecumseh (AP/Wide World Photos)

TECUMSEH   1768–1813

Shawnee Tribal Leader

Featured Documents
◆ Speech to Governor William Henry Harrison at Fort Vincennes (1810)
◆ Speech to Major General Henry Procter at Fort Malden (1813)

Overview

Tecumseh was born on March 9, 1768, at a Shawnee Indian village probably near the modern city of Xenia, Ohio. His name most likely referred to a stellar constellation conceived of in Shawnee lore as a cougar, giving rise to translations as either "Shooting Star" or "Crouching Panther." His father, Puckeshinwa, patron of Tecumseh's panther clan, was a war chief who fought against European expansion west of the Appalachians but was killed in 1774 at the Battle of Point Pleasant, a defeat that resulted in a treaty forcing the Shawnee to give up any claims to Kentucky. Two of Tecumseh's older brothers were also killed fighting against the Americans.

Tecumseh rose to prominence fighting against renewed American westward expansion after the Revolutionary War. The Indians were led by the Shawnee war chief Blue Jacket, who was ultimately defeated at the Battle of Fallen Timbers in 1794. The battle itself was not so disastrous, but the retreating Indians had expected to be protected by their British allies. However, the British did not wish to provoke open war with the United States and so turned their retreating allies away from the gates of Fort Miami, in Ohio, a demoralizing setback that caused most of Blue Jacket's war band to disperse. Blue Jacket had led a multitribal force known to Americans as the Western Lakes Confederacy, which was the largest and most powerful Indian resistance movement ever organized in North America. The Shawnee were forced to yield most of Ohio in the subsequent Treaty of Greenville of 1795, which also began the practice whereby subsidies in cash and trade goods were paid to prominent Indian leaders by the Americans on the understanding that they would redistribute that wealth to promote American interests. Tecumseh never accepted this treaty, leaving the way open for him to lead renewed resistance.

Following the Treaty of Fort Wayne of 1809, by which a large number of chiefs gave up southern Indiana to the United States in exchange for trade goods, and until the War of 1812, Tecumseh traveled extensively, even beyond the traditional Shawnee area of the Old Northwest (Ohio, Indiana, Michigan, Illinois, and Wisconsin). Throughout the region between the Appalachians and Mississippi and into Missouri, within the newly Americanized Louisiana Territory, he spoke against the United States and in favor of Indian unity, attempting to create a united Indian resistance to American expansion. His fiery oratory was the only tool at his disposal for this task, since the necessary legal

and institutional framework for such an organization did not exist in Indian culture, the structure of which was based largely on personal loyalties.

Tecumseh was never able to enact his hopes for an Indian confederacy, because the military commander William Henry Harrison's destruction of his base at Prophetstown on the Tippecanoe River in Indiana spoiled the Indian leader's reputation for victory. After this defeat, he was able to lead only a small war band in revolt against the United States during the War of 1812. His hopes in this case were never realized either, because the British had no interest in detaching the Ohio Valley from the United States but only in defending Canada. Arguably, the British sacrificed Tecumseh and his warriors to that defense once it became clear that the Indian and British war aims differed. Tecumseh was killed at the Battle of the Thames, in Ontario, in 1813.

Explanation and Analysis of Documents

Tecumseh directly addressed William Henry Harrison, the governor of the Indiana Territory and the American military commander in the Old Northwest, in 1810 (the speech included here) and 1811, demanding the revocation of the Treaty of Fort Wayne and even the Treaty of Greenville. In November 1811, Harrison humiliated the brothers' new movement by defeating a small Indian force at their village of Prophetstown (as the Americans called the settlement that was their center of operations), on the Tippecanoe River, and burning the village while Tecumseh was away conducting negotiations with various tribes south of the Ohio River. As a result, when war came in 1812 with open hostilities between Great Britain and the United States, Tecumseh was able to lead not a unified Indian nation or confederation but only a war band composed of warriors personally loyal to him. The Battle of the Thames, in which he died, was provoked by his formal speech to the British commander, Major General Henry Procter, in which he threatened that his contingent would desert if the army did not stand and fight the Americans.

◆ Speech to Governor William Henry Harrison at Fort Vincennes

In 1810 Tecumseh and a small band of his warriors visited William Henry Harrison, the territorial governor of Indiana who was to become Tecumseh's military antagonist for the rest of his life. Tecumseh had been invited to Fort Vin-

Time Line

1768

- **March 9**
  Tecumseh is born near the present site of Xenia, Ohio.

1794

- **August 20**
  Tecumseh fights under Blue Jacket against the United States in the Battle of Fallen Timbers, near the present-day site of Toledo, Ohio.

1795

- **August 3**
  Blue Jacket and other war chiefs, not including Tecumseh, sign the Treaty of Greenville, yielding most of Ohio to American settlement.

1805

- **May**
  Tecumseh's brother Tenskwatawa begins a religious revival.

1808

- Tenskwatawa and Tecumseh found Prophetstown on the Tippecanoe River.

1809

- **September 30**
  The Treaty of Fort Wayne cedes large tracts of Indian lands to the United States, sending Tecumseh on a "speaking tour" of various Indian tribes in an attempt to forge an alliance against America.

1810

- **August 12**
  Tecumseh delivers a major speech to William Henry Harrison at Fort Vincennes, demanding that the Treaty of Fort Wayne be nullified.

1811

- **November 7**
  Harrison defeats Tenskwatawa in the Battle of Tippecanoe, destroying Tecumseh's base of Prophetstown.

cennes to discuss the possibility of his going to Washington, D.C., to negotiate directly with President James Madison. Instead, Tecumseh focused the meeting on demanding the abrogation of the treaty of Fort Wayne, claiming that only then could negotiations take place in good faith. His initial speech lasted several hours, and he and Harrison negotiated for most of a week. Only a few passages were preserved, in Harrison's correspondence to the secretary of war.

After the military defeat of the Western Lakes Confederacy at the Battle of Fallen Timbers (so called because it was fought on a field littered with trees uprooted by a tornado), the Treaty of Greenville opened most of Ohio to American settlement. Tecumseh, who had fought at Fallen Timbers, never agreed to the treaty and maintains in this speech that it ought to be revoked, unlikely as that was considering the large and growing American population of Ohio. But his more pressing concern with Harrison was the Treaty of Fort Wayne. Harrison had concluded this treaty the previous year with a large number of chiefs, who had ceded southern Indiana and part of Illinois in return for about $5,000 in trade goods, so-called gifts in the polite language of diplomacy. These gifts consisted of manufactured products such as whiskey and gunpowder (in addition to items like metal cooking pots) that Indian civilization could not manufacture for itself. Such presents were vitally important to chiefs because, in this era, the loyalty of followers increasingly depended on a chief's ability to redistribute such goods among them. Although Tecumseh wanted to refuse these gifts from Harrison to demonstrate to his followers his contempt for the Americans, he nevertheless finally reached a rhetorical position that allowed him to accept them; he, too, desperately needed them.

Tecumseh begins by arguing that Harrison in particular and the white community in general worked to seize control of Indian land by driving wedges between the Indian tribes. By fomenting distrust and division among the tribes, whites are able to prevent the tribes from uniting in resistance to the spread of white settlers. After maintaining that negotiations with whites should be conducted by "warriors" rather than chiefs, Tecumseh turns his attention to one in particular, the Potawatomi chief Winnemac, who had been instrumental in persuading his colleagues to sign the Treaty of Fort Wayne and who was now present in Harrison's retinue dressed in American clothes and sporting an arsenal of American pistols. Tecumseh stood in clear distinction, dressed in traditional clothing and opposing the American governor. Despite all the support that Harrison had bought, the Treaty of Fort Wayne was widely unpopular in the larger Indian community, and Tecumseh insists that the chief had no authority to sell Indian land. Tecumseh used this resentment as the base of his political program both to preach resistance to the Americans and "to destroy village chiefs, by whom all mischief is done." As he puts it, "It is they who sell our lands to the Americans." In this way, Tecumseh sought to create a new form of political authority among Indians.

Tecumseh then takes up the issue of "presents." He tells Harrison, "Brother, do not believe that I came here to get presents from you. If you offer us any, we will not take. By taking goods from you, you will hereafter say that with them you purchased another piece of land from us." Later he relents and says, "If you think proper to give us any presents, and we can be convinced that they are given through friendship alone, we will accept them." He concludes by asking Harrison to take pity on the "red people" and asking Harrison how the Indians can possibly trust the white man, who killed his own leading religious figure, Christ, on a cross and who ridicules the religious beliefs of groups such as the Shakers.

The issue of religion was important to Tecumseh and one on which he based his resistance to white expansion. The most important element of his plans for the future of the Indian community was the new religion preached by his brother Lalawethika. In 1805 Lalawethika, while in a trance, received a revelation from a being he called the Master of Life to the effect that Indians who continued to sin after hearing his message would be punished in the afterlife. So as not to sin, Indians had to avoid foods (including alcohol) that were not native to North America and renounce the use of firearms (except for self-defense against the Americans). They could not become Christians and also had to give up traditional religious practices and the consultation of shamans not connected with the new movement. Further, while land use practices among Indian communities had never corresponded to American ideas about private ownership, from then on all land had to be held in common, and all violence, whether wars or vendettas, within the greater Indian community had to end. Last, the Master of Life revealed to Lalawethika that Americans were not human beings but had been created by an evil power. They were inherently wicked and unjust. Indians needed not only to yield no more land but also to discontinue dealings with them. (This mandate did not apply to the British and Spanish.) Lalawethika was commanded to change his name to Tenskwatawa, "the Open Door," because the new revelation passed through him.

Tecumseh's own program was to make the reformed way of life of Tenskwatawa's revelation a political reality for the Indians of the Old Northwest. He tells Harrison that he wished the Indians "to unite, and…consider their lands as the common property of the whole." He also wants to do away with the village chiefs whose rivalries could lead to internal conflict (which would be encouraged by the Americans). Tecumseh's ideas about the potential form of Indian government were far reaching. He aimed to enforce peace by creating a kind of military dictatorship. As for who had the right to sell territory under the Treaty of Fort Wayne, he tells Harrison, "It was me." Because he considered all Indian lands to be held in common, his authority as the leading Indian war chief gave him absolute territorial rights. Viewing himself as possessed of supreme executive power over a confederation of Indian tribes, Tecumseh intended to rule in consultation with "a great council, at which all the tribes will be present." The model for all this, again somewhat ironically, was the government of the United States. Tecumseh claims for himself the executive pow-

Time Line

1812	■ **August**
	Tecumseh starts to cooperate with the British forces from Canada, now at war with the United States, and quickly aids in capturing Detroit.

1813	■ **September**
	Tecumseh delivers a speech addressing sharp criticism to the British commander Henry Procter about his conduct of the war.
	■ **October 5**
	Tecumseh is killed in the defeat of the Anglo-Indian army at the Battle of the Thames, in Canada.

ers of commander in chief as well as the authority to make treaties. He imagines the tribes as regular constituent entities of a confederation like the Union. In fact, "Great Council" was the usual Indian term for the U.S. Congress. In sum, Tecumseh claims to Harrison, "I am authorized by all the tribes.…I am the head of them all; I am a warrior, and all the warriors will meet together." Indeed, he envisions a sort of mirror of the United States, complete with a president and a congress.

Tecumseh no doubt believed that he was making his vision of a greater Indian nation a reality through his constant tours of the various Indian tribes that, in general, received him favorably. The local chiefs and communities of elders agreed to support him in time of war, but the fact is that the Indians lacked the political infrastructure to carry out Tecumseh's vision. Whatever enthusiasm Tecumseh generated through his presence in a village, local leaders had little power to do more than agree to fight under his leadership if he came to defend their particular community should the Americans attack. In the end, Tecumseh could do no more than a traditional war chief and convince individual warriors that it was in their own interest to fight for him.

When war came in 1812, Tecumseh proved far less successful in attracting followers than his mentor Blue Jacket had been in the early 1790s. This was thanks in no small part to Harrison's destroying with impunity Tenskwatawa and Tecumseh's settlement of Prophetstown, on the Tippecanoe River in northern Indiana, on November 7, 1811. Tenskwatawa had promised his followers that their new faith would make them immune to American bullets, but they were easily crushed by Harrison's force. Tecumseh was never able to mobilize whole tribes, let alone all of the tribes of the Northwest, to fight the Americans, and no meeting of his great council to do away with the village chiefs ever came about. Tecumseh ultimately could speak not for a unified Indian nation in the Northwest but only, as he had to admit

Battle of the Thames and the death of Tecumseh (Library of Congress)

to Harrison, for "all the red people that listen to me." In any case, no Indian confederacy that could not at least manufacture its own gunpowder could have realistically hoped for any but the most fleeting victories against the advance of an industrial nation like the United States.

◆ Speech to Major General Henry Procter at Fort Malden

In August 1812 Tecumseh and his war band joined the British against the United States in the War of 1812. For a time the war was going well for Great Britain and its allies in the Old Northwest. Ironically, the Potawatomi chief Winnemac, who had often seemed to favor the Americans over the British and had been a political enemy of Tecumseh's, now fought with him as a British ally. But after initially capturing Detroit and for a time outmaneuvering Harrison, the British and Tecumseh were eventually forced out of that city and driven back to Ontario. In the early fall of 1813 they camped at Fort Malden, the Canadian base of the British Great Lakes squadron, with an American force approaching while being harassed every step of the way by Tecumseh's followers. By then, relations between Tecumseh and the British had become very tense. Tecumseh concluded that he had to make a public address to the new British commander Major General Henry Procter rather than speak to him privately. The motive for such an action was probably to demonstrate to his own followers that he was acting in their interest in his dealings with the British.

The text of this speech was first published in 1813 in a Washington, D.C., newspaper, the *National Intelligencer*, with a note saying it had been found among Procter's papers after his defeat by American forces. The language Tecumseh uses is simple and direct. He refers to Procter as his and his people's "father" and they as Procter's "children." He recites a litany of British betrayals of the Indians, dating back to the Battle of Fallen Timbers (1794), and airs complaints that Procter did not share intelligence and decision making with him. He notes that the Indians had been defeated earlier, as had the British, and he worries that just as the British had once made peace with the Americans ("took them by the hand"), they will do so again. The British at times had intervened to restrain Tecumseh's actions until the allied groups could act in concert. When they had incited the Indians to war ("gave the hatchet" to them), the British had promised to restore Indiana and Ohio to the native peoples ("get us our lands back, which the Americans had taken from us"). Now, however, Tecumseh laments that Harrison's army had driven them back to Canada, past any point where the British could conceivably protect the families of their Indian allies. Tecumseh knew that the British Great Lakes squadron had recently fought a battle on Lake Erie. But Procter told Tecumseh nothing about its outcome and seemed to be preparing to abandon the fleet's base to the advancing Americans. As Tecumseh puts it, "Our ships have gone one way, and we are much astonished to see our father tying up everything and preparing to run away the other, without letting his red children know what his intentions are."

Tecumseh chastises Procter for his apparent plans to withdraw. He reminds Procter that the general promised that he "would never draw [his] foot off British ground" but laments that Procter is now "drawing back" without "seeing the enemy." He summarizes his assessment of Procter's conduct of the war with characteristic humor: "We must compare our father's conduct to a fat animal that carries its tail upon its back, but when affrighted it drops it between its legs and runs off." In his concluding remarks, Tecumseh asks the general to leave behind the arms that had been promised to the Indians, for, he says, "We are determined to defend our lands, and if it is His will we wish to leave our bones upon them."

Tecumseh was correct to be suspicious of his British partner. In fact, Procter knew by this time that the British squadron had been destroyed; he was anxious to retreat because he feared American landings to his company's rear. However, since Tecumseh made clear in his speech that he and his Indian followers would desert unless the British stood and offered battle to the Americans, Procter decided to give them what they wanted. In that sense, Tecumseh's speech achieved its purposes: forcing the British to make the strategic decisions he wanted and reassuring his followers that he was still independent of the British and acting on their behalf. But Procter used the battle to punish Tecumseh for what he considered rebelliousness. Accepting battle on the Thames River on October 5, he stationed Tecumseh and his Indians in a screen in front of his British troops and the Canadian militia, to withdraw once they were engaged by the Americans, leaving the Indians to be slaughtered and Tecumseh killed. This action was too reprehensible for the British government, and Procter was court-martialed and relieved of duty. The remainder of Tecumseh's war band made a formal surrender to the Americans at Detroit a few days later.

Impact and Legacy

Tecumseh has been badly served in being presented to modern readers through nineteenth-century American and British eyes. His speeches were shaped by their reporters into the forms of popular American rhetoric of the day. Students of history can never trust that what was recorded is very close to what he said. Tecumseh is cast as a hero—even an American hero—by his enemies. He is regularly described as being handsome and, in particular, light skinned and more refined in his features than most Indians. True or not, these details have been signals to American readers that Tecumseh was a sort of noble savage, fit to be admired by American society as a valorous enemy and even a role model of fairness and justice.

The American historian's urge to present Tecumseh in this light calls into question many anecdotes. For instance, during the fighting in early 1813, when the British and Tecumseh still had the upper hand, Tecumseh ambushed

and captured an American regiment near Fort Meigs. He personally intervened to stop his followers from slaughtering American prisoners and then criticized British officers who had failed to do so. The story may be true, but it was reported mainly because of its heroic portrayal of Tecumseh's honor. From the viewpoint of correctly assessing Tecumseh's place in history, his efforts to organize the tribes of the Old Northwest into a confederacy, modeled as far as they went on his understanding of the United States, allowed contemporary American writers to cast him as a sort of native George Washington, struggling to unify and defend his country and founding a new nation—an image from the sources that cannot now be easily separated from reality. Harrison himself described Tecumseh as "one of those uncommon geniuses which spring up occasionally to produce revolutions and overturn the established order of things" (Calloway, p. 127), directly inviting a comparison to the leader of the American Revolution.

Spiritually, Tecumseh is presented by American writers as a deist, in accord with the form of religion common among the educated elite Americans of his time, holding that God does not intervene in history and is not to be approached through revealed religion. In his preserved speech to Harrison, Tecumseh merely claims, "The Great Spirit has inspired me, and I speak nothing but the truth to you," in order to guarantee the veracity of his statements. In the speech to Procter he uses the phrase "our lives are in the hand of the Great Spirit" as a metaphor meaning that the outcome of battle is uncertain. This is the same way that Washington, Thomas Jefferson, and Thomas Paine spoke about God. The ideal Tecumseh presented in the sources is, like those American figures, rational and modern in his detachment from superstition. Tecumseh's brother Tenskwatawa, in contrast, is presented as a religious fanatic, a drunken Indian deceived by alcoholic delusions into believing he had visions, and a coward and an incompetent besides. These archetypes must be understood as projections of American ideas and beliefs onto Indians as the "other," receptive to whatever mold American observers wished to employ. The legacy of Tecumseh is an image of every virtue nineteenth-century America admired (as evidenced, for instance, by the naming of the future Civil War general William Tecumseh Sherman and of several American warships after him), creating a giant in whose shadow the real Tecumseh is obscured.

Key Sources

Tecumseh's oratory is reflected in three important documentary collections, none of which, however, represents versions of his speeches as they were actually delivered or as he might have prepared them for publication. In fact, the two most important sources for Tecumseh are the military, diplomatic, and political records kept by his enemies, the Americans, and his never very loyal or sympathetic allies, the British. Harrison's dispatches to Washington concerning Tecumseh are collected among his general papers as governor of the Indiana Territory and have been edited by Logan Esarey, as *Messages and Letters of William Henry Harrison* (1922; rpt. 1975). The correspondence of British officers concerning Tecumseh and the records of Procter's court-martial are kept in the War Office section of the National Archives in London; these documents have not been published. Another unpublished collection is the Lyman C. Draper Manuscript Collection held by the State Historical Society in Madison, Wisconsin. This collection grew in the 1840s from Draper's personal interest in the history of the Old Northwest and includes any relevant documents he was able to copy, along with interviews and letters solicited from surviving eyewitnesses to the period's history, including many Indians who knew and even fought under Tecumseh, most of whom had by then been transported to the designated Indian Territory (Oklahoma). This collection has not yet been digitized, but many research libraries hold microfilm copies of it. Reels 118–120 contain documents

Essential Quotes

"You have taken our land from us, and I do not see how we can remain at peace if you continue to do so."

(Speech to Governor William Henry Harrison at Fort Vincennes)

"You want, by your distinctions of Indian tribes in allotting to each a particular tract of land, to make them to war with each other. You never see an Indian come and endeavor to make the white people do so."

(Speech to Governor William Henry Harrison at Fort Vincennes)

"Everything I have said to you is the truth. The Great Sprit has inspired me, and I speak nothing but the truth to you."

(Speech to Governor William Henry Harrison at Fort Vincennes)

"Our ships have gone one way, and we are much astonished to see our father tying up everything and preparing to run away the other, without letting his red children know what his intentions are."

(Speech to Major General Henry Procter at Fort Malden)

"We must compare our father's conduct to a fat animal that carries its tail upon its back, but when affrighted it drops it between its legs and runs off."

(Speech to Major General Henry Procter at Fort Malden)

"For us, our lives are in the hands of the Great Spirit. We are determined to defend our lands, and if it is His will we wish to leave our bones upon them."

(Speech to Major General Henry Procter at Fort Malden)

directly dealing with Tecumseh, but no index exists listing any mentions of him elsewhere in the collection.

Further Reading

■ Articles
Bluff, Rachel. "Tecumseh and Tenskwatawa: Myth, Historiography and Popular Memory." *Historical Reflections* 21 (1995): 277–299.

Edmunds, R. David. "Tecumseh, the Shawnee Prophet, and American History: A Reassessment." *Western Historical Quarterly* 14, no. 3 (July 1983): 261–276.

■ Books
Calloway, Colin G. *The Shawnees and the War for America.* New York: Viking, 2007.

Cave, Alfred A. *Prophets of the Great Spirit: Native American Revitalization Movements in Eastern North America.* Lincoln: University of Nebraska Press, 2006.

Dowd, Gregory Evans. *A Spirited Resistance: The North American Indian Struggle for Unity, 1745–1815.* Baltimore: Johns Hopkins University Press, 1992.

Eggleston, Edward. *Tecumseh and the Shawnee Prophet.* New York: Dodd, Mead, 1878.

Klinck, Carl F., ed. *Tecumseh: Fact and Fiction in Early Records: A Book of Primary Source Materials.* Englewood Cliffs, N.J.: Prentice-Hall, 1961.

Sugden, John. *Tecumseh: A Life.* New York: Henry Holt, 1998.

Turner, Frederick W., III, ed. *The Portable North American Indian Reader.* 3rd ed. New York: Viking Press, 1986.

■ Web Sites
"Techumseh." Ohio History Central Web site. http://www.ohiohistorycentral.org/entry.php?rec=373.

—Bradley A. Skeen

Questions for Further Study

1. Examine the approach Tecumseh applied in his speeches to William Henry Harrison in 1810 and Major General Henry Procter in 1813, including both his tone and the manner of his delivery. What does it say about his negotiation style that, in the case of the Harrison speech, he adopted a line of discussion other than that which he had been expected to take or that he opted to deliver a public speech directed at Procter rather than engage in a private discussion? Would he have been more or less likely to achieve his purposes if he had taken a more accommodating approach in each case?

2. A key factor in negotiations between Native American leaders and the federal government was the issue of "presents," products of white industry that provided U.S. officials with a powerful means of influencing chiefs. To what extent was the use of "presents" unfair, and to what extent was it simply a reflection of reality—an advantage that the whites would have been foolish not to employ? How much were Indian chiefs to blame for this situation, and what was Tecumseh's view of the subject?

3. Discuss Tecumseh's relationship with his brother Lalawethika, who renamed himself Tenskwatawa after receiving a putative spiritual revelation that led to the establishment of a new religion. What were the central aspects of this new faith, and how did they serve Tecumseh's aims? What were Tecumseh's own spiritual views, and how were these influenced by his brother's teachings? Evaluate Tenskwatawa in terms of his sincerity or lack thereof: Was he a madman, a charlatan, or a true believer?

4. Consider the question of Tecumseh's place within the history of the United States. How did his admirers—including his enemies—recast him in the role of a distinctly American hero, and how would Tecumseh, who continually pursued a policy of separation from the whites, have viewed this adulation? On the other hand, how much was he a product of the white culture he despised? Most notably, how were his ideas on the organization and direction of the Native American peoples modeled on the principles of the U.S. system?

SPEECH TO GOVERNOR WILLIAM HENRY HARRISON AT FORT VINCENNES (1810)

Brother: I wish you to listen to me well. As I think you do not clearly understand what I before said to you, I will explain it again....

Brother, since the peace was made, you have killed some of the Shawnees, Winnebagoes, Delawares, and Miamis, and you have taken our land from us, and I do not see how we can remain at peace if you continue to do so. You try to force the red people to do some injury. It is you that are pushing them on to do mischief. You endeavor to make distinctions. You wish to prevent the Indians doing as we wish them—to unite, and let them consider their lands as the common property of the whole; you take tribes aside and advise them not to come into this measure; and until our design is accomplished we do not wish to accept of your invitation to go and see the President. The reason I tell you this, you want, by your distinctions of Indian tribes in allotting to each a particular tract of land, to make them to war with each other. You never see an Indian come and endeavor to make the white people do so. You are continually driving the red people; when, at last, you will drive them into the Great Lake, where they can't either stand or walk.

Brother, you ought to know what you are doing with the Indians. Perhaps it is by direction of the President to make those distinctions. It is a very bad thing, and we do not like it. Since my residence at Tippecanoe we have endeavored to level all distinctions—to destroy village chiefs, by whom all mischief is done. It is they who sell our lands to the Americans. Our object is to let our affairs be transacted by warriors.

Brother, this land that was sold and the goods that were given for it were only done by a few. The treaty was afterwards brought here, and the Weas were induced to give their consent because of their small numbers. The treaty at Fort Wayne was made through the threats of Winnemac; but in future we are prepared to punish those chiefs who may come forward to propose to sell the land. If you continue to purchase of them it will produce war among the different tribes, and at last, I do not know what will be the consequence to the white people.

Brother, I was glad to hear your speech. You said that if we could show that the land was sold by people that had no right to sell, you would restore it. Those that did sell did not own it. It was me. These tribes set up a claim, but the tribes with me will not agree with their claim. If the land is not restored to us you will see, when we return to our homes, how it will be settled. We shall have a great council, at which all the tribes will be present, when we shall show to those who sold that they had no right to the claim that they set up; and we will see what will be done to those chiefs that did sell the land to you. I am not alone in this determination; it is the determination of all the warriors and red people that listen to me. I now wish you to listen to me. If you do not, it will appear as if you wished me to kill all the chiefs that sold you the land. I tell you so because I am authorized by all the tribes to do so. I am the head of them all; I am a warrior, and all the warriors will meet together in two or three moons from this; then I will call for those chiefs that sold you the land and shall know what to do with them. If you do not restore the land, you will have a hand in killing them.

Brother, do not believe that I came here to get presents from you. If you offer us any, we will not take. By taking goods from you, you will hereafter say that with them you purchased another piece of land from us.... It has been the object of both myself and brother to prevent the lands being sold. Should you not return the land, it will occasion us to call a great council that will meet at the Huron village, where the council-fire has already been lighted, at which those who sold the lands shall be called, and shall suffer for their conduct.

Brother, I wish you would take pity on the red people and do what I have requested. If you will not give up the land and do cross the boundary of your present settlement, it will be very hard, and produce great troubles among us. How can we have confidence in the white people? When Jesus Christ came on earth, you killed him and nailed him on a cross. You thought he was dead, but you were mistaken. You have Shakers among you, and you laugh and make light of their worship. Everything I have said to you is the truth. The Great Spirit has inspired me, and I speak nothing but the truth to you.... Brother, I hope you will confess that you ought not to have listened to those bad birds who bring you bad news. I have declared myself freely to you, and if any explanation should be required from our town, send a man who can speak to us. If you think proper to give us any presents, and we can be convinced that they are given through friendship alone, we will accept them. As we intend to hold our council at the Huron village, that is near the British, we may probably make them a visit. Should they offer us any presents of goods, we will not take them; but should they offer us powder and the tomahawk, we will take the powder and refuse the tomahawk. I wish you, brother, to consider everything I have said as true, and that it is the sentiment of all the red people that listen to me.

Glossary

Shakers	members of a Protestant religious group, more formally the United Society of Believers in Christ's Second Appearing, so called because their worship included emotional singing, dancing, shaking, and trembling
Tippecanoe	the name of a county in Indiana where the Battle of Tippecanoe was fought between Harrison and Tecumseh's forces on November 7, 1811
Winnemac	a Potawatomi chief who persuaded the Potawatomi and the Miami Indian tribes to agree to the Treaty of Fort Wayne

SPEECH TO MAJOR GENERAL HENRY PROCTER AT FORT MALDEN (1813)

FATHER, listen to your children! you have them now all before you. The war before this, our British father gave the hatchet to his red children when old chiefs were alive. They are now dead. In that war our father was thrown on his back by the Americans, and our father took them by the hand without our knowledge; and we are afraid that our father will do so again at this time.

Summer before last, when I came forward with my red brethren and was ready to take up the hatchet in favor of our British father, we were told not to be in a hurry; that he had not yet determined to fight the Americans.

Listen! When war was declared, our father stood up and gave us the tomahawk, and told us that he was ready to strike the Americans; that he wanted our assistance, and that he would certainly get us our lands back, which the Americans had taken from us.

Listen! You told us at that time to bring forward our families to this place, and we did so; and you promised to take care of them, and that they should want for nothing while the men would go and fight the enemy. That we need not trouble ourselves about the enemy's garrisons; that we knew nothing about them, and that our father would attend to that part of the business. You also told your red children that you would take good care of your garrison here, which made our hearts glad.

Listen! When we were last at the Rapids, it is true we gave you little assistance. It is hard to fight people who live like ground-hogs.

Father, listen! Our fleet has gone out; we know they have fought; we have heard the great guns, but know nothing of what has happened to our father with one arm. Our ships have gone one way, and we are much astonished to see our father tying up everything and preparing to run away the other, without letting his red children know what his intentions are. You always told us to remain here and take care of our lands. It made our hearts glad to hear that was your wish. Our great father, the king, is the head, and you represent him. You always told us that you would never draw your foot off British ground; but now, father, we see you are drawing back, and we are sorry to see our father doing so without seeing the enemy. We must compare our father's conduct to a fat animal that carries its tail upon its back, but when affrighted it drops it between its legs and runs off.

Listen, father! The Americans have not yet defeated us by land; neither are we sure that they have done so by water; we therefore wish to remain here and fight our enemy should they make their appearance. If they defeat us, we will then retreat with our father.

At the Battle of the Rapids, last war, the Americans certainly defeated us; and when we retreated to our fathers fort in that place the gates were shut against us. We were afraid that it would now be the case, but instead of that we now see our British father preparing to march out of his garrison.

Father! You have got the arms and ammunition which our great father sent for his red children. If you have an idea of going away, give them to us, and you may go and welcome; for us, our lives are in the hands of the Great Spirit. We are determined to defend our lands, and if it is His will we wish to leave our bones upon them.

Glossary

Battle of the Rapids	reference to the rapids of the Maumee River in Ohio and an alternate name for the Battle of Fallen Timbers that took place on August 20, 1794
British father	the British king, George III, at the time of both the American Revolution and the War of 1812

Strom Thurmond (AP/Wide World Photos)

STROM THURMOND   1902–2003

Governor and U.S. Senator

Featured Documents
◆ Keynote Address at the States' Rights Democratic Conference (1948)
◆ Southern Manifesto (1956)

Overview

Born on December 5, 1902, in Edgefield, South Carolina, James Strom Thurmond would serve in the U.S. Senate for nearly fifty years, from 1954 to 2003. Beginning his career in education, Thurmond went on to practice law. He then served in the South Carolina Senate and also the state's judiciary. During World War II, he served as a lieutenant colonel in the U.S. Army, rising to the rank of major general in the reserve force. Following the war, he won the 1946 South Carolina gubernatorial election as a Democrat, to serve from 1947 to 1951. In 1948 Thurmond ran for president of the United States on the ticket of the States' Rights Democratic Party, known as the Dixiecrats, in protest of President Harry Truman's position on civil rights. Thurmond next sought a seat in the U.S. Senate from South Carolina, but after losing his first bid for the office in 1950, he went on to complete his term as governor and then practiced law from 1951 through 1955. In 1952 he broke with the Democratic Party by endorsing Dwight D. Eisenhower, the Republican Party's candidate for president. In retaliation, the Democrats in South Carolina ensured his primary loss in the race for the U.S. Senate in 1954. Thurmond responded, however, by winning the seat through a write-in campaign. He took office early when he was appointed senator following the resignation of Charles E. Daniel, whom he had defeated in the election. Thurmond duly served until his promised resignation in 1956, but he won back the seat in a special election to fill the vacancy that he left. Thurmond was then repeatedly reelected to the Senate, serving until January 2003. He died a few months later, on June 26, 2003.

Thurmond was the first national figure in the post–World War II era to oppose integration. After taking office as governor of South Carolina in 1947, Thurmond increasingly turned his attention to the growing civil rights agenda of the Truman administration. In 1946 he had opposed the establishment of the President's Committee on Civil Rights. In December 1947 the committee produced a civil rights report titled *To Secure These Rights*, which then shaped much of Truman's agenda. In 1948 the U.S. district court judge Julius Waties Waring ordered the state of South Carolina to allow African Americans to vote in primary elections. In all, these civil rights developments persuaded Thurmond to mount a national campaign to preserve segregation in the South. Joining like-minded southern politicians in Jackson, Mississippi, in May 1948, Thurmond delivered a speech to the States' Rights Democratic Conference. He attended the Democratic National Convention held in Philadelphia in July 1948, but later that month he accepted the nomination to run for president of the United States on the States' Rights Democratic Party ticket. This provided Thurmond and other southern politicians who opposed integration with a national platform, even though Truman won the election for the presidency.

During the 1950s Thurmond fully launched his political career as a staunch defender of states' rights. After losing his first run for the U.S. Senate in 1950, Thurmond went on to win a seat in the U.S. Senate in 1954 through a write-in campaign. In 1956 Thurmond successfully led an effort to produce what became known as the Southern Manifesto. This document was signed by all southern senators except the majority leader Lyndon B. Johnson (Texas), Estes Kefauver (Tennessee), and Albert Gore, Sr. (Tennessee). The Southern Manifesto proclaimed the "clear abuse of judicial power" of the U.S. Supreme Court in *Brown v. Board of Education* (1954). Thurmond continued in his leadership role opposing integration in the name of states' rights by setting a filibuster record during Senate debates on the 1957 civil rights bill.

Thurmond solidified his movement away from Democratic positions on civil rights by switching parties in 1964, officially declaring his new political affiliation with the Republican Party and campaigning for Barry Goldwater, the party's presidential candidate. In 1968 Thurmond published a book titled *The Faith We Have Not Kept*, which summarized his conservative positions on law and order, values and morals, and the cold war against Communism, effectively outlining the conservative agenda for decades to come. In 1968 Thurmond played an important role in the "southern strategy" used by Richard Nixon to win the presidential election.

Thurmond continued to serve South Carolina and conservative America in the U.S. Senate until 2003. During the intervening years, he shifted his views on segregation and civil rights to more supportive positions, yet he maintained his strong support of states' rights in opposition to federalism. He also continued to lead the nation in matters of national defense. In 1998 Congress passed Public Law 105-261, entitled the Strom Thurmond National Defense Authorization Act for Fiscal Year 1999; members of Congress named the act in honor of Thurmond's many years of distinguished service in the military and as a member of the Senate Armed Services Committee. Overall, as a southern-

Time Line

1902
- **December 5**
  James Strom Thurmond is born in Edgefield, South Carolina.

1923
- Thurmond graduates from South Carolina's Clemson Agricultural College (now Clemson University), majoring in horticulture.

1929
- Thurmond is appointed superintendent of Edgefield County schools.

1930
- Thurmond is admitted to the bar in South Carolina and becomes Edgefield's town and county attorney.

1933
- Thurmond is elected to the South Carolina Senate.

1938
- Thurmond becomes a South Carolina circuit court judge.

1942
- Thurmond serves in World War II as a lieutenant colonel, eventually rising to major general in the U.S. Army Reserve.

1947
- **January 21**
  Thurmond takes office as governor of South Carolina.

1948
- **May 10**
  At the States' Rights Democratic Conference in Jackson, Mississippi, Thurmond delivers the keynote address.

- **November 2**
  Running for president from the States' Rights Democratic Party, Thurmond loses to Harry Truman.

1954
- **December 24**
  Having won a write-in campaign for the South Carolina seat, Thurmond is appointed to the U.S. Senate to replace the resigning Charles E. Daniel.

er who maintained steadfast antagonism to civil rights for decades, Thurmond long reflected the region and era in which he came to political prominence.

Explanation and Analysis of Documents

Thurmond emerged as a national political leader following World War II, in which the United States led a successful effort against racism in Europe and similar extremism in Asia. Thurmond fought in the war, yet unlike many of his fellow veterans, he then led efforts to preserve the societal status quo in the South based upon racial theories of white supremacy. This status quo depended upon the separation of the races through "Jim Crow" segregation laws written into state constitutions and local codes. In reaction to the civil rights agenda set by the Truman administration, Thurmond delivered a keynote address in May 1948 to like-minded southerners meeting at the States' Rights Democratic Conference in Jackson, Mississippi. Thurmond emerged from the conference as the party's presidential candidate and thus the spokesperson for states' rights, particularly the perceived right to preserve segregation in the South. Following his unsuccessful run for the presidency, Thurmond won a seat in the U.S. Senate, where he took up the mantle of states' rights and spearheaded massive resistance to complying with the 1954 U.S. Supreme Court decision in *Brown v. Board of Education*. Thurmond wrote drafts and collaborated with southern colleagues in the Senate on a document that became known as the Southern Manifesto. The broad resistance to the *Brown* decision delayed integration of the nation's schools for years to come.

◆ Keynote Address at the States' Rights Democratic Conference

In 1948 the nation saw growing opposition to President Truman's civil rights agenda, especially in the South. Emerging as the leader of southern resistance to Truman and his agenda, Thurmond essentially led a revolt against the president and the Democratic Party, with the States' Rights Democratic Party he represented, better known as the Dixiecrats, intending to preserve the right of states to maintain segregation. The Truman administration faced an additional revolt from the left in the Democratic Party with the candidacy of Henry Wallace, who was running for president on the Progressive Party ticket. Strong opposition also came from Thomas E. Dewey, the Republican Party candidate. Thurmond delivered his keynote speech to the States' Rights Democratic Conference on May 10, 1948.

Thurmond took the opportunity in his keynote speech to outline age-old grievances held by southerners against perceived northern domination in all three branches of the federal government. He points out the responsibility of the Democratic Party to protect the constitutional government, especially as outlined in the reserved powers clause found in the Tenth Amendment. In essence, Thurmond argues the case for the right of states to challenge laws emanating from the federal government and in particular from the executive branch, then under the control of the Democratic Party and the Truman administration. He states, "We are going to fight, as long as we have breath, for the rights of our states and our people under the American Constitution; and come what may, we are going to preserve our civilization in the South." He goes on to point out how the South had suffered during the years following the Civil War. In essence, he describes the South as emerging from the Civil War as an economic and social colony of the North. Specifically, he points to the freight-rate battles fought between railroads and southern farmers through the Interstate Commerce Commission. The nation's two sections are described as having developed a "crown colony" relationship, with the South providing "raw materials for the industrial East." Thurmond uses all of this background to frame the present-day grievances of the South against a federal government claimed to be dominated by northerners, an assertion many southerners believed. He does concede that the freight-rate battle was won by the southerners in 1947. Nonetheless, he uses this history to demonstrate the forced economic dependency of the South on the industrial North, as established through cripplingly high freight rates and tariffs.

It was clear to Thurmond that Truman was using civil rights as a pretext to continue "Federal encroachment on state sovereignty." Thurmond did not understand why people in other sections of the country did not stand up against proposed legislation by the Truman administration. If civil rights were to be enacted, Thurmond believed all rights would be threatened no matter where people lived, North or South. In his defense of states' rights, Thurmond cites George Washington's farewell address, Thomas Jefferson's first inaugural address, and even a statement by Franklin D. Roosevelt.

In the ensuing portion of his keynote address, Thurmond outlines specific areas under attack by the federal government and the Truman administration. He points to the anti–poll tax law, stating,

> We all know that the poll tax does not burden the right to vote. It is a minor revenue measure yielding comparatively little money, and I have advocated that we repeal it in my State. Only seven states now have a poll-tax voting requirement, and the proposed Federal law would accomplish so little that many think it harmless legislation.

The real danger, he says, is "the Congressional assertion of the right to pass this law." Such congressional intervention, he asserts, threatens states' rights, which are protected in the Tenth Amendment. With the precedent of the poll tax ban, Congress could then "exercise control over the ballot boxes of the Nation." Invoking images of the military occupation of the South during Reconstruction, he predicts the use of the military to enforce federal laws governing the states' rightful domain of voting and suffrage.

Next, Thurmond addresses proposed federal antilynching legislation. "The Federal government does not have the

Thurmond, Strom

Time Line

1956

■ **March 12**
Walter F. George, senator from Georgia, reads the Declaration of Constitutional Principles, better known as the Southern Manifesto, into the *Congressional Record*, as based upon drafts written by Thurmond in opposition to *Brown v. Board of Education* (1954).

■ **April 4**
Thurmond resigns from the U.S. Senate, having promised this to the voters from South Carolina.

■ **November 7**
After being specially reelected to fill the vacancy that he created, Thurmond resumes his seat in the Senate.

1957

■ **August 29**
Thurmond sets the Senate record for filibustering, speaking for twenty-four hours and eighteen minutes in his opposition to the pending Civil Rights Act of 1957.

1964

■ **September 16**
Thurmond switches his political affiliation from the Democratic Party to the Republican Party.

1968

■ Thurmond assists Richard M. Nixon in formulating his "southern strategy," used in his successful run for the U.S. presidency.

1970

■ Thurmond appoints Thomas Moss to his staff, becoming the first southern member of Congress to hire an African American.

1998

■ **October 17**
Congress passes Public Law 105-261, naming the National Defense Authorization Act for Fiscal Year 1999 in honor of Strom Thurmond.

Time Line

2003

■ **January 3**
Thurmond leaves the U.S. Senate, having not run for reelection.

■ **June 26**
Thurmond dies at the age of one hundred in Edgefield, South Carolina.

constitutional right to deal with crimes occurring within the states" he says. He points out that all states have laws against murder and that some specifically address lynching. Thurmond goes so far as to declare that antilynching laws are unnecessary because "enlightened public opinion" has sufficiently stopped the crime. He then claims that Congress would nonetheless take advantage of emotions stemming from the horror of such crimes to "assert the power to deal with any crime within the states," thereby radically invading local authority.

The other pending dangers to states' rights, according to Thurmond, are agencies and commissions that create laws by fiat, yet he fails to recognize that the freight-rate problems that he pointed to earlier in his speech were settled by one of these commissions, the Interstate Commerce Commission. Nevertheless, he uses this agency as a symbol of federal intervention into race relations within the South, in particular through laws governing segregation. He states,

> We in the South know that the laws dealing with the separation of the races are necessary to maintain the public peace and order, where the races live side by side in large numbers. We know that they are essential to the racial integrity and purity of the white and Negro races alike.

He is alarmed by the creation of a "Federal police system to enforce" Truman's civil rights program. Advocating the status quo, he remarks, "We are working and living side by side in peace and understanding." In so doing, Thurmond tells his audience, "We are struggling together for a bigger and better South, with greater educational and economic opportunity for all of our citizens, regardless of race, creed, or color."

Thurmond encourages his audience to attend the Democratic National Convention to exercise their rights by choosing a presidential candidate who would represent their own interests in states' rights. If the Democratic Party failed to nominate such a candidate, he says, then "the Electoral College affords us a powerful weapon to restore the prestige of the South in the political affairs of this Nation and preserve the American system of free constitutional government." In a portentous statement, he asks his listeners to vote for others who would protect state sovereignty if the Democrats did not select a presidential candidate who would do so.

Thurmond and other southern Democratic leaders indeed attended the Democratic National Convention from July 12 to 14, 1948; a number walked out after Hubert Humphrey sought to shift the party's focus away from states' rights. Delegates nominated Truman as the party's presidential candidate, and many southern Democrats met in protest on July 17 in a separate convention to select Thurmond to run for president from the States' Rights Democratic Party. Unexpectedly—as amid the competition Dewey, the Republican, seemed poised for victory—Truman managed to win the 1948 presidential election.

◆ **Southern Manifesto**

In 1954 the U.S. Supreme Court rendered its decision in *Brown v. Board of Education*, ruling that "in the field of public education, the doctrine of 'separate but equal' has no place." The Court asserted that "separate educational facilities are inherently unequal" and ordered the end of segregation in the public schools. The *Brown* decision in many ways rejuvenated Thurmond's run for the U.S. Senate in South Carolina. He pointed to his opposition of the decision and gained support from the state's branches of the White Citizens' Council, an organization formed throughout the South in opposition to *Brown*. The council was inspired by the earlier Dixiecrat movement, opposed to the encroachment of the federal government on the domain of the states in enforcing legislation passed to achieve civil rights. Claiming state sovereignty, the White Citizens' Council clamored for political action to stop integration. Nonetheless, in 1955, the Court stated that integration must occur "with all deliberate speed." Soon after his arrival in Washington, D.C., Senator Thurmond took up the mantle of states' rights, as he challenged the Court's ruling on the integration of public education and immediately began drafting a response to the *Brown* decision. Walter F. George, from Georgia, introduced this Declaration of Constitutional Principles, also called the Southern Manifesto, to the U.S. Senate on March 12, 1956. Although other southern senators contributed to the document, the essence of the states' rights manifesto remained Thurmond's.

The Southern Manifesto declares opposition to what nineteen senators and seventy-seven members of the House of Representatives believed to have been "the unwarranted decision of the Supreme Court in the public school cases." The essence of their argument revolved around the Tenth Amendment to the U.S. Constitution. Thurmond and other members of Congress argued that the U.S. Constitution did not mention education, and neither did the Fourteenth Amendment, upon which the *Brown* argument is said, incorrectly, to have relied. Through the Southern Manifesto, Thurmond and his southern allies declare,

> Though there has been no constitutional amendment or act of Congress changing this established legal principle almost a century old, the Supreme Court of the United States, with no legal basis for such action, undertook to exercise their naked judicial power and substituted their personal political and social ideas for the established law of the land.

"We in the South know that the laws dealing with the separation of the races are necessary to maintain the public peace and order, where the races live side by side in large numbers. We know that they are essential to the racial integrity and purity of the white and Negro races alike."

(Keynote Address at the States' Rights Democratic Conference)

"One of the most astounding theories ever advanced is that the Federal government by passing a law can force the white people of the South to accept into their businesses, their schools, their places of amusement, and in other public places, those they do not want to accept."

(Keynote Address at the States' Rights Democratic Conference)

"We know, and the enemies of state sovereignty know, that the Electoral College affords us a powerful weapon to restore the prestige of the South in the political affairs of this Nation and preserve the American system of free constitutional government."

(Keynote Address at the States' Rights Democratic Conference)

"We regard the decisions of the Supreme Court in the school cases as a clear abuse of judicial power. It climaxes a trend in the Federal Judiciary undertaking to legislate, in derogation of the authority of Congress, and to encroach upon the reserved rights of the States and the people."

(Southern Manifesto)

"Though there has been no constitutional amendment or act of Congress changing this established legal principle almost a century old, the Supreme Court of the United States, with no legal basis for such action, undertook to exercise their naked judicial power and substituted their personal political and social ideas for the established law of the land."

(Southern Manifesto)

"We pledge ourselves to use all lawful means to bring about a reversal of this decision which is contrary to the Constitution and to prevent the use of force in its implementation."

(Southern Manifesto)

The congressmen add that because of this "unwarranted exercise of power by the Court," irreparable damage is being done to race relations between whites and blacks in the South. The Court, they argue, "has planted hatred and suspicion where there has been heretofore friendship and understanding." They go on to assert, "Without regard to the consent of the governed, outside mediators are threatening immediate and revolutionary changes in our public schools systems." The Southern Manifesto then warns, "If done, this is certain to destroy the system of public education in some of the States." To preserve the rule of law and the Constitution, Thurmond and the document's other signatories declare that they would "resist forced integration by any lawful means." They understood that they were a minority in Congress, but they remained confident that they represented the "majority of the American people" who would oppose the "judicial usurpation" of the "reserved rights of the States and of the people."

Thurmond and the others who endorsed the Southern Manifesto led a decade-long challenge to the integration of public education in the country. The southern strategy of massive state-level resistance came in the form of delays through court challenges and violent intimidation in its more extreme forms. Thus, the Southern Manifesto accurately outlined the challenges that would delay the implementation of the *Brown* decision, emphasizing deliberation and persistence.

Impact and Legacy

The impact of Thurmond's articulation of states' rights during the civil rights struggle of the mid-twentieth century was dramatic. Thurmond formulated a strategy of southern resistance to the claimed federal power to introduce and enforce civil rights legislation protecting minorities and their rights over states' rights, which often threatened them. He based his modern theory of states' rights on the theories of Thomas Jefferson and James Madison established in the Kentucky and Virginia Resolutions, which were responses to what the authors deemed tyrannical powers of the federal government. Thurmond also refined John C. Calhoun's theory of state nullification of federal legislation into what he described in the Southern Manifesto as legitimate interposition over the *Brown* decision, opposing the "judicial usurpation" of "the rights reserved to the States and to the people, contrary to established law, and to the Constitution." Thurmond and the allied southern congressmen vowed in that document to resist the implementation of the *Brown* decision by any legal means.

Thurmond continued to adhere to his theory of interposition by employing the filibuster to challenge the passage of the Civil Rights Act of 1957; in so doing, he set a record that still stands in the U.S. Senate. Thurmond eventually concluded that the Democratic Party had abandoned him

Questions for Further Study

1. Examine the historical arguments Thurmond makes, both in his address to the States' Rights Democratic Conference and in the Southern Manifesto, regarding alleged northern oppression of the South. What are his key points, and what facts does he present to support them? How justifiable is his contention that the South had been victimized by the North, and how does he use that putative victimization to support his positions on states' rights and segregation?

2. In both of the documents presented here, Thurmond employs a line of reasoning familiar to many southerners: the idea that theirs is a unique region with its own way of life and that meddling outsiders could only cause harm by attempting to impose solutions on its racial problems. In fact, Thurmond—in another argument often employed by southern segregationists of the time—claimed that there was no problem between the races in the South and that northern interference could only strain otherwise peaceful relations. How does he defend southern race policy in general as well as southern resistance to attempts at reforming poll tax and lynching laws? Although his views conflict sharply with modern opinions on race relations, how might he have considered himself justified in claiming, as he did in the Southern Manifesto, that outside attempts at battling segregation had "planted hatred and suspicion where there has been heretofore friendship and understanding" between the races?

3. Discuss the evolution of Thurmond's political and racial views, from his early "Dixiecrat" stance to the relatively more tolerant attitudes of his later years. (Note, for instance, the fact that in 1970 he became the first southern congressman to hire an African American for his staff.) How much was this shift simply a reflection of changes within the South and the nation as a whole, and how much did it reflect an underlying change in his own opinions?

and thus changed his affiliation, joining the Republicans in 1964. In fact, Thurmond led the political shift from the Democratic Party to the Republican Party in the South primarily over the issue of civil rights. Later, he softened his views on civil rights while continuing his staunch support of conservatism. He committed much of the conservative agenda to posterity in his 1968 book titled *The Faith We Have Not Kept*, detailing the essence of conservatism in America as being predicated on the preservation of states' rights. Thurmond also helped formulate the "southern strategy" adopted by Richard Nixon in his successful run for the presidency in 1968. Thurmond additionally dedicated much of his career in the U.S. Senate to military affairs. His efforts culminated in 1998 with the naming of the National Defense Authorization Act in his honor. Thurmond died in 2003 after serving longer than any other member of the U.S. Senate.

Key Sources

The Special Collections of Clemson University, South Carolina, contain about 3,000 cubic feet of J. Strom Thurmond papers. The Strom Thurmond Collection, 1940–2003, is also available on microfilm at Clemson. There are additional related documents in the Paul Quattlebaum papers, 1860–1964; the Floyd Drayton Johnson papers, 1939–1984; the Edward Lunn Young papers, 1929–1980; and the James Evan Duffy papers, 1960–1973. The Strom Thurmond Institute of Government and Public Affairs at Clemson University also has resources. At the South Car-

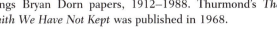

oliniana Library at the University of South Carolina, materials related to Thurmond can be found in the William Jennings Bryan Dorn papers, 1912–1988. Thurmond's *The Faith We Have Not Kept* was published in 1968.

Further Reading

■ Books

Bass, Jack, and Marilyn W. Thompson. *Ol' Strom: An Unauthorized Biography of Strom Thurmond*. Atlanta, Ga.: Longstreet, 1998.

Black, Earl, and Merle Black. *The Rise of Southern Republicans*. Cambridge, Mass.: Harvard University Press, 2002.

Cohodas, Nadine. *Strom Thurmond and the Politics of Southern Change*. Macon, Ga.: Mercer University Press, 1993.

Frederickson, Kari. *The Dixiecrat Revolt and the End of the Solid South, 1932–1968*. Chapel Hill: University of North Carolina Press, 2001.

McGirr, Lisa. *Suburban Warriors: The Origins of the New American Right*. Princeton, N.J.: Princeton University Press, 2001.

■ Web Sites

"Thurmond, James Strom, 1902–2003." Biographical Directory of the United States Congress Web site. http://bioguide.congress.gov/scripts/guidedisplay.pl?index=t000254.

—Bradley Skelcher

KEYNOTE ADDRESS AT THE STATES' RIGHTS DEMOCRATIC CONFERENCE (1948)

Governor Wright, Governor Laney, and Fellow Democrats of the South:

We have gathered here today because the American system of free constitutional government is in danger.

We are here because we have been betrayed in the house of our fathers, and we are determined that those who committed this betrayal shall not go unpunished.

We intend to meet the challenge and save constitutional government in the United States.

We shall discharge our responsibility as Democrats true to the principles of our Party, and demonstrate to the Nation that the spirit which kindled this Republic still lives in the South.

Whenever a great section of this country is regarded as so politically impotent that one major political party insults it because it is "in the bag", and the other party scorns it because there is no chance of victory, then the time has arrived for corrective and concerted action....

We want no one to be mistaken or misled. We are going to fight, as long as we have breath, for the rights of our states and our people under the American Constitution; and come what may, we are going to preserve our civilization in the South....

From the Southern states first came the call for a declaration of Independence, It was the great Southerner Thomas Jefferson, who wrote that immortal document. What the sage of Monticello proclaimed by pen, another Southerner, George Washington, won with his sword.

After we had won our independence we were without the machinery of government to preserve and perpetuate it. From the South came the movement that resulted in the Constitutional Convention of 1787. Over that Convention Washington presided. The main principles which the delegates wrote into the Constitution were taken from plans drawn up by James Madison of Virginia and Charles Pinckney of South Carolina.

We have only to read the proceedings of the Constitutional Convention to know the part played by the states we represent in creating our government.

We do not forget that of the first 25 Presidents, the South contributed 10. In those critical formative years of our Republic, Southern Presidents held the reins of government for 53 years.

Not only in the affairs of government, but in economics, in science, in social development, in education, in religion, and in every field of endeavor that contributes to human progress, the South has made its full contribution in the building of our country.

Our progress was set back many decades by the War Between the States. We are not here to fight that war over again. It is only fair to say, however, that even in those days the South suffered from vicious propaganda. No effort was spared to make it appear that we fought to perpetuate human slavery, and thereby obscure the fundamental constitutional and economic issues which brought on that unhappy conflict.

When the war was over, we were subjected to the bitter Reconstruction period. We experienced first hand the ordeal of a conquered and occupied land. Our economy was destroyed, and we had to rebuild on the foundation of a shattered civilization. The slaves who had been freed as a war measure were left as a millstone around our neck. The burden of recovery was made more difficult by the necessity of caring for these former slaves while overcoming the dislocation and destruction left in the path of war.

Throughout the whole period which has elapsed since that time, we of the South, and we alone, have earned and provided for the Negroes in our midst, and the progress which has been made by that race is a tribute to the efforts of Southerners, and of Southerners alone. The "emancipators" have done absolutely nothing to make this task easier.

On the contrary, both races have suffered in the economic struggle to overcome artificial barriers to our recovery and growth imposed upon this part of the Nation from without. The wonder is, not how little we have done, but how much we have been able to do for our people under such crushing handicaps.

It was not long after Reconstruction that a freight rate structure was instituted with discriminatory sectional differentials. The industrial progress of the Southeast, for instance, was thwarted by a 39% rate differential on manufactured goods as compared with the Eastern section of the country. The effect of these discriminatory freight rates was to keep the South in a "crown colony" status, producing raw materials for the industrial East, but unable to compete in the establishment of industries to raise our own economic level.

It was not until 1947, after the Southern Governors won their freight rate fight in the Interstate Commerce Commission and the courts, that we began to get some measure of relief from the destructive effect of this situation.

Our economy was also subjected to another hard blow. In Benjamin Harrison's administration, when the Republicans had to make good their campaign promises to the industrialists of the East who had financed their election, the high tariff was enacted. By means of this device, we in the South were buying our finished goods from the Eastern manufacturers who were protected against price competition from the rest of the world, while at the same time the raw materials which we raised were not so protected; and we had to sell them to the Eastern manufacturers at a price kept lower by foreign competition.

It is of interest here to recall that when the high tariff was proposed in Congress, there also appeared in that body another Force or "Civil Rights" bill, having for its purpose the renewal of reconstruction activities in the Southern states.

Propaganda designed to convince the country that the Southerners were remiss in the discharge of their duty to the Negroes, was heard throughout the land. There was strong Southern resistance to the high tariff legislation, because it would be ruinous to the economic progress of the South in our efforts to increase the level of life of both the white and the colored races alike. Finally, however, the tariff was passed and the Force bill pigeon-holed. Economic advantages were given to the East at the expense of the South, but we escaped the Force bill.

Under the galling yoke of freight rates and tariff, the South has struggled on to regain its rightful economic position in the Nation. While progress has necessarily been slow, it has been steady. Today industry has learned of the many advantages of climate, native labor, industrial peace, favorable taxation, natural resources, and stable government, which our states have to offer. We see giant factories and plants being constructed on all sides. We also hear the wails of other sections over the loss of industries which they possessed for so many years as a result of our defeat in war.

Now, once again, Force bills have made their appearance in the national Congress. Again the American people are being propagandized to believe that Southerners have been mistreating the Negroes in our midst, and that we are unfit for local self-government. Again, there is the stirring of old embers, the arousing of old fears, the laceration of old wounds....

We hear not a word of the tremendous efforts which we have made through the years to give both races in the South the opportunity to improve and progress.

We hear not a word of the undeniable fact that economic under-privilege in the South has known no color line, and that it has fallen heavily on both races alike.

We hear not a word of recognition of the progress which the Negro in this country has made since slavery days as a result of the efforts of the Southern people.

We are given no credit for the rebuilding of our once devastated section, accomplished without the aid of anything faintly resembling a Marshall Plan.

We are once again disturbing the economic status quo of the industrial East, and this does not suit some people.

Once again legislation is being promoted in the Congress calculated to throw us into confusion and distract our attention from our industrial program, in which our efforts have been succeeding so markedly in recent years....

It is the forward-looking and the liberal-thinking men and women of the South who will carry to a conclusion the solution of our racial as well as our economic and political problems....

In our fight against Federal encroachment on state sovereignty, we are sustained by the highest precedent and the best considered opinion which American history has known....

In his Farewell Address, George Washington, the first President of the United States, stated our case:

> The necessity of reciprocal checks in the exercise of political power, by dividing and distributing it into different depositories, and constituting each the guardian of the public weal against invasions of the others, has been evinced by experiments ancient and modern; some of them in our country, and under our own eyes. To preserve them must be as necessary as to institute them. If, in the opinion of the people, the distribution, or modification of the constitutional powers be in any particular wrong, let it be corrected by an amendment to the way which the Constitution designates. But let there be no change by usurpation; for though this, in one instance, may be the instrument of good, it is the customary weapon by which free governments are destroyed....

Thomas Jefferson, in his first Inaugural Address, stated the creed of the Democratic Party to which it has adhered consistently until this very day, in these words: "The support of the State governments in all their rights, as the most competent administrations for our domestic concerns and the surest bulwarks against anti-republican tendencies." Coming down to our own day and generation, it is peculiarly appropriate to remember the eloquent statement by the late President Franklin D. Roosevelt, who gave this forceful warning: "…to bring about government by oligarchy masquerading as democracy, it is fundamentally essential that practically all authority and control be centralized in our National Government. The individual sovereignty of our states must first be destroyed, except in mere minor matters of legislation. We are safe from the danger of any such departure from the principles on which this country was founded just so long as the individual home rule of the states is scrupulously preserved and fought for whenever it seems in danger."…He [Truman] has claimed to be carrying out a Roosevelt policy, and yet neither Franklin D. Roosevelt nor any other American President ever sent to the Congress any such message as the so-called Civil Rights proposals of President Truman.…

It has been said that the South is in revolt against the Democratic Party.

That is not true. The South is in revolt against the present leadership of the Democratic Party which has repudiated the historic principles upon which the Party was founded and has flourished.…

One of the proposals is the anti-poll tax law. We all know that the poll tax does not burden the right to vote. It is a minor revenue measure yielding comparatively little money, and I have advocated that we repeal it in my State. Only seven states now have a poll-tax voting requirement, and the proposed Federal law would accomplish so little that many think it harmless legislation.

The danger is the precedent which would be set by the Congressional assertion of the right to pass this law. If Congress can use this law to establish the power to deal with the right of the American people to vote, it can establish a form of Federal suffrage. It can exercise control over the ballot boxes of the Nation.…

When this occurs, the states could lose their effective voice in the national legislative halls as surely as did the Southern states in Reconstruction days when our ballot boxes were surrounded by Federal soldiers.…

Such power was deliberately withheld from the Federal Government when the Constitution was adopted. It has always been felt that the right of local self-government depended upon state regulation of the right of suffrage.

When the Senate Rules Committee a few days ago voted 7 to 2, to allow the pending poll-tax legislation to be considered by the Senate, the majority of the Committee admitted that its constitutionality presented a serious question, but stated that the Congress has already decided the point by passing the voting law.…

Another law recommended is an anti-lynching law. The Federal government does not have the constitutional right to deal with crimes occurring within the states. It can deal only with Federal crimes.…

The states, in governing themselves, are responsible for public peace and order. All the states have laws against murder. Many have specific laws against lynching, which is a cowardly form of murder.

This proposed law is unnecessary because enlightened public opinion has virtually stamped out this crime. It has never been a sectional crime, although some would create the contrary impression for propaganda purposes. In one year, 75% of the persons lynched throughout the United States were white.

Taking advantage of the emotional appeal springing from the horror felt for this crime by every decent person in every section of the Nation, the proposal is made that the Congress assert the power to deal with any crime within the states. This would be a radical invasion of the right of local self-government. It would be a bold extension of the power of the Federal government over the individual citizens.… The division of powers between the Federal government and the states, provided in the Constitution, would be virtually destroyed.…

Another proposal is the legislation regulating employment, promotion and discharge of the employees of private business and industry within the several states, commonly referred to as the FEPC law.… It would enable the Federal government to invade a local field clearly foreclosed to it by the Constitution. The bureaus and commissions created by it would be given power to intrude into the policies and practices of labor unions.…

Every man's private business would almost be made a public one. If he exercised his right to employ whom he pleased, he would always face the possibility of a call from a government agent, inquiring into why he did not hire someone else; he could be hauled before a Federal commission to explain himself; he could be ordered to stop choosing his employees as he saw fit, and to hire someone he did not want; he would not be allowed a jury on the issues of fact between him and the government....

Another phase of the President's proposals deals with the field of the separation of races.

We in the South know that the laws dealing with the separation of the races are necessary to maintain the public peace and order, where the races live side by side in large numbers. We know that they are essential to the racial integrity and purity of the white and Negro races alike. We know that their sudden removal would do great injury to the very people sought to be benefited....

The most alarming part of the President's program is the creation of a Federal police system to enforce it. The concept of a Federal police working within the states is utterly foreign to the Constitution of the United States. Gestapo-like, its agents would rove throughout the Nation; policing elections; meddling with private businesses; intervening in private lawsuits; breeding litigation; keeping the people in a state of duress and intimidation; and bringing to our people all the potential evils of a so-called police state....

One of the most astounding theories ever advanced is that the Federal government by passing a law can force the white people of the South to accept into their businesses, their schools, their places of amusement, and in other public places, those they do not want to accept....

Glossary

Benjamin Harrison	twenty-third U.S. president
Charles Pinckney	governor of South Carolina, U.S. congressman, U.S. senator, and signer of the Declaration of Independence
Electoral College	the set of electors representing each state and the District of Columbia, who elect the president of the United States
FEPC	Federal Employment Practices Commission
Force bill	an 1833 law that authorized the president to use force to enforce tariff laws and was used by later presidents for similar purposes
Franklin D. Roosevelt	thirty-second U.S. president
Gestapo	the state secret police of Nazi Germany
Governor Laney	Benjamin Travis Laney, Jr., governor of Arkansas
Governor Wright	Fielding L. Wright, governor of Mississippi and Strom Thurmond's vice presidential running mate on the Dixiecrat ticket
Interstate Commerce Commission	the federal regulatory agency founded in 1887 with the goal, among others, of regulating the railroad industry
James Madison	fourth president of the United States
Marshall Plan	the common name given to the economic aid the United States gave to Europe in the wake of World War II, named after its creator, General George Marshall
Reconstruction	the period following the Civil War during which the Confederate states were restored to the Union
sage of Monticello	a common nickname given to Thomas Jefferson, whose home in Virginia was named Monticello
"to bring about government by oligarchy..."	quotation from an address Franklin Roosevelt gave on March 3, 1930, while governor of New York
weal	welfare

And here and now I want to pay tribute to the colored people of the South.

During the influx of racial agitators, our colored people are continuing with their daily tasks, and are not following off after these false prophets who want to create misunderstanding in the South.

We are working and living side by side in peace and understanding. We are struggling together for a bigger and better South, with greater educational and economic opportunity for all of our citizens, regardless of race, creed, or color....

In general, I recommend to you that the procedure proposed by the Southern Governors' Conference be carried out as far as possible....

We should recommend that the State Democratic organizations see to it that the credentials of their delegates contain a proviso setting forth the reservations under which they will participate in that convention, or that notice of such reservations be given in writing to the National Committee before they take their seats.

Such a proviso should clearly set forth that the people of the state will not be bound to support the nominees for President and Vice-President if such nominees or the Party itself should advocate the so-called Federal Civil Rights Program.

If we do this, no one will be able to say that we are bolting or breaking faith with the Party if our people shall subsequently cast their electoral votes for others than such nominees.

Should the National convention choose nominees who do not meet this test, or should the Party itself favor such program, then the State Democratic organizations of the several states should immediately take action to see that the electoral votes of the Southern states shall be jointly cast in such manner as shall carry out the manifest will of the people of their states.

We know, and the enemies of state sovereignty know, that the Electoral College affords us a powerful weapon to restore the prestige of the South in the political affairs of this Nation and preserve the American system of free constitutional government.

Make no mistake about it, the South is prepared to use this weapon. Already, Alabama and Florida have spoken. Other states will take similar action. The leadership of the Democratic Party may as well realize that the South's electoral votes are no longer "in the bag" for the Democratic nominee.

The party bosses and ward heelers who have kidnapped the Democratic Party and deserted its principles may force the nomination of Harry Truman, but they cannot force the South or the Nation to accept him. Harry S. Truman has never been elected President of the United States and he never will be. True to the Party's principles, we must and shall see that our electoral votes are cast for those who adhere to those principles, and there are many distinguished men in the South and in the Nation from whom we can choose those we shall center upon.

When we shall have done this we shall restore our people to their rightful place in the political life of the Nation, which they lost through blind political faith in the Party leadership.

We shall have broken the chains binding us to those who have betrayed our trust.

We shall re-establish our autonomy and self-respect, so that no one will ever again assume that we have none.

We shall attest our faith in governmental principles which can never be willingly surrendered by a people who intend to be and remain free and self-governing.

We shall place our sound case before the people of the Nation, Democrat and Republican alike, so that we shall no longer fight alone in resisting encroachments upon the fundamental rights of the people by power-seeking Federal bureaucrats.

We shall win again the struggle for free constitutional government in America which was won before at Yorktown. We shall uphold, protect and defend the way of life which the Constitution of the United States was ordained to guarantee to the American people throughout our Nation.

SOUTHERN MANIFESTO (1956)

The Decision of the Supreme Court in the School Cases—Declaration of Constitutional Principles

Mr. [Walter F.] GEORGE. Mr. President, the increasing gravity of the situation following the decision of the Supreme Court in the so-called segregation cases, and the peculiar stress in sections of the country where this decision has created many difficulties, unknown and unappreciated, perhaps, by many people residing in other parts of the country, have led some Senators and some Members of the House of Representatives to prepare a statement of the position which they have felt and now feel to be imperative.

I now wish to present to the Senate a statement on behalf of 19 Senators, representing 11 States, and 77 House Members, representing a considerable number of States likewise....

Declaration of Constitutional Principles

The unwarranted decision of the Supreme Court in the public school cases is now bearing the fruit always produced when men substitute naked power for established law.

The Founding Fathers gave us a Constitution of checks and balances because they realized the inescapable lesson of history that no man or group of men can be safely entrusted with unlimited power. They framed this Constitution with its provisions for change by amendment in order to secure the fundamentals of government against the dangers of temporary popular passion or the personal predilections of public officeholders.

We regard the decisions of the Supreme Court in the school cases as a clear abuse of judicial power. It climaxes a trend in the Federal Judiciary undertaking to legislate, in derogation of the authority of Congress, and to encroach upon the reserved rights of the States and the people.

The original Constitution does not mention education. Neither does the 14th Amendment nor any other amendment. The debates preceding the submission of the 14th Amendment clearly show that there was no intent that it should affect the system of education maintained by the States.

The very Congress which proposed the amendment subsequently provided for segregated schools in the District of Columbia.

When the amendment was adopted in 1868, there were 37 States of the Union....

Every one of the 26 States that had any substantial racial differences among its people, either approved the operation of segregated schools already in existence or subsequently established such schools by action of the same law-making body which considered the 14th Amendment.

As admitted by the Supreme Court in the public school case (*Brown v. Board of Education*), the doctrine of separate but equal schools "apparently originated in *Roberts v. City of Boston* (1849), upholding school segregation against attack as being violative of a State constitutional guarantee of equality." This constitutional doctrine began in the North, not in the South, and it was followed not only in Massachusetts, but in Connecticut, New York, Illinois, Indiana, Michigan, Minnesota, New Jersey, Ohio, Pennsylvania and other northern states until they, exercising their rights as states through the constitutional processes of local self-government, changed their school systems.

In the case of *Plessy v. Ferguson* in 1896 the Supreme Court expressly declared that under the 14th Amendment no person was denied any of his rights if the States provided separate but equal facilities. This decision has been followed in many other cases. It is notable that the Supreme Court, speaking through Chief Justice Taft, a former President of the United States, unanimously declared in 1927 in *Lum v. Rice* that the "separate but equal" principle is "within the discretion of the State in regulating its public schools and does not conflict with the 14th Amendment."

This interpretation, restated time and again, became a part of the life of the people of many of the States and confirmed their habits, traditions, and way of life. It is founded on elemental humanity and commonsense, for parents should not be deprived by Government of the right to direct the lives and education of their own children.

Though there has been no constitutional amendment or act of Congress changing this established legal principle almost a century old, the Supreme

Court of the United States, with no legal basis for such action, undertook to exercise their naked judicial power and substituted their personal political and social ideas for the established law of the land.

This unwarranted exercise of power by the Court, contrary to the Constitution, is creating chaos and confusion in the States principally affected. It is destroying the amicable relations between the white and Negro races that have been created through 90 years of patient effort by the good people of both races. It has planted hatred and suspicion where there has been heretofore friendship and understanding.

Without regard to the consent of the governed, outside mediators are threatening immediate and revolutionary changes in our public schools systems. If done, this is certain to destroy the system of public education in some of the States.

With the gravest concern for the explosive and dangerous condition created by this decision and inflamed by outside meddlers:

We reaffirm our reliance on the Constitution as the fundamental law of the land.

We decry the Supreme Court's encroachment on the rights reserved to the States and to the people, contrary to established law, and to the Constitution.

We commend the motives of those States which have declared the intention to resist forced integration by any lawful means.

We appeal to the States and people who are not directly affected by these decisions to consider the constitutional principles involved against the time when they too, on issues vital to them may be the victims of judicial encroachment.

Even though we constitute a minority in the present Congress, we have full faith that a majority of the American people believe in the dual system of government which has enabled us to achieve our greatness and will in time demand that the reserved rights of the States and of the people be made secure against judicial usurpation.

We pledge ourselves to use all lawful means to bring about a reversal of this decision which is contrary to the Constitution and to prevent the use of force in its implementation.

In this trying period, as we all seek to right this wrong, we appeal to our people not to be provoked by the agitators and troublemakers invading our States and to scrupulously refrain from disorder and lawless acts.

Signed by:

Members of the United States Senate

Walter F. George, Richard B. Russell, John Stennis, Sam J. Ervin, Jr., Strom Thurmond, Harry F. Byrd, A. Willis Robertson, John L. McClellan, Allen J. Ellender, Russell B. Long, Lister Hill, James O. Eastland, W. Kerr Scott, John Sparkman, Olin D. Johnston, Price Daniel, J. W. Fulbright, George A. Smathers, Spessard L. Holland.

Members of the United States House of Representatives

Alabama: Frank W. Boykin, George M. Grant, George W. Andrews, Kenneth A. Roberts, Albert Rains, Armistead I. Selden, Jr., Carl Elliott, Robert E. Jones, George Huddleston, Jr.

Arkansas: E. C. Gathings, Wilbur D. Mills, James W. Trimble, Oren Harris, Brooks Hays, W.F. Norrell.

Florida: Charles E. Bennett, Robert L. F. Sikes, A.S. Herlong, Jr., Paul G. Rogers, James A. Haley, D. R. Matthews.

Georgia: Prince H. Preston, John L. Pilcher, E. L. Forrester, John James Flynt, Jr., James C. Davis, Carl Vinson, Henderson Lanham, Iris F. Blitch, Phil M. Landrum, Paul Brown.

Louisiana: F. Edward Hebert, Hale Boggs, Edwin E. Willis, Overton Brooks, Otto E. Passman, James H. Morrison, T. Ashton Thompson, George S. Long.

Mississippi: Thomas G. Abernathy, Jamie L. Whitten, Frank E. Smith, John Bell Williams, Arthur Winstead, William M. Colmer.

North Carolina: Herbert C. Bonner, L. H. Fountain, Graham A. Barden, Carl T. Durham, F. Ertel Carlyle, Hugh Q. Alexander, Woodrow W. Jones, George A. Shuford.

South Carolina: L. Mendel Rivers, John J. Riley, W. J. Bryan Dorn, Robert T. Ashmore, James P. Richards, John L. McMillan.

Tennessee: James B. Frazier, Jr., Tom Murray, Jere Cooper, Clifford Davis.

Glossary

Chief Justice Taft	William Howard Taft, twenty-seventh U.S. president and later chief justice of the United States
derogation	the act of detracting from or taking away

Harry S. Truman (Library of Congress)

HARRY S. TRUMAN   1884–1972

Thirty-third President of the United States

Featured Documents
- ◆ **Statement Announcing the Use of the A-Bomb on Hiroshima (1945)**
- ◆ **Truman Doctrine Address to Congress (1947)**
- ◆ **Address to the National Association for the Advancement of Colored People (1947)**
- ◆ **Inaugural Address (1949)**
- ◆ **Report to the American People on Korea (1951)**

Overview

Harry S. Truman was born in Lamar, Missouri, on May 8, 1884. He graduated from Independence High School but never attended college. He worked as a clerk and then served as an artillery officer in the U.S. Army during World War I. On his return from the war, Truman settled in Kansas City, Missouri, and opened a haberdashery. Active in the Democratic Party, Truman was elected as an administrator of Jackson County, Missouri, in 1922, a position he lost in the election of 1924 but regained two years later. In 1934 he ran for the U.S. Senate and won. During his tenure in the Senate, Truman developed a reputation as a reformer by opposing government waste and corruption. For the 1944 election, President Franklin D. Roosevelt chose Truman as his vice presidential running mate to replace the incumbent vice president, Henry Wallace. Wallace was thought to be too liberal by many, and in view of Roosevelt's failing health, Wallace's possible ascendancy to the presidency was considered a risk.

Roosevelt and Truman were elected, but the president died in office on April 12, 1945. Truman faced daunting challenges, foreign and domestic, after he assumed office. Thrust into the role of wartime president (in the final days of World War II) and successor to the highly popular Roosevelt, Truman attempted to craft a balance between continuing his predecessor's policies and developing and implementing his own. His first challenge came when he made the decision to use the newly developed atomic bomb against Japan in order to end the conflict in the Pacific and avoid the casualties associated with an invasion of Japan. He announced the implementation of his decision to the American public on August 6, 1945. The Japanese surrender followed quickly.

With the end of World War II, the United States was confronted by a growing threat from the Soviet Union. Truman endeavored to contain Soviet expansion through a mixture of economic and military aid to non-Communist states. In March 1947 the president issued the Truman Doctrine, which pledged assistance to those states threatened by Communist insurgencies and provided more than $400 million to Greece and Turkey. The following year, the administration unveiled the European Recovery Plan (commonly known as the Marshall Plan), which provided $13 billion to

west European democracies to help them rebuild. Meanwhile, on the domestic front, Truman became the first U.S. president to address the National Association for the Advancement of Colored People, articulating his views of civil rights in a speech delivered in June 1947. His Executive Order 9981, issued on July 26, 1948, integrated the U.S Armed Services.

After a close campaign in 1948, Truman was reelected, and in his inaugural address he outlined specific policy efforts that would be the focus of his second term. Apart from the foreign policy he outlined there, in his second term he hoped to fulfill the potential of Roosevelt's New Deal through a package of domestic programs that he titled the Fair Deal. Although Republicans and conservative Democrats blocked the passage of most of the Fair Deal programs, Truman was able to expand Social Security, increase the minimum wage, and enact public housing reforms. He soon also reorganized the nation's security agencies to create a unified Department of Defense and new intelligence bodies, including the Central Intelligence Agency. In April 1949 the North Atlantic Treaty was signed in Washington, D.C., and brought into being the North Atlantic Treaty Organization (NATO), a collective defense organization formed to contain both Germany and the Soviet Union.

Truman's popularity began to be undermined in 1950 by the outbreak of the Korean War, a war that began when Communist North Korea invaded its southern neighbor. In June of that year, Truman ordered U.S. troops to join the conflict, seeing intervention as necessary to the global containment of Communism. In April 1951, in a radio address to the American people, he defended the continued U.S. presence in the region. At the same time, Truman faced the so-called red scare at home—a period of intense anti-Communist hysteria when accusations were rife that Soviets had infiltrated the State Department and other parts of the federal government. Many of the attacks of Wisconsin Senator Joe McCarthy, chief instigator of the red scare, were directed at members of the Truman administration, and the accusations weakened public confidence in the president. Truman could have run for a third term but chose to retire. He left office in 1953 as one of the most unpopular presidents in U.S. history. Nevertheless, today he is considered one of the ten most effective presidents. His personal motto, "The Buck Stops Here," emblazoned on a sign on

1884
- **May 8**
  Harry S. Truman is born in Lamar, Missouri.

1916–1919
- Truman serves in the U.S. Army during World War I.

1922
- Truman is elected an administrator in Jackson County, Missouri.

1934
- Truman wins a seat in the U.S. Senate.

1944
- **November 7**
  Truman is elected vice president of the United States.

1945
- **April 12**
  Franklin D. Roosevelt dies in office, and Truman is sworn in as president.

- **August 6**
  The first atomic bomb is dropped on Hiroshima, Japan; Truman delivers a radio address to the American people, announcing the bombing.

- **August 14**
  World War II ends with the Japanese surrender.

1947
- **March 12**
  Truman announces the Truman Doctrine in an address to Congress.

- **June 29**
  Truman addresses the National Association for the Advancement of Colored People—the first president ever to do so.

1948
- **November 2**
  Truman is reelected to the presidency.

1949
- **January 20**
  Truman is inaugurated as president and delivers his inaugural address.

---

his desk, came to symbolize his political courage and fortitude. In retirement he remained active in public life and campaigned on behalf of successive Democratic presidential candidates. Truman died on December 26, 1972.

Explanation and Analysis of Documents

Truman was known for his plainspoken and straightforward speaking style. From his early days in office, he developed a reputation as an honest and extremely hard-working politician, and his public comments reflected these traits. Humorous and warm in person and in small groups, Truman could appear stiff when giving formal addresses. He generally disliked public speaking and had the distinct disadvantage of following Roosevelt, one of the best public speakers who ever sat in the Oval Office. But Truman was an enthusiastic campaigner, capable of passionate delivery, especially when speaking extemporaneously. He relied on a team of speechwriters led by Clark Clifford and including George Elsey, Charles S. Murphy, and Ken Hechler—all of whom served him well. The five documents highlighted here provide an overview of Truman's political philosophy and the way in which he reacted to the challenges that he faced as president: his announcement of the use of the atomic bomb against Japan; the promulgation of the Truman Doctrine; an address to the National Association for the Advancement of Colored People on civil rights policies; his 1949 inaugural address, highlighting his plans on foreign policy; and a report that he delivered to the American people on U.S. involvement in the Korean War.

◆ Statement Announcing the Use of the A–Bomb on Hiroshima

On May 8, 1945, Germany surrendered, ending World War II in Europe, but fighting against Japan continued in the Pacific. At the end of July, Truman attended a conference in Potsdam, Germany, with the leaders of the United States' main wartime allies, Great Britain and the Soviet Union. At this summit the leaders agreed to accept only an unconditional surrender by Japan. Meanwhile, U.S. military planners prepared for an invasion of the Japanese islands. Casualties were expected to be very high, based on previous military operations in the Pacific, including the Battle of Iwo Jima (1945) and the invasion of Okinawa (1945).

On April 24, 1945, shortly after taking office, Truman had been briefed on the existence of the Manhattan Project, a secret program to develop an atomic weapon. He was warned that the Soviet Union also had a nuclear program, but it was several years behind that of the United States. On July 16 the Manhattan Project scientists triggered the world's first nuclear bomb detonation. When Japan refused to surrender unconditionally, Truman ordered the military to use the weapon against Japan. The first atomic bomb was dropped on Hiroshima on August 6. Japan still would not surrender, and Truman authorized a second nuclear attack that targeted Nagasaki three days later. The attacks killed more than two hundred thousand people and injured many more. Japan surrendered on August 14.

On August 6, Truman delivered a radio address to the American people announcing the use of the atomic bomb. He notes that the bomb had the power of more than twenty thousand tons of TNT and was by far the most potent weapon ever used in warfare. Truman says that more such weapons were in production and that they had "added a new and revolutionary increase in destruction to supplement the growing power of our armed forces." He describes the new weapon as "harnessing ... the basic power of the universe" and goes on to provide an overview of the Manhattan Project. The president explains that U.S. scientists were in a "race" to develop nuclear weapons before Germany and that the country had worked with its ally Great Britain. He also tells Americans that the program had cost $2 billion and employed some sixty-five thousand people.

The president asserts that the three Allied powers had issued their ultimatum on unconditional surrender in order to "spare" the Japanese from "utter destruction." But he warns that the United States was "prepared to obliterate more rapidly and completely every productive enterprise the Japanese have above ground in any city." Truman declares that the United States was prepared to use more atomic weapons against Japan and to follow those strikes with further air, land, and sea operations. He concludes the address by speaking about the potential peaceful uses of nuclear energy and states that eventually nuclear power could "supplement" oil and coal to help meet the demands of the nation. The president tells Americans that he intended to ask Congress to create a commission to explore how atomic energy could be harnessed for peaceful purposes.

For Truman, the decision to use the atomic bomb was a difficult one, but he defended his choice throughout his life. The president sincerely believed that its use saved countless American lives and shortened the war. Truman was also well aware of growing tensions with the Soviet Union and realized that a demonstration of the potency of the new American weapon could help bolster the nation's postwar position in the nascent cold war struggle. The president and his advisers further understood how negative the public reaction would probably be if Americans learned that the government had atomic weapons but failed to use them and instead conducted an invasion at the cost of American lives. The overwhelming majority of Americans supported the use of these nuclear strikes at the time, even though few, including Truman, understood the long-term consequences of the attack—such as damage to the environment and an increase in diseases like cancer caused by exposure to radiation. In 1946 the U.S. Atomic Energy Commission was created to help develop peaceful uses for nuclear energy. The commission also oversaw the nation's continuing nuclear weapons program. In 1949 the Soviet Union detonated its own atomic weapon, formalizing the arms race between the two nations. Truman authorized the development of a more powerful hydrogen bomb, which the country tested in 1954.

Time Line

1950

- **June 25**
  The Korean War begins.

1951

- **April 11**
  In a radio address to the American people, Truman defends the U.S. presence in Korea.

1953

- **January 20**
  Truman leaves office.

- **July 27**
  An armistice is signed, ending the Korean War.

1972

- **December 26**
  Truman dies in Kansas City, Missouri.

◆ Truman Doctrine Address to Congress

Relations between the United States and the Soviet Union deteriorated in the waning days of World War II. Tensions increased after the war when the Soviets refused to withdraw forces from areas of eastern and central Europe. Communist insurgencies, supported by Moscow, threatened pro-U.S. governments in such countries as Greece, Iran, and Turkey. Meanwhile, Great Britain notified the United States that it could no longer serve as the main bulwark against Soviet expansion in the Mediterranean. Consequently, Truman and his advisers crafted a new security policy designed to contain the Soviets. The basis of this policy was laid out by George F. Kennan, deputy head of the U.S. mission in Moscow, in a note that became known as the Long Telegram; in it Kennan argued that the Soviet Union was a direct threat to the economic and political system of the United States and that the country needed to stop the spread of Soviet expansion.

On March 12, 1947, before a joint session of Congress, the president announced what came to be known as the Truman Doctrine. In the address, Truman discusses the threats to Greece and Turkey and asks Congress for more than $400 million in aid for the two countries and the authorization to deploy U.S. military advisers to the region. He notes that the United States had received a request from the Greek government for aid and that he did not think that the "American people and the Congress wish to turn a deaf ear" to the Greeks. Truman explains that the principal threat came from Communist insurgents and that the British could no longer support Greece or maintain other commitments in the region. Truman notes that the United Nations was not suited to address the current situation or provide the kind of assistance needed. The president assures Americans that U.S. aid would not come in the form of a blank check and says that the United States

Truman, Harry S.

had "condemned in the past, and we condemn now, extremist measures of the right or the left." He informs Americans that Turkey also faced threats of possible Soviet aggression (since Turkey bordered the Soviet Union) and needed U.S. economic assistance in the form of military aid and to improve its standard of living.

Truman describes his request as part of the broader framework of U.S. foreign policy. Just as the United States had fought to ensure that people were free from domination by Germany or Japan, Truman argues that the United States had to help countries facing threats from Communism. The president ties U.S. security to the security of other countries. He states that "totalitarian regimes imposed on free peoples, by direct or indirect aggression, undermine the foundations of international peace and hence the security of the United States." Truman also casts the emerging cold war as a struggle between freedom and authoritarianism. One system was marked by open government and individual liberty, and the other was dominated by oppression and tyranny. The president declares firmly "that it must be the policy of the United States to support free peoples who are resisting attempted subjugation by armed minorities or by outside pressures." Drawing upon points developed by Kennan in his Long Telegram, Truman indicates a desire to avoid direct military conflict. Instead, he argues that the United States should first try to oppose the expansion of totalitarianism through economic support and assistance. He concludes by reminding Congress and the American people that the world looked to the United States for leadership and that global events necessitated a quick response.

The Truman Doctrine was the cornerstone of U.S. foreign and security policy through the cold war. Later presidential doctrines, including that of Truman's successor, Dwight D. Eisenhower, built directly on the Truman Doctrine. Working with leading Republicans, Truman crafted a bipartisan consensus on foreign policy that remained throughout the cold war. Meanwhile, Truman's address helped secure domestic support for the cold war and U.S. policy initiatives such as the Marshall Plan and the formation of NATO.

◆ Address to the National Association for the Advancement of Colored People

Truman's attitudes on race were complicated and often contradictory. The president's racial views reflected many of the biases of the period. However, after World War II, Truman was genuinely shocked and horrified at the treatment of African American veterans in a series of brutal and vicious attacks in some southern states. He was aware that the United States could not be the champion of freedom to the outside world if it still had discriminatory policies at home. Truman and his advisers also understood the importance of the African American vote in the upcoming 1948 presidential election, although some aides argued that the president could not afford to alienate white southerners by embracing civil rights. He appointed a presidential commission on civil rights in 1946 and charged it to develop specific recommendations. Truman also began a public campaign to press for civil rights.

On June 29, 1947, Truman became the first U.S. president to address the National Association for the Advancement of Colored People. In one of his more passionate public addresses, Truman speaks to the crowd of the importance of equality and how "recent events," a reference to both World War II and the growing cold war, had reaffirmed the importance that every American have the same rights and freedoms. He asserts that the contemporary civil rights laws were designed to protect individuals against the federal government but that such measures needed to be reevaluated and expanded. Truman argues that history had shown that civil rights laws had to offer not "protection of the people against the Government, but protection of the people by the Government." Race should not inhibit citizens or restrict their opportunities. The president declares that a person should be limited only by "his ability, his industry and his character." All Americans should have equal rights to employment, home ownership, and political participation and should be treated equally by the justice system.

Truman ties civil rights in the United States to the larger effort by the country to promote freedom and liberty around the world. He strongly asserts that the United States had to demonstrate the "superiority of democracy" to the world. In pressing other countries to liberalize, the president states that U.S. foreign policy "should rest on practical evidence that we have been able to put our house in order." The national government had to lead the way on civil rights, Truman argues, in recognition of the fact that state and local governments had been able to erode or undermine equal rights without significant federal opposition. The president notes that he had appointed a civil rights commission and that the body would produce recommendations for the administration. Truman reminds the crowd that he had asked Congress to extend civil rights protections to citizens in U.S. territories such as Guam and American Samoa. He concludes by tying current civil rights efforts to past milestones, such as the Declaration of Independence and the Emancipation Proclamation, and states that the United States supported the initiative to create a global bill of rights. (The result of that initiative would be the United Nation's 1948 Universal Declaration of Human Rights.)

Truman followed his address with concrete action. In February 1948 he sent a message to Congress asking for comprehensive civil rights legislation. In July the president signed Executive Order 9981 to integrate the military, after repeated efforts to pass such legislation in Congress were blocked by southerners in the Senate. Although it took several years for the armed services to integrate, Truman's efforts helped launch the modern civil rights movement. Truman paid a steep political price for his actions. At the Democratic National Convention in 1948, southern delegates walked out in protest over Truman's civil rights policies. South Carolina Governor Strom Thurmond subsequently launched a third party bid as a Dixiecrat.

◆ Inaugural Address

Truman faced a close reelection campaign in 1948. The Democratic Party was split by Thurmond's Dixiecrats and a left-wing grouping, the Progressive Party, led by Henry Wallace. Many pundits predicted that Republican Thomas E. Dewey would defeat Truman. However, Truman ran a spirited campaign and won with 49.6 percent of the vote to Dewey's 45.1 percent, while Thurmond and Wallace each received 2.4 percent of the vote. In his inaugural address on January 20, 1949, Truman chose to avoid contentious domestic issues and instead concentrate on foreign affairs. Clifford and Elsey had strongly argued for this approach, and Clifford gained Truman's permission in December 1948 while the president and his close staff were in Key West. Truman and his advisers hoped to unify the country by emphasizing the consensus that existed on foreign policy. The resultant speech was a mixture of broad ideological themes and an overview of specific policy efforts.

The president begins by discussing U.S. global leadership. Truman argues that other nations looked to the United States for leadership because the nation had been founded on principles of freedom, equality, and opportunity. However, the United States was opposed by a system that was its direct opposite, Communism. He describes Communism as a "false philosophy" that promised equality and freedom but provided only "deceit and mockery, poverty and tyranny."

Truman discusses four major policy areas for his administration over the next four years. First, he notes that the United States would endeavor to strengthen the United Nations and increase the capabilities of that world body. Second, Truman tells Americans that his administration would continue to support "world economic recovery," which included the Marshall Plan as well as efforts to remove trade barriers around the globe. Third, the United States would endeavor to develop a system of collective defense agreements to deter aggression and contain Soviet expansion. He mentions efforts to form an alliance in the Atlantic region (which would culminate in the creation of NATO, the first permanent peacetime military alliance in U.S. history) and the 1947 Inter-American Treaty of Reciprocal Assistance, also known as the Rio Treaty. Fourth and finally, Truman calls for a new antipoverty program to share technological assistance and enhance both industrial and agricultural protection among less-developed countries. Truman declares that "old imperialism—exploitation for foreign profit—has no place in our plans"; instead, the United States sought to enhance the economic capabilities of other countries to help humanity, deter Communism, and bolster trade and investment opportunities for Americans.

While the first three of Truman's four policy recommendations were well established, the fourth point on technical assistance was a new concept initially developed by Benjamin H. Hardy, a press officer in the State Department who had argued strongly for its inclusion in the address. The initiative would become the Point Four Program (a reference to the inaugural address). Congress approved the Point Four Program in 1950 and authorized $35 million to provide technical aid to such countries as Brazil, Indonesia, and Iran. The program was the forerunner of the Peace Corps.

Residents from Pyongyang, North Korea, and refugees from other areas crawl over shattered girders of the city's bridge on December 4, 1950, as they flee south across the Taedong River to escape the advance of Chinese Communist troops. (AP/Wide World Photos)

◆ **Report to the American People on Korea**

Truman had ordered the U.S. military to fight the North Korean forces that invaded South Korea on June 25, 1950. The Korean War quickly expanded, and the UN Security Council authorized military action to defend South Korea. (The Soviet Union was in the midst of a boycott of the Security Council and therefore did not veto the measure.) Led by the United States, UN forces from sixteen nations drove the North Koreans back across the thirty-eighth parallel and came close to the Chinese border. China then launched a surprise attack in November and drove the UN forces back into South Korea. Meanwhile, the allied commander, World War II hero General Douglas MacArthur, argued for an expansion of the conflict, including air attacks on China. Truman refused to escalate the war and dismissed the popular MacArthur after the general publicly called for attacks when he had been ordered not to do so by the president.

On April 11, 1951, Truman spoke to the American people in a televised address to defend his policies in Korea. The president delivered a measured speech that emphasized the ideological and practical reasons he wanted to limit the war. He also explained his decision to remove MacArthur from command. Truman argues in the address that his policies were consistent and had not changed since the war began. Specifically, he maintains that the United States and its allies wanted to contain the war and prevent World War III. Consequently, he had rejected calls to bomb China or otherwise expand military operations. Truman contends that the invasion of Korea was the boldest effort yet by the Communist bloc to expand its influence and part of a larger effort to take control of Asia. He asserts that by preventing the fall of South Korea, the United States and its allies demonstrated the resolve of the West. He further argues that successes in Korea helped in other areas where there were Communist insurgencies, including Indochina.

The president explains that his dismissal of MacArthur was based on a disagreement over war aims. MacArthur thought the conflict should be expanded, which was counter to Truman's policy. The president notes that he felt compelled to act so that there would be no doubt by others around the world as to the goals of the United States. The commander in chief praises MacArthur as one of the nation's great military leaders but points out that the "cause of world peace is much more important than any individual." Truman concludes his address by telling the American people that his administration sought peace and was ready to negotiate. He is emphatic, however, that the United States would "not engage in appeasement." Instead, Truman sought a resolution to the conflict that reflected American values and principles and one that was in line with the nation's foreign policy goals.

Most Americans opposed Truman's decision to remove MacArthur. The Korean War and the growing attacks on Truman's administration by Senator Joseph McCarthy had already undermined the president's popularity. The dismissal of the popular war hero was perceived as an indication of weakness on the part of Truman. The president understood this and was prepared to accept the consequences of his action. MacArthur had directly challenged the president's authority as commander in chief, and Truman made the correct decision. With historically low public opinion ratings (just 22 percent), Truman decided not to run for another term. He instead endorsed the eventual Democratic nominee, Adlai Stevenson. Another war hero, Dwight D. Eisenhower, was nominated by the Republicans, and he easily won the election of 1952.

Impact and Legacy

Truman left office highly unpopular, but his political courage, as demonstrated by the decision to drop the atomic bomb to end the war in the Pacific and to fire MacArthur, was eventually recognized. History has rehabilitated Truman. Most presidential rankings now place the man from Missouri among the top ten chief executives of the nation. Many of Truman's decisions set the framework for U.S. foreign and security policy throughout the cold war and beyond. NATO, for example, remains the cornerstone of U.S. security in the transatlantic region. Truman understood the dangers of the cold war and effectively balanced the challenges faced by the country with the resources available to the United States. He was not a great

orator, and he generally disliked public speaking. Lacking the eloquence and style of Roosevelt, Truman became known as a plainspoken and earnest speaker who was nevertheless able to communicate his points directly to the American people in a manner that had broad appeal. He spoke regularly on the radio, and he was also the first president to appear on the then-new medium of television. Truman did not seek personal fame or glory but believed himself to be a servant of the American people, and his addresses and actions reflected this conviction.

Key Sources

The National Archives published an eight-volume set of Truman's papers produced while he was president, *Public Papers of the Presidents: Harry S. Truman 1945–1953* (1966). The Harry S. Truman Presidential Library and Museum in Independence, Missouri, has a vast collection of presidential documents, personal papers, and other items from Truman's life and presidency. Much of its collection is available online at http://www.trumanlibrary.org/. The Miller Center of Public Affairs at the University of Virginia (http://millercenter.org/academic/americanpresident/truman) also provides a substantial amount of information on Truman's presidency. Truman's *Memoirs* were published in two volumes (1955–1956). Robert H. Ferrell edited a compilation of autobiographical writings composed by Truman between 1934 and 1972, *The Autobiography of Harry S. Truman* (1980).

Further Reading

■ Books

Ferrell, Robert H. *Harry S. Truman and the Modern American Presidency*. Boston: Little, Brown, 1983.

Hogan, Michael J. *A Cross of Iron: Harry S. Truman and the Origins of the National Security State*. New York: Cambridge University Press, 1998.

Maddox, Robert James. *From War to Cold War: The Education of Harry S. Truman*. Boulder, Colo.: Westview Press, 1988.

McCullough, David. *Truman*. New York: Simon & Schuster, 1992.

Offner, Arnold A. *Another Such Victory: President Truman and the Cold War, 1945–1953*. Stanford, Calif.: Stanford University Press, 2002.

Pearlman, Michael D. *Truman and MacArthur: Policy, Politics, and the Hunger for Honor and Renown*. Bloomington: Indiana University Press, 2008.

Spalding, Elizabeth Edwards. *The First Cold Warrior: Harry Truman, Containment, and the Remaking of Liberal Internationalism*. Lexington: University Press of Kentucky, 2006.

"*The force from which the sun draws its power has been loosed against those who brought war to the Far East.*"

(Statement Announcing the Use of the A-Bomb on Hiroshima)

"*We are now prepared to obliterate more rapidly and completely every productive enterprise the Japanese have above ground in any city.*"

(Statement Announcing the Use of the A-Bomb on Hiroshima)

"*The free peoples of the world look to us for support in maintaining their freedoms. If we falter in our leadership, we may endanger the peace of the world—and we shall surely endanger the welfare of our own nation.*"

(Truman Doctrine Address to Congress)

"*The extension of civil rights today means, not protection of the people against the Government, but protection of the people by the Government.*"

(Address to the National Association for the Advancement of Colored People)

"*The peoples of the earth face the future with grave uncertainty, composed almost equally of great hopes and great fears. In this time of doubt, they look to the United States as never before for good will, strength, and wise leadership.*"

(Inaugural Address)

"*Communism holds that the world is so deeply divided into opposing classes that war is inevitable. Democracy holds that free nations can settle differences justly and maintain lasting peace.*"

(Inaugural Address)

"*In the simplest terms, what we are doing in Korea is this: We are trying to prevent a third world war.*"

(Report to the American People on Korea)

"*We are ready, at any time, to negotiate for a restoration of peace in the area. But we will not engage in appeasement. We are only interested in real peace.*"

(Report to the American People on Korea)

Wainstock, Dennis D. *The Decision to Drop the Atomic Bomb.*
Westport, Conn.: Praeger, 1996.

—Tom Lansford

Questions for Further Study

1. Discuss the historical background of Truman's 1945 statement on the dropping of the atomic bomb. Assess the difficulty of the task before him: announcing to the American people that a terrifying new weapon, developed secretly over the preceding years, had just been employed against an enemy. How does Truman weigh the advantages of the bombing—which would bring about a speedy and (in his view and that of many others) relatively humane end to the war—against its obvious disadvantages? Compare his statement with comments by Robert Oppenheimer on the same event. Who, in your opinion, makes a better case for his position on the bomb and why?

2. Explain the Truman Doctrine both within the context of its time and with regard to its effect on the national security and defense policies of Truman's and subsequent administrations. To what extent can Truman's predecessor, Franklin D. Roosevelt—who failed to appreciate either the scope of Soviet dictator Joseph Stalin's territorial ambitions or the ruthlessness with which he was willing to pursue them—be blamed for the conditions that necessitated the adoption of the containment policy? Did Truman have any reasonable alternative to the stance he took in 1947? How did the Truman Doctrine shape U.S. conduct in the cold war? Particularly, how did it bring about the massive increase in defense spending, overseas involvements, and covert operations that followed? Be sure to cite not only his 1947 address to Congress but also his 1949 inaugural speech, in which he outlined his approach to foreign policy.

3. How great was the significance of Truman's address to the National Association for the Advancement of Colored People, both as a symbolic statement and as evidence of substantive presidential support for civil rights? Discuss the historical significance of the event and what Truman's presence before the NAACP showed about the importance he placed on winning black votes for his administration and the Democratic Party in general. To what extent were his actions in this regard politically motivated, and to what extent did they reflect a sincere commitment to redressing social injustices? What were the political consequences for him and for the Democrats?

4. In making his 1951 report to the American people on the situation in Korea, Truman faced a number of challenges. He had dismissed General Douglas MacArthur, a national hero, and the conflict itself seemed to have no foreseeable end. How does Truman defend his actions regarding MacArthur and the war in general? What points does he make in explaining how and why he chose to take America into the war, and how does he explain his position with regard to China?

5. Although Truman left office with the lowest public approval rating of any president since such polls were instituted, he is today remembered as one of America's greatest leaders. How did this change come about, and in your opinion is it justified? Pretend you are Truman, offering advice to another president—one born, in fact, during Truman's administration—who likewise left office in the middle of a war, with abysmal public opinion ratings: George W. Bush. What would you tell him? What parallels and differences would you observe between your (that is, Truman's) experience and that of the forty-third president?

STATEMENT ANNOUNCING THE USE OF THE A-BOMB ON HIROSHIMA (1945)

Sixteen hours ago an American airplane dropped one bomb on Hiroshima, an important Japanese Army base. That bomb had more power than 20,000 tons of TNT. It had more than 2,000 times the blast power of the British "Grand Slam," which is the largest bomb ever yet used in the history of warfare.

The Japanese began the war from the air at Pearl Harbor. They have been repaid manyfold. And the end is not yet. With this bomb we have now added a new and revolutionary increase in destruction to supplement the growing power of our armed forces. In their present form these bombs are now in production, and even more powerful forms are in development.

It is an atomic bomb. It is a harnessing of the basic power of the universe. The force from which the sun draws its power has been loosed against those who brought war to the Far East….

The battle of the laboratories held fateful risks for us as well as the battles of the air, land, and sea, and we have now won the battle of the laboratories as we have won the other battles.

Beginning in 1940, before Pearl Harbor, scientific knowledge useful in war was pooled between the United States and Great Britain, and many priceless helps to our victories have come from that arrangement. Under that general policy the research on the atomic bomb was begun. With American and British scientists working together we entered the race of discovery against the Germans.

The United States had available the large number of scientists of distinction in the many needed areas of knowledge. It had the tremendous industrial and financial resources necessary for the project, and they could be devoted to it without undue impairment of other vital war work. In the United States the laboratory work and the production plants, on which a substantial start had already been made, would be out of reach of enemy bombing, while at that time Britain was exposed to constant air attack and was still threatened with the possibility of invasion. For these reasons Prime Minister Churchill and President Roosevelt agreed that it was wise to carry on the project here.

We now have two great plants and many lesser works devoted to the production of atomic power. Employment during peak construction numbered 125,000 and over 65,000 individuals are even now engaged in operating the plants. Many have worked there for two and a half years. Few know what they have been producing. They see great quantities of material going in and they see nothing coming out of these plants, for the physical size of the explosive charge is exceedingly small. We have spent $2 billion on the greatest scientific gamble in history—and won.

But the greatest marvel is not the size of the enterprise, its secrecy, nor its cost, but the achievement of scientific brains in putting together infinitely complex pieces of knowledge held by many men in different fields of science into a workable plan. And hardly less marvelous has been the capacity of industry to design, and of labor to operate, the machines and methods to do things never done before so that the brainchild of many minds came forth in physical shape and performed as it was supposed to do. Both science and industry worked under the direction of the United States Army, which achieved a unique success in managing so diverse a problem in the advancement of knowledge in an amazingly short time. It is doubtful if such another combination could be got together in the world. What has been done is the greatest achievement of organized science in history. It was done under high pressure and without failure.

We are now prepared to obliterate more rapidly and completely every productive enterprise the Japanese have above ground in any city. We shall destroy their docks, their factories, and their communications. Let there be no mistake; we shall completely destroy Japan's power to make war.

It was to spare the Japanese people from utter destruction that the ultimatum of July 26 was issued at Potsdam. Their leaders promptly rejected that ultimatum. If they do not now accept our terms they may expect a rain of ruin from the air, the like of which has never been seen on this earth. Behind this air attack will follow sea and land forces in such numbers and power as they have not yet seen and with the fighting skill of which they are already well aware….

The fact that we can release atomic energy ushers in a new era in man's understanding of nature's forces. Atomic energy may in the future supplement the power that now comes from coal, oil, and falling water, but at present it cannot be produced on a basis to compete with them commercially. Before that comes there must be a long period of intensive research….

I shall recommend that the Congress of the United States consider promptly the establishment of an appropriate commission to control the production and use of atomic power within the United States. I shall give further consideration and make further recommendations to the Congress as to how atomic power can become a powerful and forceful influence towards the maintenance of world peace.

Glossary

Churchill	Winston Churchill, British prime minister during World War II
Pearl Harbor	the site of a U.S. naval base in Hawaii that was attacked by the Japanese on December 7, 1941, drawing the United States into World War II
Potsdam	a German city southwest of Berlin, Germany, and the site of a major peace conference among the Allied powers after World War II
Roosevelt	Franklin D. Roosevelt, thirty-second U.S. president and president during most of World War II
TNT	abbreviation for 2,4,6-trinitrotoluene, a chemical whose explosive power is often the standard by which other explosives are measured

TRUMAN DOCTRINE ADDRESS TO CONGRESS (1947)

The United States has received from the Greek Government an urgent appeal for financial and economic assistance....

I do not believe that the American people and the Congress wish to turn a deaf ear to the appeal of the Greek Government....

The very existence of the Greek state is today threatened by the terrorist activities of several thousand armed men, led by Communists, who defy the government's authority at a number of points, particularly along the northern boundaries....

The British Government, which has been helping Greece, can give no further financial or economic aid after March 31. Great Britain finds itself under the necessity of reducing or liquidating its commitments in several parts of the world, including Greece.

We have considered how the United Nations might assist in this crisis. But the situation is an urgent one requiring immediate action and the United Nations and its related organizations are not in a position to extend help of the kind that is required....

The Greek Government has been operating in an atmosphere of chaos and extremism. It has made mistakes. The extension of aid by this country does not mean that the United States condones everything that the Greek Government has done or will do. We have condemned in the past, and we condemn now, extremist measures of the right or the left. We have in the past advised tolerance, and we advise tolerance now.

Greece's neighbor, Turkey, also deserves our attention.

The future of Turkey as an independent and economically sound state is clearly no less important to the freedom-loving peoples of the world than the future of Greece. The circumstances in which Turkey finds itself today are considerably different from those of Greece. Turkey has been spared the disasters that have beset Greece. And during the war, the United States and Great Britain furnished Turkey with material aid.

Nevertheless, Turkey now needs our support....

One of the primary objectives of the foreign policy of the United States is the creation of conditions in which we and other nations will be able to work out a way of life free from coercion. This was a fundamental issue in the war with Germany and Japan. Our victory was won over countries which sought to impose their will, and their way of life, upon other nations.

To ensure the peaceful development of nations, free from coercion, the United States has taken a leading part in establishing the United Nations. The United Nations is designed to make possible lasting freedom and independence for all its members. We shall not realize our objectives, however, unless we are willing to help free peoples to maintain their free institutions and their national integrity against aggressive movements that seek to impose upon them totalitarian regimes. This is no more than a frank recognition that totalitarian regimes imposed on free peoples, by direct or indirect aggression, undermine the foundations of international peace and hence the security of the United States.

The peoples of a number of countries of the world have recently had totalitarian regimes forced upon them against their will. The Government of the United States has made frequent protests against coercion and intimidation, in violation of the Yalta agreement, in Poland, Rumania, and Bulgaria. I must also state that in a number of other countries there have been similar developments.

At the present moment in world history nearly every nation must choose between alternative ways of life. The choice is too often not a free one.

One way of life is based upon the will of the majority, and is distinguished by free institutions, representative government, free elections, guarantees of individual liberty, freedom of speech and religion, and freedom from political oppression.

The second way of life is based upon the will of a minority forcibly imposed upon the majority. It relies upon terror and oppression, a controlled press and radio; fixed elections, and the suppression of personal freedoms.

I believe that it must be the policy of the United States to support free peoples who are resisting attempted subjugation by armed minorities or by outside pressures.

I believe that we must assist free peoples to work out their own destinies in their own way.

I believe that our help should be primarily through economic and financial aid which is essential to economic stability and orderly political processes....

It would be an unspeakable tragedy if these countries, which have struggled so long against overwhelming odds, should lose that victory for which they sacrificed so much. Collapse of free institutions and loss of independence would be disastrous not only for them but for the world. Discouragement and possibly failure would quickly be the lot of neighboring peoples striving to maintain their freedom and independence.

Should we fail to aid Greece and Turkey in this fateful hour, the effect will be far reaching to the West as well as to the East.

We must take immediate and resolute action....

The seeds of totalitarian regimes are nurtured by misery and want. They spread and grow in the evil soil of poverty and strife. They reach their full growth when the hope of a people for a better life has died. We must keep that hope alive.

The free peoples of the world look to us for support in maintaining their freedoms.

If we falter in our leadership, we may endanger the peace of the world—and we shall surely endanger the welfare of our own nation.

Great responsibilities have been placed upon us by the swift movement of events.

Glossary

Yalta	a city in southern Ukraine that was the site of a major Allied conference in 1945 attended by President Franklin Roosevelt, Prime Minister Winston Churchill of Britain, and Premier Joseph Stalin of the Soviet Union and held with the purpose of dealing with postwar Europe

ADDRESS TO THE NATIONAL ASSOCIATION FOR THE ADVANCEMENT OF COLORED PEOPLE (1947)

I should like to talk to you briefly about civil rights and human freedom. It is my deep conviction that we have reached a turning point in the long history of our country's efforts to guarantee a freedom and equality to all our citizens. Recent events in the United States and abroad have made us realize that it is more important today than ever before to insure that all Americans enjoy these rights.

And when I say all Americans—I mean all Americans.

The civil rights laws written in the early years of our republic, and the traditions, which have been built upon them, are precious to us. Those laws were drawn up with the memory still fresh in men's minds of the tyranny of an absentee government. They were written to protect the citizen against any possible tyrannical act by the new government in this country.

But we cannot be content with a civil liberties program, which emphasizes only the need of protection against the possibility of tyranny by the Government.

We cannot stop there.

We must keep moving forward, with new concepts of civil rights to safeguard our heritage. The extension of civil rights today means, not protection of the people against the Government, but protection of the people by the Government.

We must take the Federal Government a friendly, vigilant defender of the rights and equalities of all Americans. And again I mean all Americans.

As Americans, we believe that every man should be free to live his life as he wishes. He should be limited only by his responsibility to his fellow countrymen. If this freedom is to be more than a dream, each man must be guaranteed equality of opportunity. The only limit to an American's achievement should be his ability, his industry and his character. The rewards for his effort should be determined only by these truly relevant qualities.

Our immediate task is to remove the last remnants of the barriers, which stand between millions of our citizens and their birthright. There is no justifiable reason for discrimination because of ancestry, or religion. Or race, or color.

We must not tolerate such limitations on the freedom of any of our people and on their enjoyment of the basic rights, which every citizen in a truly democratic society must possess.

Every man should have the right to a decent home, the right to an education, the right to adequate medical care, the right to a worthwhile job, the right to an equal share in the making of public decisions through the ballot, and the right to a fair trial in a fair court.

We must insure that these rights—on equal terms—are enjoyed by every citizen.

To these principles I pledge my full and continued support.

Many of our people still suffer the indignity of insult, the harrowing fear of intimidation, and, I regret to say, the threat of physical injury and mob violence. The prejudice and intolerance in which these evils are rooted still exist. The conscience of our nation, and the legal machinery which enforces it, have not yet secured to each citizen full freedom from fear....

The support of desperate populations of battle-ravaged countries must be won for the free way of life. We must have them as allies in our continuing struggle for the peaceful solution of the world's problems. Freedom is not an easy lesson to teach, nor an easy cause to sell, to peoples beset by every kind of privation. They may surrender to the false security offered so temptingly by totalitarian regimes unless we can prove the superiority of democracy.

Our case for democracy should be as strong as we can make it. It should rest on practical evidence that we have been able to put our house in order.

For these compelling reasons, we can no longer afford the luxury of a leisurely attack upon prejudice and discrimination. There is much that state and local governments can do in providing positive safeguards for civil rights. But we cannot, any longer, await the growth of a will to action in the slowest state of the most backward community.

Our national government must show the way.

This is a difficult and complex undertaking. Federal laws and administrative machineries must be improved and expanded. We must provide the government with better tools to do the job. As a first step, I appointed an Advisory Committee on Civil Rights last December. Its members, fifteen distinguished private citizens, have been surveying our civil rights difficulties and needs for several months. I am confident that the product of their work will be a sensible and vigorous program for action by all of us.

We must strive to advance civil rights wherever it lies within our power. For example, I have asked the Congress to pass legislation extending basic civil rights to the people of Guam and American Samoa so that these people can share our ideals of freedom and self-government. This step, with others which will follow, is evidence to the rest of the world of our confidence in the ability of all men to build free institutions.

The way ahead is not easy. We shall need all the wisdom, imagination and courage we can muster. We must and shall guarantee the civil rights of all our citizens. Never before has the need been so urgent for skillful and vigorous action to bring us closer to our ideal.

We can reach the goal. When past difficulties faced our Nation, we met the challenge with inspiring charters of human rights—the Declaration of Independence, the Constitution, the Bill of Rights and the Emancipation Proclamation. Today our representatives, and those of other liberty-loving countries on the United Nations Commission on Human Rights, are preparing an International Bill of Rights.

With these noble charters to guide us, and with faith in our hearts, we shall make our land a happier home for our people, a symbol of hope for all men, and a rock of security in a troubled world.

Glossary

Guam and American Samoa	Pacific islands that are U.S. territories

Inaugural Address (1949)

Each period of our national history has had its special challenges. Those that confront us now are as momentous as any in the past. Today marks the beginning not only of a new administration, but of a period that will be eventful, perhaps decisive, for us and for the world.

It may be our lot to experience, and in a large measure bring about, a major turning point in the long history of the human race. The first half of this century has been marked by unprecedented and brutal attacks on the rights of man, and by the two most frightful wars in history. The supreme need of our time is for men to learn to live together in peace and harmony.

The peoples of the earth face the future with grave uncertainty, composed almost equally of great hopes and great fears. In this time of doubt, they look to the United States as never before for good will, strength, and wise leadership.

The American people stand firm in the faith which has inspired this Nation from the beginning. We believe that all men have a right to equal justice under law and equal opportunity to share in the common good. We believe that all men have the right to freedom of thought and expression. We believe that all men are created equal because they are created in the image of God.

From this faith we will not be moved....

In the pursuit of these aims, the United States and other like-minded nations find themselves directly opposed by a regime with contrary aims and a totally different concept of life.

That regime adheres to a false philosophy which purports to offer freedom, security, and greater opportunity to mankind. Misled by this philosophy, many peoples have sacrificed their liberties only to learn to their sorrow that deceit and mockery, poverty and tyranny, are their reward.

That false philosophy is communism....

Communism holds that the world is so deeply divided into opposing classes that war is inevitable.

Democracy holds that free nations can settle differences justly and maintain lasting peace....

We have sought no territory and we have imposed our will on none. We have asked for no privileges we would not extend to others....

In the coming years, our program for peace and freedom will emphasize four major courses of action.

First, we will continue to give unfaltering support to the United Nations and related agencies, and we will continue to search for ways to strengthen their authority and increase their effectiveness....

Second, we will continue our programs for world economic recovery.

This means, first of all, that we must keep our full weight behind the European recovery program.... In addition, we must carry out our plans for reducing the barriers to world trade and increasing its volume. Economic recovery and peace itself depend on increased world trade.

Third, we will strengthen freedom-loving nations against the dangers of aggression.

We are now working out with a number of countries a joint agreement designed to strengthen the security of the North Atlantic area. Such an agreement would take the form of a collective defense arrangement within the terms of the United Nations Charter.

We have already established such a defense pact for the Western Hemisphere by the treaty of Rio de Janeiro....

In addition, we will provide military advice and equipment to free nations which will cooperate with us in the maintenance of peace and security.

Fourth, we must embark on a bold new program for making the benefits of our scientific advances and industrial progress available for the improvement and growth of underdeveloped areas....

Our aim should be to help the free peoples of the world, through their own efforts, to produce more food, more clothing, more materials for housing, and more mechanical power to lighten their burdens....

The old imperialism—exploitation for foreign profit—has no place in our plans. What we envisage is a program of development based on the concepts of democratic fair-dealing....

We are aided by all who wish to live in freedom from fear—even by those who live today in fear under their own governments.

We are aided by all who want relief from the lies of propaganda—who desire truth and sincerity.

We are aided by all who desire self-government and a voice in deciding their own affairs.

We are aided by all who long for economic security—for the security and abundance that men in free societies can enjoy.

We are aided by all who desire freedom of speech, freedom of religion, and freedom to live their own lives for useful ends.

Our allies are the millions who hunger and thirst after righteousness.

In due time, as our stability becomes manifest, as more and more nations come to know the benefits of democracy and to participate in growing abundance, I believe that those countries which now oppose us will abandon their delusions and join with the free nations of the world in a just settlement of international differences.

Events have brought our American democracy to new influence and new responsibilities. They will test our courage, our devotion to duty, and our concept of liberty.

But I say to all men, what we have achieved in liberty, we will surpass in greater liberty.

Steadfast in our faith in the Almighty, we will advance toward a world where man's freedom is secure.

To that end we will devote our strength, our resources, and our firmness of resolve. With God's help, the future of mankind will be assured in a world of justice, harmony, and peace.

Glossary

treaty of Rio de Janeiro	more formally, the Inter-American Treaty of Reciprocal Assistance, a defense pact ratified in 1947 by numerous South and Central American countries as well as the United States

REPORT TO THE AMERICAN PEOPLE ON KOREA (1951)

In the simplest terms, what we are doing in Korea is this: We are trying to prevent a third world war....

It is right for us to be in Korea now. It was right last June. It is right today....

If they had followed the right policies in the 1930's—if the free countries had acted together to crush the aggression of the dictators, and if they had acted in the beginning when the aggression was small—there probably would have been no World War II.

If history has taught us anything, it is that aggression anywhere in the world is a threat to the peace everywhere in the world. When that aggression is supported by the cruel and selfish rulers of a powerful nation who are bent on conquest, it becomes a clear and present danger to the security and independence of every free nation.

This is a lesson that most people in this country have learned thoroughly. This is the basic reason why we joined in creating the United Nations. And, since the end of World War II, we have been putting that lesson into practice—we have been working with other free nations to check the aggressive designs of the Soviet Union before they can result in a third world war....

The aggression against Korea is the boldest and most dangerous move the Communists have yet made.

The attack on Korea was part of a greater plan for conquering all of Asia....

This plan of conquest is in flat contradiction to what we believe. We believe that Korea belongs to the Koreans, we believe that India belongs to the Indians, we believe that all the nations of Asia should be free to work out their affairs in their own way. This is the basis of peace in the Far East, and it is the basis of peace everywhere else....

So far, we have prevented World War III.

So far, by fighting a limited war in Korea, we have prevented aggression from succeeding, and bringing on a general war. And the ability of the whole free world to resist Communist aggression has been greatly improved.

We have taught the enemy a lesson. He has found that aggression is not cheap or easy, Moreover, men all over the world who want to remain free have been given new courage and new hope. They know now that the champions of freedom can stand up and fight, and that they will stand up and fight.

Our resolute stand in Korea is helping the forces of freedom now fighting in Indochina and other countries in that part of the world. It has already slowed down the timetable of conquest....

But you may ask why can't we take other steps to punish the aggressor. Why don't we bomb Manchuria and China itself? Why don't we assist the Chinese Nationalist troops to land on the mainland of China?

If we were to do these things we would be running a very grave risk of starting a general war. If that were to happen, we would have brought about the exact situation we are trying to prevent....

If we were to do these things, we would become entangled in a vast conflict on the continent of Asia and our task would become immeasurably more difficult all over the world.

Our aim is to avoid the spread of the conflict....

I believe that we must try to limit the war to Korea for these vital reasons: to make sure that the precious lives of our fighting men are not wasted; to see that the security of our country and the free world is

Glossary

Indochina	a region in Southeast Asia that includes Vietnam, Cambodia, and Laos
MacArthur	General Douglas MacArthur, a prominent American general in the Pacific Theater during World War II, in Japan during the postwar years, and during the Korean War
Manchuria	a region of Asia whose boundaries are variously defined but which lies largely in mainland China

not needlessly jeopardized; and to prevent a third world war.

A number of events have made it evident that General MacArthur did not agree with that policy. I have therefore considered it essential to relieve General MacArthur so that there would be no doubt or confusion as to the real purpose and aim of our policy.

It was with the deepest personal regret that I found myself compelled to take this action. General MacArthur is one of our greatest military commanders. But the cause of world peace is much more important than any individual.

The change in commands in the Far East means no change whatever in the policy of the United States. We will carry on the fight in Korea with vigor and determination in an effort to bring the war to a speedy and successful conclusion....

We are ready, at any time, to negotiate for a restoration of peace in the area. But we will not engage in appeasement. We are only interested in real peace....

We do not want to widen the conflict. We will use every effort to prevent that disaster. And in so doing, we know that we are following the great principles of peace, freedom, and justice.

Earl Warren (Library of Congress)

EARL WARREN 1891–1974

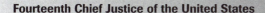

Fourteenth Chief Justice of the United States

Featured Documents
- *Brown v. Board of Education of Topeka* (1954)
- *Reynolds v. Sims* (1964)
- Warren Commission Report (1964)
- *Miranda v. Arizona* (1966)

Overview

As governor of California and chief justice of the United States, Earl Warren defied political categorization, confounding his supporters and critics alike. Although he proved to be a notoriously "liberal" judge, he had been head of the Republican Party in California and had won the vice presidential nomination on the Republican ticket in 1948. Prominent in California politics during the reformist Progressive Era, Warren pursued an agenda as district attorney and later as governor that included elimination of corruption within law enforcement, cracking down on gambling rings, and prison reform. Under his leadership as chief justice, the Supreme Court issued several landmark rulings, among them, decisions on religious freedom, criminal law procedure, civil rights and equal protection under the law, and freedom of speech and obscenity. With a long career spanning the years of the Progressive Era, the Great Depression, World War II, the cold war, and the civil rights movement, Warren epitomizes the American struggle to answer many of the moral questions of the twentieth century.

Warren was born on March 19, 1891, and grew up in the booming oil town of Bakersfield, California, where his father worked as a handyman. He graduated from Kern County High School in 1908 and enrolled at the University of California, Berkeley, where he earned both a bachelor's and a law degree. Following President Woodrow Wilson's call for a congressional declaration of war against Germany on April 2, 1917, Warren joined the army and completed officer training. In 1919 a college friend helped him secure a position as clerk of the California State Assembly Judiciary Committee. Warren soon became deputy city attorney of Oakland, working his way up to the position of district attorney of Alameda County in 1925.

His professional reputation growing, Warren was elected state chairman of the Republican Party in 1934, despite his belief in nonpartisanship; he repeatedly campaigned as a political independent. In 1938 he was elected attorney general and, in 1942, governor of California. As governor, Warren irked the Republican right when he called for compulsory medical insurance, but his record of fiscal responsibility pleased most conservatives. Under Warren's watch, the University of California system expanded, the teachers' retirement fund regained solvency, and the state began developing its massive highway system. Perhaps the most notorious act of Warren's gubernatorial stint was his support for the evacuation and internment of Japanese residents, including U.S. citizens, following the attack on Pearl Harbor, Hawaii.

After his decisive reelection victory in 1946, Warren was considered a candidate for president. He was nominated for vice president on the Republican ticket in the 1948 election, in which the Republican Thomas Dewey lost to the Democrate Harry Truman. He then lost the presidential nomination to Dwight Eisenhower in 1952. When Chief Justice Fred Vinson died of a heart attack in 1953, Eisenhower named Warren as Vinson's replacement. Under Warren's leadership, the Supreme Court handed down several historic decisions. One of the first and most important of these cases was *Brown v. Board of Education of Topeka* (1954), which paved the way for school desegregation. The chief justice wrote dissenting opinions in four separate obscenity cases, arguing that pornographers did not deserve First Amendment protection. Nevertheless, decisions such as *Engel v. Vitale* (1962), which ruled school prayer unconstitutional, fueled public outcry against the liberal nature of the Warren Court. The Court addressed the issue of voting rights in *Baker v. Carr* (1962) and the subsequent case, *Reynolds v. Sims* (1964), handing down the famous "one man, one vote" edict, which essentially extended the Court's power to the legislative branch of government. The obligation of law enforcement officials to advise criminal suspects of their rights was confirmed by the Court's 1966 ruling in *Miranda v. Arizona*. Perhaps Warren's most well-known activity, however, was his investigation into the 1963 assassination of President John F. Kennedy. The President's Commission on the Assassination of President Kennedy, popularly known as the Warren Commission, produced a report that received enormous public scrutiny and has been the subject of ongoing debate into the twenty-first century. Warren retired from the Court in 1969. He died on July 9, 1974, in Washington, D.C.

Explanation and Analysis of Documents

Earl Warren led the U.S. Supreme Court during the turbulent years of the 1950s and 1960s. Driven by his own moral compass rather than politics, Warren shocked those on the left and right as he made the transition from crime-

Time Line

1891
- ■ **March 19**
  Earl Warren is born in Los Angeles, California.

1914
- ■ **May**
  Warren graduates from the University of California, Berkeley, with a Juris Doctor degree.

1917
- ■ **September 5**
  Warren leaves for Camp Lewis, Washington, as acting first sergeant of I Company, U.S. Army.

1919
- ■ Warren returns to civilian life as a clerk of the California State Assembly Judiciary Committee.
- ■ **April**
  Warren is named deputy city attorney of Oakland, California.

1925
- ■ **January 12**
  Warren becomes district attorney of Alameda County.

1934
- ■ **September 28**
  Warren is elected state chairman of the Republican Party in California.

1938
- ■ **November 8**
  Warren is elected attorney general of California.

1942
- ■ **November 3**
  Warren is elected governor of California.

1948
- ■ **November**
  Warren unsuccessfully runs for vice president on the Republican ticket with Thomas Dewey.

1953
- ■ **October 5**
  Warren is sworn in as chief justice of the United States.

---

fighting district attorney to liberal chief justice. He became known as a protector of the rights of minorities and the oppressed, a stance reflected in many of his rulings. Warren's ability to communicate legal concepts in concise language free from emotion and accessible to the public is demonstrated in his decisions in *Brown v. Board of Education of Topeka*, *Reynolds v. Sims*, and *Miranda v. Arizona* and in the Warren Commission Report on the assassination of President John F. Kennedy.

◆ *Brown v. Board of Education of Topeka*

Brown v. Board was one of Warren's first decisions as chief justice and was arguably his most high-profile case. The landmark decision overturned the 1896 Court ruling in *Plessy v. Ferguson* and paved the way for the national ascent of the leaders of the civil rights movement, such as Rosa Parks and Martin Luther King, Jr. In the 1896 case, Homer Plessy, who was of European and African descent, challenged a Louisiana law that required blacks and whites to ride in separate railroad cars. Plessy, who was by law black, sat in a "whites only" car and was subsequently arrested when he refused to change his seat. His case ended up in the Supreme Court, where the majority ruled that state laws enforcing segregation, or the provision of "separate but equal" facilities, were constitutional. After the decision in *Plessy v. Ferguson*, laws establishing separate public areas for whites and blacks, known as Jim Crow laws, proliferated in the South.

Blacks in America continued to live under this omnipresent system of apartheid through the early decades of the twentieth century, although the National Association for the Advancement of Colored People (NAACP) launched several legal challenges, with marginal success. Racial attitudes changed dramatically following World War II, as theories of scientific racism that had been almost universally accepted by the public and academia were debunked and the evidence of Hitler's implementation of racial ideology horrified the world. This new climate reenergized the NAACP, which began to pursue a number of school segregation lawsuits throughout the country. Several of these cases ended up in the Supreme Court; one such case was *Brown v. Board of Education*. The NAACP had organized several families, including Oliver Brown and his daughter, Linda, who agreed to sue the Board of Education of Topeka, Kansas, for access to schools closer to their homes. Topeka provided eighteen schools for white children but only four for black children.

Brown v. Board was first heard by the Supreme Court, under the leadership of Chief Justice Fred Vinson, in December 1952. A cautious jurist, Vinson shied away from the kinds of groundbreaking decisions that would epitomize Warren's term as chief justice. Vinson did not want to overturn *Plessy v. Ferguson*, and for various reasons three of his fellow justices agreed with him. The other five judges thought that the "separate but equal" edict should be overturned. With such a divided opinion, the Vinson Court tabled the case. Warren thus inherited both the case and a divided Court when he took over Vinson's position. Personally convinced on moral grounds that segregation was wrong, Warren began to develop a consensus among his fellow judges, knowing that only a unanimous decision would send a strong enough message. Through his efforts and those of other jurists, particularly Felix Frankfurter, Warren pulled the Supreme Court together to deliver a nine-to-zero decision in favor of the plaintiffs.

In *Brown*, as well as in the later cases *Reynolds v. Sims* and *Miranda v. Arizona*, Chief Justice Warren voted with the majority and assigned the majority opinion to himself. Warren often assigned himself the particularly controversial cases or the ones about which he had especially strong personal beliefs or feelings. *Brown v. Board* was certainly both controversial and deeply personal for Warren. Yet it was a unanimous decision, and Warren was careful to craft a document that reflected the beliefs of all the judges, not just his own.

Warren opens his opinion with an overview of the case. As he explains, *Brown v. Board* was one of four segregation cases that the Court considered together. The Supreme Court often consolidates a number of related cases under one lead case; this was the situation in *Miranda v. Arizona* as well. In *Brown* all of the cases concerned children who were denied admission to white public schools, and all plaintiffs claimed that their Fourteenth Amendment rights had been violated. Section 1 of the Fourteenth Amendment to the Constitution guarantees "all persons born or naturalized within the United States ... equal protection of the laws." Warren clearly states that this case hinges on the Court's conclusion as to whether separate, or segregated, schools can ever be considered equal.

Following a brief reference to the 1952 hearing by the Vinson Court, Warren addresses a concern that surfaced early in the reargument. One of the reasons the Vinson Court had been so divided was that the judges could not agree on the intent behind the Fourteenth Amendment. Were its authors, in 1868, in favor of segregation, and, if so, could that intent be clearly established? Warren knew that this question needed to be addressed if he hoped to achieve a unanimous decision. Justice Felix Frankfurter, who favored striking down *Plessy v. Ferguson*, researched the history of the Fourteenth Amendment and found that there was no clear intent on behalf of the framers of the amendment either against or in support of segregation. Warren states that the Court can never truly know the intent of the Fourteenth Amendment's authors—"We cannot turn the clock back to 1868"—but that this is not the important question. In effect, Frankfurter and Warren took the constitutional question off the table and changed the nature of the discussion. The Court's decision would hang no longer on a legal issue but on a social and moral matter: the nature and role of public education in modern America.

Once he changed the nature of the debate from a legal one to a question of social justice, Warren sums up the importance of education to a functioning society. He emphasizes that education is crucial to "democratic society," meeting "basic public responsibilities," preparing citizens for "service in the armed forces," and fostering "good citizen-

Time Line

1954

■ **May 17**
Warren delivers the Supreme Court's decision in the case *Brown v. Board of Education*.

1964

■ **June 15**
Warren reads his majority opinion for *Reynolds v. Sims*.

■ **September 24**
Warren presents President Lyndon B. Johnson with the findings of the Warren Commission on the assassination of President Kennedy.

1966

■ **June 13**
Warren delivers the Court's ruling in the case of *Miranda v. Arizona*.

1969

■ **June 23**
Warren retires from the Supreme Court.

1974

■ **July 9**
Warren dies in Washington, D.C.

ship." By linking public education to American values and civic ideals, Warren persuasively argues for the importance of equal opportunity in language accessible to the public.

Warren succinctly delivers the judgment of the Court regarding whether segregation deprives children of equal educational opportunities: "We believe that it does." He then makes his case for why "separate" cannot be "equal," even if the actual school facilities are the same for black and white children. Here, Warren turns to past Supreme Court decisions to justify the current ruling. *Sweatt v. Painter* was the 1950 case of a black man who was denied admission to the University of Texas Law School. The Court ruled unanimously that Sweatt must be admitted, finding that the segregation of black students in a separate school would in and of itself have a negative impact on their potential to succeed as lawyers. *McLaurin v. Oklahoma State Regents*, another case decided in 1950, had to do with a black student admitted to the University of Oklahoma's graduate school who was assigned a special seat designated for black students in his classroom, in the school cafeteria, and in the library. Warren notes that the Court ruled that such treatment hindered the plaintiff's ability to learn. Interestingly, he also cites specific wording from an earlier lower-court ruling and references "modern authority," which included sociological and psychological publications of the time. Thus, Warren not only draws on specific cases in which the Court ruled against segregation but also invokes language used in prior court arguments against the *Brown* plaintiffs as well as opinions of experts outside the legal community.

Having decided that the concept of "separate but equal" cannot exist in public education, Warren next had to argue as to how to solve the problem of desegregating educational facilities. His language changes markedly in this section of the decision, as Warren and the other judges believed that it was not the Court's place to mandate the schedule or methods for desegregation. Warren states that the situation "presents problems of considerable complexity," which signals that the Court believes that each case will need to be readdressed by the lower courts. He articulates the Supreme Court's role in this decision very clearly: The question of "appropriate relief was necessarily subordinated" to the larger question of the constitutionality of segregated public education. As such, the cases aggregated under *Brown v. Board* were "restored to the docket," or referred back to the lower courts in which they were originally argued, so that the solutions could be worked out there.

Driven by his personal feelings, Warren argued the immorality and social injustice of segregation rather than dwelling on the technical aspects of constitutional law to reach a unanimous decision in *Brown*. As southern schools fought the mandate to desegregate, the Court eventually issued another decision in 1955, known as *Brown II*. Also written by Warren, this decision reiterated the principles of the first decision and furthermore stated that the courts and schools must act with "all deliberate speed" to end segregation. Warren's language inflamed many, but his decisions had propelled a movement. In December 1955, Rosa Parks would refuse to move from the white section of a public bus in Montgomery, Alabama, and what had started in public education would spread to still other public spaces in America.

◆ Reynolds v. Sims

Despite the protections of the Fourteenth Amendment, black voters continued to be disenfranchised in the South through the 1950s. Disenfranchisement took many forms, including literacy tests and poll taxes. The process of apportionment, which determined the boundaries of congressional districts, also effectively disenfranchised voters, particularly those who lived in urban areas. Even though many states' populations were shifting from the country to the city, most states continued to allocate representatives by county, which effectively robbed urban voters of proportional representation in their legislatures. Rural interests thus governed increasingly urban populations.

In 1959 Charles Baker and nine other urban residents sued the Tennessee secretary of state, Joe C. Carr, noting that the state had not reapportioned its districts since 1901 and had thus effectively denied its urban voters their Fourteenth Amendment rights. *Baker v. Carr* represented a challenge to the Warren Court. First of all, the courts had traditionally shied away from matters involving political

districting, concerned that judicial rulings in this area could be construed as a violation of separation of powers; legislative questions were considered political matters not appropriate for Court involvement. Furthermore, the right to vote is not clearly established by the Constitution. The Founders had a restrictive view of who should be able to vote: Slaves, women, and unpropertied males were not considered eligible. In considering *Baker v. Carr*, the Court was entering new territory. Written by William J. Brennan, the 1962 *Baker* decision was carefully worded, stating only that reapportionment could be taken up in the courts. The ruling thus let individual federal district courts decide how they would solve problems of malapportionment. Soon after the decision was announced, attorneys filed cases challenging apportionments in several states. By the end of 1962, the Supreme Court had twelve cases pending that related to redistricting. These state cases were decided collectively under *Reynolds v. Sims* on June 15, 1964.

In *Reynolds v. Sims*, several voters in Alabama sued state election officials, charging that their Fourteenth Amendment rights, as well as their rights under the Alabama Constitution, had been violated by the state's existing legislative apportionment. The case also involved a dispute over proposed reapportionment plans, which the plaintiffs argued were unconstitutional. Having established in *Baker v. Carr* that the courts did, in fact, have jurisdiction over such matters, the Warren Court now needed to address specific cases handed up by the federal district courts.

In the first paragraph of the excerpt of Warren's decision, he makes clear his opinion that the Court has jurisdiction over questions of redistricting. One of the roles of the Supreme Court is to evaluate the constitutionality of state and federal laws; by stating that the Constitution protects the right of qualified voters, Warren establishes the Court's role in striking down laws that violate those rights.

As was the case in *Brown v. Board*, Warren's decision in this case was strongly influenced by his attitude toward racial discrimination. He mentions the practice of "gerrymandering," which is the manipulation of election district boundaries in order to influence election results. The term derives from Elbridge Gerry, governor of Massachusetts from 1810 to 1812, who redistricted the state to benefit his political party. Warren refers to racial gerrymandering, which was practiced in both southern and northern states; by redrawing legislative district lines, politicians could create segregated, all-black districts or, in some cases, eliminate black voters from an area when it was expedient. Warren points out that malapportionment disenfranchises voters just as effectively as prohibiting them from voting at all.

Warren's decisions are noteworthy for their clear, straightforward language. This particular document contains an especially unusual and oft-quoted passage: "Legislators represent people, not trees or acres. Legislators are elected by voters, not farms or cities or economic interests." This verbiage was actually crafted by the law clerk Francis X. Beytagh, who worked on the case with Warren. Warren read this in the draft statement and thought that the language captured the essence of his "one man, one

PHOTOGRAPH FROM ZAPRUDER FILM

PHOTOGRAPH FROM RE-ENACTMENT

PHOTOGRAPH THROUGH RIFLE SCOPE

DISTANCE TO STATION C	181.9 FT.
DISTANCE TO RIFLE IN WINDOW	218.0 FT.
ANGLE TO RIFLE IN WINDOW	18°03′
DISTANCE TO OVERPASS	307.1 FT.
ANGLE TO OVERPASS	+0°44′

FRAME 255

Exhibit 901 in the Warren Commission Report of the assassination of John F. Kennedy (AP/Wide World Photos)

vote" argument. The passage stands out for the very reason that its tone differs from that of the rest of the document.

A key component of Warren's decision is his statement that "seats in both houses of a bicameral state legislature must be apportioned on a population basis." Important here is the assertion that both houses had to use population as a means of determining representation. Following *Baker v. Carr*, many states refused to reapportion their districts, instead using what was known as the "federal plan," in which one house of the legislature was apportioned geographically and the other by population. *Reynolds v. Sims* made clear that the federal plan was no longer an option. Warren allowed for some flexibility in redistricting in order to prevent gerrymandering or to provide for fair representation in more rural states with many counties. However, he reiterates in his decision that population is the overriding factor that should determine the number of representatives.

Reynolds v. Sims was a much broader decision than *Baker v. Carr* in the sense that it had a dramatic and lasting impact on the political landscape. By specifically defining constitutional districting plans in terms of population rather

than geography, Warren summarily eliminated the jobs of many powerful rural senators and assemblymen; rural districts disappeared as states redrew boundaries to conform to the new requirements. *Reynolds v. Sims* thus helped end one method of black voter disenfranchisement in America.

◆ **Warren Commission Report**

On November 22, 1963, President John F. Kennedy was shot while riding in a motorcade in Dallas, Texas. Lee Harvey Oswald, an employee of the Texas School Book Depository, was arrested for the murder of Kennedy and of a police officer who had attempted to stop him. Oswald claimed that he was innocent. Two days later, while police were transferring Oswald to jail, Jack Ruby, a Dallas nightclub operator, shot and killed Oswald.

The Kennedy assassination was devastating to the American public, and the details of the crime and Oswald's murder fostered rumors of a conspiracy. In the early 1960s America was embroiled in the cold war, and tense showdowns with Cuba and the Soviet Union left Americans fearful of the threat of nuclear attack as well as the spread of Communism. As speculation grew that Kennedy's death was the result of either a right-wing conspiracy or a plot hatched by the Kremlin, President Lyndon B. Johnson appointed Warren to head a commission to investigate the details of the assassination.

The Warren Commission Report begins with a description of the commission's charge and then lists the conclusions reached by the investigation. Warren refers to the cooperation of government agencies in the inquiry; one of the criticisms of the Warren Commission was that it relied on the reports of agencies such as the Central Intelligence Agency and the Federal Bureau of Investigation rather than unearthing its own evidence through independent investigations. This feature of the commission and its report fueled later speculation that the government covered up evidence in the Kennedy assassination.

The report's conclusions reflect the commission's goals of providing an objective analysis of the Kennedy assassination and of quashing rumors. One of the questions circulating was whether Kennedy had been killed by a single gunman; many argued that a second gunman had to have been involved. The document specifically addresses the issue of a second shooter, clearly concluding that a single assassin was responsible. Warren states that the killer fired from the Texas School Book Depository; the commission's evidence included the fact that witnesses saw a rifle being fired from the sixth-floor window, and police found a rifle on the sixth floor of the building. A factor leading to the multiple-shooter theory was the fact that John B. Connally, Jr., the governor of Texas, was riding in the motorcade with Kennedy and was also shot and wounded. Some speculated that it was impossible for a single bullet to account for the governor's wounds. The Warren Commission Report's language is rather vague with respect to this, referring to a "difference of opinion" as to the probability that one bullet could cause injury to both Kennedy and Connally. This vagueness also bolstered critics who suspected government involvement in covering up evidence. Part of the problem was that Warren decided not to include photographs or radiographs in the final report, as he believed that including these materials would have been offensive to the Kennedy family and an invasion of their privacy. Unfortunately, the omission became an issue and undermined the credibility of the final report.

Having determined that a lone gunman in the Texas School Book Depository was responsible for the crime, Warren then concludes that the gunman was Lee Harvey Oswald. Oswald was employed by the book depository and owned the rifle found on the sixth floor. Warren furthermore states that Oswald (and also Ruby) acted alone. As noted in the report, Oswald had lived in the Soviet Union for about three years and was involved in Communist political activity; this detail, of course, led to the rumors about an international conspiracy in Kennedy's death. Jack Ruby, in turn, had traveled to Cuba, which led some to speculate that Ruby and Oswald were part of a plot hatched by Cuba's dictator, Fidel Castro. On the other hand, Oswald had the name and telephone number of a Federal Bureau of Investigation agent in his notebook, which gave rise to rumors that Oswald was a government agent; Warren addresses this concern in the report as well, using very careful language. As was the case with the decision in *Brown v. Board*, Warren knew that he needed a unanimous conclusion by the commission. Some members refused to approve the final report unless it acknowledged the possibility of a Communist plot; Gerald Ford, then a representative and later president, believed that Castro was responsible for the assassination. In order to achieve unanimity, Warren used wording that allowed for the possibility that future evidence would substantiate a conspiracy or plot.

The Warren Commission Report was well received by the public, becoming a best-selling book. Nevertheless, conspiracy theories continued to emerge, spawning books and movies, further government inquiries, and even the exhumation of Oswald's body in 1981. The shocking, public nature of Kennedy's assassination and of Ruby's murder of Oswald, occurring at a time of heightened political concern, partially explains the skepticism surrounding the commission's report. Yet the open-ended nature of the document's conclusions, written to accommodate the different opinions of the commission's members, helped to spur on conspiracy theorists.

◆ *Miranda v. Arizona*

During the 1960s the Supreme Court received several appeals concerning confessions obtained by questionable methods. One such case was *Escobedo v. Illinois* (1964). The Chicago laborer Danny Escobedo was arrested for the murder of his brother-in-law. Police handcuffed him and took him into a separate room for interrogation. Escobedo then asked to see his attorney, who was in the police station waiting to confer with his client. The police denied Escobedo's request, however, and interrogated him for hours. Escobedo eventually admitted that he had paid an accomplice to kill his brother-in-law; he was convicted of murder and sentenced to twenty years in prison. The case ended up on appeal in the Supreme Court, which overturned Escobedo's conviction on the basis that his Fifth Amendment right against self-incrimination had been violated.

The decision in *Escobedo v. Illinois* applied only to cases where the suspect's attorney was present at the time of the interrogation. For this reason, the Court continued to receive appeals cases involving suspects who had been questioned before a lawyer was present. By November 1965, the Supreme Court faced 170 appeals concerning such questions. The Warren Court narrowed the 170 appeals to four representative cases, grouped together under *Miranda v. Arizona*.

Chief Justice Warren begins his decision with an assessment of "American criminal jurisprudence," or the balance between prosecuting suspected criminals in society and preserving the constitutional rights of those suspected criminals. He refers to *Escobedo v. Illinois* and the role of the Fifth Amendment, which prohibits a person from being "compelled in any criminal case to be a witness against himself." Warren reviews the fact that the *Escobedo* decision was open to wide interpretation by the lower courts, prosecutors, and police officers; he notes that the Supreme Court had already "granted certiorari" to several related cases, meaning they had been accepted for review. Finally, Warren reinforces his belief that both *Escobedo v. Illinois* and *Miranda v. Arizona* are cases whose rulings do not break new ground in terms of the Court's role but rather merely reinforce individuals' rights as stated in the Constitution. Warren quotes the decision in *Cohens v. Virginia* (1821), in which Chief Justice John Marshall asserted the Court's authority to rule in lower court cases involving the violation of individuals' constitutional rights, to further make this point.

One of the controversial aspects of Warren's decision was his inclusion of specific guidelines for advising suspects of their rights. Justice Brennan asked Warren to allow state legislatures to develop their own language, but Warren declined to remove the instructions from the decision. Warren gives the states room for "creative rulemaking" but provides specific language to be used; this is the origin of the commonly known phrase "You have the right to remain silent." It is clear from his language that Warren's primary interest is in achieving balance of power between the suspect and his or her interrogators. Knowledge of one's rights, he notes, helps to combat the "inherent pressures of the interrogation atmosphere."

Warren then turns to the four cases grouped together under the label *Miranda v. Arizona.* He explains how the cases are similar: The defendants were not advised of their rights while being questioned in a "police-dominated atmosphere." Warren emphasizes the psychological impact of the interrogation process, particularly the nature of "incommunicado" questioning, where the suspect is isolated from any outside influence. From his years in law enforcement, Warren was highly sensitive to the potential for interrogators to abuse their power, and his language reveals his concern for protecting suspects from questionable interview tactics.

Having established that *Escobedo v. Illinois* set the precedent for protecting the Fifth Amendment rights of suspects in custody and that the nature of police interrogation lends itself to the potential for self-incrimination, Warren concludes that the accused must be explicitly advised of his or her rights and must be allowed to exercise those rights. He then addresses a criticism of the *Escobedo* decision, which was also an issue with the cases considered under *Miranda v. Arizona.* Many, particularly prosecutors and the police, believed that advising suspects of their rights hindered the efforts of law enforcement to combat crime: Notifying detainees that they could retain counsel or refrain from answering questions might result in guilty criminals going free. Warren cites a previous Court decision, *Chambers v. Florida*, in his response to this concern. *Chambers v. Florida* was a 1940 case in which the Supreme Court reversed the conviction and associated death sentences of four black tenant farmers whose confessions were coerced by their interrogators. Announcing the unanimous decision in the case, Justice Hugo Black specifically dismissed law enforcement's argument that the well-being of the community outweighed the negative aspects of the

questioning tactics. Warren also quotes Justice Louis Brandeis, a member of the Supreme Court who, like Warren, is known for many decisions that advanced causes of social justice. The quotation is from Brandeis's dissenting opinion in *Olmstead v. United States*, a 1928 case in which the Court ruled that evidence obtained from secret wiretaps planted in the building of Roy Olmstead, a bootlegger, was admissible in court. In his dissent, Brandeis argued that such government activity "breeds contempt for law." Warren uses these two examples as evidence of legal precedent for his own decision in this case.

Warren briefly reviews the details of the *Miranda* case before rendering his decision to reverse Miranda's conviction. Ernesto Miranda was a poor, uneducated man with limited English skills. Diagnosed with a sociopathic personality disorder, he had a string of prior arrests for rape and lewd conduct. Police arrested Miranda when they found a vehicle outside Miranda's home that was identical to that owned by a woman who had been raped and kidnapped. The victim identified Miranda as the perpetrator of the crime. As Warren notes, Miranda signed a written admission of guilt stating that he confessed with complete understanding of his rights, despite the fact that the arresting officers admitted that they had not advised him. As an unsophisticated, mentally ill defendant, Miranda was the very kind of person who, Warren believed, needed protection from the sophisticated methods of law-enforcement interrogation. Guilty or not, Miranda was entitled to his constitutional rights.

Law enforcement and many politicians howled over the decision in *Miranda v. Arizona*, promising that guilty criminals would go free. The public reaction was also not entirely favorable; the Warren Court's reputation for liberal rulings was only reinforced by this decision. Ever the champion of individual rights, Warren stood by his decision. Today, the concept of a "Miranda warning," or notification of one's right to remain silent, is a cornerstone of the American criminal justice system.

Impact and Legacy

Historians typically comment on the seeming contradictions in Warren's career and personality; his apparent transformation from a conservative state politician to a liberal chief justice confounded his peers as well. The crime-fighting district attorney became the champion of the accused. The advocate of Japanese internment fought against segregation. In one sense, Warren's life and career reflect the fundamental shifts that occurred in American society during the 1950s and 1960s, as changing racial attitudes began to radically alter the ways in which minorities and underprivileged groups were viewed.

Warren's impact on the role of the Supreme Court is also reflective of these broader changes in American society and has been the source of much criticism leveled against him, today and in his own time. Never much of a student, he based his legal decisions not on carefully argued theory but

"To separate [children] from others of similar age and qualifications solely because of their race generates a feeling of inferiority as to their status in the community that may affect their hearts and minds in a way unlikely ever to be undone."

(*Brown v. Board of Education*)

"We conclude that, in the field of public education, the doctrine of 'separate but equal' has no place. Separate educational facilities are inherently unequal."

(*Brown v. Board of Education*)

"Legislators represent people, not trees or acres. Legislators are elected by voters, not farms or cities or economic interests."

(*Reynolds v. Sims*)

"The Commission has found no evidence that either Lee Harvey Oswald or Jack Ruby was part of any conspiracy, domestic or foreign, to assassinate President Kennedy."

(Warren Commission Report)

"The cases before us raise questions which go to the roots of our concepts of American criminal jurisprudence: the restraints society must observe consistent with the Federal Constitution in prosecuting individuals for crime."

(*Miranda v. Arizona*)

"We have concluded that, without proper safeguards, the process of in-custody interrogation of persons suspected or accused of crime contains inherently compelling pressures which work to undermine the individual's will to resist and to compel him to speak where he would not otherwise do so freely. In order to combat these pressures and to permit a full opportunity to exercise the privilege against self-incrimination, the accused must be adequately and effectively apprised of his rights, and the exercise of those rights must be fully honored."

(*Miranda v. Arizona*)

on his own belief system, what one historian has referred to as "a simple moral compass" (Cray, p. 11). As a result, the Supreme Court justices under Warren's leadership became the defenders of the oppressed and, in many cases, the most despised members of American society. Fellow jurist Felix Frankfurter increasingly despaired at Warren's judicial activism, fearing that the Court was overstepping its authority, particularly with respect to the state's jurisdiction in criminal matters. For Warren, however, the Court had a responsibility to protect individuals from those very state authorities, and in many cases the individuals most in need of protection were the ones least able to defend themselves: minorities and the poor.

Warren revolutionized Americans' view of the Supreme Court, situating it as an advocate for social justice. Many of his decisions affected the most sensitive areas of daily life, including religion, race, marriage, and free speech. His often controversial rulings earned Warren the ire of many but established his pivotal importance in American political and legal history.

Key Sources

Papers related to Warren's service as district attorney of Alameda County and as governor of California are housed

---

Questions for Further Study

1. Warren was among the most controversial figures ever to hold the seat of Supreme Court chief justice. Among the criticisms leveled at him was that in his penchant for judicial activism he had overstepped the bounds of the Constitution, essentially granting to the judicial branch of government powers that had been set aside for the legislative branch. Furthermore, his emphasis, in *Miranda* and other cases, on protecting the rights of the accused seemed to open the way for increasing lawlessness. Discuss these criticisms of Warren, using specific cases as examples, and evaluate the net effect of his contribution to American jurisprudence. In the long run, did he provide necessary corrections to past injustices, or did he go too far in shaping the Court as an institution actively working to change the structure of American society? Explain your answer, citing examples from his rulings.

2. Another controversial aspect of Warren's Supreme Court opinions is the fact that they were not always based purely on constitutional law. Rather, he often argued from his personal convictions regarding morality and, to support his positions, was almost as likely to refer to findings of social scientists as to the history of legal proceedings in U.S. court. Were these approaches appropriate to his role as Supreme Court chief justice? To what extent did he use supporting evidence aside from legal case histories in making his points, and did he adequately establish the legal background for his positions? How important is it for the highest judge in the land to stick purely to constitutional law as a basis for his reasoning?

3. Explain the history of the "separate but equal" notion established in *Plessy v. Ferguson* and later struck down by perhaps the most important case in the history of the Warren Court, *Brown v. Board of Education*. Briefly review the history of Jim Crow laws and institutionalized segregation, not just in the South but—as *Brown* itself showed—in the Midwest and other parts of the country as well, and explain the background of the *Brown* case. How did Warren make his argument that separate institutions were by their very nature unequal? Be sure to cite his references to *Sweatt v. Painter* and *McLaurin v. Oklahoma State Regents*.

4. Evaluate Warren's role in overseeing the investigation of the Kennedy assassination. Pay special attention to those aspects of his work on the Warren Commission that, in the eyes of many observers, seemed to suggest a cover-up: his refusal to include photographs, for instance, or his reliance on the reports of government agencies instead of conducting a full and separate investigation. What were Warren's reasons for taking these actions, and do you think he acted rightly? Why or why not? How important was his concern for unanimity on the part of the commission, and how did that influence the final shape of the report? What could he have done to allay Americans' fears of a conspiracy or cover-up regarding the assassination?

---

in the California State Archives, with an inventory available online (http://www.oac.cdlib.org/findaid/ark:/13030/tf4b69 n6gc). Documents generated during his term as chief justice of the United States are located in the Library of Congress and are also inventoried online (http://www.loc.gov/ rr/mss/text/warren.html). *The Memoirs of Earl Warren* was published in 1977.

Further Reading

■ Books

Cray, Ed. *Chief Justice: A Biography of Earl Warren*. New York: Simon & Schuster, 1997.

Schwartz, Bernard. *Super Chief: Earl Warren and His Supreme Court: A Judicial Biography*. New York: New York University Press, 1983.

Weaver, John D. *Warren: The Man, the Court, the Era*. Boston: Little, Brown, 1967.

White, G. Edward. *Earl Warren: A Public Life*. New York: Oxford University Press, 1982.

■ Web Sites

"Earl Warren." Governors of California Web site. http://www.californiagovernors.ca.gov/h/biography/governor_30.html.

"Earl Warren." Oyez Web site. http://www.oyez.org/justices/earl_warren/.

"Earl Warren (1891–1974)." Landmark Supreme Court Cases Web site. http://www.landmarkcases.org/brown/warren.html.

—Karen Linkletter

BROWN V. BOARD OF EDUCATION OF TOPEKA (1954)

These cases come to us from the States of Kansas, South Carolina, Virginia, and Delaware. They are premised on different facts and different local conditions, but a common legal question justifies their consideration together in this consolidated opinion.

In each of the cases, minors of the Negro race, through their legal representatives, seek the aid of the courts in obtaining admission to the public schools of their community on a nonsegregated basis. In each instance, they had been denied admission to schools attended by white children under laws requiring or permitting segregation according to race. This segregation was alleged to deprive the plaintiffs of the equal protection of the laws under the Fourteenth Amendment. In each of the cases other than the Delaware case, a three-judge federal district court denied relief to the plaintiffs on the so-called "separate but equal" doctrine announced by this Court in *Plessy v. Ferguson*. Under that doctrine, equality of treatment is accorded when the races are provided substantially equal facilities, even though these facilities be separate. In the Delaware case, the Supreme Court of Delaware adhered to that doctrine, but ordered that the plaintiffs be admitted to the white schools because of their superiority to the Negro schools.

The plaintiffs contend that segregated public schools are not "equal" and cannot be made "equal," and that hence they are deprived of the equal protection of the laws. Because of the obvious importance of the question presented, the Court took jurisdiction. Argument was heard in the 1952 Term, and reargument was heard this Term on certain questions propounded by the Court.

Reargument was largely devoted to the circumstances surrounding the adoption of the Fourteenth Amendment in 1868. It covered exhaustively consideration of the Amendment in Congress, ratification by the states, then-existing practices in racial segregation, and the views of proponents and opponents of the Amendment. This discussion and our own investigation convince us that, although these sources cast some light, it is not enough to resolve the problem with which we are faced. At best, they are inconclusive. The most avid proponents of the post-War Amendments undoubtedly intended them to remove all legal distinctions among "all persons born or naturalized in the United States." Their opponents, just as certainly, were antagonistic to both the letter and the spirit of the Amendments and wished them to have the most limited effect. What others in Congress and the state legislatures had in mind cannot be determined with any degree of certainty.

An additional reason for the inconclusive nature of the Amendment's history with respect to segregated schools is the status of public education at that time. In the South, the movement toward free common schools, supported by general taxation, had not yet taken hold. Education of white children was largely in the hands of private groups. Education of Negroes was almost nonexistent, and practically all of the race were illiterate. In fact, any education of Negroes was forbidden by law in some states. Today, in contrast, many Negroes have achieved outstanding success in the arts and sciences, as well as in the business and professional world. It is true that public school education at the time of the Amendment had advanced further in the North, but the effect of the Amendment on Northern States was generally ignored in the congressional debates. Even in the North, the conditions of public education did not approximate those existing today. The curriculum was usually rudimentary; ungraded schools were common in rural areas; the school term was but three months a year in many states, and compulsory school attendance was virtually unknown. As a consequence, it is not surprising that there should be so little in the history of the Fourteenth Amendment relating to its intended effect on public education.

In the first cases in this Court construing the Fourteenth Amendment, decided shortly after its adoption, the Court interpreted it as proscribing all state-imposed discriminations against the Negro race. The doctrine of "separate but equal" did not make its appearance in this Court until 1896 in the case of *Plessy v. Ferguson, supra*, involving not education but transportation. American courts have since labored with the doctrine for over half a century. In this Court, there have been six cases involving the "separate but equal" doctrine in the field of public education. In *Cumming v. County Board of Education* and *Gong Lum v. Rice*, the validity of the doctrine itself was not challenged. In more recent cases, all on the graduate school level, inequality was found in that specific benefits enjoyed by white students were denied to Negro students of the same educational qualifications. *Missouri ex rel. Gaines v. Canada, Sipuel v. Oklahoma, Sweatt v. Painter, McLaurin v. Oklahoma State Regents*. In none of these cases was it necessary to reexamine the doctrine to grant relief to the Negro plaintiff. And in *Sweatt v. Painter, supra*, the Court expressly reserved decision on the question whether *Plessy v. Ferguson* should be held inapplicable to public education.

In the instant cases, that question is directly presented. Here, unlike *Sweatt v. Painter*, there are findings below that the Negro and white schools involved have been equalized, or are being equalized, with respect to buildings, curricula, qualifications and salaries of teachers, and other "tangible" factors. Our decision, therefore, cannot turn on merely a comparison of these tangible factors in the Negro and white schools involved in each of the cases. We must look instead to the effect of segregation itself on public education.

In approaching this problem, we cannot turn the clock back to 1868, when the Amendment was adopted, or even to 1896, when *Plessy v. Ferguson* was written. We must consider public education in the light of its full development and its present place in American life throughout the Nation. Only in this way can it be determined if segregation in public schools deprives these plaintiffs of the equal protection of the laws.

Today, education is perhaps the most important function of state and local governments. Compulsory school attendance laws and the great expenditures for education both demonstrate our recognition of the importance of education to our democratic society. It is required in the performance of our most basic public responsibilities, even service in the armed forces. It is the very foundation of good citizenship. Today it is a principal instrument in awakening the child to cultural values, in preparing him for later professional training, and in helping him to adjust normally to his environment. In these days, it is doubtful that any child may reasonably be expected to succeed in life if he is denied the opportunity of an education. Such an opportunity, where the

state has undertaken to provide it, is a right which must be made available to all on equal terms.

We come then to the question presented: does segregation of children in public schools solely on the basis of race, even though the physical facilities and other "tangible" factors may be equal, deprive the children of the minority group of equal educational opportunities? We believe that it does.

In *Sweatt v. Painter, supra*, in finding that a segregated law school for Negroes could not provide them equal educational opportunities, this Court relied in large part on "those qualities which are incapable of objective measurement but which make for greatness in a law school." In *McLaurin v. Oklahoma State Regents, supra*, the Court, in requiring that a Negro admitted to a white graduate school be treated like all other students, again resorted to intangible considerations: "…his ability to study, to engage in discussions and exchange views with other students, and, in general, to learn his profession."

Such considerations apply with added force to children in grade and high schools. To separate them from others of similar age and qualifications solely because of their race generates a feeling of inferiority as to their status in the community that may affect their hearts and minds in a way unlikely ever to be undone. The effect of this separation on their educational opportunities was well stated by a finding in the Kansas case by a court which nevertheless felt compelled to rule against the Negro plaintiffs:

"Segregation of white and colored children in public schools has a detrimental effect upon the colored children. The impact is greater when it has the sanction of the law, for the policy of separating the races is usually interpreted as denoting the inferiority of the negro group. A sense of inferiority affects the motivation of a child to learn. Segregation with the sanction of law, therefore, has a tendency to [retard] the educational and mental development of negro children and to deprive them of some of the benefits they would receive in a racial[ly] integrated school system."

Whatever may have been the extent of psychological knowledge at the time of *Plessy v. Ferguson*, this finding is amply supported by modern authority. Any language in *Plessy v. Ferguson* contrary to this finding is rejected.

We conclude that, in the field of public education, the doctrine of "separate but equal" has no place. Separate educational facilities are inherently unequal.…

Because these are class actions, because of the wide applicability of this decision, and because of the great variety of local conditions, the formulation of decrees in these cases presents problems of considerable complexity. On reargument, the consideration of appropriate relief was necessarily subordinated to the primary question—the constitutionality of segregation in public education. We have now announced that such segregation is a denial of the equal protection of the laws. In order that we may have the full assistance of the parties in formulating decrees, the cases will be restored to the docket, and the parties are requested to present further argument on Questions 4 and 5 previously propounded by the Court for the reargument this Term.

REYNOLDS V. SIMS (1964)

Undeniably, the Constitution of the United States protects the right of all qualified citizens to vote, in state as well as in federal, elections. A consistent line of decisions by this Court in cases involving attempts to deny or restrict the right of suffrage has made this indelibly clear. It has been repeatedly recognized that all qualified voters have a constitutionally protected right to vote, *Ex parte Yarbrough*, and to have their votes counted, *United States v. Mosley*. In *Mosley*, the Court stated that it is "as equally unquestionable that the right to have one's vote counted is as open to protection…as the right to put a ballot in a box." The right to vote can neither be denied outright, *Guinn v. United States, Lane v. Wilson*, nor destroyed by alteration of ballots, *see United States v. Classic*, nor diluted by ballot box stuffing, *Ex parte Siebold, United States v. Saylor*. As the Court stated in *Classic*, "Obviously included within the right to choose, secured by the Constitution, is the right of qualified voters within a state to cast their ballots and have them counted."

Racially based gerrymandering … and the conducting of white primaries,…both of which result in denying to some citizens their right to vote, have been held to be constitutionally impermissible. And history has seen a continuing expansion of the scope of the right of suffrage in this country. The right to vote freely for the candidate of one's choice is of the essence of a democratic society, and any restrictions on that right strike at the heart of representative government. And the right of suffrage can be denied by a debasement or dilution of the weight of a citizen's vote just as effectively as by wholly prohibiting the free exercise of the franchise.

In *Baker v. Carr*, we held that a claim asserted under the Equal Protection Clause challenging the constitutionality of a State's apportionment of seats in its legislature, on the ground that the right to vote of certain citizens was effectively impaired, since debased and diluted, in effect presented a justiciable controversy subject to adjudication by federal courts. The spate of similar cases filed and decided by lower courts since our decision in *Baker* amply shows that the problem of state legislative malapportionment is one that is perceived to exist in a large number of the States. In *Baker*, a suit involving an attack on the apportionment of seats in the Tennessee Legislature, we remanded to the District Court, which had dismissed the action, for consideration on the merits. We intimated no view as to the proper constitutional standards for evaluating the validity of a state legislative apportionment scheme. Nor did we give any consideration to the question of appropriate remedies. Rather, we simply stated: "Beyond noting that we have no cause at this stage to doubt the District Court will be able to fashion relief if violations of constitutional rights are found, it is improper now to consider what remedy would be most appropriate if appellants prevail at the trial."

We indicated in *Baker*, however, that the Equal Protection Clause provides discoverable and manageable standards for use by lower courts in determining the constitutionality of a state legislative apportionment scheme, and we stated:

"Nor need the appellants, in order to succeed in this action, ask the Court to enter upon policy determinations for which judicially manageable standards are lacking. Judicial standards under the Equal Protection Clause are well developed and familiar, and it has been open to courts since the enactment of the Fourteenth Amendment to determine if, on the particular facts they must, that a discrimination reflects no policy, but simply arbitrary and capricious action."

Subsequent to *Baker*, we remanded several cases to the courts below for reconsideration in light of that decision.…

Legislators represent people, not trees or acres. Legislators are elected by voters, not farms or cities or economic interests. As long as ours is a representative form of government, and our legislatures are those instruments of government elected directly by and directly representative of the people, the right to elect legislators in a free and unimpaired fashion is a bedrock of our political system. It could hardly be gainsaid that a constitutional claim had been asserted by an allegation that certain otherwise qualified voters had been entirely prohibited from voting for members of their state legislature. And, if a State should provide that the votes of citizens in one part of the State should be given two times, or five times, or 10 times the weight of votes of citizens in another part of the State, it could hardly be contended that the right to vote of those residing in the disfavored areas had not been effectively diluted. It would appear extraordinary to suggest that a State could be constitutionally permitted to enact a law providing that certain of the State's voters could vote two, five, or 10 times for their legislative representatives, while voters living elsewhere could vote only once. And it is inconceivable that a state law to the effect that, in counting votes for legislators, the votes of citizens in one part of the State would be multiplied by two, five, or 10, while the votes of persons in another area would be counted only at face value, could be constitutionally sustainable. Of course, the effect of state legislative districting schemes which give the same number of representatives to unequal numbers of constituents is identical. Overweighting and overvaluation of the votes of those living here has the certain effect of dilution and undervaluation of the votes of those living there. The resulting discrimination against those individual voters living in disfavored areas is easily demonstrable mathematically. Their right to vote is simply not the same right to vote as that of those living in a favored part of the State. Two, five, or 10 of them must vote before the effect of their voting is equivalent to that of their favored neighbor. Weighting the votes of citizens differently, by any method or means, merely because of where they happen to reside, hardly seems justifiable. One must be ever aware that the Constitution forbids "sophisticated, as well as simpleminded, modes of discrimination."…

State legislatures are, historically, the fountainhead of representative government in this country. A number of them have their roots in colonial times, and substantially antedate the creation of our Nation and our Federal Government. In fact, the first formal stirrings of American political independence are to be found, in large part, in the views and actions of several of the colonial legislative bodies. With the birth of our National Government, and the adoption and ratification of the Federal Constitution, state legislatures retained a most important place in our Nation's governmental structure. But representative government is, in essence, self-government through the medium of elected representatives of the people, and each and every citizen has an inalienable right to full and effective participation in the political processes of his State's legislative bodies. Most citizens can achieve this participation only as qualified voters through the election of legislators to represent them. Full and effective participation by all citizens in state government requires, therefore, that each citizen have an equally effective voice in the election of members of his state legislature. Modern and viable state government needs, and the Constitution demands, no less.

Logically, in a society ostensibly grounded on representative government, it would seem reasonable that a majority of the people of a State could elect a majority of that State's legislators. To conclude differently, and to sanction minority control of state legislative bodies, would appear to deny majority rights in a way that far surpasses any possible denial of minority rights that might otherwise be thought to result. Since legislatures are responsible for enacting laws by which all citizens are to be governed, they should be bodies which are collectively responsive to the popular will. And the concept of equal protection has been traditionally viewed as requiring the uniform treatment of persons standing in the same relation to the governmental action questioned or challenged. With respect to the allocation of legislative representation, all voters, as citizens of a State, stand in the same relation regardless of where they live. Any suggested criteria for the differentiation of citizens are insufficient to justify any discrimination, as to the weight of their votes, unless relevant to the permissible purposes of legislative apportionment. Since the achieving of fair and effective representation for all citizens is concededly the basic aim of legislative apportionment, we conclude that the Equal Protection Clause guarantees the opportunity for equal participation by all voters in the election of state legislators. Diluting the weight of votes because of place of residence impairs basic constitutional rights under the Fourteenth Amendment just as much as invidious discriminations based upon factors such as race, *Brown v. Board of Education*, or economic status, *Griffin v. Illinois, Douglas v. California*. Our constitutional system amply provides for the protection of minorities by means other than giving them majority control of state legislatures. And the democratic ideals of equality and majority rule, which have served this Nation so well in the past, are hardly of any less significance for the present and the future.

We are told that the matter of apportioning representation in a state legislature is a complex and many-faceted one. We are advised that States can rationally consider factors other than population in apportioning legislative representation. We are admonished not to restrict the power of the States to impose differing views as to political philosophy on their citizens. We are cautioned about the dangers of entering into political thickets and mathematical quagmires. Our answer is this: a denial of constitutionally protected rights demands judicial protection; our oath and our office require no less of us....

We hold that, as a basic constitutional standard, the Equal Protection Clause requires that the seats in both houses of a bicameral state legislature must be apportioned on a population basis. Simply stated, an individual's right to vote for state legislators is unconstitutionally impaired when its weight is in a substantial fashion diluted when compared with votes of citizens living in other parts of the State....

By holding that, as a federal constitutional requisite, both houses of a state legislature must be apportioned on a population basis, we mean that the Equal Protection Clause requires that a State make an honest and good faith effort to construct districts, in both houses of its legislature, as nearly of equal population as is practicable....

History indicates, however, that many States have deviated, to a greater or lesser degree, from the equal population principle in the apportionment of seats in at least one house of their legislatures. So long as the divergences from a strict population standard are based on legitimate considerations incident to the effectuation of a rational state policy, some deviations from the equal population principle are constitutionally permissible with respect to the apportionment of seats in either or both of the two houses of a bicameral state legislature. But neither history alone, nor economic or other sorts of group interests, are permissible factors in attempting to justify disparities from population-based representation. Citizens, not history or economic interests, cast votes.

Glossary

bicameral	consisting of two legislative bodies, generally one made up of statewide representatives and the other of local representatives
concededly	admittedly
gainsaid	denied
gerrymandering	the act of drawing congressional boundary lines for the purpose of giving an advantage to a party, group of constituents, or candidate in an election
justiciable	able to be evaluated and ruled on in the courts
remanded	returned to a lower court for further consideration

WARREN COMMISSION REPORT (1964)

Conclusions

This Commission was created to ascertain the facts relating to the preceding summary of events and to consider the important questions which they raised. The Commission has addressed itself to this task and has reached certain conclusions based on all the available evidence. No limitations have been placed on the Commission's inquiry; it has conducted its own investigation, and all Government agencies have fully discharged their responsibility to cooperate with the Commission in its investigation. These conclusions represent the reasoned judgment of all members of the Commission and are presented after an investigation which has satisfied the Commission that it: has ascertained the truth concerning the assassination of President Kennedy to the extent that a prolonged and thorough search makes this possible.

1. The shots which killed President Kennedy and wounded Governor Connally were fired from the sixth floor window at the southeast corner of the Texas School Book Depository....

3. Although it is not necessary to any essential findings of the Commission to determine just which shot hit Governor Connally, there is very persuasive evidence from the experts to indicate that the same bullet which pierced the President's throat also caused Governor Connally's wounds. However, Governor Connally's testimony and certain other factors have given rise to some difference of opinion as to this probability but there is no question in the mind of any member of the Commission that all the shots which caused the President's and Governor Connally's wounds were fired from the sixth floor window of the Texas School Book Depository.

4. The shots which killed President Kennedy and wounded Governor Connally were fired by Lee Harvey Oswald....

9. The Commission has found no evidence that either Lee Harvey Oswald or Jack Ruby was part of any conspiracy, domestic or foreign, to assassinate President Kennedy. The reasons for this conclusion are:

(a) The Commission has found no evidence that anyone assisted Oswald in planning or carrying out the assassination....

(b) The Commission has found no evidence that Oswald was involved with any person or group in a conspiracy to assassinate the President, although it has thoroughly investigated, in addition to other possible leads, all facets of Oswald's associations, finances, and personal habits, particularly during the period following his return from the Soviet Union in June 1962.

(c) The Commission has found no evidence to show that Oswald was employed, persuaded, or encouraged by any foreign government to assassinate President Kennedy or that he was an agent of any foreign government, although the Commission has reviewed the circumstances surrounding Oswald's defection to the Soviet Union, his life there from October of 1959 to June of 1962 so far as it can be reconstructed, his known contacts with the Fair Play for Cuba Committee and his visits to the Cuban and Soviet Embassies in Mexico City during his trip to Mexico from September 26 to October 3, 1963, and his known contacts with the Soviet Embassy in the United States.

(d) The Commission has explored all attempts of Oswald to identify himself with various political groups, including the Communist Party, U.S.A., the Fair Play for Cuba Committee, and the Socialist Workers Party, and has been unable to find any evidence that the contacts which he initiated were related to Oswald's subsequent assassination of the President.

(e) All of the evidence before the Commission established that there was nothing to support the speculation that Oswald was an agent, employee, or informant of the FBI, the CIA, or any other governmental agency. It has thoroughly investigated Oswald's relationships prior to the assassination with all agencies of the U.S. Government. All contacts with Oswald by any of these agencies were made in the regular exercise of their different responsibilities.

(f) No direct or indirect relationship between Lee Harvey Oswald and Jack Ruby has been discovered by the Commission, nor has it been able to find any credible evidence that either knew the other, although a thorough investigation was made of the many rumors and speculations of such a relationship.

(g) The Commission has found no evidence that Jack Ruby acted with any other person in the killing of Lee Harvey Oswald....

Because of the difficulty of proving negatives to a certainty the possibility of others being involved with either Oswald or Ruby cannot be established categorically, but if there is any such evidence it has been beyond the reach of all the investigative agencies and resources of the United States and has not come to the attention of this Commission....

11. On the basis of the evidence before the Commission it concludes that Oswald acted alone.

MIRANDA V. ARIZONA (1966)

The cases before us raise questions which go to the roots of our concepts of American criminal jurisprudence: the restraints society must observe consistent with the Federal Constitution in prosecuting individuals for crime. More specifically, we deal with the admissibility of statements obtained from an individual who is subjected to custodial police interrogation and the necessity for procedures which assure that the individual is accorded his privilege under the Fifth Amendment to the Constitution not to be compelled to incriminate himself. We dealt with certain phases of this problem recently in *Escobedo v. Illinois* (1964). There, as in the four cases before us, law enforcement officials took the defendant into custody and interrogated him in a police station for the purpose of obtaining a confession. The police did not effectively advise him of his right to remain silent or of his right to consult with his attorney. Rather, they confronted him with an alleged accomplice who accused him of having perpetrated a murder. When the defendant denied the accusation and said "I didn't shoot Manuel, you did it," they handcuffed him and took him to an interrogation room. There, while handcuffed and standing, he was questioned for four hours until he confessed. During this interrogation, the police denied his request to speak to his attorney, and they prevented his retained attorney, who had come to the police station, from consulting with him. At his trial, the State, over his objection, introduced the confession against him. We held that the statements thus made were constitutionally inadmissible.

This case has been the subject of judicial interpretation and spirited legal debate since it was decided two years ago. Both state and federal courts, in assessing its implications, have arrived at varying conclusions. A wealth of scholarly material has been written tracing its ramifications and underpinnings. Police and prosecutor have speculated on its range and desirability. We granted certiorari in these cases, 382 U.S. 924, 925, 937, in order further to explore some facets of the problems thus exposed of applying the privilege against self-incrimination to in-custody interrogation, and to give concrete constitutional guidelines for law enforcement agencies and courts to follow.

We start here, as we did in *Escobedo*, with the premise that our holding is not an innovation in our jurisprudence, but is an application of principles long recognized and applied in other settings. We have undertaken a thorough reexamination of the *Escobedo* decision and the principles it announced, and we reaffirm it. That case was but an explication of basic rights that are enshrined in our Constitution—that "No person...shall be compelled in any criminal case to be a witness against himself," and that "the accused shall ... have the Assistance of Counsel"—rights which were put in jeopardy in that case through official overbearing. These precious rights were fixed in our Constitution only after centuries of persecution and struggle. And, in the words of Chief Justice Marshall, they were secured "for ages to come, and ... designed to approach immortality as nearly as human institutions can approach it."...

The constitutional issue we decide in each of these cases is the admissibility of statements obtained from a defendant questioned while in custody or otherwise deprived of his freedom of action in any significant way. In each, the defendant was questioned by police officers, detectives, or a prosecuting attorney in a room in which he was cut off from the outside world. In none of these cases was the defendant given a full and effective warning of his rights at the outset of the interrogation process. In all the cases, the questioning elicited oral admissions, and in three of them, signed statements as well which were admitted at their trials. They all thus share salient features—incommunicado interrogation of individuals in a police-dominated atmosphere, resulting in self-incriminating statements without full warnings of constitutional rights.

An understanding of the nature and setting of this in-custody interrogation is essential to our decisions today. The difficulty in depicting what transpires at such interrogations stems from the fact that, in this country, they have largely taken place incommunicado....

Today, then, there can be no doubt that the Fifth Amendment privilege is available outside of criminal court proceedings, and serves to protect persons in all settings in which their freedom of action is curtailed in any significant way from being compelled to incriminate themselves. We have concluded that, without proper safeguards, the process of in-custody interrogation of persons suspected or accused of crime contains

inherently compelling pressures which work to undermine the individual's will to resist and to compel him to speak where he would not otherwise do so freely. In order to combat these pressures and to permit a full opportunity to exercise the privilege against self-incrimination, the accused must be adequately and effectively apprised of his rights, and the exercise of those rights must be fully honored.

It is impossible for us to foresee the potential alternatives for protecting the privilege which might be devised by Congress or the States in the exercise of their creative rulemaking capacities. Therefore, we cannot say that the Constitution necessarily requires adherence to any particular solution for the inherent compulsions of the interrogation process as it is presently conducted. Our decision in no way creates a constitutional straitjacket which will handicap sound efforts at reform, nor is it intended to have this effect. We encourage Congress and the States to continue their laudable search for increasingly effective ways of protecting the rights of the individual while promoting efficient enforcement of our criminal laws. However, unless we are shown other procedures which are at least as effective in apprising accused persons of their right of silence and in assuring a continuous opportunity to exercise it, the following safeguards must be observed.

At the outset, if a person in custody is to be subjected to interrogation, he must first be informed in clear and unequivocal terms that he has the right to remain silent. For those unaware of the privilege, the warning is needed simply to make them aware of it—the threshold requirement for an intelligent decision as to its exercise. More important, such a warning is an absolute prerequisite in overcoming the inherent pressures of the interrogation atmosphere. It is not just the subnormal or woefully ignorant who succumb to an interrogator's imprecations, whether implied or expressly stated, that the interrogation will continue until a confession is obtained or that silence in the face of accusation is itself damning, and will bode ill when presented to a jury. Further, the warning will show the individual that his interrogators are prepared to recognize his privilege should he choose to exercise it....

A recurrent argument made in these cases is that society's need for interrogation outweighs the privilege. This argument is not unfamiliar to this Court. See, e.g., *Chambers v. Florida* (1940). The whole thrust of our foregoing discussion demonstrates that the Constitution has prescribed the rights of the individual when confronted with the power of government when it provided in the Fifth Amendment that an individual cannot be compelled to be a witness against himself. That right cannot be abridged. As Mr. Justice Brandeis once observed:

"Decency, security and liberty alike demand that government officials shall be subjected to the same rules of conduct that are commands to the citizen. In a government of laws, existence of the government will be imperiled if it fail to observe the law scrupulously. Our Government is the potent, the omnipresent teacher. For good or for ill, it teaches the whole people by its example. Crime is contagious. If the Government becomes a lawbreaker, it breeds contempt for law; it invites every man to become a law unto himself; it invites anarchy. To declare that, in the administration of the criminal law, the end justifies the means …would bring terrible retribution. Against that pernicious doctrine this Court should resolutely set its face."…

Because of the nature of the problem and because of its recurrent significance in numerous cases, we have to this point discussed the relationship of the Fifth Amendment privilege to police interrogation without specific concentration on the facts of the cases before us. We turn now to these facts to consider the application to these cases of the constitutional principles discussed above. In each instance, we have concluded that statements were obtained from the defendant under circumstances that did not meet constitutional standards for protection of the privilege....

On March 13, 1963, petitioner, Ernesto Miranda, was arrested at his home and taken in custody to a Phoenix police station. He was there identified by the complaining witness. The police then took him to "Interrogation Room No. 2" of the detective bureau. There he was questioned by two police officers. The officers admitted at trial that Miranda was not advised that he had a right to have an attorney present. Two hours later, the officers emerged from the interrogation room with a written confession signed by Miranda. At the top of the statement was a typed paragraph stating that the confession was made voluntarily, without threats or promises of immunity and "with full knowledge of my legal rights, understanding any statement I make may be used against me."

At his trial before a jury, the written confession was admitted into evidence over the objection of defense counsel, and the officers testified to the prior oral confession made by Miranda during the interrogation. Miranda was found guilty of kidnapping and rape. He was sentenced to 20 to 30 years' imprisonment on each count, the sentences to run concurrently. On appeal, the Supreme Court of Arizona held that Miranda's constitutional rights were not violated in obtaining the confession, and affirmed the conviction.... In reaching its decision, the court emphasized heavily the fact that Miranda did not specifically request counsel.

We reverse. From the testimony of the officers and by the admission of respondent, it is clear that Miranda was not in any way apprised of his right to consult with an attorney and to have one present during the interrogation, nor was his right not to be compelled to incriminate himself effectively protected in any other manner. Without these warnings, the statements were inadmissible. The mere fact that he signed a statement which contained a typed-in clause stating that he had "full knowledge" of his "legal rights" does not approach the knowing and intelligent waiver required to relinquish constitutional rights.

Glossary

certiorari	a writ issued by a higher court ordering a lower court to deliver a case record for review; more generally, the granting of a right to appeal a case
Chief Justice Marshall	John Marshall, the fourth chief justice of the United States
holding	a legal term referring to a court's decision about a matter of law based on the issues a particular case presents
jurisprudence	the theory and philosophy of law
Justice Brandeis	Louis Brandeis, associate justice of the U.S. Supreme Court in the early twentieth century

Booker T. Washington (Library of Congress)

BOOKER T. WASHINGTON   1856–1915

Educator and Civil Rights Leader

Featured Documents
- ◆ Atlanta Exposition Address (1895)
- ◆ "Statement on Suffrage" (1903)
- ◆ "A Protest against Lynching" (1904)
- ◆ Letter to William Howard Taft (1908)
- ◆ Letter to C. Elias Winston (1914)

Overview

Booker Taliaferro Washington was born on a farm near Hale's Ford in the foothills of the Blue Ridge Mountains in Franklin County, Virginia, most likely on April 5, 1856. Washington spent the first eight years of his childhood as a slave. Following emancipation he moved with his mother, brother, and sister to join his stepfather, who had found employment in the saltworks in Malden, West Virginia. Emancipation did not significantly raise the economic well-being of the family. The young Washington alternated between working in the saltworks and attending school.

At the age of sixteen, Washington left home for Virginia to further his education at Hampton Institute, under the influence of General Samuel C. Armstrong and his theory of industrial education. Three years later he graduated as one of the school's top students and a protégé of General Armstrong. After a short stint as a schoolteacher in Malden, Washington returned to Hampton as a member of the faculty and for additional education. In May 1881, Armstrong arranged for his prize student to be named principal of a recently authorized Alabama state normal and industrial school for black students.

When Washington arrived in Tuskegee, he discovered that the school existed only on paper. Despite his youth and inexperience he managed to create the school—acquiring land, erecting the buildings, and recruiting the faculty. More impressively, he mastered the political, administrative, and financial skills that he needed to form a black institution in the inhospitable hills of northern Alabama. By the early 1890s Tuskegee Institute was a success, and Washington was beginning to address the broader political and economic issues that confronted African Americans.

In 1895 Washington was asked to speak at the opening ceremonies of the Atlanta Exposition. This speech was a phenomenal success and transformed Washington from a southern educator to the most influential and powerful African American in the United States. He consulted with presidents and corporate leaders and headed a political machine that dispersed funds and political patronage throughout the black community. In 1901 his status brought him an invitation to lunch at the White House with President Theodore Roosevelt.

Washington confronted the task of devising a strategy for blacks to successfully move from slavery to citizenship,

a process made more difficult by the rise in racism, discrimination, and violence characterizing the beginning of the twentieth century. Washington's strategy addressed the needs of the vast majority of African Americans who resided in the South. It focused on education, self-reliance, hard work, and economic success. While his critics accused him of accepting discrimination and white supremacy, Washington consistently spoke out against segregation, lynching, and the restrictions placed on black suffrage. Nevertheless, in the early twentieth century W. E. B. Du Bois and other African American leaders, especially in the North, became increasingly dissatisfied with Washington's program and his political power. The Niagara Movement founded in 1905 and, later, the National Association for the Advancement of Colored People (NAACP) founded in 1909 challenged his leadership. Still, at the time of his death in November 1915, Washington was still the most widely known and respected African American leader in the United States.

Explanation and Analysis of Documents

Following his success as principal of Tuskegee Institute, Washington began to address the issues confronting African Americans in the South. Washington was an astute politician. He developed associations with northern business leaders and southern politicians that enabled him to operate Tuskegee as a black educational institution. As he addressed the concerns of his race, he balanced his attack on the injustice of segregation and racial violence with his need to survive in an increasingly racist and violent South. The significant point is that Washington was not silent. He spoke out about the injustice of discrimination and biased suffrage laws and the horror of lynching. But his language was more moderate than shrill. He retained the belief that logic would prevail and that if they were shown that it was in their interest to promote the development of blacks, the leadership of the South and educated and cultured southerners would support the cause of racial justice.

Washington used a variety of means to express his views. His most famous statements were public speeches, but he also published "letters to the editor" in southern and northern newspapers, gave interviews, and wrote articles

1865

■ **August**
Washington is freed by the defeat of the South in the Civil War; Washington and his family move to Malden, West Virginia.

1872

■ **October 5**
Washington leaves home and enrolls in Hampton Institute.

1881

■ **July 4**
Washington opens the Tuskegee Institute in Tuskegee, Alabama, modeling the school's curriculum on the Hampton Institute.

1895

■ **September 18**
Washington delivers an address at the opening ceremonies of the Cotton States and International Exposition, commonly called the Atlanta Exposition.

1896

■ **May 18**
In *Plessy v. Ferguson*, the Supreme Court rules that a Louisiana law segregating passengers on railroads is legal because it provides *separate but equal* facilities—validating a number of laws segregating African Americans.

1898

■ **April 25**
In *Williams v. State of Mississippi*, the Supreme Court rules that a Mississippi law that allows poll taxes and literacy tests to be used as voter qualifications is legal, legitimizing the tactics used by southern states to deny African Americans the right to vote.

1901

■ **March**
Washington publishes his best-known autobiography, *Up from Slavery*.

and private letters to powerful and influential white men to express his political and racial views. The five documents discussed here illustrate Washington's positions on race issues and his efforts to alter the policies and the violence that oppressed African Americans. The first document is a public address to a mixed, but largely white audience; the next two are published letters to the editors of white newspapers; and the last two are private letters.

◆ **Atlanta Exposition Address**

On September 18, 1895, in Atlanta's Exposition Park, Booker T. Washington, in a brief speech during the opening ceremonies of the Cotton States and International Exposition, established himself as the most prominent African American of his generation. This speech is one of the two or three best-known addresses ever made by blacks. In it Washington defines his plan for an alliance between blacks and whites that would bring into reality the prosperous and progressive "New South" that the exposition in Atlanta celebrated. Fundamental to the plan is Washington's argument that the fate of black and white southerners was forever bound together; both would prosper, or both would perish. The speech is so carefully crafted to reach the potentially hostile white majority in the audience that the complexity and details of Washington's argument may have been lost.

Washington opens his speech praising the organizers for involving African Americans in the exhibition and the opening ceremonies. He then moves into one of his best-known parables, about a ship lost at sea and sighting another vessel. Signaling the other ship for fresh water, the captain receives the reply "'Cast down your bucket where you are.'" So the captain "cast down his bucket, and it came up full of fresh, sparkling water from the mouth of the Amazon River." Washington admonishes both the blacks and whites in the audience to cast down their buckets where they were—blacks to cast it down in the South, among southerners, rather than seeking their future in the North or abroad, and whites to cast it down among blacks, rather than turning to immigrant labor as their workforce. Together, both races would prosper, blacks in "agriculture, mechanics, in commerce, in domestic service, and in the professions" and whites by gaining a loyal and faithful workforce. Washington was criticized by some blacks for endorsing a system that relegated blacks to unskilled and oppressed labor in the South. However, he was careful to enunciate a range of black occupations and depict an economic relationship that benefited both races.

Washington concludes this address with the most quoted and most reviled statement in the speech: "In all things that are purely social we can be as separate as the fingers, yet one as the hand in all things essential to mutual progress." Black critics accused Washington of acquiescing to segregation; white segregationists applauded the statement. Supporting segregation was not Washington's intent. In the sentence previous to this quote he describes blacks "interlacing our industrial, commercial, civil, and religious life with yours in a way that shall make the interests of both races one." In the following paragraph he quotes a verse from a poem by the abolitionist poet John Greenleaf Whittier that again asserts that the two races, oppressor and oppressed, would share the same fate. Washington then describes graphically the options that whites faced: They could assist blacks, and together the two races would make the South bloom; if oppression continued, he warns, blacks would drag down the South to its ruin. As he puts it, "Nearly sixteen millions of hands will aid you in pulling the load upward, or they will pull against you the load downward."

The Atlanta Exposition address presented Washington's views and his argument for racial cooperation. Over time, however, his friends and enemies took from the speech what they wanted to hear, and the heart of the message was lost. Nevertheless, Washington emerged from Atlanta victorious. For the next two decades his voice would dominate.

◆ **"Statement on Suffrage"**

In the years that followed the Atlanta address, Washington's power grew. In 1901 he lunched with President Theodore Roosevelt at the White House. He counted many top industrialists, such as Andrew Carnegie, as his supporters. Nonetheless, racial conditions grew steadily worse as segregation became entrenched and southern states deprived black citizens of their right to vote. Washington's prestige allowed him access to the media to voice his concerns about these developments, and he did so repeatedly. In June 1903 he addressed the suffrage issue in a letter published in the Philadelphia *North American*.

Washington begins his letter by asserting that blacks should refrain from the full exercise of their political rights until they established themselves economically and acquired property and education. To Washington, this did not mean that blacks should not vote; instead, he saw the exercise of the right to vote as essential to the political education of blacks. He advises blacks to cooperate with respectable and informed whites in the exercise of the right to vote, much as they did in their economic endeavors.

The focus of this letter is the injustice of suffrage laws. These laws had proliferated across the South in the years between 1895 and 1903 and been upheld by the Supreme Court in *Williams v. Mississippi* in 1898. Washington labels these laws as "unjust" and attacks them because they were implemented in a way that discriminated against African Americans. He acknowledges that the states had the right to prevent the ignorant from voting, but he insists that the literacy tests employed by southern states were used to disfranchise only black voters. As he puts it, "I believe in universal, free suffrage,…but whatever tests are required they should be made to apply with equal and exact justice to both races." He further contends that cheating the black man at the ballot box undermines the entire democratic process and ultimately would lead to the denial of the right to vote to whites as well.

As was his style, Washington here presents logical arguments appealing to both the reason and the self-interest of his white audience. He is not confrontational. While this approach displeased many of his black critics, it allowed

Time Line

1901

■ **July 16**
Controversy arises after Washington dines at the White House while consulting President Theodore Roosevelt about political appointments in the South.

1903

■ **April 18**
W. E. B. Du Bois begins his criticism of Washington's leadership with the publication of the essay, "Of Mr. Booker T. Washington and Others," in his book *The Souls of Black Folk*.

■ **June 7**
Washington outlines his views on suffrage in an essay "Statement on Suffrage," which he publishes in the Philadelphia *North American*.

1904

■ **February 22**
Washington writes "A Protest against Lynching," one of his strongest arguments against lynching.

1905

■ **July 10**
Twenty-nine African Americans, including W. E. B. Du Bois meet in Fort Erie, Ontario, to create the Niagara Movement, a new civil rights organization that directly challenges Booker T. Washington's leadership and policies.

1908

■ **June 4**
Washington writes a letter to William Howard Taft in which he advises the Republican candidate for the presidency on political issues related to the South and to African Americans.

1909

■ **May 31**
The National Negro Conference establishes the National Association for the Advancement of Colored People, a biracial organization challenging Washington's approach to civil rights.

1913

■ **March 4**
The inauguration of Democrat Woodrow Wilson as president of the United States significantly reduces Washington's political influence.

1914

■ **October 2**
Washington responds to a letter from the Reverend C. Elias Winston in which he clarifies his position on segregation.

1915

■ **November 14**
Washington dies at home in Tuskegee, Alabama.

him to make his arguments in a way that did not undermine his position among whites and protected the security of Tuskegee and his family in rural Alabama. As persuasive as his arguments were, they did not have any immediate impact on the movement to deny blacks their political rights. However, even more aggressive attacks on disfranchisement did not bear fruit for many years.

◆ **"A Protest against Lynching"**

Segregation and restrictions on suffrage were major affronts to the civil rights of African Americans, but the most brutal reality of American racism was the epidemic of racial violence that destroyed black lives. Between 1895 and 1904 almost a thousand African Americans were tortured and killed by lynch mobs. Washington addressed lynching on a number of occasions. His 1904 letter to the Birmingham *Age Herald* was reprinted in several newspapers and quoted in the *New York Times*. The passion with which Washington writes in this piece indicates his frustration and dismay with the worsening racial climate. He opens his letter bluntly with these provocative words: "Within the last fortnight three members of my race have been burned at the stake; of these one was a woman." With this clear and concise statement Washington attacks the fundamental myth of lynching: that it was the necessary execution of a black man who raped a white woman. Washington depicts a harsher reality. It was his contention that rape was seldom the crime that lynching avenged and that black women also were victims.

Washington continues his assault on the myths of lynching. It was not always carried out in the dark of night by masked men at hidden locations. He notes that the three recent burnings "took place in broad daylight and two of them occurred on Sunday afternoon in sight of a Christian church." The fundamental issue that he raises in this protest is that the barbarism of these public burnings undermined civil authority, destroyed any possibility of

peaceful race relations, and made an obscene mockery of American churches and their program of "sending missionaries to Africa and China and the rest of the so-called heathen world."

After establishing the inhumanity of lynching, Washington returns to logical argument when he outlines a remedy. He argues the absurdity of lynching when the white-controlled legal system rarely failed to mete out justice to black criminals: "The laws are as a rule made by the white people and their execution is in the hands of the white people; so that there is little probability of any guilty colored man escaping." He further says, "If the law is disregarded when a Negro is concerned, it will soon be disregarded when a white man is concerned." He urges white newspaper editors, preachers and ministers, and political leaders to use their moral authority to make such outrages unacceptable. In the short term, Washington's appeals fell on deaf ears. Lynching continued unabated until it began to decline in the late 1920s.

◆ **Letter to William Howard Taft**

Washington's lunch at the White House in the summer of 1901 reflected the political influence he had acquired in the years following the Atlanta speech. Presidents William McKinley, Theodore Roosevelt, and William Howard Taft sought his advice on issues affecting African Americans, and he controlled much of the patronage that went to blacks. In June 1908 Washington wrote a "personal and very confidential" letter to Taft on the eve of the Republican National Convention that would nominate Taft for the presidency. Washington notes that he is including a suggested plank for the Republican platform. In the letter itself he mentions two issues: the reduction of southern representation, which he opposes, and the use of the term "Lily-Whiteism." The first item refers to the never-utilized Section 2 of the Fourteenth Amendment to the Constitution, which authorized Congress to reduce the representation in Congress of any state that disfranchised a proportion of their otherwise eligible adult male voters. Washington opposes placing it in the platform because Republicans had never acted on previous platform promises to enforce the provision. The second item refers to a movement by the "Lily-White" faction of most southern Republican groups to purge from the party African Americans and their supporters. Washington's letter is respectful but also rather casual, suggesting his comfortable relationship with the Republican nominee-to-be.

The attachment, "Suggested Plank for Platform," is a concise outline of Washington's political views. First, he reminds the Republican Party that its roots lie in its commitment to equal rights, and he urges the party to continue its efforts to "secure equal justice to all men" regardless of race or color. Second, he applauds the efforts of President Theodore Roosevelt to enforce equal accommodations for blacks and whites on railroads and other public transportation carriers. Next he demands that any law affecting political or civil rights be applied equally to all races and that the voting rights of African Americans be protected.

A mob gathers at the gallows in Nacogdoches, Texas, in October 1902 for the hanging of Jim Buchanan, a nineteen-year-old who had been seen in the neighborhood where a family of three had been killed. (AP/Wide World Photos)

Finally, he condemns the actions of "Lily-White" Republicans for violating the Republican Party's commitment to equality. Washington concludes his suggestions with a statement on the "Rights of the Negro," which reiterates the demand for "equal justice for all men, without regard to race or color"; the full enforcement of the Thirteenth, Fourteenth, and Fifteenth Amendments; and the condemnation of efforts to disfranchise blacks "for reasons of color alone, as…un-American and repugnant to the supreme law of the land."

This private statement is the fullest exposition of Washington's beliefs, expressed more strongly than in his more public communications. Taft won the nomination and the election, but Washington's political influence was by then declining. The 1913 inauguration of a Democrat, Woodrow Wilson, ended Washington's access to the White House.

◆ Letter to C. Elias Winston

In the second decade of the twentieth century, Washington and his ideas, especially his approach to racial problems, increasingly came under attack from within the African American community. The establishment of the biracial NAACP added legitimacy, financial support, and a forum for Washington's most significant critics, while the continued deterioration of civil rights undermined Washington's popu-

larity. Nevertheless, Washington still exercised significant power and influence, and he attempted to answer his foes as he continued to pursue his civil rights agenda.

In October 1914 Washington explained his position on segregation to C. Elias Winston. Winston, a prominent minister and civil rights advocate in St. Louis, had written to ask whether Washington had told blacks to stop fighting segregation. Washington denies that he had ever made the remark that Winston cited and notes that he had recently persuaded the city council of Birmingham, Alabama, to reject a segregation ordinance they were considering. While not endorsing segregation, he admits that he frequently tried to "urge upon the railroads throughout this country to provide more equal, more just, more clean and up-to-date railroad facilities for the black people of this country, wherever the law requires" segregation. He also acknowledges that he encouraged blacks in segregated communities to maintain, upgrade, and beautify their communities despite segregation. He goes on to say that while he joins with those condemning segregation in all its forms, he also believes that condemnation is not enough. He cites the "danger of our spending too much time and strength in mere condemnation without attempting to aid our cause by progressive, constructive work." It was his belief that "in proportion as we go forward in all parts of the country,

"'Cast down your bucket where you are.' Cast it down among the eight millions of Negroes whose habits you know, whose fidelity and love you have tested in days when to have proved treacherous meant the ruin of your firesides."

(Atlanta Exposition Address)

"In all things that are purely social we can be as separate as the fingers, yet one as the hand in all things essential to mutual progress."

(Atlanta Exposition Address)

"I do not believe that any State should make a law that permits an ignorant and poverty-stricken white man to vote and prevents a black man in the same condition from voting."

("Statement on Suffrage")

"Within the last fortnight three members of my race have been burned at the stake; of these one was a woman. Not one of the three was charged with any crime even remotely connected with the abuse of a white woman."

("A Protest against Lynching")

"If the law is disregarded when a Negro is concerned, it will soon be disregarded when a white man is concerned."

("A Protest against Lynching")

"The Republican Party had its origin in an effort to secure equal justice to all men. Above the tariff, above the currency question, is the matter of justice between man and man and as between race and race.... If the party anywhere has drifted from its original moorings, it should as speedily as possible get back to the original starting point and demand justice for all men regardless of race and regardless of color."

(Letter to William Howard Taft)

"I have always opposed the passing of any law to segregate the Negro, either in city, town or country district.... Segregation is unnecessary, unjust, unwise, and from my point of view, illegal."

(Letter to C. Elias Winston)

making real progress and asking for fair and just treatment by the hands of all people, North and South, our race is going to command the respect and confidence of all the people of all classes."

Washington's views on segregation remained relatively constant throughout his career. He saw injustice when blacks were denied equal quality and value for the dollar they paid, and he believed that segregation always meant that blacks received inferior accommodations. Nevertheless, he also advised blacks to work to improve their inferior accommodations even as they protested the injustice of segregation.

Impact and Legacy

From the mid-1890s until 1915 Washington was the best-known and most powerful African American leader. For two decades he helped define the African American response to the challenges blacks faced as segregation and discrimination hardened. Washington's perspective was that of the southern black, but during his life the vast majority of African Americans lived in the rural South. His Atlanta Exposition address and the rest of his political writings and speeches assumed that the future of African Americans was in the South and that the issues of race must be addressed with the white southerner. Against this reality, Washington devised his somewhat oblique approach, prioritizing education and acquisition of property and wealth while pursuing a nonconfrontational struggle for equal rights and racial justice. It was his misfortune that the times were against him and that the irrational forces of racism and white supremacy overwhelmed his arguments based on the rational self-interest of whites. This does not diminish the power of Washington's words. His Atlanta address stands with Martin Luther King, Jr.'s "I have a dream" speech at the pinnacle of black oratory. The strategy that he outlined in his attacks on discrimination ultimately bore fruit when combined with

Questions for Further Study

1. According to Washington, the keys to full equality for African Americans lay in hard work and self-reliance, with an emphasis on education and economic success. He placed considerably less emphasis on the use of purely political means to bring about an end to segregation, disenfranchisement, lynching, and other injustices visited upon blacks in his time. In later decades, many African American leaders would refute his ideas, and in the 1950s and 1960s the political approach Washington had eschewed—marches, sit-ins, boycotts, and other means of attracting attention and applying pressure to national leaders—took the forefront. Evaluate the merits of Washington's approach and the arguments of his detractors. Who do you think was right and why? Would it have been possible to pursue the economic objectives Washington outlined while also working for political solutions, and how might this have taken place?

2. Examine Washington's 1895 Atlanta Exposition address as a piece of literature and history, and set it within the context not only of race relations but also of southern recovery from the Civil War. The speech was delivered at the Cotton States and International Exposition, an event of great symbolic importance: In another memorable speech at a similar exposition just a few years earlier, the *Atlanta Constitution* editor Henry Grady had proclaimed that the South, led by the city of Atlanta, was rising again. How did these aspects of the setting, combined with the harsh realities of racism, make Washington's job more difficult in delivering his speech? How successful was the oration, both at the time and later? The speech is sometimes called "The Atlanta Compromise," and Washington was later attacked for statements in it that seemed to uphold the status quo of segregation: Should—or could—he have taken a stronger position?

3. Compare and contrast Washington with his contemporary W. E. B. Du Bois. What were the principal areas of difference in their approaches to the problems facing African Americans, and who, in your opinion, had the more justifiable position? Be sure to support your ideas with facts and quotes from both men, particularly Washington. To what extent did Washington and Du Bois represent two differing strains of thought within the African American community that would continue to be argued by other leaders in time to come? For instance, what parallels might be drawn between the two men's disagreements and those of Martin Luther King, Jr., and Malcolm X fifty years later?

the NAACP's legal strategy and the sit-ins and freedom marches of the 1960s.

When Washington died in 1915, the African American civil rights struggle was at its nadir, and the somewhat more confrontational approach to civil rights of W. E. B. Du Bois and the NAACP was coming into ascendancy. Over time Washington's reputation suffered, especially among African American intellectuals, who equated his leadership with the spread of discrimination and racial violence. By the 1960s Washington's criticism of segregation, disfranchisement, and lynching was largely overlooked, and he was condemned, especially by civil rights and Black Power activists, as an accommodationist or worse. Nevertheless, Washington's influence was considerable and durable. His concepts of economic advancement and the development of African American institutions were echoed by twentieth-century leaders like Marcus Garvey and other advocates of black nationalism. Even Du Bois, once one of Washington's harshest critics, adapted a portion of Washington's economic self-help agenda during the Great Depression of the 1930s.

Key Sources

From 1972 through 1989 *The Booker T. Washington Papers*, edited by Louis R. Harlan and Raymond W. Smock, was published in fourteen volumes. Washington's papers are also available online in searchable form at the University of Illinois Press Web site (http://www.historycooperative. org/btw/info.html). Washington wrote two autobiographies, the 1901 classic *Up from Slavery* and the lesser-known *An Autobiography: The Story of My Life and Work* (1901).

Further Reading

■ Books

Brundage, W. Fitzhugh, ed. *Booker T. Washington and Black Progress: Up from Slavery 100 Years Later*. Gainesville: University of Florida Press, 2003.

Harlan, Louis R. *Booker T. Washington: The Making of a Black Leader, 1856–1901*. New York: Oxford University Press, 1972.

———. *Booker T. Washington: The Wizard of Tuskegee, 1901–1915*. New York: Oxford University Press, 1983.

Meier, August. *Negro Thought in America, 1880–1915*. Ann Arbor: University of Michigan Press, 1988.

Moore, Jacqueline H. *Booker T. Washington, W. E. B. Du Bois, and the Struggle for Racial Uplift*. Wilmington, Del.: Scholarly Resources, 2003.

Norrell, Robert J. *Up from History: The Life of Booker T. Washington*. Cambridge, Mass.: Belknap Press, 2009.

West, Michael Rudolph. *The Education of Booker T. Washington: American Democracy and the Idea of Race Relations*. New York: Columbia University Press, 2006.

Wolters, Raymond. *Du Bois and His Rivals*. Columbia: University of Missouri Press, 2002.

—Cary D. Wintz

ATLANTA EXPOSITION ADDRESS (1895)

Mr. President and Gentlemen of the Board of Directors and Citizens: One-third of the population of the South is of the Negro race. No enterprise seeking the material, civil, or moral welfare of this section can disregard this element of our population and reach the highest success. I but convey to you, Mr. President and Directors, the sentiment of the masses of my race when I say that in no way have the value and manhood of the American Negro been more fittingly and generously recognized than by the managers of this magnificent Exposition at every stage of its progress. It is a recognition that will do more to cement the friendship of the two races than any occurrence since the dawn of our freedom.

Not only this, but the opportunity here afforded will awaken among us a new era of industrial progress. Ignorant and inexperienced, it is not strange that in the first years of our new life we began at the top instead of at the bottom; that a seat in Congress or the state legislature was more sought than real estate or industrial skill; that the political convention or stump speaking had more attractions than starting a dairy farm or truck garden.

A ship lost at sea for many days suddenly sighted a friendly vessel. From the mast of the unfortunate vessel was seen a signal, "Water, water; we die of thirst!" The answer from the friendly vessel at once came back, "Cast down your bucket where you are." A second time the signal, "Water, water; send us water!" ran up from the distressed vessel, and was answered, "Cast down your bucket where you are." And a third and fourth signal for water was answered, "Cast down your bucket where you are." The captain of the distressed vessel, at last heeding the injunction, cast down his bucket, and it came up full of fresh, sparkling water from the mouth of the Amazon River. To those of my race who depend on bettering their condition in a foreign land or who underestimate the importance of cultivating friendly relations with the Southern white man, who is their next-door neighbour, I would say: "Cast down your bucket where you are"—cast it down in making friends in every manly way of the people of all races by whom we are surrounded.

Cast it down in agriculture, mechanics, in commerce, in domestic service, and in the professions. And in this connection it is well to bear in mind that whatever other sins the South may be called to bear, when it comes to business, pure and simple, it is in the South that the Negro is given a man's chance in the commercial world, and in nothing is this Exposition more eloquent than in emphasizing this chance. Our greatest danger is that in the great leap from slavery to freedom we may overlook the fact that the masses of us are to live by the productions of our hands, and fail to keep in mind that we shall prosper in proportion as we learn to dignify and glorify common labour, and put brains and skill into the common occupations of life; shall prosper in proportion as we learn to draw the line between the superficial and the substantial, the ornamental gewgaws of life and the useful. No race can prosper till it learns that there is as much dignity in tilling a field as in writing a poem. It is at the bottom of life we must begin, and not at the top. Nor should we permit our grievances to overshadow our opportunities.

To those of the white race who look to the incoming of those of foreign birth and strange tongue and habits for the prosperity of the South, were I permitted I would repeat what I say to my own race, "Cast down your bucket where you are." Cast it down among the eight millions of Negroes whose habits you know, whose fidelity and love you have tested in days when to have proved treacherous meant the ruin of your firesides. Cast down your bucket among these people who have, without strikes and labour wars, tilled your fields, cleared your forests, builded your railroads and cities, and brought forth treasures from the bowels of the earth, and helped make possible this magnificent representation of the progress of the South. Casting down your bucket among my people, helping and encouraging them as you are doing on these grounds, and to education of head, hand, and heart, you will find that they will buy your surplus land, make blossom the waste places in your fields, and run your factories. While doing this, you can be sure in the future, as in the past, that you and your families will be surrounded by the most patient, faithful, law-abiding, and unresentful people that the world has seen. As we have proved our loyalty to you in the past, in nursing your children, watching by the sick-bed of your mothers and fathers, and often following them with tear-dimmed eyes to their graves, so in the future, in our humble way, we shall stand by you with a devotion that no foreigner can approach, ready to lay down our lives, if need be, in defense of yours, interlacing our industrial, commercial, civil, and religious life with yours in a way that shall make the interests of both races one. In all things that are purely social we can be as separate as the fingers, yet one as the hand in all things essential to mutual progress.

There is no defense or security for any of us except in the highest intelligence and development of all. If anywhere there are efforts tending to curtail the fullest growth of the Negro, let these efforts be turned into stimulating, encouraging, and making him the most useful and intelligent citizen. Effort or means so invested will pay a thousand per cent interest. These efforts will be twice blessed "blessing him that gives and him that takes."

There is no escape through law of man or God from the inevitable:

"The laws of changeless justice bind
Oppressor with oppressed;
And close as sin and suffering joined
We march to fate abreast."

Nearly sixteen millions of hands will aid you in pulling the load upward, or they will pull against you the load downward. We shall constitute one-third and more of the ignorance and crime of the South, or one-third its intelligence and progress; we shall contribute one-third to the business and industrial prosperity of the South, or we shall prove a veritable body of death, stagnating, depressing, retarding every effort to advance the body politic.

Gentlemen of the Exposition, as we present to you our humble effort at an exhibition of our progress, you must not expect overmuch. Starting thirty years ago with ownership here and there in a few quilts and pumpkins and chickens (gathered from miscellaneous sources), remember the path that has led from these to the inventions and production of agricultural implements, buggies, steam-engines, newspapers, books, statuary, carving, paintings, the management of drug stores and banks, has not been trodden without contact with thorns and thistles. While we take pride in what we exhibit as a result of our independent efforts, we do not for a moment forget that our part in this exhibition would fall far short of your expectations but for the constant help that has come to our educational life, not only from the Southern states, but especially from Northern philanthropists, who have made their gifts a constant stream of blessing and encouragement.

The wisest among my race understand that the agitation of questions of social equality is the extremest folly, and that progress in the enjoyment of all the privileges that will come to us must be the result of severe and constant struggle rather than of artificial forcing. No race that has anything to contribute to the markets of the world is long in any degree ostracized. It is important and right that all privileges of the law be ours, but it is vastly more important that we be prepared for the exercise of these privileges. The opportunity to earn a dollar in a factory just now is worth infinitely more than the opportunity to spend a dollar in an opera-house.

In conclusion, may I repeat that nothing in thirty years has given us more hope and encouragement, and drawn us so near to you of the white race, as this opportunity offered by the Exposition; and here bending, as it were, over the altar that represents the results of the struggles of your race and mine, both starting practically emptyhanded three decades ago, I pledge that in your effort to work out the great and intricate problem which God has laid at the doors of the South, you shall have at all times the patient, sympathetic help of my race; only let this be constantly in mind, that, while from representations in these buildings of the product of field, of forest, of mine, of factory, letters, and art, much good will come, yet far above and beyond material benefits will be that higher good, that, let us pray God, will come, in a blotting out of sectional differences and racial animosities and suspicions, in a determination to administer absolute justice, in a willing obedience among all classes to the mandates of law. This, coupled with our material prosperity, will bring into our beloved South a new heaven and a new earth.

Glossary

gewgaws	trinkets, showy but worthless toys
The laws of changeless justice bind...	from "At Point Royal" (1862) by American poet John Greenleaf Whittier

"STATEMENT ON SUFFRAGE" (1903)

Negro and the White

I believe it is the duty of the negro—as the greater part of the race is already doing—to deport himself modestly in regard to political claims, depending on the slow but sure influences that proceed from the possession of property, intelligence and high character for the full recognition of his political rights.

I think that the according of the full exercise of political rights is going to be a matter of natural, slow growth, not an over-night, gourd-vine affair. I do not believe that the negro should cease voting, for a man cannot learn the exercise of self-government by ceasing to vote, any more than a boy can learn to swim by keeping out of the water; but I do believe that in his voting he should more and more be influenced by those of intelligence and character who are his next-door neighbors.

I know colored men who, through the encouragement, help and advice of Southern white people, have accumulated thousands of dollars worth of property, but who, at the same time, would never think of going to those same persons for advice concerning the casting of their ballots. This, it seems to me, is unwise and unreasonable, and should cease. In saying this, I do not mean that the negro should truckle, or not vote from principle, for the instant he ceases to vote from principle he loses the confidence and respect of the Southern white man even.

Suffrage Laws Unjust

I do not believe that any State should make a law that permits an ignorant and poverty-stricken white man to vote and prevents a black man in the same condition from voting.

Such a law is not only unjust, but it will react, as all unjust laws do, in time; for the effect of such a law is to encourage the negro to secure education and property, and at the same time it encourages the white man to remain in ignorance and poverty. I believe that in time, through the operation of intelligence and friendly race relations, all cheating at the ballot-box in the South will cease.

It will become apparent that the white man who begins by cheating a negro out of his ballot soon learns to cheat a white man out of his, and that man who does this ends his career of dishonesty by the theft of property or by some equally serious crime.

In my opinion, the time will come when the South will encourage all of its citizens to vote. It will see that it pays better, from every standpoint, to have healthy, vigorous life than to have that political stagnation which always results when one-half the population has no share and no interest in the government.

As a rule, I believe in universal, free suffrage, but I believe that in the South we are confronted with peculiar conditions that justify the protection of the ballot in many of the States, for a while at least, either by an educational test, a property test, or by both combined; but whatever tests are required they should be made to apply with equal and exact justice to both races.

Glossary

gourd-vine affair	possibly a reference to the biblical book of Jonah, chapter 4, in which God provides Jonah with the shade of a gourd vine to ease his discomfort
truckle	submit, yield

"A Protest against Lynching" (1904)

Within the last fortnight three members of my race have been burned at the stake; of these one was a woman. Not one of the three was charged with any crime even remotely connected with the abuse of a white woman. In every case murder was the sole accusation. All of these burnings took place in broad daylight and two of them occurred on Sunday afternoon in sight of a Christian church.

In the midst of the nation's busy and prosperous life few, I fear, take time to consider where these brutal and inhuman crimes are leading us. The custom of burning human beings has become so common as scarcely to excite interest or attract unusual attention.

I have always been among those who condemned in the strongest terms crimes of whatever character committed by members of my race, and I condemn them now with equal severity; but I maintain that the only protection of our civilization is a fair and calm trial of all people charged with crime and in their legal punishment if proved guilty.

There is no shadow of excuse for departure from legal methods in the cases of individuals accused of murder. The laws are as a rule made by the white people and their execution is in the hands of the white people; so that there is little probability of any guilty colored man escaping.

These burnings without a trial are in the deepest sense unjust to my race; but it is not this injustice alone which stirs my heart. These barbarous scenes followed, as they are, by publication of the shocking details are more disgraceful and degrading to the people who inflict the punishment than those who receive it.

If the law is disregarded when a Negro is concerned, it will soon be disregarded when a white man is concerned; and, besides, the rule of the mob destroys the friendly relations which should exist between the races and injures and interferes with the material prosperity of the communities concerned.

Worst of all these outrages take place in communities where there are Christian churches; in the midst of people who have their Sunday schools, their Christian Endeavor Societies and Young Men's Christian Associations, where collections are taken up for sending missionaries to Africa and China and the rest of the so-called heathen world.

Is it not possible for pulpit and press to speak out against these burnings in a manner that shall arouse a public sentiment that will compel the mob to cease insulting our courts, our Governors and legal authority; cease bringing shame and ridicule upon our Christian civilization?

Booker T. Washington

Glossary

Christian Endeavor Societies	a group of Christian religious orders founded in 1881
lynching	the execution of a person by a mob, without trial, often done by hanging but also done by burning and other means

Letter to William Howard Taft (1908)

Personal and Very Confidential

My dear Mr. Secretary: Enclosed I send you some suggestions for a plank in the Chicago platform. Of course, I presume the wording will be changed, but I have tried to make my meaning clear. I think I know the situation pretty well among the colored people and I do think the substance of what is stated in this suggestion ought to go in the platform in some form. I have put it in plain language as the situation demands plain language, something which cannot be misunderstood or misinterpreted.

My own view is that something like the enclosed would do more good than the meaningless platform about reducing Southern representation. That was in the last platform and made no impression because it did not mean anything, and if another plank goes into the platform about reducing Southern representation I do not believe it will make the least impression, but what I have suggested, in my opinion, if put in some form would help the situation tremendously.

The words "Lily Whitism" may seem inelegant, but the meaning will be clear to all. Yours very truly,

Booker T. Washington

Suggested Plank for Platform:

The Republican Party had its origin in an effort to secure equal justice to all men. Above the tariff, above the currency question, is the matter of justice between man and man and as between race and race. The Republican Party, as now constituted, cannot afford to deviate in any degree from the principles of its founders. If the party anywhere has drifted from its original moorings, it should as speedily as possible get back to the original starting point and demand justice for all men regardless of race and regardless of color.

In this connection we applaud and commend the efforts of President Roosevelt to secure equal accommodations on railroads and other public carriers for the white and black races.

The Republican Party demands that wherever any law relating to the civil or political conduct or rights of individuals is framed and promulgated, that that law shall apply with equal and exact justice to all races; especially is this true in regard to the exercise of the franchise. The weak need the protection which the ballot affords. No color line should be recognized in the American ballot. The provision known as the "grandfather clause" in some state constitutions is an insult to American manhood and we condemn and oppose it as unwarranted and un-American.

The National Republican Party unequivocally records itself as opposed to the recognition of any party organization which excludes or discourages men from joining county, state or national organizations because of their race or color; and especially does the party record itself as being opposed to the doctrine known in some parts of the country as "Lily Whiteism." This departure from Republican principles must find no place in the plans or policies of the Republican Party.

◆ **Rights of the Negro:**

The Republican party has been for more than fifty years the consistent friend of the American Negro. It granted to him the freedom & the citizenship which he earned by his valor & service. It wrote into the organic law of the land the declarations that proclaim his civil and political rights, and it believes today that his noteworthy progress in intelligence, industry and good citizenship has earned the respect and encouragement of the Nation. We demand equal justice for all men, without regard to race or color; we approve the efforts of President Roosevelt and the vote of the Republican majority in Congress, over a solid Democratic opposition, to secure equal accommodations on railroads and other public carriers for all citizens,

Glossary

promulgated	distributed, proclaimed
Roosevelt	Theodore Roosevelt, twenty-sixth U.S. president

whether white or black; we declare once more, and without reservation, for the enforcement in spirit and letter of all those amendments to the Constitution which were designed for the protection and advancement of the Negro, and we condemn all devices like the so-called "grandfather clause" that have for their real aim his disfranchisement for reasons of color alone, as unfair, un-American and repugnant to the supreme law of the land.

Letter to C. Elias Winston (1914)

My dear Mr. Winston: I regret the delay in answering your letter owing to the fact that I have been off on a fishing trip for a week.

In your case, I am doing something which I very rarely do, and that is to attempt to correct a misrepresentation of my words. I have found by some experience in public life that if one spends his time in attempting to correct false reports, he will rarely do anything in the way of constructive work, and that the time spent in trying to make such corrections could be better spent, in most cases, in some direct effort in the way of progress.

I am making exception in your case, because you have been kind and thoughtful enough to do that which very few people think of doing, and that is to try to find out directly from the individual, himself, the facts concerning his utterances. In most cases, persons simply hear a rumor, or read a garbled report of one's address and then this report or rumor is passed from one hand to another without anyone taking the precaution to get first-hand, direct information from the person most concerned.

You say that I am quoted in both the white and colored press as making the following remarks: "The Negro should stop fighting segregation and lend his forces towards beautifying the neighborhood in which he lives." Let me say that I have made no such remarks at any time or at any place. On the other hand, I have always opposed the passing of any law to segregate the Negro, either in city, town or country district. I have always said, especially when speaking to Southern white people, that such segregation is unnecessary, unjust, unwise, and from my point of view, illegal, and I have been often surprised at the number of white people in the South who have agreed with my position.

A few weeks ago, when an attempt was made to pass a law segregating colored people in Birmingham, I, in connection with a number of other colored people in Alabama, took the matter up directly with the city commissioners and the law was not passed.

When speaking on the subject of railroad accommodations in Muskogee, I made the following direct remarks to the white people who composed a large part of the audience, "Let us urge upon the railroads throughout this country to provide more equal, more just, more clean and up-to-date railroad facilities for the black people of this country, wherever the law requires such separation. And there is no white man in the United States, no matter where he lives, North or South, who will not agree with us in the statement that, whenever and wherever a Negro pays a railroad fare that is equal to that paid by a white man, he should have accommodations that are just as just and equal, and that are just as clean and decent, as those furnished the white man for the same amount of money. You would not permit the white merchants in Muskogee to sell so many pounds of flour to a Negro customer at a certain price and then sell better flour and more flour to a white customer for the same money; no more should a railroad be permitted to furnish one kind of accommodation to the Negro passenger and another kind of accommodation to the white passenger for the same money."

What I did attempt to say in Muskogee, and what I have attempted on numerous occasions to say when speaking in public, was to urge our people not to become discouraged or disheartened in communities where they were segregated, but notwithstanding such segregation, go forward and make progress. In a word, to overcome evil with good; to make so much progress in the beauty, comfort and convenience of their surroundings that those who have treated them unjustly will be made to blush with shame because of the progress that the colored people are making. In a word, I try to impress upon our people the idea that they should keep a cheerful heart and a strong will and not permit themselves to be continually on the defensive side of life, but to make such progress that the world will admire the rapid strides with which they are going forward.

I realize fully the importance of condemning wrong—such wrongs as segregation,—but I realize, too, the danger of our spending too much time and strength in mere condemnation without attempting to aid our cause by progressive, constructive work as well as condemnation. Condemnation is easy; construction is difficult. The constructive action should employ the major portion of our time. The two lines of thought and work must go hand in hand; condemnation of wrong and constructive effort; overcoming injustice through evidences of progress. On this platform we can make an appeal to every white man in the South and in the North whose goodwill and influence is worth having. More and more, throughout the South, the number of white people who feel and see that it never helps to yield to the temptation of mistreating a black man is increasing; throughout this country, the number of black people who feel and see that it never helps a black man to yield to the temptation of mistreating a white man is increasing.

In proportion as we go forward in all parts of the country, making real progress and asking for fair and just treatment by the hands of all people, North and South, our race is going to command the respect and confidence of all the people of all classes.

You are at liberty to make any use of this letter that your judgment dictates.

Yours very truly,

Booker T. Washington

George Washington (Library of Congress)

GEORGE WASHINGTON

1732–1799

First President of the United States

Featured Documents
- ◆ Address to Congress on Resigning His Commission (1783)
- ◆ Proclamation of Neutrality (1793)
- ◆ Farewell Address (1796)

Overview

As both soldier and statesman, George Washington played a pivotal role in the establishment of the United States of America, from the 1750s until his death in 1799. Washington could be found at the center of events during both the French and Indian War (1754–1763) and the American Revolution. As commander in chief of the Continental army during the Revolutionary War (1775–1783), he led the fledgling country through years of dismal, often uncertain conflict. After a brief retirement, Washington presided over the Constitutional Convention in 1787. Following two terms as the nation's first president, he retired to his plantation of Mount Vernon, dying on December 14, 1799.

Washington was born in 1732 in Westmoreland County, Virginia. As a native Virginian, Washington envisioned his beloved Potomac River as the gateway to the West. As a young man he surveyed western lands, and he continued to take an interest in the West throughout his life. As a commander of militia troops in 1754, scouting western Pennsylvania, Washington was defeated by French forces at Fort Necessity, which helped spark the conflict that became the French and Indian War. In 1758 Washington, by then a colonel, won an important victory at Fort Duquesne. That year he also won election for the first time to Virginia's House of Burgesses. The next year, he married the wealthy widow Martha Dandridge Custis.

At the onset of the Revolutionary War, Washington stood out as the obvious choice to be commander in chief of the Continental army. Although he lost more battles than he won against the superior British force during the war, events like the crossing of the Delaware River became legendary; by keeping the army alive, he kept the Revolution alive. Finally, at the Battle of Yorktown in 1781, Washington, with French allies, defeated the British under General Charles Cornwallis, effectively bringing the war to a close.

In 1783 Washington resigned his army post and retired to Mount Vernon. Meanwhile, in the wake of the war, the United States faced severe financial problems, ineffective government under the Articles of Confederation, and violent unrest. By 1787 Washington was among those who thought the articles insufficient to preserve liberty and provide order. Washington's reputation for fairness and prudence placed him in the presider's chair at the Constitutional Convention in Philadelphia from May 25 to September 17, 1787. In the end, the convention discarded the articles and proposed instead a wholly new constitution for the Union, one delineating a stronger central government. Having proved during the Revolutionary War that he could be trusted with great power, Washington soon became the nation's first president under the U.S. Constitution.

As president, Washington realized that every action he undertook would produce a lasting precedent. In choosing his political course, he drew from a well of wisdom, fortitude, and judiciousness that few of his contemporaries seemed to possess. He did his best to balance conflicting commercial and agrarian interests in the country, the former being represented in his cabinet by the New Yorker Alexander Hamilton and the latter by the Virginian Thomas Jefferson. By the middle of Washington's second term, both men had resigned and could be found leading the Federalist and Republican factions against each other. Washington, however, managed to stay above party politics, and he is the only president to have done so successfully.

Having published his farewell address in a Philadelphia newspaper on September 19, 1796, Washington retired to Mount Vernon the following spring. Several years later, after a riding tour of his plantation in unusually cold and damp weather, Washington's health rapidly deteriorated. He died of a respiratory illness on December 14, 1799. In his will, he freed those slaves he personally owned.

Explanation and Analysis of Documents

A few days after Washington's death in 1799, Henry Lee eulogized him with these now famous words: "First in war, first in peace and first in the hearts of his countrymen." In addition, said Lee, Washington was "pious, just, humane, temperate and sincere." The development of what Lee and his contemporaries referred to as Washington's "public character," or reputation, as a virtuous man began well before the American Revolution. But his reputation as a person who could be trusted with power is traceable directly to December 23, 1783, the day Washington issued his address to Congress on resigning his commission. Rather than seek greater power or set himself up as a military dictator, Washington instead voluntarily resigned as general in chief of the Continental Army. In so doing, he surprised many while setting the important precedent in the United States for civilian authority over the military.

1732
■ **February 22**
George Washington is born in Westmoreland Country, Virginia.

1748
■ Washington helps survey Virginia's Shenandoah Valley.

1754
■ **July 3**
Following a short battle, Washington surrenders to the French at Fort Necessity.

1755
■ **April**
Washington is appointed aide-de-camp to the British general Edward Braddock.

■ **August**
Washington is appointed colonel and commander of the Virginia Militia.

1758
■ **November**
Washington helps capture Fort Duquesne.

■ Washington is elected to the Virginia House of Burgesses.

1774
■ **July 18**
The Fairfax County Resolves, coauthored by Washington to protest the "Intolerable Acts," are promulgated.

■ **September 5–October 26**
Washington serves as a Virginia delegate to the First Continental Congress in Philadelphia.

1775
■ **June 15**
The Second Continental Congress appoints Washington commander in chief of the Continental army.

1781
■ **October 19**
Washington defeats the British general Charles Cornwallis at Yorktown, Virginia, effectively ending the Revolutionary War.

This prudent leadership likewise can be seen in Washington's Proclamation of Neutrality, which he issued in 1793 shortly into his second presidential administration. In the face of much public opposition and without consulting Congress, Washington concluded that neutrality in the war between France and Great Britain was the only prudent course of action if the fledgling United States was to survive and prosper. This policy headed off pro-French militancy in the United States even as it avoided war with Great Britain. A not unintended consequence was great economic growth, as American trade with European nations increased.

In his farewell address (1796), imitating his famous resignation of 1783, Washington announced that he would retire rather than seek the presidency a third time. He did so at a time when he once again stood accused of monarchical ambitions. This address also contained timely admonitions about dangers posed by factionalism and regionalism to the future of the United States as well as governing principles that most Americans ever since have considered to be timeless. In all three documents, Washington modeled how one ought to wield power under republican government: with temperance, prudence, and a sense of public duty.

◆ **Address to Congress on Resigning His Commission**

Washington's resignation as commander in chief of the Continental army following the Revolutionary War was one of his most significant acts. More than the retirement of a general, it set the important precedent in U.S. political culture of civilian authority over the military at the very time the new republic was being born. Washington had been the only leader and singular symbol of unity that the disparate, newly independent states had had during the Revolution. In ongoing contact with the Continental Congress and the state governors or legislatures throughout the war, he thus served as the de facto commander in chief of the country when no national government or chief executive existed. His resignation from the army also set a precedent regarding power—how to wield it and the necessity in a republic that leaders be willing to relinquish it—that he himself would later follow when as president he declined to run for a third term.

In July 1783, Washington sent a farewell letter to state governors, imploring them to remain united. To notify Congress officially, he arrived in Annapolis, Maryland, in mid-December 1783; he acceded to Congress's request that the resignation be done in a public ceremony rather than merely in writing. The general begins his speech by noting that the recent "great events" have ended, making "the trust committed to me" no longer necessary. Washington thus begs "the indulgence of retiring from the Service of my Country." This carefully crafted, humble language was important, making clear that the civilian government, not the general, was in charge. Just nine months earlier, certain leading army officers had complained to Congress about their continued lack of pay, among other things. Implicit in their complaint was the possibility of a military coup if congressional inaction were to continue. When Washington learned of this unrest, he headed off the potential revolt. This event came to be known as the Newburgh conspiracy.

He could resign, Washington tells Congress, because he confidently believed that the "Independence and Sovereignty" of the United States were secure. Indeed, three weeks after his resignation, the Congress of the Confederation, representing the new nation under its first constitution, the Articles of Confederation, approved the Treaty of Paris, officially ending hostilities with Great Britain. Washington continues in the self-effacing, humble tones of an eighteenth-century Virginia gentleman, recalling his own "diffidence in my abilities." In fact, after some of his early defeats, the Congress and some generals lacked confidence in his abilities as well. Washington says that he had placed his trust in "the rectitude of our Cause, the support of the Supreme Power of the Union, and the patronage of Heaven"; since the cause of liberty always is just, and because the people of the several states had unified to oppose tyranny, God had blessed American arms. A problem with this statement, as the Congress and Washington well knew, was that the general had faced resistance when seeking funding, assistance, and troops from the states and Congress throughout the war. By not mentioning this, Washington allowed his resignation to become an even stronger statement of civilian control over the military, for his final obeisance as general is offered to essentially the same Congress with which he had had so much trouble.

Having asserted his submission to Congress, Washington next addresses his "obligations to the Army in general." That he squelched the Newburgh conspiracy did not mean that Washington failed to understand his officers' complaints; nor did it mean that in his last official act as commander in chief of the Continental army he would fail to sing the praises of his men and ask for their just recognition and due from Congress. In particular, he compliments "the peculiar Services and distinguished merits of the Gentlemen" who have served on his staff. He recommends "as worthy of the favorable notice and patronage of Congress" those still in the army.

Washington closes his speech by "commending the Interests of our dearest Country to the protection of Almighty God." For Washington, who as a Freemason spoke often of Providence or the Divine Architect but rarely of God and never of Jesus Christ, this was a rare but pointed choice of words. As he would state in his more famous retirement announcement, his presidential farewell address, without religion a republic is doomed to decline rapidly.

There is a legend that when King George III heard that Washington would resign his commission, the king said that if he did so, he would be the greatest man in the world. Not only in Europe but also in the United States, many expected and some even hoped that Washington would instead name himself military ruler. That he did not do so earned him the title "American Cincinnatus," after the Roman farmer Lucius Quinctius Cincinnatus, who answered the call of Rome to lead its armies as dictator and then, immediately after defeating the Aequians, relinquished power and returned to his farm.

Time Line

1783
- **December 23**
  Washington resigns as commander in chief of the Continental army.

1787
- **May 25– September 17**
  Washington presides over the Constitutional Convention at Philadelphia.

1789
- **April 30**
  Washington is inaugurated for his first term as president of the United States.

1790
- **July 16**
  Washington signs the bill creating the District of Columbia, where the nation's capital, already being called "Washington City," will be located.

1793
- **March 4**
  Washington is inaugurated as president for his second and final term.
- **April 22**
  Washington issues his Proclamation of Neutrality.

1795
- **August 18**
  Washington signs the Jay Treaty with Great Britain.

1796
- **September 19**
  Washington's farewell address is published.

1798
- **July**
  Washington is named commander of the U.S. Army, but war with France is averted.

1799
- **December 14**
  Washington dies at Mount Vernon.

Washington's final words in his resignation speech remain famous: "Having now finished the work assigned me, I retire from the great theatre of Action." In his view, to retain his position any longer would have been unseemly and an abuse of power. To relinquish it would be the greatest support he could offer to the new government, in which civilians were to have authority over the military. Thus did Washington take his "leave of all the employments of public life," thinking that he was retiring to Mount Vernon forever.

◆ Proclamation of Neutrality

As commander in chief of the Continental army during the Revolutionary War, Washington grasped the necessity and utility of establishing a Franco-American alliance. In 1778 France and the United States signed two accords, the Treaty of Amity and Commerce and the Treaty of Alliance. This U.S.-French military alliance proved instrumental to American victories during the war, and following a nearly monthlong siege in 1781 at Yorktown, Virginia, the British under General Cornwallis surrendered to a combined American and French army. It was the strength of the newly arrived French fleet that ultimately forced Cornwallis's hand. Two years later, the Treaty of Paris officially ended the war.

Whether the abolition of the monarchy and the establishment of a French Republic in 1792 ended American treaty obligations to France soon became a subject for debate in the United States. Meanwhile, Washington was reelected president in November 1792. When revolutionaries executed King Louis XVI on January 21, 1793, and soon after declared war on Great Britain and much of continental Europe, the administration's interpretation of U.S. treaty obligations to France became critical. The administration's response to these events in Europe—a response that helped split the president's cabinet and create the new nation's first political parties—successfully kept the United States out of a widening European war and sustained the still-fragile Union. Also, in the long term, the manner in which Washington asserted his presidential authority established the lasting precedent of executive dominance in the formulation and discharge of foreign policy.

The Proclamation of Neutrality, issued by Washington on April 22, 1793, was the fruit of much contemplation on the part of the president and among his cabinet. At this time, Washington's cabinet retained its original members: Thomas Jefferson as secretary of state, Edmund Randolph as attorney general, Alexander Hamilton as secretary of treasury, and Henry Knox as secretary of war. Using these men as a council of advisers rather than simply as executors of the president's policies or as independent European-style ministers proved to be one of the most enduring precedents established by Washington. On occasion, the president even took a majority vote, counting his own among the five cast; most of the time, however, he sought advice to guide his decision making. This was the case with the cabinet meetings leading up to his neutrality proclamation.

In February 1793 Washington and his cabinet began to discuss several matters relating to revolutionary France,

such as the extant debt to France, whether to extend a loan to its new government, and whether to receive Edmond Genet, the minister to the United States newly appointed by France. On April 1, Jefferson received news that revolutionary France had declared war against several countries, including Great Britain. Within days some Americans, particularly in South Carolina, were seeking to outfit privateers to prey on British shipping, action that Washington immediately opposed and which, if left unchecked, promised to drag the United States into the European conflict. To address with finality the many loose ends of American policy toward France that had become even more entangled owing to pro-French public opinion, Washington sent each cabinet member thirteen questions dealing with Franco-American relations. First on the list was this: "Shall a proclamation issue for the purpose of preventing interferences of the Citizens of the United States in the War between France & Great Britain &ca? Shall it contain a declaration of Neutrality or not? What shall it contain?" (Patrick and Pinheiro, p. 452).

The next day Washington called a meeting with his cabinet to explore these questions. Disagreement ensued, largely with the two northerners, Knox and Hamilton, opposing the two Virginians, Jefferson and Randolph. Hamilton was pro-British in sentiment, not least because his whole vision of a commercial, centralized United States hinged on a close relationship with Great Britain and stability in Europe. Jefferson had been in favor of the French Revolution from the beginning and was intensely anti-British, seeing Hamilton's commercialism as deadly to his own desire for a decentralized, agrarian republic. Randolph typically sided with Jefferson but often proved to be the voice of compromise on critical issues. Washington, as usual, was to mediate between these competing views, based not only on contrasting principles but also on each man's personal experience and on sectionalism.

The cabinet did agree that "a Proclamation shall issue forbidding our Citizens to take part in any hostilities on the seas with or against any of the belligerent Powers ... and enjoining them from all acts & proceedings inconsistent with the duties of a friendly nation towards those at War" (Patrick and Pinheiro, p. 459). Randolph would write the document, and president and cabinet would meet again on April 22 to approve a final draft and to address Washington's eleven remaining questions. In the end, the cabinet meeting of April 22 produced no answers to any of the president's other questions, so intense was the disagreement among the men; each secretary sent Washington written answers. The meeting did, however, produce the now-famous Proclamation of Neutrality. Prudently, Washington conducted these deliberations while Congress was in recess so as to avoid any prolongation of the issue.

The most telling fact about the proclamation is that it does not contain the word *neutrality*. Rather, the short document declares it the "duty and interest" of all Americans to "pursue a conduct friendly and impartial toward the belligerent Powers." Washington, as president, is declaring that this is now the official policy of the United States. He wanted as much to inform Europe of U.S. intentions as he did to restrain and head off pro-French militarism among Americans. Indeed, the bulk of the proclamation is spent explicitly warning Americans that if they are caught "committing, aiding, or abetting hostilities against any of the said Powers" or smuggling "contraband," the United States will not defend them or secure their release from foreign nations. In fact, perpetrators were to be punished under U.S. law if caught within the United States.

In various ways the proclamation effectively dealt with the immediate concerns about privateers, Genet, and trade with Europe. Jefferson criticized the American neutrality as effectively pro-British, since the larger English navy could easily blockade France, stopping trade between it and the United States; Hamilton recognized this fact, and happily so. Ultimately, however, Washington's neutrality policy gave a major boost to the American economy in the 1790s by substantially increasing the amount of American goods carried on American ships. These immediate benefits contributed to this proclamation's being one of the key policy statements issued by Washington.

The carefully formulated and shrewdly promulgated Proclamation of Neutrality put into action Washington's primary goal as the nation's first president: to preserve the new, still-tenuous Union while creating conditions in which it could flourish. The proclamation also revealed Washington's remarkable ability to exert power in the arena of foreign affairs at a time when the relationship between the executive and legislative branches was still under debate. The president realized that tying the United States permanently either to France or to Great Britain would be a grave mistake, in the short run and in the long run. European wars come and go, Washington knew, and it would be prudent to stay out of them. Three years later, in his farewell address, Washington reiterated and expanded upon the principles on which the Proclamation of Neutrality was based.

♦ **Farewell Address**

Toward the end of his first administration, George Washington expressed an intense interest in retiring to what he familiarly referred to as his "vine and fig tree." Indeed, once before he had voluntarily relinquished power with fond hopes of farming and retirement from public life—in 1783, when he stepped down as commander in chief of the Continental army. Having forgone retirement to serve as president, Washington by 1792 was ready once again to return to Mount Vernon. Thus, he asked James Madison to pen for him a farewell address to the nation, and Madison did so. Yet when Hamilton and Jefferson, among others, informed Washington that the new republic might quickly disintegrate were he to leave the post of president, Washington relented and shelved Madison's draft.

By 1796 Washington was more determined than ever not to run for another term. The growing partisanship and factionalism over foreign affairs that by then had driven Hamilton and Jefferson from his administration only increased his desire to retire to his plantation. Washington also realized that in so rabid a political atmosphere, accusations that he had grown monarchical in his sentiments could best be met, and met with finality, not through words only but through action as well—a voluntary relinquishing of power combining the symbolic and the real as only Washington could. Perhaps most important, he realized that if he died in office he would be setting the worst precedent of all: The first president of the United States would have been president for life, thus offering to posterity the apparent example of an autocrat unwilling to relinquish power, even if he had wielded it without abuse.

Having made his decision, Washington this time tapped Hamilton to write the address. Hamilton worked from Madison's older version but also used an outline written by Washington. After a few months of revisions, with the president working to temper Hamilton's own ideas and partisanship, the farewell address was ready for publication. Unlike his 1783 address to Congress on resigning his commission, Washington's farewell address would be published rather than delivered as a speech; only in doing so could he directly address the people. The farewell address appeared first on September 19, 1796, in Philadelphia's Federalist *American Daily Advertiser* and then soon after in newspapers around the country. The historian Joseph Ellis, in his essay "The Farewell," succinctly explains the mixed authorship of the address: "Some of the words were Madison's; most of the words were Hamilton's; all the ideas were Washington's" (Higginbotham, p. 234).

Washington opens the address with a salutation to "Friends and Citizens," thus framing his announcement from the beginning as an address to the people and not to the states or to the Congress. He will "decline being considered among the number of those out of whom a choice is to be made" for the next presidential election. Responding to those critics who had accused him of monarchical ambitions, he pointedly notes, "I constantly hoped that it would have been much earlier in my power…to return to that retirement from which I had been reluctantly drawn." He informs Americans that he had indeed been determined to retire in 1792, but duty and patriotism had prevented him. Now, however, "patriotism does not forbid it."

Once finished with this brief announcement of retirement, Washington proceeds to the largest portion of the address, an attempt to frame the political questions of the 1790s. He comments on the importance of the U.S. Constitution, the Union, piety, and national sentiment for the liberty and prosperity of the United States. Although it is partly a defense of his administration, this also is the portion of the address to which later generations of Americans would look for advice on domestic unity, national security, and foreign policy.

The "main pillar in the edifice of your real independence," Washington states, is the Union of the states under the Constitution. He implores Americans to recognize "the immense value" of their "national union," connected as it is by "sacred ties." Indeed, he leaves no doubt about his own nationalism: "The name of American … must always exalt the just pride of patriotism more than any appellation

Surrender of the British general Charles Cornwallis at Yorktown, Virginia (Library of Congress)

derived from local discriminations." The crucible of the Revolutionary War, along with common "religion, manners, habits, and political principles," ought to long be the foundation for a real sense of national brotherhood. In other words, Washington is urging Americans to think of themselves primarily as Americans rather than just as Virginians or New Yorkers and to remain constantly vigilant against the forces of disunion. This was a tall order in 1796 and would continue to be so throughout the period ending in the Civil War, but Washington was convinced that a strong Union did not threaten liberty and prosperity but rather preserved the former and promoted the latter.

Echoing the content of Federalist 10, written by James Madison, Washington proceeds to argue that while the regions of the United States are diverse, this variety makes them strong and interdependent. This argument appeals to individual self-interest rather than merely seeking to motivate Americans through the lofty rhetoric of brotherhood forged in battle. The increasingly commercial, industrial, and maritime North, Washington asserts, needs "the productions" of the South, and this relationship helps to expand the South's agriculture and commerce. The East, in turn, can serve as a conduit of imports and its own "productions" to the West, while the West is likewise dependent

on the East for "supplies requisite to its growth and comfort" as well as for "indispensable outlets" for its products. The Union, therefore, "ought to be considered as a main prop of your liberty, and … the love of the one ought to endear to you the preservation of the other."

Having told Americans what they have in common, Washington next offers a warning against particular "causes which may disturb our Union." He begins with political organizations, such as parties, that are based on a mistaken belief that "there is a real difference of local interests and views." Regional parties, which rather arise from "jealousies" and "misrepresentations," do not reflect the reality that "fraternal affection" and interdependence bind the country. The U.S. government "has a just claim to your confidence and your support," Washington states, because it represents equally all parts of the nation. He observes, "The very idea of the power and the right of the people to establish government presupposes the duty of every individual to obey the established government." The United States provides ordered liberty under the law, and the duty to obey this law applies to all equally, not least because the nation is governed by popular consent. Moreover, the Constitution is, after all, amendable. Thus, any willful obstructions of the law by "combinations and associations," even well meaning ones, undermine liberty and order because in time, once in the hands of "cunning, ambitious, and unprincipled men" such organizations "become potent engines" destructive to the nation's ideals.

As to how often and to what extent Americans should be willing to amend their Constitution, Washington warns that a constant "spirit of innovation" driven by an addiction "to perpetual change" would enervate the whole system, subverting "what cannot be directly overthrown." Reflecting the political philosophy of the contemporary Anglo-Irish statesman Edmund Burke, Washington explains the importance of prudence and patience: "Time and habit are…necessary to fix the true character of governments," while "experience is the surest standard by which to test the real tendency of the existing constitution of a country." The best policy, then, is to let natural development, not "mere hypothesis and opinion," dictate the pace and level of reform. In effect, Washington is assuring Americans that even without him as head of state, time will prove the Constitution's principles strong enough to "maintain all in the secure and tranquil enjoyment of the rights of person and property."

If regional parties are the most dangerous of all factions, owing to their increasing the likelihood of disunion and civil war, even "the spirit of party generally" is dangerous to a republic's health. But "this spirit," Washington concedes, "is inseparable from our nature." As Jefferson's Democratic-Republicans and Hamilton's Federalists were gathering their forces for the election of 1796, this was a timely warning indeed. Perhaps parties are necessary bulwarks of liberty in some countries, Washington muses, but not in nations "of the popular character." Parties end up serving neither the state nor the people, instead engorging themselves "on the ruins of public liberty."

More dangerous still, partisanship, growing as it does out of weaknesses in human nature, "kindles the animosity" of citizens and regions against one another, enshrining demagoguery in political practice. Alluding to the debate over the proper American policy toward the war in Europe, Washington warns that partisanship also "opens the door to foreign influence and corruption." Although Washington's Federalist supporters would have interpreted this last point as a jab at the Francophile Democratic-Republican Party, he was speaking to the pro-British Federalists as well. (So important is this point that Washington later addresses foreign policy more fully.) Since 1796 these injunctions against "the spirit of party" have been the least followed of all the allegedly timeless advice in Washington's farewell address, other than in platitudes proffered by normally rabid partisans or in more serious wartime attempts at national unity.

The Constitution and prescriptive laws, Washington continues, can do only so much to guard against the dark but ineradicable aspects of human nature. If Americans really are to cultivate a sense of fraternity and national sentiment, "religion and morality are indispensable." Washington believed that morality issues from religion, not the other way around, and he condemns abstract theorizing about whether "morality can be maintained without religion," as "reason and experience both forbid us to expect that national morality can prevail in exclusion of religious principle." This need for "virtue or morality," that is, for piety, applies equally to the governors as well as to the governed. Indeed, piety is deemed "a necessary spring of popular government." Even as piety acts as a key ingredient in ensuring the vitality of popular government, so, too, does education. "Public opinion," Washington asserts, "should be enlightened." One of his dreams for the new capital city on the Potomac River was a national university. Although he does not say as much here, the implication would have been hard for readers of the address to miss.

Having briefly drawn the connection between education and self-government, Washington next, with only a little less brevity, discusses economics. He implores his readers to "cherish public credit," by which he means the good financial standing of the U.S. government. He criticizes the carrying of a national debt as "ungenerously throwing upon posterity the burden which we ourselves ought to bear." Military disbursements composed the bulk of U.S. government expenditures in 1796, and so Washington concludes that the surest way to avoid significant debt is by "cultivating peace." However, he very typically strikes a tone of moderation, adding that "timely disbursements to prepare for danger frequently prevent much greater disbursements to repel it." Weakness and ill-preparedness could end up costing more in the long run, so a balanced view of preparation would be necessary. In times of peace, he says, the proper duty of the U.S. government is to pay its debts as quickly as possible.

Washington's admonitions on public credit serve as an effective introduction to the second-longest portion of the farewell address, that concerning foreign relations. This part of the address is best understood in the context of divisions among Americans over U.S.-French and U.S.-British relations in 1796. Later Americans would come to see in this portion timeless advice on the wisdom of noninterventionism and even isolationism.

Washington's thoughts on foreign relations in his farewell address are largely an explication of the philosophy behind the Proclamation of Neutrality of 1793. The political atmosphere remained tense, with Democratic-Republicans desiring to support France and possibly war against Great Britain. These tensions were exacerbated by that party's lingering mistrust of Washington as a result of his support for the pro-British Jay Treaty, which had finally gone into effect earlier in 1796. Yet, as with neutrality, Washington had seen the Jay Treaty as the most prudent course of action for the young country to take. Thus in his address he advises Americans to deal honestly and "cultivate peace" with all nations—and to Democratic-Republicans, this meant toward Great Britain. But unmistakably this also was a message to those Federalists who so clearly wished to wage war on France. He remarks, "Religion and morality enjoin this conduct; and can it be, that good policy does not equally enjoin it?" Good policy, that is, ought to flow from morality, which finds its source in religion. "The permanent felicity of a nation," Washington claims, is connected by Providence with its virtue.

Much like the Roman orator Marcus Tullius Cicero in his *On Duties*, Washington is arguing here that advantage and right always go together, even in foreign policy. He deems that "in the course of time and things...any temporary advantages" will more than be outweighed by a just, benevolent foreign policy. Although he was speaking in generalities, Washington is clear: "Inveterate antipathies" and "passionate attachments" to certain nations "should be excluded," to be replaced by "just and amicable feelings towards all." "Habitual hatred" and "habitual fondness" equally enslave a nation by leading it "astray from its duty and its interest." Calling on historical lessons from the Roman Republic, the decline of which Cicero had done so much to forestall, Washington maintains that "foreign influence is one of the most baneful foes of republican government" because under it "tools and dupes" come to surrender their own interests unknowingly.

So, then, how ought the American Republic conduct its foreign relations? According to Washington, "the great rule of conduct" is to have as much commerce and "as little political connection as possible" with other nations. He recognizes the connections between the United States and Europe but points out that geographical isolation affords America advantages, the greatest of which is that only by choice will the United States become involved in the "frequent controversies" in Europe. "Why forego the advantages of so peculiar a situation?" Washington asks. "Why... entangle our peace and prosperity in the toils of European ambition, rivalship, interest, humor or caprice?" The United States, for the sake of its "peace and prosperity," should "steer clear of permanent alliances." Notably, nowhere does Washington use the term "entangling alliances," although Americans have long attributed it to him; ironically, the first to use that phrase would be Thomas Jefferson at his 1801 presidential inauguration. Yet the idea is surely present here: Washington asserts that "interweaving our destiny with that of any part of Europe" will lead only to disaster, now and in the future.

Thanking his "countrymen" for taking the time to read "these counsels of an old and affectionate friend," Washington closes with an explicit endorsement of his Proclamation of Neutrality, saying, "the spirit of that measure has continually governed me, uninfluenced by any attempts to deter or divert me from it." His overriding motivation during his administration, and specifically with the proclamation (and by extension, with the Jay Treaty), "has been to endeavor to gain time to our country to settle and mature its yet recent institutions." Washington hopes that his farewell address "will make the strong and lasting impression I could wish." Unstated is his hope that Americans will see his allegedly pro-British policies in the same light that he does: that of prudence, piety, and patriotism.

Impact and Legacy

George Washington retired from the presidency as a relatively unpopular leader. Yet in a few short years, even Thomas Jefferson was to praise the nation's first head of state and his conduct. By the early decades of the nineteenth century the Washington of history became the Washington of pious myth, as the printer and author Mason Locke Weems and others began to use his life to educate children in character. But Washington needs no myth or legend to retain his traditional importance as the key Founding Father, given his real accomplishments and his remarkable ability to maintain a prudent and temperate public character.

As soldier and general, Washington kept the dream of an independent United States alive by keeping the Continental army intact during the Revolutionary War. For this alone Washington might have earned the title "Father of His Country," but he went on to win the nickname of "American Cincinnatus" as well for resigning his generalcy and refusing to preside over some sort of military state. In so doing, he installed at the very birth of the United States the principle of civilian authority over the military.

As president, Washington secured the trans-Appalachian West and Great Lakes region through Indian wars and treaties; oversaw the development of the State, Treasury, and War departments; and kept the United States out of a destructive European war. He also negotiated the establishment of the new national capital not far from his plantation of Mount Vernon, which overlooked the Potomac. The locale, he hoped, would place the capital at the center of the expanding, prosperous, and westward-looking country that he believed would develop in time. In all these accomplishments, Washington established important precedents regarding the relationship between the executive and legislative branches, the president's role in foreign policy and treaty making, the use of the veto power, the use of a cabinet, and, down to a minute level, how the president of the Republic behaves while in office.

The impact of Washington's farewell address has lain in its symbolism as much as in its content. The content proved even more important later in American history, and into the twenty-first century American politicians continue to cite Washington's admonitions about foreign policy as relevant axioms. The modern applicability of these principles is debated, but the address's symbolism is not. Once again Washington had wielded great power, and once again he had relinquished it willingly. In so doing he demonstrated that in a republic the presidency is an office one occupies for a limited time in order to serve one's country, not an office one owns in order to serve oneself. This was perhaps Washington's most important precedent of all.

Key Sources

Immediately after retiring from the presidency George Washington worked to preserve his voluminous papers—some 135,000 documents in all (though Martha Washington burned all but two of their personal letters). The bulk of Washington's papers are held at the Library of Congress and the National Archives, but a great number can be

"I consider it an indispensable duty to close this last solemn act of my Official life, by commending the Interests of our dearest Country to the protection of Almighty God, and those who have the superintendence of them, to his holy keeping."

(Address to Congress on Resigning His Commission)

"And I do hereby also make known that whosoever of the citizens of the United States shall render himself liable to punishment and forfeiture under the law of nations, by committing, aiding or abetting hostilities against any of the said powers, or by carrying to any of them those articles, which are deemed contraband by the modern usage of nations, will not receive the protection of the United States, against such punishment or forfeiture."

(Proclamation of Neutrality)

"The name of American, which belongs to you in your national capacity, must always exalt the just pride of patriotism more than any appellation derived from local discriminations."

(Farewell Address)

"The Constitution which at any time exists, till changed by an explicit and authentic act of the whole people, is sacredly obligatory upon all. The very idea of the power and the right of the people to establish government presupposes the duty of every individual to obey the established government."

(Farewell Address)

"Observe good faith and justice towards all nations; cultivate peace and harmony with all. Religion and morality enjoin this conduct; and can it be, that good policy does not equally enjoin it?"

(Farewell Address)

"It is our true policy to steer clear of permanent alliances with any portion of the foreign world."

(Farewell Address)

found in smaller public and private repositories. Two multivolume editions of select Washington documents were published during the 1800s. Between 1931 and 1944 John C. Fitzpatrick published thirty-nine volumes of *The Writings of George Washington*, containing most of Washington's outgoing correspondence; this otherwise valuable edition thus presented only about half the story. With more sophisticated editorial methods, the University of Virginia has been working since 1969 to transcribe, edit, annotate, and publish all of Washington's papers, including his incoming correspondence, as *The Papers of George Washington*, in five series, with fifty-two of ninety planned vol-

Questions for Further Study

1. Discuss the importance of Washington's role as America's first president, whose every action would set a precedent. How aware was Washington himself of the importance of that role, and how did he attempt to set the pace for future presidents? Areas to address include his use of the cabinet as a genuine advisory board, his subordination of the military to civilian government, his cautious approach in foreign affairs, and (perhaps most important of all) his willing relinquishment of power. Be sure to quote from the speeches excerpted here as they relate to these and other important precedents of his administration.

2. What was the role of religion in Washington's worldview? Examine his religious beliefs and the manner in which he applied them to the public discourse, in particular within his 1783 resignation address and his 1796 farewell. How did his views differ from traditional Christianity, and in what ways were they aligned with it? Pay special attention to his statements on the importance of morality to the civil order and the role of religion in sustaining morality. How would he regard the relationship between religion and government in the America of present times?

3. Washington's time was an age when many people looked to the classical past of Greece and Rome for guidance and examples. Thus he quotes Cicero in his farewell address, and thus admirers called him "the American Cincinnatus," comparing him to a great leader of the early Roman Republic. His career could also be contrasted with that of another Roman, a man who like Washington was "father of his country": Augustus Caesar, who founded the Roman Empire. How did the two leaders differ in their approach to power, their regard for the people under their leadership, and their establishment of precedents for leaders who would follow them? Consider Washington's ideas on the peaceful and democratic transition of power, as opposed to Augustus's establishment of a royal dynasty over a state that remained a republic in name only. On the other hand, how apt was the comparison to Cincinnatus? Finally, what lessons did Washington draw from Cicero on the challenges of preserving republican government?

4. Explain the historical setting and significance of the 1793 Proclamation of Neutrality. Begin by explaining the circumstances that brought it about, including the specific difficulties Washington faced in gaining agreement from his cabinet. Go on to assess the precedent it established for later U.S. foreign policy. Why did Washington believe that past agreements with the French were no longer binding, and how justified do you think this position was? Examine the differences between the American and French revolutions and how they might have played into Washington's approach. What was the effect of the neutrality proclamation in the short term, as it related to American trade, and in the long term, as it regarded foreign affairs in general and particularly the role of the executive branch in conducting diplomacy?

5. Review Washington's farewell address in detail, examining its significance with respect to both the political environment of 1796 and its continuing legacy and influence. How did Washington use the address to emphasize his views on the importance of national union and of control by the people over the government? What threats does he warn against, and what advice does he give to preserve peace and prosperity? How have his words served as a guide to later generations, and to what extent do you believe that the leaders of today remain faithful to Washington's vision for the newborn republic from whose presidency he was retiring?

umes published thus far. In 2007 this project launched a fully searchable digital edition of the papers (http://gwpapers.virginia.edu/). See, in particular, Christine S. Patrick and John C. Pinheiro, eds. *The Papers of George Washington*, Presidential Series, Vol. 12: *January–May 1793* (2005).

Further Reading

■ Books

Ellis, Joseph. *His Excellency: George Washington*. New York: Vintage Books, 2005.

Higginbotham, Don, ed. *George Washington Reconsidered*. Charlottesville: University Press of Virginia, 2001.

Longmore, Paul K. *The Invention of George Washington*. Charlottesville: University Press of Virginia, 1999.

Sharp, James Roger. *American Politics in the Early Republic: The New Nation in Crisis*. New Haven, Conn.: Yale University Press, 1993.

—John C. Pinheiro

ADDRESS TO CONGRESS ON RESIGNING HIS COMMISSION (1783)

Mr. President: The great events on which my resignation depended having at length taken place; I have now the honor of offering my sincere Congratulations to Congress and of presenting myself before them to surrender into their hands the trust committed to me, and to claim the indulgence of retiring from the Service of my Country.

Happy in the confirmation of our Independence and Sovereignty, and pleased with the opportunity afforded the United States of becoming a respectable Nation, I resign with satisfaction the Appointment I accepted with diffidence. A diffidence in my abilities to accomplish so arduous a task, which however was superseded by a confidence in the rectitude of our Cause, the support of the Supreme Power of the Union, and the patronage of Heaven.

The Successful termination of the War has verified the most sanguine expectations, and my gratitude for the interposition of Providence, and the assistance I have received from my Countrymen, increases with every review of the momentous Contest.

While I repeat my obligations to the Army in general, I should do injustice to my own feelings not to acknowledge in this place the peculiar Services and distinguished merits of the Gentlemen who have been attached to my person during the War. It was impossible the choice of confidential Officers to compose my family should have been more fortunate. Permit me Sir, to recommend in particular those, who have continued in Service to the present moment, as worthy of the favorable notice and patronage of Congress.

I consider it an indispensable duty to close this last solemn act of my Official life, by commending the Interests of our dearest Country to the protection of Almighty God, and those who have the superintendence of them, to his holy keeping.

Having now finished the work assigned me, I retire from the great theatre of Action; and bidding an Affectionate farewell to this August body under whose orders I have so long acted, I here offer my Commission, and take my leave of all the employments of public life.

PROCLAMATION OF NEUTRALITY (1793)

Whereas it appears that a state of war exists between Austria, Prussia, Sardinia, Great Britain, and the United Netherlands, of the one part, and France on the other; and the duty and interest of the United States require, that they should with sincerity and good faith adopt and pursue a conduct friendly and impartial toward the belligerent Powers.

I have therefore thought fit by these presents to declare the disposition of the United States to observe the conduct aforesaid towards those Powers respectfully; and to exhort and warn the citizens of the United States carefully to avoid all acts and proceedings whatsoever, which may in any manner tend to contravene such disposition.

And I do hereby also make known, that whatsoever of the citizens of the United States shall render himself liable to punishment or forfeiture under the law of nations, by committing, aiding, or abetting hostilities against any of the said Powers, or by carrying to any of them those articles which are deemed contraband by the modern usage of nations, will not receive the protection of the United States, against such punishment or forfeiture; and further, that I have given instructions to those officers, to whom it belongs, to cause prosecutions to be instituted against all persons, who shall, within the cognizance of the courts of the United States, violate the law of nations, with respect to the Powers at war, or any of them.

In testimony whereof, I have caused the seal of the United States of America to be affixed to these presents, and signed the same with my hand. Done at the city of Philadelphia, the twenty-second day of April, one thousand seven hundred and ninety-three, and of the Independence of the United States of America the seventeenth.

George Washington
April 22, 1793

Glossary

by these presents	in the present document

FAREWELL ADDRESS (1796)

Friends and Citizens:

The period for a new election of a citizen to administer the executive government of the United States being not far distant, and the time actually arrived when your thoughts must be employed in designating the person who is to be clothed with that important trust, it appears to me proper, especially as it may conduce to a more distinct expression of the public voice, that I should now apprise you of the resolution I have formed, to decline being considered among the number of those out of whom a choice is to be made....

The acceptance of, and continuance hitherto in, the office to which your suffrages have twice called me have been a uniform sacrifice of inclination to the opinion of duty and to a deference for what appeared to be your desire. I constantly hoped that it would have been much earlier in my power, consistently with motives which I was not at liberty to disregard, to return to that retirement from which I had been reluctantly drawn. The strength of my inclination to do this, previous to the last election, had even led to the preparation of an address to declare it to you; but mature reflection on the then perplexed and critical posture of our affairs with foreign nations, and the unanimous advice of persons entitled to my confidence, impelled me to abandon the idea....

I have the consolation to believe that, while choice and prudence invite me to quit the political scene, patriotism does not forbid it....

If benefits have resulted to our country from these services, let it always be remembered to your praise, and as an instructive example in our annals, that under circumstances in which the passions, agitated in every direction, were liable to mislead, amidst appearances sometimes dubious, vicissitudes of fortune often discouraging, in situations in which not unfrequently want of success has countenanced the spirit of criticism, the constancy of your support was the essential prop of the efforts, and a guarantee of the plans by which they were effected. Profoundly penetrated with this idea, I shall carry it with me to my grave, as a strong incitement to unceasing vows that heaven may continue to you the choicest tokens of its beneficence; that your union and brotherly affection may be perpetual; that the free Constitution, which is the work of your hands, may be sacred-

ly maintained; that its administration in every department may be stamped with wisdom and virtue; that, in fine, the happiness of the people of these States, under the auspices of liberty, may be made complete by so careful a preservation and so prudent a use of this blessing as will acquire to them the glory of recommending it to the applause, the affection, and adoption of every nation which is yet a stranger to it.

Here, perhaps, I ought to stop. But a solicitude for your welfare, which cannot end but with my life, and the apprehension of danger, natural to that solicitude, urge me, on an occasion like the present, to offer to your solemn contemplation, and to recommend to your frequent review, some sentiments which are the result of much reflection, of no inconsiderable observation, and which appear to me all-important to the permanency of your felicity as a people. These will be offered to you with the more freedom, as you can only see in them the disinterested warnings of a parting friend, who can possibly have no personal motive to bias his counsel. Nor can I forget, as an encouragement to it, your indulgent reception of my sentiments on a former and not dissimilar occasion.

Interwoven as is the love of liberty with every ligament of your hearts, no recommendation of mine is necessary to fortify or confirm the attachment.

The unity of government which constitutes you one people is also now dear to you. It is justly so, for it is a main pillar in the edifice of your real independence, the support of your tranquility at home, your peace abroad; of your safety; of your prosperity; of that very liberty which you so highly prize. But as it is easy to foresee that, from different causes and from different quarters, much pains will be taken, many artifices employed to weaken in your minds the conviction of this truth; as this is the point in your political fortress against which the batteries of internal and external enemies will be most constantly and actively (though often covertly and insidiously) directed, it is of infinite moment that you should properly estimate the immense value of your national union to your collective and individual happiness; that you should cherish a cordial, habitual, and immovable attachment to it; accustoming yourselves to think and speak of it as of the palladium of your political safety and prosperity; watching for its preservation with jealous anxiety; discountenancing whatever may suggest even a suspicion that it can in any event be abandoned; and indignantly frowning upon the first dawning of every attempt to alienate any portion of our country from the rest, or to enfeeble the sacred ties which now link together the various parts.

For this you have every inducement of sympathy and interest. Citizens, by birth or choice, of a common country, that country has a right to concentrate your affections. The name of American, which belongs to you in your national capacity, must always exalt the just pride of patriotism more than any appellation derived from local discriminations. With slight shades of difference, you have the same religion, manners, habits, and political principles. You have in a common cause fought and triumphed together; the independence and liberty you possess are the work of joint counsels, and joint efforts of common dangers, sufferings, and successes....

The North, in an unrestrained intercourse with the South, protected by the equal laws of a common government, finds in the productions of the latter great additional resources of maritime and commercial enterprise and precious materials of manufacturing industry. The South, in the same intercourse, benefiting by the agency of the North, sees its agriculture grow and its commerce expand. Turning partly into its own channels the seamen of the North, it finds its particular navigation invigorated; and, while it contributes, in different ways, to nourish and increase the general mass of the national navigation, it looks forward to the protection of a maritime strength, to which itself is unequally adapted. The East, in a like intercourse with the West, already finds, and in the progressive improvement of interior communications by land and water, will more and more find a valuable vent for the commodities which it brings from abroad, or manufactures at home. The West derives from the East supplies requisite to its growth and comfort, and, what is perhaps of still greater consequence, it must of necessity owe the secure enjoyment of indispensable outlets for its own productions to the weight, influence, and the future maritime strength of the Atlantic side of the Union, directed by an indissoluble community of interest as one nation. Any other tenure by which the West can hold this essential advantage, whether derived from its own separate strength, or from an apostate and unnatural connection with any foreign power, must be intrinsically precarious.

While, then, every part of our country thus feels an immediate and particular interest in union, all the parts combined cannot fail to find in the united mass of means and efforts greater strength, greater resource, proportionably greater security from external danger, a less frequent interruption of their peace by foreign nations; and, what is of inestimable value, they must derive from union an exemption from those broils and wars between themselves, which so frequently afflict neighboring countries not tied together by the same governments, which their own rival ships alone would be sufficient to produce, but which opposite foreign alliances, attachments, and intrigues would stimulate and embitter. Hence, likewise, they will avoid the necessity of those overgrown military establishments which, under any form of government, are inauspicious to liberty, and which are to be regarded as particularly hostile to republican liberty. In this sense it is that your union ought to be considered as a main prop of your liberty, and that the love of the one ought to endear to you the preservation of the other.

These considerations speak a persuasive language to every reflecting and virtuous mind, and exhibit the continuance of the Union as a primary object of patriotic desire. Is there a doubt whether a common government can embrace so large a sphere? Let experience solve it. To listen to mere speculation in such a case were criminal. We are authorized to hope that a proper organization of the whole with the auxiliary agency of governments for the respective subdivisions, will afford a happy issue to the experiment. It is well worth a fair and full experiment. With such powerful and obvious motives to union, affecting all parts of our country, while experience shall not have demonstrated its impracticability, there will always be reason to distrust the patriotism of those who in any quarter may endeavor to weaken its bands.

In contemplating the causes which may disturb our Union, it occurs as matter of serious concern that any ground should have been furnished for characterizing parties by geographical discriminations, Northern and Southern, Atlantic and Western; whence designing men may endeavor to excite a belief that there is a real difference of local interests and views. One of the expedients of party to acquire influence within particular districts is to misrepresent the opinions and aims of other districts. You cannot shield yourselves too much against the jealousies and heartburnings which spring from these misrepresentations; they tend to render alien to each other those who ought to be bound together by fraternal affection. The inhabitants of our Western country have lately had a useful lesson on this head; they have seen, in the negotiation by the Executive, and in the unanimous ratification by the Senate, of the treaty with Spain, and in the universal satisfaction at that event, throughout the United States, a decisive proof how unfounded were the suspicions propagated among them of a policy in the General Government and in the Atlantic States unfriendly to their interests in regard to the Mississippi; they have been witnesses to the formation of two treaties, that with Great Britain, and that with Spain, which secure to them everything they could desire, in respect to our foreign relations, towards confirming their prosperity. Will it not be their wisdom to rely for the preservation of these advantages on the Union by which they were procured? Will they not henceforth be deaf to those advisers, if such there are, who would sever them from their brethren and connect them with aliens?

To the efficacy and permanency of your Union, a government for the whole is indispensable. No alliance, however strict, between the parts can be an adequate substitute; they must inevitably experience the infractions and interruptions which all alliances in all times have experienced. Sensible of this momentous truth, you have improved upon your first essay, by the adoption of a constitution of government better calculated than your former for an intimate union, and for the efficacious management of your common concerns. This government, the offspring of our own choice, uninfluenced and unawed, adopted upon full investigation and mature deliberation, completely free in its principles, in the distribution of its powers, uniting security with energy, and containing within itself a provision for its own amendment, has a just claim to your confidence and your support. Respect for its authority, compliance with its laws, acquiescence in its measures, are duties enjoined by the fundamental maxims of true liberty. The basis of our political systems is the right of the people to make and to alter their constitutions of government. But the Constitution which at any time exists, till changed by an explicit and authentic act of the whole people, is sacredly obligatory upon all. The very idea of the power and the right of the people to establish government presupposes the duty of every individual to obey the established government.

All obstructions to the execution of the laws, all combinations and associations, under whatever plausible character, with the real design to direct, control, counteract, or awe the regular deliberation and action of the constituted authorities, are destructive of this fundamental principle, and of fatal tendency. They serve to organize faction, to give it an artificial and extraordinary force; to put, in the place of the delegated will of the nation the will of a party, often

a small but artful and enterprising minority of the community; and, according to the alternate triumphs of different parties, to make the public administration the mirror of the ill-concerted and incongruous projects of faction, rather than the organ of consistent and wholesome plans digested by common counsels and modified by mutual interests.

However combinations or associations of the above description may now and then answer popular ends, they are likely, in the course of time and things, to become potent engines, by which cunning, ambitious, and unprincipled men will be enabled to subvert the power of the people and to usurp for themselves the reins of government, destroying afterwards the very engines which have lifted them to unjust dominion.

Towards the preservation of your government, and the permanency of your present happy state, it is requisite, not only that you steadily discountenance irregular oppositions to its acknowledged authority, but also that you resist with care the spirit of innovation upon its principles, however specious the pretexts. One method of assault may be to effect, in the forms of the Constitution, alterations which will impair the energy of the system, and thus to undermine what cannot be directly overthrown. In all the changes to which you may be invited, remember that time and habit are at least as necessary to fix the true character of governments as of other human institutions; that experience is the surest standard by which to test the real tendency of the existing constitution of a country; that facility in changes, upon the credit of mere hypothesis and opinion, exposes to perpetual change, from the endless variety of hypothesis and opinion; and remember, especially, that for the efficient management of your common interests, in a country so extensive as ours, a government of as much vigor as is consistent with the perfect security of liberty is indispensable. Liberty itself will find in such a government, with powers properly distributed and adjusted, its surest guardian. It is, indeed, little else than a name, where the government is too feeble to withstand the enterprises of faction, to confine each member of the society within the limits prescribed by the laws, and to maintain all in the secure and tranquil enjoyment of the rights of person and property....

Let me now take a more comprehensive view, and warn you in the most solemn manner against the baneful effects of the spirit of party generally.

This spirit, unfortunately, is inseparable from our nature, having its root in the strongest passions of the human mind. It exists under different shapes in all governments, more or less stifled, controlled, or repressed; but, in those of the popular form, it is seen in its greatest rankness, and is truly their worst enemy.

The alternate domination of one faction over another, sharpened by the spirit of revenge, natural to party dissension, which in different ages and countries has perpetrated the most horrid enormities, is itself a frightful despotism. But this leads at length to a more formal and permanent despotism. The disorders and miseries which result gradually incline the minds of men to seek security and repose in the absolute power of an individual; and sooner or later the chief of some prevailing faction, more able or more fortunate than his competitors, turns this disposition to the purposes of his own elevation, on the ruins of public liberty....

[The spirit of Party] serves always to distract the public councils and enfeeble the public administration. It agitates the community with ill-founded jealousies and false alarms, kindles the animosity of one part against another, foments occasionally riot and insurrection. It opens the door to foreign influence and corruption, which finds a facilitated access to the government itself through the channels of party passions. Thus the policy and the will of one country are subjected to the policy and will of another.

There is an opinion that parties in free countries are useful checks upon the administration of the government and serve to keep alive the spirit of liberty. This within certain limits is probably true; and in governments of a monarchical cast, patriotism may look with indulgence, if not with favor, upon the spirit of party. But in those of the popular character, in governments purely elective, it is a spirit not to be encouraged. From their natural tendency, it is certain there will always be enough of that spirit for every salutary purpose. And there being constant danger of excess, the effort ought to be by force of public opinion, to mitigate and assuage it. A fire not to be quenched, it demands a uniform vigilance to prevent its bursting into a flame, lest, instead of warming, it should consume.

It is important, likewise, that the habits of thinking in a free country should inspire caution in those entrusted with its administration, to confine themselves within their respective constitutional spheres, avoiding in the exercise of the powers of one department to encroach upon another. The spirit of encroachment tends to consolidate the powers of all the departments in one, and thus to create, whatever the form of government, a real despotism. A just estimate of that love of power, and proneness to abuse it, which predominates in the human heart, is sufficient to satisfy us of the truth of this position.

The necessity of reciprocal checks in the exercise of political power, by dividing and distributing it into different depositaries, and constituting each the guardian of the public weal against invasions by the others, has been evinced by experiments ancient and modern; some of them in our country and under our own eyes. To preserve them must be as necessary as to institute them. If, in the opinion of the people, the distribution or modification of the constitutional powers be in any particular wrong, let it be corrected by an amendment in the way which the Constitution designates. But let there be no change by usurpation; for though this, in one instance, may be the instrument of good, it is the customary weapon by which free governments are destroyed. The precedent must always greatly overbalance in permanent evil any partial or transient benefit, which the use can at any time yield.

Of all the dispositions and habits which lead to political prosperity, religion and morality are indispensable supports. In vain would that man claim the tribute of patriotism, who should labor to subvert these great pillars of human happiness, these firmest props of the duties of men and citizens. The mere politician, equally with the pious man, ought to respect and to cherish them. A volume could not trace all their connections with private and public felicity. Let it simply be asked: Where is the security for property, for reputation, for life, if the sense of religious obligation desert the oaths which are the instruments of investigation in courts of justice? And let us with caution indulge the supposition that morality can be maintained without religion. Whatever may be conceded to the influence of refined education on minds of peculiar structure, reason and experience both forbid us to expect that national morality can prevail in exclusion of religious principle.

It is substantially true that virtue or morality is a necessary spring of popular government. The rule, indeed, extends with more or less force to every species of free government. Who that is a sincere friend to it can look with indifference upon attempts to shake the foundation of the fabric?

Promote then, as an object of primary importance, institutions for the general diffusion of knowledge. In proportion as the structure of a government gives force to public opinion, it is essential that public opinion should be enlightened.

As a very important source of strength and security, cherish public credit. One method of preserving it is to use it as sparingly as possible, avoiding occasions of expense by cultivating peace, but remembering also that timely disbursements to prepare for danger frequently prevent much greater disbursements to repel it, avoiding likewise the accumulation of debt, not only by shunning occasions of expense, but by vigorous exertion in time of peace to discharge the debts which unavoidable wars may have occasioned, not ungenerously throwing upon posterity the burden which we ourselves ought to bear....

Observe good faith and justice towards all nations; cultivate peace and harmony with all. Religion and morality enjoin this conduct; and can it be, that good policy does not equally enjoin it? It will be worthy of a free, enlightened, and at no distant period, a great nation, to give to mankind the magnanimous and too novel example of a people always guided by an exalted justice and benevolence. Who can doubt that, in the course of time and things, the fruits of such a plan would richly repay any temporary advantages which might be lost by a steady adherence to it? Can it be that Providence has not connected the permanent felicity of a nation with its virtue? The experiment, at least, is recommended by every sentiment which ennobles human nature. Alas! Is it rendered impossible by its vices?

In the execution of such a plan, nothing is more essential than that permanent, inveterate antipathies against particular nations, and passionate attachments for others, should be excluded; and that, in place of them, just and amicable feelings towards all should be cultivated. The nation which indulges towards another a habitual hatred or a habitual fondness is in some degree a slave. It is a slave to its animosity or to its affection, either of which is sufficient to lead it astray from its duty and its interest....The nation, prompted by ill-will and resentment, sometimes impels to war the government, contrary to the best calculations of policy....The peace often, sometimes perhaps the liberty, of nations, has been the victim.

So likewise, a passionate attachment of one nation for another produces a variety of evils. Sympathy for the favorite nation, facilitating the illusion of an imaginary common interest in cases where no real common interest exists, and infusing into one the enmities of the other, betrays the former into a participation in the quarrels and wars of the latter without adequate inducement or justification. It leads also to concessions to the favorite nation of privileges denied to others which is apt doubly to injure the nation making the concessions; by unnecessarily parting with what ought to have been retained, and by exciting jealousy, ill-will, and a disposition to retaliate, in the parties from whom equal privileges are withheld. And it gives to ambitious, corrupted, or deluded citizens (who devote themselves to the favorite nation), facility to betray or sacrifice the interests of their own country, without odium, sometimes even with popularity; gilding, with the appearances of a virtuous sense of obligation, a commendable deference for public opinion, or a laudable zeal for public good, the base or foolish compliances of ambition, corruption, or infatuation.

As avenues to foreign influence in innumerable ways, such attachments are particularly alarming to the truly enlightened and independent patriot. How many opportunities do they afford to tamper with domestic factions, to practice the arts of seduction, to mislead public opinion, to influence or awe the public councils. Such an attachment of a small or weak towards a great and powerful nation dooms the former to be the satellite of the latter.

Against the insidious wiles of foreign influence (I conjure you to believe me, fellow-citizens) the jealousy of a free people ought to be constantly awake, since history and experience prove that foreign influence is one of the most baneful foes of republican government....Excessive partiality for one foreign nation and excessive dislike of another cause those whom they actuate to see danger only on one side, and serve to veil and even second the arts of influence on the other. Real patriots who may resist the intrigues of the favorite are liable to become suspected and odious, while its tools and dupes usurp the applause and confidence of the people, to surrender their interests.

The great rule of conduct for us in regard to foreign nations is in extending our commercial relations, to have with them as little political connection as possible. So far as we have already formed engagements, let them be fulfilled with perfect good faith. Here let us stop. Europe has a set of primary interests which to us have none; or a very remote relation. Hence she must be engaged in frequent controversies, the causes of which are essentially foreign to our concerns. Hence, therefore, it must be unwise in us to implicate ourselves by artificial ties in the ordinary vicissitudes of her politics, or the ordinary combinations and collisions of her friendships or enmities.

Our detached and distant situation invites and enables us to pursue a different course. If we remain one people under an efficient government, the period is not far off when we may defy material injury from external annoyance; when we may take such an attitude as will cause the neutrality we may at any time resolve upon to be scrupulously respected; when belligerent nations, under the impossibility of making acquisitions upon us, will not lightly hazard the giving us provocation; when we may choose peace or war, as our interest, guided by justice, shall counsel.

Why forgo the advantages of so peculiar a situation? Why quit our own to stand upon foreign ground? Why, by interweaving our destiny with that of any part of Europe, entangle our peace and prosperity in the toils of European ambition, rivalship, interest, humor or caprice?

It is our true policy to steer clear of permanent alliances with any portion of the foreign world; so far, I mean, as we are now at liberty to do it; for let me not be understood as capable of patronizing infidelity to existing engagements. I hold the maxim no less applicable to public than to private affairs, that honesty is always the best policy. I repeat it, therefore, let those engagements be observed in their genuine sense. But, in my opinion, it is unnecessary and would be unwise to extend them.

Taking care always to keep ourselves by suitable establishments on a respectable defensive posture, we may safely trust to temporary alliances for extraordinary emergencies.

Harmony, liberal intercourse with all nations, are recommended by policy, humanity, and interest. But even our commercial policy should hold an equal and impartial hand; neither seeking nor granting exclusive favors or preferences; consulting the natural course of things; diffusing and diversifying by gentle means the streams of commerce, but forcing nothing; establishing (with powers so disposed, in order to give trade a stable course, to define the rights of our merchants, and to enable the govern-

ment to support them) conventional rules of intercourse, the best that present circumstances and mutual opinion will permit, but temporary, and liable to be from time to time abandoned or varied, as experience and circumstances shall dictate; constantly keeping in view that it is folly in one nation to look for disinterested favors from another; that it must pay with a portion of its independence for whatever it may accept under that character; that, by such acceptance, it may place itself in the condition of having given equivalents for nominal favors, and yet of being reproached with ingratitude for not giving more. There can be no greater error than to expect or calculate upon real favors from nation to nation. It is an illusion, which experience must cure, which a just pride ought to discard.

In offering to you, my countrymen, these counsels of an old and affectionate friend, I dare not hope they will make the strong and lasting impression I could wish; that they will control the usual current of the passions, or prevent our nation from running the course which has hitherto marked the destiny of nations. But, if I may even flatter myself that they may be productive of some partial benefit, some occasional good; that they may now and then recur to moderate the fury of party spirit, to warn against the mischiefs of foreign intrigue, to guard against the impostures of pretended patriotism; this hope will be a full recompense for the solicitude for your welfare, by which they have been dictated.

Glossary

apostate	exhibiting disloyalty or abandonment
batteries	here, groups of guns or artillery, or fire from those guns
discountenancing	looking on with disapproval
essay	attempt
gilding	making deceptively pleasing, as in applying a thin layer of gold to baser metals
humor	here, disposition
palladium	something on which the welfare of the community depends; derived from Greek mythology, which held that the safety of Troy depended on the preservation of a statue of the goddess Pallas Athena
specious	deceptive
suffrages	votes
tenure	form of ownership
weal	good, welfare

How far in the discharge of my official duties I have been guided by the principles which have been delineated, the public records and other evidences of my conduct must witness to you and to the world. To myself, the assurance of my own conscience is, that I have at least believed myself to be guided by them.

In relation to the still subsisting war in Europe, my proclamation of the twenty-second of April, 1793, is the index of my plan. Sanctioned by your approving voice, and by that of your representatives in both houses of Congress, the spirit of that measure has continually governed me, uninfluenced by any attempts to deter or divert me from it.

After deliberate examination, with the aid of the best lights I could obtain, I was well satisfied that our country, under all the circumstances of the case, had a right to take, and was bound in duty and interest to take, a neutral position. Having taken it, I determined, as far as should depend upon me, to maintain it, with moderation, perseverance, and firmness....

The inducements of interest for observing that conduct will best be referred to your own reflections and experience. With me a predominant motive has been to endeavor to gain time to our country to settle and mature its yet recent institutions, and to progress without interruption to that degree of strength and consistency which is necessary to give it, humanly speaking, the command of its own fortunes.

Though, in reviewing the incidents of my administration, I am unconscious of intentional error, I am nevertheless too sensible of my defects not to think it probable that I may have committed many errors. Whatever they may be, I fervently beseech the Almighty to avert or mitigate the evils to which they may tend. I shall also carry with me the hope that my country will never cease to view them with indulgence; and that, after forty five years of my life dedicated to its service with an upright zeal, the faults of incompetent abilities will be consigned to oblivion, as myself must soon be to the mansions of rest.

Relying on its kindness in this as in other things, and actuated by that fervent love towards it, which is so natural to a man who views in it the native soil of himself and his progenitors for several generations, I anticipate with pleasing expectation that retreat in which I promise myself to realize, without alloy, the sweet enjoyment of partaking, in the midst of my fellow-citizens, the benign influence of good laws under a free government, the ever-favorite object of my heart, and the happy reward, as I trust, of our mutual cares, labors, and dangers.

Geo. Washington.

Daniel Webster (Library of Congress)

DANIEL WEBSTER   1782–1852

U.S. Congressman, Senator, and Secretary of State

Featured Documents
◆ Second Reply to Robert Hayne (1830)
◆ Speech to the Senate on the Preservation of the Union (1850)

Overview

Born on January 18, 1782, in Salisbury, New Hampshire, Daniel Webster was the son of a Revolutionary War officer. At fourteen he went off to Phillips Exeter Academy, a preparatory school; a year later he entered Dartmouth College, graduating near the top of his class in 1801. Admitted to the bar in 1805, Webster soon embarked on a career in politics as a member of the Federalist Party, which advocated a strong central government and a diverse, integrated economy. Elected to Congress from New Hampshire in 1812, Webster opposed the decision by James Madison's administration to go to war against Great Britain that year, saying that it would damage New England economically. Federalists risked being portrayed as unpatriotic for opposing the war; when Americans believed that they had prevailed in the conflict owing to Andrew Jackson's astonishing victory in New Orleans, most Federalists found themselves struggling to survive in public life. As for Webster, after moving to Boston in 1816, he would win election to Congress as a representative from Massachusetts in 1822.

Webster first gained renown as a lawyer. Admitted to practice before the Supreme Court in 1814, he played important roles in two critical cases five years later. Representing his alma mater in *Trustees of Dartmouth College v. Woodward*, he successfully argued for the sanctity of public contracts from subsequent unilateral modification by the state. Representing the Second Bank of the United States in *McCulloch v. Maryland*, he effectively fended off the state's attempt to tax the federally chartered bank, building upon established notions of national supremacy. In 1824, in *Gibbons v. Ogden*, he successfully argued that the Constitution gave the authority to regulate interstate commerce, broadly defined to include transportation, exclusively to the federal government through Congress.

In 1827 Webster was elected a U.S. senator from Massachusetts. On the Senate floor three years later, he offered a celebrated attack upon the doctrine of nullification, by which states were held to have the right to defy federal legislation that they deemed unconstitutional. However, Webster failed in 1832 to secure the recharter of the Second Bank of the United States, and his showing in the 1836 presidential contest, which pitted four different Whig candidates against Martin Van Buren, proved an embarrassing failure. By 1840 he found himself committed to supporting the presidential ambitions of William Henry Harrison, and he was rewarded by being appointed Harrison's secretary of

state in 1841. As a diplomat, he is perhaps best remembered for his role in negotiating the Webster-Ashburton Treaty, which demarcated the border between the United States and Canada west to the territory of Oregon, provided for use of the Great Lakes by American and British shipping, and moved to end the international slave trade.

Retiring from the cabinet in 1843, Webster returned to public life two years later when he was again elected to the Senate. He opposed the Mexican-American War of 1846–1848; in 1850 he found himself in the middle of a political debate occasioned in part by the legacy of that conflict, over issues including the future of slavery in the United States. Once more Webster took up the cause of Union and Constitution, most notably in what became known as his seventh of March speech. His disparagements of antislavery and abolitionist northerners on this occasion subjected him to much criticism from former supporters and admirers. Joining the cabinet again as secretary of state under Millard Fillmore, Webster made one more bid for his party's presidential nomination in 1852; after falling short once more, he returned to his home in Massachusetts, where he died on October 24, 1852.

Explanation and Analysis of Documents

Although he enjoyed a long and successful career as an elected official and a diplomat, Webster is best remembered for his achievements as an orator and a lawyer. In these roles he labored to establish the U.S. Constitution as the law of the land, claiming for himself the title of the document's foremost and authoritative interpreter. While his accomplishments as a lawyer endure in the form of critical Supreme Court rulings framed by Chief Justice John Marshall, as an orator Webster attained a form of immortality, for schoolchildren in the North in the nineteenth century often found themselves declaiming the Massachusetts senator's words for classroom exercises in public address.

As seen in two speeches—his second reply to the South Carolina senator Robert Hayne (1830) and the seventh of March speech (1850), on the preservation of the Union—Webster combined logic and passion in framing his discussions of the Constitution. In these and other speeches he sought to forge Americans' attachment to the Constitution as a birthright of the Revolutionary War and a cornerstone of American identity. By emphasizing how the Constitution was a living legacy of the founding generation of the United States and the best guarantee of a united and harmonious republic, he hoped to appeal to the hearts as well as the minds of his audience. His approach was especially important with regard to countering southern claims about how states might defy, or nullify, federal measures or perhaps even secede. By declaring that the Constitution was a creation of the American people and not of the individual states, Webster hoped to circumvent the dry and legalistic arguments of his opponents by appealing to common sense and patriotic fervor as well as plain logic.

The key difference between the two speeches rests in the author's handling of the slavery issue. The second reply to Hayne preceded by nearly a year the publication of the first number of William Lloyd Garrison's *Liberator*, the prime abolitionist newspaper for decades to come. People linked Webster's fiery denunciation of nullification to an antisouthern position, since many people believed that at the heart of southern claims embracing states' rights was a desire to protect the institution of slavery from federal interference. However, Webster avoided saying anything about slavery as a cause of sectional division, focusing instead squarely on southern chatter and threats about nullification and disunion. He would not be drawn into a discussion of slavery's morality. Two decades later, with the federal government's policy toward slavery at the center of political controversy, Webster chose to embrace compromise over sectional confrontation. He hoped to appease southern Whigs to attract their support for a possible presidential bid; to that point he gave the impression of being only mildly antislavery, yet enough so that he remained the favorite of many New Englanders who saw him as a warrior against the southern separatism being fueled by the desire to protect slavery. It was not his advocacy of compromise that offended other supporters nearly so much as his open denunciation of abolitionists and antislavery agents for their failure to enforce existing fugitive slave legislation and their continuous agitation of the slavery issue.

◆ **Second Reply to Robert Hayne**

During the 1820s South Carolinians began discussing ways by which the Palmetto State could resist what they believed to be federal intrusions into state affairs. Much of this argument ostensibly concerned federal tariff policy. As South Carolina relied upon agricultural exports (cotton and rice) as the basis of its prosperity, its leaders came to oppose protective tariffs on imported goods, because they believed that the resulting higher prices implicitly supported the growth of northern industrial enterprises. Lurking just beneath the surface, however, was an ever-growing concern that the federal government might use its powers, including that of controlling interstate commerce, to restrict or even eventually abolish slavery. Northern efforts to restrict the spread of slavery in 1820 resulted in the Missouri Compromise, which placed limits on slavery's westward expansion; the freed slave Denmark Vesey's attempt to incite a slave insurrection in Charleston in 1822 alerted white South Carolinians to what the future might hold if they did not take sufficient steps to protect themselves.

Vice President John C. Calhoun, a former South Carolina congressman, took the lead in framing the doctrine of nullification. In 1828 he composed a protest against the so-called Tariff of Abominations (part of a series of taxes upon imported goods), which had passed Congress earlier that year. He claimed that such a protective tariff unfairly favored manufacturing over agricultural interests and was thus an unconstitutional measure. Calhoun set forth nullification as a proposed remedy, asserting that as states had agreed to the contract known as the Constitution, each contracting party—each state—could judge for itself whether any federal measure was constitutional and could choose to nullify it (that is, block its implementation within the state's borders).

Long a strong supporter of federal power and economic development, Webster found nullification objectionable. New England manufacturing benefited from protective tariffs, so he was also defending the interests of many of his constituents and contributors. A debate over public land policy in the Senate brought the issue of nullification to the nation's attention. The occasion was a resolution to look into placing limitations upon the sale of public lands, mostly in the West. Several senators from western states rose up in opposition to the proposal; Senator Robert Hayne of South Carolina, a close confidant of Calhoun's, seized the moment to try to forge common cause between the South and the West and at the same time advance the principle of nullification. Hayne argued that once more the Northeast was trying to use the federal government to benefit its own interests at the expense of the South and the West by twisting the Constitution to serve its needs. Hayne believed that the time had come for the South and the West to join political forces by rejecting such misinterpretations of the Constitution, and he advanced nullification as one means of safeguarding sectional interests. Webster countered Hayne's first foray into the debate; Hayne's response was to outline, more explicitly and with more care, the doctrine of nullification, this time in direct opposition to Webster's initial speech. Webster squarely met this argument in what would become known as his second reply to Hayne, which he delivered on January 26 and 27, 1830, with Calhoun himself looking on from his position as president of the Senate.

In the portion of his speech addressing nullification, Webster first outlines Hayne's main propositions and then wrestles with their underlying assumptions. The Constitution, he argues, was not a contract concluded between the states but was the direct expression of the popular will, to serve as the supreme law of the land. Since states were not the contracting agents, it was incorrect to treat them as such. The American people themselves approved of the Constitution as the law of the land. State governments could not overrule the federal government, as the Constitution established the federal government as sovereign on matters properly belonging to it. As for nullification, Webster declares that the theory is in effect nonsense, for it was not left to the individual states to pass judgment on the constitutionality of measures passed by Congress. The

Webster, Daniel

Time Line

1841

■ **March 6**
Under William Henry Harrison, Webster begins a two-year stint as secretary of state.

1842

■ **August 9**
Webster completes the negotiation of the Webster-Ashburton Treaty.

1845

■ Webster is again elected a U.S. senator from Massachusetts.

1850

■ **March 7**
Webster delivers his speech on the preservation of the Union on the floor of the Senate.

■ **July 23**
Webster begins a second term as secretary of state under Millard Fillmore.

1852

■ Webster runs unsuccessfully for the Whig presidential nomination.

■ **October 24**
Webster dies in Marshfield, Massachusetts.

Constitution specifies within itself the proper remedy for determining the constitutionality of any measures or policies pursued by the federal government, namely, judicial review as exercised by the Supreme Court. No state could exercise that power, and thus there was no legal or constitutional basis for nullification. But Webster cannot stop there. Having set forth his intellectual argument, he ends on an emotional note, declaring disunion unimaginable. His closing comment—"Liberty and Union, now and for ever, one and inseparable!"—was widely quoted and endorsed in years to come.

A close reading of the speech reveals that Webster combined a set of logical assertions with an appeal to the emotions of his audience. The speech offers little in the way of detailed constitutional explication or careful consideration of the specific intents of the Constitution's framers. He offers no references to any writings of the framers outside the founding document itself. By declaring that the Constitution drew its power from the people, he implies that nullification would thus challenge rule by the people. In closing with images of a nation rent by division and thrust into civil war, he paints a powerful picture of the chaos that would ensue should nullification be embraced, for it would be but the first step leading toward disunion.

Three years later, Webster would return to this argument in a speech given in the wake of the nullification crisis of 1832–1833, declaring as misguided and flawed Calhoun's insistence that the Constitution remained a compact contracted between the states. By that time, Calhoun had taken charge of making his own case, having resigned as vice president to fulfill his election to the Senate from South Carolina. Although Webster's efforts to prevent the passage of a compromise tariff bill proved futile, his address was a more concrete and grounded logical refutation of Calhoun's theories than he had set forth three years before. The relative absence of passionate oratorical flourishes and direct appeals to patriotism meant that the later speech would be more studied than quoted or fondly remembered.

◆ Speech to the Senate on the Preservation of the Union

In 1850, some two decades after Webster first battled a South Carolina senator over constitutional issues with the threat of disunion in the air, he did so again. Senator Henry Clay of Kentucky had introduced a bill that he hoped would resolve a number of outstanding issues related to slavery and its expansion, including the status of slavery in the West and in the District of Columbia. Clay's bill contained several components. It would admit California as a free state. It provided for the organization of the remainder of the land acquired from Mexico as a result of the Mexican-American War into a new territory, called New Mexico, without determining whether slavery would be allowed there. It resolved a border dispute between the territory of New Mexico and Texas in favor of the territory (thus reducing the amount of land unquestionably reserved for slavery, as Texas was a slave state), promising to compensate Texas by having the federal government assume responsibility for the debts incurred by Texas as an independent republic (1836–1845). It established that while the federal government would not interfere with slavery in the District of Columbia, the trading and selling of slaves would come to an end in the nation's capital. And it set forth a more powerful fugitive slave act. On March 4, 1850, Calhoun, persisting as a senator in what would be the last month of his life, had his colleague James M. Mason of Virginia deliver what was to be his own Senate speech, in which he advised secession should the North not submit to the South's demands and provide lasting safeguards for slavery in part by rejecting Clay's proposal, which he deemed insufficiently pro-slavery.

Three days later Webster commenced his reply in most memorable fashion: "I wish to speak to-day, not as a Massachusetts man, nor as a Northern man, but as an American, and a member of the Senate of the United States." He explicitly states that "the preservation of the Union" is at stake in this debate. Calling upon his fellow senators to support Clay's proposal, Webster advocates compromise, striving to walk a middle path between extremists on both sides. He chastises those northerners who refuse to comply with constitutional provisions for the return of fugitive slaves to their masters, and he charges abolitionists with needlessly interfering in the affairs of white southerners to the point of perhaps discouraging southern efforts on behalf of abolition. It remains the responsibility of "the sober and sound minds at the North" to arrest such irresponsible extremism. But Webster also warns southerners that secession is not the answer. As before, he insists that such a measure would be unconstitutional; this time, furthermore, he stresses the impracticability of secession and roundly dismisses any idea that secession can be accomplished peacefully. As he did in 1830, he again uses powerful imagery to stir the emotions of his audience, painting a vivid picture of the potential impact of disunion and civil war upon the hopes and dreams of the Founders' Republic. Complete catastrophe would ensue should compromise fail.

Once more, Webster took on Calhoun over the issues of the Constitution, the Union, secession, and slavery. In this case, however, he also placed himself in opposition to antislavery forces in the North. As such, many who had once celebrated Webster's replies to Hayne and Calhoun now derided him as a traitor to the cause of freedom. They attributed the stance of the speech to Webster's desire to curry favor among southern Unionists in anticipation of a final run for the presidency in 1852. It appeared to them that he had sold his soul for one last bid at the presidential chair.

In the 1830s, Webster confronted the advocates of secession and slavery and emerged victorious, at least in the minds of most northerners. In 1850, however, his speech proved to be more memorable than effective. Other senators, including New York's William Henry Seward and Mississippi's Jefferson Davis, also took to the Senate floor to plead the causes of their sections. Clay was unable to secure the passage of his proposal on its own merits; it took the death of President Zachary Taylor and the legislative skill of the Illinois senator Stephen A. Douglas to achieve the passage of the constituent parts of Clay's original proposal. The resulting legislation, however, not only did little to allay fears about the growing sectional divide but also, in the case of the new fugitive slave law, actually exacerbated the situation. Nor did the speech serve Webster's political ambitions. Although most northern conservatives welcomed his words, many antislavery northerners, including people who had once celebrated Webster's oratory and passionate Unionism, now deplored his attacks upon abolitionists and antislavery advocates. In turn, Webster's words failed to soothe those southerners who still harbored reservations about his suitability as a presidential possibility, and he failed to gain much support. In July 1850, Webster gave up his seat in the Senate to serve as secretary of state for the new president, Millard Fillmore. He continued to press for sectional compromise and a return to national harmony, but such was not to be. Thus, if the second reply to Hayne demonstrated the power of Webster's oratory, the seventh of March speech suggested its limits, including its failure to secure for Webster the Whig presidential nomination in 1852.

Satire on the presidential election of 1852, showing Winfield Scott, Daniel Webster, and Franklin Pierce competing in a footrace before a crowd of onlookers for a $100,000 prize (the four-year salary for a president). (Library of Congress)

Impact and Legacy

During his lifetime Daniel Webster was renowned for his oratorical and legal skills. However, observers were also aware of his burning ambition, his love of the good things in life, and his sense of ethics, by which he often blurred the line between private gain and the public interest. At no time was public awareness of his private flaws more evident than when critics claimed that his speech of March 7, 1850, was little more than an appeasement of southern interests in preparation for a run at the presidency; thus his foes called him "Black Dan," in contrast to one of his admirers, who called him "the Godlike Daniel."

Webster's abilities as a lawyer were especially critical in the cases he argued before the Supreme Court, where he helped establish the judicial foundations of national supremacy and the fostering of economic development. Webster's legal career helped lay the basis for his reputation as an earnest advocate of federal power. He built upon that reputation by employing his considerable rhetorical skill, both in public presentations and on the floor of the U.S. Senate. In speech after speech he declaimed in favor of the supremacy of the federal government and challenged the assertions put forth by advocates of states' rights, state sovereignty, nullification, and secession. Even as Webster deployed his considerable reasoning skill in pursuit of his arguments, what rendered his orations distinctive was their powerful appeal to one's heart as well as one's head. In the

senatorial discussions on the nature of the federal system, Webster's speeches on behalf of the Union and the Constitution—though they contain more than their share of intellectual substance—were far more memorable than the dry and legalistic offerings of his counterpart, John C. Calhoun. This was in large part because of the force and emotion with which Webster delivered his speeches and because of his willingness to appeal to sentiment, memory, and allegiance as well as to legal logic and common sense.

At a time when American politics was evolving into a party system in which candidates curried favor with voters, brokered compromises between competing factions, and engaged in a political style that emphasized their being one of the people, Webster tried a different tack. Claiming that the proper way to proceed as a nation could be determined through an understanding of first principles, as manifested in interpreting the meaning of the Constitution, Webster sought to position himself as the nation's foremost expounder of that founding document. Attaining that goal, he believed, would make simple his case for national leadership and perhaps the presidency. For years to come, biographers would celebrate the powerful nationalist while questioning the private emotions and ambitions of the senator from Massachusetts. In *Profiles in Courage* (1956), John F. Kennedy, himself then a Massachusetts senator, chose Webster's seventh of March speech as a prime example of political courage by a man who knowingly committed political suicide in speaking on behalf of the Union and

"It is, Sir, the people's Constitution, the people's government, made for the people, made by the people, and answerable to the people."

(Second Reply to Robert Hayne)

"While the Union lasts, we have high, exciting, gratifying prospects spread out before us and our children.... When my eyes shall be turned to behold for the last time the sun in heaven, may I not see him shining on the broken and dishonored fragments of a once glorious Union; on States dissevered, discordant, belligerent; on a land rent with civil feuds, or drenched, it may be, in fraternal blood!"

(Second Reply to Robert Hayne)

"Liberty and Union, now and for ever, one and inseparable!"

(Second Reply to Robert Hayne)

"I wish to speak to-day, not as a Massachusetts man, nor as a Northern man, but as an American, and a member of the Senate of the United States.... I am looking out for no fragment upon which to float away from the wreck, if wreck there must be, but for the good of the whole, and the preservation of all;... I speak to-day for the preservation of the Union."

(Speech to the Senate on the Preservation of the Union)

"I put it to all the sober and sound minds at the North as a question of morals and a question of conscience. What right have they, in their legislative capacity or any other capacity, to endeavor to get round this Constitution, or to embarrass the free exercise of the rights secured by the Constitution to the persons whose slaves escape from them? None at all; none at all."

(Speech to the Senate on the Preservation of the Union)

"There can be no such thing as peaceable secession.... Is the great Constitution under which we live, covering this whole country, is it to be thawed and melted away by secession, as the snows on the mountain melt under the influence of a vernal sun, disappear almost unobserved, and run off? No, Sir! No, Sir!"

(Speech to the Senate on the Preservation of the Union)

criticizing antislavery and abolitionist advocates. The truth was somewhat more complex, as Webster was in fact seeking to maintain support in the South for his final presidential bid, which ended in failure at the Whig nominating convention in 1852.

While he has been the subject of several significant scholarly biographies, Webster's popular image has faded over time. Nonetheless, examining his rhetoric remains essential for students who are interested in understanding the nature of nineteenth-century American nationalism and the arguments against state sovereignty, nullification, and secession.

Key Sources

The Writings and Speeches of Daniel Webster (1903), edited by James W. McIntyre, offers a far larger collection of Webster's speeches than can be found in the more modern *Papers of Daniel Webster* (1974–1989), compiled by a team under the general editorship of Charles M. Wiltse in four series totaling fifteen volumes. Wiltse also supervised the publication of the *Microfilm Edition of the Papers of Daniel Webster* (1971), comprising some forty-one reels as well as a guide. Webster's documents are spread across several dozen repositories, including the Boston Public Library, Brandeis University Library, Chicago Historical Society, Dartmouth College, Harvard University, Massachusetts Historical Society, and New Hampshire Historical Society.

Further Reading

■ Articles
Simpson, Brooks D. "Daniel Webster and the Cult of the Constitution." *Journal of American Culture* 15 (Spring 1992): 15–23.

■ Books
Bartlett, Irving H. *Daniel Webster*. New York: W. W. Norton, 1978.

Baxter, Maurice G. *One and Inseparable: Daniel Webster and the Union*. Cambridge, Mass.: Harvard University Press, 1984.

Current, Richard Nelson. *Daniel Webster and the Rise of National Conservatism*. Boston: Little, Brown, 1955.

Questions for Further Study

1. Discuss the similarities and differences between the 1830 and 1850 speeches of Webster excerpted here, not only in terms of the positions Webster took in each but also with regard to the political situation in the United States as it changed over those turbulent years. Consider the conflict between Webster and Calhoun, with their differing beliefs and rhetorical styles. What accounted for the changes in Webster's position between the two speeches, most notably his opposition to abolitionism in the later speech? What justification for his position might Webster have offered, based on his desire to preserve the Union and the Constitution at all costs?

2. Examine Webster as an orator and rhetorician. How did he differ from Calhoun and others, with his emphasis on emotional appeals over purely intellectual arguments? How effective was his style, and how deserved was his later reputation as an exemplary thinker and speaker whose addresses schoolchildren learned by heart?

3. Read the chapter on Webster in John F. Kennedy's *Profiles in Courage* and evaluate the future president's appraisal of another great Massachusetts senator. How accurate is Kennedy's portrayal, and how valid is his claim that Webster sacrificed his chances at the presidency by making a principled stance in his 1850 speech on preservation of the Union?

4. Despite his many efforts in several elections, Webster never achieved the highest office in the land. Why, in your opinion, did he fail to do so, and what kind of president would he have made? Do you agree or disagree with those critics who claimed that in his 1850 speech, he betrayed his principles in order to win southern votes? Why or why not?

5. What does Stephen Vincent Benét's short story "The Devil and Daniel Webster," written a century after Webster's heyday, say about his continuing status as an American hero? How has Webster's reputation changed since 1937, when the story was published, and what accounts for this change?

Dalzell, Robert F., Jr. *Daniel Webster and the Trial of American Nationalism, 1843–1852*. Boston: Houghton Mifflin, 1973.

Nathans, Sydney. *Daniel Webster and Jacksonian Democracy*. Baltimore: Johns Hopkins University Press, 1973.

Peterson, Merrill D. *The Great Triumvirate: Webster, Clay, and Calhoun*. New York: Oxford University Press, 1987.

Remini, Robert V. *Daniel Webster: The Man and His Time*. New York: W. W. Norton, 1997.

Shewmaker, Kenneth E., ed. *Daniel Webster: "The Completest Man."* Hanover, N.H.: University Press of New England, 1990.

—Brooks D. Simpson

SECOND REPLY TO ROBERT HAYNE (1830)

I understand the honorable gentleman from South Carolina to maintain, that it is a right of the State legislatures to interfere, whenever, in their judgment, this government transcends its constitutional limits, and to arrest the operation of its laws.

I understand him to maintain this right, as a right existing *under* the Constitution, not as a right to overthrow it on the ground of extreme necessity, such as would justify violent revolution.

I understand him to maintain an authority, on the part of the States, thus to interfere, for the purpose of correcting the exercise of power by the general government, of checking it, and of compelling it to conform to their opinion of the extent of its powers.

I understand him to maintain that the ultimate power of judging of the constitutional extent of its own authority is not lodged exclusively in the general government, or any branch of it: but that, on the contrary, the States may lawfully decide for themselves, and each State for itself, whether, in a given case, the act of the general government transcends its power.

I understand him to insist, that, if the exigency of the case, in the opinion of any State government, require it, such State government may, by its own sovereign authority, annul an act of the general government which it deems plainly and palpably unconstitutional....

This leads us to inquire into the origin of this government and the source of its power. Whose agent is it? Is it the creature of the State legislatures, or the creature of the people? If the government of the United States be the agent of the State governments, then they may control it, provided they can agree in the manner of controlling it; if it be the agent of the people, then the people alone can control it, restrain it, modify, or reform it. It is observable enough, that the doctrine for which the honorable gentleman contends leads him to the necessity of maintaining, not only that this general government is the creature of the States, but that it is the creature of each of the States severally, so that each may assert the power for itself of determining whether it acts within the limits of its authority. It is the servant of four-and-twenty masters, of different will and different purposes and yet bound to obey all. This absurdity (for it seems no less) arises from a misconception as to the origin of this government and its true character. It is, Sir, the people's Constitution, the people's government, made for the people, made by the people, and answerable to the people. The people of the United States have declared that the Constitution shall be the supreme law. We must either admit the proposition, or dispute their authority. The States are, unquestionably, sovereign, so far as their sovereignty is not affected by this supreme law. But the State legislatures, as political bodies, however sovereign, are yet not sovereign over the people. So far as the people have given the power to the general government, so far the grant is unquestionably good, and the government holds of the people, and not of the State governments. We are all agents of the same supreme power, the people. The general government and the State governments derive their authority from the same source. Neither can, in relation to the other, be called primary, though one is definite and restricted, and the other general and residuary. The national government possesses those powers which it will be shown the people have conferred upon it, and no more. All the rest belongs to the State governments, or to the people themselves. So far as the people have restrained State sovereignty, by the expression of their will, in the Constitution of the United States, so far, it must be admitted. State sovereignty is effectually controlled. I do not contend that it is, or ought to be, controlled farther. The sentiment to which I have referred propounds that State sovereignty is only to be controlled by its own "feeling of justice": that is to say, it is not to be controlled at all, for one who is to follow his own feelings is under no legal control. Now, however men may think this ought to be, the fact is, that the people of the United States have chosen to impose control on State sovereignties. There are those, doubtless, who wish they had been left without restraint; but the Constitution has ordered the matter differently. To make war, for instance, is an exercise of sovereignty; but the Constitution declares that no State shall make war. To coin money is another exercise of sovereign power, but no State is at liberty to coin money. Again, the Constitution says that no sovereign State shall be so sovereign as to make a treaty. These prohibitions, it must be confessed, are a control on the State sovereignty of South Carolina, as well as of the other

States, which does not arise "from her own feelings of honorable justice." The opinion referred to, therefore, is in defiance of the plainest provisions of the Constitution....

I must now beg to ask, Sir, Whence is this supposed right of the States derived? Where do they find the power to interfere with the laws of the Union? Sir the opinion which the honorable gentleman maintains is a notion founded in a total misapprehension, in my judgment, of the origin of this government, and of the foundation on which it stands. I hold it to be a popular government, erected by the people; those who administer it, responsible to the people; and itself capable of being amended and modified, just as the people may choose it should be. It is as popular, just as truly emanating from the people, as the State governments. It is created for one purpose; the State governments for another. It has its own powers; they have theirs. There is no more authority with them to arrest the operation of a law of Congress, than with Congress to arrest the operation of their laws. We are here to administer a Constitution emanating immediately from the people, and trusted by them to our administration. It is not the creature of the State governments. It is of no moment to the argument, that certain acts of the State legislatures are necessary to fill our seats in this body. That is not one of their original State powers, a part of the sovereignty of the State. It is a duty which the people, by the Constitution itself, have imposed on the State legislatures; and which they might have left to be performed elsewhere, if they had seen fit. So they have left the choice of President with electors; but all this does not affect the proposition that this whole government, President, Senate, and House of Representatives, is a popular government. It leaves it still all its popular character. The governor of a State (in some of the States) is chosen, not directly by the people, but by those who are chosen by the people, for the purpose of performing, among other duties, that of electing a governor. Is the government of the State, on that account, not a popular government? This government, Sir, is the independent offspring of the popular will. It is not the creature of State legislatures; nay, more, if the whole truth must be told, the people brought it into existence, established it, and have hitherto supported it, for the very purpose, amongst others, of imposing certain salutary restraints on State sovereignties. The States cannot now make war; they cannot contract alliances; they cannot make, each for itself, separate regulations of commerce; they cannot lay imposts; they cannot coin money. If this Constitu-

tion, Sir, be the creature of State legislatures, it must be admitted that it has obtained a strange control over the volitions of its creators.

The people, then, Sir, erected this government. They gave it a Constitution, and in that Constitution they have enumerated the powers which they bestow on it. They have made it a limited government. They have defined its authority. They have restrained it to the exercise of such powers as are granted; and all others, they declare, are reserved to the States or the people. But, Sir, they have not stopped here. If they had, they would have accomplished but half their work. No definition can be so clear, as to avoid possibility of doubt; no limitation so precise, as to exclude all uncertainty. Who, then, shall construe this grant of the people? Who shall interpret their will, where it may be supposed they have left it doubtful? With whom do they repose this ultimate right of deciding on the powers of government? Sir, they have settled all this in the fullest manner. They have left it with the government itself, in its appropriate branches. Sir, the very chief end, the main design, for which the whole Constitution was framed and adopted, was to establish a government that should not be obliged to act through State agency, or depend on State opinion and State discretion. The people had had quite enough of that kind of government under the Confederation. Under that system, the legal action, the application of law to individuals, belonged exclusively to the States. Congress could only recommend; their acts were not of binding force, till the States had adopted and sanctioned them. Are we in that condition still? Are we yet at the mercy of State discretion and State construction? Sir, if we are, then vain will be our attempt to maintain the Constitution under which we sit.

But, Sir, the people have wisely provided, in the Constitution itself, a proper, suitable mode and tribunal for settling questions of Constitutional law. There are in the Constitution grants of powers to Congress, and restrictions on these powers. There are, also, prohibitions on the States. Some authority must, therefore, necessarily exist, having the ultimate jurisdiction to fix and ascertain the interpretation of these grants, restrictions, and prohibitions. The Constitution has itself pointed out, ordained, and established that authority. How has it accomplished this great and essential end? By declaring, Sir, that "the Constitution, and the laws of the United States made in pursuance thereof, shall be the supreme law of the land, any thing in the constitution or laws of any State to the contrary notwithstanding."...

I have not allowed myself, Sir, to look beyond the Union, to see what might lie hidden in the dark recess behind. I have not coolly weighed the chances of preserving liberty when the bonds that unite us together shall be broken asunder. I have not accustomed myself to hang over the precipice of disunion, to see whether, with my short sight, I can fathom the depth of the abyss below; nor could I regard him as a safe counsellor in the affairs of this government, whose thoughts should be mainly bent on considering, not how the Union may be best preserved, but how tolerable might be the condition of the people when it should be broken up and destroyed. While the Union lasts, we have high, exciting, gratifying prospects spread out before us and our children. Beyond that I seek not to penetrate the veil. God grant that in my day, at least, that curtain may not rise! God grant that on my vision never may be opened what lies behind! When my eyes shall be turned to behold for the last time the sun in heaven, may I not see him shining on the broken and dishonored fragments of a once glorious Union; on States dissevered, discordant, belligerent; on a land rent with civil feuds, or drenched, it may be, in fraternal blood! Let their last feeble and lingering glance rather behold the gorgeous ensign of the republic, now known and honored throughout the earth, still full high advanced, its arms and trophies streaming in their original lustre, not a stripe erased or polluted, not a single star obscured, bearing for its motto, no such miserable interrogatory as "What is all this worth?" nor those other words of delusion and folly, "Liberty first and Union afterwards"; but everywhere, spread all over in characters of living light, playing on all it sample folds, as they float over the sea and over the land, and in every wind under the whole heavens, that other sentiment, dear to every true American heart,˜Liberty and Union, now and forever, one and inseparable!

Glossary

construction	interpretation
ensign of the republic	the American flag
exigency	urgent situation
four-and-twenty masters	the states, numbering twenty-four at the time
imposts	tariffs on imported goods
residuary	that which remains, as in a will, where specific bequests are made but the remainder of the deceased's estate is the residuary

SPEECH TO THE SENATE ON THE PRESERVATION OF THE UNION (1850)

I wish to speak to-day, not as a Massachusetts man, nor as a Northern man, but as an American, and a member of the Senate of the United States. It is fortunate that there is a Senate of the United States; a body not yet moved from its propriety, not lost to a just sense of its own dignity and its own high responsibilities, and a body to which the country looks, with confidence, for wise, moderate, patriotic, and healing counsels. It is not to be denied that we live in the midst of strong agitations, and are surrounded by very considerable dangers to our institutions and our government. The imprisoned winds are let loose. The East, the North, and the stormy South combine to throw the whole sea into commotion, to toss its billows to the skies, and disclose its profoundest depths. I do not affect to regard myself, Mr. President, as holding, or as fit to hold, the helm in this combat with the political elements; but I have a duty to perform, and I mean to perform it with fidelity, not without a sense of existing dangers, but not without hope. I have a part to act, not for my own security or safety, for I am looking out for no fragment upon which to float away from the wreck, if wreck there must be, but for the good of the whole, and the preservation of all; and there is that which will keep me to my duty during this struggle, whether the sun and the stars shall appear, or shall not appear for many days. I speak to-day for the preservation of the Union. "Hear me for my cause." I speak to-day, out of a solicitous and anxious heart for the restoration to the country of that quiet and harmonious harmony which make the blessings of this Union so rich, and so dear to us all. These are the topics I propose to myself to discuss; these are the motives, and the sole motives, that influence me in the wish to communicate my opinions to the Senate and the country; and if I can do any thing, however little, for the promotion of these ends, I shall have accomplished all that I expect....

Mr. President, in the excited times in which we live, there is found to exist a state of crimination and recrimination between the North and South. There are lists of grievances produced by each; and those grievances, real or supposed, alienate the minds of one portion of the country from the other, exasperate the feelings, and subdue the sense of fraternal affection, patriotic love, and mutual regard. I shall bestow a little attention, Sir, upon these various grievances existing on the one side and on the other. I begin with complaints of the South. I will not answer, further than I have, the general statements of the honorable Senator from South Carolina, that the North has prospered at the expense of the South in consequence of the manner of administering this government, in the collecting of its revenues, and so forth. These are disputed topics, and I have no inclination to enter into them. But I will allude to the other complaints of the South, and especially to one which has in my opinion just foundation; and that is, that there has been found at the North, among individuals and among legislators, a disinclination to perform fully their constitutional duties in regard to the return of persons bound to service who have escaped into the free States. In that respect, the South, in my judgment, is right, and the North is wrong. Every member of every Northern legislature is bound by oath, like every other officer in the country, to support the Constitution of the United States; and the article of the Constitution which says to these States that they shall deliver up fugitives from service is as binding in honor and conscience as any other article. No man fulfills his duty in any legislature who sets himself to find excuses, evasions, escapes from this constitutional obligation. I have always thought that the Constitution addressed itself to the legislatures of the States or to the States themselves. It says that those persons escaping to other States "shall be delivered up," and I confess I have always been of the opinion that it was an injunction upon the States themselves. When it is said that a person escaping into another State, and coming therefore within the jurisdiction of that State, shall be delivered up, it seems to me the import of the clause is, that the State itself, in obedience to the Constitution, shall cause him to be delivered up. That is my judgment. I have always entertained that opinion, and I entertain it now. But when the subject, some years ago, was before the Supreme Court of the United States, the majority of the judges held that the power to cause fugitives from service to be delivered up was a power to be exercised under the authority of this government. I do not know, on the whole, that it may not have been a fortunate decision. My habit is to respect the result of judicial deliberations and the solemnity of judicial decisions. As it now stands, the business of seeing that these fugitives are delivered up resides in the power of Congress and the national judicature, and my friend at the head of the Judiciary Committee has a bill on the subject now before the Senate, which, with some amendments to it, I propose to support, with all its provisions, to the fullest extent. And I desire to call the attention of all sober-minded men at the North, of all conscientious men, of all men who are not carried away by some fanatical idea or some false impression, to their constitutional obligations. I put it to all the sober and sound minds at the North as a question of morals and a question of conscience. What right have they, in their legislative capacity or any other capacity, to endeavor to get round this Constitution, or to embarrass the free exercise of the rights secured by the Constitution to the persons whose slaves escape from them? None at all; none at all. Neither in the forum of conscience, nor before the face of the Constitution, are they, in my opinion, justified in such an attempt. Of course it is a matter for their consideration. They probably, in the excitement of the times, have not stopped to consider of this. They have followed what seemed to be the current of thought and of motives, as the occasion arose, and they have neglected to investigate fully the real question, and to consider their constitutional obligations; which, I am sure, if they did consider, they would fulfil with alacrity. I repeat, therefore, Sir, that here is a well-founded ground of complaint against the North, which ought to be removed, which it is now in the power of the different departments of this government to remove; which calls for the enactment of proper laws authorizing the judicature of this government, in the several States, to do all that is necessary for the recapture of fugitive slaves and for their restoration to those who claim them. Wherever I go, and whenever I speak on the subject, and when I speak here I desire to speak to the whole North, I say that the South has been injured in this respect, and has a right to complain; and the North has been too careless of what I think the Constitution peremptorily and emphatically enjoins upon her as a duty....

Then, Sir, there are the Abolition societies, of which I am unwilling to speak, but in regard to which I have very clear notions and opinions. I do not think them useful. I think their operations for the last twenty years have produced nothing good or valuable. At the same time, I believe thousands of their members to be honest and good men, perfectly well-meaning men. They have excited feelings; they think they must do something for the cause of liberty; and, in their sphere of action, they do not see what else they can do than to contribute to an Abolition press, or an Abolition society, or to pay an Abolition lecturer. I do not mean to impute gross motives even to the leaders of these societies, but I am not blind to the consequences of their proceedings. I cannot but see what mischiefs their interference with the South has produced. And is it not plain to every man?...

It is said, I do not know how true it may be, that they sent incendiary publications into the slave States; at any rate, they attempted to arouse, and did arouse, a very strong feeling; in other words, they created great agitation in the North against Southern slavery. Well, what was the result? The bonds of the slave were bound more firmly than before, their rivets were more strongly fastened. Public opinion, which in Virginia had begun to be exhibited against slavery, and was opening out for the discussion of the question, drew back and shut itself up in its castle. I wish to know whether any body in Virginia can now talk openly as Mr. Randolph, Governor McDowell, and others talked in 1832 and sent their remarks to the press? We all know the fact, and we all know the cause; and every thing that these agitating people have done has been, not to enlarge, but to restrain, not to set free, but to bind faster the slave population of the South....

I hear with distress and anguish the word "secession," especially when it falls from the lips of those who are patriotic, and known to the country, and known all over the world, for their political services. Secession! Peaceable secession! Sir, your eyes and mine are never destined to see that miracle. The dismemberment of this vast country without convulsion! The breaking up of the fountains of the great deep without ruffing the surface! Who is so foolish, I beg every body's pardon, as to expect to see any such thing? Sir, he who sees these States, now revolving in harmony around a common centre, and expects to see them quit their places and fly off without convulsion, may look the next hour to see heavenly bodies rush from their spheres, and jostle against each other in the realms of space, without causing the wreck of the universe. There can be no such thing as peaceable secession. Peaceable secession is an utter impossibility. Is the great Constitution under which we live, covering this whole country, is it to be thawed and melted away by secession, as the snows on the mountain melt under the influence of a vernal sun, disappear almost unobserved, and run off? No, Sir! No, Sir! I will not state what might produce the disruption of the Union; but, Sir,

I see as plainly as I see the sun in heaven what that disruption itself must produce; I see that it must produce war, and such a war as I will not describe, in its twofold character.

Peaceable secession! Peaceable secession! The concurrent agreement of all the members of this great republic to separate! A voluntary separation, with alimony on one side and on the other. Why, what would be the result? Where is the line to be drawn? What States are to secede? What is to remain American? What am I to be? An American no longer? Am I to become a sectional man, a local man, a separatist, with no country in common with the gentlemen who sit around me here, or who fill the other house of Congress? Heaven forbid! Where is the flag of the republic to remain? Where is the eagle still to tower? or is he to cower, and shrink, and fall to the ground? Why, Sir, our ancestors, our fathers and our grandfathers, those of them that are yet living amongst us with prolonged lives, would rebuke and reproach us; and our children and our grandchildren would cry out shame upon us, if we of this generation should dishonor these ensigns of the power of the government and the harmony of that Union which is every day felt among us with so much joy and gratitude. What is to become of the army? What is to become of the navy? What is to become of the public lands? How is each of the thirty States to defend itself? I know, although the idea has not been stated distinctly, there is to be, or it is supposed possible that there will be, a Southern Confederacy. I do not mean, when I allude to this statement, that any one seriously contemplates such a state of things. I do not mean to say that it is true, but I have heard it suggested elsewhere, that the idea has been entertained, that, after the dissolution of this Union, a Southern Confederacy might be formed. I am sorry, Sir, that it has ever been thought of, talked of, or dreamed of, in the wildest flights of human imagination. But the idea, so far as it exists, must be of a separation, assigning the slave States to one side and the free States to the other. Sir, I may express myself too strongly, perhaps, but there are impossibilities in the natural as well as in the physical world, and I hold the idea of a separation of these States, those that are free to form one government, and those that are slave-holding to form another, as such an impossibility. We could not separate the States by any such line, if we were to draw it. We could not sit down here to-day and draw a line of separation that would satisfy any five men in the country. There are natural causes that would keep and tie us together, and there are social and domestic relations which we could not break if we would, and which we should not if we could....

I would rather hear of natural blasts and mildews, war, pestilence, and famine, than to hear gentlemen talk of secession. To break up this great government! to dismember this glorious country! to astonish Europe with an act of folly such as Europe for two centuries has never beheld in any government or any people! No, Sir! no, Sir! There will be no secession! Gentlemen are not serious when they talk of secession.

Glossary

"Hear me for my cause"	quotation from Shakespeare's *Julius Caesar*, spoken by Brutus in act 3, scene 2
injunction	command
judicature	judicial branch of government; the courts
McDowell	Governor James McDowell of Virginia
Randolph	Thomas Jefferson Randolph, a member of the Virginia legislature, who gave an abolitionist speech in 1832
vernal	pertaining to spring

IDA B. WELLS   1862–1931

Civil Rights Activist and Journalist

Featured Documents
- "Eight Men Lynched" (1892)
- *The Red Record* (1895)
- "Lynching and the Excuse for It" (1901)
- "Booker T. Washington and His Critics" (1904)
- "Lynching: Our National Crime" (1909)

Overview

Ida B. Wells was born a slave in Holly Springs, Mississippi, on July 16, 1862. When her parents and a younger brother died in a yellow fever epidemic in 1878, she accepted the first of several jobs as a rural schoolteacher to help support her six younger brothers and sisters. Success as a freelance writer eventually led to a career as a newspaper journalist and editor. Through newspaper articles and lectures, she quickly gained fame as a crusader against lynching. In addition to numerous newspaper and magazine articles, Wells is known for two pamphlets published in the 1890s—*Southern Horrors* and *The Red Record*. After marrying Ferdinand Lee Barnett, a Chicago newspaperman and civil rights advocate in 1895, Wells devoted much of her time to civic reform work. She also gained notoriety as an investigator into the causes of race riots. Wells disagreed philosophically with the accommodationist program advocated by Booker T. Washington. Although she was a signer of "The Call," a document inviting prominent black and white Americans to a conference that led to the formation of the National Association for the Advancement of Colored People (NAACP), and was a founding member of that organization, she found it too accommodating to whites. Ida Wells-Barnett died in Chicago of uremia on March 25, 1931.

Wells confronted a racially divided South on numerous occasions. While traveling to her job as a schoolteacher, she experienced segregation firsthand when a railway conductor ordered her to move to a car reserved for "colored" passengers even though she had purchased a first-class ticket. She took her case to court and won, only to have the Tennessee Supreme Court overturn that decision. She lost her teaching job in 1891 because she wrote articles criticizing the poor quality of education given to black children in segregated schools. When three friends of hers were lynched in Memphis, Tennessee, in 1892 and Wells publicly denounced their murders, the newspaper office of the Memphis *Free Speech*, of which she was editor and part owner, was destroyed by an angry white mob.

After the Memphis incident, Wells began a lifelong crusade against lynching. Through newspaper articles in the *New York Age* and later in the Chicago *Conservator* and in lectures in the United States and Great Britain, she demanded that the United States confront lynching, which

she termed "our national crime." Her two major pamphlets, *Southern Horrors* and *The Red Record*, offered detailed statistical information on lynching as well as her own controversial interpretation of the data presented. As Wells continued her public crusade against lynching, she began to investigate the causal factors behind race riots that seemed to be on the rise in a number of the nation's major cities. She also began to devote much of her time to civic reform in Chicago and worked to persuade black women to become directly involved in organizational work for racial justice.

Defiant and confrontational throughout her life, Wells challenged the racial policies of both the Woman's Christian Temperance Union and the National American Woman Suffrage Association, openly debated Booker T. Washington on the proper course for black progress, and withdrew from the NAACP because she was not comfortable with its liberal white leadership. During the 1920s, a decade that saw a rebirth of the Ku Klux Klan, Wells became increasingly disillusioned with the state of race relations in America. Never a black separatist, she was drawn to Marcus Garvey's Universal Negro Improvement Association during the 1920s because of his call for black self-help and economic independence and for instilling a new racial consciousness among African Americans. Feeling that she had lost her influence as a spokesperson for racial issues, Wells began writing her *Autobiography*. She was at work on the project when she died.

Explanation and Analysis of Documents

Ida Wells was deeply affected by racism and the violence inflicted by whites upon blacks in the United States in the late nineteenth and early twentieth centuries. In an attempt to arouse the nation to confront its racial prejudices and barbaric actions, she began to write articles and pamphlets and to lecture widely both in this country and in Great Britain. Her vivid depictions of the horrors of lynching and her statistically supported discussion of that practice began the slow, arduous process toward public rejection of those crimes. Pulling no punches in her comments, Wells criticized both blacks and whites. Black elites, shielded by their wealth from many of the indignities of discrimination, ignored the problems of others in their communi-

1862

■ **July 16**
Ida B. Wells is born in Holly Springs, Mississippi.

1878

■ Wells's parents die in a yellow fever epidemic and Wells begins a teaching career.

1884

■ Wells sues Chesapeake, Ohio & Southwestern Railroad over segregated seating policy.

1889

■ Wells becomes co-owner of the Memphis *Free Speech and Headlight*.

1891

■ Wells criticizes the Memphis school board for its segregated educational policies, loses her teaching position, and starts a career as a full-time journalist.

1892

■ **May 21**
Wells publishes the editorial "Eight Men Lynched" in the Memphis *Free Speech*, challenging the rape myth behind lynching; the newspaper's office is torched.

1895

■ Wells publishes *The Red Record*.

1901

■ **May**
Wells publishes "Lynching and the Excuse for It" in the *Independent*.

1904

■ **April**
Wells publishes "Booker T. Washington and His Critics" in the *World To-Day*.

1909

■ Wells presents "Lynching: Our National Crime" at the conference that led to the creation of the National Association for the Advancement of Colored People.

ties. Black clergymen did not speak out strongly enough against segregation. Black politicians betrayed their race to seek the favor of whites. Whites accepted social myths and cultural stereotypes that allowed them to excuse inexcusable crimes against humanity.

Wells took it upon herself to wage a public crusade against the sufferings, indignities, and wrongs of an oppressed race. Five documents, which include one editorial, one public address, and three published writings, demonstrate Wells's nuanced narrative style and her uncompromising tone: her editorial in the Memphis *Free Press*, "Eight Men Lynched," in which she boldly challenges the rape myth; an excerpt from her pamphlet *The Red Record* in which she analyzes white-on-black violence in terms of power and control; her article in the *Independent*, "Lynching and the Excuse for It," in which she disputes the "accepted" excuse for lynching; her article in the *World To-Day* in which she contests Booker T. Washington's accommodationist philosophy; and her address before the convention that led to the creation of the NAACP in which she labels lynching "our national crime" and calls for federal intervention.

◆ "Eight Men Lynched"

Ida Wells had written newspaper editorials that attacked the practice of lynching prior to the killing of three black men in Memphis, Tennessee, in March 1892. As the topic of lynching began to occupy more of her attention, she became increasingly curious about the alleged causes of those crimes. Searching through newspaper accounts, she had expected to find that rape was the most common charge. To her surprise, she learned that was not the case. But if rape was not the overriding explanation for the increase in the number of lynchings, then what was? The conclusion she drew was that southern whites were becoming increasingly alarmed by evidence of African American advancement in the post-Reconstruction era. Whites did not want competition from educated and enterprising black men and used racial terrorism to prevent it. She was learning that perceived challenges to white supremacy came in many forms.

The incident that caused Wells to deepen her understanding of lynching as a form of intimidation and to enter into a lifelong crusade against that practice occurred when three friends were murdered by a white mob in her hometown of Memphis, Tennessee. One method open to blacks hoping for advancement in the years following Reconstruction was black capitalism. In pursuit of that dream, three black men had opened the People's Grocery in direct competition with a white store owner. Desperate for a way to eliminate his competition, the white store owner persuaded the police to raid the People's Grocery and arrest its three owners. Taken from jail several days later by an angry mob, the three men were brutally murdered.

The Memphis murders affected Wells on a deeply personal level and made her rethink her assumptions. She found herself questioning the dominant cultural assumption about lynching in the South—that the rape of white women by black men was the root of lynching and that it was the outrage of that offense that provoked mobs to act. But the three black store owners had not committed any crime against white women, nor were they accused of one. For Wells, the event cast a new light on lynching. She understood it as an excuse to eliminate blacks who were starting to acquire property and improve themselves economically; it was intended to keep the race terrorized and to hold the black man down.

Having grasped this new dynamic behind lynching, Wells boldly decided to challenge the rape myth in an editorial in the Memphis *Free Speech*. After detailing eight recent lynchings in Arkansas, Louisiana, Alabama, and Georgia, Wells calls the rape excuse a lie and warns that if "Southern white men are not careful, they will overreach themselves and public sentiment will have a reaction; a conclusion will then be reached which will be very damaging to the moral reputation of their women." The implied meaning of her editorial was that white women often encouraged liaisons with black men. Her comments had the impact of an explosion. The offices and presses of the *Free Speech* were destroyed. Forced to flee the South, Wells joined the editorial staff of the *New York Age* and immediately began to write a series on lynching. When her seven-column article signed "Exiled" appeared on June 25, 1892, it created a sensation. Providing detailed statistics on lynching and again challenging the rape myth, the article was such a forceful indictment of lynching and its dominant rationale that ten thousand copies were distributed to the public. The article served as the basis for her first pamphlet, *Southern Horrors*, published later that year.

◆ The Red Record

Several years after Wells began her crusade against lynching, she published *The Red Record*, an eighty-five-page pamphlet in which she provided detailed statistics on the number of lynchings in the United States and their alleged causes from 1892 to 1894. She hoped that the shocking information, especially the most recent report for the year 1894 noting that 197 persons had been murdered by angry mobs with no opportunity for a legal defense of the charges against them, would trigger a popular demand for remedies that would prevent lynchings, end anarchy (mob activity), and promote law and order by ensuring a fair trial to those accused of a crime. Convinced that charges against black men for assaulting white women were historically based on falsehoods, she also asked readers to send resolutions to Congress in support of a bill proposed by Senator Henry W. Blair, a Maine Republican. The so-called Blair bill advocated creating a committee to investigate the number of assaults by men upon women for the previous ten years and establish in an official report the true circumstances and facts relating to the alleged assaults. Such data could be crucial in breaking long-standing racial stereotypes that had provided a rationale for lynch law.

To present an intellectual context for her statistics and to underscore the fallacy of the southern defense of white-on-black violence, Wells begins her pamphlet with a discussion of the excuses that white southerners have historically given

Time Line

1931

■ **March 25**
Wells dies in Chicago.

to justify their actions. Borrowing an argument that had recently been made by Frederick Douglass, Wells argues that there had been three distinct stages of southern barbarism and three distinct, although erroneous, southern excuses to account for them. The first excuse for the murder of defenseless blacks in the South, she argues, had been the need of the white man, in the years immediately succeeding the Civil War, to stamp out planned black insurrections. But no insurrection or riot had ever occurred. When that argument had proved to be patently false, a second rationale had been put forth. The second excuse had gained popularity during Reconstruction when black males had been given the right to vote and the protection of citizenship. But in the southern mind the vote had become equated with "Negro Domination." To nullify its effect, racist organizations such as the Ku Klux Klan and lawless mobs had justified violence to intimidate blacks from voting.

With the eventual decline in the black vote, however, the rationale that excused the violence no longer carried any weight. To maintain an environment in which whippings, shootings, torture, and lynchings could continue and the black man could be kept in his place, a new justification was needed. The third excuse that white southerners used to legitimize their actions was that black men had to be killed to avenge their assaults on white women. Such a charge, if left uncontested, would continue to paint the black man as a monster and place him "beyond the pale of human sympathy." It was the goal of Wells to refute this latest southern falsehood. In her mind, white-on-black violence was all about maintaining power and control. Lynching was the newest form of intimidation and rape the latest metaphor in the mind of the white southerner for any challenge to white supremacy.

◆ "Lynching and the Excuse for It"

Wells had hoped that her crusade against lynching would gain support from other prominent reformers and their organizations. Unfortunately, her unwillingness to tolerate expediency over principle alienated her from many of the leading reformers she had hoped to win to her cause. She publicly quarreled with Frances Willard, president of the Woman's Christian Temperance Union, charging that Willard accepted the southern rape myth and was willing to subordinate the race issue to win the backing of southern whites for prohibition. Similarly, she criticized Susan B. Anthony for tolerating segregation in the South in order to win white southern support for woman suffrage.

Wells's uncompromising position on racial questions also caused her to take issue with an article written by Jane Addams, the noted settlement house worker and cofounder of Hull-House in Chicago. Wells and Addams had much in common as it related to concern for urban social problems, and Addams had a reputation for being a white racial liberal. Nevertheless, Wells felt it to be her duty to challenge "an unfortunate presumption used as a basis for her argument [that] works so serious, tho doubtless unintentional, an injury to the memory of thousands of victims of mob law." The presumption referred to came from an article Addams had written for the January 1901 issue of the *Independent* in which she had strongly condemned lynching. Addams had rhetorically accepted some of the southern assertions about "a certain class of crimes" (black-on-white rape) to argue that even if they had validity there could still be no justification for lynching. The enforcement of the law, not lynching, could stop rape. To Wells, however, even a rhetorical acceptance of the southern rape myth was unacceptable.

In her response to Addams, which appeared as a separate article in the same issue of the magazine, Wells starts with a conciliatory note that she appreciates Addams's helpful protest against lynching. But she is quick to point out that it is "this assumption, this absolutely unwarrantable assumption, that vitiates every suggestion which it inspires Miss Addams to make." Wells supports her argument with statistics to show a low correlation between charges of rape and actual lynchings. She contends that when African Americans were lynched, "the mobs' incentive was race prejudice." To Wells, the error of Addams and the vast majority of white liberals was that they accepted the ingrained notions that black men were prone to criminality and defined as violators of white women. They refused to examine lynching statistics critically, unlink lynching from sexual crime, and see that the cause of lynching was race prejudice. In the end, Wells can only lament that it "is strange that an intelligent, law-abiding and fair minded people should so persistently shut their eyes to the facts in the discussion of what the civilized world now concedes to be America's national crime."

◆ "Booker T. Washington and His Critics"

Wells's most significant public debate resulted from philosophical disagreements she had with Booker T. Washington. Washington had attracted attention for the success of his school, the Tuskegee Institute in Alabama. The educational program at Tuskegee stressed black self-reliance and taught skills in agriculture and the trades that would allow blacks to become economically independent. Emerging as the dominant black leader in America after the death of Frederick Douglass in 1895, Washington broadened his reputation as a forward-looking black educator in speeches in which he advanced his prescription for black progress. He strongly believed that black education should concentrate on teaching industrial skills as the primary means for black economic advancement. If southern whites would provide the jobs that would enable black opportunity, whites would be repaid with increased economic growth and greater prosperity. He also believed that if blacks would defer demands for social and political equality, whites could be assured that the mutual cooperation he proposed could take place in a climate of racial harmony. Such cooperation would, in time, prepare the way for broader civil rights.

Wells also wanted to see blacks advance economically but disagreed with Washington's program. Where Washington contended that black advancement would come through patient effort that would win white acceptance, Wells saw lynching as a white contrivance designed to prevent black progress. Where Washington tolerated inequality to foster racial cooperation and economic uplift, Wells demanded immediate equality as a fundamental right. Where Washington believed that economic power could be gained by conforming to the status quo, Wells thought blacks should use their economic potential against white control. As an untapped labor force, Wells thought blacks could be an industrial factor in an industrializing South. If blacks would recognize that reality, they could gain economic leverage with both southern employers and northern investors. An understanding of that power and its judicious use in areas where lynching was prevalent could do much to halt that practice. Both Washington and Wells agreed that white elites held the key to social and economic change in the South. But unlike Washington, Wells was more concerned about redirecting their self-interest than appealing to their good graces.

By the turn of the century Washington had gained notice for the success of his school and for his ability to raise money from northern white philanthropists. But to Wells, Washington's success had exacted a cost. Because Washington had placed such a pronounced emphasis on vocational as opposed to higher education, those who listened to his speeches and financially supported his school had concluded that college education was unnecessary for blacks. The impact of that general assumption, argues Wells, had been detrimental to black education in general. Northern donations to support black colleges had dwindled, while northern colleges had reduced the number of black students they admitted. Citing Washington's educational theory as its guide for doing so, the Board of Education of New Orleans had limited the curriculum in the public schools for black children to the fifth grade. By his avoidance of the broader aspects of the topic, Wells says, Washington had enhanced the image of blacks as being inferior if not uneducable. To counter the Washington position, Wells states at the end of the document that the black man understands that industrial education alone "will not stand him in place of political, civil and intellectual liberty, and he objects to being deprived of fundamental rights of American citizenship to the end that one school for industrial training shall flourish. To him it seems like selling a race's birthright for a mess of pottage."

◆ "Lynching: Our National Crime"

When William Monroe Trotter and W. E. B. Du Bois, two other dissenters from Booker T. Washington's point of view, joined efforts to form a new organization for racial protest in 1905, Ida Wells quickly joined it. Known as the Niagara Movement, the association condemned segregation, the disenfranchisement of black voters, lynching, and any suggestion that the demand for immediate civil rights be deferred. This new body gained strength as a result of a race riot in Springfield, Illinois, in the summer of 1908. The riot had started when a white woman accused a black man of trying to rape her. That charge triggered two nights of violence. Eventually, local officials had to call in the state militia to restore order. Several days after the riot, the white woman recanted her charge. That a major race riot could occur in a northern city that also happened to be the hometown of Abraham Lincoln showed that racially motivated white mob violence was not a problem unique to the South.

One of those who had been shocked by the violence in Springfield was William English Walling, a noted social activist. In the aftermath of the riot, Walling concluded that a new national organization was needed to fight racial oppression. His idea quickly caught the attention of white liberals. In 1909 Walling and his supporters sent out an invitation known as "The Call" to other like-minded individuals of both races to attend a conference for the discussion of ways in which social and political equality might be obtained for African Americans. The petition, issued on the one-hundredth anniversary of Abraham Lincoln's birth, contained the signatures of sixty activists, including Wells. The conference, which took place in New York City on May 31 and June 1, 1909, led to the creation of the NAACP.

Given an opportunity to speak at the conference, Wells gave a short address entitled "Lynching: Our National Crime." In her address, she repeats earlier arguments that lynching is "color line murder" and that crimes against women are the excuses rather than the causes of such actions. On this occasion, in light of the Springfield riot, Wells calls lynching a national crime that requires a national solution. Agitation to stop lynching has to be supported by the force of antilynching legislation that would provide for federal prosecution of offenders in cases where states fail to act. It is the only way, she contends, "to make life, liberty, and property secure against mob rule."

Because of her reputation for being fiercely independent, Wells's relationship with the organizers of the conference proved to be problematic. Feeling slighted at being omitted from the Committee of Forty, a body charged with creating the new organization, Wells walked out of the meeting. Although she was later added to the executive committee of the NAACP, she would never play a significant role in its operation. Offended by her treatment and distrustful of the predominantly white leadership that controlled the new body, she retreated to her home base in Chicago to focus on organizing new civic programs of black self-help that she could direct.

Impact and Legacy

As Wells pursued a career in journalism, she developed a writing style that was, at all times, passionate. As part owner and editor of the *Free Press*, she wrote editorials that increasingly focused on the topic of racial injustice, and her style became bolder and more censorious. She was unafraid to condemn the actions of powerful groups, black or white, if she thought their actions contributed to racial

Ku Klux Klan members parade down Pennsylvania Avenue, Washington, D.C., in 1926. (Library of Congress)

discrimination. Wells quickly established her own voice as a writer, but in refusing to compromise principle for expediency she often undercut her support base in both the black community and among liberal white reformers and their organizations. Her confrontational style also precluded any dialogue with southern whites. While on an antilynching speaking tour in Great Britain, she mailed copies of her speeches and public endorsements to leading newspapers in the country. Southern newspapers responded in kind by attacking her character, questioning her statistical data, and challenging her basic assertion regarding the rape myth and her charge that the southern legal system was so racially biased that it made a mockery of the rule of law.

As Wells gained notice as a writer, she never retreated from her initial position. Lynching was more than a punishment for the alleged crime of rape; it was a conscious act of intimidation and oppression motivated by racial prejudice. Deeply affected by racial injustice, Wells devoted her life to what was seemingly a single-handed crusade to interpret and express the indignities, wrongs, and sufferings being inflicted upon African Americans. Her vivid depictions of the horrors of lynching and statistically grounded discussion of that practice attracted national attention for the first time and started the slow process toward public rejection of those crimes. Ida Wells broke the silence and in doing so challenged deeply rooted cultural assumptions. By steadfastly refusing to condone racial prejudice and tolerate lynching, she undercut her effectiveness as an orga-

"Nobody in this section of the country believes the old thread-bare lie that Negro men rape white women. If Southern white men are not careful, they will overreach themselves, and public sentiment will have a reaction; a conclusion will then be reached which will be very damaging to the moral reputation of their women."

("Eight Men Lynched")

"Scourged from his home; hunted through the swamps; hung by midnight raiders, and openly murdered in the light of day, the Negro clung to his right of franchise with a heroism which would have wrung admiration from the hearts of savages."

(*The Red Record*)

"It is strange that an intelligent, law-abiding and fair minded people should so persistently shut their eyes to the facts in the discussion of what the civilized world now concedes to be America's national crime."

("Lynching and the Excuse for It")

"It is indeed a bitter pill to feel that much of the unanimity with which the nation to-day agrees to Negro disfranchisement comes from the general acceptance of Mr. [Booker T.] Washington's theories."

("Booker T. Washington and His Critics")

"They [Negroes] know that the white South has labored ever since reconstruction to establish and maintain throughout the country a color line in politics, in civil rights and in education, and they feel that with Mr. [Booker T.] Washington's aid the South has largely succeeded in her aim."

("Booker T. Washington and His Critics")

"Lynching is color line murder."

("Lynching: Our National Crime")

"No other nation, civilized or savage, burns its criminals; only under the stars and stripes is the human holocaust possible."

("Lynching: Our National Crime")

nizational leader, but her determination to keep those issues before the public forced others, white and black, to confront them. She was, during her lifetime, the racial conscience of the nation.

Key Sources

The Ida B. Wells Papers at the University of Chicago Library Special Collections Research Center are indexed on the library's Web site (http://ead.lib.uchicago.edu/view. xqy?id=ICU.SPCL.IBWELLS&q=Ida+B.+Wells&page=1). Much of Wells's published writings appeared in newspapers such as the Memphis *Free Press*, the *New York Age*, and the Chicago *Conservator* and in popular periodicals such as the *Arena*, the *Independent*, and the *World To-Day*. A collection of Wells's early writings has been compiled by Miriam Decosta-Willis in *The Memphis Diary of Ida B. Wells: An Intimate Portrait of the Activist as a Young Woman* (1995). A collection of her major writings, with a lengthy introduction, can be found in Jacqueline Jones Royster, ed., *Southern Horrors and Other Writings: The Anti-Lynching Campaign of Ida Wells, 1892–1900* (1997). Wells's two best-known works, *Southern Horrors* and *The Red Record*, can also be accessed online at Project Gutenberg (www.gutenberg.org/etext/14975 and www.gutenberg.org/etext/14977, respectively). Wells's autobiography, *Crusade for Justice* (1970) includes an introduction by her daughter Alfreda M. Duster. Another helpful resource is the film "Ida B. Wells: A Passion for Justice" (1989), which tells her story through her own words as read by the Nobel Prize–winning author Toni Morrison.

Further Reading

■ Articles

Tucker, David M. "Miss Ida B. Wells and Memphis Lynching." *Phylon* 32 (Summer 1971): 112–122.

■ Books

Giddings, Paula J. *Ida: A Sword among Lions: Ida B. Wells and the Campaign against Lynching*. New York: Amistad, 2008.

Holt, Thomas C. "The Lonely Warrior: Ida B. Wells-Barnett and the Struggle for Black Leadership." In *Black Leaders of the Twentieth Century*, eds. John Hope Franklin and August Meier. Urbana: University of Illinois Press, 1982.

McMurray, Linda O. *To Keep the Waters Troubled: The Life of Ida B. Wells*. New York: Oxford University Press, 1998.

Schechter, Patricia A. *Ida B. Wells-Barnett and American Reform, 1880–1930*. Chapel Hill: University of North Carolina Press, 2001.

—Steven L. Piott

Questions for Further Study

1. Compare and contrast Wells with the leading African American figure of the period 1895–1915, Booker T. Washington. What are her major points of disagreement with Washington, as expressed not only in her 1904 critique but also in other writings? On what issues did they agree—for example, about the myths associated with lynching, or the need for blacks to achieve economic independence—and to what extent was Wells willing or unwilling to admit these points of agreement?

2. Discuss the meaning and history of lynching in the United States, particularly as it was used against African Americans in the century following the end of the Civil War. What effect did Wells's work have on bringing an end to this shameful practice?

"Eight Men Lynched" (1892)

Eight negroes lynched since last issue of the *Free Speech* one at Little Rock, Ark., last Saturday morning where the citizens broke into the penitentiary and got their man; three near Anniston, Ala., one near New Orleans; and three at Clarksville, Ga., the last three for killing a white man, and five on the same old racket—the new alarm about raping white women. The same programme of hanging, then shooting bullets into the lifeless bodies was carried out to the letter.

Nobody in this section of the country believes the old thread-bare lie that Negro men rape white women. If Southern white men are not careful, they will overreach themselves and public sentiment will have a reaction; a conclusion will then be reached which will be very damaging to the moral reputation of their women.

THE RED RECORD (1895)

"The Case Stated"

Not all nor nearly all of the murders done by white men, during the past thirty years in the South, have come to light, but the statistics as gathered and preserved by white men, and which have not been questioned, show that during these years more than ten thousand Negroes have been killed in cold blood, without the formality of judicial trial and legal execution....

Naturally enough the commission of these crimes began to tell upon the public conscience, and the Southern white man, as a tribute to the nineteenth-century civilization, was in a manner compelled to give excuses for his barbarism. His excuses have adapted themselves to the emergency, and are aptly outlined by that greatest of all Negroes, Frederick Douglass, in an article of recent date, in which he shows that there have been three distinct eras of Southern barbarism, to account for which three distinct excuses have been made.

The first excuse given to the civilized world for the murder of unoffending Negroes was the necessity of the white man to repress and stamp out alleged "race riots." For years immediately succeeding the war there was an appalling slaughter of colored people, and the wires usually conveyed to northern people and the world the intelligence, first, that an insurrection was being planned by Negroes, which, a few hours later, would prove to have been vigorously resisted by white men, and controlled with a resulting loss of several killed and wounded. It was always a remarkable feature in these insurrections and riots that only Negroes were killed during the rioting, and that all the white men escaped unharmed.

From 1865 to 1872, hundreds of colored men and women were mercilessly murdered and the almost invariable reason assigned was that they met their death by being alleged participants in an insurrection or riot. But this story at last wore itself out. No insurrection ever materialized; no Negro rioter was ever apprehended and proven guilty, and no dynamite ever recorded the black man's protest against oppression and wrong. It was too much to ask thoughtful people to believe this transparent story, and the southern white people at last made up their minds that some other excuse must be had.

Then came the second excuse, which had its birth during the turbulent times of reconstruction. By an amendment to the Constitution the Negro was given the right of franchise, and, theoretically at least, his ballot became his invaluable emblem of citizenship. In a government "of the people, for the people, and by the people," the Negro's vote became an important factor in all matters of state and national politics. But this did not last long. The southern white man would not consider that the Negro had any right which a white man was bound to respect, and the idea of a republican form of government in the southern states grew into general contempt. It was maintained that "This is a white man's government," and regardless of numbers the white man should rule. "No Negro domination" became the new legend on the sanguinary banner of the sunny South, and under it rode the Ku Klux Klan, the Regulators, and the lawless mobs, which for any cause chose to murder one man or a dozen as suited their purpose best. It was a long, gory campaign; the blood chills and the heart almost loses faith in Christianity when one thinks of Yazoo, Hamburg, Edgefield, Copiah, and the countless massacres of defenseless Negroes, whose only crime was the attempt to exercise their right to vote.

But it was a bootless strife for colored people. The government which had made the Negro a citizen found itself unable to protect him. It gave him the right to vote, but denied him the protection which should have maintained that right. Scourged from his home; hunted through the swamps; hung by midnight raiders, and openly murdered in the light of day, the Negro clung to his right of franchise with a heroism which would have wrung admiration from the hearts of savages. He believed that in that small white ballot there was a subtle something which stood for manhood as well as citizenship, and thousands of brave black men went to their graves, exemplifying the one by dying for the other.

The white man's victory soon became complete by fraud, violence, intimidation and murder. The franchise vouchsafed to the Negro grew to be a "barren ideality," and regardless of numbers, the colored people found themselves voiceless in the councils of those whose duty it was to rule. With no longer the fear of "Negro Domination" before their eyes, the white man's second excuse became valueless. With the Southern governments all subverted and the Negro actually eliminated from all participation in state and national elections, there could be no longer an excuse for killing Negroes to prevent "Negro Domination."

Brutality still continued; Negroes were whipped, scourged, exiled, shot and hung whenever and wherever it pleased the white man so to treat them, and as the civilized world with increasing persistency held the white people of the South to account for its outlawry, the murderers invented the third excuse—that Negroes had to be killed to avenge their assaults upon women. There could be framed no possible excuse more harmful to the Negro and more unanswerable if true in its sufficiency for the white man.

Humanity abhors the assailant of womanhood, and this charge upon the Negro at once placed him beyond the pale of human sympathy. With such unanimity, earnestness and apparent candor was this charge made and reiterated that the world has accepted the story that the Negro is a monster which the Southern white man has painted him. And today, the Christian world feels, that while lynching is a crime, and lawlessness and anarchy the certain precursors of a nation's fall, it can not by word or deed, extend sympathy or help to a race of outlaws, who might mistake their plea for justice and deem it an excuse for their continued wrongs.

The Negro has suffered much and is willing to suffer more. He recognizes that the wrongs of two centuries can not be righted in a day, and he tries to bear his burden with patience for today and be hopeful for tomorrow. But there comes a time when the veriest worm will turn, and the Negro feels today that after all the work he has done, all the sacrifices he has made, and all the suffering he has endured, if he did not, now, defend his name and manhood from this vile accusation, he would be unworthy even of the contempt of mankind. It is to this charge he now feels he must make answer.

Glossary

bootless	fruitless
Frederick Douglass	a prominent nineteenth-century African American abolitionist and former slave
Ku Klux Klan	a white supremacist organization, formed in 1866, that mounted a campaign of violence and intimidation against African Americans, Jews, and others
reconstruction	the period following the Civil War when the states of the Confederacy were brought back under U.S. control
Regulators	an organization similar to the Ku Klux Klan in using violence and intimidation against African Americans after the Civil War
sanguinary	bloody
veriest	truest, most actual or real
vouchsafed	given, granted
wires	telegraphs
Yazoo, Hamburg, Edgefield, Copiah	communities throughout the American South where notorious lynchings occurred

"Lynching and the Excuse for It" (1901)

It was eminently befitting that *The Independent's* first number in the new century should contain a strong protest against lynching. The deepest dyed infamy of the nineteenth century was that which, in its supreme contempt for law, defied all constitutional guarantees of citizenship, and during the last fifteen years of the century put to death two thousand men, women and children, by shooting, hanging and burning alive. Well would it have been if every preacher in every pulpit in the land had made so earnest a plea as that which came from Miss [Jane] Addams's forceful pen.

Appreciating the helpful influences of such a dispassionate and logical argument as that made by the writer referred to, I earnestly desire to say nothing to lessen the force of the appeal. At the same time an unfortunate presumption used as a basis for her argument works so serious, tho doubtless unintentional, an injury to the memory of thousands of victims of mob law, that it is only fair to call attention to this phase of the writer's plea. It is unspeakably infamous to put thousands of people to death without a trial by jury; it adds to that infamy to charge that these same victims were moral monsters, when, in fact, four-fifths of them were not so accused even by the fiends who murdered them.

Almost at the beginning of her discussion, the distinguished writer says:

"Let us assume that the Southern citizens who take part in and abet the lynching of negroes honestly believe that that is the only successful method of dealing with a certain class of crimes."

It is this assumption, this absolutely unwarrantable assumption, that vitiates every suggestion which it inspires Miss Addams to make. It is the same baseless assumption which influences ninety-nine out of every one hundred persons who discuss this question. Among many thousand editorial clippings I have received in the past five years, ninety-nine per cent discuss the question upon the presumption that lynchings are the desperate effort of the Southern people to protect their women from black monsters, and while the large majority condemn lynching, the condemnation is tempered with a plea for the lyncher—that human nature gives way under such awful provocation and that the mob, insane for the moment, must be pitied as well as condemned. It is

strange that an intelligent, law-abiding and fair minded people should so persistently shut their eyes to the facts in the discussion of what the civilized world now concedes to be America's national crime.

This almost universal tendency to accept as true the slander which the lynchers offer to civilization as an excuse for their crime might be explained if the true facts were difficult to obtain. But not the slightest difficulty intervenes. The Associated Press dispatches, the press clipping bureau, frequent book publications and the annual summary of a number of influential journals give the lynching record every year. This record, easily within the reach of every one who wants it, makes inexcusable the statement and cruelly unwarranted the assumption that negroes are lynched only because of their assaults upon womanhood....

It would be supposed that the record would show that all, or nearly all, lynchings were caused by outrageous assaults upon women; certainly that this particular offense would outnumber all other causes for putting human beings to death without a trial by jury and the other safeguards of our Constitution and laws.

But the record makes no such disclosure. Instead, it shows that five women have been lynched, put to death with unspeakable savagery, during the past five years. They certainly were not under the ban of the outlawing crime. It shows that men, not a few, but hundreds, have been lynched for misdemeanors, while others have suffered death for no offense known to the law, the causes assigned being "mistaken identity," "insult," "bad reputation," "unpopularity," "violating contract," "running quarantine," "giving evidence," "frightening child by shooting at rabbits," etc. Then, strangest of all, the record shows that the sum total of lynchings for these offenses—not crimes—and for the alleged offenses which are only misdemeanors, greatly exceeds the lynchings for the very crime universally declared to be the cause of lynching....

In the case of the negroes lynched the mobs' incentive was race prejudice. Few white men were lynched for any such trivial offenses as are detailed in the causes for lynching colored men. Negroes are lynched for "violating contracts," "unpopularity," "testifying in court" and "shooting at rabbits." As only negroes are lynched for "no offense," "unknown offenses," offenses not criminal, misdemeanors and crimes not capital, it must be admitted that the real cause of lynching in all such cases is race prejudice, and should be so classified....

No good result can come from any investigation which refuses to consider the facts. A conclusion that is based upon a presumption, instead of the best evidence, is unworthy of a moment's consideration. The lynching record, as it is compiled from day to day by unbiased, reliable and responsible public journals, should be the basis of every investigation which seeks to discover the cause and suggest the remedy for lynching. The excuses of lynchers and the spe-

cious pleas of their apologists should be considered in the light of the record, which they invariably misrepresent or ignore. The Christian and moral forces of the nation should insist that misrepresentation should have no place in the discussion of this all important question, that the figures of the lynching record should be allowed to plead, trumpet tongued, in defense of the slandered dead, that the silence of concession be broken, and that truth, swift-winged and courageous, summon this nation to do its duty to exalt justice and preserve inviolate the sacredness of human life.

Glossary

Associated Press	an organization that disseminates news stories to newspapers throughout the country
clipping bureau	an organization that provides clippings of stories and articles from newspapers and magazines
vitiates	invalidates, diminishes

"Booker T. Washington and His Critics" (1904)

Industrial education for the Negro is Booker T. Washington's hobby. He believes that for the masses of the Negro race an elementary education of the brain and a continuation of the education of the hand is not only the best kind, but he knows it is the most popular with the white South. He knows also that the Negro is the butt of ridicule with the average white American, and that the aforesaid American enjoys nothing so much as a joke which portrays the Negro as illiterate and improvident; a petty thief or a happy-go-lucky inferior....

[Booker T. Washington] knows, as do all students of sociology, that the representatives which stand as the type for any race, are chosen not from the worst but from the best specimens of that race; the achievements of the few rather than the poverty, vice and ignorance of the many, are the standards of any given race's ability. There is a Negro faculty at Tuskegee, some of whom came from the masses, yet have crossed lances with the best intellect of the dominant race at their best colleges. Mr. Washington knows intimately the ablest members of the race in all sections of the country and could bear testimony as to what they accomplished before the rage for industrial schools began. The Business League, of which he is founder and president, is composed of some men who were master tradesmen and business men before Tuskegee was born. He therefore knows better than any man before the public to-day that the prevailing idea of the typical Negro is false....

The men and women of to-day ... know that the leaders of the race, including Mr. Washington himself, are the direct product of schools of the Freedmen's Aid Society, the American Missionary Association and other such agencies which gave the Negro his first and only opportunity to secure any kind of education which his intellect and ambition craved. Without these schools our case would have been more hopeless indeed than it is; with their aid the race has made more remarkable intellectual and material progress in forty years than any other race in history. They have given us thousands of teachers for our schools in the South, physicians to heal our ailments, druggists, lawyers and ministers....

That one of the most noted of their own race should join with the enemies to their highest progress in condemning the education they had received, has been to them a bitter pill. And so for a long while they keenly, though silently, resented the jibes against the college-bred youth which punctuate Mr. Washington's speeches. He proceeds to draw a moral therefrom for his entire race. The result is that the world which listens to him and which largely supports his educational institution, has almost unanimously decided that college education is a mistake for the Negro. They hail with acclaim the man who has made popular the unspoken thought of that part of the North which believes in the inherent inferiority of the Negro, and the always outspoken southern view to the same effect.

This gospel of work is no new one for the Negro. It is the South's old slavery practice in a new dress. It was the only education the South gave the Negro for two and a half centuries she had absolute control of his body and soul. The Negro knows that now, as then, the South is strongly opposed to his learning anything else but how to work.

No human agency can tell how many black diamonds lie buried in the black belt of the South, and the opportunities for discovering them become rarer every day as the schools for thorough training become more cramped and no more are being established. The presidents of Atlanta University and other such schools remain in the North the year round, using their personal influence to secure funds to keep these institutions running. Many are like the late Collis P. Huntington, who had given large amounts to Livingston College, Salisbury, North Carolina. Several years before his death he told the president of that institution that as he believed Booker Washington was educating Negroes in the only sensible way, henceforth his money for that purpose would go to Tuskegee. All the schools in the South have suffered as a consequence of this general attitude, and many of the oldest and best which have regarded themselves as fixtures now find it a struggle to maintain existence....

Admitting for argument's sake that its system is the best, Tuskegee could not accommodate one-hundredth part of the Negro youth who need education. The Board of Education of New Orleans cut the curriculum in the public schools for Negro children down to the fifth grade, giving Mr. Washington's theory as an inspiration for so doing. Mr. Washington denied in a letter that he had ever advocated such a thing, but the main point is that this is the deduction the New Orleans school board made from his frequent statement that previous systems of education were a mistake and that the Negro should be taught to work. Governor Vardaman, of Mississippi, the other day in his inaugural address, after urging the legislature to abolish the Negro public school and substitute manual training therefor, concluded that address by saying that all other education was a curse to the Negro race.

This is the gospel Mr. Washington has preached for the past decade. The results from this teaching then would seem to be, first, a growing prejudice in northern institutions of learning against the admission of Negro students; second, a contracting of the number and influence of the schools of higher learning so judiciously scattered through all the southern states by the missionary associations, for the Negroes benefit; third, lack of a corresponding growth of industrial schools to take their places; and fourth, a cutting down of the curriculum for the Negro in the public schools of the large cities of the South, few of which ever have provided high schools for the race.

Mr. Washington's reply to his critics is that he does not oppose the higher education, and offers in proof of this statement his Negro faculty. But the critics observe that nowhere does he speak for it, and they can remember dozens of instances when he has condemned every system of education save that which teaches the Negro how to work. They feel that the educational opportunities of the masses, always limited enough, are being threatened by this retrogression....

There are many who can never be made to feel that it was a mistake thirty years ago to give the unlettered freedmen the franchise, their only weapon of defense, any more than it is a mistake to have fire for cooking and heating purposes in the home, because ignorant or careless servants sometimes burn themselves. The thinking Negro knows it is still less a mistake to-day when the race has had thirty years of training for citizenship. It is indeed a bitter pill to feel that much of the unanimity with which the nation to-day agrees to Negro disfranchisement comes from the general acceptance of Mr. Washington's theories.

Does this mean that the Negro objects to industrial education? By no means. It simply means that he knows by sad experience that industrial education will not stand him in place of political, civil and intellectual liberty, and he objects to being deprived of fundamental rights of American citizenship to the end that one school for industrial training shall flourish. To him it seems like selling a race's birthright for a mess of pottage.

They believe it is possible for Mr. Washington to make Tuskegee all it should become without sacrificing or advocating the sacrifice of race manhood to do it. They know he has the ear of the American nation as no other Negro of our day has, and he is therefore molding public sentiment and securing funds for his educational theories as no other can. They know that the white South has labored ever since reconstruction to establish and maintain throughout the country a color line in politics, in civil rights and in education, and they feel that with Mr. Washington's aid the South has largely succeeded in her aim.

Glossary

birthright	an inheritance one is entitled to by birth
mess of pottage	literally, a single meal ("mess") of soup; an allusion to the story of Esau, recounted in the biblical book of Genesis, who sold his inheritance in exchange for something of little value
reconstruction	the period following the Civil War, when the states of the Confederacy were brought back under U.S. control
Vardaman	James Kimble Vardaman, governor of Mississippi in the early twentieth century

"LYNCHING: OUR NATIONAL CRIME" (1909)

The lynching record for a quarter of a century merits the thoughtful study of the American people. It presents three salient facts:

First: Lynching is color line murder.

Second: Crimes against women is the excuse, not the cause.

Third: It is a national crime and requires a national remedy.

Proof that lynching follows the color line is to be found in the statistics which have been kept for the past twenty-five years. During the few years preceding this period and while frontier lynch law existed, the executions showed a majority of white victims. Later, however, as law courts and authorized judiciary extended into the far West, lynch law rapidly abated and its white victims became few and far between.

Just as the lynch law régime came to a close in the West, a new mob movement started in the South. This was wholly political, its purpose being to suppress the colored vote by intimidation and murder. Thousands of assassins banded together under the name of Ku Klux Klans, "Midnight Raiders," "Knights of the Golden Circle," etc., spread a reign of terror, by beating, shooting and killing colored people by the thousands. In a few years, the purpose was accomplished and the black vote was suppressed. But mob murder continued.

From 1882, in which year 52 were lynched, down to the present, lynching has been along the color line. Mob murder increased yearly until in 1892 more than 200 victims were lynched and statistics show that 3,284 men, women and children have been put to death in this quarter of a century. During the last ten years from 1899 to 1908 inclusive the number lynched was 959. Of this number 102 were white while the colored victims numbered 857. No other nation, civilized or savage, burns its criminals; only under the stars and stripes is the human holocaust possible. Twenty-eight human beings burned at the stake, one of them a woman and two of them children, is the awful indictment against American civilization—the gruesome tribute which the nation pays to the color line.

Why is mob murder permitted by a Christian nation? What is the cause of this awful slaughter? This question is answered almost daily—always the same shameless falsehood that "Negroes are lynched to protect womanhood." Standing before a Chautauqua assemblage, John Temple Graves, at once champion of lynching and apologist for lynchers, said: "The mob stands to-day as the most potential bulwark between the women of the South and such a carnival of crime as would infuriate the world and precipitate the annihilation of the Negro race." This is the never varying answer of lynchers and their apologists. All know it is untrue. The cowardly lyncher revels in murder, then seeks to shield himself from public execration by claiming devotion to woman. But truth is mighty and the lynching record discloses the hypocrisy of the lyncher as well as his crime.

The Springfield, Illinois, mob rioted for two days, the militia of the entire state was called out, two men were lynched, hundreds of people driven from their homes, all because a white woman said a Negro had assaulted her. A mad mob went to the jail, tried to lynch the victim of her charge and, not being able to find him, proceeded to pillage and burn the town and to lynch two innocent men. Later, after the police had found that the woman's charge was false, she published a retraction, the indictment was dismissed and the intended victim discharged. But the lynched victims were dead. Hundreds were homeless and Illinois was disgraced....

Various remedies have been suggested to abolish the lynching infamy, but year after year, the butchery of men, women and children continues in spite of plea and protest....

The only certain remedy is an appeal to law. Lawbreakers must be made to know that human life is sacred and that every citizen of this country is first a citizen of the United States and secondly a citizen of the state in which he belongs. This nation must assert itself and defend its federal citizenship at home as well as abroad. The strong arm of the government must reach across state lines whenever unbridled lawlessness defies state laws....

Federal protection of American citizenship is the remedy for lynching....

[This] ... has been more than once suggested in Congress. Senator Gallinger of New Hampshire in a resolution introduced in Congress called for an investigation "with the view of ascertaining whether there is a remedy for lynching which Congress may apply." The Senate Committee has under consideration a bill drawn by A. E. Pillsbury, formerly Attorney-General of Massachusetts, providing for federal prosecution of lynchers in cases where the state fails to protect citizens or foreigners. Both of these resolutions indicate that the attention of the nation has been called to this phase of the lynching question....

In a multitude of counsel there is wisdom. Upon the grave question presented by the slaughter of innocent men, women and children there should be an honest, courageous conference of patriotic, law-abiding citizens anxious to punish crime promptly, impartially and by due process of law, also to make life, liberty, and property secure against mob rule.

Time was when lynching appeared to be sectional, but now it is national—a blight upon our nation, mocking our laws and disgracing our Christianity. "With malice toward none but with charity for all" let us undertake the work of making the "law of the land," effective and supreme upon every foot of American soil—a shield to the innocent and to the guilty punishment swift and sure.

Glossary

Chautauqua	an educational institution, founded in New York State, that provides nontraditional educational opportunities and forums for discussion of public issues
Gallinger	Jacob Harold Gallinger, a U.S. senator
holocaust	mass murder, usually directed against a racial, ethnic, or religious group
John Temple Graves	newspaper editor and politician from Georgia
Ku Klux Klan	a white supremacist organization, formed in 1866, that mounted a campaign of violence and intimidation against African Americans, Jews, and others
"With malice toward none but with charity for all"	a quotation from President Abraham Lincoln's second inaugural address

Woodrow Wilson (Library of Congress)

WOODROW WILSON

1856–1924

Twenty-eighth President of the United States

Featured Documents
- ◆ Address at Gettysburg (1913)
- ◆ Address to a Joint Session of Congress on Trusts and Monopolies (1914)
- ◆ Address in Support of a World League for Peace (1917)
- ◆ Second Inaugural Address (1917)
- ◆ War Message to Congress (1917)
- ◆ Fourteen Points Speech (1918)

Overview

Woodrow Wilson was born in Staunton, Virginia, in 1856 and grew up in Augusta, Georgia, and Columbia, South Carolina. He overcame a learning disability to become a lawyer in 1882 and earned a doctorate from Johns Hopkins in history and political science four years later. He had a distinguished academic career, becoming president of Princeton University in 1902. While leading the university, Wilson developed a reputation as a reformer. He won New Jersey's gubernatorial election in 1910 and oversaw enactment of a number of Progressive measures. Wilson secured the Democratic presidential nomination in 1912. With the Republican Party split between the incumbent William H. Taft and former President Theodore Roosevelt, Wilson won the election and became the first Democratic president elected since 1892 and the first southerner in the White House since just after the Civil War. In one of his earliest addresses as president, on the fiftieth anniversary of the Battle of Gettysburg, Wilson sought to soften regional tensions and unite the country.

During the 1912 campaign Wilson had titled his ambitious program of domestic policies "New Freedom." The president supported various reforms during his first term. He worked with Congress to undertake tariff reductions through the 1913 Underwood-Simmons Act. Wilson was the first president to benefit from the ratification of the Sixteenth Amendment, which authorized a federal income tax; the new, progressive tax allowed him to offset any revenue losses from lower tariffs. He also endorsed the 1913 Federal Reserve Act, which created the modern system to oversee monetary policy, including credit and currency supplies and regulation of banks. The president likewise benefited from the adoption of the Seventeenth Amendment in 1913, which mandated the direct election of U.S. senators. The result was an increasing number of Progressive senators who endorsed Wilson's reforms. The Department of Labor was created under Wilson, as was the Federal Trade Commission. The president was instrumental in the passage of the 1914 Clayton Antitrust Act, which further regulated business practices to prevent monopolies.

Wilson adopted an idealistic foreign policy that emphasized free trade, self-determination, and democracy. He

was credited with ending the brief age of American imperialism that had begun in the 1890s. For instance, he persuaded Congress to grant the Philippines greater political control over their affairs. Puerto Rico became a territory, with its people being granted U.S. citizenship. Under Wilson, the United States was the first country to offer diplomatic recognition to the Chinese Republic. Wilson was willing to use force to promote democracy. The result was a series of military interventions in Latin America and the Caribbean, including Nicaragua (1914), Haiti (1915), and the Dominican Republic (1916). He also intervened in the Mexican Revolution, sending troops to occupy Vera Cruz in 1914 and dispatching five thousand soldiers to northern Mexico in 1916. That year, Wilson bought the Danish Virgin Islands for $25 million.

The president tried to keep the United States neutral in World War I, but by his second term the county began to be drawn into the global conflict, which he acknowledged in his second inaugural address. In January of 1917, he spoke to Congress about the terms of a possible negotiated peace. He personally supported the Allied forces and endorsed U.S. sales of weapons, foodstuffs, and industrial products to France and Great Britain. Unrestricted German submarine warfare and the publication of the famous Zimmermann telegram, in which Germany promised to aid Mexico in recapturing territories lost during the Mexican-American War, led the United States to enter the war in 1917. During the war Wilson supported curtailments to civil liberties through the Espionage Act of 1917 and the Sedition Act of 1918. He managed the largest military and industrial mobilization that the country has witnessed to date, with industrial output increasing 20 percent between 1917 and 1919.

The entry of the United States into the war led to the defeat of Germany and the Central powers. At war's end Wilson was one of the architects of the Treaty of Versailles, but isolationist sentiment within the United States constrained his postwar foreign policy. He hoped that the nations of the world would adopt new measures, outlined in what became known as his "fourteen points proposal," which prevented another global conflict by encouraging self-determination and creating a League of Nations to resolve disputes. His program was weakened, however, by

1856

■ **December 28**
Woodrow Wilson is born in
Staunton, Virginia.

1886

■ Wilson earns his doctorate
degree in history and
political science from
Johns Hopkins University.

1902

■ Wilson becomes president
of Princeton University.

1910

■ **November 8**
Wilson is elected governor
of New Jersey.

1912

■ **November 5**
Wilson is elected president
of the United States.

1913

■ **July 4**
Wilson delivers a speech
at Gettysburg during the
commemoration of fiftieth
anniversary of the Civil
War battle.

1914

■ **January 20**
Wilson gives an address
to a joint session of
Congress on trusts and
monopolies.

1916

■ **November 7**
Wilson is reelected
president of the United
States.

1917

■ **January 22**
Wilson gives a speech in
support of a world league
for peace.

■ **March 5**
Wilson delivers his second
inaugural address.

■ **April 2**
Wilson's requests that
Congress declare war on
the Central powers.

■ **April 6**
The United States enters
World War I.

---

the victorious Allied forces, who sought to punish Germany. Meanwhile, Republicans took control of Congress in 1918 and blocked several of Wilson's initiatives, including U.S. membership in the League of Nations. Wilson supported the Eighteenth Amendment (1919), which banned alcohol, and, after initially opposing women's suffrage, endorsed the Nineteenth Amendment (1920), which granted women the vote. In 1920 the president received the Nobel Peace Prize. He suffered a stroke that left him incapacitated during the final months of his presidency. After he left office, Wilson retired from public life and died on February 3, 1924.

Explanation and Analysis of Documents

Wilson was a gifted orator whose public addresses embodied the main stylistic elements of his day. He was one of a new generation of orators who emphasized plain language and avoided the classical allusions used by older, noted speakers such as William Jennings Bryan. Nonetheless, he was able to relate contemporary issues to larger philosophical themes. As a lawyer and academic, Wilson had spent most of his life speaking in front of audiences, and he was very comfortable before crowds. He usually spoke extemporaneously, which allowed him to develop eye contact with his audience. Wilson revived the practice of appearing before Congress to deliver the annual message, beginning with his 1913 address. A scholar of history and politics, Wilson appreciated the success that Theodore Roosevelt had garnered by taking his message directly to the American people and sought to replicate that success. Six speeches illustrate Wilson's style and highlight the president's policy priorities: his address at the commemoration of the Battle of Gettysburg; an address to a joint session of Congress on trusts and monopolies; the 1917 speech in support of a world league for peace, delivered on the eve of U.S. entry into World War I; his second inaugural address; the war declaration request to Congress; and his fourteen points speech.

◆ Address at Gettysburg

As the first southerner to serve as president since Andrew Johnson, Wilson was aware of the continuing regional cleavages that existed within the country. During his presidential campaign, Wilson had sought to appeal to northern and midwestern Progressives as well as southern conservatives. He was acutely aware that although he had won 435 electoral votes to his opponents' ninety-six in the 1912 election, he had garnered only 41.8 percent of the popular vote. Wilson sought to ameliorate the regional tensions and unite the country.

In one of his first major addresses as president, Wilson chose to speak at the site of the 1863 Battle of Gettysburg during the fiftieth anniversary commemoration of the epic battle that turned the tide of the Civil War. Many veterans of the battle and the Civil War attended the commemoration. The president deliberately spoke on July 4, 1913, the anniversary of the signing of the Declaration of Independence. He begins his address by noting the sacrifices made by both sides and by emphasizing the courage and heroism of both Union and Confederate soldiers. He points out that the battle site had become a place of reconciliation and that Americans had "found one another again as brothers and comrades in arms, enemies no longer." Wilson discusses in broad terms the progress made by the United States, including its prosperity and the addition of new states. He explains that for the men buried on the battlefield the struggle was over. But the nation was not complete, and the new generations owed a debt to those who had fallen to continue forward. He declares that "the days of sacrifice and cleansing are not closed" and that the nation faced even more difficult tasks because the issues confronting the United States were less clear than those of the Civil War.

Wilson goes on to assert that he had been chosen president to represent not one people or one area of the nation but all of the United States. Using the battle as an allusion, the president argues that he is the commander of a new army of Americans. The new force did not distinguish between rich or poor or on the basis of race or national origin. Wilson asserts that the Constitution and the nation's laws were the "articles of enlistment" and the "orders of the day" for Americans. He states that the new force sought to ensure for Americans "their freedom, their right to lift themselves from day to day and behold the things they have hoped for, and so make way for still better days for those whom they love who are to come after them."

Wilson's election and his subsequent efforts at national reconciliation were part of a larger trend in the United States. In many ways, the 1898 Spanish-American War had healed many of the nation's divisions by presenting the country with a common foe. Wilson sought to go further and fuse the Progressive and southern conservative wings of the Democratic Party. However, some of his domestic policies expanded divisions within the nation. Wilson allowed the civil service to be resegregated. In July 1913, he refused to create a commission to examine race relations in the United States. And he appointed the segregationist James McReynolds to the Supreme Court in 1914. As a result, the president developed a tense relationship with prominent African American leaders of the day, including W. E. B. Du Bois and William Monroe Trotter. Some of these figures, including Du Bois, had broken with the African American community's traditional support for the Republicans and endorsed Wilson in the 1912 election; however, most subsequently supported the Republican candidate in the 1916 presidential election and future balloting until the 1932 election of Franklin D. Roosevelt.

◆ **Address to a Joint Session of Congress on Trusts and Monopolies**

As part of his Progressive reforms, Wilson sought to further curb the power and influence of trusts and monopolies in the United States. In 1913 he achieved one of his economic objectives when a special session of Congress dramatically reduced the nation's tariffs through the Underwood-

Time Line

1918

■ **January 8**
  Wilson delivers his fourteen points speech.

■ **November 11**
  World War I ends.

1919

■ Wilson attends the Paris Peace Conference.

1920

■ Wilson receives the Nobel Peace Prize for 1919.

1924

■ **February 3**
  Wilson dies in Washington, D.C.

Simmons Act. Tariff reduction was opposed by many businesses, which perceived the taxes on imports as a means to protect domestic industries. Meanwhile, that same year, the Federal Reserve Act ushered in banking reform and created the Federal Reserve System of twelve regional banks, instead of one national or central bank. Wilson was actively involved in the negotiations surrounding both measures, and he sought to replicate these successes with another special session of Congress, focusing on cartels and monopolies. In late 1913 and into 1914 the country was in the midst of an economic downturn, and Wilson hoped that by breaking up monopolies the government could open the way for new businesses and economic growth. He was also aware that Theodore Roosevelt had garnered substantial public approval for his efforts to break up trusts and monopolies. Wilson did not want radical changes, since he was afraid of further depressing the country's economy; instead, he strove for a balanced approach that would redefine government-business relations under his administration and curry favor with industrialists and financiers generally opposed to increased government oversight of the private sector.

In his address to the special session on trusts and monopolies, Wilson declares that "the antagonism between business and government is over" and that "Government and business men are ready to meet each other half-way." He argues that all understood that trusts and monopolies slowed economic growth and prevented innovation and new ventures by concentrating markets under the control of a single company or grouping. He emphasizes that his administration did not seek radical changes but only minor steps to improve competition.

Wilson's efforts culminated in Congress with the passage of the Clayton Antitrust Act in June 1914. The act expanded on the provisions of the 1890 Sherman Antitrust Act, which was the first U.S. law that restricted the ability of companies and corporations to form monopolies or trusts. Monopolies and trusts limited economic competition and generally resulted in increased prices. The new law forbade exclusive sales contracts that required buyers to purchase from only one supplier. It also prohibited certain rebates and concessions between businesses. It did away with the then-common practice of creating interlocking corporate boards that formed de facto trusts. In his address Wilson argues that by forcing corporate boards to open their memberships, the government could prompt businesses to bring "new men, new energies, a new spirit of initiative, new blood, into the management of our great business enterprises." In a nod to organized labor, the act authorized strikes and picketing, and it reduced the ability of companies to seek injunctions against unions or union activity.

In this address Wilson also proposes measures to strengthen the power of the Interstate Commerce Commission, which regulated the nation's railroads, and he sought the creation of a new interstate trade commission. The president argues that the new body should not be deeply involved in the regulation of business but that it should serve as an "indispensable instrument of information and publicity, as a clearing house for the facts by which both the public mind and the managers of great business undertakings should be guided." Congress formalized Wilson's proposal through the creation of the Federal Trade Commission in September 1914. The commission was charged with overseeing consumer protection for Americans. It also emerged as the agency to enforce the provisions of the nation's antitrust measures, including the Clayton Act. The Federal Trade Commission is an independent agency of the federal government whose board is appointed by the president but is empowered to act autonomously. It superseded the Bureau of Corporations, which was seen as inefficient and powerless to compel businesses to follow federal laws.

Wilson also asks Congress in his speech to allow him to waive statute-of-limitations provisions for private individuals and corporations that sought to file suit against corporations that had been successfully sued by the federal government. The president contends that it was "not fair that the private litigant should be obliged to set up and establish again the facts which the Government has proved." Wilson's speech and his role in the negotiations on the Clayton Act and the creation of the Federal Trade Commission reaffirmed his effort to balance consumer rights with limited government intrusion into private industry.

◆ **Address in Support of a World League for Peace**

After World War I began in August 1914, Wilson and his administration diligently endeavored to avoid U.S. involvement in the conflict. Nonetheless, the United States also prepared for war and increased military spending. The conflict pitted most of the countries of Europe and their empires against one another. On one side were the Allied forces, led by France, Great Britain, and Russia; on the other were the Central powers, led by Germany, the Austro-Hungarian Empire, and the Ottoman Empire. During the conflict, Germany used submarines in an effort to create a naval blockade of Great Britain. Wilson staunchly defended

the privileges of neutral Americans, including the right to travel to and from the countries at war, such as Great Britain and France. In 1915 a German submarine sank the British passenger liner *Lusitania*, killing 1,195 people, including 123 Americans. Wilson demanded an end to unrestricted submarine warfare, and Germany, eager to prevent the United States from entering the conflict, pledged to change tactics. During the 1916 presidential campaign Wilson's slogan was "He kept us out of war!" The president won reelection with 49.4 percent of the vote to his Republican challenger Charles Evans Hughes's 46.2 percent.

On January 20, 1917, Wilson delivered an address to the U.S. Senate, wherein he suggested the terms of a negotiated peace. The war had stalemated in the West with neither the Central powers nor the Allied forces able to gain a decisive victory. Wilson began his speech by asserting that when the war ended, the resultant peace had to be developed in such a way as to prevent future global conflicts. He contends that even though the United States was not at that time a participant in the conflict, it had to be part of the settlement to ensure a lasting peace. The president argues that "only a tranquil Europe can be a stable Europe" and that any settlement had to prevent the great power rivalries that had initiated the war.

Wilson advances the radical argument that neither side should declare victory, since it would alienate the other side and sow the seeds for future conflict. The president argues that if either side believed it was victorious, the result would be "a sting, a resentment, a bitter memory upon which terms of peace would rest, not permanently, but only as upon quicksand." Wilson asserts that the best way to counter such problems would be to ensure that all participants believed that any peace settlement was among "equals" and that individual states perceived that their main interests were preserved by the peace settlement.

The president goes on to contend that any lasting peace could be achieved only if the governments involved were democratic. He also makes a strong argument in favor of self-determination and condemns the common practice whereby colonies were transferred from one state to another. Wilson cites the example of Poland to illustrate his point: Poland had been divided among various warring powers since the 1700s, and prior to World War I its territory had been split among Germany, Russia, and the Austro-Hungarian Empire. He states his assumption that an independent Poland will emerge from the war. The president proposes that the world adopt the main anticolonial principles of the Monroe Doctrine, which took effect in 1824, so that no country would attempt to gain territory without the consent of the governed.

One underlying factor that led to World War I was a system of secret alliances that emerged in Europe. These accords compelled various countries to come to the aid of their allies once war broke out. When fighting began in 1914, a succession of nations, on both sides, were thus drawn into the war. Wilson asserts that the world needed to end such "entangling alliances" to prevent this type of conflict escalation. He also argues strongly in favor of freedom of the seas. The main thrust of Wilson's speech was the creation of what he would term a world league of peace whereby nations would develop a system to facilitate the peaceful settlement of disputes. These proposals formed the core of Wilson's fourteen points initiative that became the core of U.S. goals once the United States entered World War I.

The president's initiatives were rebuffed by the belligerent powers. While there were sentiments on both sides in favor of a negotiated peace, neither the Allied forces nor the Central powers were willing to concede the loss of territory or national pride. Meanwhile, the worsening military situation of the Central powers led Germany to adopt a more aggressive stance toward the United States. Stalemated on the western front, German military leaders hoped to be able to choke Great Britain into surrender by cutting off shipments of food, industrial resources, and other commodities. On January 31, 1917, Germany announced the resumption of unrestricted submarine warfare, to begin on February 1, and notified the Wilson administration that any ships, including those of neutral states traveling to Great Britain would be subject to attack.

◆ **Second Inaugural Address**

Wilson's second inaugural speech, delivered on March 5, 1917, was relatively short compared with the inaugural addresses of other presidents. Yet it was extremely significant, in that it was part of a broader effort by the administration to prepare the country for war. In response to Germany's resumption of unrestricted submarine warfare, the president broke diplomatic relations with Germany in February. Wilson hoped the action would prompt the Germans to respect the rights of neutral vessels, but the government in Berlin refused to change its policy. In addition, on February 23, the British government turned over to Wilson a telegram that had been sent by Germany's foreign minister, Arthur Zimmermann, in which Germany proposed an alliance with Mexico in the event that the United States entered the war. In exchange for Mexican military action against the United States, Germany promised military and financial support and pledged to help Mexico regain Texas, New Mexico, and Arizona, lost during the Mexican-American War. When the telegram became public, it created an uproar in the United States and increased pressure on Wilson to take stronger action against Germany.

In the address, Wilson briefly acknowledges the domestic accomplishments of his first term but notes that the ongoing international conflict had forced the nation to reevaluate its priorities and focus on foreign affairs. Wilson states that it had "been impossible to avoid" the ramifications of Word War I and that the results of the conflict had "shaken men everywhere with a passion and an apprehension they never knew before." The president recognized the cleavages within the United States that the global conflict had engendered. He exclaims that "we are of the blood of all the nations that are at war." At the time, one in eight Americans had been born overseas, and many had ties to the countries involved in the war. There was a large German American community in the United States and an even larger community of immigrants and descendants of immigrants from the British Isles (although this group was split with many Irish Americans supporting the Central powers, while others backed the Allied forces). Aware that U.S. involvement in the conflict was increasingly likely, Wilson sought to unify the nation. He expresses his belief that the war had not pushed Americans apart but rather had brought them together, stating that "despite many divisions, we have drawn closer together."

Wilson declares that although the United States had suffered "intolerable" actions by the Central powers, the nation still sought peace over war. He affirms that the country stood "firm in armed neutrality" and that it was willing to use force to protect its interests. Wilson acknowledges that the nation's efforts to remain neutral might not be successful and that the United States could be drawn into the war. He asserts that if the United States did become involved in the war, the nation's wartime goals would remain consistent with its principles. He states that the United States desired "neither conquest nor advantage." Instead, he reiterates the main principles of his address in support of a world league for peace and argues that the United States sought only a resolution to the war that would prevent future conflicts and grant people around the globe the right to choose their own government.

With an eye to the future, Wilson also contends that nations had "the duty of seeing to it that all influences proceeding from its own citizens meant to encourage or assist revolution in other states should be sternly and effectually suppressed and prevented." This was a reference to German efforts to encourage revolution in Russia. Exhausted and bankrupt from the war, Russia saw a series of revolutions sweep the country by March 1917. The czar was overthrown, and eventually a Communist government was established under Vladimir Lenin.

The president exclaims that Americans were "provincials no longer" and that the nation increasingly understood the nature of the war, even if they were horrified by its brutality. He sees it as "imperative that we should stand together" and that the nation was "being forged into a new unity amidst the fires that now blaze throughout the world." He finishes the address by reminding Americans of the need to be "true to ourselves"; by doing so, the nation could serve as a beacon for those who sought justice and democracy around the world.

Although the speech was part of a public effort to prepare the nation for war, the administration had already begun preparations. The 1916 National Defense Act increased the size of the peacetime Army to 175,000 regular troops and quadrupled the National Guard to 450,000. It also authorized further increases in the size of the military in the event of war. The National Defense Act also gave the president the authority to compel industries to produce arms and wartime supplies, and it created the Council of National Defense, comprising industrialists, labor leaders, and politicians to oversee wartime production. The administration undertook other actions as well to begin the transition to a wartime economy.

Docked German World War I submarines (AP/Wide World Photos)

◆ **War Message to Congress**

Although Wilson continued to prefer a peaceful resolution of the tensions between the United States and Germany, war became inevitable. German submarines were sinking an increasing number of American merchant vessels. Four U.S. merchant ships were sunk in March, with the loss of fifteen Americans. These losses and the Zimmermann telegram had finally swayed public and congressional opinion. On April 2, 1917, Wilson addressed a special session of Congress and asked for a declaration of war. He begins by condemning Germany's use of unrestricted submarine warfare. He notes that ships from neutral countries, including the United States, had been attacked in violation of international law, and he describes the practice as "warfare against mankind." The president states that he had initially hoped that armed neutrality would deter German aggression, but that effort had failed. Consequently, Wilson explains that he had no choice but to ask Congress for a declaration of war.

Wilson then speaks about the effect of the war on the United States, both domestically and in terms of the nation's external affairs. He states that the United States would have to embark on a major mobilization of both its military forces and industrial capacity. The president also stresses the need for the United States to help its allies by granting them credits and by providing supplies and armaments. Wilson strongly cautions the country not to finance the war through loans and instead asks Congress to enact "well-conceived taxation" to pay for the coming expenses.

The president reminds Americans that the war should be considered a fight not against the German people but rather against a tyrannical government that did not faith-

fully represent the interests of Germans. Wilson cites the Zimmermann telegram as an example of the unscrupulous nature of the German regime. To preserve national unity, Wilson also warns Americans not to mistrust their fellow citizens of German origin. In the most famous quote from the address, the president declares that "the world must be made safe for democracy" to prevent future global wars. The line became one of the nation's wartime slogans. He asserts that the United States did not seek territorial or other gain from involvement in the conflict. Instead, the country sought only to secure the rights and freedoms of all people, including democracy, self-determination, and the sovereignty of "small nations."

Congress declared war on April 6. The United States entered the war at a critical time and had a major impact on the conflict. Germany and Austria had inflicted major defeats on the British and Italians, and Russia's involvement in the war was tenuous. (Russia's Communist regime would negotiate a separate peace with Germany in 1918.) Within a few months of America's entry into the conflict, losses from German submarine warfare had been cut in half and badly needed supplies were flowing into Great Britain. The United States embarked on a massive wartime industrial program that included dramatic increases in shipbuilding and armaments production. Congress authorized conscription, and the U.S. military forces grew to more than 4.3 million. U.S. troops were instrumental in stopping a major German offensive in March 1918 and had a hand in the Allied counteroffensive that inflicted a major defeat on German forces. By the autumn the Central powers sought a negotiated end to the war.

◆ Fourteen Points Speech

On January 8, 1918, Wilson again addressed a joint session of Congress to detail what he believed were the nation's war aims. He had developed fourteen specific recommendations. The address refined and detailed many of Wilson's earlier initiatives, including his call for self-determination and the creation of a world league to resolve future disputes. Wilson begins with a justification of American participation in the war and an assertion that U.S. goals were the same as those of other nations. The president then provides an overview of each of his fourteen points. Wilson reiterates his call for an end to secret treaties and entangling alliances and places emphasis on public diplomacy. He also repeats his demand for freedom of the seas and calls for reductions in trade barriers and "equality of trade conditions" among the nations of the world. To maintain peace in the future, the president sought arms control and the reduction of military capabilities "to the lowest point consistent with domestic safety."

In line with earlier calls for self-determination, Wilson contends that all colonial issues should be decided on the basis of self-determination. He also stipulates that foreign troops should leave Russia. (U.S. and other Allied forces had occupied parts of the country in 1918 during the civil war that followed the Communist takeover.) Wilson further proposes the removal of all foreign forces from Belgium. In an effort to redress past transfers of territory within Europe, the president puts forward several ideas. First, he suggests that the province of Alsace-Lorraine, which had been captured by Germany in the 1871 Franco-Prussian War, be returned to France. Second, Wilson wants Italy's borders to be redefined in a way that would be consistent "along clearly recognizable lines of nationality." Third, he asks that the people of the Austro-Hungarian Empire be granted self-determination. Fourth, Wilson calls for foreign troops to leave Romania, Serbia, and Montenegro; he recommends that the borders of those countries be adjusted to follow historical divisions and that "international guarantees" be made to respect the autonomy of those countries. Fifth, Wilson seeks self-determination for the peoples of the Ottoman Empire. Sixth, the president repeats his demand for an independent Poland.

Wilson's last point laid the foundation for the League of Nations. He sought to create the collective security organization by establishing "specific covenants for the purpose of affording mutual guarantees of political independence and territorial integrity to great and small states alike." Wilson endeavored to make his "fourteen points" the basis of peace negotiations that began after an armistice was established in November 1918. However, at the 1919 Paris Peace Conference, France and Great Britain opposed Wilson's calls for self-determination because of their extensive colonies. In addition, despite Wilson's opposition, the Allied forces sought to punish Germany for its role in the war and demanded that the country pay significant reparations as part of the peace settlement, the Treaty of Versailles. Nonetheless, many of Wilson's points were adopted in the final peace accord, including an independent Poland and the creation of new states from the Austro-Hungarian and Ottoman empires. The treaty also established the League of Nations.

Wilson returned to the United States and launched a nationwide tour to rally support for the Treaty of Versailles. Notwithstanding the president's vigorous efforts, the Republican-controlled Senate refused to ratify the treaty. Republicans and conservative Democrats opposed U.S. involvement in the league, seeing it as a violation of George Washington's long-standing admonishment to avoid "permanent alliances." The suffering and brutality of World War I led to an era of isolationism in the United States when there was little public support for internationalism. Some U.S. leaders also decried the reparations required of Germany. As a result, the United States never ratified the Treaty of Versailles and never joined the League of Nations (which dramatically undermined its effectiveness). The country had to negotiate separate peace treaties with the Central powers in the 1920s. Exhausted, Wilson suffered a stroke and was partially incapacitated for the remainder of his presidency.

Impact and Legacy

Wilson was a transitional figure in public political speaking. A gifted extemporaneous orator, he bridged the classical style used by American politicians of the 1800s and early 1900s with the more modern techniques of such successors as Franklin D. Roosevelt. Wilson's addresses were marked by plain speech interwoven with the broad themes and ideals of American politics. As president, he used his speaking abilities to rally Americans on both domestic and international issues, though his powers of persuasion were overcome by isolationist sentiment in the aftermath of World War I.

Although he left office unpopular and humiliated by the failure of the United States to ratify the Treaty of Versailles, Wilson has come to be regarded as one of the more effective presidents in U.S. history. His early domestic programs, including the creation of the Federal Reserve System and the Federal Trade Commission, remain important components of the contemporary U.S. government. Wilson's greatest legacy was in the realm of foreign policy. He sought to create a global international system marked by democracy and self-determination, international law, and collective security. He correctly foresaw that the spread of democracy would ameliorate conflict and lead to economic and political stability in Europe. His proposal for the League of Nations would be refined and developed more fully in the aftermath of World War II with the establishment of the United Nations. His main diplomatic principles would lay the foundation for U.S. foreign policy throughout the twentieth century.

Key Sources

The Woodrow Wilson Presidential Library, located in Staunton, Virginia, features an online collection of search-

"Come, let us be comrades and soldiers yet to serve our fellow-men in quiet counsel, where the blare of trumpets is neither heard nor heeded and where the things are done which make blessed the nations of the world in peace and righteousness and love."

(Address at Gettysburg)

"The antagonism between business and government is over."

(Address to a Joint Session of Congress on Trusts and Monopolies)

"Only a tranquil Europe can be a stable Europe."

(Address in Support of a World League for Peace)

"As some of the injuries done us have become intolerable we have still been clear that we wished nothing for ourselves that we were not ready to demand for all mankind—fair dealing, justice, the freedom to live and to be at ease against organized wrong."

(Second Inaugural Address)

"We are provincials no longer. The tragic events of the thirty months of vital turmoil through which we have just passed have made us citizens of the world."

(Second Inaugural Address)

"The present German submarine warfare against commerce is a warfare against mankind. It is a war against all nations."

(War Message to Congress)

"The world must be made safe for democracy."

(War Message to Congress)

"A general association of nations must be formed under specific covenants for the purpose of affording mutual guarantees of political independence and territorial integrity to great and small states alike."

(Fourteen Points Speech)

able transcriptions of letters, speeches, notes, and other documents as well as scans of original manuscripts and images (http://www.woodrowwilson.org/). The most significant and complete collection of Wilson's papers and documents is the sixty-nine-volume set *The Papers of Woodrow Wilson* (1966–1994). The American Presidency Project, through the University of California at Santa Barbara, has a large collection of Wilson's addresses and documents available online at http://www.presidency.ucsb.edu/wood row_wilson.php. The documentary *Woodrow Wilson* was produced for the PBS series *The American Experience* (2001).

Further Reading

■ Articles

Ferrell, Robert H. "Woodrow Wilson: Man and Statesman." *Review of Politics* 18, no. 2 (April 1956): 131–145.

Martin, Daniel W. "The Fading Legacy of Woodrow Wilson." *Public Administration Review* 48, no. 2 (March–April 1988): 631–636.

Stid, Daniel D. "Woodrow Wilson and the Problem of Party Government." *Polity* 26, no. 4 (Summer 1994): 553–578.

Questions for Further Study

1. Compare and contrast Wilson's address at Gettysburg with the much more famous one delivered by Abraham Lincoln fifty years earlier. How had the national situation changed from the time of the Civil War, and in what ways did the effects of that conflict still linger? How prevalent were regional and racial tensions in Wilson's time, and how did he attempt to deal with those problems?

2. Examine the areas of continuity and difference between Wilson and Theodore Roosevelt. How did Wilson set out to emulate Roosevelt, particularly in the areas of trust busting and foreign policy? What areas of disagreement existed between the two leaders, and did they arise primarily from differences of political party or of personality?

3. Today Wilson is regarded as an early representative of modern liberalism, yet many of his views were reactionary by today's standards. Discuss his support for segregation, eugenics, and other racist policies as well as his oft-quoted comments praising D. W. Griffith's cinematic masterpiece *Birth of a Nation*, which glorified the Ku Klux Klan. Additionally, he favored Prohibition, curtailed civil liberties during World War I, and took an aggressive stance in dealing with revolutions in Latin America. On the other hand, his foreign policy—with its emphasis on self-determination for all nations, an end to colonialism, an equitable peace for all sides, and the formation of an organization to guarantee world peace—seems to prefigure the views of Franklin D. Roosevelt and other classic liberals who followed. Would you judge Wilson to have been, on balance, a "Progressive" or a reactionary? Use statements from the speeches excerpted here as well as other of his works to support your position.

4. Discuss the particulars of Wilson's foreign policy as exemplified in the four documents from 1917 and 1918 included here. How are his views aligned with historic American positions, most notably in the Monroe Doctrine and the principle (attributed to Washington but actually phrased by Jefferson) of "avoiding entangling alliances"? Were his interventions in Latin America consistent with his efforts to enable self-determination and an end to colonialism (including American colonialism) elsewhere in the world? How was his foreign policy guided by the fact that a large portion of the U.S. population in his time was made up of recent immigrants from Europe?

5. How did Wilson envision the postwar world, and how successful was he in making that vision a reality? In answering this question, review his fourteen points in detail, particularly his suggestions for the settlement of boundaries and the dismantling of empires. How did his promise of "peace without victory" serve to encourage the German leadership to lay down their arms, and why did those hopes fail to be realized? What role did the other Allies, particularly France and Britain, play in overruling him? Consider also the opposition at home from Senator Henry Cabot Lodge and others, and evaluate their arguments against the Treaty of Versailles and the League of Nations. How justified were Wilson's critics in blaming him for failing to bring about a truly successful peace settlement?

Walker, Larry. "Woodrow Wilson, Progressive Reform, and Public Administration." *Political Science Quarterly* 104, no. 3 (Autumn 1989): 509–525.

■ **Books**

Brands, H. W. *Woodrow Wilson*. New York: Times Books, 2003.

Clements, Kendrick A. *The Presidency of Woodrow Wilson*. Lawrence: University Press of Kansas, 1992.

Cooper, John Milton. *Breaking the Heart of the World: Woodrow Wilson and the Fight for the League of Nations*. New York: Cambridge University Press, 2001.

Heckscher, August. *Woodrow Wilson*. New York: Scribners, 1991.

Knock, Thomas. *To End All Wars: Woodrow Wilson and the Quest for a New World Order*. New York: Oxford University Press, 1992.

Link, Arthur S., ed. *Woodrow Wilson and a Revolutionary World*. Chapel Hill: University of North Carolina Press, 1982.

—Tom Lansford

ADDRESS AT GETTYSBURG (1913)

I need not tell you what the Battle of Gettysburg meant. These gallant men in blue and gray sit all about us here. Many of them met upon this ground in grim and deadly struggle. Upon these famous fields and hillsides their comrades died about them. In their presence it were an impertinence to discourse upon how the battle went, how it ended, what it signified! But fifty years have gone by since then, and I crave the privilege of speaking to you for a few minutes of what those fifty years have meant.

What have they meant? They have meant peace and union and vigor, and the maturity and might of a great nation. How wholesome and healing the peace has been! We have found one another again as brothers and comrades in arms, enemies no longer, generous friends rather, our battles long past, the quarrel forgotten, except that we shall not forget the splendid valor, the manly devotion of the men then arrayed against one another, now grasping hands and smiling into each other's eyes. How complete the union has become and how dear to all of us, how unquestioned, how benign and majestic, as State after State has been added to this our great family of free men! How handsome the vigor, the maturity, the might of the great Nation we love with undivided hearts; how full of large and confident promise that a life will be wrought out that will crown its strength with gracious justice and with a happy welfare that will touch all alike with deep contentment! We are debtors to those fifty crowded years; they have made us heirs to a mighty heritage.

But do we deem the Nation complete and finished? These venerable men crowding here to this famous field have set us a great example of devotion and utter sacrifice. They were willing to die that the people might live. But their task is done. Their day is turned into evening. They look to us to perfect what they established. Their work is handed on to us, to be done in another way, but not in another spirit. Our day is not over; it is upon us in full tide.

Have affairs paused? Does the Nation stand still? Is what the fifty years have wrought since those days of battle finished, rounded out, and completed? Here is a great people, great with every force that has ever beaten in the lifeblood of mankind. And it is secure.... The days of sacrifice and cleansing are not closed. We have harder things to do than were done in the heroic days of war, because harder to see clearly, requiring more vision, more calm balance of judgment, a more candid searching of the very springs of right.

Look around you upon the field of Gettysburg! Picture the array, the fierce heats and agony of battle, column hurled against column, battery bellowing to battery! Valor? Yes! Greater no man shall see in war; and self-sacrifice, and loss to the uttermost; the high recklessness of exalted devotion which does not count the cost. We are made by these tragic, epic things to know what it costs to make a nation, the blood and sacrifice of multitudes of unknown men lifted to a great stature in the view of all generations by knowing no limit to their manly willingness to serve. In armies thus marshaled from the ranks of free men you will see, as it were, a nation embattled, the leaders and the led, and may know, if you will, how little except in form its action differs in days of peace from its action in days of war.

May we break camp now and be at ease? Are the forces that fight for the Nation dispersed, disbanded, gone to their homes forgetful of the common cause? Are our forces disorganized, without constituted leaders and the might of men consciously united because we contend, not with armies, but with principalities and powers and wickedness in high places? Are we content to lie still? Does our union mean sympathy, our peace contentment, our vigor right action, our maturity self-comprehension and a clear confidence in choosing what we shall do? War fitted us for action, and action never ceases.

I have been chosen the leader of the Nation. I cannot justify the choice by any qualities of my own, but so it has come about, and here I stand. Whom do I command? The ghostly hosts who fought upon these battlefields long ago and are gone? These gallant gentlemen stricken in years whose fighting days are over, their glory won? What are the orders for them, and who rallies them? I have in my mind another host, whom these set free of civil strife in order that they might work out in days of peace and settled order the life of a great Nation. That host is the people themselves, the great and the small, without class or difference of kind or race or origin; and undivided in interest, if we have but the vision to guide and direct them and order their lives aright in what we do. Our constitutions are their articles of enlistment. The orders of the day are the laws upon our statute books. What we strive for is their freedom, their right to lift themselves from day to day and behold the things they have hoped for, and so make way for still better days for those whom they love who are to come after them. The recruits are the little children crowding in....

Come, let us be comrades and soldiers yet to serve our fellow-men in quiet counsel, where the blare of trumpets is neither heard nor heeded and where the things are done which make blessed the nations of the world in peace and righteousness and love.

principalities	territories ruled by a monarch or prince; "principalities and powers" also suggests the names of orders of angels in traditional Christian theology and is a reference to Romans 8:38 and Ephesians 6:12

ADDRESS TO A JOINT SESSION OF CONGRESS ON TRUSTS AND MONOPOLIES (1914)

What we are purposing to do, therefore, is, happily, not to hamper or interfere with business as enlightened business men prefer to do it, or in any sense to put it under the ban. The antagonism between business and government is over. We are now about to give expression to the best business judgment of America, to what we know to be the business conscience and honor of the land. The Government and business men are ready to meet each other half-way in a common effort to square business methods with both public opinion and the law....

We are all agreed that "private monopoly is indefensible and intolerable," and our program is founded upon that conviction. It will be a comprehensive but not a radical or unacceptable program and these are its items, the changes which opinion deliberately sanctions and for which business waits:

It waits with acquiescence, in the first place, for laws which will effectually prohibit and prevent such interlockings of the personnel of the directorates of great corporations, banks and railroads, industrial, commercial, and public service bodies, as in effect result in making those who borrow and those who lend practically one and the same, those who sell and those who buy but the same persons trading with one another under different names and in different combinations, and those who affect to compete in fact partners and masters of some whole field of business....

Such a prohibition will work much more than a mere negative good by correcting the serious evils which have arisen because, for example, the men who have been the directing spirits of the great investment banks have usurped the place which belongs to independent industrial management working in its own behoof. It will bring new men, new energies, a new spirit of initiative, new blood, into the management of our great business enterprises. It will open the field of industrial development and origination to scores of men who have been obliged to serve when their abilities entitled them to direct....

In the second place, business men as well as those who direct public affairs now recognize, and recognize with painful clearness, the great harm and injustice which has been done to many, if not all, of the great railroad systems of the country by the way in which they have been financed and their own distinctive interests subordinated to the interests of the men who financed them and of other business enterprises which those men wished to promote. The country is ready, therefore, to accept, and accept with relief as well as approval, a law which will confer upon the Interstate Commerce Commission the power to superintend and regulate the financial operations by which the railroads are henceforth to be supplied with the money they need for their proper development to meet the rapidly growing requirements of the country for increased and improved facilities of transportation. We cannot postpone action in this matter without leaving the railroads exposed to many serious handicaps and hazards; and the prosperity of the railroads and the prosperity of the country are inseparably connected. Upon this question those who are chiefly responsible for the actual management and operation of the railroads have spoken very plainly and very earnestly, with a purpose we ought to be quick to accept. It will be one step, and a very important one, toward the necessary separation of the business of production from the business of transportation....

And the business men of the country desire something more than that the menace of legal process in these matters be made explicit and intelligible. They desire the advice, the definite guidance and information which can be supplied by an administrative body, an interstate trade commission.

The opinion of the country would instantly approve of such a commission. It would not wish to see it empowered to make terms with monopoly or in any sort to assume control of business, as if the Government made itself responsible. It demands such a commission only as an indispensable instrument of information and publicity, as a clearing house for the facts by which both the public mind and the managers of great business undertakings should be guided, and as an instrumentality for doing justice to business where the processes of the courts or the natural forces of correction outside the courts are inadequate to adjust the remedy to the wrong in a way that will meet all the equities and circumstances of the case....

Other questions remain which will need very thoughtful and practical treatment. Enterprises, in these modern days of great individual fortunes, are oftentimes interlocked, not by being under the control of the same directors, but by the fact that the greater part of their corporate stock is owned by a single person or group of persons who are in some way ultimately related in interest....

There is another matter in which imperative considerations of justice and fair play suggest thoughtful remedial action. Not only do many of the combinations effected or sought to be effected in the industrial world work an injustice upon the public in general; they also directly and seriously injure the individuals who are put out of business in one unfair way or another by the many dislodging and exterminating forces of combination. I hope that we shall agree in giving private individuals who claim to have been injured by these processes the right to found their suits for redress upon the facts and judgments proved and entered in suits by the Government where the Government has upon its own initiative sued the combinations complained of and won its suit, and that the statute of limitations shall be suffered to run against such litigants only from the date of the conclusion of the Government's action. It is not fair that the private litigant should be obliged to set up and establish again the facts which the Government has proved.

Glossary

behoof	benefit or advantage
directorates	the directors of corporations or other large institutions
litigants	parties to a legal dispute

ADDRESS IN SUPPORT OF A WORLD LEAGUE FOR PEACE (1917)

In every discussion of the peace that must end this war it is taken for granted that that peace must be followed by some definite concert of power which will make it virtually impossible that any such catastrophe should ever overwhelm us again. Every lover of mankind, every sane and thoughtful man must take that for granted....

The present war must first be ended; but we owe it to candor and to a just regard for the opinion of mankind to say that, so far as our participation in guarantees of future peace is concerned, it makes a great deal of difference in what way and upon what terms it is ended. The treaties and agreements which bring it to an end must embody terms which will create a peace that is worth guaranteeing and preserving, a peace that will win the approval of mankind, not merely a peace that will serve the several interests and immediate aims of the nations engaged....

No covenant of cooperative peace that does not include the peoples of the New World can suffice to keep the future safe against war; and yet there is only one sort of peace that the peoples of America could join in guaranteeing.

The elements of that peace must be elements that engage the confidence and satisfy the principles of the American governments, elements consistent with their political faith and with the practical convictions which the peoples of America have once for all embraced and undertaken to defend....

If the peace presently to be made is to endure, it must be a peace made secure by the organized major force of mankind.

The terms of the immediate peace agreed upon will determine whether it is a peace for which such a guarantee can be secured. The question upon which the whole future peace and policy of the world depends is this:

Is the present war a struggle for a just and secure peace, or only for a new balance of power? If it be only a struggle for a new balance of power, who will guarantee, who can guarantee, the stable equilibrium of the new arrangement?

Only a tranquil Europe can be a stable Europe. There must be, not a balance of power, but a community of power; not organized rivalries, but an organized common peace....

I am seeking only to face realities and to face them without soft concealments. Victory would mean peace forced upon the loser, a victor's terms imposed upon the vanquished. It would be accepted in humiliation, under duress, at an intolerable sacrifice, and would leave a sting, a resentment, a bitter memory upon which terms of peace would rest, not permanently, but only as upon quicksand.

Only a peace between equals can last. Only a peace the very principle of which is equality and a common participation in a common benefit. The right state of mind, the right feeling between nations, is as necessary for a lasting peace as is the just settlement of vexed questions of territory or of racial and national allegiance.

The equality of nations upon which peace must be founded if it is to last must be an equality of rights; the guarantees exchanged must neither recognize nor imply a difference between big nations and small, between those that are powerful and those that are weak.

Right must be based upon the common strength, not upon the individual strength, of the nations upon whose concert peace will depend....

And there is a deeper thing involved than even equality of right among organized nations. No peace can last, or ought to last, which does not recognize and accept the principle that governments derive all their just powers from the consent of the governed, and that no right anywhere exists to hand peoples about from sovereignty to sovereignty as if they were property.

I take it for granted, for instance, if I may venture upon a single example, that statesmen everywhere are agreed that there should be a united, independent, and autonomous Poland, and that henceforth inviolable security of life, of worship, and of industrial and social development should be guaranteed to all peoples who have lived hitherto under the power of governments devoted to a faith and purpose hostile to their own....

And in holding out the expectation that the people and Government of the United States will join the other civilized nations of the world in guaranteeing the permanence of peace upon such terms as I have named I speak with the greater boldness and confidence because it is clear to every man who can think that there is in this promise no breach in either our traditions or our policy as a nation, but a fulfilment, rather, of all that we have professed or striven for.

I am proposing, as it were, that the nations should with one accord adopt the doctrine of President Monroe as the doctrine of the world: that no nation should seek to extend its polity over any other nation or people, but that every people should be left free to determine its own polity, its own way of development, unhindered, unthreatened, unafraid, the little along with the great and powerful.

I am proposing that all nations henceforth avoid entangling alliances which would draw them into competitions of power, catch them in a net of intrigue and selfish rivalry, and disturb their own affairs with influences intruded from without. There is no entangling alliance in a concert of power. When all unite to act in the same sense and with the same purpose all act in the common interest and are free to live their own lives under a common protection.

I am proposing government by the consent of the governed; that freedom of the seas which in international conference after conference representatives of the United States have urged with the eloquence of those who are the convinced disciples of liberty; and that moderation of armaments which makes of armies and navies a power for order merely, not an instrument of aggression or of selfish violence.

These are American principles, American policies. We could stand for no others. And they are also the principles and policies of forward looking men and women everywhere, of every modern nation, of every enlightened community. They are the principles of mankind and must prevail.

Glossary

governments derive all their just powers from the consent of the governed	an allusion to the American Declaration of Independence
Monroe	James Monroe, fifth U.S. president and author of the Monroe Doctrine in opposition to European meddling in the affairs of the Americas
polity	form of government

Second Inaugural Address (1917)

Although we have centered counsel and action with such unusual concentration and success upon the great problems of domestic legislation to which we addressed ourselves four years ago, other matters have more and more forced themselves upon our attention—matters lying outside our own life as a nation and over which we had no control, but which, despite our wish to keep free of them, have drawn us more and more irresistibly into their own current and influence.

It has been impossible to avoid them. They have affected the life of the whole world. They have shaken men everywhere with a passion and an apprehension they never knew before. It has been hard to preserve calm counsel while the thought of our own people swayed this way and that under their influence. We are a composite and cosmopolitan people. We are of the blood of all the nations that are at war. The currents of our thoughts as well as the currents of our trade run quick at all seasons back and forth between us and them. The war inevitably set its mark from the first alike upon our minds, our industries, our commerce, our politics and our social action. To be indifferent to it, or independent of it, was out of the question.

And yet all the while we have been conscious that we were not part of it. In that consciousness, despite many divisions, we have drawn closer together. We have been deeply wronged upon the seas, but we have not wished to wrong or injure in return; have retained throughout the consciousness of standing in some sort apart, intent upon an interest that transcended the immediate issues of the war itself.

As some of the injuries done us have become intolerable we have still been clear that we wished nothing for ourselves that we were not ready to demand for all mankind—fair dealing, justice, the freedom to live and to be at ease against organized wrong.

It is in this spirit and with this thought that we have grown more and more aware, more and more certain that the part we wished to play was the part of those who mean to vindicate and fortify peace. We have been obliged to arm ourselves to make good our claim to a certain minimum of right and of freedom of action. We stand firm in armed neutrality since it seems that in no other way we can demonstrate what it is we insist upon and cannot forget. We may even be drawn on, by circumstances, not by our own purpose or desire, to a more active assertion of our rights as we see them and a more immediate association with the great struggle itself. But nothing will alter our thought or our purpose. They are too clear to be obscured. They are too deeply rooted in the principles of our national life to be altered. We desire neither conquest nor advantage. We wish nothing that can be had only at the cost of another people. We always professed unselfish purpose and we covet the opportunity to prove our professions are sincere.

There are many things still to be done at home, to clarify our own politics and add new vitality to the industrial processes of our own life, and we shall do them as time and opportunity serve, but we realize that the greatest things that remain to be done must be done with the whole world for stage and in cooperation with the wide and universal forces of mankind, and we are making our spirits ready for those things.

We are provincials no longer. The tragic events of the thirty months of vital turmoil through which we have just passed have made us citizens of the world. There can be no turning back. Our own fortunes as a nation are involved whether we would have it so or not....

These, therefore, are the things we shall stand for, whether in war or in peace:

That all nations are equally interested in the peace of the world and in the political stability of free peoples, and equally responsible for their maintenance; that the essential principle of peace is the actual equality of nations in all matters of right or privilege; that peace cannot securely or justly rest upon an armed balance of power; that governments derive all their just powers from the consent of the governed and that no other powers should be supported by the common thought, purpose or power of the family of nations; that the seas should be equally free and safe for the use of all peoples, under rules set up by common agreement and consent, and that, so far as practicable, they should be accessible to all upon equal terms; that national armaments shall be limited to the necessities of national order and domestic safety; that the community of interest and of power upon which peace must henceforth depend imposes upon each nation the duty of seeing to it that all influences proceeding from its own citizens meant to encourage or assist revolution in other states should be sternly and effectually suppressed and prevented....

Upon this as a platform of purpose and of action we can stand together. And it is imperative that we should stand together. We are being forged into a new unity amidst the fires that now blaze throughout the world. In their ardent heat we shall, in God's Providence, let us hope, be purged of faction and division, purified of the errant humors of party and of private interest, and shall stand forth in the days to come with a new dignity of national pride and spirit. Let each man see to it that the dedication is in his own heart, the high purpose of the nation in his own mind, ruler of his own will and desire....

The shadows that now lie dark upon our path will soon be dispelled, and we shall walk with the light all about us if we be but true to ourselves—to ourselves as we have wished to be known in the counsels of the world and in the thought of all those who love liberty and justice and the right exalted.

Glossary

governments derive their just powers from the consent of the governed	an allusion to the American Declaration of Independence
provincials	backward rural people

WAR MESSAGE TO CONGRESS (1917)

The present German submarine warfare against commerce is a warfare against mankind. It is a war against all nations. American ships have been sunk, American lives taken in ways which it has stirred us very deeply to learn of; but the ships and people of other neutral and friendly nations have been sunk and overwhelmed in the waters in the same way. There has been no discrimination. The challenge is to all mankind....

When I addressed the Congress on the 26th of February last, I thought that it would suffice to assert our neutral rights with arms, our right to use the seas against unlawful interference, our right to keep our people safe against unlawful violence. But armed neutrality, it now appears, is impracticable. Because submarines are in effect outlaws when used as the German submarines have been used against merchant shipping, it is impossible to defend ships against their attacks as the law of nations has assumed that merchantmen would defend themselves against privateers or cruisers, visible craft giving chase upon the open sea....

With a profound sense of the solemn and even tragical character of the step I am taking and of the grave responsibilities which it involves, but in unhesitating obedience to what I deem my constitutional duty, I advise that the Congress declare the recent course of the Imperial German government to be in fact nothing less than war against the government and people of the United States....

What this will involve is clear. It will involve the utmost practicable cooperation in counsel and action with the governments now at war with Germany and, as incident to that, the extension to those governments of the most liberal financial credits, in order that our resources may so far as possible be added to theirs. It will involve the organization and mobilization of all the material resources of the country to supply the materials of war and serve the incidental needs of the nation in the most abundant and yet the most economical and efficient way possible. It will involve the immediate full equipment of the Navy in all respects but particularly in supplying it with the best means of dealing with the enemy's submarines....

It will involve also, of course, the granting of adequate credits to the government, sustained, I hope, so far as they can equitably be sustained by the pres-

ent generation, by well-conceived taxation....It is our duty, I most respectfully urge, to protect our people so far as we may against the very serious hardships and evils which would be likely to arise out of the inflation which would be produced by vast loans....

We have no quarrel with the German people. We have no feeling toward them but one of sympathy and friendship. It was not upon their impulse that their government acted in entering this war. It was not with their previous knowledge or approval. It was a war determined upon as wars used to be determined upon in the old, unhappy days when peoples were nowhere consulted by their rulers and wars were provoked and waged in the interest of dynasties or of little groups of ambitious men who were accustomed to use their fellowmen as pawns and tools....

Even in checking these things and trying to extirpate them, we have sought to put the most generous interpretation possible upon them because we knew that their source lay, not in any hostile feeling or purpose of the German people toward us (who were no doubt as ignorant of them as we ourselves were) but only in the selfish designs of a government that did what it pleased and told its people nothing. But they have played their part in serving to convince us at last that that government entertains no real friendship for us and means to act against our peace and security at its convenience. That it means to stir up enemies against us at our very doors the intercepted note to the German minister at Mexico City is eloquent evidence....

The world must be made safe for democracy. Its peace must be planted upon the tested foundations of political liberty. We have no selfish ends to serve. We desire no conquest, no dominion. We seek no indemnities for ourselves, no material compensation for the sacrifices we shall freely make. We are but one of the champions of the rights of mankind. We shall be satisfied when those rights have been made as secure as the faith and the freedom of nations can make them....

We have borne with their present government through all these bitter months because of that friendship—exercising a patience and forbearance which would otherwise have been impossible. We shall, happily, still have an opportunity to prove that friendship in our daily attitude and actions toward the millions of men and women of German birth and native sympathy who live among us and share our life, and we shall be proud to prove it toward all who are in fact loyal to their neighbors and to the government in the hour of test. They are, most of them, as true and loyal Americans as if they had never known any other fealty or allegiance....

There are, it may be, many months of fiery trial and sacrifice ahead of us. It is a fearful thing to lead this great peaceful people into war, into the most ter- rible and disastrous of all wars, civilization itself seeming to be in the balance. But the right is more precious than peace, and we shall fight for the things which we have always carried nearest our hearts— for democracy, for the right of those who submit to authority to have a voice in their own governments, for the rights and liberties of small nations, for a uni- versal dominion of right by such a concert of free peoples as shall bring peace and safety to all nations and make the world itself at last free.

Glossary

fealty	fidelity, allegiance
indemnities	payments, compensation
privateers	privately owned warships

FOURTEEN POINTS SPEECH (1918)

We entered this war because violations of right had occurred which touched us to the quick and made the life of our own people impossible unless they were corrected and the world secure once for all against their recurrence. What we demand in this war, therefore, is nothing peculiar to ourselves. It is that the world be made fit and safe to live in; and particularly that it be made safe for every peace-loving nation which, like our own, wishes to live its own life, determine its own institutions, be assured of justice and fair dealing by the other peoples of the world as against force and selfish aggression. All the peoples of the world are in effect partners in this interest, and for our own part we see very clearly that unless justice be done to others it will not be done to us. The program of the world's peace, therefore, is our program; and that program, the only possible program, as we see it, is this:

I. Open covenants of peace, openly arrived at, after which there shall be no private international understandings of any kind but diplomacy shall proceed always frankly and in the public view.

II. Absolute freedom of navigation upon the seas, outside territorial waters, alike in peace and in war, except as the seas may be closed in whole or in part by international action for the enforcement of international covenants.

III. The removal, so far as possible, of all economic barriers and the establishment of an equality of trade conditions among all the nations consenting to the peace and associating themselves for its maintenance.

IV. Adequate guarantees given and taken that national armaments will be reduced to the lowest point consistent with domestic safety.

V. A free, open-minded, and absolutely impartial adjustment of all colonial claims, based upon a strict observance of the principle that in determining all such questions of sovereignty the interests of the populations concerned must have equal weight with the equitable claims of the government whose title is to be determined.

VI. The evacuation of all Russian territory and such a settlement of all questions affecting Russia as will secure the best and freest cooperation of the other nations of the world in obtaining for her an unhampered and unembarrassed opportunity for the independent determination of her own political development and national policy and assure her of a sincere welcome into the society of free nations under institutions of her own choosing; and, more than a welcome, assistance also of every kind that she may need and may herself desire. The treatment accorded Russia by her sister nations in the months to come will be the acid test of their good will, of their comprehension of her needs as distinguished from their own interests, and of their intelligent and unselfish sympathy.

VII. Belgium, the whole world will agree, must be evacuated and restored, without any attempt to limit the sovereignty which she enjoys in common with all other free nations. No other single act will serve as this will serve to restore confidence among the nations in the laws which they have themselves set and determined for the government of their relations with one another. Without this healing act the whole structure and validity of international law is forever impaired.

VIII. All French territory should be freed and the invaded portions restored, and the wrong done to France by Prussia in 1871 in the matter of Alsace-Lorraine, which has unsettled the peace of the world for nearly fifty years, should be righted, in order that peace may once more be made secure in the interest of all.

IX. A readjustment of the frontiers of Italy should be effected along clearly recognizable lines of nationality.

X. The peoples of Austria-Hungary, whose place among the nations we wish to see safeguarded and assured, should be accorded the freest opportunity to autonomous development.

XI. Rumania, Serbia, and Montenegro should be evacuated; occupied territories restored; Serbia accorded free and secure access to the sea; and the relations of the several Balkan states to one another determined by friendly counsel along historically established lines of allegiance and nationality; and international guarantees of the political and economic independence and territorial integrity of the several Balkan states should be entered into.

XII. The Turkish portion of the present Ottoman Empire should be assured a secure sovereignty, but the other nationalities which are now under Turkish rule should be assured an undoubted security of life and an absolutely unmolested opportunity of autonomous development, and the Dardanelles should be permanently opened as a free passage to the ships and commerce of all nations under international guarantees.

XIII. An independent Polish state should be erected which should include the territories inhabited by indisputably Polish populations, which should be assured a free and secure access to the sea, and whose political and economic independence and territorial integrity should be guaranteed by international covenant.

XIV. A general association of nations must be formed under specific covenants for the purpose of affording mutual guarantees of political independence and territorial integrity to great and small states alike....

For such arrangements and covenants we are willing to fight and to continue to fight until they are achieved; but only because we wish the right to prevail and desire a just and stable peace such as can be secured only by removing the chief provocations to war, which this program does remove. We have no jealousy of German greatness, and there is nothing in this program that impairs it. We grudge her no achievement or distinction of learning or of pacific enterprise such as have made her record very bright and very enviable. We do not wish to injure her or to block in any way her legitimate influence or power. We do not wish to fight her either with arms or with hostile arrangements of trade if she is willing to associate herself with us and the other peace-loving nations of the world in covenants of justice and law and fair dealing. We wish her only to accept a place of equality among the peoples of the world,—the new world in which we now live,—instead of a place of mastery.

Glossary

acid test	a rigorous judgment or appraisal; a figure of speech derived from the process of identifying minerals using chemicals
Dardanelles	a strait in northwestern Turkey
Ottoman Empire	the empire that encompassed Turkey and surrounding territories until the end of World War I
quick	sensitive tissue, such as that under the fingernails or toenails

VICTORIA WOODHULL   1838–1927

Woman's Rights Activist and Presidential Candidate

Featured Documents
◆ Lecture on Constitutional Equality (1871)
◆ "'And the Truth Shall Make You Free': A Speech on the Principles of Social Freedom" (1871)

Overview

Victoria Woodhull (née Claflin) was born on September 23, 1838, on an Ohio farm. She was married to the physician Canning Woodhull at the age of fourteen, acquiring the name she would use professionally throughout her life. Her husband, an alcoholic, never provided for her or their two children. By the time of the Civil War, Woodhull's parents were in the business of promoting her younger sister, Tennessee (or Tennie C.) Claflin, as a "magnetic healer," claiming that she could cure disease through mesmerism, or hypnosis. The family dispersed after the indictment of Claflin for manslaughter following the death of Rebecca Howe, whom she was treating for breast cancer. Woodhull and Claflin struck out for a time on their own, establishing practices in various cities, including Cincinnati, St. Louis, and Chicago. Claflin continued her magnetic healing, to which service Woodhull added consultations as a spirit medium, claiming that she could talk to the spirits of her clients' dead relatives. The sisters were periodically run out of town either by the authorities or by popular hostility. During these intervals they would travel around frontier towns selling patent medicine—drugs that had little or no actual medical effect. In 1866 Woodhull married Colonel James Harvey Blood in Dayton, Ohio. In 1868 Woodhull settled in New York City together with her husband, her sister, and the rest of her family.

In 1870 the shipping and railroad tycoon Cornelius Vanderbilt consulted the sisters, probably in the hope of contacting his dead son. Vanderbilt came to establish the two as heads of a brokerage firm he capitalized, making them the first female stockbrokers in America. Using their new income, the sisters started their own newspaper (with Blood acting as editor) to promote their radical political beliefs, which included suffrage for women. Woodhull became only the second woman to address Congress, arguing that the Fourteenth and Fifteenth Amendments—which granted citizenship and voting rights to freed slaves following the Civil War—by their terms also gave women the right to vote. Woodhull began to promote her own idea of free love, a far more radical conception of gender equality than mere universal suffrage. In 1870 she announced her candidacy for the presidency of the United States in the 1872 election. She would be formally nominated by the Equal Rights Party in 1872, with the abolitionist and former slave Frederick Douglass as her running mate. In 1871 she was elected president of the American Association of Spiritualists, the main professional organization for spirit mediums.

By 1872 it had become clear that Woodhull had become too radical for her own good; she was damaging the public image of her causes and as such was forfeiting the support of Vanderbilt and of other suffragettes, such as Susan B. Anthony. Woodhull responded to her declining stature, on instructions from the spirit world, so she claimed, by attacking various prominent public figures with charges of immorality, including the nationally prominent Protestant preacher Henry Ward Beecher (a notable critic of free love). Woodhull published evidence of Beecher's adultery in her newspaper. A number of legal and ecclesiastical trials followed, constituting perhaps the greatest scandal in nineteenth-century America. Woodhull spent many weeks in prison and saw her personal finances ruined by prosecution brought about by the postal censor Anthony Comstock over the publication of the Beecher story, though the case against her was thrown out on a technicality. After these proceedings, Woodhull was viewed as a martyr and was able to begin a national lecture tour that largely restored her fortunes. In 1876, Woodhull divorced Blood. The next year she moved to England, where she married the wealthy banker John Biddulph Martin. She continued to promote changing the circumstances of family life, though in a far less radical vein, until about 1905, when she retired to a country estate. She died on June 9, 1927.

Explanation and Analysis of Documents

Any analysis of Woodhull's writings is complicated by the many uncertainties that exist about her work. Even scholars who have studied her documents closely cannot decide whether she wrote them or whether they were written by male intellectuals in the radical political circles she associated with, for her to deliver as speeches or publish under her more famous name. Many examples of the manuscripts that she read for her lectures exist, and they certainly are not in her handwriting, but she may yet have dictated them. While she had little formal education that would have prepared her to compose the elegant speeches she delivered, she would have heard hundreds of public speeches—especially sermons—throughout her youth and could well have picked up a working knowledge of rhetoric in that way. In any case, Woodhull's experience as a patent medicine saleswoman, which involved moving from town to town, holding the attention of crowds on the street, and persuading people to buy essentially worthless medicines purely through

1838

- **September 23**
  Woodhull is born Victoria Claflin in Homer, Ohio.

1870

- **January 19**
  Woodhull's Wall Street firm, Woodhull, Claflin & Co., opens.

- **April 2**
  Woodhull announces her candidacy for the presidency of the United States.

- **May 14**
  Woodhull & Claflin's Weekly begins its six-year run of publication.

1871

- **January 11**
  Woodhull presents her memorial—as her statement about women's voting rights was termed— to the House Judiciary Committee.

- **February 16**
  Woodhull gives a lecture on constitutional equality in Washington, D.C.

- **September 12**
  Woodhull is elected president of the American Association of Spiritualists.

- **November 20**
  Woodhull delivers a lecture in New York City entitled "'And the Truth Shall Make You Free': A Speech on the Principles of Social Freedom"

- **December 30**
  Woodhull & Claflin's Weekly presents the first publication of Karl Marx's *Communist Manifesto* in the United States.

1877

- Woodhull moves permanently to England.

1927

- **June 9**
  Woodhull dies in Bredon's Norton, England.

her engaging power as a speaker, would have given her ample opportunity to polish her rhetorical skills. Little clarification is to be gleaned from the numerous drafts of her autobiography. She seems to have obsessively rewritten her life story every few years, preparing for her daughter to publish a final version (never realized) after her death. The changes between the various versions are so marked that these documents can be judged only as highly fictionalized.

◆ **Lecture on Constitutional Equality**

With this February 1871 lecture in Washington, D.C., Woodhull announced and expanded upon her address to Congress on the subject of woman suffrage. She had been given the privilege of a congressional audience mostly because she had gained a celebrity status shunned by other suffragettes. Woodhull was regularly featured in sensationalist newspaper stories relating to her roles as a newspaper publisher, as the first female owner of a stock brokerage, and as an announced presidential candidate. The scandal attached to her background made her more interesting to reporters than the staid personas of respectable middle-class suffragettes like Susan B. Anthony and Elizabeth Cady Stanton. In fact, a wide variety of suffragettes looked to Woodhull to make their case to the public and government. One advantage that Woodhull possessed as a spokeswoman for the woman suffrage movement was that, as an outsider, she had not taken part in the contentious split over the Fifteenth Amendment. The movement for woman suffrage had always been closely aligned with that for the abolition of slavery. When the Fifteenth Amendment, granting the right to vote to freed slaves, was being written, some more radical suffragettes, such as Anthony, campaigned for the same amendment to explicitly grant women the right to vote also, a position eventually advocated by the National Woman Suffrage Association. Meanwhile, conservatives such as Lucy Stone, a founder of the American Woman Suffrage Association, did not want to risk losing suffrage for former slaves by trying to then gain suffrage for all.

The argument that Woodhull delivered to Congress and later reprised for popular consumption in New York (even after her proposals had been rejected by a two-thirds vote of Congress's joint Judiciary Committee) was essentially based on traditional suffragist thought going back to the 1848 Seneca Falls Convention on women's rights. Woodhull begins the main part of her argument by adapting the language of the Declaration of Independence: "I come before you, to declare that my sex are entitled to the inalienable right to life, liberty and the pursuit of happiness." This pattern of adaptation had been established by the Declaration of Sentiments produced at Seneca Falls. The essence of Woodhull's argument is that the right to personal freedom attaches to the condition of being human and that if the full exercise of freedom, including the right to vote, is denied women, it is a tyranny worse than that exercised by George III over the American colonies or by slave owners over slaves. In particular, Woodhull considers the legal position of women in America up until 1871 to be a "previous condition of servitude," which, according to the newly passed Fifteenth Amendment, could not be used as a bar to voting rights.

Again following the Declaration of Sentiments, Woodhull moves on to a specific list of grievances against women's freedoms, also based insofar as possible on the Declaration of Independence. Women are subject to laws over whose making they have no control because they neither vote for nor serve as legislators. In particular, women must pay taxes that they have no role in levying, a point echoing the colonial American grievance against taxation without representation. Listing the taxes she must pay, she says, "Of what it is my fortune to acquire each year I must turn over a certain per cent." This does not refer to the current income tax, begun in 1913, which is now the chief source of government revenue, but to the short-lived 3 percent income tax levied between 1861 and 1872 to help pay the cost of the Civil War.

Woodhull moves on to the main part of her argument, an analysis of the Fourteenth and Fifteenth Amendments to the Constitution, which after the Civil War established the newly freed slaves as citizens and specifically granted them the right to vote. She contends that if there was any doubt about the equality of women's citizenship before, the broadly inclusive language of the Fourteenth Amendment should settle it: "All persons, born or naturalized in the United States, and subject to the jurisdiction thereof, are citizens of the United States and of the State wherein they reside." She does not, however, directly address the second clause of the amendment, which expressly prohibits states from denying suffrage to any male citizens only. Yet she insists that the inclusive language must be read in the broadest possible meaning, to comprehend everyone not specifically excluded. In such a reading, the specific mention of males indicates nothing about females. Woodhull might also have found in the amendment's second clause support for her argument about taxation being a basis for voting rights, since the amendment excludes "Indians" from voting for the specifically stated reason that they are not taxed.

It was the very brief and general language of the Fifteenth Amendment, however, that was the main support of suffragette hopes. Woodhull quotes the text in full: "The right of citizens of the United States to vote shall not be denied or abridged by the United States or by any State on account of race, color or previous condition of servitude." She regards this text as clearly supporting her cause: "Nothing could be more explicit than this language, and nothing more comprehensive." She presents two arguments for the inclusion of women within the language of the amendment. Since gender is a larger and more inclusive category than any of those specifically mentioned in the amendment, she supposes that it must be inferred that gender also cannot be used to deny the right to vote. Her second, and more powerful, argument, is actually the opposite of the first. She quite rightly reads the amendment as not referring exclusively to the "black" race but as applying equally to all races and to people of all colors. Since, insofar as race is a legal category, all women belong to some race, the guarantee of rights to members of any race includes the female members

of the races unless, as the amendment does not do, they are specifically excluded. As she reasons, "A race is composed of two sexes. If you speak of a race you include both sexes. If you speak of a *part* of a race, you must designate *which* part in order to make yourselves intelligible."

Thus far, Woodhull has more or less followed the mainstream of suffragist thought on the relevance of the Reconstruction amendments to women's voting rights. None of these arguments is original to her, as they had long been developed by Anthony and other leaders of the movement. In fact, in the 1872 elections Anthony and hundreds of other suffragettes voted or attempted to vote, knowing that they would be arrested and could eventually present their arguments in court. (Woodhull herself was in jail on Election Day of 1872 on trumped-up charges of sending obscene material through the mail.) Irrespective of suffragettes' arguments and efforts, the 1874 Supreme Court decision in *Minor v. Happersett* settled the matter, ruling that no part of the Constitution, including the Reconstruction amendments, granted women the right to vote. Women would not gain suffrage until the ratification of the Nineteenth Amendment in 1920.

The remainder of Woodhull's address departs from the mainstream of the suffrage movement. Most suffragettes were middle-class women from conservative backgrounds, and while they thought it just that women be granted the vote and other legal rights of citizens, they distanced themselves from the more radical political ideologies embraced by Woodhull (such as Socialism), both because they did not find them appealing and because they did not want their movement to be perceived as a general threat to the existing social order. Woodhull had no such scruples, and her further proposals here are of a piece with her radical decision to run for the presidency. She states that if women are not granted full equality by Congress to elect and be elected in 1872, women will start a new American revolution and create a new constitution based on freedom rather than tyranny:

> We mean treason; we mean secession, and on a thousand times grander scale than was that of the South. We are plotting revolution; we will overthrow this bogus republic and plant a government of righteousness in its stead, which shall not only profess to derive its power from the consent of the governed, but shall do so in reality.

This, of course, was a sensationalistic, if not fantastic, assertion that had no potential of being realized. Although it presents itself as an extension of the suffragettes' echoing of the Declaration of Independence, it rather belongs to the rhetoric of revolution found in Woodhull's Socialist politics. Later in 1871 her weekly would issue the first publication of the *Communist Manifesto* in the United States.

◆ "'And the Truth Shall Make You Free': A Speech on the Principles of Social Freedom"

In this speech Woodhull addresses the subject of free love, presenting an argument that is more nearly her own

Cartoon depicting Victoria Woodhull as Mrs. Satan, advocating free love (Library of Congress)

In explaining what she means by social freedom, Woodhull turns, as she did in the case of woman suffrage, to the Declaration of Independence. She claims that social freedom will exist only when "certain inalienable rights, among which are life, liberty and the *pursuit* of happiness," are granted to all. When an individual exercises his or her freedom by exerting control over another person, without government restraint, then that other person's freedom is taken away, and the usurper becomes a tyrant. The tyrant cannot live in freedom but must live the life of an oppressor. The tyrannical institution that Woodhull is alluding to is legal marriage as it existed in 1871, which gave the husband control over the wife's property, custody of their children, and many other rights denied the woman.

Woodhull then shifts her allusions from the Declaration of Independence to another document that many of her contemporaries would have considered foundational to American civilization, the Christian Bible. She quotes the Tenth Commandment from Exodus 20, "Thou shalt not covet thy neighbor's wife." She argues that Jesus interpreted the meaning of the commandment by spiritualizing the terms *neighbor* and *adultery*. Woodhull takes this as a warrant to read the term *wife* in the same way, such that marriage is transformed from a legal contract to a spiritual love that she calls free love. The recognition of this new relationship of free love is seen as a natural consequence of social justice. Woodhull asserts,

> Yes, I am a Free Lover. I have an inalienable, constitutional and natural right to love whom I may, to love as long or as short a period as I can; to change that love every day if I please, and with that right neither you nor any law you can frame have any right to interfere.

She then digresses somewhat into a long aside in which she defends her doctrine of free love against its detractors: "The press have stigmatized me to the world as an advocate, theoretically and practically, of the doctrine of Free Love, upon which they have placed their stamp of moral deformity; the vulgar and inconsequent definition which they hold makes the theory an abomination." She never spells out the false and distorted versions of free love attacked by her critics, but those versions related the term to promiscuity and prostitution.

For Woodhull, free love is, rather, the antidote to the "*insidious* form of slavery" of legal marriage, which transfers women's freedom to the control of their husbands. Without the control of such laws, Woodhull believes, men and women could approach each other as equal partners. To be in a position to express their love freely, women must be as economically independent as men, otherwise they would inevitably be devalued in exchanging love for finan-

than were those for woman suffrage that she accepted. She advances her argument for free love much as she advanced that for suffrage, perceptively invoking the context of the general growth of freedom in Western society since the Renaissance, as culminated politically in the American Revolution. She positions free love as an inevitable extension of this process. In her view, the battle for religious freedom of the Reformation gave rise to the idea of freedom of conscience that found its expression in both the French Revolution and, more perfectly, the American Revolution. In this way society gained religious and political freedoms; Woodhull considers that another revolution is necessary for the gain of what she calls social freedom.

Woodhull believed that the coming of social freedom is a teleological process, meaning that the entire history of Western civilization has been moving toward and will inevitably reach the goal of social freedom. She declares that "the spirit of the age...will *not* admit all civilization to be a failure" but must in the end produce the fullest measures of freedom. This kind of thinking was intimately connected to Woodhull's practice of spiritualism, including communication with the dead; the spiritualist movement held that the combination of new technologies, the appear-

Illustrations of the Henry Ward Beecher scandal (Library of Congress)

cial support, which Woodhull considers to be as disgraceful inside marriage as out. Woodhull hated prostitution but nevertheless wanted to see it legalized to protect women whose poverty forced them to pursue such work from exploitation. This analysis of marriage, with its conclusion that women must become financially independent, is the most radical part of Woodhull's construct of social freedom; she goes far beyond the calls of the suffragettes and anticipates the linchpin of the entire feminist program of the second half of the twentieth century. Hers is a call to utterly revolutionize society. The creation of social equality through free love is what Woodhull considered to be the certain fulfillment of history. In fact, Woodhull's embrace of Socialism was directly connected to her desire for the economic empowerment of women.

Woodhull's final theme concerns women's reproductive rights under her doctrine of free love. Under legal marriage, women had no right to refuse to procreate either through abstinence or birth control; those decisions rested with the husband. Woodhull found this an unacceptable condition, indeed, a form of slavery: "It is a *fearful* respon-

sibility with which women are intrusted by nature, and the very *last* thing that they should be compelled to do is to *perform* the office of that responsibility against their will, under improper conditions or by disgusting means." This was a practical issue that Woodhull frequently addressed, especially in her newspaper and even in her later life, when she abandoned much of her radicalism. She opposed abortion because she considered it murder, but she also had in mind the dangers of the procedure to the mother's life under the primitive medical conditions of the day, especially when performed illegally by nonphysicians. She advocated birth control, probably principally meaning what today would be called the rhythm method. In any case, she insisted that women alone should decide whether and when to have children.

While Woodhull cites the broader circumstance that reproductive decisions all lay with the husband under the laws and social customs of the 1870s, it is not hard to see her own life experience reflected in her views. Married at the age of fourteen to a man who turned out to be a physically abusive alcoholic, Woodhull had two children by him

"I come before you, to declare that my sex are entitled to the inalienable right to life, liberty and the pursuit of happiness."

(Lecture on Constitutional Equality)

"I make the plain and broad assertion, that the women of this country are as much subject to men as the slaves were to their masters."

(Lecture on Constitutional Equality)

"We mean treason; we mean secession, and on a thousand times grander scale than was that of the South. We are plotting revolution; we will overthrow this bogus republic and plant a government of righteousness in its stead, which shall not only profess to derive its power from the consent of the governed, but shall do so in reality."

(Lecture on Constitutional Equality)

"Yes, I am a Free Lover. I have an inalienable, constitutional and natural right to love whom I may, to love as long or as short a period as I can; to change that love every day if I please, and with that right neither you nor any law you can frame have any right to interfere."

("'And the Truth Shall Make You Free': A Speech on the Principles of Social Freedom")

"If the law be required to enforce virtue, its real presence is wanting."

("'And the Truth Shall Make You Free': A Speech on the Principles of Social Freedom")

"I protest against this form of slavery, I protest against the custom which compels women to give the control of their maternal functions over to anybody. It should be theirs to determine when, and under what circumstances, the greatest of all constructive processes—the formation of an immortal soul—should be begun."

("'And the Truth Shall Make You Free': A Speech on the Principles of Social Freedom") in quick succession. The second of these children was intellectually impaired, a condition that Woodhull believed (quite wrongly) came about because her husband was drunk at the time of conception. Her husband did nothing to support her or the children but was nonetheless able, whenever he wished, to take any money that she herself earned to support the family. What compelled Woodhull to tolerate these conditions was the marriage law. Even when she was finally driven to obtain a divorce, she risked losing custody of her children and suffered a social stigma that prevented her from ever being considered a "respectable" woman in the dominant culture of nineteenth-century America. She might never have remarried if not for the fact that her second and third husbands were likewise political radicals who disregarded ordinary social norms. Woodhull wanted to separate love and reproduction from legal compulsion and social judgment. Her idea of free love seems to have aptly arisen as the answer to the misfortunes of her own life, and she naturally then saw free love as the answer to the problems of civilization as well.

Impact and Legacy

Woodhull's brief celebrity between 1870 and 1872 derived from a profoundly radical position that effectively polarized both the spiritualist and suffragette movements into conservative factions that wished to pursue only their most immediate concerns and liberal factions that could approach her more radical ideas. Woodhull called for the complete destruction and re-creation of society, combining not only such diverse movements as women's rights and spiritualism but also her free love concept, eugenics (founded on the idea that unfit people should not be allowed to have children), Socialism, and anarchism to create an ideology for a new millennial age in which social freedom could be realized in secular terms to supplement preexisting religious and political freedoms. Indeed, in many ways, Woodhull anticipated later societal developments.

While her historically premature candidacy for the presidency certainly in no sense led to the prominent roles played by women in twenty-first century politics, it did distantly prefigure accomplishments by later women politicians. Woodhull's political beliefs, in fact, were more like those of second-wave feminism in the late twentieth century than they were like those of her contemporary suffragettes. She obtained full independence from men by becoming economically self-sufficient and disregarding traditional social conventions, and she wanted to change women's education and revolutionize society so that all women could envision such a transformation for themselves and do the same. Her concern with a woman's control of her own fertility as an essential aspect of true equality is another late feminist idea. Woodhull eventually real-

---

Questions for Further Study

1. How much effect did Woodhull's past have on her later career, particularly as she emerged into the national spotlight in the 1870s? Key areas to consider include her rather checkered family history, her early marriage to an abusive husband, her experience as a young mother to a child with special needs, and her role as a promoter of patent medicines. How did these aspects of her background prepare her for her later career, and in what ways might they have served to diminish her effectiveness as a political leader?

2. What do the two addresses excerpted here say about Woodhull's uniqueness as a feminist leader in the latter half of the nineteenth century? On the one hand, much of what she has to say on constitutional equality draws from the traditions of the suffragist movement, most notably the Seneca Falls Declaration of Sentiments, which in turn borrowed from that most foundational of American documents, the Declaration of Independence. Yet her lecture on free love and her call for revolution in the address before Congress suggest a radical departure from the mainstream. To what extent was Woodhull "her own woman," and to what extent was she a product of her time? How well did her varied mixture of ideas—feminism, free love, Socialism, spiritualism, and eugenics—fit together?

3. Evaluate Woodhull from the standpoint of modern views on gender equality and sexuality. How might her argument for free love be relevant today, most notably in discussions regarding gay rights? In what ways did she, to a much greater degree than most of her feminist contemporaries, serve as a forerunner to feminists of the late twentieth century and beyond? What aspects of her worldview have caused latter-day feminists to judge her harshly? How justified is this appraisal? How and why do you think Woodhull is treated differently from the birth-control advocate Margaret Sanger, who also supported eugenics?

---

ized that her positions were unrealistic for her era, and in midlife she abandoned the American political scene entirely. Even today Woodhull is not warmly embraced by feminists, perhaps because of her opposition to abortion and her interest in the discredited pseudoscience of eugenics.

Key Sources

Woodhull's books are rare in American libraries, but her 1871 work *The Origin, Tendencies and Principles of Government* has been placed online by the University of California (http://www.archive.org/details/origintendencies00wood rich). A collection of her papers, including letters and autobiographical drafts, exists at Southern Illinois University, in Carbondale. A few articles from *Woodhull & Claflin's Weekly* have been archived online (http://victoria-woodhull.com/wcwarchive.htm). Given the rarity of other Woodhull resources, Madeleine B. Stern's 1974 collection of texts, *The Victoria Woodhull Reader*, is indispensable. A collection of Woodhull's writings on eugenics was edited in 2005 by Michael W. Perry as *Lady Eugenist: Feminist Eugenics in the Speeches and Writings of Victoria Woodhull*.

Further Reading

■ Articles

Blanchard, Margaret A., and John E. Semonche. "Anthony Comstock and His Adversaries: The Mixed Legacy of This Battle for Free Speech." *Communication Law and Policy* 11, no. 3 (2006): 317–366.

Gutierrez, Cathy. "Sex in the City of God: Free Love and the American Millennium." *Religion and American Culture* 15, no. 2 (Summer 2005): 187–208.

Horowitz, Helen Lefkowitz. "Victoria Woodhull, Anthony Comstock, and Conflict over Sex in the United States in the 1870s." *Journal of American History* 87, no. 2 (September 2000): 403–434.

Ray, Angela G. "The Rhetorical Ritual of Citizenship: Women's Voting as Public Performance, 1868–1875." *Quarterly Journal of Speech* 93, no. 1 (February 2007): 1–26.

Robb, George. "Women and White-Collar Crime: Debates on Gender, Fraud and the Corporate Economy in England and America, 1850–1930." *British Journal of Criminology* 46, no. 6 (2006): 1058–1072.

■ Books

Doyle, J. E. P., ed. *Plymouth Church and Its Pastor; or, Henry Ward Beecher and His Accusers*. Hartford, Conn.: Park Publishing, 1874.

Frisken, Amanda. *Victoria Woodhull's Sexual Revolution: Political Theater and the Popular Press in Nineteenth-Century America*. Philadelphia: University of Pennsylvania Press, 2004.

Gabriel, Mary. *Notorious Victoria: The Life of Victoria Woodhull, Uncensored*. Chapel Hill, N.C.: Algonquin Books, 1998.

Goldsmith, Barbara. *Other Powers: The Age of Suffrage, Spiritualism, and the Scandalous Victoria Woodhull*. New York: Knopf, 1998.

Stinchcombe, Owen. *American Lady of the Manor, Bredon's Norton: The Later Life of Victoria Woodhull Martin, 1901–1927*. Cheltenham, U.K.: O. Stinchcombe, 2000.

Tilton, Theodore. *Victoria C. Woodhull: A Biographical Sketch*. New York: Golden Age, 1871.

Underhill, Lois Beachy. *The Woman Who Ran for President: The Many Lives of Victoria Woodhull*. New York: Penguin, 1996.

■ Web Sites

"Victoria Woodhull, the Spirit to Run the White House." Victoria Woodhull Web site. http://www.victoria-woodhull.com/.

—Bradley A. Skeen

Lecture on Constitutional Equality (1871)

I have no doubt it seems strange to many of you that a woman should appear before the people in this public manner for political purposes, and it is due both to you and myself that I should give my reasons for so doing.

On the 19th of December, 1870, I memorialized Congress, setting forth what I believed to be the truth and right regarding Equal Suffrage for all citizens. This memorial was referred to the Judiciary Committees of Congress. On the 12th of January I appeared before the House Judiciary Committee and submitted to them the Constitutional and Legal points upon which I predicated such equality. January 20th Mr. Bingham, on behalf of the majority of said Committee, submitted his report to the House in which, while he admitted all my basic propositions, Congress was recommended to take no action. … I assumed and recommended that Congress *should* pass a Declaratory Act, forever settling the mooted question of suffrage.

Thus it is seen that equally able men differ upon a simple point of Constitutional Law, and it is fair to presume that Congress will also differ *when* these Reports come up for action. That a proposition involving such momentous results as this, should receive a one-third vote upon first coming before Congress has raised it in importance, which spreads alarm on all sides among the opposition. So long as it was not made to appear that women were denied Constitutional rights, no opposition was aroused; but now that new light is shed, by which it is seen that such is the case, all the Conservative weapons of bitterness, hatred and malice are marshalled in the hope to extinguish it, before it can enlighten the masses of the people, who are always true to freedom and justice.

Public opinion is against Equality, but it is simply from prejudice, which requires but to be informed to pass away. No greater prejudice exists against equality than there did against the proposition that the world was a globe. This passed away under the influence of better information, so also will present prejudice pass, when better informed upon the question of equality.…

I come before you, to declare that my sex are entitled to the inalienable right to life, liberty and the pursuit of happiness. The first two I cannot be deprived of except for cause and by due process of law; but upon the last, a right is usurped to place restrictions so general as to include the whole of my sex, and for which no reasons of public good can be assigned. I ask the right to pursue happiness by having a voice in that government to which I am accountable. I have not forfeited that right, still I am denied. Was assumed arbitrary authority ever more arbitrarily exercised? In practice, then, our laws are false to the principles which we profess. I have the right to life, to liberty, unless I forfeit it by an infringement upon others' rights, in which case the State becomes the arbiter and deprives me of them for the public good. I also have the right to pursue happiness, unless I forfeit it in the same way, and am denied it accordingly. It cannot be said, with any justice, that my pursuit of happiness in voting for any man for office, would be an infringement of one of his rights as a citizen or as an individual. I hold, then, that in denying me this right without my having forfeited it, that departure is made from the principles of the Constitution, and also from the true principles of government, for I am denied a right born with me, and which is inalienable.…

If freedom consists in having an *actual share* in appointing those who frame the laws, are not the women of this country in absolute *bondage*, and can government, in the face of the XV Amendment, assume to deny them the right to vote, being in this "condition of servitude?" According to Franklin we are absolutely enslaved, for there *are* "governors set over us by other men," and we are "subject to the laws" they make. Is *not* Franklin good authority in matters of freedom? Again, rehearsing the arguments that have emanated from Congress and applying them to the present case, we learn that "It is idle to show that, in certain instances, the fathers failed to apply the sublime principles which they declared. Their failure can be *no* apology for those on whom the duty is now cast." Shall it be an apology *now*? Shall the omission of others to do justice keep the government from measuring it to those who now cry out for it?…

I *am* subject to tyranny! I am taxed in every conceivable way. For publishing a paper I must pay—for engaging in the banking and brokerage business I must pay—of what it is my fortune to acquire each year I must turn over a certain per cent—I must pay high prices for tea, coffee and sugar: to *all* these must I submit, that *men's* government may be maintained, a government in the administration of which I am denied a voice, and from its edicts there is no appeal. I must submit to a heavy advance upon the first cost of *nearly everything I wear* in order that industries in which I have no interest may exist at my expense. I am compelled to pay extravagant rates of fare wherever I travel, because the franchises, extended to gigantic corporations, enable them to *sap* the vitality of the country, to make their *managers money kings*, by means of which they boast of being able to control not only legislators but even a State judiciary.

To be compelled to submit to *these* extortions that *such* ends may be gained, upon *any* pretext or under *any* circumstances, is bad enough: but to be compelled to submit to them, and also denied the right to cast my vote *against* them, is a tyranny *more* odious than that which, being rebelled against, gave this country independence....

Therefore it is, that instead of growing in republican liberty, we are departing from it. From an unassuming, acquiescent part of society, woman has gradually passed to an individualized human being, and as she has advanced, one after another evident right of the common people has been accorded to her. She has now become so *much* individualized as to demand the full and unrestrained exercise of *all* the rights which can be predicated of a people constructing a government based on individual sovereignty. She asks it, and shall Congress deny her?

The formal abolition of slavery created several millions of male negro citizens, who, a portion of the acknowledged citizens assumed to say, were *not* entitled to equal rights with themselves. To get over this difficulty, Congress in its wisdom saw fit to propose a XIV Amendment to the Constitution, which passed into a law by ratification by the States. Sec. I. of the Amendment declares: "All persons, born or naturalized in the United States, and subject to the jurisdiction thereof, are citizens of the United States and of the State wherein they reside. No State shall make or enforce any law which shall abridge the privileges and immunities of citizens of the United States. Nor shall any State deprive any person of life, liberty and property without due process of law, nor deny any person within its jurisdiction the equal protection of the law."...

After the adoption of the XIV Amendment it was found that still more legislation [XV Amendment] was required to secure the exercise of the right to vote to all who by it were declared to be citizens, and the following comprehensive amendment was passed by Congress and ratified by the States: "The right of citizens of the United States to vote shall not be denied or abridged by the United States or by any State on account of race, color or previous condition of servitude." Nothing could be more explicit than this language, and nothing more comprehensive. "But," says the objector, ever on the alert, "it may be denied on account of sex." It must be remembered "that is law which is written," and that all *inferences* drawn must be in accord with the *general intent* of the instrument involved by the inference. *If* the right to vote cannot be denied on account of race, *how* can it be denied on account of a constituent part of race, unless the power of denial is specially *expressed*. The larger *always* includes the smaller, which, if reserved, the reservation that it has no *broader* application. Whoever it may include, under logical construction, to them the right to vote shall not be denied. Take the African race and the black color and the previous slaves out of the way, and what application would this Amendment then have? This is the way to test these things, the way to arrive at what they mean. *Who* will pretend to say this Amendment would mean nothing were there no negroes, and there had been no Southern slaves? Who will pretend to say that the Amendment would mean nothing in the coming election, provided that there never before had been an election under the Constitution? If you provide a Constitutional amendment, having *one* race specially in view, it must not be forgotten that there are *other* races besides. Thirty-seven States constitute the United States. If you speak of the United States you speak of all the States, for they are all included. If you speak of a *part* of the United States, you must designate *what* part, in order that it may be known what you mean. A race is composed of two sexes. If you speak of a race you include both sexes. If you speak of a *part* of a race, you must designate *which* part in order to make yourselves intelligible....

I make the plain and broad assertion, that the women of this country are as *much* subject to men as the slaves were to their masters. The extent of the subjection may be less and its severity milder, but it is a complete subjection nevertheless. What can women do that men deny them? What could not the slave have done if not denied?

It is not the women who are happily situated, whose husbands hold positions of honor and trust, who are blessed by the bestowal of wealth, comforts and ease that I plead for. These do not feel their condition of servitude any more than the happy, well-treated slave felt her condition. Had slavery been of this kind it is at least questionable if it would not still have been in existence; but it was not all of this kind. Its barbarities, horrors and inhumanities roused the blood of some who were free, and by their efforts the male portion of a race were elevated by Congress to the exercise of the rights of citizenship. Thus would I have Congress regard woman, and shape their action, *not* from the condition of those who are so well cared for as not to wish a change to enlarge their sphere of action, but for the *toiling female millions*, who have human rights which should be respected....

We are now prepared to dispose of the sex argument. If the right to vote shall not be denied to any person of any race, how shall it be denied to the female part of all races? Even if it could be denied on account of sex, I ask, what warrant men have to presume that it is the *female* sex to whom such denial can be made instead of the *male* sex? Men, you are wrong, and you stand convicted before the world of denying me, a woman, the right to vote, not by any right of law, but simply because you have usurped the power so to do, just as all other tyrants in all ages have, to rule their subjects. The extent of the tyranny in either case being limited only by the power to enforce it....

Under such glaring inconsistencies, such unwarrantable tyranny, such unscrupulous despotism. What is there left women to do but to become the mothers of the future government.

We will have our rights. We say no longer by your leave. We have besought, argued and convinced, but we have failed; *and we will not* fail.

We will try you *just once more*. If the very next Congress refuse women all the legitimate results of citizenship; if they indeed merely so much as fail by a proper declaratory act to withdraw every obstacle to the most ample exercise of the franchise, then we give here and now, deliberate notification of what we will do next.

There is one alternative left, and we have resolved on that. This convention is for the purpose of this declaration. As surely as one year passes, from this day, and this right is not fully, frankly and unequivocally considered, we shall proceed to call another convention expressly to frame a new constitution and to erect a new government, complete in all its parts, and to take measures to maintain it as effectually as men do theirs.

If for people to govern themselves is so unimportant a matter as men now assert it to be, they could not justify themselves in interfering. If, on the contrary, it is the important thing we conceive it to be, they can but applaud us for exercising our right.

We mean treason; we mean secession, and on a thousand times grander scale than was that of the South. We are plotting revolution; we will overthrow this bogus republic and plant a government of righteousness in its stead, which shall not only profess to derive its power from the consent of the governed, but shall do so in reality.

Glossary

besought	asked for, begged for
Bingham	John Bingham, Ohio congressman
Franklin	Benjamin Franklin, one of the nation's founders
mooted	having no legal significance, already settled

"And the Truth Shall Make You Free": A Speech on the Principles of Social Freedom" (1871)

Religious freedom does, in a measure, exist in this country, but not yet perfectly; that is to say, a person is not entirely independent of public opinion regarding matters of conscience. Though since Political freedom has existed in theory, every person has the *right* to entertain any religious theory he or she may conceive to be true, and government can take no cognizance thereof—he is *only* amenable to *society*—despotism. The necessary corollary to Religious and Political freedom is Social freedom, which is the third term of the trinity; that is to say, if Religious and Political freedom exist, *perfected*, Social freedom is at that very moment guaranteed, since Social freedom is the fruit of that condition.

We find the principle of Individual freedom was quite dormant until it began to speak against the right of religious despots, to determine what views should be advocated regarding the relations of the creature to the Creator. Persons began to find ideas creeping into their souls at variance with the teachings of the clergy; which ideas became so *strongly* fixed that they were compelled to protest against Religious Despotism. Thus, in the sixteenth century, was begun the battle for Individual freedom. The claim that rulers had *no right* to control the consciences of the people was boldly made, and right nobly did the fight continue until the *absolute* right to individual opinion was wrung from the despots, and even the *common* people found themselves entitled to not only entertain but also to promulgate *any* belief or theory of which they could conceive.

With yielding the control over the *consciences* of individuals, the despots had no thought of giving up any right to their *persons*. But Religious freedom naturally led the people to question the right of this control, and in the eighteenth century a new protest found expression in the French Revolution, and it was baptized by a deluge of blood yielded by thousands of lives. But not until an enlightened people freed themselves from English tyranny was the right to self-government acknowledged in theory, and *not yet* even is it fully accorded in practice, as a legitimate result of that theory....

King George III, and his Parliament denied our forefathers the right to make their own laws; they rebelled, and being successful, inaugurated this government. But men do not seem to comprehend that they are now pursuing toward *women* the *same* despotic course that King George pursued toward the American colonies....

Now, the individual *is* either self-owned and self-possessed or *is not* so self-possessed. If he be self-owned, he is so because he has an *inherent* right to self, which right cannot be delegated to any second person; a right—as the American Declaration of Independence has it—which is "inalienable." The individual must be responsible to self and God for his acts. If he be owned and possessed by some second person, then there is *no such thing* as individuality: and that for which the world has been striving these thousands of years is the merest myth.

But against this irrational, illogical, inconsequent and irreverent theory I boldly oppose the spirit of the age—that spirit which will *not* admit all civilization to be a failure, and all past experience to count for nothing; against that demagogism, I oppose the plain principle of freedom in its *fullest, purest, broadest, deepest* application and significance—the freedom which we see exemplified in the starry firmament, where whirl innumerable worlds, and never one of which is made to lose its individuality, but each performs its part in the grand economy of the universe, giving and receiving its natural repulsions and attractions; we also see it exemplified in every department of nature about us: in the sunbeam and the dewdrop; in the storm-cloud and the spring shower; in the driving snow and the congealing rain—all of which speak more eloquently than can human tongue of the heavenly *beauty, symmetry and purity* of the spirit of freedom which in them reigns untrammeled.

Our government is based upon the proposition that: All men and women are born free and equal and entitled to certain inalienable rights, among which are life, liberty and the *pursuit* of happiness. Now what we, who demand social freedom, ask, is simply that the government of this country shall be administered in accordance with the spirit of this proposition. *Nothing* more, *nothing* less. If that proposition means *anything*, it means *just what* it says, without qualification, limitation or equivocation. It means that *every* person who comes into the world of outward existence is of *equal* right as an individual, and is free as an individual, and that he or she is entitled to pursue *happiness* in whatever direction he or she may choose. Now this is absolutely true of all men and all women. But just here the wise-acres stop and tell us that *everybody* must *not* pursue happiness in his or her own way; since to do so absolutely, would be to have no protection against the action of individual. These good and well-meaning people only see *one-half* of what is involved in the proposition. They look at a single individual and for the time lose sight of all others. They do not take into their consideration that every other individual beside the one whom they contemplate is *equally* with him entitled to the *same* freedom; and that each is free within the area of his or her individual sphere; and *not* free within the sphere of any other individual whatever. They do not seem to recognize the fact that the moment one person gets out of *his* sphere into the sphere of *another*, that other must protect him or herself against such invasion of rights. They do not seem to be able to comprehend that the moment one person encroaches upon another person's rights he or she ceases to be a *free* man or woman and becomes a *despot*. To all such persons we assert: that it is *freedom* and *not* despotism which we advocate and demand; and we will as rigorously demand that individuals be restricted to *their* freedom as any person dare to demand; and as rigorously demand that people who are predisposed to be *tyrants* instead of free men or women shall, by the government, be so restrained as to make the exercise of their proclivities impossible....

The tenth commandment of the Decalogue says: "Thou shalt not covet thy neighbor's wife." And Jesus, in the beautiful parable of the Samaritan who fell among thieves, asks: "Who is thy neighbor?" and answers his own question in a way to lift the conception wholly out of the category of mere local proximity into a sublime spiritual conception. In other words, he spiritualizes the word and sublimates the morality of the commandment. In the same spirit I ask now, Who is a *wife*? And I answer, not the woman who, ignorant of her own feelings, or with lying lips, has promised, in hollow ceremonial, and before the law, to love, but *she who really loves most*, and *most truly*, the man who commands her affections, and who in turn loves her, with or without the ceremony of marriage; and the man who holds the heart of such a woman in such a relation is "thy *neighbor*," and *that woman is "thy neighbor's wife" meant in the commandment*; and whosoever, though he should have been a hundred times married to her by the law, shall claim, or *covet* even, the possession of that woman as against the true lover and husband in the spirit, sins against the commandment.

We know positively that Jesus would have answered in that way. He has defined for us "the neighbor," not in the paltry and commonplace sense, but spiritually. He has said, "He that looketh on a woman to lust after her hath committed adultery with her already in his heart." So, therefore, he spiritualized the idea of adultery. In the kingdom of heaven, to be prayed for daily, to come on earth, there is to be no "marrying or giving in marriage," that is to say, formally and legally; but spiritual marriage must always exist, and had Jesus been called on to define a wife, can anybody doubt that he would, in the same spirit, the spiritualizing tendency and character of all his doctrine, have spiritualized the marriage relation as absolutely as he did the breach of it? that he would, in other words, have said in meaning precisely what I now say? And when Christian ministers are no longer afraid or ashamed *to be Christians* they will embrace this doctrine. Free Love will be an integral part of the religion of the future.

It can now be asked: What is the legitimate sequence of Social Freedom? To which I unhesitatingly reply: Free Love, or freedom of the affections. "And are you a Free Lover?" is the almost incredulous query.

I repeat a frequent reply: "I am; and I can honestly, in the fullness of my soul, raise on my voice to my Maker, and thank Him that *I am*, and that I have had the strength and the devotion to truth to stand before this traducing and vilifying community in a manner representative of that which shall come with healing on its wings for the bruised hearts and crushed affections of humanity."

And to those who denounce me for this I reply: "Yes, I am a Free Lover. I have an *inalienable, constitutional* and *natural* right to love whom I may, to love *as long* or as *short* a period as I can; to change that love *every day* if I please, and with *that* right neither *you* nor any *law* you can frame have *any* right to interfere. And I have the *further* right to demand a free and unrestricted exercise of that right, and it is *your duty* not only to *accord* it, but, as a community, to see that I am protected in it. I trust that I am fully understood, for I mean *just* that, and nothing less!

To speak thus plainly and pointedly is a *duty I owe* to myself. The press have stigmatized me to the world as an advocate, theoretically and practically, of the doctrine of Free Love, upon which they have placed their stamp of moral deformity; the vulgar and inconsequent definition which they hold makes the theory an abomination. And though this conclusion is a no more legitimate and reasonable one than that would be which should call the Golden Rule a general license to all sorts of debauch, since Free Love bears the *same* relations to the moral deformities of which it stands accused as does the Golden Rule to the Law of the Despot, yet it obtains among many intelligent people. But they claim, in the language of one of these exponents, that "Words belong to the people; they are the common property of the mob. Now the common use, among the mob, of the term Free Love, is a synonym for promiscuity." Against this absurd proposition I oppose the assertion that words *do not* belong to the mob, but to that which they represent. Words are the exponents and interpretations of ideas. If I use a word which exactly interprets and represents what I would be understood to mean, shall I go to the *mob* and *ask of them* what interpretation *they* choose to place upon it? If lexicographers, when they prepare their dictionaries, were to go to the mob for the rendition of words, what kind of language would we have?

I claim that freedom means *to be free*, let the mob claim to the contrary as strenuously as they may. And I claim that love means an exhibition of the affections, let the mob claim what they may. And therefore, in compounding these words into Free Love, I claim that united they mean, and should be used to convey, their united definitions, the mob to the contrary notwithstanding. And when the term Free Love finds a place in dictionaries, it will prove my claim to have been correct, and that the mob have not received the attention of the lexicographers, since it will not be set down to signify sexual debauchery, and that only, or in any governing sense....

The false and hollow relations of the sexes are thus resolved into the mere question of the *dependence* of women upon men for support, and women, whether married or single, are supported *by* men because they *are* women and their opposites in sex. I can see no moral difference between a woman who marries and lives with a man because he can provide for her wants, and the woman who is *not* married, but who is provided for at the same price. There is a *legal* difference, to be sure, upon one side of which is set the seal of respectability, but there is no virtue in law. In the *fact* of law, however, is the evidence of the lack of virtue, since if the law be *required* to enforce virtue, its real presence is wanting; and women need to comprehend this truth.

The sexual relation, must be rescued from this *insidious* form of slavery. Women must rise from their position as *ministers* to the passions of men to be their equals. Their entire system of education must be changed. They must be trained to be *like* men, permanent and independent individualities, and not their mere appendages or adjuncts, with them forming but one member of society. They must be the companions of men from *choice, never* from necessity....

I protest against this form of slavery, I *protest* against the custom which compels women to give the control of their maternal functions over to anybody. It should be *theirs* to determine *when*, and under what circumstances, the greatest of all constructive processes—the formation of an immortal soul—should be begun. It is a *fearful* responsibility with which women are intrusted by nature, and the very *last* thing that they should be compelled to do is to *perform* the office of that responsibility against their will, under improper conditions or by disgusting means.

Glossary

Decalogue	the Ten Commandments in Judeo-Christian tradition
demagogism	condition of being a demagogue, or one who panders to others for selfish ends
Golden Rule	the concept, found in many world religions, that people should treat others as they themselves would wish to be treated
"He that looketh on a woman..."	a slight paraphrase from the Gospel of Matthew 5:28
Samaritan	a member of a religious group that was generally despised at the time of Christ
untrammeled	not limited or restrained

Brigham Young (Library of Congress)

BRIGHAM YOUNG

1801–1877

Religious Leader

Featured Documents
◆ Sermon on Mormon Governance (1859)
◆ Sermon on Race and Slavery (1859)

Overview

Brigham Young was an early convert to the Mormon Church, which was founded in 1830 by Joseph Smith, Young's relative by marriage. Young quickly advanced within the Mormon hierarchy, becoming president of the Quorum of the Twelve Apostles (the governing body of the church). After Smith's death in 1844, various leaders asserted their claims to become his successor. Rather than settling on a single candidate, the Mormon Church splintered into sects, each with its own leader. Young became the president of the largest faction, then centered in the Mormon city of Nauvoo, Illinois. This faction became the modern-day Church of Jesus Christ of Latter-day Saints (LDS). In 1846 conflict with the local population made the Mormon position in Illinois untenable, so Young ordered the church members to move westward, as many Americans were doing at the time. They established a new LDS center in the Utah Valley around the Great Salt Lake. There Young became the autocratic ruler of a Mormon state whose isolation made it in its early days a virtually independent country.

Young and Joseph Smith both came from poor families and had struggled to find some kind of economic stability prior to the foundation of Mormonism. Although they both had been born in Vermont, their families had moved to the "burnt-over" counties of Upstate New York, so called because the intensity and frequency of fundamentalist religious revivals had left almost no one "unsaved" during the period that was called the Second Great Awakening. Young was typical of many people in this environment. He converted to more than one sect of the Baptist Church and then became a Methodist before encountering the Book of Mormon, the church's sacred scripture, in 1832. Young himself first became accustomed to public speaking as the leader of a series of Bible-reading groups. He was a nervous speaker at first, but he was determined to perfect his skills through practice and rapidly did so. Smith had at one time worked as a treasure hunter, taking fees from landowners in exchange for using his methods of spiritual divination to discover buried treasure on their land. His supposed discovery of the golden tablets on which the Book of Mormon was written, buried on his own land, was an extension of this trade.

Young's work as a Mormon missionary and leader in the 1830s and 1840s accustomed him to addressing very large crowds, both of the converted and of those who had come to hear him with the possibility of becoming Mormons. He regularly spoke before crowds in eastern cities such as Boston or New York and in London. His manner of preaching was very much that of a fundamentalist preacher of that time. He supported his rhetoric with frequent biblical citations and appeals to his own authority and that of the hierarchy and "'tradition" he represented. Once he was in control of the LDS Church and was the unquestioned leader of the Mormon community in Utah, he maintained this style, also supporting his political decisions and dictates with an appeal to his own authority as a prophet. He created a carefully crafted public image as a wise and holy authority. As such he made several addresses each week, technically classed as sermons, but given the theocratic nature of his rule, the religious and political functions of his speeches cannot be disentangled. Because Young was a national political figure from at least the late 1830s and increasingly so after Smith's death, his speeches were commonly reproduced and analyzed in national newspapers.

Explanation and Analysis of Documents

Once the LDS community became established in Utah, Young ordered the publication of the *Journal of Discourses*, which collected the public speeches of Mormon leaders. The vast majority of its contents during his lifetime are by Young. The texts were published as a monthly magazine starting in January 1853 (continuing through 1886) and then were reprinted as hardbound annual collections the following year. The texts were compiled by stenographers present at the sermons rather than from revised reading scripts. Young did not speak from prepared notes. The historian Stanley Hirshson suggests that this might have been because Young was semiliterate, for the economic circumstances of his early family life allowed him to attend school for less than a year. This was not unusual at the time. Many popular church leaders learned rhetoric and memorized the text of the Bible through a lifetime of hearing sermons, without necessarily knowing how to read. Young's brothers became Methodist ministers despite a complete lack of literacy. This would also tend to explain the high ratio of Young's allusions to and quotations from the Bible as opposed to the Book of Mormon, which he did not hear read repeatedly during his youth. The texts in the *Journal* embody Young's opinions and decisions at the height of his career, when he was the highest authority in the LDS

Time Line

1801	■ **June 1** Brigham Young is born in Whitingham, Vermont.
1832	■ Young converts to Mormonism and begins to work as a missionary and community leader.
1835	■ **February 14** Young is ordained in the initial creation of the Quorum of the Twelve Apostles of the Mormon Church.
1839	■ **February** Young leads Mormon refugees to Illinois and founds the city of Nauvoo.
1840–1841	■ Young works as a missionary in England.
1844	■ **August 8** At a meeting of the Mormon Church Council to select a successor to the lynched prophet Joseph Smith, Young is made president of the Church of Jesus Christ of Latter-day Saints.
1847	■ **July 24** Young founds Salt Lake City, then part of Mexico.
1848	■ As a result of the Mexican War, Salt Lake City and the huge Mormon-claimed area of "Deseret" are incorporated into the United States.
1849	■ **February 13** Young excludes blacks from the priesthood of the Mormon Church.
1850	■ Young founds the University of Deseret, now the University of Utah.

Church and the virtual dictator of Utah. Although Young classed these talks as sermons, his discourses were as often political as religious, for in the Mormon view these two strands were inextricably intertwined.

◆ **Sermon on Mormon Governance**

From Henry David Thoreau's retreat at Walden Pond to organized communes such as the Oneida Community, many Americans in the mid-nineteenth century experimented with moving away from mainstream society to find a new way of living in complete independence. The early Mormon movement had much in common with other utopian communes, moving ever farther west to found new settlements. The establishment of the first Mormon community came with the mass conversion of an already-existing Baptist commune in Kirtland, Ohio. But friction with local non-Mormons eventually led to the abandonment of that community and the foundation of new centers at Far West, Missouri (1836), and Nauvoo, Illinois (1839). After the failure of these Mormon centers but the eventual success of the community in Salt Lake City (1847), Young defined the characteristics of the Mormon political ideal. In a sermon delivered on July 31, 1859, he outlines his theoretical understanding of what the government of the Mormon community should be. As with other Utopian movements, Young calls for isolation from the rest of society: "Let us alone, and we will build up the kingdom of God." This statement is most likely conditioned by the history of conflict between Mormon communes and adjacent non-Mormon communities.

The precise form of the government did not matter much to Young, but it had to be theocratic, that is, based on the rule of God. He said: "But few, if any, understand what a theocratic government is. In every sense of the word, it is a republican government, and differs but little in form from our National, State, and Territorial Governments; but its subjects will recognize the will and dictation of the Almighty." A republic or democratic form of government can assume a theocratic character, Young says, when "the power of the Holy Ghost" acts through the voters. Since this power is, in Mormon belief, present only in Mormon "saints," its exercise requires limiting the right to vote to Mormons. In practice Mormons had always voted en bloc following the advice of their prophet, whether Smith or Young. Young thought that the current American government was excellent, but an even better model was "the government of the children of Israel to the time when they elected a king." In his view it was unnecessary to change the executive every four or eight years: "Would it not be better to extend that period during life or good behaviour; and when the people have elected the best man to that office, continue him in it as long as he will serve them?" He is talking about his own rule over the Mormon commune as president and prophet, elected offices that he held for life, though he was ready to apply the same principle to the American presidency should it ever become established as a theocracy. His complaint against the American government was not its form but the fact that the laws "are too often administered in unrighteousness." He meant that laws can be justly administered only by "saints," or Mormons.

In Utah, Young found the isolation that his movement needed, though after Utah came under the authority of the United States in 1848, he and the Mormons found themselves at odds with the federal government until Young resigned as Utah's governor. He retained his position within the LDS Church, however, and thereafter relied on economic measures, such as boycotts, to keep non-Mormons out of Utah. Young tells his audience that non-Mormons inevitably hate and fear Mormons and will act to destroy them. He posits a psychological explanation for this enmity, explaining what he conceives of as the thinking of non-Mormons: "If we had the power to destroy you [Mormons], we would do it; and we are afraid that if you are let alone, you will have the power to destroy us and will do as we would under like circumstances."

Young goes on to emphasize the religious tolerance of Mormonism:

> All denominations and communities would be alike protected in their rights, whether they worshipped the Supreme Author of our existence, or the sun, or the moon, or, as do some of our aborigines [native Americans], a white dog; and none will be permitted to infringe upon their neighbours.... The Hindoos would have the privilege of erecting their temples and of worshipping as they pleased; but they would not be permitted to compel other worshippers to conform to their mode of worship, nor to burn their companions upon the funeral pyre; for that would interfere with individual rights.

Young's rhetoric of religious tolerance served many purposes. It was meant to reassure the federal government that the Mormons would not take steps to exclude non-Mormons from Utah. But Young is also speaking to the most cherished Mormon beliefs when he envisions a situation in which Mormons dominate a state including Hindus and Muslims, in other words, a global state. He still has in mind the same vision of a single theocratic state that impelled Joseph Smith to aim for the presidency of the United States.

It should be emphasized, though, that while Young boasts of Mormon respect for the religions of other communities, in the same speech he constantly emphasizes that his desired theocracy would be run exclusively by "Saints of the Most High...established upon the earth." So while other religious communities might be tolerated, they would be denied all political rights. Although Young realized by 1859 that he could not directly prohibit the immigration of non-Mormon American citizens into Utah, his actions in regard to religious tolerance were far different from his words. When the Mormons arrived in the Utah basin, they found it inhabited by the Ute Indians. Young imagined that these "Lamanites," as he called them based on the mythology of the Book of Mormon, could be easily converted to Mormonism and integrated into the general community, for the Book of Mormon states that preaching

Time Line

1851
- ■ **February 9**
  Young becomes governor of the Territory of Utah.

1857–1858
- ■ Young leads an uprising against the United States (the Utah War) and is replaced as governor of Utah.

1859
- ■ **July 31**
  Young delivers a sermon outlining the Mormon philosophy of government.
- ■ **October 9**
  Young delivers a sermon stating his position on slavery and race relations.

1875
- ■ Young founds the Brigham Young Academy, now Brigham Young University.

1877
- ■ **August 29**
  Young dies in Salt Lake City, Utah.

the gospel to Native Americans would make them become "white," since their racial identity is a punishment for past sins. But by 1859 it was clear that the Utes had no interest in conversion and were prepared to resist the Mormon seizure of their land. Accordingly, Young had Mormon militias drive them onto reservations in remote areas of Utah.

◆ **Sermon on Race and Slavery**

In the fall of 1859, no one familiar with the American political scene could fail to see the crisis looming before the Republic, though few even then imagined that open civil war would be the result of that crisis. Young's address on the Mormon attitude toward blacks and slavery came less than two weeks before the raid by the abolitionist John Brown on Harpers Ferry, Virginia, intended to spark an uprising among the southern slave population. Although the Mormons in Utah did not hold slaves, Young supported the position of the Democratic Party, which hoped that continuing compromise between the slave and free states could keep the situation under control. In this sermon Young shapes a Mormon position on the issue of race and slavery based on the Bible and the Book of Mormon.

Young begins his sermon by stating his subject as "the intelligence given to the children of men." His point of departure is the Psalm of the Hebrew Bible: "What is man, that thou art mindful of him?... For thou hast made him a little lower than the angels, and hast crowned him with

Mormon pioneers on their way to Utah Territory in July 1847 (Library of Congress)

glory and honour." For Young, this text means that human intelligence is a "great mystery." He supposes that the nature of human intelligence—in particular, its distribution among individual races of humankind—cannot be understood by rational inquiry but only from revealed scripture. Young, however, rejects the creation myth of the second chapter of Genesis, in which God forms man from earth, deeming it "an idle tale." He advances instead an idea that is consistent with the Book of Mormon, which holds that God created many planets throughout the universe along with inhabitants for them.

Young, however, goes further: "Mankind are here because they are the offspring of parents who were first brought here from another planet." The significance of this momentous statement has generally been overlooked. As far as Mormon theology goes, it was Young's original idea. Although it has never been officially incorporated as a Mormon doctrine, Young may have justified the idea as a special revelation to himself, as he reportedly did his belief that the sun and moon were inhabited by creatures similar to human beings. It was not unusual for astronomers in the nineteenth century to put forward the notion either that planets orbited other stars or that planets (including the planets of our solar system) were inhabited and even that

life on the earth may have originated elsewhere in the universe. Young may have picked up the idea from popular scientific literature, which already speculated on not only the plurality of worlds but also the existence of extraterrestrial life. Elsewhere in the *Journal of Discourses* (vol. 11, June 17, 1866, p. 249), Young speaks of God living on another planet. He passes on to a description of how the salvation of human souls depends upon the Mormon founder Joseph Smith, whom Young says now rules over the "celestial kingdom" and the "spirit-world."

Young then turns to the history of humankind on the earth, which he presents as controlled by the Hebrew patriarch Abraham (whom he conceives as a preexistent figure incarnated on the earth) in much the same way Smith supposedly controls human beings after they depart from the earth. In this way, Young brings the discussion back around to his original subject of racial differences in intelligence. Humankind is divided into the various races based on skin color (a pseudoscientific concept almost universally embraced in the nineteenth century), which in turn is based on particular events described in the biblical book of Genesis. In this way blacks have become different from the other races. "You see some classes of the human family … are black, uncouth, un-comely, disagreeable and low in their habits, wild, and seemingly deprived of nearly all the blessings of the intelligence that is generally bestowed upon mankind." Young claims that blacks are the descendants of individuals cursed by God for their sins. In the first instance, the descendants of Cain, the son of Adam and Eve whom God punished for the murder of his brother, Abel, were cursed with "the flat nose and black skin." Following the biblical Flood, after which all of the human race descended from Noah, this curse is continued on blacks, who are now also given a second curse, that of being slaves by nature. This doubtless refers to Noah's son Ham, who was cursed by God for seeing his father's nakedness and who was widely accepted in Christian thought as the ancestor of the inhabitants of Africa.

This discourse is related to the theological position of blacks within Mormonism. Joseph Smith had ordained blacks to the Mormon priesthood (meaning admittance to the church as an ordinary member, since all male Mormons are held to be priests) and even as elders. But in 1849 Young had become so outraged when he learned that a black Mormon elder, Enoch Lewis, had married a white Mormon woman that he publicly stated he would kill them both if he could. Young then ruled that no black could hold the Mormon priesthood, citing the mark of Cain as the justification. This effectively excluded blacks from equal participation within the LDS Church. The views of this sermon also position Mormonism in terms of the national controversy over slavery. If blacks are inherently inferior (not only to whites but to Native Americans and other races as well) and are cursed by God with the condition of slavery, the efforts of the abolitionists are not only misguided but indeed blasphemous because they are working against God's will. As Young says, blacks "should be the 'servant of servants;' and they will be, until that curse is removed; and the Abolitionists cannot help it, nor in the least alter that decree." This removal of the curse will come about only after all the other races have been completely converted to Mormonism. This sermon suggests that Young, as a national political figure, was content to tolerate the institution of slavery as a means of preserving the Union.

Young's views on race, abhorrent as they seem today, were not far from the mainstream views of his contemporaries, even among abolitionists. They closely echo, for example, words Abraham Lincoln used in debates with Stephen Douglas, his opponent in the campaign for a seat in the Illinois Senate in 1858. Additionally, Thomas Huxley, a staunch supporter of abolition and, after Charles Darwin, the world's leading evolutionary biologist, constantly tried to debunk pseudoscientific attempts to deny that blacks were less than full human beings. Even Huxley, though, did not accept the full equality of the races but insisted that blacks were physically inferior, with smaller brains than whites, though he did not consider this to be a justification for slavery.

Young, then, used Mormon theology to defend slavery, a position usually found only among southern apologists. It was not held even by the great Democratic compromiser Stephen Douglas, who believed that slavery depended on the right of states to make their own laws rather than on

the innate characteristics of blacks. Young's views on race, entrenched by his authority as LDS prophet, held sway in Mormonism far into the twentieth century.

Impact and Legacy

Brigham Young is still today revered by the LDS Church as a great prophet and its second founder. As such, the church has produced a large number of works promoting his saintly image while resisting efforts by academic historians to investigate his life and career. At the same time, Young and the Mormon movement generally have become the subject of what the historian Stanley Hirshson terms hate literature. Such literature is useful in preserving testimony from persons who knew Young and published unfavorable impressions of him, drawing a picture that has always been systematically denied by the LDS authorities. More often, Mormon literature and that of Mormonism's opponents agree on the basic facts at issue and differ only in their interpretations. Young's negative popular image among contemporaries is epitomized by his appearance in Arthur Conan Doyle's first Sherlock Holmes novel, *A Study in Scarlet* (1887), whose mystery depends on the Danites (the Mormon paramilitary) and the institution of polygamy and whose main villain is Brigham Young himself. Eastern newspaper editorials regularly denounced Young as a murderous tyrant whose rule was based on fraud.

Young, however, did succeed in realizing the Mormon dream of establishing a separate Mormon civilization largely independent and self-supporting economically. This goal had developed over time through trial and error in the Mormon settlements in Ohio, Missouri, and Illinois of Joseph Smith's lifetime. Only Young's more extreme experiment of migration to the Far West succeeded. To this day the majority of Utah's population is Mormon, but the ideal of an isolated utopia has been replaced by a worldwide mission of conversion. Young made the LDS Church over from a religion of constantly renewed revelation, in which each member could receive divine communications prone to fragmenting the church and challenging Young's authority, into a conservative social structure devoted to increasing the wealth of the Mormon community. The church, as had so many American Protestant sects, adopted the idea of the sixteenth-century theologian John Calvin, that material prosperity was a sign of divine favor.

Key Sources

The LDS Church has a vast archive of documents concerning its early history and figures like Smith and Young. Yale University, the New York Public Library, and the National Archives have large collections of materials relevant to Mormon history. But perhaps the most important sources on early Mormon history, especially for the period in which Young became the Mormon president, are the archives of newspapers, both national papers such as the

New York Times and local papers such as the Springfield *Republican* or the Warsaw (Illinois) *Signal* for events in Nauvoo. The *Journal of Discourses*, which in the 1850s began to record all the public utterances of Mormon leaders, especially Young, is an important source. The Mormon Brigham Young University maintains a scan of the twenty-six volumes of the *Journal* online at http://contentdm.lib. byu.edu/cdm4/browse.php?CISOROOT=%2FJournalOf Discourses3.

Further Reading

■ Articles

Hunter, Milton R. "Brigham Young, Colonizer." *Pacific Historical Review* 6 (1937): 341–360.

■ Books

Bagley, Will. *Blood of the Prophets: Brigham Young and the Massacre at Mountain Meadows*. Norman: University of Oklahoma Press, 2002.

Essential Quotes

"The Constitution and laws of the United States resemble a theocracy more closely than any government; now on the earth."
(Sermon on Mormon Governance)

"People are afraid of 'Mormonism,' as they call it. They are afraid of the Gospel of salvation, and say that we have something that others have not— that we have an almighty influence, and that influence is a mystery."
(Sermon on Mormon Governance)

"The world seem to be afraid of the power of God, or rather, as I observed not long since, afraid that we are not in possession of it. They need not borrow trouble upon that point; for if we are not what we profess to be, we shall certainly fail, and they will no longer be disturbed about 'Mormonism.'"
(Sermon on Mormon Governance)

"Mankind are here because they are the offspring of parents who were first brought here from another planet, and power was given them to propagate their species, and they were commanded to multiply and replenish the earth."
(Sermon on Race and Slavery)

"The first man that committed the odious crime of killing one of his brethren will be cursed the longest of any one of the children of Adam. Cain slew his brother...and the Lord put a mark upon him, which is the flat nose and black skin. Trace mankind down to after the flood, and then another curse is pronounced upon the same race—that they should be the 'servant of servants;' and they will be, until that curse is removed; and the Abolitionists cannot help it, nor in the least alter that decree."
(Sermon on Race and Slavery)

Brodie, Fawn M. *No Man Knows My History: The Life of Joseph Smith, the Mormon Prophet.* New York: Knopf: 1945.

Brooke, John L. *The Refiner's Fire: The Making of Mormon Cosmology.* New York: Cambridge University Press, 1996.

Burton, Richard Francis. *The City of the Saints and across the Rocky Mountains to California* (1861), ed. Fawn M. Brodie. New York: Knopf, 1963.

Farmer, Jared. *On Zion's Mount: Mormons, Indians, and the American Landscape.* Cambridge, Mass.: Harvard University Press, 2008.

Hirshson, Stanley. *The Lion of the Lord: A Biography of Brigham Young.* New York: Knopf, 1969.

Sutton Robert P. *Communal Utopias and the American Experience: Secular Communities 1824–2000.* Westport, Conn.: Praeger, 2004.

■ **Web Sites**
"Young, Brigham." Brigham Young University Web site. http://unicomm.byu.edu/about/brigham.aspx.

    —Bradley A. Skeen

Questions for Further Study

1. Discuss Young's religious and educational background and how it influenced his later work as a spiritual and political leader. Examine the fact that he may have been semiliterate as it relates to his extemporaneous speaking style and his reliance primarily on quotes from the Bible rather than the Book of Mormon. In addition, how might his lack of education have played a role in some of his views on history, politics, and society?

2. How effectively does Young present the case for a Mormon theocratic state in his sermon on Mormon governance? Is he successful in resolving the apparent contradiction between theocracy and republican and democratic values? How, in his view, is it possible for religious tolerance to exist in a state governed by a single religion, and how does he propose to preserve the liberties of individuals, minorities, and opposition groups under such a system? To what extent are his claims supported by the actual experience of non-Mormons in Utah during the period of Mormon theocracy?

3. Examine Young's views on the races as discussed in the second of the two sermons excerpted here. How does he use a unique account of history to justify his positions, and what effect did those positions have on the Mormon response to the national crisis brewing in 1859? Discuss the changing Mormon views on blacks, both in Young's time and later, and how it has affected the church's missionary activities as well as Young's attempts to present Mormonism as a religion capable of providing national or even international leadership.

SERMON ON MORMON GOVERNANCE (1859)

Erroneous traditions and the powers of darkness have such sway over mankind, that, when we speak of a theocracy on the earth, the people are frightened. The government of the "Holy Catholic Church," from which all the Protestant churches are offshoots, is professedly theocratic, though it is directly opposed to the theocracy described in the Bible.

But few, if any, understand what a theocratic government is. In every sense of the word, it is a republican government, and differs but little in form from our National, State, and Territorial Governments; but its subjects will recognize the will and dictation of the Almighty. The kingdom of God circumscribes and comprehends the municipal laws for the people in their outward government, to which pertain the Gospel covenants, by which the people can be saved; and those covenants pertain to fellowship and faithfulness.

The Gospel covenants are for those who believe and obey; municipal laws are for both Saint and sinner.

The Constitution and laws of the United States resemble a theocracy more closely than any government; now on the earth, or that ever has been, so far as we know, except the government of the children of Israel to the time when they elected a king.

All governments are more or less under the control of the Almighty, and, in their forms, have sprung from the laws that he has from time to time given to man. Those laws, in passing from generation to generation, have been more or less adulterated, and the result has been the various forms of government now in force among the nations; for, as the Prophet says of Israel, "They have transgressed the laws, changed the ordinances, and broken the everlasting covenant."

Whoever lives to see the kingdom of God fully established upon the earth will see a government that will protect every person in his rights. If that government was now reigning upon this land of Joseph, you would see the Roman Catholic, the Greek Catholic, the Episcopalian, the Presbyterian, the Methodist, the Baptist, the Quaker, the Shaker, the Hindoo, the Mahometan, and every class of worshippers most strictly protected in all their municipal rights and in the privilege of worshipping who, what, and when they pleased, not infringing upon the rights of others. Does any candid person in his sound judgment desire any greater liberty?

The Lord has thus far protected and preserved the human family under their various forms and administrations of government, notwithstanding their wickedness, and is still preserving them; but if the kingdom of God, or a theocratic government, was established on the earth, many practices now prevalent would be abolished.

One community would not be permitted to array itself in opposition to another to coerce them to their standard; one denomination would not be suffered to persecute another because they differed in religious belief and mode of worship. Every one would be fully protected in the enjoyment of all religious and social rights, and no state, no government, no community, no person would have the privilege of infringing on the rights of another one Christian community would not rise up and persecute another.

I will here remark that we are generally looked upon as a dangerous people, and for the reason that there are thousands and millions of people who are afraid that justice will be meted out to them; and they say, to use Scripture language, that "if the Saints are let alone, they will take away our place and nation, and will measure to us what we have measured to them." They conclude thus because they estimate others by themselves, realizing that if they had the power to deprive us of our rights, they would exercise it. "We will judge you Latter-day Saints by ourselves. If we had the power to destroy you, we would do it; and we are afraid that if you are let alone, you will have the power to destroy us and will do as we would under like circumstances." If this people had that power to-day, they would not infringe in the least upon the rights of any person; neither could they, without ceasing to be Saints.

When the Saints of the Most High are established upon the earth, and are prepared to receive the kingdom of God in its fulness, as foretold by the Prophet Daniel, they will have power to protect themselves and all the sons and daughters of Adam in their rights. Then, when a person or community says, "I do not want to believe your religion," they will enjoy liberty to believe as they please, as fully as we shall....

People are afraid of "Mormonism," as they call it. They are afraid of the Gospel of salvation, and say that we have something that others have not—that we have an almighty influence, and that influence is a mystery....

It is recorded in the Bible that in the last days the God of heaven will set up a kingdom. Will that kingdom destroy the human family? No: it will save every person that will and can be saved. The doctrines of the Saviour reveal and place the believers: in possession of principles whereby saviours will come upon Mount Zion to save the house of Esau, which is the Gentile nations, from sin and death,—all except those who have sinned against the Holy Ghost. Men and women will enter into the temples of God, and be, in comparison, pillars there, and officiate year after year for those who have slept thousands of years. The doctrine of the Christian world, which I have already said I was familiar with, sends them to hell irretrievably, which to me is the height of folly. They do not understand what the Lord is doing, nor what he purposes to do.

It is alleged and reiterated that we do not love the institutions of our country. I say, and have so said for many years, that the Constitution and laws of the United States combine the best form of Government in force upon the earth. But does it follow that each officer of the Government administers with justice? No; for it is well known throughout our nation that very many of our public officers are as degraded, debased, corrupt, and regardless of right as men well can be.

I repeat that the Constitution, laws, and institutions of our Government; are as good as can be, with the intelligence now possessed by the people. But they, as also the laws of other nations, are too often administered in unrighteousness; and we do not and cannot love and respect the acts of the administrators of our laws, unless they act justly in their offices.

Jehovah has decreed and plainly foretold the establishment of his kingdom upon this earth; and it will prove to me a shield to the ordinances of his house, in the endowments, and in all the gifts and graces of the Spirit of God with which the Priesthood, so to speak, is clothed. The municipal laws of that kingdom are designed for the protection of all classes of people in their legitimate rights; and were it now in its fulness upon the earth, and the New Jerusalem built upon this continent, which is the land of Zion, the Latter-day Saints would not alone enjoy its blessings, but all denominations and communities would be alike protected in their rights, whether they worshipped the Supreme Author of our existence, or the sun, or the moon, or, as do some of our aborigines, a white dog; and none will be permitted to infringe upon their neighbours, though every

knee shall bow and every tongue confess that Jesus is the Christ. The Hindoos would have the privilege of erecting their temples and of worshipping as they pleased; but they would not be permitted to compel other worshippers to conform to their mode of worship, nor to burn their companions upon the funeral pyre; for that would interfere with individual rights.

The kingdom of God will be extended over the earth; and it is written, "I will make thine officers peace, and thine exactors righteousness." Is that day ever coming? It is; and the doctrine we preach leads to that point. Even now the form of the Government of the United States differs but little from that of the kingdom of God.

In our Government a President is elected for four years, and can be reelected but once, thus limiting the time of any one person to but eight years at most. Would it not be better to extend that period during life or good behaviour; and when the people have elected the best man to that office, continue him in it as long as he will serve them?

Would it not be better for the States to elect their Governors upon the same principle; and if they officiate unjustly, hurl them from office? If a good man is thus elected and continues to do his duty, he will keep in advance of the people; and if he does not, he does not magnify his office. Such is the kingdom of God, in comparison.

When the best man is elected President, let him select the best men he can find for his counsellors or cabinet; and let all the officers within the province of the Chief Magistrate to appoint be selected upon the same principle to officiate wisely in different parts of the nation. Our Father in heaven does not visit every place in person to guide and administer the law to the people, and to do this, that, and the other: he never did and never will; but he has officers, whom he sends when and where he pleases, giving to them their credentials and missions, as does our Government to our fellow-men here....

The kingdom that the Almighty will set up in the latter days will have its officers, and those officers will be peace. Every man that officiates in a public capacity will be filled with the Spirit of God, with the light of God, with the power of God, and will understand right from wrong, truth from error, light from darkness, that which tends to life and that which tends to death. They will say, "We offer you life; will you receive it?" "No," some will say. "Then you are at perfect liberty to choose death: the Lord does not, neither will we control you in the least in the exercise of your agency. We place the principles of life before you. Do as you please, and we will protect you in your rights, though you will learn that the system you have chosen to follow brings you to dissolution— to being resolved to native element."

When the government of God is in force upon the earth, there will be many officers and branches to that government, as there now are to that of the United States. There will be such helps, governments, &c., as the people require in their several capacities and circumstances; for the Lord will not administer everywhere in person.

The world seem to be afraid of the power of God, or rather, as I observed not long since, afraid that we are not in possession of it. They need not borrow trouble upon that point; for if we are not what we profess to be, we shall certainly fail, and they will no longer be disturbed about "Mormonism."…

I know that the kingdom of God is in its youth upon this earth, and that the principles of life and salvation are freely proffered to the people all over the world.…

When the kingdom of God is established upon the earth, people will find it to be very different from what they now imagine. Will it be in the least degree tyrannical and oppressive towards any human being? No, it will not; for such is not the kingdom of God.

I believe in a true republican theocracy, and also in a true democratic theocracy, as the term democratic is now used; for they are to me, in their present use, convertible terms.

What do I understand by a theocratic government? One in which all laws are enacted and executed in righteousness, and whose officers possess that power which proceedeth from the Almighty. That is the kind of government I allude to when I speak of a theocratic government, or the kingdom of God upon the earth. It is, in short, the eternal powers of the Gods.

What do the world understand theocracy to be? A poor, rotten government of man, that would say, without the shadow of provocation or just cause, "Cut that man's head off; put that one on the rack; arrest another, and retain him in unlawful and unjust duress while you plunder his property and pollute his wife and daughters; massacre here and there." The Lord Almighty does nothing of that kind, neither does any man who is controlled by his Spirit.

Again, the theocracy I speak of is the power of the Holy Ghost within you—that living and eternal principle that we do not possess in the fulness that we are seeking. When we talk about heavenly things, and see the world grovelling in their sin and misery, and loving iniquity and corruption, the heavens weep over the people, and still they will not infringe upon

their rights. God has created them so far perfectly independent as to be able to choose death or life; and he will not infringe upon this right.

And then to see people running after this and that which is calculated to destroy them spiritually and temporally—to bring upon them the first death, and then the second, so that they will be as though they had not been—is enough to make the heavens weep.

When his kingdom is established upon the earth, and Zion built up, the Lord will send his servants as saviours upon Mount Zion. The servants of God who have lived on the earth in ages past will reveal where different persons have lived who have died without the Gospel, give their names, and say, "Now go forth, ye servants of God, and exercise your rights and privileges; go and perform the ordinances of the house of God for those who have passed their probation without the law, and for all who will receive any kind of salvation: bring them up to inherit the celestial, terrestial and telestial kingdoms," and probably many other kingdoms not mentioned in the Scriptures; for every person will receive according to his capacity and according to the deeds done in the body, whether good or bad, much or little.

What will become of the rest? Jesus will reign until he puts all enemies under his feet, and will destroy the death that we are afflicted with, and will also destroy him that hath the power of death; and one eternal life will spread over the earth. Then it will be exalted and become as a sea of glass, as seen by John the Revelator, and become the eternal habitation of those who are so happy as to gain eternal life and live in the presence of our Father and Saviour.

There are millions and millions of kingdoms that the people have no conception of. The Christians of the day have no knowledge of God, of godliness, of eternity, of the worlds that are, that have been, and that are coming forth. There are myriads of people pertaining to this earth who will come up and receive a glory according to their capacity.

A man apostatizes and comes back, and there is a place prepared for him; and so there is for all persons, to suit their several capacities and answer to the lives they have lived in the flesh.

There are many who swear occasionally; others get drunk, &c. Do you not know it? O fools and slow of heart to understand your own existence! But many indulge in such practices, and some will stumble here and there; and we must keep pulling them out of the mire and washing them all the time.

Will they be consigned to eternal damnation for such conduct? No; for those who drink too much will make good servants, if you can get them where whisky will not cloud their brains, or where there is none. Make servants of such characters and set them to work in their different departments, and they can do something: they are not useless. They are the workmanship of God's hands—brothers to Jesus, flesh of his flesh and bone of his bone. The same Father that begat the tabernacle of Jesus on the earth brought forth the world of mankind; and we are all his children, whether we do wickedly or not. We are the offspring of one common Father.

Brother Kimball says that it is a pity there is such a quarrel in the family. In the flesh we are the sons and daughters of Father Adam and Mother Eve: we are all one family; and yet we are contending and quarrelling, and have arrived at such a pass that many do not know whether they belong to one kingdom and family, or not....

With you, my brethren, I have the principles of eternal salvation; and for this cause they quarrel with us. The world say that we have principles that really lay the axe at the roots of the trees of all false creeds; and if we are let alone, their creeds will cease having followers. If they let us alone, and we are wrong and corrupt, as they say we are, we shall come to an end.

Why do they prefer to be corrupt? They do not understand true principles, otherwise they would say, "Praise God! I am thankful that you are here. Do right, prosper, and bring salvation to all the house of Israel, and to the Gentile world so far as you can."

Let us alone, and we will build up the kingdom of God. We are striving for what all Christendom professes to be, and we will bring it forth. If they persecute us, we will bring it forth the sooner. Could all the Elders of Israel have given "Mormonism" the

Glossary

adulterated	corrupted, mixed with impurities
apostatizes	abandons beliefs
begat	to father, or make children
Chief Magistrate	the president
covenants	agreements, specifically between God and his people
Gentile	a Christian (as opposed to a Jew)
house of Esau	possibly the Edomites, the descendants of the biblical figure Esau, who, according to the biblical book of Obadiah, incur God's wrath for their sins
"if the Saints are let alone..."	a very loose quotation from the Gospel of John 11:47–49
"I will make thine officers peace..."	quotation from Isaiah 60:17
Jehovah	God
John the Revelator	also called John of Patmos, the author of the biblical Book of Revelation
Mahometan	Muslim
Mount Zion	a hill just outside of Jerusalem in Israel, with Zion becoming a figure of speech for all of Israel
New Jerusalem	literally or figuratively, the city God will prepare for his saints
telestial	the lowest of the three heavenly kingdoms
theocracy	rule by God through a state-instituted church
"They have transgressed the laws..."	from Isaiah 24:5

same impetus that the last quarrel has done? No. The Lord will bring more out of that than all the Elders could have done by any performance of theirs.

If the Devil and his servants are permitted to persecute us, why should we complain? Has not the Prophet; said that the servants of the Devil would make lies their refuge, and hide themselves under falsehood? Poor, miserable, lying curses here can write lies and publish them and send them forth in every direction. Traders take our money for goods, and all the time stir up every destructive element in their power to sell our blood, destroy our lives, and pollute our society.

Should the Lord reveal to me that my work on this earth is finished, I am ready to depart this life at any moment he may require. But the time has not yet come, and I expect to live until the Lord is willing that I should die.

I expect to live until I finish my work; and what is that? To promote the welfare of mankind, and save as many of the sons and daughters of Adam as I can prevail upon to be saved. How many I shall prevail upon to be saved is not for me to say.

When I get through my work here, my body will have the privilege to rest; and I understand where my spirit will go, and who will be my associates in the spirit world.

We have more friends behind the vail than on this side, and they will hail us more joyfully than you were ever welcomed by your parents and friends in this world; and you will rejoice more when you meet them than you ever rejoiced to see a friend in this life; and then we shall go on from step to step, from rejoicing to rejoicing, and from one intelligence and power to another, our happiness becoming more and more exquisite and sensible as we proceed in the words and powers of life.

God bless you! Amen.

SERMON ON RACE AND SLAVERY (1859)

I shall address you this morning upon a subject that is more interesting to me than any other pertaining to the life of man. It is a subject of deep study and research, and has been from age to age among the reflecting and philosophical portions of the human family. The intelligence given to the children of men is the subject to which I allude, and upon which has been expended more intellectual labour and profound thought than upon any other that has ever attracted the attention of man.

The Psalmist has written, "What is man, that thou art mindful of him? and the son of man that thou visitest him? For thou hast made him a little lower than the angels, and hast crowned him with glory and honour." This passage is but one of many which refer to the organization of man as though it were a great mystery—something that could not be fully comprehended by the greatest minds while dwelling in earthly tabernacles. It is a matter of vital interest to each of us, and yet it is often farthest from the thoughts of the greater portion of mankind. Instead of reflecting upon and searching for hidden things of the greatest value to them, they rather wish to learn how to secure their way through this world as easily and as comfortably as possible. The reflections what they are here for, who produced them, and where they are from, far too seldom enter their minds....

When we view mankind collectively, or as nations, communities, neighbourhoods, and families, we are led to inquire into the object of our being here and situated as we find ourselves to be. Did we produce ourselves, and endow ourselves with that knowledge and intelligence we now possess? All are ready to acknowledge that we had nothing to do with the origin of our being—that we were produced by a superior Power, without either the knowledge or the exercise of the agency we now possess. We know that we are here. We know that we live, breathe, and walk upon the earth. We know this naturally, as the brute creation knows. …Who can define and point out the particularities of the wonderful organization of man?…

Here let me state to all philosophers of every class upon the earth, When you tell me that father Adam was made as we make adobies from the earth, you tell me what I deem an idle tale. When you tell me that the beasts of the field were produced in that manner, you are speaking idle words devoid of meaning. There

is no such thing in all the eternities where the Gods dwell. Mankind are here because they are the offspring of parents who were first brought here from another planet, and power was given them to propagate their species, and they were commanded to multiply and replenish the earth. The offspring of Adam and Eve are commanded to take the rude elements, and, by the knowledge God has given, to convert them into everything required for their life, health, adornment, wealth, comfort, and consolation. Have we the knowledge to do this? We have. Who gave us this knowledge? Our Father who made us; for he is the only wise God, and to him we owe allegiance; to him we owe our lives. He has brought us forth and taught us all we know. We are not indebted to any other power or God for all our great blessings....

Joseph Smith holds the keys of this last dispensation, and is now engaged behind the vail in the great work of the last days. I can tell our beloved brother Christians who have slain the Prophets and butchered and otherwise caused the death of thousands of Latter-day Saints, the priests who have thanked God in their prayers and thanksgiving from the pulpit that we have been plundered, driven, and slain, and the deacons under the pulpit, and their brethren and sisters in their closets, who have thanked God, thinking that the Latter-day Saints were wasted away, something that no doubt will mortify them—something that, to say the least, is a matter of deep regret to them—namely, that no man or woman in this dispensation will ever enter into the celestial kingdom of God without the consent of Joseph Smith. From the day that the Priesthood was taken from the earth to the winding-up scene of all things, every man and woman must have the certificate of Joseph Smith, junior, as a passport to their entrance into the mansion where God and Christ are—I with you and you with me. I cannot go there without his consent. He holds the keys of that kingdom for the last dispensation—the keys to rule in the spirit-world; and he rules there triumphantly, for he gained full power and a glorious victory over the power of Satan while he was yet in the flesh, and was a martyr to his religion and to the name of Christ, which gives him a most perfect victory in the spirit-world. He reigns there as supreme a being in his sphere, capacity, and calling, as God does in heaven. Many will exclaim—"Oh, that is very disagreeable! It is preposterous! We cannot bear the thought!" But it is true.

I will now tell you something that ought to comfort every man and woman on the face of the earth. Joseph Smith, junior, will again be on this earth dictating plans and calling forth his brethren to be baptized for the very characters who wish this was not so, in order to bring them into a kingdom to enjoy, perhaps, the presence of angels or the spirits of good men, if they cannot endure the presence of the Father and the Son; and he will never cease his operations, under the directions of the Son of God, until the last ones of the children of men are saved that can be, from Adam till now....

Abraham was ordained to be the father of the faithful,—that is, he was ordained to come forth at a certain period; and when he had proved himself faithful to his God, and would resist the worship of idols, and trample them under his feet in the presence of their king, and set up the worship of the true God, he obtained the appellation of "father of the faithful." "For whom he did foreknow he also did predestinate to be conformed to the image of his Son." He knew, millions of years before this world was framed, that Pharaoh would be a wicked man. He saw—he understood; his work was before him, and he could see it from the beginning to the end. And so scrutinizing, penetrating, and expanded are his visions and knowledge, that not even a hair of our head can fall to the ground unnoticed by him. He foreknew what Joseph, who was sold into Egypt, would do. Joseph was foreordained to be the temporal Saviour of his father's house, and the seed of Joseph are ordained to be the spiritual and temporal saviours of all the house of Israel in the latter days.

Joseph's seed has mixed itself with all the seed of man upon the face of the whole earth. The great majority of those who are now before me are the descendants of that Joseph who was sold. Joseph Smith, junior, was foreordained to come through the loins of Abraham, Isaac, Jacob, Joseph, and so on down through the Prophets and Apostles; and thus he came forth in the last days to be a minister of salvation, and to hold the keys of the last dispensation of the fulness of times.

The whole object of the creation of this world is to exalt the intelligences that are placed upon it, that they may live, endure, and increase for ever and ever. We are not here to quarrel and contend about the things of this world, but we are here to subdue and beautify it. Let every man and woman worship their God with all their heart. Let them pay their devotions and sacrifices to him, the Supreme, and the Author of their existence. Do all the good you can to your fellow-creatures. You are flesh of my flesh and bone of my bone. God has created of one blood all the nations and kingdoms of men that dwell upon all the face of the earth: black, white, copper-coloured, or whatever their colour, customs, or religion, they have all sprung from the same origin; the blood of all is from the same element. Adam and Eve are the parents of all pertaining to the flesh, and I would not say that they are not also the parents of our spirits.

You see some classes of the human family that are black, uncouth, un-comely, disagreeable and low in their habits, wild, and seemingly deprived of nearly all the blessings of the intelligence that is generally bestowed upon mankind. The first man that committed the odious crime of killing one of his brethren will be cursed the longest of any one of the children

Abraham	the founding patriarch of the nation of Israel, featured in the biblical book of Genesis
Apostles	the twelve chosen disciples of Christ
Cain slew his brother	recounted in Genesis 4, as well as in the Islamic Qur'an, Sura, chapter 5
dispensation	a fate ordained by God
earthly tabernacles	human bodies
Joseph, who was sold into Egypt	recounted in Genesis 37
Pharaoh	the ruler of Egypt
Psalmist	author of the biblical book of Psalms; quotation Psalm 8:4–5

of Adam. Cain slew his brother. Cain might have been killed, and that would have put a termination to that line of human beings. This was not to be, and the Lord put a mark upon him, which is the flat nose and black skin. Trace mankind down to after the flood, and then another curse is pronounced upon the same race—that they should be the "servant of servants;" and they will be, until that curse is removed; and the Abolitionists cannot help it, nor in the least alter that decree. How long is that race to endure the dreadful curse that is upon them? That curse will remain upon them, and they never can hold the Priesthood or share in it until all the other descendants of Adam have received the promises and enjoyed the blessings of the Priesthood and the keys thereof. Until the last ones of the residue of Adam's children are brought up to that favourable position, the children of Cain cannot receive the first ordinances of the Priesthood. They were the first that were cursed, and they will be the last from whom the curse will be removed. When the residue of the family of Adam come up and receive their blessings, then the curse will be removed from the seed of Cain, and they will receive blessings in like proportion.

I have but just commenced my remarks, and have presented you a few texts; and it is now time to adjourn. The exertion required to speak to you somewhat at length seems to injure me. I will therefore stop.

I bless you all, inasmuch as you have desired and striven to do right, to revere the name of Deity, and to exalt the character of his Son on the earth. I bless you in the name of Jesus Christ! Amen.

Correspondence and Diaries

Abigail Adams's Letter to John Adams (1774)

Abigail Adams's Letter to John Adams (1776)

Abigail Adams's Letter to John Quincy Adams (1780)

Abigail Adams's Letter to Lucy Cranch (1784)

Abigail Adams's Letter to Thomas Boylston Adams (1796)

John Quincy Adams's Diary Entries on the Adams-Onís Treaty (1819)

John Quincy Adams's Diary Entries on the Monroe Doctrine (1823)

Samuel Adams's Letter to James Warren (1776)

Samuel Adams's Letter to Noah Webster (1784)

Samuel Adams's Letter to Richard Henry Lee (1787)

Susan B. Anthony's Letters concerning Casting a Vote in the 1872 Federal Election (1872–1873)

Aaron Burr's Deciphered Letter to General James Wilkinson (1806)

Aaron Burr's *The Private Journal of Aaron Burr* (1808–1812)

Henry Clay's Letter to the Editors of the *Washington National Intelligencer* on Texas Annexation (1844)

Grover Cleveland's "Principles above Spoils" Letter (1890)

Everett Dirksen's Definition of Freedom (ca. 1965)

Frederick Douglass's Letter "To My Old Master" (1848)

Elbridge Gerry's Letter to the Massachusetts Legislature on the U.S. Constitution (1787)

Elbridge Gerry's First Reply to "A Landholder" (1788)

Elbridge Gerry's Second Reply to "A Landholder" (1788)

Elbridge Gerry's Letter to the Electors of Middlesex (1788)

Ulysses S. Grant's Letter to William Tecumseh Sherman (1864)

Ulysses S. Grant's Letter to Daniel H. Chamberlain (1876)

Alexander Hamilton's Letter to Harrison Gray Otis on Westward Expansion (1799)

Patrick Henry's Letter to Robert Pleasants, a Quaker, Concerning Slavery (1773)

J. Edgar Hoover's Letter to Harry Truman's Special Consultant, Sidney Souers (1950)

J. Edgar Hoover's Memo on Martin Luther King (1965)

J. Edgar Hoover's Memo on the Leak of Vietnam War Information (1965)

J. Edgar Hoover's Memo on Abbott Howard Hoffman (1970)

John Jay's Letter to George Washington (1779)

John Jay's "Circular-Letter from Congress to Their Constituents" (1779)

George F. Kennan's "Long Telegram" (1946)

Martin Luther King, Jr.'s "Letter from a Birmingham Jail" (1963)

Robert E. Lee's Letter to Mary Lee (1856)

Robert E. Lee's Letter to Custis Lee (1861)

Robert E. Lee's Letter to Jefferson Davis (1862)

Robert E. Lee's Letter to Jefferson Davis (1863)

Robert E. Lee's Letter to Jefferson Davis (1864)

Robert E. Lee's Letter to Andrew Hunter (1865)

George Mason's Letter to the Committee of Merchants in London (1766)

Joseph McCarthy's Telegram to President Harry S. Truman (1950)

Joseph McCarthy's Letter to President Dwight Eisenhower (1953)

J. Robert Oppenheimer's Memorandum to Brigadier General Thomas Farrell on the Radiological Dangers of a Nuclear Detonation (1945)

Ely Parker's Letter of Resignation as Commissioner of Indian Affairs (1871)

Ely Parker's Letter to Harriet Maxwell Converse about Indian Policy Reform (1885)

Ronald Reagan's Letter to the American People about Alzheimer's Disease (1994)

Eleanor Roosevelt's Resignation from the Daughters of the American Revolution (1939)

Theodore Roosevelt's Letter to Oliver Wendell Holmes (1903)

John Ross's Memorial to Congress (1829)

John Ross's Letter to Martin Van Buren (1837)

John Ross's Letter to David Crockett (1831)

William Henry Seward's Memorandum to President Abraham Lincoln (1861)
Joseph Story's Letter to Samuel P. P. Fay as "Matthew Bramble" (1807)
Booker T. Washington's Letter to William Howard Taft (1908)
Booker T. Washington's Letter to C. Elias Winston (1914)

Essays, Reports, and Manifestos

John Adams's "Letters of Novanglus" (1775)
John Adams's *Thoughts on Government* (1776)
John Adams's *The Report of a Constitution, or Form of Government, for the Commonwealth of Massachusetts* (1779)
John Adams's *A Defence of the Constitutions of Government of the United States of America* (1787–1788)
Samuel Adams's Instructions to Boston's Representatives (1764)
Samuel Adams's "CANDIDUS" (1771)
Jane Addams's "Passing of the War Virtues" (1907)
Jane Addams's "Why Women Should Vote" (1910)
Susan B. Anthony's "The Status of Woman, Past, Present, and Future" (1897)
Ella Baker's "Bigger Than a Hamburger" (1960)
Louis D. Brandeis's "The Greatest Life Insurance Wrong" (1906)
John C. Calhoun's "On the Relation Which the States and General Government Bear to Each Other" (1831)
Salmon P. Chase's *Reclamation of Fugitives from Service* (1847)
Salmon P. Chase's "Appeal of the Independent Democrats in Congress to the People of the United States" (1854)
Henry Clay's Letter to the Editors of the *Washington National Intelligencer* on Texas Annexation (1844)
Jefferson Davis's Preface to *The Rise and Fall of the Confederate Government* (1881)
Eugene V. Debs's "How I Became a Socialist" (1902)
Frederick Douglass's *Narrative of the Life of Frederick Douglass* (1845)
Frederick Douglass's Letter "To My Old Master" (1848)
W. E. B. Du Bois's "Strivings of the Negro People" (1897)
W. E. B. Du Bois's "The Parting of the Ways" (1904)
W. E. B. Du Bois's "Agitation" (1910)
W. E. B. Du Bois's "Returning Soldiers" (1919)
W. E. B. Du Bois's "Marxism and the Negro Problem" (1933)
Benjamin Franklin's "A Proposal for Promoting Useful Knowledge among the British Plantations in America" (1743)
Benjamin Franklin's "Exporting of Felons to the Colonies" (1751)
Benjamin Franklin's "The Way to Wealth" (1758)
Benjamin Franklin's "Rules by Which a Great Empire May Be Reduced to a Small One" (1773)
Benjamin Franklin's "The Sale of the Hessians" (1777)
Benjamin Franklin's "An Address to the Public" (1789)
Benjamin Franklin's *Autobiography* (1771–1790)
Margaret Fuller's "A Short Essay on Critics" (1840)
Margaret Fuller's *Summer on the Lakes, in 1843* (1844)
Margaret Fuller's *Woman in the Nineteenth Century* (1845)
William Lloyd Garrison's "To the Public" (1831)
William Lloyd Garrison's "The Triumph of Mobocracy in Boston" (1835)
William Lloyd Garrison's "Declaration of Sentiments Adopted by the Peace Convention" (1838)
William Lloyd Garrison's "Address to the Friends of Freedom and Emancipation in the United States" (1844)
William Lloyd Garrison's Speech Relating to the Execution of John Brown (1859)
William Lloyd Garrison's Valedictory Editorial (1865)
Elbridge Gerry's First Reply to "A Landholder" (1788)
Elbridge Gerry's Second Reply to "A Landholder" (1788)
Emma Goldman's "Anarchism: What It Really Stands For" (1917)
Emma Goldman's "The Psychology of Political Violence" (1917)
Emma Goldman's "Marriage and Love" (1917)
Samuel Gompers's Editorial on the Pullman Strike (1894)
Samuel Gompers's Editorial on the Supreme Court Ruling in the Danbury Hatters' Case (1908)
Samuel Gompers's Circular to the Organizers of the American Federation of Labor (1915)
Al Gore's "From Red Tape to Results: Creating a Government That Works Better and Costs Less" (1993)
Billy Graham's "The Flame of Political Dilemma" (1965)
Billy Graham's "The Coming Storm" (1981)

Billy Graham's "The Winds of Change" (1992)
Billy Graham's "When Life Turns against Us" (2006)
Billy Graham's "A Final Word from Billy Graham" (2006)
Alexander Hamilton's Federalist 84 (1788)
Alexander Hamilton's "First Report on Public Credit" (1790)
Alexander Hamilton's "Against an Alliance with France" (1794)
Oliver Wendell Holmes's "Early Forms of Liability" (1881)
Charles Hamilton Houston's "Educational Inequalities Must Go!" (1935)
Jesse Jackson's "The Fight for Civil Rights Continues" (2005)
John Jay's Federalist Papers 2–5 and 64 (1787–1788)
Thomas Jefferson's Declaration of Independence (1776)
George F. Kennan's "The Sources of Soviet Conduct" (1947)
George F. Kennan's "PPS/23: Review of Current Trends in U.S. Foreign Policy" (1948)
George F. Kennan's "Introducing Eugene McCarthy" (1968)
George F. Kennan's "A Modest Proposal" (1981)
Martin Luther King, Jr.'s "Letter from a Birmingham Jail" (1963)
Robert La Follette's Platform of the Conference for Progressive Political Action (1924)
James Madison's "Memorial and Remonstrance against Religious Assessments" (1785)
James Madison's Federalist 10 (1787)
James Madison's "Advice to My Country" (1834)
George Mason's Fairfax County Resolves (1774)
George Mason's "Objections to This Constitution of Government" (1787)
J. Robert Oppenheimer's Memorandum to Brigadier General Thomas Farrell on the Radiological Dangers of a
    Nuclear Detonation (1945)
J. Robert Oppenheimer's Report on the International Control of Atomic Energy (1946)
J. Robert Oppenheimer's General Advisory Committee's Report on the Building of the H-Bomb (1949)
Thomas Paine's *The Crisis* No. 1 (1776)
Thomas Paine's *The Crisis* No. 4 (1777)
Ely Parker's Report on Indian Affairs to the War Department (1867)
Ely Parker's Annual Report of the Commissioner of Indian Affairs (1869)
Frances Perkins's "City Diets and Democracy" (1941)
Frances Perkins's "Three Decades: A History of the Department of Labor" (1943)
Adam Clayton Powell's "Black Power: A Form of Godly Power" (1967)
Adam Clayton Powell's "Black Power and the Future of Black America" (1971)
Colin Powell's "U.S. Forces: Challenges Ahead" (1992/1993)
Eleanor Roosevelt's "Women Must Learn to Play the Game as Men Do" (1928)
Eleanor Roosevelt's Resignation from the Daughters of the American Revolution (1939)
Theodore Roosevelt: An Autobiography (1913)
Theodore Roosevelt's Statements Pertaining to Conservation (1903–1916)
Margaret Sanger's "Sexual Impulse—Part II" (1912)
Margaret Sanger's "The Prevention of Conception" (1914)
Margaret Sanger's "Birth Control and Racial Betterment" (1919)
Roger Sherman's "A Caveat against Injustice; or, An Inquiry into the Evils of a Fluctuating Medium of Exchange"
    (1752)
Roger Sherman's "Letters of a Countryman" (November 14, 1787)
Roger Sherman's "Letters of a Countryman" (November 22, 1787)
Elizabeth Cady Stanton's Declaration of Sentiments (1848)
Joseph Story's "Privileges of Citizens—Fugitives—Slaves" (1833)
Robert A. Taft's "The Place of the President and Congress in Foreign Policy" (1951)
Strom Thurmond's Southern Manifesto (1956)
Earl Warren's Warren Commission Report (1964)
Booker T. Washington's "Statement on Suffrage" (1903)
Booker T. Washington's "A Protest against Lynching" (1904)
Ida B. Wells's "Eight Men Lynched" (1892)
Ida B. Wells's *The Red Record* (1895)
Ida B. Wells's "Lynching and the Excuse for It" (1901)
Ida B. Wells's "Booker T. Washington and His Critics" (1904)

Interviews

Ella Baker's "Developing Community Leadership" (1970)
"Ella Baker: Organizing for Civil Rights" (1980)
Allen Dulles's Television Interview on the Soviets' Intentions (1956)
"Conversations with Alice Paul: Woman Suffrage and the Equal Rights Amendment" (1972–1973)

Legal

Hugo Black's opinion in *Korematsu v. United States* (1944)
Hugo Black's dissent in *Adamson v. California* (1947)
Hugo Black's opinion in *Youngstown Sheet & Tube Co. v. Sawyer* (1952)
Hugo Black's opinion in *Gideon v. Wainwright* (1963)
Hugo Black's dissent in *Griswold v. Connecticut* (1965)
Harry Blackmun's opinion in *Roe v. Wade* (1973)
Harry Blackmun's dissent in *Beal v. Doe* (1977)
Harry Blackmun's dissent in *Bowers v. Hardwick* (1986)
Harry Blackmun's dissent in *DeShaney v. Winnebago County Department of Social Services* (1989)
Harry Blackmun's dissent in *Callins v. Collins* (1994)
Louis D. Brandeis's concurrence in *Whitney v. California* (1927)
Louis D. Brandeis's dissent in *Olmstead v. United States* (1928)
William J. Brennan, Jr.'s opinion in *Baker v. Carr* (1962)
William J. Brennan, Jr.'s opinion in *New York Times Co. v. Sullivan* (1964)
William J. Brennan, Jr.'s opinion in *Craig v. Boren* (1976)
William J. Brennan, Jr.'s opinion in *Texas v. Johnson* (1989)
Warren E. Burger's dissent in *Bivens v. Six Unknown Named Agents of the Federal Bureau of Narcotics* (1971)
Warren E. Burger's opinion in *United States v. Nixon* (1974)
Warren E. Burger's opinion in *Milliken v. Bradley* (1974)
Salmon P. Chase's *Reclamation of Fugitives from Service* (1847)
Salmon P. Chase's opinion *Texas v. White* (1869)
William O. Douglas's dissent in *Dennis v. United States* (1951)
William O. Douglas's concurrence in *Mapp v. Ohio* (1961)
William O. Douglas's opinion in *Griswold v. Connecticut* (1965)
William O. Douglas's dissent in *Sierra Club v. Morton* (1972)
William O. Douglas's concurrence in *Furman v. Georgia* (1972)
Stephen J. Field's opinion in *Cummings v. Missouri* (1867)
Stephen J. Field's dissent in *Munn v. Illinois* (1876)
Stephen J. Field's opinion in *Ho Ah Kow v. Nunan* (1879)
Felix Frankfurter's opinion in *Minersville School District v. Gobitis* (1940)
Felix Frankfurter's opinion in *Colegrove v. Green* (1946)
Felix Frankfurter's concurrence in *Cooper v. Aaron* (1958)
Felix Frankfurter's opinion in *Gomillion v. Lightfoot* (1960)
Ruth Bader Ginsburg's opinion in *United States v. Virginia* (1996)
Ruth Bader Ginsburg's opinion in *Friends of the Earth, Inc. et al. v. Laidlaw Environmental Services, Inc.* (2000)
Ruth Bader Ginsburg's concurrence in *Stenberg, Attorney General of Nebraska, et al. v. Carhart* (2000)
Ruth Bader Ginsburg's opinion in *Eldred v. Ashcroft* (2003)
John Marshall Harlan's dissent in the Civil Rights Cases (1883)
John Marshall Harlan's dissent in *Hurtado v. California* (1884)
John Marshall Harlan's dissent in *Pollock v. Farmers' Loan & Trust Co.* (1895)
John Marshall Harlan's dissent in *Plessy v. Ferguson* (1896)
Oliver Wendell Holmes's dissent in *Lochner v. New York* (1905)
Oliver Wendell Holmes's opinion in *Schenck v. United States* (1919)
Oliver Wendell Holmes's dissent in *Abrams v. United States* (1919)
Oliver Wendell Holmes's opinion in *Buck v. Bell* (1927)
Charles Hamilton Houston's petition in *Missouri ex rel Gaines v. Canada* (1938)
Charles Hamilton Houston's brief in *Hurd v. Hodge* (1948)
Robert H. Jackson's opinion in *West Virginia State Board of Education v. Barnette* (1943)
John Jay's "Charge to the Grand Juries" (1790)
John Marshall's opinion in *Marbury v. Madison* (1803)

John Marshall's opinion in *McCulloch v. Maryland* (1819)
John Marshall's opinion in *Gibbons v. Ogden* (1824)
Thurgood Marshall's opinion in *Grayned v. City of Rockford* (1972)
Thurgood Marshall's concurrence in *Furman v. Georgia* (1972)
Thurgood Marshall's separate opinion in *Regents of the University of California v. Bakke* (1978)
Thurgood Marshall's dissent in *Florida v. Bostick* (1991)
Sandra Day O'Connor's concurrence in *Webster v. Reproductive Health Services* (1989)
Sandra Day O'Connor's dissent in *Metro Broadcasting, Inc. v. Federal Communications Commission* (1990)
Sandra Day O'Connor's concurrence in *Zelman v. Simmons-Harris* (2002)
Sandra Day O'Connor's opinion in *Grutter v. Bollinger* (2003)
William Rehnquist's dissent in *Roe v. Wade* (1973)
William Rehnquist's opinion in *United States v. Lopez* (1995)
William Rehnquist's opinion in *George W. Bush et al. v. Albert Gore, Jr., et al.* (2000)
Joseph Story's opinion in *United States v. Coolidge* (1813)
Roger B. Taney's opinion in *Charles River Bridge v. Warren Bridge* (1837)
Roger B. Taney's opinion in License Cases (1847)
Roger B. Taney's opinion in *Dred Scott v. Sandford* (1857)
Earl Warren's opinion in *Brown v. Board of Education of Topeka* (1954)
Earl Warren's opinion in *Reynolds v. Sims* (1964)
Earl Warren's opinion in *Miranda v. Arizona* (1966)

Legislative

Susan B. Anthony's Nineteenth Amendment (1920)
Jefferson Davis's Resolutions to the U.S. Senate on the Relations of States (1860)
Al Gore's High-Performance Computing Act of 1991
Patrick Henry's Resolutions in Opposition to the Stamp Act (1765)
J. Edgar Hoover's Testimony before the House Un-American Activities Committee (1947)
John Jay's Draft of the Proclamation of Neutrality (1793)
Thomas Jefferson's Virginia Act for Establishing Religious Freedom (1786)
James Madison's Virginia Resolutions (1798)
George Mason's Virginia Declaration of Rights (1776)
Alice Paul's Testimony before the House Judiciary Committee (1915)
Alice Paul's Equal Rights Amendment (1921)

Military

Ulysses S. Grant's Letter to William Tecumseh Sherman (1864)
Ulysses S. Grant's Final Report of Military Operations (1865)
Robert E. Lee's General Order No. 9 (1865)

Presidential/Executive

John Adams's Inaugural Address (1797)
John Quincy Adams's First Annual Message to Congress (1825)
James Buchanan's Inaugural Address (1857)
James Buchanan's Fourth Annual Message to Congress (1860)
George W. Bush's Remarks on Signing the Economic Growth and Tax Relief Reconciliation Act (2001)
George W. Bush's Address on the Terrorist Attacks of September 11 (2001)
George W. Bush's Second State of the Union Address (2002)
George W. Bush's Address to the Nation on Military Operations in Iraq (2003)
George W. Bush's Second Inaugural Address (2005)
Grover Cleveland's First Inaugural Address (1885)
Grover Cleveland's Special Session Message to Congress on the Economic Crisis (1893)
Grover Cleveland's Message to Congress on Hawaiian Sovereignty (1893)
Grover Cleveland's Fourth Annual Message to Congress (1896)
Bill Clinton's First Inaugural Address (1993)
Bill Clinton's Remarks on Signing the North American Free Trade Agreement (1993)

Bill Clinton's Remarks on Signing the Personal Responsibility and Work Opportunity Reconciliation Act (1996)
Bill Clinton's Remarks at Annual Prayer Breakfast (1998)
Bill Clinton's Farewell Address (2001)
Dwight D. Eisenhower's First Inaugural Address (1953)
Dwight D. Eisenhower's "Cross of Iron" Speech (1953)
Dwight D. Eisenhower's Atoms for Peace Speech (1953)
Dwight D. Eisenhower's Special Message to Congress on the Eisenhower Doctrine (1957)
Dwight D. Eisenhower's Second Inaugural Address (1957)
Dwight D. Eisenhower's Farewell Address (1961)
Ulysses S. Grant's First Inaugural Address (1869)
Ulysses S. Grant's Special Message to Congress Announcing Ratification of the Fifteenth Amendment (1870)
Ulysses S. Grant's Sixth Annual Message to Congress (1874)
Ulysses S. Grant's Special Message to the Senate on Unrest in Louisiana (1875)
Ulysses S. Grant's Letter to Daniel H. Chamberlain (1876)
Herbert Hoover's Inaugural Address (1929)
Herbert Hoover's Kellogg-Briand Pact Proclamation (1929)
Herbert Hoover's Annual Message to Congress (1931)
Herbert Hoover's "The Consequences of the Proposed New Deal" (1932)
Andrew Jackson's Proclamation Regarding the Opening of U.S. Ports to British Vessels (1830)
Andrew Jackson's Second Annual Message to Congress (1830)
Andrew Jackson's Veto of the Bill to Limit the Power of the Bank of the United States (1832)
Andrew Jackson's Proclamation to the People of South Carolina Regarding Nullification (1832)
Thomas Jefferson's First Inaugural Address (1801)
Thomas Jefferson's Second Inaugural Address (1805)
Andrew Johnson's First Annual Message to Congress (1865)
Andrew Johnson's Veto of the Freedmen's Bureau Bill (1866)
Andrew Johnson's Veto of the Civil Rights Act (1866)
Lyndon Baines Johnson's Speech to a Joint Session of Congress on Assuming the Presidency (1963)
Lyndon Baines Johnson's Commencement Address at the University of Michigan (1964)
Lyndon Baines Johnson's Remarks on the Gulf of Tonkin Incident (1964)
Lyndon Baines Johnson's Speech to a Joint Session of Congress on Civil Rights (1965)
John F. Kennedy's Inaugural Address (1961)
John F. Kennedy's Report to the American People on the Soviet Arms Buildup in Cuba (1962)
John F. Kennedy's Report to the American People on Civil Rights (1963)
Abraham Lincoln's "House Divided" Speech (1858)
Abraham Lincoln's First Inaugural Address (1861)
Abraham Lincoln's Gettysburg Address (1863)
Abraham Lincoln's Second Inaugural Address (1865)
William McKinley's Message to Congress about Intervention in Cuba (1898)
William McKinley's "Benevolent Assimilation" Proclamation (1898)
William McKinley's Home Market Club Speech (1899)
William McKinley's Last Speech (1901)
James Monroe's Second Annual Message to Congress (1818)
James Monroe's Second Inaugural Address (1821)
James Monroe's Seventh Annual Message to Congress (1823)
James Monroe's Special Message to the Senate on the Slave Trade Convention with Great Britain (1824)
Richard M. Nixon's Resignation Address to the Nation (1974)
James Polk's Inaugural Address (1845)
James Polk's Message to Congress on War with Mexico (1846)
James Polk's Farewell Message to Congress (1848)
Ronald Reagan's First Inaugural Address (1981)
Ronald Reagan's "Evil Empire" Speech (1983)
Franklin Delano Roosevelt's First Inaugural Address (1933)
Franklin Delano Roosevelt's "Four Freedoms" Message to Congress (1941)
Franklin Delano Roosevelt's "Second Bill of Rights" Message to Congress (1944)
Theodore Roosevelt's Letter to Oliver Wendell Holmes (1903)
Theodore Roosevelt's Special Message to Congress (1908)
Theodore Roosevelt's Statements Pertaining to Conservation (1903–1916)

Harry S. Truman's Statement Announcing the Use of the A-Bomb on Hiroshima (1945)
Harry S. Truman's Truman Doctrine Address to Congress (1947)
Harry S. Truman's Address to the National Association for the Advancement of Colored People (1947)
Harry S. Truman's Inaugural Address (1949)
Harry S. Truman's Report to the American People on Korea (1951)
George Washington's Proclamation of Neutrality (1793)
George Washington's Farewell Address (1796)
Woodrow Wilson's Address at Gettysburg (1913)
Woodrow Wilson's Address to a Joint Session of Congress on Trusts and Monopolies (1914)
Woodrow Wilson's Address in Support of a World League for Peace (1917)
Woodrow Wilson's Second Inaugural Address (1917)
Woodrow Wilson's War Message to Congress (1917)
Woodrow Wilson's Fourteen Points Speech (1918)

Speeches/Addresses

John Adams's Inaugural Address (1797)
John Quincy Adams's First Annual Message to Congress (1825)
John Quincy Adams's Jubilee of the Constitution Address (1839)
John Quincy Adams's Congressional Debate over Motion for Censure (1842)
John Quincy Adams's Address to Constituents at Braintree (1842)
Samuel Adams's Massachusetts Ratifying Convention Speeches (1788)
Samuel Adams's Address to the Massachusetts Legislature (1795)
Jane Addams's "The Subjective Necessity for Social Settlements" (1892)
Jane Addams's "A Modern Lear" (1896)
Susan B. Anthony's "Is It a Crime for a Citizen of the United States to Vote?" (1873)
Ella Baker's "The Black Woman in the Civil Rights Struggle" (1969)
Louis D. Brandeis's "The Opportunity in the Law" (1905)
Louis D. Brandeis's "The Jewish Problem: How to Solve It" (1915)
William Jennings Bryan's Speech to Congress on Tariff Reform (1892)
William Jennings Bryan's "Cross of Gold" Speech (1896)
William Jennings Bryan's Speech at the Scopes Trial (1925)
James Buchanan's Remarks to Congress on Slavery (1836)
James Buchanan's Inaugural Address (1857)
James Buchanan's Fourth Annual Message to Congress (1860)
Aaron Burr's Farewell Address to the U.S. Senate (1805)
Aaron Burr's Address to the Court on Innocence of Treason (1807)
Aaron Burr's Motion to the Court to Limit Prosecution Evidence (1807)
George W. Bush's Remarks on Signing the Economic Growth and Tax Relief Reconciliation Act (2001)
George W. Bush's Address on the Terrorist Attacks of September 11 (2001)
George W. Bush's Second State of the Union Address (2002)
George W. Bush's Address to the Nation on Military Operations in Iraq (2003)
George W. Bush's Second Inaugural Address (2005)
Robert C. Byrd's Line-Item Veto Speech XIV (1993)
Robert C. Byrd's "We Stand Passively Mute" Speech (2003)
Robert C. Byrd's "The Emperor Has No Clothes" Speech (2003)
John C. Calhoun's "On the Second Resolution Reported by the Committee on Foreign Relations" (1811)
John C. Calhoun's "To the People of the United States" (1832)
John C. Calhoun's "On the Reception of Abolition Petitions" (1837)
John C. Calhoun's "On His Resolutions in Reference to the War with Mexico" (1848)
John C. Calhoun's "On the Slavery Question" (1850)
César Chávez's Plan of Delano (1966)
César Chávez's Address to the Seventh Constitutional Convention of the United Farm Workers of America (1984)
César Chávez's Wrath of Grapes Speech (1986)
Shirley Chisholm's Speech in Favor of the Equal Rights Amendment (1970)
Shirley Chisholm's Announcement of Candidacy for the Democratic Nomination for President (1972)
Shirley Chisholm's "The Black Woman in Contemporary America" (1974)
Henry Clay's Speech on the Bill to Raise an Additional Military Force (1813)

Patrick Henry's Election Speech at Charlotte Court House (1799)
Oliver Wendell Holmes's "Early Forms of Liability" (1881)
Herbert Hoover's "Rugged Individualism" Campaign Speech (1928)
Herbert Hoover's Inaugural Address (1929)
Herbert Hoover's Kellogg-Briand Pact Proclamation (1929)
Herbert Hoover's Annual Message to Congress (1931)
Herbert Hoover's "The Consequences of the Proposed New Deal" (1932)
Sam Houston's Inaugural Address as President of the Republic of Texas (1836)
Sam Houston's Speech Supporting the Compromise of 1850 (1850)
Sam Houston's Speech Opposing the Kansas-Nebraska Act (1854)
Sam Houston's Speech on Refusal to Take the Oath of Loyalty to the Confederacy (1861)
Andrew Jackson's Proclamation Regarding the Opening of U.S. Ports to British Vessels (1830)
Andrew Jackson's Second Annual Message to Congress (1830)
Andrew Jackson's Proclamation to the People of South Carolina Regarding Nullification (1832)
Jesse Jackson's "The Struggle Continues" (1988)
Robert H. Jackson's "The Federal Prosecutor" (1940)
Robert H. Jackson's Opening Statement before the International Military Tribunal, Nuremberg, Germany (1945)
Robert H. Jackson's Closing Statement before the International Military Tribunal, Nuremberg, Germany (1946)
Thomas Jefferson's First Inaugural Address (1801)
Thomas Jefferson's Second Inaugural Address (1805)
Andrew Johnson's First Annual Message to Congress (1865)
Lyndon Baines Johnson's Speech to a Joint Session of Congress on Assuming the Presidency (1963)
Lyndon Baines Johnson's Commencement Address at the University of Michigan (1964)
Lyndon Baines Johnson's Remarks on the Gulf of Tonkin Incident (1964)
Lyndon Baines Johnson's Speech to a Joint Session of Congress on Civil Rights (1965)
Barbara Jordan's "The Constitutional Basis for Impeachment" (1974)
Barbara Jordan's "Who Then Will Speak for the Common Good?" (1976)
Barbara Jordan's "Change: From What to What?" (1992)
John F. Kennedy's Inaugural Address (1961)
John F. Kennedy's Report to the American People on the Soviet Arms Buildup in Cuba (1962)
John F. Kennedy's Report to the American People on Civil Rights (1963)
Robert F. Kennedy's Tribute to John F. Kennedy at the Democratic National Convention (1964)
Robert F. Kennedy's Day of Affirmation Address at the University of Cape Town (1966)
Robert F. Kennedy's Address at the University of California, Berkeley (1966)
Robert F. Kennedy's Remarks on the Death of Martin Luther King (1968)
Martin Luther King, Jr.'s "I Have a Dream" Speech (1963)
Martin Luther King, Jr.'s Speech in Opposition to the Vietnam War (1967)
Robert La Follette's Speech on the Amendment of National Banking Laws (1908)
Robert La Follette's Speech Opposing War with Germany (1917)
Abraham Lincoln's "House Divided" Speech (1858)
Abraham Lincoln's First Inaugural Address (1861)
Abraham Lincoln's Gettysburg Address (1863)
Abraham Lincoln's Second Inaugural Address (1865)
Henry Cabot Lodge's Speech on the Retention of the Philippine Islands (1900)
Henry Cabot Lodge's Speech on Mexico (1915)
Henry Cabot Lodge's Speech on President Woodrow Wilson's Plan for a World Peace (1917)
Henry Cabot Lodge's Speech Opposing the League of Nations (1919)
Huey Long's "Every Man a King" Address (1934)
Huey Long's "Share Our Wealth" Address (1935)
Huey Long's "Our Growing Calamity" Address (1935)
James Madison's Speech on the New Jersey Plan to the Constitutional Convention (1787)
James Madison's Speech to the House of Representatives Proposing a Bill of Rights (1789)
Malcolm X's "Message to the Grass Roots" (1963)
Malcolm X's "The Ballot or the Bullet" Speech (1964)
George Marshall's Speech to the American Historical Association on the National Organization for War (1939)
George Marshall's Speech to the Graduating Class of the U.S. Military Academy (1942)
George Marshall's Washington's Birthday Remarks at Princeton University (1947)
George Marshall's Marshall Plan Speech (1947)

Elizabeth Cady Stanton's "Solitude of Self" (1892)

Robert A. Taft's "Equal Justice under Law: The Heritage of the English-Speaking Peoples and Their Responsibility" (1946)

Robert A. Taft's "The Sound Basis for Federal Aid to Education" (1947)

Tecumseh's Speech to Governor William Henry Harrison at Fort Vincennes (1810)

Tecumseh's Speech to Major General Henry Procter at Fort Malden (1813)

Strom Thurmond's Keynote Address at the States' Rights Democratic Conference (1948)

Harry S. Truman's Statement Announcing the Use of the A-Bomb on Hiroshima (1945)

Harry S. Truman's Truman Doctrine Address to Congress (1947)

Harry S. Truman's Address to the National Association for the Advancement of Colored People (1947)

Harry S. Truman's Inaugural Address (1949)

Harry S. Truman's Report to the American People on Korea (1951)

Booker T. Washington's Atlanta Exposition Address (1895)

George Washington's Address to Congress on Resigning His Commission (1783)

George Washington's Farewell Address (1796)

Daniel Webster's Second Reply to Robert Hayne (1830)

Daniel Webster's Speech to the Senate on the Preservation of the Union (1850)

Ida B. Wells's "Lynching: Our National Crime" (1909)

Woodrow Wilson's Address at Gettysburg (1913)

Woodrow Wilson's Address to a Joint Session of Congress on Trusts and Monopolies (1914)

Woodrow Wilson's Address in Support of a World League for Peace (1917)

Woodrow Wilson's Second Inaugural Address (1917)

Woodrow Wilson's War Message to Congress (1917)

Woodrow Wilson's Fourteen Points Speech (1918)

Victoria Woodhull's Lecture on Constitutional Equality (1871)

Victoria Woodhull's "'And the Truth Shall Make You Free': A Speech on the Principles of Social Freedom" (1871)

Brigham Young's Sermon on Mormon Governance (1859)

Brigham Young's Sermon on Race and Slavery (1859)

Volume numbers are indicated before each page number. Bold page numbers indicate the primary entry about the topic.